Helping People Change:
A Textbook of Methods

Edited by

Frederick H. Kanfer
University of Illinois

and

Arnold P. Goldstein
Syracuse University

PERGAMON GENERAL PSYCHOLOGY SERIES

Editors: Arnold P. Goldstein, *Syracuse University*
Leonard Krasner, *SUNY, Stony Brook*

PGPS - 52

PERGAMON PRESS INC.

New York · Toronto · Oxford · Sydney · Braunschweig

PERGAMON PRESS INC.
Maxwell House, Fairview Park, Elmsford, N.Y. 10523

PERGAMON OF CANADA LTD.
207 Queen's Quay West, Toronto 117, Ontario

PERGAMON PRESS LTD.
Headington Hill Hall, Oxford

PERGAMON PRESS (AUST.) PTY. LTD.
Rushcutters Bay, Sydney, N.S.W.

PERGAMON GmbH
D - 3300 Braunschweig, Burgplatz 1

Library of Congress Cataloging in Publication Data

Kanfer, Frederick H   1925–
    Helping people change.

    (Pergamon general psychology series, 52)
    1. Personality change. I. Goldstein, Arnold P.,
joint author. II. Title.
BF698.2.K36   158   74-19027
ISBN 0-08-018272-0
ISBN 0-08-018271-2 (pbk.)

"Bond of Union," a lithograph by M. C. Escher.

Reproduction courtesy of Vorpal Galleries, San Francisco and Chicago

Printed in the United States of America

To Ruby, Ruth, and Larry for their infinite patience,
encouragement, and affection

and

To Susan with love and admiration for her concern
with helping others

The Editors

Frederick H. Kanfer (Ph.D., Indiana University) is Professor of Psychology at the University of Illinois. His primary interest is in developing the necessary conceptualizations and methods to provide a broad behavioral framework for application to personal and social problems.

He was awarded a Diplomate in Clinical Psychology from the American Board of Examiners in Professional Psychology. He is a Fellow of the American Psychological Association and has held offices in the Division of Clinical Psychology and in the Association for the Advancement of Behavior Therapy.

Dr. Kanfer has taught at Washington University, St. Louis; at Purdue University; in the Department of Psychiatry at the University of Oregon Medical School; and at the University of Cincinnati. He was a Fullbright scholar to Europe in 1968 and has been Visiting Professor and Consultant to various agencies dealing with psychological problems, both in the United States and in Europe. In addition, he has served on editorial boards of several psychological journals and has published over 90 articles. He is co-author of a book on *Learning Foundations of Behavior Therapy*. His experimental work is primarily in the area of self-control, self-reinforcement, and vicarious learning.

Arnold P. Goldstein (Ph.D., Pennsylvania State University) is Professor of Psychology at Syracuse University. His primary interest is in behavior modification, skill training, and interpersonal relationships. He is a Fellow of the American Psychological Association and a member of the Association for the Advancement of Behavior Therapy and the Society for Psychotherapy Research.

Dr. Goldstein has taught at the University of Pittsburgh Medical School and served as a research psychologist at the VA outpatient research laboratory in Washington, D.C. He was a Visiting Professor at the Free University of Amsterdam, Holland, in 1970 and at the University of Hawaii in the summer of 1972. He has published over forty articles and is author, co-author, or editor of *Therapist-Patient Expectancies in Psychotherapy*; *Psychotherapy and the Psychology of Behavior Change*; *The Investigation of Psychotherapy*; *Psychotherapeutic Attraction*; *The Lonely Teacher*; *Structured Learning Therapy*; and *Changing Supervisor Behavior*.

Contents

Contributors

Linda G. Buckner, M.A.
Fresno, California

William C. Coe, Ph.D.
Psychology Department
California State University
Fresno, California

David L. Elwood, Ph.D.
Psychology Laboratory
Quinco Consulting Center
Columbus, Indiana

John Flowers, Ph.D.
Program in Social Ecology
University of California
Irvine, California

Anita P. Goldfried, M.A.
East Setauket, New York

Marvin R. Goldfried, Ph.D.
Psychology Department
State University of New York
Stony Brook, New York

Arnold P. Goldstein, Ph.D.
Psychology Department
Syracuse University
Syracuse, New York

David W. Johnson, Ph.D.
Psychological Foundations
University of Minnesota
Minneapolis, Minnesota

Frederick H. Kanfer, Ph.D.
Psychology Department
University of Illinois
Champaign, Illinois

Paul Karoly, Ph.D.
Psychology Department
University of Cincinnati
Cincinnati, Ohio

Morton A. Lieberman, Ph.D.
Department of Behavioral Sciences
(Human Development) and Department of
Psychiatry
University of Chicago
Chicago, Illinois

G. Alan Marlatt, Ph.D.
Psychology Department
University of Washington
Seattle, Washington

Ronald P. Matross, Ph.D.
Student Life Studies
University of Minnesota
Minneapolis, Minnesota

Donald Meichenbaum, Ph.D.
Psychology Department
University of Waterloo
Waterloo, Ontario, Canada

Richard J. Morris, Ph.D.
Psychology Department
Syracuse University
Syracuse, New York

Martha Perry, Ph.D.
Psychology Department
University of Washington
Seattle, Washington

Jack Sandler, Ph.D.
Psychology Department
University of South Florida
Tampa, Florida

Preface

For many years in the United States, persons in need of help for psychological problems could seek the aid of only a very restricted range of highly trained and specialized helpers. Other types of helpers, while they existed, were rarely acknowledged and thus often difficult to find. The helping procedures typically used by the formal helpers were also few in number and rather elaborate in content. These situations have changed dramatically in recent years. There now are many, many types of helpers and a very broad range of helping techniques. Helping others change is no longer the sole preserve of the psychiatrist, psychologist, and social worker, but also of the aide, mental health technician, foster grandparent, behavioral analyst, peer counselor, and the like. The present book is written for all of these helpers, professional and paraprofessional, undergraduate and graduate, novice and experienced.

The chapters which follow are each devoted to a major set of procedures for helping people change. These procedures may be viewed as the components or active ingredients which constitute all forms of psychotherapy, guidance, counseling, and related efforts by one person to assist another with his psychological problems. Significant helping procedures have been included, if there existed sound research evidence that the procedure was in fact helpful in effecting change. We have quite intentionally avoided inclusion of fad-like, glamorous procedures whose purpose is actually "fun and games" or aggrandizement of its developer, and not lasting client change.

We have been most fortunate in this effort in having the participation of contributors of outstanding quality, persons able to reflect in their writing a joint concern for human suffering and scientific rigor. Their efforts, taken together, yield in this book a comprehensive and accurate presentation of behavioral, cognitive, attitudinal, group, and related change procedures. Emphasis is on the specific content of these procedures and how to use them. It is our hope and expectation that this book will prove to be of significant value in helping people change.

This is a book for students, professionals, and paraprofessionals and, as such, we have sought and received wise counsel and criticism from persons of each type. Their thoughtful efforts have added significantly to almost every chapter. Our sincerest thanks are thus extended to Susan Goldstein, Larry Grimm, Bryce Kaye, Marina Kolb, Charles Spates, and Andrew Ursino.

CHAPTER 1

Introduction

FREDERICK H. KANFER AND ARNOLD P. GOLDSTEIN

Perhaps the most characteristic feature of our lives during the last few decades has been the rapid increase in the rate of change—in the physical environment, in our technology, and in our social, political, and moral institutions. Bombarded by mass media, by a wealth of available goods and ideas, and by the ever changing scene to which our senses are exposed, each of us finishes the day having changed for better or worse, even if ever so slightly. A conversation with a friend, an interesting movie or book, a new emotional experience, a political rally, a work of art, or a breathtaking natural scene may all make a deep impression on us and can alter our attitudes about ourselves and about the world. If an experience is sufficiently intense, it may alter our behavior to the extent that our families and friends are surprised at the change. Yet, many persons go through their daily routine given the same exposure to ideas, images, and people as others, but remain unable to change their view of themselves or others, and unable to give up self-defeating patterns of behavior even though solutions and opportunities for growth are at an arm's length. Others meet their world in rigid, fearful, or aggressive ways, finding little happiness or satisfaction, yet unable to break the vicious circles they seem to engender. It is these populations, persons who are stymied in resolving their personal and interpersonal problems, who are the focus of our attention as professional helpers.

This book is about psychological methods designed to help people change for the better, so that they can fully develop their potentials and capitalize on the opportunities available in their social environment. The helping methods we will examine share the common goal of promoting change in ways which can lead to greater personal happiness, competence, and satisfaction. Our point of view stresses that a professional or paraprofessional helper can serve as both a consultant and an expert teacher or guide to persons whose discomforts, psychological disabilities, and social inefficiencies have been of sufficient concern to them, or to others in their environment, that the assistance of a trained outsider is deemed necessary.

People help one another in numerous ways in everyday life and, indeed, people do change as a result of such informal assistance. However, several distinct

1

characteristics consistently differentiate the professional or paraprofessional helping relationship from friendship or other helpful interactions. Whether the helping relationship is called psychotherapy, counseling, guidance, behavior modification, or Gestalt therapy, and whether it is conducted by a physician, a psychiatrist, a psychologist, a social worker, a child care worker, a mental health technician, or a hospital nurse or aide, the same features are found in all professional or paraprofessional helping relationships: they are unilateral, systematic, formal, and time limited.

The *unilateral* aspect of the helping relationship reflects the fact that the participants agree that one person is defined as the helper and the other as the client. It is also agreed, explicitly or implicitly, that the focus of the relationship and all its activities is on solving the problems of the client. In this respect, the change process is unlike most other interpersonal interactions. The personal problems, the private affairs, the worries and the wishes of one person, the helper, are intentionally not focused upon. Treatment, therapy, or whatever the helping relationship may be called, is one-sided and concentrates exclusively on the client.

The professional or paraprofessional helping relationship is *systematic* in that the participants typically agree at the outset on the purposes and objectives of their interaction, and the helper attempts to plan and carry out procedures that move in an organized fashion toward resolution of his client's problems.

The relationship is *formal*, in that the interaction between helper and client is usually confined to specified times and places. While the interaction need not always be conducted at the same time of day and in the same office, clinic, or hospital, this usually is the case. The times and places are arranged in such a way that the helper has no other role or duty during his meetings with his client. At times, the helper may intentionally provide an informal atmosphere. For example, a helping interaction can occur when a child care worker plays checkers or ping pong, or takes a walk with a child, or when an adult client is seen in his home. However, under these circumstances the child care worker's concern is not with winning the game or getting physical exercise out of his walk, nor is the visit in a client's home a social occasion for mutual enjoyment. These are, instead, examples of formal treatment in an informal setting.

Helping relationships are *time limited*. The relationship terminates when the stated objectives and goals are reached. The termination is always considered as the final outcome of the relationship and can be based on mutual agreement or on either the helper's or the client's initiative.

If you consider a friendship or an interaction with a colleague or a neighbor for a moment, it will become clear that none of the features listed is common in such relationships. Social relationships are formed for mutual benefit of the participants, there is usually no fixed agenda for what is to be accomplished, the relationship is typically enjoyed for what it is rather than for what it may accomplish, and it is terminated for numerous reasons other than completion of a task.

The history of professional helpers goes back over many centuries. In each age, the predominant theory of human nature determined which professional group was considered the most competent to relieve people's discomforts and psychological problems. In societies in which theological explanations of man dominated, priests, shamans, or witch-doctors were given the task of assisting people with their personal problems or rectifying behavioral deviations. More recently, the assumption was accepted in western societies that behavioral disorders were manifestations of disturbances of the nervous system, or the biological structure of the individual. As a result, major responsibility for dealing with psychological problems was given to physicians and, in particular, psychiatrists. Indeed, early suspicions that brain damage or weak nervous system structures were the causes of many behavior disorders resulted in rigorous search for the specific roots of what was then called "mental diseases." Even Freud's comprehensive theory of human behavior was based on the assumption that the driving energy underlying human activity, psychic libido, developed by conversion from physical energy via the nervous system.

In the last three decades there has been increasing disenchantment with the view that behavioral problems represent mental illnesses associated with the organism's biological or psychic structures. Alternate models of psychological disturbances have been based on ideas derived from philosophical systems and, increasingly, from scientific psychology. Congruent with this trend, there has also been the recognition that relief of psychological problems can be offered by persons with expertise in nonmedical specialties. Further, the erosion in belief in the infallibility of the authoritative professional has hastened the development of brief training programs that permit many lay persons to participate in the treatment or behavior change process. This expansion of the helper manpower pool has helped to reduce the scarcity of assistance available, caused by the small number of highly trained professionals and the large number of persons in need of help. This greatly expanded use of paraprofessional personnel, parents, volunteer workers, and many others as helpers is a development we strongly endorse. Their success with many types of clients with a broad range of problems is already evident.

WHO IS QUALIFIED TO HELP?

Many different professions have as one of their goals the accomplishment of behavior change in their clients. Teachers, physicians, clergymen, social workers, psychologists, and probation officers are among the professionals who offer services designed to change human behavior. Even if enduring changes in the client's behavior are not the immediate focus of the professional service, they may still play a role in the total context of the services offered. Attorneys, nurses, dentists, and financial advisors are among those who can achieve their specifically stated goals more easily if they can influence their clients to change in ways ranging from minor accommodations to sweeping changes in their life patterns. For example, the more effective dentist is one who not only restores tooth damage or applies preventive treatment in the office, but who is also able to persuade his patient to alter his daily oral hygiene behaviors and, perhaps, even his eating habits sufficiently so that future damage is prevented or retarded. However, not all professionals are equally qualified to deal effectively with psychological problems. Currently, the most acceptable criteria for qualification in the helping professions has been evidence of successful completion of specified training programs. Generally, the successful completion of a study program is certified by a degree and the holder is regarded as competent to carry out a specified range of professional duties. Of course, the distinction between meeting requirements in academic courses and showing the skills needed for professional practice is not clearly made by degree-granting institutions. In fact, frequent and heated debates have centered on the type of training that qualifies persons best for helping professions.

The most widely accepted criteria of professional level competence are doctoral degrees with specialties in clinical psychology or counseling psychology, medical degrees with residency training in psychiatry, or advanced degrees in social work. However, there has been a growing recognition that the management of behavior change programs is not the province of any single discipline, nor is it necessary to expect every practitioner to be able to function in all areas within the given discipline. In fact, as treatment methods for psychological problems have moved away from their earlier foundations in religious, philosophical, or biological concepts of man, to encompass psychological, social, economic, and political components as well, there has been a parallel development that has facilitated the delivery of effective behavior change programs by persons with much shorter and less complex formal training than the mastery of four to six years of post graduate training which is required of psychologists or psychiatrists. As noted earlier, such persons can and do make significant contributions to helping people change. In part, this change in requirements is a result of the division of labor now possible because of clearer specification of the ways in which behavior change techniques can be applied. Traditional psychotherapeutic techniques were based primarily on complex and abstract personality theories, and the interpersonal relationship between helper and client was considered to be the primary instrument of change. As a result, it was necessary to train a person first, in depth, in the theories and assumptions of the therapy system. The development of treatment skills was a slow process, mainly by apprenticeship and close individual supervision. In many disciplines, e.g., in psychoanalysis, the training period might extend until the trainee was in his forties. With the realization that many components of a behavior change program can be learned rather quickly and that complete mastery of the entire field is not essential for participating in some stages of the total program, there has been the increased effort noted earlier to train persons with limited knowledge of change methods (paraprofessionals) to work under the direction of more extensively trained persons.

In a recent survey of leading writers in the field of behavior modification, Sulzer-Azaroff, Thaw, and Olsen (1974) asked respondents to indicate the type of competency expected of four levels of helpers: behavior analyst, behavior technology coordinator, behavior technologist engineer, and behavior co-technician. The expectations were quite consistent for the highest level (behavior analyst) who was seen as a person who develops programs, research, and new methods. The lowest level (behavior co-technician) was not expected to have very specific competencies; most of his skills could be obtained in on-the-job training or in relatively few college courses. The behavior technology coordinator was described generally as a skilled person, at the pre-doctoral level, who could conduct helping programs in schools, institutions, and other facilities, but who was not expected to assume research and administrative roles. The survey clearly showed that persons at different training and skill levels might collaborate successfully in the helping effort.

Supervisors must have skills in evaluating the nature and scope of a person's problems. They must understand the social, biological, and economic context of the problem. They must be skilled in making decisions that would permit them to select among available helping techniques in order to construct a therapeutic program. They must know the methods by which progress in a program can be monitored and under what conditions the helping program can be changed. Finally, they must know the limitations of both their own skills and those of their helpers and they must have knowledge of resources that can be called upon when the problem falls beyond the limits of their own competence or the resources of their agencies. In this sense, a pyramid operation can be developed with a supervisor or consultant whose role is greatest at the beginning of treatment, who can monitor progress of treatment, and who can offer to the paraprofessional any supervision and advice needed. This concept, developing a team of helpers varying in skill and competence, is also useful because it permits the delivery of psychological services to large numbers of people who previously could not have afforded expensive individual psychotherapy. Thus, qualifications for offering psychological help differ for different levels of helpers. While it is possible for a person to carry out a well planned and structured change program under supervision after only a few weeks of training, the total management of a client requires consultation or supervision by a person with thorough familiarity of psychological principles, clinical methods, and an awareness of the limitations of his and others' skills.

A totally different qualification for a helper concerns his personal characteristics. As already indicated, and later discussed in detail in a following section on ethics, it is essential that the helper be motivated primarily by the goal of helping his client rather than furthering his own interest. In addition, the helper must be able to discern cues about the impact of his own behavior on his client. Which other particular helper characteristics are desirable has been the subject of research and theory for many years. They seem to include, at minimum, helper empathy, warmth, honesty, and expertness. These and other apparently desirable helper characteristics are examined in depth in Chapters 2 and 3.

Although the helping methods described in the following chapters have been tested and validated to some extent, it cannot be stressed too often that the methods themselves do not guarantee success. It is both the skillful *application* (i.e., the judgment of when to apply what methods to which clients) and knowledge about when to *change* a technique or an objective that is essential for successful helping programs. Most of the techniques described in the following chapters are not tied to specific client problems. Thus, they can be used in ameliorating a wide variety of personal, social, sexual, or other problems. When skillfully applied, they are likely to bring about beneficial changes in the client's behavior. But mere acquaintance with a catalog of available therapeutic techniques is insufficient preparation for competent psychological helping.

The problems and dangers of use of psychological helping techniques by persons without proper qualifications are legion. For example, operant techniques applied to continuing physical complaints may reduce the frequency of the complaints. However, such a change may also mask the inroads of a serious medical illness. Increasing assertiveness or feelings of independence in one marriage partner may indeed change the partner's behavior. However, without a thorough assessment and appreciation of the interpersonal context of the problem, an unskilled therapist may also find himself contributing to increasing problems between marriage partners, and perhaps divorce or abandonment by a partner. Treatment for homosexual behavior, even though the client wishes to change his sexual orientation, might fail simply because the client may not have a sufficiently strong repertoire of heterosexual behaviors to explore new sexual directions, or to achieve sufficient success in sexual and nonsexual activities that can take the place of his previous pleasurable experiences. The helper, therefore, must have full awareness of the range of factors that go into designing a treatment program, be aware of his own limitations, and work closely with others who can provide the necessary guidance. Premature, clumsy, or ignorant application of behavior change techniques may be wasteful and inefficient at best, and harmful at worst.

Summarizing our discussion on the necessary qualifications of the helper, it should be clear that the paraprofessional, including students, human service aides, mental health technicians, attendants, nurses, and many other persons without prolonged professional training in psychological services can make major contributions to helping people change. In fact, they are often the persons who can put a conceptual program into actual operation best. In many settings, a paraprofessional worker spends more time with a client than any professional and has, by far, more influence in his extensive contact with the client than a senior professional might have in the short time of a diagnostic or therapeutic interview. However, execution and not design is the task of the paraprofessional. Continuous self-monitoring and feedback to a consultant or supervisor are necessary to maintain the efficiency of the program and to protect the client.

WHAT IS A PSYCHOLOGICAL PROBLEM?

Psychological problems, in general terms, are difficulties in a person's relations with others, in his perception of the world about him or in his attitudes toward himself. Psychological problems can be characterized by a person's feelings of anxiety or tension, dissatisfaction with his own behavior, excessive attention to the problem area, inefficiency in reaching his desired goals, or inability to function effectively in psychological areas. Psychological problems may at times also be characterized by the fact that while the client himself has no complaint, others in his social environment are adversely affected by his behavior or judge him to be ineffective, destructive, unhappy, disruptive, or in some other way acting contrary to his best self-interest or the best interest of the social community in which he lives. Thus the major characteristics of a psychological problem may include: (1) The client suffers subjective discomfort, worry, or fears that are not easily removable by some action that he can perform without assistance; (2) The client shows a behavioral deficiency or excessively engages in some behavior that interferes with functioning described as adequate either by himself or by others; (3) The client engages in activities which are objectionable to those around him and which lead to negative consequences either for himself or for others; and (4) The client shows behavioral deviations that result in severe social sanctions by those in his immediate environment.

Psychological problems sometimes are related to problems in other areas. For example, an automobile accident may cause physical disability which in turn leads to psychological difficulties. A person who has lost his job, his marital partner, or his savings may temporarily face psychological difficulties. Socio-political climates such as discriminatory practices against a minority member, economic problems, sexual, moral, or religious demands by the environment that are inconsistent with the person's past history, all may cause psychological problems. Very frequently, transient psychological problems can be resolved not by psychological helpers but by resolution of the "source" problem. For example, concern about a medical disability or serious illness is better treated, if treatable, by medical care than by psychological help. Unhappiness over loss of a job may be more easily remedied by finding a new job than by resolving psychological problems about the loss. It is incumbent upon the psychological helper, therefore, to analyze the total problem to determine if dealing successfully with at least some aspects of it can be more effectively carried out by somebody who is not a psychological helper, while those components which comprise the person's attitudes, behaviors, or interactions remain the proper domain for mental health helpers.

THE GOALS AND OBJECTIVES OF HELPING RELATIONSHIPS

A good treatment program is built with a clear conception of treatment goals, hopefully developed jointly by the helper and the client. It is possible to differentiate among five long-term treatment objectives: (1) Change of a particular problem behavior, such as poor interpersonal skills; (2) Insight or a clear rational and emotional understanding of one's problems; (3) Change in a person's subjective emotional comfort, including changes in anxiety or tension; (4) Change in one's self-perceptions, including goals, self-confidence, and sense of adequacy; and (5) Change in the person's lifestyle or "personality restructuring," an objective aimed at a sweeping change in the client's way of living. The selection of any one of these goals does not eliminate the secondary achievement of other objectives. For example, while many of the techniques described in this book are oriented toward change of particular behaviors, such changes often bring with them changes in the person's insights into his own actions, modification of his attitudes toward himself, and in some cases, a rather sweeping alteration of the person's total lifestyle. At the same time, therapists who aim for improved insight and major personality changes in their clients may also achieve, during the helping process, change in social behaviors or self-reactions. Thus, treatment objectives are not mutually exclusive and the listing above is simply intended to indicate that primary emphasis can be given to a particular goal, without sacrificing the achievement of others as by-products or secondary outcomes of the change process.

Behavior Change

If the goal of a helping effort is to change a particular behavior, a thorough evaluation of the person's life circumstances is required in order to be sure not only that the target behavior is amenable to change, but also that such a change will lead to a significant improvement in the person's total life situation. A more detailed description of the steps necessary prior to beginning the change program is given below in our discussion of the diagnostic process.

Insight

Insight as a goal has been most characteristic of psychoanalysis and its variations. These helping methods are not covered in the present volume, first because the assumptions underlying psychoanalytic therapy are extensive, and thorough training of therapists in psychoanalytic methods, including personal analysis and long supervision of cases, is usually required. Secondly, the therapeutic benefits of psychoanalytic and other insight seeking methods are currently not well substantiated by empirical research and laboratory findings. They are excessively time consuming and, in our view, rarely represent the treatment of choice. The arguments in the psychological and psychiatric literature concerning the utility of insight versus behavior change, however, have sometimes been overstated. When a motivated client establishes a relationship between his current behavior problems and his past history, whether or not such a relationship is in fact accurate, the satisfaction of having achieved an explanation for his own behavior, and the new labels he can then attach to his emotional experiences, may serve as a beginning for change in his actual daily behaviors.

Emotional Relief

The reduction of anxiety has long been considered as the most critical problem in the management of neurotic disorders.* In general, when anxiety reduction or relief of chronic emotional tension is the primary objective of a helping effort, it is assumed that the client will later be able to conduct himself more effectively because: (1) he already has in his repertoire the skills necessary to deal with life situations; and (2) his use of these skills was previously inhibited by anxiety. If this is not the case (i.e., if the problem involves not only inhibition due to anxiety, but

---

*The techniques for reduction of anxiety are described in Chapter 8 of this volume.

also incompetence due to skill deficiency), changes in particular skill behaviors might be set up as the next goal in the change program. If the problem is both partly emotional and partly related to particular behavior deficiencies, then both the reduction of emotional tension and behavioral skill training may be dual treatment objectives.

Change in the Client's Self-Perception

Techniques for changing a person's self-perceptions and evaluations of his own behavior are found in several chapters in this volume. In general, the application of such procedures assumes that a person's improved self-image is sufficient to help him perform the constructive behaviors of which he is capable. For example, once a person sees himself as competent or perceives himself more realistically in relation to others, he may be able to plan and act with greater self-confidence, a greater sense of direction, and greater social effectiveness.

Lifestyle Changes

The most ambitious objective for a change program is the attempt to alter the person's total pattern of living. Frequently, this requires not only a change in the client's behavior, but also plans for changing the environment in which he lives, his circle of friends, his place of employment, and so forth. One example might be the client who is a drug addict and whose entire daily routine is subordinated to the procurement of an illegal narcotic.

DESIGNING A CHANGE PROGRAM

This volume is not intended to provide the helper with in-depth knowledge about diagnostic methods for analyzing the client's problem and designing a treatment program on the basis of this assessment. Nevertheless, the reader should be aware of the importance of an early analysis of the problem as the absolutely essential foundation for the application of any treatment technique. At this time there are few widely accepted principles that can guide a helper through the evaluation and assessment process. There are several books and articles that summarize available psychological tests; some also discuss the most critical features of the person's life situation that should be examined before a decision is made concerning an objective and its associated treatment technique (e.g., Goldfried and Pomeranz, 1968; Gottman and Leiblum, 1974; Kanfer and Saslow, 1969; Lanyon and Goodstein, 1971). As a minimum requirement for deciding upon the choice of helping methods, the helper must make a thorough analysis of the context in which the problem behavior occurs, the form and severity of the problem behavior, the consequences both to the client and to his environment of the problem behavior, the resources of the client and of his environment for the promotion of change, and the effects which a change in his behavior would have on the client and others. These and other factors comprise the content of what has been called a *functional analysis* of the problem situation. The information necessary to complete such an analysis may come from interviews, from observations, from knowledge of the client's past history, from reports of other persons who know the client, or from any other source that yields reliable information. In some cases, especially when the problem behavior has some physiological components, information about the medical status and physical health of the client is absolutely necessary.

A good functional analysis reveals factors that have contributed to the problem behavior and those that currently maintain it. It also gives some information about what particular stresses and demands are placed upon the client by the environment in which he lives. For example, for a complete assessment it is not sufficient to know what a person does and what effects his actions have. It is also necessary to have an understanding of what requirements are placed upon him by his immediate circle of friends, his job situation, his community, and by persons who are important in his life. Further, a good functional analysis also yields a list of problematic behaviors that may require attention and information that would assist the helper to set priorities so that he can better decide which particular problem(s) to attack. Which items are placed high on the priority list would depend on the individual's life circumstances and his initial responses to the change program. For example, any behavior that is self-destructive or has serious social consequences would be the most central initial target. However, in some cases, several problems may have equal priority. In this instance, a decision might rest on which of these problem behaviors are more amenable to solution by the available techniques. The client's conviction that he can change, and the degree of support from other persons in his environment to assist in the change program, must also be taken into account.

Another important aspect of the assessment procedure lies in the establishment of some methods and criteria for assessing the client's progress throughout the program. For example, the operant behavior change methods described in Chapter 7 are usually applied in conjunction with quantitative records of the frequency, intensity, or duration of the behavior being changed before, during, and after the change program. With other techniques, the evaluation component is not so readily built into the treatment program. For example, relationship methods, group techniques, and attitude change methods often aim to alter more complex behavior patterns and typically do not incorporate a quantitative measurement or monitoring process into the treatment. Nevertheless, the helper should have some record of the patient's problem behaviors, complaints and expectations prior to the onset of any change program. It is only with such documentation that helper and client can decide whether the change program has been effective, and further decisions about shifting to other objectives or terminating the relationship can be made. The evaluation component of the treatment program is of importance not only for assisting the helper and client in making decisions about progress and termination. It also serves as an incentive for both client and helper by giving them some objective evidence of the progress that has been achieved, and it enables the helper to specify more clearly the areas in which the program may have failed, and the reasons for this failure.

ETHICAL CONSIDERATIONS

A helper makes a number of demands on his clients. He expects them to be frank in discussing their problems, to be involved in the change program, and to commit themselves to certain requirements of the program such as keeping appointments, paying bills, and carrying out contracted exercises or activities. Because of the very nature of the helping relationship, it is quite obvious that the client's interests must be protected to avoid damage or grief resulting from a helper's ignorance, his unscrupulousness, his self-serving manipulation of the client, or his exploitation of the client's vulnerability.

The use of the helping techniques described in this book should be restricted to situations in which a person *seeks* help from others in a formal way. Thus, the change techniques should not be applied in informal settings in which a person is unaware of the fact that attempts are being made to change his behavior; they should not be applied casually in personal relationships with friends or family members; they should not be applied when a client denies the existence of a problem even though it has been pointed out to him by others. In the latter case, more complex treatment programs would have to be used, even though the change techniques presented here may ultimately comprise part of the total treatment package.

In our discussion of professional qualifications, we pointed to the importance of the helper's training and background for the protection of the client. In this section we will consider a series of ethical considerations that a helper must abide by if he is to be helpful to the client and be accepted by the community in which he practices. On some of the matters which follow, there is debate concerning the breadth of action open to the helper. Therefore, the following items range in importance from those for which a breech of ethics may lead to expulsion from professional societies to those items which are primarily a matter of individual conscience.

Exploitation by the Helper

There is no disagreement concerning the absolute requirement that the helper must not utilize the relationship in order to gain social, sexual, or other personal advantage. The self-serving functions of a helper, however, may extend from the slight extension of a treatment program beyond its absolutely necessary limits, in order to provide a helper with financial resources, to the flagrant financial, moral, or sexual exploitation of a client. The helper has access to confidential information that may embarrass or hurt the client. Even subtle pressure implying the use of such information for self-serving purposes is equivalent to blackmail and is clearly unethical.

Deception

The purposes and goals of the interaction should be clear to the client or his guardian. For example, it is improper to discuss the achievements or objectives of a change program with a third party, be it a marital partner, a parent, or an employer, without communicating such intentions to the client himself. Similarly, advice and guidance which would force the client into a situation over which he has no control would constitute unethical behavior. Advice to engage in illegal behaviors, or suggestions of actions that would expose the client to hazards or predictable untoward consequences are examples of deceptive helper maneuvers.

Competence and Appropriate Treatment

It is the responsibility of the helper not only to offer the highest level of service, but also to be aware of his own limitations so that he can refer the client to someone else when necessary. In addition to referrals to others in the mental health field, it is also the helper's responsibility to be certain that problems outside the area of psychological treatment be properly referred. For example, referral to a physician for medical difficulties, to an attorney for legal problems, or to a social service agency for economic assistance should be made when these problems are evident or likely. Since the helper sometimes may not be fully aware of the limitations in his own training, it is advisable for a helper to have some professional affiliation that will enable him to obtain assistance from colleagues regarding difficult cases. Persons who have paraprofessional training should discuss such problems with their supervisor under whose direction the change program is conducted.

Principle of Least Intervention

While it is obvious that almost any person might benefit from psychological counseling or a helping relationship, it is essentially the task of the helper to intervene in the client's everyday life only to the extent that the client desires a change. Once the jointly agreed upon objective is reached, the helper should either terminate the relationship or discuss in detail with the client the possibility of future change programs. Only if the client agrees to additional programs should they be undertaken. A prior problem concerns the question of whether any treatment should take place at all. In some instances, clients will seek assistance for problems that actually turn out to be common difficulties in everyday life. In such cases, for example, when a client is experiencing a grief reaction after the death of a close relative, information and reassurance may be sufficient. Similarly, parents may refer their children for assistance when, in fact, the child's behavior is not unusual for his age group. In such instances, behavior change programs would not be undertaken and it may be possible to terminate the interaction when reassurance and information are given to the client.

Some techniques of behavior change, especially those that rest heavily on the alteration of the client's social environment (discussed in Chapter 7), may involve the participation of other persons in channeling the client's behavior in a desired direction through the use of rewards and punishments. Programs in institutions such as hospitals, schools, or prisons may involve deprivation of certain privileges in order that they may be used later as rewards for appropriate behaviors. There is intense dispute concerning the appropriateness of such techniques because of their nonvolitional and manipulative aspects. As a result, special caution must be exercised to assure that the client's civil rights are not infringed upon and that the client can make the kind of choices about participating in a program that would normally be considered reasonable in the institutional setting in which they are introduced. The utilization of aversive stimuli is especially questionable when the client's permission is not obtained. Ethical problems associated with this method are discussed in detail in Chapter 9.

In general, the helper needs to assure himself continuously that he is maintaining the dignity of his client, that he is guarding the confidentiality of information obtained in the helping relationship, and that his therapeutic program does not have detrimental effects either on the client or on others. It is the helper's responsibility to protect the client's rights and interests so that the change program clearly contributes to the client's welfare, rather than creates new problems and conflicts for him.

WHAT IS CONTAINED IN THE FOLLOWING CHAPTERS?

The chapters in this book provide detailed descriptions of different behavior change techniques by professionals who are expert in their respective fields. The techniques are generally appropriate for treatment of persons who show no gross social disorganization or such serious disturbances in their social or personal behavior that they require institutionalization. The techniques are, therefore, most applicable to persons who have difficulties in some areas of their life but who can function at least marginally well in other areas. The techniques presented here are by no means exhaustive of the field of behavior change. They do constitute the most important methods that have been applied in the treatment of psychological problems. In selecting treatment approaches and techniques, we have chosen only those which are based on psychological theory that is widely accepted, and which have as their foundation at least some laboratory research and evidence of effectiveness in application. Many of the methods mentioned here are quite new or still in the exploratory stage. However, we have eliminated from presentation a large number of methods now practiced that are based only on the belief of the practitioner that they are effective but which have no other empirical evidence or theoretical rationale behind them. Anecdotal observation or limited clinical experience that has not been substantiated by research or field studies is insufficient grounds for use of a method. We have eliminated techniques which clients have reported have made them feel better, unless some independent evidence of change is also available. All of the methods that are discussed in the following chapters have been described at considerable length in the professional literature. The reader will find references at the end of each chapter that will guide him to additional reading in order to strengthen his knowledge of each technique and, consistent with the ultimate goal of this book, more fully aid the helper in helping people change.

REFERENCES

Goldfried, N. R. and Pomeranz, D. M. The role of assessment in behavior therapy. *Psychological Reports*, 1968, **23**, 75–87.

Gottman, J. M. and Leiblum, S. R. *How to do psychotherapy and how to evaluate it: A manual for beginners.* New York: Holt, Rinehart and Winston, 1974.

Kanfer, F. H. and Saslow, G. Behavioral diagnosis. In C. Franks (Ed.), *Behavior therapy: Appraisal and status.* New York: McGraw-Hill, 1969.

Lanyon, R. I. and Goodstein, L. D. *Personality assessment.* New York: Wiley, 1971.

Sulzer-Azaroff, B., Thaw, J., and Olsen, C. Behavioral competencies for the evaluation of behavior modifiers. Unpublished mimeo, University of Massachusetts, Mansfield Training School, 1974.

CHAPTER 2

Relationship-Enhancement Methods

ARNOLD P. GOLDSTEIN

Barbara Harris is a 34-year-old woman, a wife, mother of two children, part time office receptionist and, every Tuesday at 10:00 A.M., a psychotherapy patient. Over the course of the past few years, Barbara had developed a number of concerns which more and more were interfering with her comfort and happiness. Backaches and a series of vague physical symptoms which seemed hard to cure were the apparent beginning of her change from a relatively problem-free and fully functioning person. Conflicts with her husband began around this time—about money, about sex, and about raising their children. Barbara's physical discomfort, her irritability, and her difficulty in getting along with people all increased as time passed. Eventually, these concerns and behaviors became so troublesome to Barbara and those around her that she contacted a psychotherapist recommended by her physician. She has been meeting with him for about a year now, and both feel she has made substantial progress in dealing effectively with her problems. Her physical complaints have decreased markedly, her relations with others are considerably more satisfying and, in general, Barbara seems well on her way to joining the two-thirds of all psychotherapy patients who apparently benefit from treatment.

In the same city in which Barbara lives there are four other women who have gone through similar difficulties and similar recovery from these difficulties. Yet none of them has ever met with a psychotherapist. What did they do? Pressed by the stress each was experiencing, each sought out a "good listener" or a "friendly problem-solver" with whom she felt she could share her burdens. For one, it was a friend; for the second, her minister; for the third, her family physician; and for the last, a "paraprofessional" helper called a "home aide." All five women changed for the better, apparently in large part because of whatever occurred between each and her helper. Barbara's recovery may or may not have been somewhat more complete, or somewhat more rapid but, for our present purposes, the significant fact is that all women improved.

These mini-case histories are fictitious, but the facts they portray are well established. Many people do find problem-relief, personal growth, and self-understanding as a result of participating in some form of psychotherapy. But many people obtain similar benefits as a result of their interactions with a wide variety of other types of helpers—friends, clergymen, bartenders, relatives, counselors, nurses, and so forth. These facts have long intrigued researchers interested in what it is that causes people to change their behavior, emotions, and attitudes. Perhaps, many of these researchers have proposed, some of the causes of such changes can be identified by determining what ingredients successful psychotherapy and successful help from others have in common. If certain procedures, circumstances, or events are clearly characteristic of successful helping of different kinds, then we have the opportunity to use them most effectively in helping others.

Dr. Jerome Frank, in his important book, *Persuasion and Healing* (1961), has made a similar point. He compared psychotherapy, "informal" psychotherapy (from a friend, clergyman, etc.), faith healing, religious revivalism, placebo effects in medical practice, and a host of other activities in which two people, a helper and a client, collaborate to bring about some sort of psychological change in the client. According to Frank, perhaps the major responsible ingredient in determining whether such change occurs is the quality of the helper-client relationship. The same conclusion emerges if one examines descriptions of almost all of the many different approaches to formal psychotherapy. These several approaches vary in many respects—therapist activity and directiveness, how much the focus is upon behavior versus the patient's inner world of feelings and attitudes, whether emphasis is placed upon the patient's present life or his childhood history, which aspects of his current difficulties are examined, and in a host of procedural ways. Yet, almost every approach to psychotherapy emphasizes the importance of the therapist-patient relationship for patient change. The better the relationship: (1) the more open is the patient about this feeling, (2) the more likely he is to explore these feelings deeply with the helper, and (3) the more likely he is to listen fully to and act upon advice offered him by the helper. That is, the more likely the patient is to change.

This remarkably consistent viewpoint, in the psychotherapies and in other approaches to psychological change, has found consistent support in other fields also. How well a variety of medications serve their intended purpose has been shown to be partly a result of the relationship between the drug giver and the drug receiver. Learning in school has been demonstrated to depend in part on the teacher-pupil relationship. The subject's behavior in the experimental laboratory may also be readily influenced by the experimenter-subject relationship. In brief, there now exists a wide variety of research evidence, from several different types of two-person interactions, to indicate that the quality of the helper-client relationship can serve as a powerful positive influence upon communication, openness, persuasibility and, ultimately, positive change in the client. This evidence is also useful in providing information which helps define the term "relationship." Our definition, it will be noted, places emphasis upon positive feelings and interpersonal attitudes reciprocally held by the helper and client: a positive or "therapeutic" relationship may be defined as feelings of liking, respect, and trust by a client toward the helper from whom he is seeking assistance, combined with similar feelings of liking, respect, and trust on the part of the helper toward the client.

A number of methods have been identified as ways of making the helper-client relationship a more positive one. Each of these relationship-enhancement methods has been the subject of considerable research. Each has added to both our understanding of what relationship is and helped explain the usefulness of the relationship for helping people change. These several methods, therefore, form the framework for the remainder of this chapter. We will, in turn, consider several concrete examples of each method, focusing upon how the relationship may be enhanced or improved to the benefit of client change. Figure 2.1 provides an overview of our viewpoint.

Relationship Enhancers	Relationship Components	Relationship Consequences	Outcome
Client structuring Client imitation Client conformity Helper expertness Helper empathy Helper warmth Helper–client matching Helper–client physical closeness and posture	Liking Respect Trust	Communication Openness Persuasibility	Client change

Fig. 2.1. Progression from relationship enhancement to client change.

The relationship enhancers listed above are the major means currently available for improving the quality of the helper-client interaction. This interaction or relationship may be defined in terms of the three components indicated: liking, respect, and trust. Successful enhancement of these components, in turn, has been shown to lead to greater influenceability and, subsequently, to greater client change. It should be noted that most psychotherapists and psychotherapy researchers view a positive relationship between helper and client as necessary, but not sufficient for client change. Without such a relationship, change is very unlikely. With it, the foundation exists for other more specific change procedures (such as those described in subsequent chapters) to yield their intended effects.

ATTRACTION

Laboratory research has developed several procedures for successfully increasing attraction of the experiment's subjects to their experimenter. The present writer (Goldstein, 1971) has shown that many of these attraction-increasing procedures are highly effective in enhancing the helper-client relationship, especially the client's liking of his helper. Three such procedures: structuring, imitation, and conformity pressure are presented below.

Structuring

It is perhaps fitting, in this book in which several dozen procedures for helping people change will be described, that the first procedure to be illustrated is probably one of the least complex. Structuring a client so that he will like or be attracted to his helper is, quite simply, a matter of: (1) telling him that he will like his helper ("direct" structuring), (2) briefly describing to him certain positive characteristics of his helper ("trait" structuring), or (3) clarifying what he may realistically anticipate will go on in his meetings with the helper (role expectancy structuring). Each of these three structuring procedures seeks to mold the client's expectations and feelings about his relationship with his helper. In one of the first uses of direct structuring to strengthen client attraction to the helper, new clients at a Counseling Center were first given certain tests which asked for information about the kind of helper they would prefer to meet with—his behavior, his expectations, his goals, etc. Shortly after this testing, clients were told by the tester:

> We have carefully examined the tests you took in order to assign you to a therapist whom you would like to work with most. We usually can't match a patient and therapist the way they want most, but for you we have almost exactly the kind of therapist you described. (The tester then showed the client how well his test results describing his preferred helper apparently matched other information purportedly indicating the actual behavior, expectations and goals of the helper with whom he would be meeting.) As a matter of fact, the matching of the kind of person you wanted to work with and the kind of person Mr. _____ is, is so close that it hardly ever happens. What's even more, he has often described the kind of patient he likes to work with most as someone just like you in many respects. You two should get along extremely well. (Goldstein, 1971, p. 21.)

It should be noted that no actual matching of client preferences with helper characteristics was done here. Clients participated in the structuring procedure we have just described, and then each was assigned to a therapist whose turn it was for a new patient. Nevertheless, such structuring led the client to actually show increased liking of their helpers and increased openness about their problems. Thus, the client's belief that the helper would be a person they would like was enough to influence their actual attraction toward him.

The enhancing effect on both attraction and openness has been shown to be even stronger when trait structuring of the client is conducted. These are instances in which specific, important qualities of the helper are described to the client before they actually meet. Once again, the effect of these procedures on the actual attraction which develops is quite strong even though the helper characteristics described may in fact not be present. Which particular helper characteristics are selected to be described to the client is an important matter. In most uses of trait structuring, the two helper traits chosen have been his "warmth" and his "experience"—the first of which tells the client something important about how comfortable he is likely to feel during the helping process, the second gives him information about the likely positive outcome of this process. Both items of information, therefore, enhance client attraction to the helper. The statement which follows is an example of trait structuring of helper warmth and experience:

> The therapist has been engaged in the practice of therapy for over 20 years and has lectured and taught at some of the country's leading universities and medical schools. Questionnaires submitted to the therapist's colleagues seem to reveal that he is a rather warm person, industrious, critical, practical and determined. (Goldstein, 1971, p. 50.)

Trait structuring has also been used successfully "in reverse" to increase helper attraction toward the client. Here, qualities of the client are emphasized which lead the helper to anticipate that the client will be "a good patient." The type of problem the client supposedly has, his diagnosis, and his motivation to work hard to improve are some examples of positively structured traits of the client which have been communicated to the helper.

A great deal of psychological research has been conducted on the effects of leading a person to believe he is similar to a stranger in important attitudes, background, or values and on his liking that person when they meet. This research convincingly shows that the greater the structured similarity, the greater the attraction to the other person. This positive effect of structured similarity on attraction has also been found to operate in the helper-client relationship. It is largely for this reason that great use has been made in recent years of certain types of "paraprofessional" helpers, that is, persons who may be lacking in certain formal training or degrees but who possess beliefs, a personal background, and a life style quite similar to that of the persons they are seeking to help. These similarities between paraprofessional helpers and the people they serve, like "structured similarity," enhance the quality of the therapeutic relationship.

We have seen thus far that direct structuring, and trait structuring for warmth, experience, and similarity each can have attraction-increasing effects. So, too, can the final type of structuring we wish to present—role expectancy structuring. Whereas direct and trait structuring mostly concern telling the client something about the kind of person his helper *is*, role expectancy structuring focuses on what the helper (and what the client himself) actually will *do* when they meet. If, because of misinformation or lack of information about what to expect, the client later experiences events during his meetings with the helper which surprise or confuse him, negative feelings will result. Events which confirm his expectancies will serve to increase his attraction to the helper. For example, many new psychotherapy patients come to therapy with expectations based primarily on their past experiences in what they judge to be similar relationships, such as what happens when they meet with their medical doctor. During those visits, the patient typically presented his physical problem briefly, was asked a series of questions by his physician, and then authoritatively told what to do. Now, however, when the client with such "medical expectations" starts psychotherapy, he is in for some surprises. The client describes his psychological problem, and sits back awaiting the helper's questions and eventual advice. The helper, unlike the general physician, wants the client to explore his feelings, to examine his history, to speculate about the causes for his problems. These are not the client's role expectations, and when such important expectations differ, the relationship clearly suffers. These are but a few of the several ways in which client and helper may differ in their anticipations of how each will behave. Prior structuring of such expectations has been shown to be an important contributor to increased attraction and a more lasting and fruitful helper-client relationship. This structuring may be provided by having new clients listen to a tape recording of a typical helper-client meeting. More commonly, role expectancy structuring has been accomplished by providing the client with a structuring interview (also called an "anticipatory socialization interview" or a "role induction interview") before his first meeting with his helper. The following is an excerpt from such an interview in which a helper explains to his prospective client what he can expect to occur in psychotherapy:

> Now, what is therapy about? What is going on? Well, for one thing, I have been talking a great deal; in treatment your doctor won't talk very much. The reason I am talking now is that I want to explain these things to you. There is equally good reason that the doctor in treatment does not say much. Everyone expects to tell the psychiatrist about his problem and then have him give advice which will solve everything just like that. This isn't true; it just doesn't work like that. . . . Before you came here you got advice from all kinds of people. . . . If all of the advice you have received had helped, odds are that you wouldn't be here. Your doctor wants to help you to figure out what you really want to do—what the best solution is for you. It's his job not to give advice but to help you find out for yourself how you are going to solve your problem.
>
> Now, what goes on in treatment itself? What is it that you talk about? What is it that you do? How does it work? Well, for one thing, you will talk about your wishes, both now and in the past . . . You will find that with your doctor you will be able to talk about anything that comes to your mind. He won't have any preconceived notions about what is right or what is wrong for you or what the best solution would be. Talking is very important because he wants to help you get at what you really want . . . The doctor's job is to help *you* make the decision . . . most of us are not honest with ourselves. We try to kid ourselves, and it's your doctor's job to make you aware of when you are kidding yourself. He is not going to try to tell you what he thinks but he will point out to you how two things you are saying just don't fit together.
>
> . . . the patient . . . sometimes feels worse and discouraged at some stages of treatment. You know, you'll feel you're not getting anywhere, your doctor is a fool, and there's no point in this, and so on. These very feelings are often good indications that you are working and that it's uncomfortable. It is very important that you don't give in to these temporary feelings when they come up.
>
> . . . say whatever comes to your mind, even if you think it is trivial or unimportant. It doesn't matter. It is still important to say it. And if you think it is going to bother your doctor, that doesn't matter either; you still say it.
>
> So, just like the [keeping of] appointments, we make an absolute rule not to think ahead about what you'll say and therefore protect yourself from facing important things. Say whatever is on the top of your mind, no matter what.*

We may note then, in summary of our presentation thus far, that structuring can lead to increased attraction by the client toward his helper whether such structuring is a simple matter of a straightforward statement of probable liking (direct structuring), a description of certain of the helper's positive qualities or of helper-client similarity (trait structuring), or an explanation of the events and behaviors one should expect in the relationship (role expectancy structuring). Whether a given structuring statement of any of these kinds actually does increase client attraction will depend in part on matters other than the structuring itself. These statements will tend to be most effective when the person doing the structuring is perceived as trustworthy, and when the client is experiencing distress or discomfort from his problems.

---

*From Orne, M. T. and Wender, P. H. Anticipatory socialization for psychotherapy. *American Journal of Psychiatry*, Vol. 124, 1968, pp. 1202–1212. Copyright © 1968 the American Psychiatric Association.

Imitation

As we have just described, attempts to increase client attraction by structuring typically rely on statements about the helper presented to the client. A second approach to attraction-enhancement, i.e., to the liking component of the helper-client relationship, has relied on different procedures, those based on research concerned with imitation. Essentially, increasing attraction to the helper through imitation involves exposing the client to a person (the "model") who plays the part of a client who likes the helper and clearly says so. This approach is also called modeling or observational learning. In the typical use of imitation, an audiotape or videotape of the attracted model client is played to the real client. The content of such tapes is usually part of an actual or constructed counseling or psychotherapy session between the model and the helper. The client simply listens to or observes the tape(s) and then later meets with the helper himself. The following is an excerpt from such an attraction-imitation tape, a tape which in its entirety contained a dozen such high attraction statements by the model client:

> How would I like my parents to be different? Well, I think mostly in the fact that they could've cared more, that they could have showed it, you know, been warmer and not so cold. That's mainly it ... You know, I guess I said this before, but *even though all you've been doing the past 5 or 10 minutes is asking me questions, I still for some reason or another feel comfortable talking to you and being honest about myself. I feel that you're warm and that you care*. (Goldstein, 1973, p. 216.)

As suggested in our discussion of structuring, a change-enhancing relationship involves *both* client attraction toward the helper, and helper attraction toward the client. The more reciprocal or mutual the positive feelings, the more likely is progress toward rapid client change. For this reason, imitation has also been used to increase helper attraction to the client. The following transcript is part of a modeling tape designed for this purpose, a tape used successfully with helpers of several kinds. Each statement in italics depicts a model helper expressing attraction, liking, or positive evaluation toward a client, i.e., expressing the behaviors we were training the listening helpers to imitate.

Therapist: Since this is our first interview, I'll be asking you about a number of different areas of your life. Why don't we start off by your telling me about your family?

Patient: My family. Well, you know sometimes—sometimes I think my family could do—just as well without me. You know. Like I'm a—a useless sort of object that sort of sits around the house. When I—come home from work it's like—like there's nothing there.

Therapist: You don't feel that your family looks forward to your coming home at night?

Patient: Sometimes it—sometimes it seems that they don't even know when I'm home. Kids'll be running around and—my wife—well sometimes the way she acts it would be better if I just stayed out. Some of the things that she gets into—MMMMMMMMMM.

Therapist: *I'm not clear why your wife would act that way. I find you a rather easy person to talk with. . . . What kind of things does your wife get into?*

Patient: —I don't know. She's always yelling and screaming—wants me to do things when I come inside—always telling me I have this to do and that to do. She doesn't realize I just wanna come home and I wanna relax a little bit. Nah—I don't know how she can push me all the time—do this—do that—all the time.

Therapist: Sounds like marriage has been a lot of trouble for you.

Patient: —Yeah. Yeah—really it—it was different before. When we first got married it was—it was nice. We went out and saw different people, did . . . did some things together. Got along pretty good too. Didn't have all this that's going on now.

Therapist: *From our meeting so far, I'm finding it rather easy to get along with you too. . . . I guess things aren't going very well with your wife now.*

Patient: No—my wife changed. She got—she got different. Things started—you know—she started not to care about things. We couldn't go out as much. Then—then the babies came and then—wow—feeding them and taking care of them and doing all those things. Never had any time to do the things that we used to do together.—You know, it's usually hard for me to talk about things like this, but it's easy talking to you. Like—you know when I'd come home from work—my wife—she'd be running around the house after the kids—and when I'd come in the door I'd get ignored you know. No one says hello—no one asks you how you are.

Therapist: —Somehow all this seemed to happen around the time the children came?

Patient: It—seems that way. Before we had the kids we didn't have these problems. Now it—it's just not the same.

Therapist: What about your parents, did your father—drink?

Patient: Oh, yeah. He—could down them with the best of them. My old lady will tell you that. Yeah, he really knew how to drink. Used to get into some terrible fights with my old lady though. Boy—he'd come home—have a little too much in him—she'd really let him have it. I'd have to—pull the pillow up over my head so I wouldn't hear the noise. Couldn't get to sleep.

Therapist: Your mother was very hard on your father then.

Patient: Yeah. She really used to get mad at him. You know, for drinking and all that. She used to yell at him. Get on his back all the time. Really be nasty to him. Maybe that's one of the reasons why he's six feet under right now.

Therapist: Sort of like the same thing your wife is doing to you?

Patient: Yeah. You're right. You really hit the nail on the head. You really understand what's going on. There's a lot of things about the two that are kind of the same. I think she's trying to do the same thing to me that my mother did to my father.—Yell and fight—the yelling and carrying on. They'll both do it. Scream at you—and call you a drunk. Telling me I can't take on any responsibility. Always yelling about something. Money. Why don't you have more of it? Why can't we buy this? Why can't we buy that? I'm working—as hard as I can—and she does—she doesn't realize that. She thinks all I have to do is work—all the time. She thinks it's—it's easy for me to—to work every day.—Always pushing me. I don't like to be pushed. I get—I'll get things done. But I have to work—at my own pace, otherwise—it just doesn't matter if I work or not, if I can't work at my own pace.

Therapist: *You seem to be really trying to make your marriage work. I respect people who really try like that. . . . It sounds like your wife and you just—don't do things the same way.*

Patient: Yeah. She's in her own world.—She doesn't care about anything that I do—or say. She doesn't care about me or anyone else. Sometimes I just feel like getting up and leaving. There's nothing there any more.

Therapist: You'd like to just go away?

Patient: Mmhmm.

Therapist: Have you ever done this?

Patient: —Not for any long time. Used to—get away for a couple of days by myself. But I always ended up coming back because I had no one else to go to.

Therapist: *Well, now when you feel like that you can come see me . . . You don't like being alone.*

Thus, imitation is a second established path to attraction-enhancement. Yet matters are not quite this simple. Each of us observes many people every day, but most of what we observe we do not imitate. We see expensively produced and expertly acted modeling displays of people buying things on television commercials, but much more often than not we do not imitate. People imitate others only under certain circumstances. We tend to imitate others with whom we can identify, thus to encourage imitation the taped model should be the same sex and approximate age as the viewing client whose attraction we are seeking to increase. We are especially prone to imitate behavior we see leading to rewards which we too desire. Therefore, the most successful attraction-enhancing modeling tapes are those on which the attracted model is rewarded by having his problems resolved. Further, it is not by accident that television commercials so frequently involve extensive repetition (particularly of the product's name), since imitation often increases with the repetition of the modeling display. Finally, imitation will be more likely if the viewer is encouraged to rehearse or practice what he has seen. In short, repetitive watching of a rewarded model of the viewer's age and sex, and rehearsing the observed behaviors, will all increase the amount of imitation which occurs.

Conformity Pressure

People with problems often have problems with people. Clients often seek help in the first place because of their difficulty in getting along with others, and these difficulties may be reflected in *low* attraction (dislike, suspiciousness, ambivalence) toward the helper. Under such circumstances, trying to increase attraction by telling him (structuring) or showing him (imitation) appropriate materials may not work. More powerful procedures may be required. If so, conformity pressure is one such possibility. In the typical use of conformity pressure in the research laboratory, a group of individuals meet and each member in turn is required to make a judgment aloud—about which of two lines is longer, or whether a dot of light moved, or which social or political viewpoint is more correct, or some other matter of judgment. However, unknown to one member of the group, all the other members are actually accomplices of the group leader and are told in advance to respond to his requests for their judgments in a predetermined and usually unanimous or near-unanimous manner. In at least a third of the groups arranged in this manner, the non-accomplice member conforms to the majority judgment—even when it is (to the outsider) obviously incorrect. Research conducted by the present writer in counseling settings indicates that similar use of conformity pressure can indeed serve as a powerful attraction-enhancer. After hearing a taped session between a helper and client, three members (accomplices) of a group of four "clients" rated aloud the helper as attractive in a variety of ways. The real client conformed to this pressure and did likewise. Of greatest interest, in other groups different real clients also rated the taped helper as highly attractive after conformity pressure from accomplices even when the taped helper being rated was (again to outside observers) highly *un*attractive in several important respects.

HELPER EXPERTNESS AND STATUS

Our definition of relationship emphasized reciprocal liking, respect, and trust. Seeking to improve the relationship by focus upon attraction-enhancement is equivalent to emphasizing the liking component of this definition. Relationship may also be enhanced by procedures relevant to the respect component. A major means for enhancing client respect for his helper concerns the helper's real or apparent expertness and status. In general, we may assume that the greater the helper's expertness, the greater is the client's respect for him.

In psychotherapy, there is much about the psychotherapist, his behavior, and his physical surroundings which testifies to his apparent expertness and authority. Haley (1963) comments in this regard:

> The context of the relationship emphasizes the therapist's position .... Patients are usually referred to him by people who point out what a capable authority he is and how much the patient needs help. Some therapists have a waiting list, so that the patient is impressed by standing in line to be treated, while others may imply that patients with similar symptoms were successfully treated. Furthermore, the patient must be willing to pay money even to talk to the therapist, and the therapist can either treat him or dismiss him, and so controls whether or not there is going to be a relationship. Not only the therapist's prestige is emphasized in the initial meeting, but also the patient's inadequacy is made clear. The patient ... must emphasize his difficulties in life to a man who apparently has none. The physical settings in which most therapists function also reinforce their superior position. In many instances the therapist sits at a desk, the symbol of authority, while the patient sits in a chair, the position of the suppliant. In psychoanalytic therapy the arrangement is more extreme. The patient lies down while the therapist sits up. His chair is also placed so that he

can observe the patient's reactions, but the patient cannot observe him. Finally, the initial interview in therapy usually makes quite explicit the fact that the therapist is in charge of the relationship by the rules for treatment he lays down. He suggests the frequency of interviews, implies he will be the one who decides when treatment will end, and he usually instructs the patient how to behave in the office. He may make a general statement about how the patient is to express himself there, or he may provide specific instructions as in the analytic situation where the patient is told he must lie down and say whatever comes to mind. (pp. 71–73.)*

What else is there that distinguishes the expert helper from the inexpert? In our own research, as will be seen shortly, the level of apparent helper expertness was varied by altering the external trappings surrounding the helper—his title, books, office, diploma, etc. Research reported by Schmidt and Strong (1970) shows that clients also judge expertness to a large extent from the observable behavior of their helper. According to their results, college students describe the expert and the inexpert counselor quite differently:

The *expert* shakes the student's hand, aligning the student with himself, and greets him with his first name. He seems interested and relaxed. He has a neat appearance but is not stuffy . . ..He talks at the student's level and is not arrogant toward him. The expert assumes a comfortable but attentive sitting position. He focuses his attention on the student and carefully listens to him. He has a warm facial expression and is reactive to the student. His voice is inflective and lively, he changes his facial expressions, and uses hand gestures. He speaks fluently with confidence and sureness. The expert has prepared for the interview. He is informed as to why the student is there and is familiar with the student's test scores, grades, and background . . .. He asks direct and to-the-point questions. His questions are thought-provoking and follow an apparently logical progression. They seem spontaneous and conversational. The expert is willing to help determine if the student's decisions are right, but does not try to change the student's ideas forcefully. He lets the student do most of the talking and does not interrupt him. The expert moves quickly to the root of the problem. He points out contradictions in reasoning, and restates the student's statements as they bear on the problem . . .. He makes recommendations and suggests possible solutions.

The *inexpert* is awkward, tense, and uneasy. He seems to be afraid of the student. He does not greet the student by name to put him at ease . . .. He is not quite sure of himself or of some of his remarks. He seems too cold, strict and dominating, and too formal in attitude and action. His gestures are stiff and overdone . . .. The inexpert slouches in his chair. He is too casual and relaxed . . .. His voice is flat and without inflection, appearing to show disinterest and boredom . . .. The inexpert comes to the interview cold. He has not cared enough about the student to acquaint himself with the student's records. The inexpert asks vague questions which are trivial and irrelevant and have no common thread or aim. His questioning is abrupt and tactless with poor transitions. He asks too many questions like a quiz session, giving the student the third degree . . .. The inexpert is slow in getting his point across and is confusing in his discussion of what the student should do . . .. The inexpert does not get to the core of the problem . . .. He just doesn't seem to be getting anywhere. (p. 117.)†

These descriptions were then used by the investigators (Strong and Schmidt, 1970) as the script outline in a study examining the effects of status on a helper's influence. Counselors taking the role of expert and inexpert were thoroughly

---

*From Haley, J. *Strategies of Psychotherapy.* New York: Grune and Stratton, 1963, Reprinted by permission of Grune & Stratton, Inc. and the author.

†From Schmidt, L. D. and Strong, S. R. Expert and inexpert counselors. *Journal of Counseling Psychology,* 1970, **17**, 115–118. Copyright 1970 by the American Psychological Association. Reprinted by permission.

rehearsed in the behaviors described above. The former were introduced to clients with the statement:

> The person you will be talking with is Dr. _____, a psychologist who has had several years of experience interviewing students.

The inexpert helper was, contrastingly, introduced with the statement:

> We had originally scheduled Dr. _____ to talk with you but unfortunately he notified us that he wouldn't be able to make it today. In his place we have Mr. _____, a student, who unfortunately has had no interviewing experience and has been given only a brief explanation of the purpose of this study. I think he should work out allright, though. (Strong and Schmidt, 1970, p. 83.)

Analysis of the helper-client interviews which were then held revealed, as predicted, greater positive change in those clients structured and in fact seen by the "expert" helper.

It thus seems that the greater the change-agent's expertness, the greater his effectiveness in altering the behavior and beliefs of his target. Laboratory research strongly supports this contention. A substantial number of investigations confirm the fact that a statement is more fully accepted and acted upon when the recipient believes it comes from an expert or high status person, than when its apparent source is a person of low or unknown expertise.

The first evidence we obtained in support of the relationship aspect of this finding was obtained almost accidentally (Goldstein, 1971). We conducted a study whose purpose was to determine if client attraction to the helper would increase if the helper went out of his way to do a small favor or extend an extra courtesy to the client. The courtesy involved was offering the client coffee and a donut, not a usual event in counseling or psychotherapy. While this procedure did improve their relationship, attraction increased even more at those times when the helper made it clear that the coffee and donut he was calling for were for himself, and not for the client! We had not predicted this result, and only half-jokingly speculated that perhaps attraction increased because anyone behaving so boorishly must be an important person. That is, perhaps attraction increased here because, in the client's eyes, the helper had increased his status. We tested this notion more directly in our next investigation (Sabalis, 1969). Sabalis had four groups of clients, two of whom were seen by what appeared to be a high-status helper, two by a low-status helper. Not all persons, we predicted, are attracted to high-status persons. Authoritarian persons, those rigidly respectful of authority, seem to be highly responsive and attracted to such persons, whereas more equalitarian individuals are less drawn to experts and similar sources. Thus, in this study it was predicted that a high-status helper would increase the attraction-to-helper of high authoritarian clients, but not equalitarian clients.

The clients (of both kinds) in the high-status groups each received a postcard indicating the time of their interview. The interviewer was "Dr. Robert Sabalis." When each client arrived for his interview, the interviewer introduced himself as "Dr. Sabalis, a member of the faculty of the Psychology Department." A "Dr. Robert Sabalis" nameplate was on the interviewer's desk, and the office itself was a large, well-furnished one belonging to a faculty member. The interviewer was neatly dressed in a business suit. The session began with some test-taking by the client, which the interviewer described as tests on which he was doing research. As the client filled out the test forms, the interviewer opened a text and began to jot down notes from it, indicating to the client as he did that he was preparing an examination for one of the classes he taught.

For the low-status groups, the interviewer's name on the postcard and in his introduction upon meeting was "Bob Sabalis." He described himself to clients as a senior undergraduate psychology major who was meeting with them as a requirement for one of his own courses. His attire was consistent with the typical undergraduate's. The interview office was quite small and sparsely furnished. As the test-taking commenced, he began note-taking from a text again, but this time indicated he was preparing for an examination he had to take.

The predicted effect of status on attraction was obtained. That is, high authoritarian clients became significantly more attracted to the interviewer after the high-status, but not the low-status procedures.

As described above, Strong and Schmidt showed the positive effect of expertness by training counselors to behave either expert or inexpert. Sabalis used one interviewer, who served as both the high- and low-status helper. The positive effect on the helper-client relationship was obtained again. Streltzer and Koch (1968) implemented expertness in yet another way. Their research concerned the effects role playing the part of lung cancer patients would have on persons needing to reduce their smoking. Participating "patients" role played a series of scenes involving meeting the doctor, the doctor giving the diagnosis, treatment plans, and advice to quit smoking immediately. Half of the "patients" enacted their role with a "doctor" who was a 21-year-old female psychology major. She used no title. The other smokers met with a 32-year-old male physician, who introduced himself as "Doctor." Both types of smokers decreased in smoking more than persons not participating in the role playing. Those role playing with the real expert, furthermore, showed by far the greatest negative change in their attitudes toward smoking.

Similar findings have been reported by other researchers. In general, it may be concluded that helper expertness and status serve to increase client respect, which in turn leads to his being more open to the helper's attempts to influence him and, subsequently, more likelihood of client change.

HELPER EMPATHY

We have just examined the positive effects on the helper-client relationship of the real or apparent expertness and status of the helper. There are several other helper qualities of importance in this regard and the present section will focus upon one of these, empathy. The level of empathy offered by the helper and its effects on the client has been the object of considerable research and theory. This research has consistently shown that a helper's empathy with his client's feelings strongly influences the quality of the helper-client relationship which develops and, subsequently, the degree of client change.

Truax and Carkhuff (1967) are two researchers who have been quite active in studying the effects of empathy on the helper-client relationship. They comment, as a beginning definition of "empathy":

> As we come to know some of his wants, some of his needs, some of his achievements and some of his failures, we find ourselves as therapists "living" with the patient much as we do with the central figure of a novel . . .. Just as with the character in the novel, we come to know the person from his own internal frame of reference, gaining some flavor of his moment-by-moment experience. We see events and significant people in his life as they appear to him—not as they "objectively are" but as he experiences them. As we come to know him from his personal vantage point we automatically come to value and like him . . .. We begin to perceive the events and experiences of his life "as if" they were parts of our own life. It is through this process that we come to feel warmth, respect and liking . . .. (p. 42.)

These same researchers have also developed a more detailed definition of empathy, which is quoted in full below. Described in the statement which follows is their Empathy Scale, consisting of levels of empathy which a helper may provide a client—graduated from very low (Level 1) to very high (Level 5).

EMPATHIC UNDERSTANDING IN INTERPERSONAL PROCESSES

A Scale for Measurement

Level 1

The verbal and behavioral expressions of the helper either do not attend to or detract significantly from the verbal and behavioral expressions of the client(s) in that they communicate significantly less of the client's feelings and experiences than the client has communicated himself.

Example. The helper communicates no awareness of even the most obvious, expressed surface feelings of the client. The helper may be bored or disinterested or simply operating from a preconceived frame of reference which totally excludes that of the client(s).

In summary, the helper does everything but express that he is listening, understanding, or being sensitive to even the most obvious feelings of the client in such a way as to detract significantly from the communications of the client.

Level 2

While the helper responds to the expressed feelings of the client(s), he does so in such a way that he subtracts noticeable affect from the communications of the client.

Example. The helper may communicate some awareness of obvious, surface feelings of the client, but his communications drain off a level of the affect and distort the level of meaning. The helper may communicate his own ideas of what may be going on, but these are not congruent with the expressions of the client.

In summary, the helper tends to respond to other than what the client is expressing or indicating.

Level 3

The expressions of the helper in response to the expressions of the client(s) are essentially interchangeable with those of the client in that they express essentially the same affect and meaning.

Example. The helper responds with accurate understanding of the surface feelings of the client but may not respond to or may misinterpret the deeper feelings.

In summary, the helper is responding so as to neither subtract from nor add to the expressions of the client. He does not respond accurately to how that person really feels beneath the surface feelings; but he indicates a willingness and openness to do so. Level 3 constitutes the minimal level of facilitative interpersonal functioning.

Level 4

The responses of the helper add noticeably to the expressions of the client(s) in such a way as to express feelings a level deeper than the client was able to express himself.

Example. The helper communicates his understanding of the expressions of the client at a level deeper than they were expressed and thus enables the client to experience and/or express feelings he was unable to express previously.

In summary, the helper's responses add deeper feeling and meaning to the expressions of the client.

Level 5

The helper's responses add significantly to the feeling and meaning of the expressions of the client(s) in such a way as to accurately express feelings levels below what the client himself was able to express or, in the event of ongoing, deep self-exploration on the client's part, to be fully with him in his deepest moments.

Example. The helper responds with accuracy to all of the client's deeper as well as surface feelings. He is "tuned in" on the client's wave length. The helper and the client might proceed together to explore previously unexplored areas of human existence.

In summary, the helper is responding with a full awareness of who the other person is and with a comprehensive and accurate empathic understanding of that individual's deepest feelings. (pp. 174–175.)*

A great deal of research has been done on the effects of high levels of helper empathy in counseling, guidance, and psychotherapy. Certain effects on the client regularly occur in these studies. Feeling understood, that someone has been able to truly perceive his deeper feelings, the client's liking of his helper increases. In a sense, the client also comes to trust himself more under these circumstances, for one regular result of high helper empathy is deeper and more persevering *self*-exploration by the client. In several of these studies, greater client change is a clear result. High levels of helper empathic responding may, therefore, be viewed as a necessary (but probably not sufficient) condition for client change. Carkhuff (1969) is, we feel, largely correct in his comment:

> Empathy is the key ingredient of helping. Its explicit communication, particularly during early phases of helping, is critical. Without an empathic understanding of the helpee's world and his difficulties as he sees them there is no basis for helping. (Carkhuff, 1969, p. 173.)

A more concrete understanding of helper empathy, and its effects upon client behavior, is provided by the specific examples which follow. The first is drawn from

---

*From Truax, Charles B. and Carkhuff, Robert R. *Toward effective counseling and psychotherapy* (Chicago: Aldine Publishing Company, 1967); copyright © by Charles B. Truax and Robert R. Carkhuff. Reprinted by permission of the authors and Aldine Publishing Company.

a psychotherapy session. Note how all helper statements are at least Level 3, and often higher:

Helper: Um, I don't know whether, whether I'm right or wrong in feeling the way I do, but, uh, I find myself withdrawing from people. I don't care to go out and socialize and play their stupid little games any more. Um, I get very anxious and come home depressed and have headaches — it seems all so superficial. There was a time when I used to get along with everybody; everybody said, "Oh, isn't she wonderful! She gets along with everybody; she's so nice and everybody likes her," and I used to think that was . . . that was something to be really proud of, but, oh, but, I think that only told how I, or who I was at that time, that I had no depth. I was sort of whatever the crowd wanted me to be, or the particular group I was with at the time. Um, I know it's important for my husband's business that we go out and socialize and meet people and make a good impression and join clubs and play all those stupid little games — Elks, and, you know, bowling banquets, and, uh, fishing trips and fraternity-type gatherings. Um, I . . . I just don't care to do it any more, and, um, I don't know if that means that I'm a . . . that there's something wrong with me psychologically, or, uh, or is this normal. I mean . . . uh . . . people don't really know who I am and they really don't care who one another, who the other person is. They . . . it's all at such a superficial level.

Helper: You're darn sure of how you feel, but you really don't know what it all adds up to. Is it you? Is it the other people? What are the implications of your husband's business? You? Where is it all going?

Helpee: Uh, huh. It's an empty life. It's, um, there's, uh, no depth to it at all. I mean, you just talk about very, very superficial things, and the first few times, it's O.K. But then after that, there's nothing to talk about. So you drink and you pretend to be happy over silly jokes and silly things that people do when they all, uh, are trying to impress one another, and they're very materialistic, and, uh, it's just not the route I want to go.

Helper: So your feelings are so strong now that you just can't fake it any more.

Helpee: That's right, so what do you do? People say, "Oh, there's something wrong with you," then, "You need to see a psychiatrist or something." because you . . . you know the thing in society is that the normal person gets along with people, and, uh, can adjust to any situation. And when you . . . when you're a little discriminating, maybe very discriminating or critical, then that means there's something wrong with you.

Helper: While you know how strongly you feel about all these things, you're not sure you can really act in terms of them and be free.

Helpee: I don't know if I'm strong enough. The implications are great. It may mean, uh, a break up of the marriage, uh, and it means going it alone, and that's too frightening. I don't think I have the courage. But I do feel like I'm in sort of a trap.

Helper: You know you can't pretend, yet you're really fearful of going it alone.

Helpee: Yes, there's nobody I can really talk to, I mean, you know, it's one thing if you have a . . . like your husband . . . if you can share these things, if he can understand it at some level, but . . . um . . . he can't.

Helper: It's like, "If I act on how I really feel, though, it frightens the people who mean most to me. They won't understand it, and I sure can't share that with them."

Helpee: (Pause) So what do you do. (Pause) I mean . . . I . . . you know. I find myself going out and telling the people who I really feel about, about different topics and getting into controversial issues, and, uh, and that's, that's too anxiety provoking for me. I can't, because then you get into arguments and I don't want to do that either, that leads nowhere. I just get frustrated and anxious and upset and angry with myself for getting myself into the situation.

Helper: You know that doesn't set you free, you know . . .

Helpee: No, it bottles me up.

Helper: That only causes you more problems, and what you're really asking about is, how you can move toward greater freedom and greater fulfillment in your own life.

Helpee: I . . . I think I know who I am now, independent of other people, and, uh, which people aren't and . . . um . . . there's no room for that kind of person in this society.

Helper: There's no room for me out there!

Helpee: (Pause) So what do I do?

Helper: We run over and over the questions that . . . you end up with. "Where do I go from here? How do I act on this? I know how I feel, but I don't know what'll happen if I act on how I feel."

Helpee: I . . . have an idea of what'll happen.

Helper: And it's not good!

Helpee: No! It means almost starting a whole new life.

Helper: And you don't know if you can make it.

Helpee: Right, I know what I've got here, and if I don't make it all the way with the other, then I'm in trouble.

Helper: While you don't know what'll happen if you act on your feelings, you know what the alternatives are if you don't. And they're not good either. They're worse.

Helpee: I . . . I don't have much choice. (pp. 219–220.)*

A second series of examples is drawn from our own research (Goldstein, 1973), in which we sought successfully to increase helper empathy by a set of training procedures rather different from Truax and Carkhuff's. Our trainees were nurses and attendants employed in state mental hospitals. Part of our training sequence involved exposing them to a number of different examples of highly empathic responses to difficult or problematic patient behaviors and statements. These examples included:†

1. *Nurse*:   Here is your medicine, Mr. _____.
   Patient: I don't want it. People here are always telling me to do this, do that, do the other thing. I'll take the medicine when *I* want to.

   Nurse: So it's not so much the medicine itself, but you feel you're bossed around all the time. You're tired of people giving you orders.

2. *Patient*:   I can't leave the hospital, I'm still sick. What will I do when I get home?

   Nurse: You just don't feel ready to go yet, and wonder if you're up to being home.

3. *Patient*:   I don't know why they keep giving me this medicine. I've taken it for weeks and I don't feel any better. I've told this to Dr. _____ twice already.

   Nurse: Not only doesn't the medicine seem to work, but the doctor doesn't seem interested in doing anything about it.

4. *Patient*:   I was in the hospital before. Things were really bothering me. Finally, I just couldn't take it anymore. I left home, didn't show up at work, and somehow ended up in the hospital.

   Nurse: Things just piled up and up, from bad to worse, and you wound up here.

5. *Patient*:   Sometimes I think my family could do just as well without me. It's like I almost don't exist as far as they're concerned. They almost never come to see me.

   Nurse: You'd really like them to visit, but they don't really seem to care about you.

---

*From Carkhuff, R. F. *Helping and human relations.* New York: Holt, Rinehart and Winston, 1969. Reprinted by permission.

†From Goldstein, A. P. *Structured learning therapy.* New York: Academic Press, 1973. Reprinted by permission.

6. *Patient*:   My father and mother used to get into terrible fights. He'd come home and they'd really go at it. I'd have to pull the pillow over my head so I wouldn't hear the noise.

   Nurse: It sounds like something that would be really upsetting, especially to a child.

7. *Patient*:   I'd really like to know about their school, their friends, things like that. You know, the things a father is interested in. My youngest son, he's on a football team, but he never invited me to a game. He never cared if I was there or not. I don't understand it.

   Nurse: It must hurt very deeply when he doesn't let you be a part of his life.

8. *Patient*:   I don't like talking to the psychologist. He's OK but I've been asked *all* the questions many times already.

   Nurse: You're just good and tired of going through the whole procedure.

9. *Patient*:   It's just not fair that I have to stay on the ward because of last weekend. My husband was nasty. He made me very nervous. It wasn't my fault. Can't I please go off the ward?

   Nurse: You feel the trouble at home was really your husband's fault, and now you're being punished for it.

10. *Patient*:   I can't stand her anymore. She never shuts up, talk, talk, talk. She talks more than any other patient here. I don't want to sit near her or be near her.

    Nurse: She's really very annoying to you. You'd like to have nothing to do with her.

A similar set of high empathy examples was used to train a different type of helper, Home Aides. These are persons trained to provide psychological and physical assistance to elderly, disabled, psychiatric outpatient, and similar persons in their own homes. Some of these examples were:

1. *Patient*:   The old age home was really different from this apartment building. All my friends are still there. I don't even know anyone here.

   Home Aide: Sounds like you're lonely in your new home. Kind of like a stranger in a new place. I can see how it's pretty depressing missing all your friends.

   Patient: I sure *am* lonely. Every friend I have is still at the home. And it's so hard living all alone with three whole rooms to myself. I even get sad listening to people's voices in the other apartments.

   Home Aide: You'd like to get out of your three lonely rooms and meet some of the other people in the building. You'd be happier if you made some new friends.

2. *Patient*:   I don't like . . . It makes me feel silly for you to wash and feed me.

   Home Aide: It makes you uncomfortable when someone takes care of you. You feel like you should be doing things on your own and you shouldn't need me.

   Patient: Mm hm. I feel like a baby when someone's helping me. But I know I can't do stuff myself now 'cause I've tried.

   Home Aide: You feel foolish when you have to rely on other people since you should be helping yourself. But you know that you need other people's help now for your own well being.

3. *Patient*:   I think about things like falling down the stairs, or dropping my cigarette in bed, or a stranger coming to my house late at night . . . I don't really know what I'd do . . .

   Home Aide: You're worried about whether you could handle an emergency all alone.

   Patient: Yeah, I worry, *a lot* . . . I remember how scary it was the time I fainted and nobody was here to help me.

   Home Aide: It would be nice to be able to count on somebody's help when something goes wrong and you're not sure you can take care of things all by yourself.

4. *Patient*:   All I seem to do is care for these kids 25 hours a day! Which is a lot for a mother to do by herself!

Home Aide: Sounds as if you'd like more time to yourself or someone to help you. That's a lot for one person to do and you seem angry about it.

Patient: Why shouldn't I be angry! It's a lot to expect one person to change diapers, tie shoelaces, fix meals, yank the kids out of the mud, wash their filthy faces, constantly run to drag their stupid toys out of the road . . .

Home Aide: You get pretty angry when you constantly have to watch over those kids. It's like the more demands they make on you, the less time you have to do things for yourself.

5. *Patient*:   My kids couldn't care less if I exist. They're only in Rochester, but somehow that's too far away to visit me.

Home Aide: You'd like them to visit, but somehow they don't seem interested enough.

Patient: Yeah, you got the idea. If they were interested in me they'd make the short trip to come see me. But they don't even call. And I'll be damned if I'll invite them one more time.

Home Aide: You're not about to beg them to visit you if they aren't interested. But you seem pretty hurt that your own children don't seem to care about you.

6. *Patient*:   (Bashfully looking down). Do you think you could maybe show me how to, um, wash myself alone, instead of you helping me. The nurses helped me in the hospital when I had arthritis . . . Well . . . I still shake so much I'm afraid I'll drop the soap or fall down.

Home Aide: It's kind of embarrassing to need someone to help you wash. Even though right now it's probably safer that way, you'd really rather do it yourself.

Patient: You're not kidding. I can't tell you how I hated bathtime in the hospital. It was so embarrassing to have the nurse see me, you know, naked. But maybe it had to be that way. Like you say, it was safer. And also a lot cleaner than if I did it myself.

Home Aide: So even though you don't like people to see you naked, maybe it would make you feel more comfortable if I helped you while the arthritis is still bothering you.

7. *Patient*:   This apartment's *nothing* like the old age home. There I had people to take care of me, and there was always something to do, and my room was arranged differently there . . .

Home Aide: It's hard getting used to a brand new home which doesn't even seem like your home yet.

Patient: But you know, I remember being afraid I wouldn't get used to the old age home, and I did. So, even if it's hard now in this new place, I guess I'll get used to it.

Home Aide: Even though it's a little hard and scary at first, it's comforting to know you got used to a new home before and you can probably do it again.

8. *Patient*:   (Annoyed) I wish you wouldn't put things away in my house any way you feel like it!

Home Aide: I'm just barging right into your house, doing whatever I want with your things—as though I don't respect you.

Patient: Yeah! I keep my things in certain places for certain reasons and I don't like anyone moving them without asking me.

Home Aide: You're used to living a certain way and all of a sudden I come in and put things where *I* think they should go. I can understand that you'd be angry with me for barging in.

9. *Patient*:   (Hectically) Oh! I'm really sorry about that chair! I was planning to reupholster it last week! And that lightbulb just blew out yesterday. (Heavily, shaking head in hand) Oh-h-h I'm sorry . . . . This place is a rathole.

Home Aide: It's kind of embarrassing when someone comes to your house for the first time and sees it looking like a mess.

Patient: Well, *you'd* be embarrassed, wouldn't you? The furniture is a wreck, the walls are shabby, some of the lights don't work . . . I don't even want you to see the kitchen . . . I feel terrible that you have to see everything like this!

Home Aide: You're ashamed that everything in your house seems to be dirty or broken and you feel like apologizing for the mess.

10. *Patient*:   The only reason I called Home Aides is that the doctor recommended it and he was standing right there. I really don't want you to take care of me. I don't need help.

Home Aide: You feel that you can take care of yourself, and you resent it when I come in and start doing things for you.

Patient: Yes, I *can* take care of myself!... Except, I guess I could use some help now that I don't see so good.

Home Aide: You still feel up to taking care of things like before, but you realize it's a little harder now... Even so, you don't like to ask for help.

The significance of helper empathy in the helping enterprise has been emphasized in our earlier discussion, and we have now provided several examples. It will be useful to close this section with a listing of the guidelines, provided by Carkhuff (1969), for helpers wishing to become proficient in offering these levels of empathic responses to clients:

1. The helper will find that he is most effective in communicating an empathic understanding when he concentrates with intensity upon the client's expressions, both verbal and nonverbal.

2. The helper will find that initially he is most effective in communicating empathic understanding when he concentrates upon responses that are interchangeable with those of the client (Level 3).

3. The helper will find that he is most effective in communicating empathic understanding when he formulates his responses in language that is most attuned to the client.

4. The helper will find that he is most effective in communicating empathic understanding when he responds in a feeling tone similar to that communicated by the client.

5. The helper will find that he is most effective in communicating empathic understanding when he is most responsive.

6. The helper will find that he is most effective in communicating empathic understanding when, having established an interchangeable base of communication (Level 3), he moves tentatively toward expanding and clarifying the client's experiences at higher levels (Levels 4 and 5).

7. The helper will find that he is most effective in communicating empathic understanding when he concentrates upon what is not being expressed by the client and, in a sense, seeks to fill in what is missing rather than simply dealing with what is present.

8. The helper will find that he is most effective in communicating empathic understanding when he employs the client's behavior as the best guideline to assess the effectiveness of his responses.

HELPER WARMTH

As was true of empathy, warmth is appropriately considered a central ingredient of the helping relationship. Whatever specific change methods the helper uses, their likelihood of success seems in large measure to be a result of the relationship base on which he and the client are interacting. Helper warmth is a highly important aspect of this base. Without it, specific helping procedures may be technically correct but therapeutically impotent.

Helper warmth is also important in relationship terms because it appears to beget reciprocal warmth from the client. Truax and Carkhuff (1967), in fact, comment that "It is a rare human being who does not respond to warmth with warmth and to hostility with hostility. It is probably the most important principle for the beginning therapist to understand if he is to be successful in the therapeutic relationship." This contention received ample support in a research program conducted by the present writer (Goldstein, 1971). When liking of A toward B (helper or client) was increased by structuring, status-enhancement, or by other procedures, B's liking of A reciprocally increased—even though we had applied no procedures whatsoever to B directly. Several other researchers have reported the same reciprocal result. The Truax and Carkhuff definition of this helper quality, and their examples of its occurrence in counseling and psychotherapy, will help clarify the nature and significance of helper warmth.

The dimension of nonpossessive warmth or unconditional positive regard ranges from a high level, where the therapist warmly accepts the patient's experience as part of that person without imposing conditions, to a low level where the therapist evaluates a patient or his feelings, expresses dislike or disapproval, or expresses warmth in a selective and evaluative way.

Level 1

The therapist is actively offering advice or giving clear negative regard. He may be telling the patient what would be "best for him," or in other ways actively approving or disapproving of his behavior. The therapist's actions make himself the locus of evaluation; he sees himself as responsible for the patient.

Example.

    Patient: ...and I don't, I don't know what sort of a job will be offered me, but—eh...

    Therapist: It might not be the best in the world.

    Patient: I'm sure it won't.

    Therapist: And, uh...

    Patient: ...but...

    Therapist: But if you can make up your mind to stomach some of the unpleasantness of things.

    Patient: Um hm.

    Therapist: ...you have to go through—you'll get through it.

    Patient: Yeah, I know I will.

    Therapist: And, ah, you'll get out of here.

    Patient: I certainly, uh, I just, I just know that I have to do it, so I'm going to do it but—it's awfully easy for me, Doctor, to (sighs) well, more than pull in my shell, I—I just hibernate. I just, uh, well, just don't do a darn-thing.

    Therapist: It's your own fault. (Severely)

    Patient: Sure it is. I know it is. (Pause) But it seems like whenever I—here—here's the thing. Whenever I get to the stage where I'm making active plans for myself, they say I'm high. An...

    Therapist: In other words they criticize you that...

    Patient: Yeah.

    Therapist: So tender little lady is gonna really crawl into her shell.

    Patient: Well, I—I'll say "okay."

    Therapist: If they're gonna throw, if they're gonna shoot arrows at me, I'll just crawl behind my shell and I won't come out of it. (Forcefully)

Patient: That's right. (Sadly)

Therapist: And that's worse. (Quickly)

Patient: (Pause) But why don't they let me be a little bit high? Why—right now I'm taking...

Therapist: (Interrupting). Because some people...

Patient: (Talking with him)...600 milligrams of malorin, whatever that is, malorin.

Therapist: ...because a lot of people here don't know you very well at all. And because people in general, at times, you have to allow that they could be stupid. You too. I mean you're stupid sometimes, so why can't other people...

Patient: So much of the time.

Therapist: Why can't other people? I mean, you're an intelligent person and are stupid. Why, why can't you allow that other intelligent people can also be stupid? When it comes to you they don't know very much.

Patient: Mmm. (Muttering)

Level 2

The therapist responds mechanically to the client, indicating little positive regard and hence little nonpossessive warmth. He may ignore the patient or his feelings, or display a lack of concern or interest. The therapist ignores the client at times when a nonpossessively warm response would be expected; he shows a complete passivity that communicates almost unconditional lack of regard.

Example.

Patient: (Speaking throughout in a woebegone voice) You don't have to sit down and, and, and write like that but I thought he'd answer my letter. I thought, I didn't think he'd answer the letter, I thought he'd come up.

Therapist: Um, hm.

Patient: ...and, and visit me; it's only 50, he hasn't been to visit me yet. It's only been about, uh, it's only about 50, 60 miles from here.

Therapist: Um, hm.

Patient: And I kind of expected him last Sunday but he didn't...

Therapist: You were just sort of looking for him but he...

Patient: (Interrupting insistently) Well, I wasn't, I wasn't, I was looking for him, I wasn't looking for him. I had a kind of a half-the-way feeling that he wouldn't be up here. I know him pretty well and he's—walks around, you know, and thinks and thinks and thinks and—maybe it'll take him two or three weeks an' all of a sudden he—he'll walk in the house (laughs)—"Let's go see—so and so." (Nervous laughter) He's a—he's a lot like I am—we're all the same, I guess. He probably—read the letter and—probably never said very much, walked out, forgot about it (laughing nervously), then all of a sudden it dawned on 'im (nervous laughter) and, ah, that's, ah, that's about, about the size of it, as far as that goes. And, uh, uh, so as I say, I—I wouldn't be, I wasn't—too overly disappointed when he, when he didn't ah, ah, ah, ah, answer it or come to see me. He probably will yet. (Laughs) I'm an optimist, I always have been, he'll probably come and visit me some day. Maybe he'll come and let me go down there 'n live. Maybe he won't, won't make much difference (laughs) one way or another.

Therapist: Hmmm. You can sort of...

Patient: Yeah.

Therapist: ...take things as they come. (Brightly)

Level 3

The therapist indicates a positive caring for the patient or client, but it is a semipossessive caring in the sense that he communicates to the client that his behavior matters to him. That is, the therapist communicates such things as "It is not all right if you act immorally," "I want you to get along at work," or "It's important to me that you get along with the ward staff." The therapist sees himself as responsible for the client.

Example.

Patient: I still, you sorta hate to give up something that you know that you've made something out of, and, and, uh, in fact, it amounts to, uh, at least, uh, what you would, uh, earn working for somebody else, so ...

Therapist: (Enthusiastically). O.K. What, well, eh, why don't—why don't we do it this way? That, uh I'll kind of give you some homework to do. (Laughs) And when you're going home these weekends, um, really talk to your wife, and, ah, think yourself about pretty specific possibilities for you, considering the location and considering what time of year it is and, what you can do and things like this, and, eh, then we can talk it out here and really do some, some working on this in earnest, and not just talk plans . . . . (Patient answers "Yeah" after every phrase or so)

Patient: (Interrupting). Well, I actually, I'd almost feel gettin' out right away but I, somethin' sort of holds me back, yet the season isn't—there (*Therapist*: Uh, huh) and I don't know if it's good for me or not (*Therapist*: Uh, huh), but I, ah ...

Therapist: O.K., but at least this next couple of months we can use in—trying at least to set something up or, or ...

Patient: Cuz I feel that I, I don't know, I—feel I just want to do things again.

Therapist: (Um, hm). Uh, 'cuz the longer you stay away from work, I was just reading about that psychologist James here the other day, an' it seems like if once you get into things and work, you feel better (*Patient*: Sure) ... and you don't uh, it seems like, uh the further you stay away from things, eh, you, well, eh, you sort'a think about it, put it that way. Um, hm. O.K. So, ah—in our thinking about it, though, that next few weeks, let's get closer to the doing of them. O.K.? (Warmly)

Patient: Well, yes, that's—what . . . .

Therapist: Sound okay to you?

Patient: Yes, It sounds okay to me.

Therapist: Good enough. (Amiably)

Level 4

The therapist clearly communicates a very deep interest and concern for the welfare of the patient, showing a nonevaluative and unconditional warmth in almost all areas of his functioning. Although there remains some conditionality in the more personal and private areas, the patient is given freedom to be himself and to be liked as himself. There is little evaluation of thoughts and behaviors. In deeply personal areas, however, the therapist may be conditional and communicate the idea that the client may act in any way he wishes—except that it is important to the therapist that he be more mature, or not regress in therapy, or accept and like the therapist. In all other areas, however, nonpossessive warmth is communicated. The therapist sees himself as responsible to the client.

Example.

> *Therapist*: One thing that occurs to me is I'm so glad you came. I was afraid you wouldn't come. I had everything prepared, but I was afraid you wouldn't come. (Pause)
>
> *Patient*: What—would you have thought of me then? I guess maybe I shouldn't have, but I did anyway. (Rapidly)
>
> *Therapist*: Is that—like saying, "Why or What?" But, partly you feel—maybe you shouldn't have come—or don't know if you shouldn't or "not should." There's something about—feeling bad that could make you—not want to come. I don't know if I got that right, but—because if you feel very bad then—then, I don't know. Is there anything in that?
>
> *Patient*: Well—I've told you before, I mean, you know, two things that, when I feel bad. I mean one that always—I feel that there's a possibility, I suppose, that you know, that they might put me back in the hospital for getting that bad.
>
> *Therapist*: Oh, I'd completely forgotten about that, yeah—yet, and that's one thing—But there is another?
>
> *Patient*: Yeah, I already told you that, too.
>
> *Therapist*: Oh, yeah, you sure did—I'd forgotten about it—and the other you've already said, too?
>
> *Patient*: I'm sure I did tell it. (Pause)
>
> *Therapist*: It doesn't come. All I have when I try to think of it is just the general sense that if you feel—very bad, then it's hard or unpleasant to—but I don't know—so I may have forgotten something—must have. (Pause)
>
> *Patient*: You talk—you always, hear what I'm saying now, are so good at evading me, you always end up making me talk anyway.
>
> *Therapist*: You're right.
>
> *Patient*: You always comment on the question or something, and it just doesn't tell me.
>
> *Therapist*: (Interjecting) Right, I just instinctively came back—to you when I wondered—what, I, well like saying, because—that's what I felt like saying. You mean to—you mean to say that a few minutes ago we had decided that I would talk ...
>
> *Patient*: Well, you—you mentioned it, but (*Therapist*: Right) that's as far as it got.
>
> *Therapist*: You're right—and I just—was thinking of what you're asking—I'm more interested in you right now than anything else.

Level 5

At stage 5, the therapist communicates warmth without restriction. There is a deep respect for the patient's worth as a person and his rights as a free individual. At this level the patient is free to be himself even if this means that he is regressing, being defensive, or even disliking or rejecting the therapist himself. At this stage the therapist cares deeply for the patient as a person, but it does not matter to him how the patient chooses to behave. He genuinely cares for and deeply prizes the patient for his human potentials, apart from evaluations of his behavior or his thoughts. He is willing to share equally the patient's joys and aspirations or depressions and failures. The only channeling by the therapist may be the demand that the patient communicate personally relevant material.

Example.

> *Patient*: .... ever recovering to the extent where I could become self-supporting and live alone. I thought that I was doomed to hospitalization for the rest of my life and seeing some of the

people over in, in the main building, some of those old people who are, who need a lot of attention and all that sort of thing, is the only picture I could see of my own future. Just one of (*Therapist*:   Mhm) complete hopelessness, that there was any—

Therapist: (Interrupting). You didn't see any hope at all, did you?

Patient: Not, not in the least. I thought no one really cared and I didn't care myself, and I seriously—uh—thought of suicide; if there'd been any way that I could end it all completely and not become just a burden or an extra care, I would have committed suicide, I was that low. I didn't want to live. In fact, I hoped that I—I would go to sleep at night and not wake up, because I, I really felt there was nothing to live for (*Therapist*:   Uh, huh [very softly]) Now I, I truly believe that this drug they are giving me helps me a lot, I think, I think it is one drug that really does me good (*Therapist*:   Uh, hm).

Therapist: But you say that, that during this time you, you felt as though no one at all cared, as to what (*Patient*:   That's right) . . . what happened to you.

Patient: And, not only that, but I hated myself so that I didn't, I, I felt that I didn't deserve to have anyone care for me. I hated myself so that I, I, I not only felt that no one did, but I didn't see any reason why they should.

Therapist: I guess that makes some sense to me now. I was wondering why it was that you were shutting other people off. You weren't letting anyone else care.

Patient: I didn't think I was worth caring for.

Therapist: So you didn't ev- maybe you not only thought you were—hopeless, but you wouldn't allow people . . . (Therapist statement is drowned out by patient).

Patient: (Interrupting and very loud). I closed the door on everyone. Yah, I closed the door on everyone because I thought I just wasn't worth bothering with. I didn't think it was worthwhile for you to bother with me. "Just let me alone and—and let me rot that's all I'm worth." I mean, that was my thought. And I, I, uh, will frankly admit that when the doctors were making the rounds on the ward, I mean the routine rounds, I tried to be where they wouldn't see me. The doctor often goes there on the ward and asks how everyone is and when she'd get about to me, I'd move to a spot that she's already covered . . .

Therapist: You really avoided people.

Patient: So that, so that she wouldn't, uh, talk with me (*Therapist*:   Uh, hm) and when—the few times that I refused to see you, it was for the same reason. I didn't think I was worth bothering with, so why waste your time—let's just . . .

Therapist: Let me ask you, ask you something about that. Do you think it would have been, uh, better if I had insisted that, uh, uh, you come and talk with me?

Patient: No, I don't believe so, doctor. (They speak simultaneously).

Therapist: I wondered about that; I wasn't sure . . . (Softly).

Patient: I don't—I, I, I . . . (Truax and Carkhuff, 1967, 58–68.)

Raush and Bordin (1957) help define warmth further. Helper warmth they hold, has three components.

Commitment. The therapist demonstrates some degree of willingness to be of assistance to the patient. This assistance may vary in degree of activity and concreteness. For example, the therapist may offer help in the form of setting limits, breaking limits, or actively collaborating with the patient in the solution of an external problem, or he may offer help only by committing his time. At any given moment, the therapist occupies some point along a continuum representing degree of commitment . . . . The therapist most typically commits a specified amount of time to the patient; he commits, for the patient's use at those times, a private meeting place which will remain relatively undisturbed by extraneous factors; he commits his skills and his efforts at understanding and aiding the patient; he also commits to the patient a relationship in which the patient's needs and interests are dominant, and in which the therapist's personal demands are minimized. For the patient also there are commitments: to honor appointments, to pay fees regularly, to avoid conscious inhibitions of associations, to discuss impending decisions, and so forth.

Effort to understand. The therapist shows his effort to understand by asking questions designed to elicit the patient's view of himself and the world, by testing with the patient the impressions that he, the therapist, has gained of these views, and by indicating, by comments or other forms of action, his interest in understanding the patient's views. At the other extreme, aside from absence of the kind of behavior we have just described, the therapist tends to act as though he had a preconceived view of the patient, his actions, and his feelings . . .. Certainly, it is the therapist's efforts at understanding which produce the first major emotional tie between patient and therapist in most forms of psychotherapy . . . this effort on the part of the therapist will be a major determinant of 'rapport' and of communication between patient and therapist. Such an effort on the part of the therapist may be communicated in many ways: by attentive and unintrusive listening, by questions indicative of interest, by sounds of encouragement, by any of the verbal or nonverbal cues which say in effect, "I am interested in what you are saying and feeling—go on." But whatever the manner of communication, the effort at understanding on the part of the therapist is communication of warmth . . .. The patient's gratification and his willingness to communicate more freely under these circumstances . . . are 'natural' responses to warmth, in the sense that both children and adults feel gratified when their serious communications are listened to seriously.

Spontaneity. The least spontaneous therapist is guarded, either consciously or unconsciously masking all of his feelings. These masked feelings may be intimately related to the underlying needs and feelings of the patient, or they may be those which occur as part of the natural interaction between any two people. Such a therapist maintains an impressive mien and is likely to be inhibited in all of his motor expressions, such as gestures. His verbal communications are marked by stereotype, formalism, and stiffness. The least spontaneous therapist may, however, seem to act impulsively. Such impulsivity will have a compelled, unnatural quality . . .. "Simply going through the motions of psychotherapy is not enough," is, and must be, emphasized by supervisors of students of the process. The therapist must be capable of expressing something of himself . . .. Observation of different therapists indicates considerable variability in the amount of affect expressed. Some therapists seems always to have a tight rein on themselves; they are or seem to be emotionless. Others seem to feel much freer to express themselves; they seem more 'natural.' (p. 352.)*

Similar behaviors represent warmth in yet other research. In one we read: "During a warm interview the interviewer smiled, nodded her head, and spoke warmly. During a cold interview she spoke unsmilingly, she did not nod her head; and she kept her voice drab and cold." As in much of this type of research, these investigators found that interviewees talked significantly† more to the warm interviewer. Another study with a similar result used a helper speaking in a "soft, melodic and pleasant voice" versus speaking in a "harsh, impersonal, and business-like voice" for the comparison of warm versus cold helpers. In a successful repeat study, the same researcher elaborated his definition of warmth in a manner akin to Raush and Bordin's "commitment" and "effort to understand." Specifically, in addition to the voice qualities, the warm helper "showed interest, concern, and attention," whereas his "cold" counterpart displayed "disinterest, unconcern, and nonattentiveness."

---

*From Raush, H. L. and Bordin, E. S. Warmth in personality development and in psychotherapy. *Psychiatry*, 1957, **20**, 351–363. Reprinted by permission.

†The term "significantly" will be used throughout this book in its common statistical usage, i.e., a statistically significant result is a "real" one, one which might happen by chance only 5 times in 100.

Though it is clear that helpers can be trained to reliably show the behavior described above, and these helper behaviors have been shown to effect what the client does, the reader must be cautioned against a too rigid adoption of "a warm stance." Smiling, a pleasant voice, and the like can indeed represent warmth. But if warmth at root is, as Raush and Bordin suggest, commitment, effort to understand and spontaneity, warmth can also be represented behaviorally by directiveness, assertiveness, autonomy-enhancing distancing, and even anger. To a large extent, it is the context and content of the helper-client interaction which will determine if a given instance of helper behavior is perceived by the client as warmth. Carkhuff and Berenson (1967) make a similar observation when they comment: ". . . it is not always communicated in warm, modulated tones of voice; it may be communicated, for example, in anger. In the final analysis, it is the client's experience of the expression that counts." (p. 28.)

MISCELLANEOUS METHODS

We have seen so far in this chapter that the helper-client relationship may be enhanced by direct statements to the client about the helper's likability (structuring); by the client's observation of a counterpart expressing attraction to a helper, or helper observation of a counterpart expressing attraction to a client (imitation); by a client hearing other clients rate a helper as attractive (conformity pressure); by describing the helper to the client as someone of considerable expertness, experience, and accomplishment, or by surrounding the helper with various signs and symbols of such expertness and achievement (status); or by the facilitative conditions or helping behaviors actually offered the client by the helper (e.g., empathy and warmth). These several approaches may be considered to be the major methods of relationship-enhancement which are currently available, because of the amount and conclusiveness of research on each. However, certain other means for improving the nature of the helper-client interaction have also appeared in the professional literature. Each of these should be viewed by the reader as somewhat more tentative or speculative than those considered above, since the amount or quality of supporting research evidence for each is still rather small.

Helper-Client Matching

This approach to the helping relationship, in contrast to those considered above, typically does not seek to alter anything in the helper or client in order to enhance the goodness of their fit. Instead, an effort is made to (a) identify real characteristics of helpers and clients which are relevant to how well they relate, (b) measure helpers and clients on these characteristics, and (c) match helpers and clients into optimal (for client change) pairs based on these measurements. Much of the research on matching is conflicting or inconclusive, but some of it does lead to useful, if tentative, conclusions. The following are frequent characteristics of an optimal helper-client match:

1. Helper and client hold congruent expectations of the role each is to play in the relationship. They understand and agree upon their respective rights and obligations regarding what each is expected to do and not to do during their interactions.

2. Helper and client are both confident of positive results from their meetings. Each anticipates at least a reasonably high likelihood of client change.

3. Helper and client come from similar social, cultural, racial, and economic backgrounds.

4. Helper and client are similar in their use of language, conceptual complexity, extroversion-introversion, objectivity-subjectivity, flexibility, and social awareness.

5. Helper and client are complementary or reciprocal in their need to offer and receive inclusion, control, and affection. The need for inclusion relates to associating, belonging, and companionship versus isolation, detachment, and aloneness. Control is a power or influence dimension, and affection refers to emotional closeness, friendliness, and the like. Helper and client are complementary or reciprocal on these dimensions if the level of inclusion, affection, or control which one member needs to offer approximates the level of that dimension which the other member needs to receive.

Obviously, no given helper and client can be paired on all of these dimensions. However, the greater the number of them reflected in a particular pairing, the more likely it is that a favorable relationship will develop.

Proxemics

Proxemics is the study of personal space and interpersonal distance. Is there a connection between how far apart two persons sit and their posture, on the one hand, and the favorableness of their relationship on the other hand? First, it does appear that liking in an interview setting will lead to physical closeness and a particular type of posture. In an experiment by Leipold (1963), one group of college students were told, "We feel that your course grade is quite poor and that you have not tried your best. Please take a seat in the next room and Mr. Leipold will be in shortly to discuss this with you." Other groups heard neutral or positive statements about their course performance. Those receiving praise subsequently sat significantly closer to the interviewer; those who were criticized chose to sit further away.

A second study also suggests that increased liking leads to decreased physical distance. Walsh (1971) used imitation procedures to successfully increase how attracted a group of patients were to an interviewer. Before their interview, the office was arranged so that the patient's chair was physically light, on wheels and located at the other end of the room eight feet from where the interviewer would be sitting. Upon entering the room, the interviewer suggested to the patient that he "pull up the chair." Attracted patients pulled the chair significantly closer to the interviewer than did unattracted patients.

Our concern, of course, is the other way around, i.e., relationship-enhancement. Does close sitting and certain posturing *lead to* a favorable relationship? This notion was tested in one of our modeling studies. For some patients, the interviewer not only sat close by (27 inches), but also assumed a posture shown in other research to reflect liking. Specifically, he leaned forward (20°) toward the patient, maintained eye contact 90 percent of the time, and faced the patient directly (shoulder orientation of 0°). Very different distance and posture were involved in the contrasting condition. The interviewer was 81 inches from the patient, leaned backward 30°, showed eye contact 10 percent of the time, and faced partially away from the patient with a shoulder orientation of 30°. Results of this research did in part show that distance and posture can indeed influence the patient liking which develops. As was true in the case of helper-client matching, relevant proxemic research is not great. Tentatively, however, we may begin to view close distance and "interested" posture as probable relationship-enhancers.

Conversational "Do's" and "Don'ts"

A step by step relationship-building "cookbook" is neither possible nor desirable. Obviously, each helper-client pair is different enough from others that what we have provided in this chapter should be read and used as *general* suggestions only. How, when, and where a given procedure is used, and what specific form it takes, must be left to the good judgment of each helper. This same proviso applies to the material which follows. Wolberg (1967) has provided a listing of what he views as helper behaviors to include or avoid when trying to build a favorable helper-client relationship. Most of this listing, and the examples he provides, are reproduced below. His suggestions should be taken as guidelines only, and not as a recipe to be applied verbatim.

Avoid exclamations of surprise.
Patient: I never go out on a date without wanting to scream.
Unsuitable responses.
Therapist: Well, for heaven's sake!
Therapist: That's awful!
Therapist: Of all things to happen!

Suitable responses.
Therapist: I wonder why?
Therapist: Scream?
Therapist: There must be a reason for this.

Avoid expressions of overconcern.
Patient: I often feel as if I'm going to die.
Unsuitable responses.
Therapist: Well, we'll have to do something about that right away.
Therapist: Why, you poor thing!
Therapist: Goodness, that's a horrible thing to go through.
Suitable responses.
Therapist: That must be upsetting to you.
Therapist: Do you have any idea why?
Therapist: What brings on this feeling most commonly?

Avoid moralistic judgments.
Patient: I get an uncontrollable impulse to steal.

Unsuitable responses.
Therapist: This can get you into a lot of trouble.
Therapist: You're going to have to put a stop to that.
Therapist: That's bad.

Suitable responses.
Therapist: Do you have any idea of what's behind this impulse?
Therapist: How far back does this impulse go?
Therapist: How does that make you feel?

Avoid being punitive under all circumstances.

Patient: I don't think you are helping me at all.

Unsuitable responses.
Therapist: Maybe we ought to stop therapy.
Therapist: That's because you aren't cooperating.
Therapist: If you don't do better, I'll have to stop seeing you.

Suitable responses.
Therapist: Let's talk about this; what do you think is happening?
Therapist: Perhaps you feel I can't help you.
Therapist: Is there anything I am doing or fail to do that upsets you?

Avoid criticizing the patient.

Patient: I just refuse to bathe and get my hair fixed.

Unsuitable responses.
Therapist: Are you aware of how unkempt you look?
Therapist: You just don't give a darn about yourself, do you?
Therapist: That's like cutting off your nose to spite your face.

Suitable responses.
Therapist: There must be a reason why.
Therapist: Do you have any ideas about that?
Therapist: How does that make you feel?

Avoid making false promises.

Patient: Do you think I'll ever be normal?

Unsuitable responses.
Therapist: Oh, sure, there's no question about that.
Therapist: In a short while you're going to see a difference.
Therapist: I have great hopes for you.

Suitable responses.
Therapist: A good deal will depend on how well we work together.
Therapist: You seem to have some doubts about that.
Therapist: Let's talk about what you mean by normal.

Avoid threatening the patient.

Patient: I don't think I can keep our next two appointments, because I want to go to a concert on those days.

Unsuitable responses.
Therapist: You don't seem to take your therapy seriously.
Therapist: If you think more of concerts than coming here, you might as well not come at all.
Therapist: Maybe you'd better start treatments with another therapist.

Suitable responses.
Therapist: I wonder why the concerts seem more important than coming here.

Therapist: Maybe it's more pleasurable going to the concerts than coming here.
Therapist: What do you feel about coming here for therapy?

Avoid burdening the patient with your own difficulties.

Patient: You look very tired today.

Unsuitable responses.
Therapist: Yes I've been having plenty of trouble with sickness in my family.
Therapist: This sinus of mine is killing me.
Therapist: I just haven't been able to sleep lately.

Suitable responses.
Therapist: I wouldn't be surprised, since I had to stay up late last night. But that shouldn't interfere with our session.
Therapist: I've had a touch of sinus, but it's not serious and shouldn't interfere with our session.
Therapist: That comes from keeping late hours with meetings and things. But that shouldn't interfere with our session.

Avoid displays of impatience.

Patient: I feel helpless and I think I ought to end it all.

Unsuitable responses.
Therapist: You better "snap out of it" soon.
Therapist: Well, that's a nice attitude, I must say.
Therapist: Maybe we had better end treatment right now.

Suitable responses.
Therapist: I wonder what is behind this feeling.
Therapist: Perhaps there's another solution for your problems.
Therapist: You sound as if you think you're at the end of your rope.

Avoid political or religious discussions.

Patient: Are you going to vote Republican or Democratic?

Unsuitable responses.
Therapist: Republican, of course; the country needs good government.
Therapist: I'm a Democrat and would naturally vote Democratic.

Suitable responses.
Therapist: Which party do you think I will vote for?
Therapist: Have you been wondering about me?
Therapist: I wonder what you'd feel if I told you I was either Republican or Democrat. Would either make a difference to you?
Therapist: I vote for whoever I think is the best person, irrespective of party, but why do you ask?

Avoid arguing with the patient.

Patient: I refuse to budge an inch as far as my husband is concerned.

Unsuitable responses.
Therapist: It's unreasonable for you to act this way.
Therapist: Don't you think you are acting selfishly?
Therapist: How can you expect your husband to do anything for you if you don't do anything for him?

Suitable responses.
Therapist: You feel that there is no purpose in doing anything for him?
Therapist: Perhaps you're afraid to give in to him?
Therapist: How do you actually feel about your husband right now?

Avoid ridiculing the patient.

Patient: There isn't much I can't do, once I set my mind on it.

Unsuitable responses.

Therapist: You don't think much of yourself, do you?

Therapist: Maybe you exaggerate your abilities.

Therapist: It sounds like you're boasting.

Suitable responses.

Therapist: That puts kind of a strain on you.

Therapist: Have you set your mind on overcoming this emotional problem?

Therapist: You feel pretty confident once your mind is made up.

Avoid belittling the patient.

Patient: I am considered very intelligent.

Unsuitable responses.

Therapist: An opinion with which you undoubtedly concur.

Therapist: The troubles you've gotten into don't sound intelligent to me.

Therapist: Even a moron sometimes thinks he's intelligent.

Suitable responses.

Therapist: How do you feel about that?

Therapist: That's all the more reason for working hard at your therapy.

Therapist: That sounds as if you aren't sure of your intelligence.

Avoid blaming the patient for his failures.

Patient: I again forgot to bring my doctor's report with me.

Unsuitable responses.

Therapist: Don't you think that's irresponsible?

Therapist: There you go again.

Therapist: When I tell you the report is important, I mean it.

Suitable responses.

Therapist: I wonder why?

Therapist: Do you know why?

Therapist: Perhaps you don't want to bring it.

Avoid rejecting the patient.

Patient: I want you to like me better than any of your other patients.

Unsuitable responses.

Therapist: Why should I?

Therapist: I don't play favorites.

Therapist: I simply don't like a person like you.

Suitable responses.

Therapist: I wonder why you'd like to be preferred by me.

Therapist: Perhaps you'd feel more secure if I told you I liked you best.

Therapist: What do you think I feel about you?

Avoid displays of intolerance.

Patient: My wife got into another auto accident last week.

Unsuitable responses.

Therapist: Those women drivers.

Therapist: Women are sometimes tough to live with.

Therapist: The female of the species is the most deadly of the two.

Suitable responses.

Therapist: How does that make you feel?

Therapist: What do you think goes on?
Therapist: How did you react when you got this news?

Avoid dogmatic utterances.

Patient: I feel cold and detached in the presence of women.

Unsuitable responses.
Therapist: That's because you're afraid of women.
Therapist: You must want to detach yourself.
Therapist: You want to destroy women and have to protect yourself.

Suitable responses.
Therapist: That's interesting; why do you think you feel this way?
Therapist: How far back does this go?
Therapist: What feelings do you have when you are with women?

Avoid premature deep interpretations.

Patient: I've told you what bothers me. Now what do you think is behind it all?

Unsuitable responses.
Therapist: Well, you seem to be a dependent person and want to collapse on a parent figure.
Therapist: You've got an inferiority complex.
Therapist: You never resolved your Oedipus complex.

Suitable responses.
Therapist: It will be necessary to find out more about the problem before I can offer a valid opinion of it.
Therapist: We'll continue to discuss your attitudes, values and particularly your feelings, and before long we should discover what is behind your trouble.
Therapist: That's for us to work on together. If I gave you the answers, it wouldn't be of help to you.

Avoid the probing of traumatic material when there is too great resistance.

Patient: I just don't want to talk about sex.

Unsuitable responses.
Therapist: You'll get nowhere by avoiding this.
Therapist: You must force yourself to talk about unpleasant things.
Therapist: What about your sex life?

Suitable responses.
Therapist: It must be hard for you to talk about sex.
Therapist: All right, you can talk about anything else you feel is important.
Therapist: Sex is always a painful subject to talk about.

Avoid unnecessary reassurance.

Patient: I think I'm the most terrible, ugly, weak, most contemptible person in the world.

Unsuitable responses.
Therapist: That's silly. I think you're very good looking and a wonderful person in many ways.
Therapist: Take it from me, you are not.
Therapist: You are one of the nicest people I know.

Suitable responses.
Therapist: Why do you think you feel that way?
Therapist: How does it make you feel to think that of yourself?
Therapist: Do others think the same way about you?

Express open-mindedness, even toward irrational attitudes.

Patient: I think that all men are jerks.

Unsuitable responses.
Therapist: That's a prejudiced attitude to hold.
Therapist: You ought to be more tolerant.
Therapist: With such attitudes you'll get nowhere.

Suitable responses.
Therapist: What makes you feel that way?
Therapist: Your experiences with men must have been disagreeable for you to have this feeling.

Therapist: Understandably you might feel this way right now, but there may be other ways of looking at the situation that may reveal themselves later on.

Respect the right of the patient to express different values and preferences from yours.
Patient: I don't like the pictures on your walls.

Unsuitable responses.
Therapist: Well, that's just too bad.
Therapist: They are considered excellent pictures by those who know.
Therapist: Maybe your taste will improve as we go on in therapy.

Suitable responses.
Therapist: Why?
Therapist: What type of pictures do you like?
Therapist: What do you think of me for having such pictures?

Make sympathetic remarks where indicated.
Patient: My husband keeps drinking and then gets violently abusive in front of the children.

Unsuitable responses.
Therapist: Why do you continue living with him?
Therapist: Maybe you do your share in driving him to drink.
Therapist: He's a no-good scoundrel.

Suitable responses.
Therapist: This must be very upsetting to you.
Therapist: It must be very difficult to live with him under these circumstances.
Therapist: You must find it hard to go on with this kind of threat over you. (pp. 584–590.)*

SUMMARY

For whom is this chapter written? Who should our helpers be? Relationship-enhancing procedures, as well as the many helper methods described in the chapters which follow, are not the private property of a chosen few who happen to have earned certain professional credentials. Certainly, such training can lead to skills of considerable positive consequence for client change. But, at least as important is the kind of person the helper is. We are in strong agreement with Strupp (1973), who

---

*From Wolberg, L. R. *The technique of psychotherapy*, 2nd ed. New York: Grune and Stratton, 1967. Reprinted by permission of Grune & Stratton, Inc. and the author.

observes:

> It seems that there is nothing esoteric or superhuman about the qualities needed by a good therapist! They are the attributes of a good parent and a decent human being who has a fair degree of understanding of himself and his interpersonal relations so that his own problems do not interfere, who is reasonably warm and empathic, not unduly hostile or destructive, and who has the talent, dedication, and compassion to work cooperatively with others. (Strupp, 1973, p. 2.)

Thus, the potential helper's personal background, degree of self-understanding, maturity, typical ways of relating, and concern for others are all as crucial to the outcome of his helping effort as is his formal training as a helper.

We have held throughout this chapter that without a favorable helper-client relationship, client change will rarely occur. With such a relationship, client change is possible, or even probable, but not inevitable. Other, more specific change measures must typically be utilized in addition. We leave to the chapters which follow the task of fully describing and illustrating these specific procedures.

REFERENCES

Carkhuff, R. F. *Helping and human relations*. New York: Holt, Rinehart and Winston, 1969.

Carkhuff, R. F. and Berenson, B. G. *Beyond counseling and therapy*. New York: Holt, Rinehart and Winston, 1967.

Frank, J. D. *Persuasion and healing*. Baltimore: Johns Hopkins Press, 1961.

Goldstein, A. P. *Psychotherapeutic attraction*. New York: Pergamon Press, 1971.

Goldstein, A. P. *Structured learning therapy*. New York: Academic Press, 1973.

Haley, J. *Strategies of psychotherapy*. New York: Grune and Stratton, 1963.

Leipold, W. E. Psychological distance in a dyadic interview. Unpublished Doctoral dissertation, University of North Dakota, 1963.

Orne, M. T. and Wender, P. H. Anticipatory socialization for psychotherapy. *American Journal of Psychiatry*, 1968, **124**, 88–98.

Raush, H. L. and Bordin, E. S. Warmth in personality development and in psychotherapy. *Psychiatry*, 1957, **20**, 351–363.

Sabalis, R. F. Subject authoritarianism, interviewer status, and interpersonal attraction. Unpublished Master's thesis, Syracuse University, 1969.

Schmidt, L. D. and Strong, S. R. Expert and inexpert counselors. *Journal of Counseling Psychology*, 1970, **17**, 115–118.

Streltzer, N. E. and Koch, G. V. Influence of emotional role-playing on smoking habits and attitudes. *Psychological Reports*, 1968, **22**, 817–820.

Strong, S. R. and Schmidt, L. D. Expertness and influence in counseling. *Journal of Counseling Psychology*, 1970, **17**, 81–87.

Strupp, H. H. On the basic ingredients of psychotherapy. *Journal of Consulting and Clinical Psychology*, 1973, **41**, 1–8.

Truax, C. B. and Carkhuff, R. R. *Toward effective counseling and psychotherapy*. Chicago: Aldine, 1967.

Walsh, W. G. The effects of conformity pressure and modeling on the attraction of hospitalized patients toward an interviewer. Unpublished Doctoral dissertation, Syracuse University, 1971.

Wolberg, L. R. *The technique of psychotherapy*, 2nd ed. New York: Grune and Stratton, 1967.

CHAPTER 3

Attitude Modification Methods

DAVID W. JOHNSON AND RONALD P. MATROSS

Attempts to influence our attitudes happen many times a day. Advertisers try to influence us to buy consumer products, professors attempt to influence college students to study, your friends may try to influence your attitudes towards drugs, a counselor tries to influence a client's attitudes towards himself. Each of us tries to change another's attitudes and each of us is influenced by another who is trying to change our attitudes. This makes the area of attitude formation and change one of the most important for individuals concerned with helping themselves and others change. The material in this chapter will attempt to answer the questions, "What kinds of attitude change will help people?" and "How can one go about producing those changes?"

How does attitude formation and change relate to helping people change? A 15-year-old girl is influenced by her friends and her boy friend to believe that she is in love; she is then persuaded to engage in sexual relations; she later becomes pregnant and must make a decision to have the child or obtain an abortion; she asks her parents, her friends, her minister, her doctor, and a counselor to help her make up her mind; each of the persons from whom she has requested help will try to influence her attitudes towards abortion or childbearing.

A 23-year-old teacher begins his career in an inner-city school in which 90 percent of the students are from a lower-class background. There is a great deal of hostility towards teachers, and the students are generally uncooperative and antagonistic. After two frustrating months the teacher becomes hopelessly convinced that he is unable to teach. He turns to several fellow teachers, former college teachers, his girl friend, his parents, and two of the students, for advice about whether to stay in teaching, to switch schools, or to resign and become an insurance salesman. Each of the persons he talks to will try to influence his attitudes towards teaching, his current students, his abilities as a teacher, and his performance during the past two months.

A liberal student prides herself on her participation in programs aimed at reducing the discrimination against Native Americans in her community. She returns to school to find that she has been placed with a Native American

51

roommate. Though she learns that they keep different hours, have completely different friends, cannot communicate on a very intimate level, and want to study at different hours, she becomes more and more hostile towards her roommate, at the same time experiencing increasing guilt about mistreating a Native American. The situation becomes unbearable because she cannot resolve the conflict caused by her wish to campaign for Native American rights and her reluctance to live with her Native American roommate. She goes to friends, a counselor, and a stranger she meets in a bar for advice. Each of the persons she talks with will try to influence her attitudes towards herself, her roommate, Native Americans, and civil rights.

When people come for help they have certain attitudes about themselves and their situations. They want to discuss their problems and receive advice and guidance. Part of any helping process is to clarify their current attitudes towards the significant people involved in their problems and towards alternative actions which can be taken to solve the problem. An integral part of many problems are attitudes which lead to self-destructive behaviors and to thought patterns which cause depression, anxiety, anger, and resentment. You, as a helper, will want to change and modify such attitudes. No psychological problem can be solved, no helping process can be conducted, without attempts to change attitudes.

What are attitudes? *Attitudes* are a combination of feelings and beliefs which result in a predisposition to respond favorably or unfavorably towards particular persons, groups, ideas, events, or objects. The affective component of attitudes consists of the evaluation, liking, or emotional response. The cognitive or belief component consists of what information the person has about the target of the attitude. When you say, "I like ice cream," you are expressing an attitude. When you leap up and run out of the room when an ex-girl friend walks in, you are expressing an attitude. Attitudes are relatively enduring predispositions which give continuity to behavior over time; they are learned rather than innate; they are susceptible to change. What is attitude change? *Attitude change* is the acquisition, reversal, or intensification of an attitude.

What purpose do attitudes serve? Why does a person have attitudes? In daily living a person is constantly confronted with a variety of regularly repeated situations. There probably is not a day in a male college student's life when he does not see an attractive girl. What he considers to be attractive, what he considers an appropriate way to meet a girl, are attitudes which affect how he behaves. Thus attitudes develop to help a person anticipate and cope with recurrent events. Attitudes give a person a simplified and practical guide for appropriate behavior. Because all experiences cannot be grasped in their uniqueness, people tend to group experiences into convenient categories and synthesize useful generalities about relationships among these abstract categories (the categories of attractiveness and girls are put together in the above example). Like any other generalization, an attitude involves an oversimplification of the complexity of an individual's life. Attitudes make certain reactions automatic, thus freeing a person to deal with the unique experiences of daily life. Reliance upon attitudes is part of a fundamental psychological economy which can be described as a "least-effort" principle: Whenever possible, apply past solutions to present problems; or, whenever possible, apply past reactions to present experiences.

Attitudes can either facilitate or frustrate the living of a satisfying and fulfilling life. *Appropriate attitudes* from a helper's point of view are attitudes which promote the ability to carry on those transactions with the environment which result in maintaining oneself, growing, and flourishing. *Inappropriate attitudes* are attitudes which make for a more painful and troubled life through decreasing such abilities. Appropriate attitudes promote feelings of happiness, satisfaction, enjoyment, joy, and even ecstasy. Inappropriate attitudes promote feelings of depression, despair, sadness, guilt, fear, anxiety, shame, and even anguish. These feelings are not only caused by attitudes; many immediate experiences can cause joy or depression. But if the feelings become long term and habitual, it is because they are sustained by attitudes. Many people learn attitudes which sustain negative and self-destructive feelings; many people are taught attitudes which lead to self-defeating and frustrating cycles of behavior. These attitudes are taught and supported by their family, peers, reference groups, society, and culture. With no opportunity for change such self-defeating attitudes affect all aspects of their lives. People with self-destructive attitudes need help in changing to more appropriate and self-enhancing ones.

ATTITUDES AND BEHAVIOR

Changing one's attitudes is often a crucial step in changing one's way of life. A change in attitudes about one's self-worth, for example, may lead to a new career, improved social relationships and a wide variety of other changes in behavior. Yet, despite the pervasive and important effects of attitudes, there is little consistent evidence supporting the hypothesis that knowledge of a person's attitudes will allow one to predict exactly the way he will behave. There are several explanations of why attitudes and behavior often seem unrelated. One is that at any time there is multiplicity of different attitudes, motives, and skills which may affect a person's behavior. In any situation the wide variety of attitudes a person has may interact or be combined in ways which result in behavior not clearly predictable from any one attitude. Attitudes about being a gentleman may affect how prejudiced attitudes are expressed towards members of a certain ethnic group. A person's verbal, intellectual, and social skills may affect how attitudes are expressed in behavior; a person may be against war and still vote for a prowar politician because he cannot understand the varied references the politician makes to his position on war; or a person may want to be friendly with another person, but not have the skills to express friendliness.

Another explanation of the lack of relationship between attitudes and behavior is that there is considerable research which demonstrates that in some situations predictions of overt behavior can be made more accurately from knowledge of the situation than from knowledge of individual characteristics such as attitudes and values (Mischel, 1968). Behavior is always some combination of a response to situational influences and one's personality, but usually it is the response to the situational influences which is more important. Who is present in the situation, what the normative prescriptions of proper behavior are, the alternative behaviors available, unforeseen extraneous events, expected and/or actual consequences of various acts, and the specificity of attitude objects will all affect a person's behavior. A person may believe that derogating other people is great fun, but not do it when his boss is present. A woman may have negative attitudes towards short men, but not express them while she is the hostess at a dinner party attended by several short men. A waiter may not want to have certain types of individuals frequent his restaurant, but when they do he may express his negative attitudes by giving poor service rather than by asking them to leave. A person may be prejudiced against Hungarians, but have a great time at a party without ever realizing that all the other people present are Hungarians. Many situational influences affect behavior and knowing the person's attitudes will not make it possible to always predict how a person will behave. Most situations are sufficiently complex so that several attitudes may be relevant to any action taken, or several actions may be relevant expressions of the same attitude. Predicting whether a student who has favorable attitudes towards a teacher will engage in friendly behavior towards the teacher at a specific time, for example, may depend upon knowing such things as how the student feels physically (he may be sick and want to avoid other people) and what behaviors are competing with the predicted behavior (he may want to study for an exam or he may want to talk with his friends more than he wants to be friendly towards the teacher).

This is not to say that attitudes are unimportant—the whole point of this chapter is to the contrary. We merely wish to suggest that behavior has many determinants, and behavior change is far from being an exact science. In helping people you may be disappointed to find that a person who says that he really looks at things differently makes no real changes in his day-to-day living. Or you may find that an apparently trivial revision in an attitude turns out to be the key to a completely new life.

The purpose of this chapter is to help you understand when and how to use the techniques and processes of attitude change in your efforts to help others.

MODELS FOR CHANGE

When a person approaches you for help there are two general models you need to have. The first is a model of psychological health which indicates what the person will be like when the changes have taken place successfully. The discussion of social competencies in the next section is an example of such a model. The second is a model of procedures you will use in helping the person. Such procedures include: (1) establishing the conditions for attitude change, (2) selecting and implementing a theory (or combination of theories) of attitude change, and (3) stabilizing the new attitudes by building supports which will maintain them. Each of these procedures will be discussed in subsequent sections. In implementing these procedures a person needs to understand the relationship between attitudes and behavior and needs to hold to basic professional ethical guidelines. Each of these issues will also be discussed.

PSYCHOLOGICAL HEALTH

Psychological health is the ability to understand and effectively manage one's overt relationships with other people. Psychological difficulties are difficulties in interpersonal relationships (Fromm-Reichman, 1950; Sullivan, 1953; Johnson, in press). Psychological health is reflected in a person's *interpersonal effectiveness* (the extent to which the consequences of a person's behavior match his intentions) and in his ability to form *humanizing relationships* (relationships which reflect the qualities of kindness, consideration, tenderness, concern, compassion, responsiveness, friendship, love, and mercy) (Johnson, 1972a, 1973a). As we are social species, and since other people are the most important aspect of our environment, the basic competencies which facilitate effective interaction with other persons form the nucleus of a normative model for the helping process. A helper can use this model to diagnose the current functioning of a client, make hypotheses about the origin of the client's difficulties, and provide a direction for the client's attempts to change. These basic social competencies may be subsumed under the concept of social effectiveness. *Social effectiveness* may be defined as the attitudes, cognitive capacities, and behavioral skills a person needs to maintain himself, grow, and flourish in his relationships with other people. Social effectiveness is necessary for the development of a psychologically healthy person who lives a productive and fulfilling life. A healthy person develops social effectiveness in the interpersonal environment created by his family and other reference groups. How a person is related to and what he is taught about relating to others affects the development of his inherent social competencies. It is within interpersonal relationships that psychological health or illness is created and helping others make constructive change is a success to the extent that it increases their social effectiveness.

The basic social competencies essential for social effectiveness consist of four attitudes, a cognitive ability, and a set of behavioral skills. The *first attitude* is the *trusting* attitude that one can rely on the effect and support of other people. Such an attitude is necessary for forming stable and fulfilling relationships characterized by effective cooperation, communication, and problem solving. A distrusting attitude, that others are harsh and undependable, results in such emotional states as withdrawal, depression, anxiety, fear, apprehension, a view of others as being critical, rejecting, and humiliating, an approach to other people characterized by shyness and suspiciousness, and generally unstable and inadequate relationships with other people. The *second attitude* is one of having *confidence* in one's capabilities and in one's capacity to effect desired changes in one's environment. Confidence in one's capabilities facilitates the development of autonomy, increases risk-taking and initiation of efforts to achieve desired goals, and results in basic satisfactions from influencing one's life.

Persons who view themselves as basically incompetent tend to become locked into cycles of self-defeating behavior. Having become convinced of their incompetence, they take few risks and initiate few attempts to achieve their goals. Consequently they seldom have the experience of seeing their actions directly result in worthwhile or outstanding achievements. Through their own actions they perpetuate and confirm their worst fears about themselves.

A *third attitude* is that there is a meaningful *purpose* and *direction* in one's life. Individuals who have directionality are characterized by intentionality (directing one's attention towards an object of significance to the person), awareness of one's choices, goal-directedness and motivation, psychological success (satisfaction from achieving meaningful goals), and self-actualization (development and utilization of one's potentials). Individuals who lack directionality are characterized by floundering from one tentative activity to another, unawareness of the choices they are making, apathy, and a stunting of their potential. They will have feelings of vague discontent, purposelessness, meaninglessness, and lostness. The *fourth attitude* is one of having an integrated and coherent *self-identity*. Persons with a consistent set of attitudes which define "who I am" are characterized by a high level of personal adjustment, mental health, self-acceptance, and a view of self as being liked, wanted, acceptable to others, capable, and worthy. They are also accepting of other people. Individuals who lack a basic self-identity typically view themselves as inadequate, unliked, unwanted, unacceptable, and unable. They show the emotions of anxiety, insecurity, depression, cynicism, and unhappiness. They tend to be contemptuous of themselves and other people. They are psychologically unstable and lack personal adjustment.

A crucial cognitive capacity for social effectiveness is *perspective taking*. Perspective taking is the ability to understand how a situation appears to another person and how that person is reacting cognitively and affectively. Current research demonstrates that such perspective taking ability is related to self-awareness, social adjustment, communication effectiveness, autonomous judgment, cooperative abilities, empathy, the ability to think reflectively in order to make sense of one's own experiences, the ability to predict the effects of one's behavior, open-mindedness, and acceptance of differences. Egocentrism (seeing situations only from one's own point of view) is related to just the opposite.

Finally, a person needs the interpersonal skills to build and maintain high quality relationships in order to be socially effective. The lack of such skills results in an inability to make and sustain contact, get along, and socialize with other people. Such individuals are usually lonely and alienated.

In summary, persons who have trusting attitudes towards others, confidence in their capabilities, directionality, an integrated and coherent self-identity, perspective taking ability, and basic interpersonal skills will be socially effective and psychologically healthy. Persons who have distrustful attitudes, who have attitudes of incompetence and inadequacy, who lack directionality, who lack an integrated and coherent self-identity, who are egocentric, and who lack basic interpersonal skills are socially ineffective and suffer from psychological illness. This basic social effectiveness model forms one basis for having a sense of direction in helping others.

CONDITIONS FOR ATTITUDE CHANGE

Within a helping relationship there are several conditions which have to be established for attitude change to take place. Trust needs to be built and maintained, defensiveness which protects current attitudes needs to be reduced, egocentrism which prevents seeing one's problems from new perspectives needs to be reduced, and demoralization which decreases a person's motivation to solve his problems needs to be reduced. Your effectiveness as a helping person will be greatly increased if you learn to build trust and reduce the obstacles to attitude change.

Kurt Lewin, a great social psychologist, observed that there are three ways to bring about change in a person: you can add forces for change, you can reduce forces currently preventing change, and you can redirect current forces to support change. Most individuals first try to add forces for change when they try to change someone's attitudes. Thus they try to persuade the person to adopt new attitudes. Adding forces for change, however, has its disadvantages. If a high school girl, for example, is afraid of potential rejection from boys and, therefore, never accepts any dates, trying to persuade her to go on a date will only increase her fear. Lewin notes that a more effective way to change attitudes is to reduce the forces currently preventing change. Thus in this case you would identify the girl's fears and try to reduce them before suggesting she accept a date (see Chapter 8, dealing with methods of fear reduction). The redirection of forces can become highly complicated and so we won't discuss it here. The essential point here is that the first stage in helping a person change his attitudes is to reduce the forces preventing such changes before advocating new and more constructive attitudes.

Building and Maintaining Trust

The first issue in helping another person is how much the other person trusts you. (See Chapter 2 for a presentation of relationship-enhancing methods.) A certain level of trust between the helper and the client has to be established and maintained in order for constructive attitude change to take place. The discussion of the client's problems and attitudes, the client's openness to influence and change, the effectiveness of communication between the client and the helper, and the success of the cooperative problem solving, all depend upon the level of trust established and maintained in their relationship (Deutsch, 1962; Friedlander, 1970; Gibb, 1964; Johnson, 1971d; Johnson and Noonan, 1972; Walton and McKersie, 1965). It is important to understand that trust is not something which exists in a person and is stable and unchanging; trust is something which exists in a relationship and is constantly changing and varying. The behavior of both the client and the helper is important in establishing and maintaining trust in their relationship.

Trust—a word everyone uses—is a very complex concept and difficult to define. Based upon the writings of Deutsch (1962) and others, trust may be defined as including the following elements:

1. You are in a situation where a choice to trust another person can lead to beneficial consequences for your needs and goals or harmful consequences. Thus, you realize there is a risk involved in trusting.
2. You realize that whether the beneficial consequences or the harmful consequences result depends upon the behavior of another person.
3. You expect to suffer more from the harmful consequences than you expect to gain from the beneficial consequences.
4. You feel relatively confident that the other person will behave in such a way that the beneficial consequences will result.

Thus, a person who is depressed over problems relating to his wife is making a trusting choice when he shares his problems with a friend because: (1) he is aware that the choice to discuss his marital problems can lead to beneficial consequences (figuring out an effective course of action to improve his marriage) or harmful consequences (being laughed at, ridiculed, rejected, and gossiped about), (2) he realizes that the consequences of his choice depend upon the behavior of the friend from whom he is asking help, (3) he would suffer more from being rejected and ridiculed than he would gain from planning a course of action to try improving things with his wife, and (4) he feels relatively confident that the friend will behave in a way that the beneficial consequences will result.

Most of what happens in helping relationships depends upon the communication between the helper and the client. Trust and communication are interdependent in the sense that trust cannot be developed without communication and communication is affected by the level of trust existing among individuals. Several studies have indicated that communication will not be as effective under low trust conditions as it is under high trust conditions (Deutsch, 1957, 1962). Trust, therefore, must be established and maintained if the effective communication necessary for helping is to take place.

Successful helping also depends upon client self-disclosure to the helper. If the client will not discuss his problems and attitudes openly and fully, it becomes difficult for helping to take place. Self-disclosure makes a person vulnerable to possible rejection, scorn, ridicule, shame, or exploitation. In a trust situation, the person initiating trust is dependent upon the other not to take advantage of his vulnerability. Vulnerability exists when a person has taken a risk which exposes him to harmful consequences. Because of the initiator's vulnerability, trust is damaged when the receiver uses his power to harm the initiator. Being trustworthy is using one's power to build a productive helping relationship by listening with acceptance and understanding to the disclosures of the client. The key to building and maintaining trust in a helping relationship is being trustworthy.

Since the disclosure of problems and feelings by the client is essential for the helper to be useful, and since the client's fears of rejection or exploitation by the helper must be minimized, the steps in building trust are:

1. The client takes a risk in disclosing his problems, feelings, behavior, and ideas.
2. The helper responds with acceptance (i.e., warmth, accurate understanding, and cooperative intentions).
3. The helper reciprocates to some extent the client's disclosures by disclosing such information as his perceptions of the client and his reactions to what is taking place within the helping situation.

There are two types of behavior which will decrease trust in a helping relationship. The first is the use of rejection, ridicule, or disrespect as a response to the other's self-disclosures; moralizing about his behavior, being evaluative in your response, or being silent and poker-faced, all communicate rejection and will effectively silence the other person and destroy some of the trust in the relationship. The second is the nonreciprocation of self-disclosures. To the extent that you are closed and the other person is open, he will not trust you. If someone discloses himself and you do not reciprocate, he will often feel overexposed and very vulnerable.

Acceptance is probably the first and deepest concern to arise in a helping relationship. Two points concerning acceptance need to be made. The first is that acceptance of others usually results from and begins with acceptance of oneself. The second is that acceptance is the key to reducing anxiety and fears about vulnerability. Defensive feelings of fear and distrust are one of the most common blocks to cooperative problem solving and the development of trust (Johnson, 1972a, 1973a; Rogers, 1951, 1965). If the client does not feel accepted, then the frequency and depth of disclosures will decrease (Colson, 1968; Johnson and Noonan, 1972; Taylor, Altman, and Sorrentine, 1969).

What is acceptance? How does a helper communicate acceptance to the client? *Acceptance* is the communication of (1) high regard for another person and (2) nonevaluative and interest responses to the other's behavior. A high regard for another person is communicated through the expression of warmth. A nonevaluative and interested orientation towards the other is communicated through the use of accurate understanding and expressing cooperative intentions. The expression of warmth, accurate understanding, and cooperative intentions conveys acceptance and increases trust in a relationship, even when there are unresolved conflicts between the two persons involved (Johnson, 1971b; Johnson and Noonan, 1972). In the following paragraphs these three types of behaviors will be discussed in more detail.

The Expression of Warmth

Warmth is a feeling and, therefore, we shall briefly review the communication of feelings while we discuss the expression of warmth. It is important that feelings be expressed clearly and unambiguously. In doing so a person needs to have a mastery of both verbal and nonverbal communication. Clearly communicating your feelings depends upon your being aware of your feelings, accepting them, and being skillful in their constructive expression. Verbally, you try to express your feelings by describing them. A description of a feeling must be a personal statement (that is, refer to "I," "me," or "my") and specify some kind of feeling by name (I feel warmly towards you), figure of speech (I feel close to you), or action urge (I feel like hugging you). Further examples of the verbal expression of warmth are statements like "I feel very comfortable around you"; "I always look forward to seeing you"; and "I feel as if you are a true friend." The more clearly one's words describe one's feelings the more effective the communication.

In communicating feelings to another person the verbal component will usually carry less than 35 percent of the social meaning and the nonverbal component will carry more than 65 percent (McCroskey, Larson, and Knapp, 1971). In addition to words, we communicate by our manner of dress, physique, posture, body tension, facial expressions, degree of eye contact, hand and body movements, tone of voice, continuities in speech (such as rate, duration, nonfluencies, and pauses), spatial distance, and touch. In order to communicate warmth to another person, therefore, you must be concerned with the nonverbal messages you are sending. The specific nonverbal cues used to communicate warmth are a soft tone of voice, a smiling and interested facial expression, a relaxed posture in which you are leaning forward slightly, direct eye contact, soft touches, open and welcoming gestures, and close spatial distance.

It is not possible to overemphasize the importance of making congruent your verbal and nonverbal messages for communicating feelings. If you wish to express warmth, your words and your nonverbal cues must all communicate warmth. Contradictory messages will only indicate to the client that you are untrustworthy or inauthentic. For a person to believe your expression of feelings is real and genuine, the verbal and nonverbal messages must be congruent.

Expressing warmth is a skill which is developed like any other skill; it is broken down into parts and practiced until you can perform the skill naturally and easily. Readers should practice both the verbal and the nonverbal messages necessary to communicate warmth until it all is a natural automatic process expressing how you feel. For specific exercises and a more thorough discussion of the expression of feelings readers are referred to Johnson (1972a).

Accurate Understanding

The second basic skill in building trust is the expression of accurate understanding. Accurate understanding is an indication of a nonevaluative and interested orientation towards the client's disclosures and behaviors. It may be defined as the taking of the perspective or frame of reference of another person and restating the content, feelings, and meaning expressed in the other's messages. Accurate understanding has often been called role reversal as it involves taking the other's role in restating his message. The basic rule to follow in accurate understanding is that you can reply to a person's message only after you have first restated the content, feelings, and meaning of the other accurately and to the other's satisfaction. The general guidelines for accurate understanding are:

1. Restate the sender's expressed content, feelings, and meanings in your own words rather than mimicking or parroting his exact words.
2. Preface restated remarks with, "You feel...," "You mean...," "You think...," "It seems to you...," and so on.
3. Avoid any indication of approval or disapproval, agreement or disagreement; your restatement must be nonevaluative.
4. Make your nonverbal messages congruent with your verbal restatement. Look attentive, interested, open to the other's ideas and feelings, and look like you are concentrating upon what the other is trying to communicate.

For specific exercises to develop your skills in accurate understanding see Johnson (1972a).

Cooperative Intentions

Cooperative intentions are the third aspect of building trust. When a person comes to you for help, you must express the willingness to give that help and the commitment to engage in the cooperative problem solving necessary to solve the person's problems or change his attitudes and feelings. Cooperative intentions will indicate that you are not going to exploit the person's vulnerability and will have a nonevaluative and interested response to the disclosures and behavior of the person seeking help. In a helping relationship, mutual goals concerning constructive changes in the client's actions, feelings, and attitudes are set, and a plan for how the relationship will facilitate the accomplishment of such goals is agreed upon. Cooperative interaction is the coordination of behavior among individuals to achieve mutual goals and, therefore, all helping relationships are based upon cooperative interaction and problem solving. Cooperative intentions are expressed through verbal and nonverbal messages that you want to help the other person, want to understand his situation, and wish to cooperate in a plan to improve the other's life. For specific exercises and procedures to build your skills in expressing cooperative intentions and in cooperative problem solving see Johnson (1972a) and Johnson and Johnson (1975a, 1975b).

Reciprocation of Disclosures

The reciprocation of disclosures is the fourth step in building and maintaining trust in a helping relationship. There is a great deal of research which indicates that the more disclosing the helper is, the more disclosing the client will be (Chittick and Himelstein, 1967; Drag, 1968; Jourard and Friedman, 1970; Murdoch, Chenowith, and Riseman, 1969; Taylor, 1964; Worthy, Gary, and Kahn, 1969). Johnson and Noonan (1972) conducted a study in which trained confederates either reciprocated or did not reciprocate a person's disclosures; they found that the subjects trusted and liked the confederates in the reciprocation condition significantly more than did the subjects in the nonreciprocation condition.

What is meant by self-disclosure? How does a helper disclose in a way which increases trust in a relationship? *Self-disclosure* is revealing how you are reacting to the present situation and giving any information about the past that is relevant to understanding how you are reacting to the present (Johnson, 1972a); it is the sharing of information, ideas, thoughts, feelings, and reactions relevant to the issue being discussed (Johnson and Johnson, 1975a). Reciprocated disclosures indicate your willingness to trust the client, thus promoting his further trust of you. Your willingness to risk being vulnerable to him increases the likelihood that he will risk being vulnerable to you. If, for example, a person confides that he is disappointed in your efforts to help him, he is risking your rejection. You will build trust if you offer your own feelings about the situation, such as your frustration in not being able to give him the kind of immediate relief that he expected.

Self-disclosure is based upon self-awareness and self-acceptance; in order to disclose your reactions, for example, you have to be aware of your reactions and accept them enough so that you will not defensively hide or misrepresent them. For specific exercises to develop skills in self-disclosure see Johnson (1972a).

Reduction of Defensiveness

When a person is feeling defensive he will protect himself by stubbornly adhering to his present attitudes and behavior and will feel threatened by other points of view. Defensiveness reduces the tolerance of ambiguity as well as one's openness to the new and unfamiliar. The tension generated by being defensive leads to rigid and stereotyped thought processes. Such feelings of threat and levels of tension lead to closed rather than open-mindedness. In order to be influenced by another person one must attend to the other's messages, accurately comprehend the messages, and finally accept the content as valid. *Open-mindedness* is the willingness to attend to, comprehend, and gain insight into attitudes which are discrepant from one's own; it is the ability to receive, evaluate, and act on relevant information on its *own* merits (as opposed to viewing it only from one's own frame of reference). *Closed mindedness* is the withdrawal (psychologically or physically) from opportunities to explore attitudes which are discrepant from one's own and the search to bolster one's attitudes by seeking out others with similar views. There is considerable research which indicates that the more defensive the person is the more he will refuse to communicate with others who have opposing points of view (Johnson, 1973b). In order for the helper to change destructive and inappropriate client attitudes he must reduce the client's defensiveness and increase the client's open-mindedness.

Client defensiveness can be reduced through the same actions which establish trust in the relationship. As trust increases, the feeling of risk in being open to other points of view decreases, thus reducing the tension and feelings of threat connected with exploring alternative attitudes and behavior.

In particular, defensiveness is reduced and open-mindedness increases through the helper's communicating that the client has been heard and clearly understood. It is important that the helper express both his *intention* of wanting to understand the client and his *actual* understanding of the client's situation.

Johnson (1971b) found that a communicator can express the *intention* of trying to accurately understand the listener's position, as well as the impression that he is an understanding person through the expression of *warmth*. Johnson also found that the expression of *accurately understanding* of the listener's position resulted in the belief that the expressor accurately understands the listener's position, is attempting to understand the listener's position, and is an understanding person. Thus the expression of warmth will communicate the *intentions* of wanting to understand the client and the expression of accurate understanding will communicate both the intentions of wanting to understand and the *actual* understanding of the client. Since both the expression of warmth and accurate understanding have been discussed previously, they will not be discussed here.

Reduction of Egocentrism

In order for a person to change his attitudes he needs to become sufficiently detached from his original viewpoints to be able to see the situation from new perspectives. The basis of rational problem solving is a clear understanding of all sides of an issue and an accurate assessment of their validity and relative merits. The helper and the client analyze the current crisis of the client in order to find more constructive patterns of thinking and behaving. To do this the client must have the capacity to understand the perspectives of other people (including the helper). A helper must facilitate the perspective taking ability of the client in order to reduce the client's egocentrism which prevents constructive problem solving and functional attitude change. *Egocentrism* is the inability to take another person's perspective. *Perspective taking* is the ability to understand how a situation appears to another person and how the person is reacting cognitively and affectively to the situation (Johnson, 1975). As was discussed earlier, the development of perspective taking ability is crucial in order for the client to view his problems and actions from a variety of points of view, which allows for insight into the destructiveness of self-defeating attitudes and the awareness of how a new set of attitudes will promote constructive thought patterns and constructive interaction with others.

The major procedures for the helper to use to increase the client's perspective taking is role reversal. Role reversal occurs when the client takes the role of another person and presents the viewpoint of that person as if the client were he. To initiate the use of role reversal the helper identifies another person involved in the client's problems. This can be a current person (such as his wife) or a past person (such as his father when the client was 10 years old). It can even be a different part of the client (such as taking the minority viewpoint in the client's ambivalence about a problem situation). Once the person has been identified the helper asks the client to present the position and attitudes of the other person. In doing so the client is to present the position and attitudes as if he were that person. Sometimes it is helpful for the client to switch back and forth between his position and viewpoint and the viewpoint and position of another significant person; in such a case having the client switch chairs as he switches viewpoints helps the process. Sometimes it is possible to have the person being role played observe and comment on the accuracy of the representation. Other times it is possible to have another person (such as oneself or a third party) to play the role of the other person and then periodically have the client and the other role player switch roles.

The use of role reversal has been found to increase a person's understanding of the content and frame of reference of others' positions (Johnson, 1966, 1967, 1968, 1971c, 1972b). The more incompatible the positions of the client and the person being role played, however, and the more defensive and committed the client is to his position and attitudes, the harder it will be to achieve insight into the positions and attitudes of others (Johnson, 1968). Many times the client, due to his defensiveness and biases, will misperceive the actions and attitudes of others with whom he is interacting. In order for successful problem solving and productive change to take place such misunderstandings and misperceptions need to be clarified. Johnson (1966, 1967, 1968) found strong support for the notion that role reversal will clarify misunderstandings and misperceptions.

Reduction of Demoralization

People's reactions towards their psychological difficulties are different from their reactions towards other kinds of problems. An engineer who daily solves extremely complex technical problems can become extremely demoralized when he finds himself unable to form lasting relationships with other people. A psychologist who is adept at helping other people solve their personal difficulties can become frustrated and discouraged when he confronts a serious difficulty in his own life. When a person finds himself continually unable to act, feel, and think as he believes he should, he usually becomes demoralized (Frank, 1973). Everyone who has personal problems which are not quickly resolved is in danger of becoming demoralized. Frank (1973) notes that to be *demoralized* is to be deprived of courage, to be disheartened, bewildered, confused, and disordered. Demoralized persons are conscious of having failed to meet their expectations or the expectations of others, or of being unable to cope with pressing problems. They feel confused and unable to change the situation or themselves. In some cases they fear that they cannot even control their own feelings, giving rise to the fear that they may "go crazy." To various degrees the demoralized person feels isolated, hopeless, and helpless.

Besides being intrinsically painful, demoralization blocks effective problem solving. First, it can compound the problem and make it worse. If the problem is one in which anxiety is hurting performance, worrying about the problem hurts even more. Sexual difficulties are good examples. A man who becomes impotent may find himself in a vicious circle. The longer his problem continues, the more he worries. Yet the more he worries, the worse the problem gets. All problems involving a large component of fear or anxiety feed and grow on demoralization.

The second destructive feature of demoralization is that it keeps people from perceiving reasonable solutions. A person who feels guilty, anxious, frustrated, and generally rotten about himself is in a very poor frame of mind for rationally developing and weighing alternative courses of action. Demoralized people are prone to plunge into drastic and rash solutions to their difficulties, such as running away or attempting suicide.

How do you reduce demoralization? The lasting cure for demoralization is success. The person who is continually able to meet his personal standards for successful living is bound to feel good about himself. Of course getting the client to this position is the end point of the helping process, and it cannot be achieved without some more immediate relief of demoralization. Recent research on causal attribution theory (Jones et al., 1971; Matross, 1974a) and some not so recent clinical observations suggest that demoralization is related to the individual's "insight" into his problems—the way he conceptualizes the nature and source of his difficulties. Some explanations of the causes of problems lead people to feel better about themselves and prospects for change. Other insights compound the distress and despair of demoralization. A short-term way to help people feel less demoralized is by shaping their explanations of their problems.

The first factor to consider in explaining psychological problems is the *stability* implied by the explanation (Blechman, 1973). Individuals feel less demoralized when they attribute their problems to *unstable* causes—things which come and go or at least had a definite beginning. Explanations in terms of attitudes, learned habits, or environmental stresses all imply instability. On the other hand, attributions of difficulties to fixed personality traits or to a malignant destiny imply stability. All too often demoralized people fear that their personality make-up has a radical and permanent defect. Others, like Job, feel that they have been singled out and fated to endure a painful existence. Neither of these attributions to stable causes will lead to change and health.

Even when a person really has suffered a permanent blow, he can be helped by attributing the majority of his difficulties to causes besides his fate. One of the authors counseled disabled veterans of the Vietnamese War. Some of these young men, vigorous and athletic before they were injured, blamed their injury for ruining their lives. They were depressed, apathetic, with no desire to find employment, or even to see other people. Part of their treatment was to get them to realize that many of their problems were due to their attitudes towards their injuries and not a necessary consequence of the injury itself. Once they understood that their depression, apathy, and shame could be attributed to their attitude of having been completely ruined by their injuries, they were able to improve. The key to this improvement was the shift from attributing their problems to an unchanging, permanent cause to an unstable, controllable cause.

The second aspect of problem explanations which you should consider is whether or not the explanation implies that the individual is *responsible* for his problems. Virtually all theories and philosophies of helping people maintain that individuals should be responsible for *changing* their own difficulties. But opinion differs as to whether it is good for people to feel that they caused their problems in the first place. It is likely that in some cases it is helpful for the person to feel as if he caused his problems, while in others it is best that the person attribute his problems to external causes, such as conditioning or job pressures. Current research and practice (Jones et al., 1971; Skilbeck, 1973) suggest that problems of phobias, sexual difficulties, depression, and any difficulty requiring crisis intervention may be helped by attributing them to external causes and avoiding making the person feel responsible for bringing on the problem. Lecturing a guilt-ridden, suicidal individual as to how he got himself into his predicament hardly seems to be the treatment of choice. On the other hand, if a person has been avoiding taking action on his difficulties, or feels generally apathetic and helpless, attributing his difficulties to his own volition may lead him to constructive action (Kirtner and Cartwright, 1958; Schroeder, 1960). Problems like smoking, losing weight, and delinquent behavior are examples of difficulties which can be helped by attributing them to personal causes.

The rationales presented by major therapy systems tend to reflect the differences in explanations and individuals we have considered above. The therapy system which most clearly emphasizes external attributions of problems, Reciprocal Inhibition Therapy, (see Chapter 8) was developed from Joseph Wolpe's experience in working with persons whose problems involved a great deal of fear and anxiety. In contrast the system most emphasizing personal responsibility for problems, Reality Therapy, was developed from William Glasser's experiences in working with juvenile delinquents.

How do you help people gain insights which will reduce their demoralization? There are two basic ways. The first is quite straightforward. You simply offer the client an interpretation of his difficulties which incorporates the qualities you want it to have. For instance, if you wanted a fearful person to attribute his problems to an impersonal, unstable cause you might follow the procedure outlined by Wolpe and Lazarus (1966):

> The behavior therapist schools the patient to realize that his unpleasant reactions are due to emotional habits that he cannot help; that they have nothing to do with moral fibre or an unwillingness to get well; that similar reactions are easily induced in animals, and that when the time comes when the experimenter decides to "cure" the neurosis, he applies to the problem methods that are determined by principles of learning. Just as the unlearning of the experimental neurosis is completely in the control of the experimenter, so the overcoming of a human neurosis is quite within the control of the therapist through techniques quite similar to those used in the laboratory (pp. 16–17.)

Although you will often find behavior therapists who want nothing to do with the concept of insight, many of them explicitly combat demoralization by reducing the client's feelings of being personally responsible for his problems.

If the client is not in the midst of an emotional crisis, and has had difficulty in confronting his real problems, you can consider attributing his problems to a personal, unstable cause. One way to do this is to use a Reality Therapy (Glasser, 1965) approach of ignoring an individual's external explanations of his behavior (e.g., "I drink because of my job pressures") and attributing his difficulties to his unwillingness to take responsibility. Point out to him that he is not taking responsibility for his current behavior, and that if he expects to change he must *choose* to commit himself to that effort. Such an explanation implies personal causation for problem behavior, as well as instability.

Of course, any explanation you give a client for his difficulties should make sense to you. You should never give an explanation which you do not find personally credible. There are enough plausible explanations for a given problem so that you need never feel that you have to lie to a person to combat his demoralization.

There is a second, more subtle way to help a person develop a useful insight into his dilemmas. This is the method of "problem elaboration" developed by George Kelly (1955). Skilled therapists have learned that diagnostic questions can be used to reduce demoralization as well as gain information. Kelly suggests that the following set of questions will accomplish both purposes:

1. For what problems do you wish help?
2. When were these problems first noticed?
3. Under what conditions did these problems first appear?
4. What corrective measures have been attempted?
5. What changes have come with treatment or the passing of time?
6. Under what conditions are the problems most noticeable?
7. Under what conditions are the problems least noticeable?

The formulation of the questions is designed to get the client (1) to see his problems as having a definite beginning and end, (2) to see them as fluid and temporary, and then (3) to interpret them as responsive to (a) treatment, (b) the passing of time, and (c) varying conditions (Kelly, 1955). Answering these questions will get the client well on his way to seeing his problems as unstable, an important step for the demoralized individual who sees his problems as everlasting features of his existence.

Anyone who finds himself falling short of his standards is likely to be demoralized. You can help remove this obstacle to change by giving the individual an explanation for his difficulties which will reduce his fears about them and give him the belief that they can be controlled.

In summary, you will be more effective in changing attitudes if you first establish conditions conducive to change. This means building a trusting relationship, which will allow you and the client to communicate effectively, and reducing factors which interfere with constructive problem solving: defensiveness, which protects inappropriate attitudes; egocentrism, which prevents seeing

Table 3.1. A Model of Attitude Change in a Helping Relationship.

1. Using a model of psychological health, diagnose the client's present situation. Identify attitudes to be changed and goals of change.
2. Establish conditions conducive to attitude change: Build a trusting relationship with the client and reduce the change obstacles of defensiveness, egocentrism, and demoralization.
3. From major theories of attitude change, select and apply appropriate attitude change methods.
4. Stabilize desirable changes and assess the client's progress.

one's problems from new perspectives; and demoralization, which decreases a person's motivation to solve his problems.

After the conditions for attitude change have been established the helper must select and implement a theory (or combination of theories) of attitude change. In the following sections the major theories of attitude change will be reviewed.

ATTITUDE ACQUISITION AND CHANGE

There are five major approaches to the area of attitude acquisition and change. For one thing, attitudes are learned and, therefore, it is possible to approach attitude acquisition and change with *learning* methods. Yet attitudes are largely composed of meanings; how two attitudes relate to each other depends upon their meaningful content, not just upon their both being learned. Thus, there is a *cognitive* approach to attitude acquisition and change. Third, attitudes are developed only if they serve a function for the person; a person develops attitudes to cope with his world by forming relatively stable orientations toward common parts of his experience. Thus, there is a *functional* approach to changing and acquiring attitudes. Most attitudes are influenced by other people with whom a person interacts and identifies. Thus, there are *social influence* methods which can be used to develop and change attitudes. Finally, the social *structure* which prescribes certain behavioral roles and the *process* of carrying out these roles influence the acquisition and stability of attitudes. Each of these five approaches to attitude acquisition and change will be discussed in the following sections with the emphasis being placed upon their use for a person helping another individual.

LEARNING THEORY APPROACHES

Since attitudes are learned all methods known to increase or decrease learning should be applicable to the acquisition or changing of attitudes. Attitude change may be simply a matter of new learning. There are three orientations to changing attitudes through learning methods: classical conditioning, operant conditioning, and the work of Carl Hovland and his associates.

Classical Conditioning

A basic principle of classical conditioning is *stimulus generalization*: when a particular response habitually follows a particular stimulus, elements similar to, or closely associated with, this stimulus also show a tendency to elicit a similar response. This process has been suggested as an explanation for the acquisition of attitudes (Staats, 1967). For example, a girl may be consistently scolded by a stern father. Her father's behavior elicits in her feelings of fear, anxiety, and anger. Through stimulus generalization other men come to elicit these same feelings in her when she is around them. As a result she develops negative attitudes towards men.

Sometimes a person will have been conditioned to have a negative response towards something he really needs to like. To help him you would use *counter-conditioning* which involves repeatedly pairing a stimulus which evokes a negative emotional response with a stimulus which evokes a positive emotional response; such a procedure will condition the positive emotional response to the negative stimulus if the positive stimulus elicits more powerful responses than the negative stimulus. Sounds complicated? It works like this: A friend of yours who is a football coach asks your help. Like many whites, he is prejudiced against blacks, yet his star football players are black and he needs to develop a positive attitude towards them. Since his original prejudiced attitudes are assumed to have developed through classical conditioning you decide they can be changed through counter-conditioning. You decide on the following plan. More than anything else your friend wants to be known as a great coach. Every time your friend sees a black person you immediately tell him what a good coach he is. If the compliment is more positive than the prejudice is negative gradually the coach will change his attitudes towards blacks! Although this example is offered somewhat in fun and is oversimplified, Litcher and Johnson (1968) did conduct a study in which the repeated pairing of pictures of blacks with middle-class characteristics significantly reduced the prejudice of white second graders. Thus, counter-conditioning can work. (See Chapter 8 for a full examination of counter-conditioning methods.)

Operant Conditioning

A basic principle of operant conditioning is *response reinforcement*, which takes place when rewards are associated with specific responses. (See Chapter 7 for a full examination of operant conditioning methods.) Responses which are rewarded are more likely to be repeated; attitudes which are rewarded are more likely to be developed and maintained. The procedures for using operant conditioning are as follows. Clearly identify the attitude you wish to strengthen and the words and behaviors which represent that attitude. Every time the person makes one of the specified statements or engages in one of the specified behaviors you reward him in some way. Very quickly the expression of the attitude will increase and you begin rewarding him for only every third expression of the attitude. In this way the attitude may be quickly strengthened and maintained for long periods of time.

For example, one of your teachers asks your help in improving his lectures. You and he identify a series of attitudes which will improve his lectures, such as the attitude that students are interested in learning and are quite fascinating people. An expression of such an attitude would be to ask students questions during class and be quite attentive when they give a reply or make a spontaneous statement about the material being covered. You enlist the aid of several students and every time the teacher asks students questions or looks attentive you all smile and nod approval. After the teacher begins to ask lots of questions and looks very attentive, you all smile and nod every other time, then every third time, and so on. Before long the teacher not only improves his lectures, but develops positive attitudes towards students. Through operant conditioning you have significantly altered the behavioral expression of his attitudes towards students, and hence the attitudes themselves.

Yale Attitude Change Program

Carl Hovland and his associates at Yale University developed a program of empirical research organized around the theme, "Who says what to whom with what effect?" This sentence is usually broken down into an examination of three components: the communicator, the message, and the audience. The Yale approach is derived from learning theory in that it assumes that people are rational in the way they process information, are motivated to attend to a message, learn its contents, and incorporate it into their attitudes. For a more complete discussion of the Yale research, see Goldstein, Heller, and Sechrest (1966), and Strong (1968).

The Communicator

Aristotle noted that an effective communicator must be a man of good sense, goodwill, and good moral character. Following Aristotle's notions, most of the research on personal characteristics of the communicator has focused on the dimension of credibility. The credibility of a communicator consists of his expertise, trustworthiness, and objectivity; that is, his perceived ability to know valid information and his motivation to communicate this knowledge without bias. More specifically, research has demonstrated that credibility consists of:

1. Expertness relevant to the topic under discussion.
2. Reliability as an information source; this refers to the perceived character of the communicator, such as his dependability, predictability, and consistency.
3. Intentions of the communicator. It is usually important for the receiver to know whether or not the motives of the communicator are entirely selfish. Whatever effect we want our message to have upon the receiver, we should be open about it.
4. The expression of warmth and friendliness.
5. Dynamism of the communicator. A dynamic communicator is perceived to be aggressive, empathic, and forceful.
6. The majority opinion of other people concerning the degree of credibility of the communicator. If all our friends tell us the communicator is an expert and trustworthy, we tend to believe it.

The more you develop your skills in each of the above areas, the more credible and effective you will become. Much of what you can do to become credible requires a serious long-term effort. Credibility involves becoming genuinely knowledgeable about help-giving through study and practice, and leading the kind of life that gives you a reputation for honesty and dependability.

Fortunately, some skills contributing to credibility can be developed and practiced fairly quickly. The techniques for expressing warmth and cooperative intentions referred to earlier in this chapter are two examples. In addition, you can learn to do some things to appear dynamic and competent to the person you are trying to help.

The first way to appear dynamic is to be responsive, both verbally and nonverbally. Look at the other person when you talk to him and vary your facial expression as he speaks. Avoid staring off into space or planting a "dead pan" expression on your face. As you speak, vary the tone of your voice and use mild and natural gestures. Try to get rid of things like nervous tics, recurring itches, bad breath, and anything else which might distract a listener from concentrating on what you are saying.

The second way to appear dynamic is to make your questions and comments logically coherent. Your questions should follow in a logical sequence and not ask for more than one piece of information at a time. When you make comments, you should get to your point quickly and confidently without rambling. You should take the lead in organizing and structuring the conversation. In short, you should make sense. People who need help are confused enough without your adding to their confusion.

A helper's knowledge and experience may have little impact if he is not dynamic. Schmidt and Strong (1970) found that students viewing video tapes of simulated counseling sessions considered an experienced psychologist and an advanced graduate student less responsive and coherent than beginning graduate students. Without knowing their backgrounds, the viewers rated the beginning students as more expert than the others. Being genuinely competent and trustworthy are the most important ways to be credible, but you will be unnecessarily handicapping yourself if you do not also learn to appear warm, cooperative, and dynamic.

The Message

The ability of the communicator to organize and phrase his message skillfully determines much of the effectiveness he has in changing the attitudes of his audience. The nature of arguments, their logical coherence, their emotional appeal, and the language used by the communicator are all important. The general results of social psychological research in this area are that two-sided arguments in which the side you are advocating is presented last is probably the most effective. Thus, if you wanted to convince a person of his competence, you would briefly mention his feelings of being incompetent and then give a detailed presentation as to why you think he is competent. Emotional appeals can be useful under certain circumstances; if you want to help a person stop smoking, arousing a great deal of fear is useful, provided that you recommend explicit and possible actions to take to avoid the dangers you are noting. Clearly you do not want to use an emotional appeal with a person who is already tense and distraught. In most cases it is helpful to state the conclusions of your arguments. However, if you are dealing with a highly intelligent person and you can offer convincing evidence, it is better to let him draw his own conclusions.

The Audience

The effectiveness of any message is assumed to be determined by how successfully it is tailored for its intended audience. Appealing to a religious value might be very persuasive to a seminary student but quite ineffective with someone without strong religious feelings. If people do not want to have their attitudes changed it is often helpful to distract them while you are presenting your message; then they can't argue effectively against it to themselves (planting the message in a story is one way to use distractions). Individuals with low self-esteem are more easily influenced than are individuals with high self-esteem. Within limits, people with problems have lowered self-esteem and are frequently highly persuadable.

COGNITIVE THEORY APPROACHES

We all have lots of attitudes and they are organized into systems according to their content and meanings. How attitudes relate to each other depends on their meaningful content. Thus, principles of cognitive organization need to be considered for understanding the acquisition and change of attitudes. Specifically, there are two principles of cognitive organization which are discussed in the attitude literature: the principle of simplicity and the principle of evaluative consistency.

Simplicity

Our senses pick up a mass of stimuli which must be organized if we are to make sense out of it. In organizing our perceptions we simplify them by placing things into categories (such as boys and girls) and then organizing the categories into conceptual systems. People tend to organize their cognitions into a framework of maximum uniformity and regularity and this is the principle of simplicity. Perceptions become organized into a "whole" or "gestalt" which is more than just the sum of its separate parts and which tends to be as well organized as prevailing conditions allow. Attitudes, as one type of cognition, are organized, therefore, into systems which are characterized by simplification in order to get a good "gestalt." In other words, people do not perceive things as unrelated isolates, but rather they organize things in the perceptual process into meaningful wholes. Attitudes become a way of simplifying one's perceptions; they become a frame of reference into which new perceptions are placed. If you see another person on campus, for example, you may immediately classify the person by sex and attractiveness and automatically have certain feelings towards that person.

The lack of simple and well-organized gestalts is a malady of our times. Rapid changes in social and religious customs have left many people without a solid core of attitudes to help them interpret the world. By spending time helping a person to clarify his values and attitudes and their effect on his life you can help the person come to terms with needed changes. One of the authors counseled a young man who was threatening suicide. Newly acquired family responsibilities and a dissatisfaction with his present job had left him demoralized and rootless. A long discussion of the young man's values and attitudes resulted in his concluding that the value of learning was one invariant factor that made life meaningful and worthwhile to him. The counselor pointed out how suicide would be shutting off all opportunities to grow and learn. With his new awareness of his values and attitudes the young man was able to give up both his thoughts of suicide and his dissatisfying job and return to college. Thus, the way in which the principle of simplicity can be used by a helper interested in changing the attitudes of the client is through discussing the client's attitudes in ways which lead to a reorganization and a new frame of reference. This can be done by discovering better "gestalts" of a simpler way of putting several attitudes together.

Besides being disorganized, "gestalts" can be incomplete or unfinished. A young lawyer once came to one of the authors on the advice of his doctors and asked whether his ulcers were being caused by unresolved psychological tensions. After a series of sessions it became apparent that the lawyer was constantly angry about the high expectations and standards his father had for his behavior, but because of his fear of his father's disapproval he was afraid to express his anger or even admit it to himself most of the time. Consequently, he would repress all awareness of his anger. This unexpected anger became an unfinished "gestalt" which may have contributed to his ulcers.

Evaluative Consistency

Closely related to the tendency to simplify our cognitions is a tendency towards an evaluative consistency. Attitudes possess an evaluative quality. The principle of evaluative consistency holds that we tend to have similar evaluations of cognitive elements which are associated together. If we closely associate two attitudes in our thinking (attitudes towards this chapter and the two authors, for example) we will tend to have similar evaluations, pro or con, in regard to them (if we like the chapter we like the authors!). And, conversely, if we have similar evaluations of two objects we will tend to organize them together.

There are several consistency theories of attitude change. Each theory postulates a basic "need" for consistency among attitudes or between attitudes and behavior. Most of the theories further assume that the presence of inconsistency produces "psychological tension," or at least is uncomfortable, and in order to reduce this tension a person "rearranges" his psychological world to produce consistency. In other words, persons will try to appear rational and consistent to themselves. The original consistency theory is Heider's (1958) and the best known consistency theory is Festinger's (1957).

The most powerful source of inconsistency is between one's self-attitudes about one's self and one's perceived behavior or one's other attitudes. A person may believe that he is absolutely worthless and when others tell him how valuable his behavior has been there will be feelings of inconsistency, imbalance, or dissonance. A feeling of consistency will be achieved by changing one's attitudes about oneself (I really am worthwhile) or about one's behavior (I fooled them; they don't realize how worthless my behavior actually was). One may help a person who has a low evaluation of himself by making his behavior so apparently and clearly of value that he has little alternative but to change his self-attitudes if he is to achieve consonance or balance. Another person may believe that he is a fair and just person, but also believe certain ethnic groups are inferior to the white majority. By highlighting these two attitudes, and emphasizing how fair and just the person is, the person will have little alternative but to change his attitudes towards the ethnic groups. The general procedure for using an evaluative consistency approach to attitude change is, therefore, to identify the self-attitudes, identify the behavior or other attitudes inconsistent with the self-attitudes, and emphasize the inconsistency while supporting the attitude or behavior which you do not want the person to change.

In focusing consistency theory on attitude change, research has been conducted on the question of inconsistency between attitudes and behavior when the person has been "forced" into the behavior. When the attitudes are important to the person and when there is little justification for allowing oneself to be forced into the behavior, a great deal of dissonance or inconsistency is felt. Most often a person will then change his attitudes as he cannot take back his behavior. A helper may use this procedure in the following way. Suppose a person comes to you for help saying he is hopelessly a leaf on the breeze, unable to provide any direction to his life or have any impact on what happens to him. You might examine with him all the effects his behavior has had and the way in which he set a goal for his behavior and carried them through. In addition you defeat all his attempts to deny that his behavior had no impact and emphasize the potency he has shown. The person will have no alternative but to change his self-attitude if he wants to achieve consistency or balance or consonance. If fact, in such a situation the very fact that he came to someone for help shows a capacity for affecting the direction and effect of his behavior.

Socrates was probably the first person to use a consistency approach to attitude change. His "Socratic Method" for changing the attitudes of his students was to question them about specific cases illustrating their definitions of the concept under question, such as friendship, justice, or piety. He structured his questions in such a way as to get the students to admit exceptions to their definitions. The inconsistency between the old definition and the newly revealed specific exceptions caused the students to evolve new and more comprehensive definitions. By no coincidence, the new definitions closely resembled Socrates' own definitions, even though Socrates did not openly state his own position. The two keys to the Socratic Method were the use of questioning and the use of inductive reasoning—deriving general statements from specific cases. Socrates stood in sharp contrast to other teachers, who deduced their opinions and then lectured their students as to why these opinions should be accepted.

Matross (1974b) developed a method of changing people's attitudes towards themselves, utilizing the principles of the Socratic Method. The logic of this approach is to use questioning to elicit a pattern of specific examples from the client's behavior which are inconsistent with the attitude you want to change. Confronted with concrete and specific evidence refuting an unhealthy self-perception, the individual will thus be encouraged to inductively arrive at a new view of himself. The steps in this method are as follows:

1. Identify the self-perception which needs to be changed, e.g., a belief that one is incompetent and unable to achieve. Then think of actions which would be inconsistent with the target attitude. In our example, actions involving hard work, extra effort, and unusual striving are likely to have resulted in genuine achievement and would be inconsistent with a perception of incompetence.

2. Start questioning the person about specific behaviors relating to the target attitude. Start with a general lead, such as, "Let's talk about your achievement. Can you think of some examples which illustrate the ways you try to achieve?"

3. Continue the questioning, asking for exactly what you want. Initially a person may give you an example which you don't want (e.g., "I goofed off and flunked biology"). Acknowledge such nontarget examples with the briefest of summaries (e.g., "So biology was bad news") and move on to a question explicitly requesting a target example, "Can you think of a time when you really put out a lot of effort and came through when you had to?"

4. Ask detailed questions about the effects of the target behavior and the effects of nontarget actions the person could have taken, e.g., "What were the results of putting out that effort on the psychology paper? Did you get a better grade? Did your teacher think it was pretty good? Did you get a sense of personal satisfaction?" Summarize the answers to these questions and then ask questions about the effects of nontarget alternatives, e.g., "Suppose you hadn't researched that paper so well. Suppose you had only read a few pages and not put out much effort at all. Do you think you would have done poorly?" Give a final summary of the example, contrasting what the person did with the things he did not do, e.g., "You could have sloughed off, spent only a couple of hours in the library, and copied a lot of that paper. If you had done that, you would have gotten a low grade, disappointed your teacher and yourself. Instead you chose to push hard, studying many hours, reading several books and giving them a lot of thought. As a consequence of this effort, you got a good grade, pleased the teacher and gained self-respect."

5. Continue asking for examples of target behaviors and going through the question sequence above. When the conversation comes to a logical conclusion, offer a final summary. Take your three or four best examples of target behaviors and emphasize how these form a consistent pattern, with only a brief nonspecific acknowledgment of contrary behavior, e.g., "On the one hand, there are times when you don't exert much effort and don't achieve. On the other hand, there are several times when you do exert a lot of effort and do very well. For example . . . ."

The success of the Socratic Method rests on its concreteness and specificity. Rather than lecturing the person as to why he should change an inappropriate attitude you are getting him to generate his own case for change. A person who is down on himself has usually been creating evidence to support his negative attitudes. By focusing his attention on examples of positive actions, you will be creating a healthy inconsistency in his views of himself. If done well, the impact of the specific examples you have elicited should be enough so that you should not have to openly state the conclusion you want the client to reach. Matross (1974b) found that additional influence attributable to an overtly stated conclusion dissipated over time. Also individuals given an overt conclusion had less confidence in their conclusions than did those who were presented only with the Socratic questions. With practice you will find that the question sequences will become quite smooth and natural.

FUNCTIONAL APPROACH

Of what use to a person are his attitudes? This question epitomizes the central focus of the functional approach to attitude acquisition and change. Two major functional approaches are those of Katz (1960) and Ellis (1962). The functional approach to attitudes views humans as striving to accomplish certain goals, and analyzes attitudes in terms of the extent to which the attitudes facilitate goal accomplishment. Katz' version of the functional approach is to specify the psychological needs individuals are trying to meet by holding the attitudes they do (Katz, 1960; Katz and Stotland, 1959; Sarnoff and Katz, 1954). Katz states there are four functions of attitudes: (1) adjustive, (2) ego-defensive, (3) knowledge, and (4) value-expressive.

The *adjustive function* of attitudes recognizes that people strive to maximize the rewards in their external environment and to minimize the penalties. Thus a person develops favorable attitudes towards the objects which are associated with the satisfaction of his needs and unfavorable attitudes towards objects which thwart or punish him. The *ego-defensive function* revolves around the notion that a person protects himself from anxiety by obliterating threatening external and internal stimuli. Thus attitudes can function like defense mechanisms to protect a person from acknowledging his conflicts and deficiencies to himself and other people. To a considerable degree, for example, prejudiced attitudes help to sustain the individual's self-concept by maintaining a sense of superiority over others. The *knowledge function* refers to the fact that people seek knowledge to give meaning to what otherwise would be an unorganized, chaotic world. People need standards or frames of reference for understanding their world, and attitudes help to supply such standards. Attitudes help people establish a degree of predictability, consistency, and stability in their perception of the world. Finally, the *value-expressive function* of attitudes involves the notion that attitudes give positive expression to an individual's central values and his self-concept. Satisfactions are derived from the expression of attitudes which reflect one's cherished beliefs and self-image.

The ways in which you can use Katz' theory are as follows. When the client comes to you for help, you identify who and what are meeting his needs and who and what are thwarting his needs; your discussion with him should be used to build positive attitudes towards the former and negative attitudes toward the latter (adjustive function). You may also identify the ways in which his attitudes are protecting him from anxiety and either increase their effectiveness or point out why they should be discarded for a set of more effective attitudes (ego-defensive function). You may identify the person's frame of reference and see how much predictability, consistency, and stability the frame of reference provides for the person; you therefore attempt to strengthen the attitudes in the frame of reference, or point out how they are ineffective and try to persuade the person to discard them for a more effective set (knowledge function). You may identify the values and self-concept of the client, and evaluate his attitudes on the basis of how well they express the values and promote a positive self-concept; again, you seek to either strengthen productive attitudes, or point out their ineffectiveness and try to persuade the client to discard them for a more effective set (value-expressive function).

Katz' theory can also help you understand resistance to change. A person may be reluctant to change an attitude which has helped him cope with the world, however inadequately. You can reduce the threat of change if you can demonstrate how a new attitude will better serve the function of the old attitude.

A second approach to the functional change of attitudes is that of Ellis (1962). Whereas Katz considers the adaptive, coping functions of attitudes, Ellis stresses the negative, self-defeating functions which attitudes can serve. He assumes that most psychological problems are rooted in certain erroneous and destructive attitudes. For instance, frustration, disappointment, and apathy can result from the attitude that everything one does must be perfect. When confronted by inevitable mistakes, the person with this attitude continually criticizes himself and reindoctrinates himself with his perfectionistic standards. The way out of this predicament is to adopt a new and more realistic set of attitudes towards performance, such as the belief that failure, while not pleasant, is not catastrophic, and that appropriate goal setting is more pleasant than demands for perfection.

To use the Ellis approach to change, you should first identify the attitudes responsible for the negative events in the client's life. You should then elaborate in considerable detail all the ways in which these attitudes serve negative and self-defeating functions. Finally, you should point out exactly how new attitudes will serve positive, self-enhancing functions. Instructions for these procedures can be found in Ellis (1962) and in Chapter 4 of the present book.

SOCIAL INFLUENCE APPROACH

The correctness of many of our attitudes cannot be checked against physical reality. There is, for example, often no way to objectively measure our personal value. When physical reality cannot be used to determine the correctness of an attitude, a person is dependent upon other people as a basis of social reality. Every person depends upon other people for information to establish the validity of their attitudes. There are two major influences within social reality which will be discussed in this section: reference groups and reference individuals.

Reference Groups

A reference group is a group of persons we use as standards to evaluate our attitudes, abilities, or current situation. A person using a reference group to evaluate his attitudes assumes his attitudes to be correct to the extent that most of the members of the group have similar attitudes. It is, of course, not necessary that all people with whom he associates agree with his attitudes, but it is important that some relevant reference group share his attitudes. There is considerable evidence that the groups we belong to have powerful influences on our attitudes and behavior. Johnson and Neale (1970), for example, found that students involved in social action activities belong to groups which have norms favorable to social action activities, and have a negative identification with groups against social action activities. Watson and Johnson (1972) summarize a great deal of research in the areas of conformity, reference groups, group norms, group decision making, and social comparison processes which demonstrates the power a group has over a person's attitudes and behavior. The implications of this research for attitude change are:

1. The attitudes of an individual are strongly influenced by the groups to which he belongs and those to which he wants to belong.
2. If a person's attitudes conform to group standards and norms he is reinforced, and he is punished for having attitudes which deviate from group standards and norms.
3. Those individuals who are most attached to the group are the least influenced by attempts to change their attitudes.
4. The support of even one other member for a minority attitude weakens the powerful effect of the group majority upon that attitude.
5. A minority of two people who are consistent in the expression of their attitudes can influence the majority of other group members.
6. Participation in group discussions and group decision making helps to overcome resistance to developing new attitudes; if a group decides to adopt new attitudes, its members will also adopt new attitudes.
7. As a person's reference groups change, so do his attitudes.

Suppose a friend comes to you and asks you to help him develop better study habits so he will not flunk out of school. You find that his friends (other than yourself) all have negative attitudes towards studying and positive attitudes towards spending every available minute in a certain bar. When the person tries to study he is teased; when he is not in the bar he is ridiculed. From a reference group standpoint, there are two ways to deal with this problem: change the reference group norms or change the person's reference groups. There are two ways to change the reference group norms: conduct a group discussion in which a group decision is made to change the group norm, or influence one or two members to change their attitudes, thus forming a solid minority. Changing a person's reference group is usually a gradual process of reducing the importance of one group while increasing the importance of another. The stabilizing effects reference groups have on attitudes point up the importance of ensuring that there will be interpersonal support for any new attitudes a client develops while you are working with him.

Another way in which reference groups can be helpful is when you are requested to help a person who has never shared his attitudes with others and who, therefore, is in a state of insulated ignorance about the appropriateness and generality of his attitudes. *Insulated ignorance* is defensiveness which prevents a person from sharing his attitudes with others or listening to attitude expressions of others in a sensitive area. Some individuals are so fearful of discussing their attitudes and feelings with others that they never do and, therefore, have distorted views of what most people believe. A person once came to one of the authors of this chapter for help in developing better sexual relationships with females. Part of his problem was that he believed that females were inherently liars, deceitful, untrustworthy, hostile towards men, uncaring, insensitive, ensnaring, and wanted only to exploit men for their bodies. He firmly believed that the vast majority of men in the United States shared his attitudes. Such ignorance of others' attitudes was insulated by his extreme defensiveness which prevented him from discussing females with any of his friends. The author encouraged the person to discuss his attitudes with others and suggested group experiences which put him in contact with men who held more favorable attitudes towards women; such experiences helped the person realize the extent to which his attitudes were unusual and should be reconsidered.

Reference Individuals

Reference individuals are individuals a person uses as standards to evaluate his attitudes, abilities, or current situation; such influence is often exercised through identification. *Identification* is a general process whereby one person takes on the attributes (such as attitudes) of another. Johnson and Neale (1970), for example, found that students involved in social action activities identified with persons within and outside their family who had attitudes favorable to such involvement. If the client identifies with the helper, and uses the helper as a reference individual, the helper will be able to exercise a great deal of influence over the client's incorporation of more appropriate and constructive attitudes and behaviors. The helping process has been described as rectifying false identifications. Bad identifications are those which result in stunting or thwarting the individual's growth or which result in destructive and self-defeating attitudes and behavior. Good identifications are those which promote satisfying experiences and goal accomplishment. Thus, you will want to encourage client identification with appropriate persons (including yourself) who have more constructive attitudes than the client now has.

How can the helper encourage a constructive identification by the client with the helper? The primary way is to establish a relationship in which the helper facilitates constructive change of the client's attitudes and expresses warmth towards the client as a person.

When a person comes to you for help he expects and hopes to receive it. You and the client become a cooperative dyad whose goals are to alleviate the client's suffering, find constructive solutions to his problems, and improve his social competencies so he can better handle future crises. With specific reference to attitudes the helper and the client cooperate to identify the current attitudes of the client, assess their impact upon his life and their current relationship to his problems, and then come to a decision about what attitudes need to be strengthened and what attitudes need to be changed or replaced. The helper then tries to facilitate these changes. The client's expectation that the helper will facilitate the accomplishment of the client's goals and the resulting cooperative problem solving produces liking for the helper (D. W. Johnson and Johnson, 1972; D. W. Johnson and Johnson, 1974; S. Johnson and Johnson, 1972). In addition there is considerable evidence that the helper's expression of warmth towards the client as a person will result in client liking for the helper (Johnson, 1971b, 1971d, Johnson and Noonan, 1972). Thus by cooperatively working towards constructive changes in the client's attitudes and by expressing warmth for the client as a person, the helper will facilitate the client's liking for and identification with the helper, which will give the helper more potential influence over the client's attitudes. That liking and identification are related is indicated by the finding that the expression of warmth also produces perceptions by the client that the helper is similar to the client in attitudes and values and as a person (Johnson, 1971b, 1971d; Johnson and Noonan, 1972); in order to keep such a perception valid, the client will often have to modify his attitudes to make them more congruent with those of the helper.

Once identification has been established, there are a variety of ways in which the helper's behavior and actions may influence the attitudes of the client. Identification will lead to potential client incorporation and imitation of the helper's attitudes without much action on the part of the helper. Yet there are four specific helper actions which have an impact upon the attitudes of the client: expression of accurate understanding, expression of cooperative intentions, expression of coldness and anger towards destructive attitudes, and structuring client role reversal.

The expression of accurate understanding has been previously discussed; when it is used in a cold manner while reflecting the destructive attitudes of the client it will result in attitude change (Johnson, 1971b). The expression of cooperative intentions will promote client attitude change (Johnson, 1971b); the procedures for doing so have also been previously discussed. While the expression of warmth does produce liking, it has an interesting relationship to the expression of coldness and anger in regard to a person's attitudes.

When warmth is expressed towards a person's attitudes he will believe that the helper agrees with and supports those attitudes (Johnson, 1971a, 1971b, 1971d). The expression of coldness and anger create the impression that the helper disagrees with and disapproves of those attitudes (Johnson, 1971b, 1971d). But anger and coldness can also produce disliking for the helper (Johnson, 1971b, 1971d). Thus there is a combination of warmth towards a person but coldness and anger towards destructive attitudes which the helper needs to be able to express in order for constructive attitude change to take place. The expression of coldness and anger is discussed below.

The expression of *coldness* is best done through nonverbal messages. A hard tone of voice, a poker-face, frowning, or disinterested facial expression, a tense posture in which you are leaning away from the client, and more closed, harsh gestures are all ways of expressing coldness. Verbally, coldness can be best expressed through ignoring (i.e., silence) the expression of destructive attitudes or simply saying coolly that you do not agree with the attitude and believe it to be destructive to the client's best interests.

The expression of *anger* can be expressed both verbally and nonverbally. Verbally, anger can be expressed by such statements as, "That attitude makes me angry," "That attitude turns me off," "That attitude angers me because of what it does to you," and so on. Nonverbally, anger can be expressed through a cold and cutting tone of voice, a tight-lipped expression, maintaining a stiff or aggressive posture, clenching fists, and leaning back while glaring. Anger is a very delicate tool for a helper to use as Johnson (1971d) found that the expresser often underestimates the negative impact it can have on the receiver. It must be used with great caution.

One of the most effective ways of influencing client attitudes is through structuring role reversal situations. In *role reversing*, a person is asked to present the attitudes, thoughts, and position of another person in an involved way. Through role reversal the person increases his understanding of the content of others' positions and the perspective or frame of reference behind their position (Johnson, 1966, 1967, 1968, 1971a, 1972b). In role reversal the client is asked to enact the behavior of another person and to assume and publicly espouse a set of attitudes with which he disagrees. By engaging in role reversal the client persuades himself to modify his attitudes. There are a number of studies which demonstrate greater modification of attitudes after active role reversal than after passive exposure to the same persuasive materials (Johnson, 1971d). Johnson (1966, 1967, 1971a) found consistent evidence that engaging in role reversal resulted in subsequent attitude change, even when taking the position of others with whom one is negotiating a conflict.

A couple who have had a close relationship for several years requests your assistance in saving their relationship. The husband insists that they move to a small, isolated town because of a better job opportunity. They argue violently about this issue, each accusing the other of failing to love enough to give in to the other's demands. A woman comes to you for help in developing more autonomy. She constantly cries about the way in which her mother treated her as a child and angrily pounds the arm of the chair as she describes the ways in which her mother has failed her. Each of these instances is an example of when you might want to use role reversal. In the first instance each partner needs to gain more understanding and attitude change about the position of the other. In the second instance, the woman needs to change her attitudes about her mother, her mother's perceptions of their relationship, and her dependence upon her mother to make her life turn out well.

The procedures for the use of role reversal are as follows. First, the persons present their attitudes or position. Second, they present the attitudes and position of someone else involved in the situation (such as spouse or mother). In taking the role of the other person they need to role play, as well as they can, the other person. A way in which this can be facilitated is through having another chair available to which a person moves when he is taking the role of the other. If the other person is in the room, the accuracy with which the person is portraying the other's position and perspective can be determined. If the other person is not in the room, the success of the role reversal depends upon the involvement the person can bring to the portrayal. To get the optimal effect it may be necessary for a person to switch back and forth between his own attitudes and perspective and the perspective and position of the other. Thus the woman in the above example may make a statement to her mother (represented by the empty chair), change seats and reply as her mother, change seats and reply as herself, and so on. This role reversal procedure can even be used when one person is ambivalent about certain of his attitudes; he can present each side of his ambivalence and argue the issue with himself while switching back and forth between chairs.

When the dramatized version of role reversal is not possible or appropriate, it is possible to use modified procedures. The use of accurate understanding is a mild form of role reversal; clients can be taught to use accurate understanding in discussing their attitudes with others who have different and more destructive attitudes. The male in the couple in the example above may be asked to describe the female's position and perspective without actually dramatizing her role by pretending to be her. Such procedures will greatly enhance communication and attitude change but perhaps not as effectively as the more involved role playing.

STRUCTURE-PROCESS-ATTITUDE APPROACH

The previous four approaches to attitude acquisition and change have primarily focused upon changing the person in order to change his attitudes and the way in which he interacts with his environment. There is another approach which focuses upon changing the environment in order to change the person. By changing the types (or objective pattern) of situations in which a person finds himself, the ways in which the person interacts with others will be changed and the person's attitudes will be modified. By changing jobs, marital status, schools, teachers, and so on, the attitudes of the person can also be changed. Every society includes a number of subunits of organized interaction which may be called social systems. A family, a school, a business, a baseball team, or a hospital is a social system. Within each social system, persons are given roles which specify generally the expected behaviors of each while interacting with other members. In a family there are the roles of father, mother, and children, each of which has expected behaviors as to how one should interact with the others. These role expectations are further supported by norms and values as to what is appropriate for a given role. A social system, therefore, has a certain pattern or *structure* establishing prescribed roles. In the *process* of carrying out these roles individuals develop corresponding outlooks, *attitudes*, and feelings. A change in the system brings changes in roles, and the changed interaction alters the members' attitudes and feelings. Thus, a social system structure leads to a process of interaction among members which leads to the acquisition of attitudes. For a full discussion of this attitude acquisition and change theory see Watson and Johnson (1972).

When a person comes to you for help, it is important to look at possibilities of changes in social systems or changes in role which will cause new patterns of interaction which in turn will lead to attitude change. A person may continually feel like a failure in one job but feel successful in another; in one group of friends a person may be given the uncomfortable role of "intellectual" which may cause him discomfort, while in another group of friends he may be expected to play the comfortable and familiar role of clown.

Table 3.2.   Approaches to Attitude Change.

I. Learning Approaches
    Classical conditioning methods
    Operant conditioning methods
    Yale program methods: communicator, message, and audience factors
II. Cognitive Approaches
    Gestalt methods
    Consistency methods
III. Functional Approaches
    Katz' functional theory
    Ellis' Rational-Emotive theory
IV. Social Influence Approaches
    Reference group methods
    Reference individual methods
V. Structure-Process-Attitude Interventions

STABILIZING NEW ATTITUDES

After you have established the conditions for attitude change and have selected and implemented a theory (or combination of theories) of attitude change in your sessions with the client, it is necessary to be concerned with stabilizing the new attitudes so that they will endure during future crises and during attempts by others to change them. New attitudes may be acquired; old attitudes can be changed. Yet, if a person is really helped, the new attitudes have to be stabilized so that they do not change back as soon as the helping stops. There are four ways in which a helper can facilitate the stabilization of new attitudes. The first is to discuss the new attitudes enough so that they become integrated into the attitude systems of the person. Since attitudes are organized into systems, a change of a few attitudes will have effects upon many additional attitudes, which will have to be modified and reorganized to accommodate the new attitudes. Changing a person's self-attitudes, for example, may necessitate the changing or modification of his attitudes about the value of other people, the type of jobs he is qualified for, the type of treatment he should expect from other people, the risks he should take in achievement related activities, the type of women he should ask for dates, the credibility he can ascribe to his parents' evaluations of him, and so on. The cognitive organization of attitudes is important and attitude change will not be permanent unless it results in new gestalts or new systems of attitude clusters.

A second way to facilitate the stabilization of new attitudes is through firmly embedding them in chains of causation with their consequences. If the new attitudes stop the old self-destructive behavior and facilitate self-enhancing behaviors the increased satisfaction, happiness, and effectiveness and the decreased pain and depression will sustain the attitudes. Such attributions, however, need to be clear to the client; new attitudes will not be sustained if their consequences are not clear.

The third method of stabilizing attitudes is through inoculation against change. Just as a person can be inoculated against physical disease a person can be, at least to some extent, inoculated against attitude change. By challenging the client's new attitudes with mild arguments against them a helper can stimulate the client to develop strong arguments supporting the new attitudes and defending them against future change attempts. Thus by preparing the client to defend his new attitudes against opposition he becomes inoculated against attitude change. A helper, for example, might structure a short role playing situation in which he takes the role of one of the people who helped build the old, self-destructive attitudes in the client and challenges the new attitudes. A mild form of this can be summarized in the question, "What will you say when x says to you, 'You do not have the ability to do y'?"

The fourth way to stabilize change is by enhancing the individual's feeling of being personally responsible for the change. If a person attributes beneficial change to his own effort, he is more likely to maintain that change than if he attributes it to external forces such as luck, a "magic" technique, or a powerful helper. You can encourage personal attribution of change throughout your dealings with the client. In the beginning of the relationship you should emphasize that the process will be a cooperative endeavor, in which the client will have to do the major work. Then, when you suggest changes, you should try to minimize the appearance of overt pressure. That is, you should not use imperative statements, commands, or very strong conclusions, unless they are only ways to accomplish your objectives. After the individual has successfully changed, you should emphasize how he *chose* to change. You can convey this attitude of personal choice by specifically pointing out all the self-defeating actions the person could have taken but did not. By taking these measures you will help the person to "own" his new attitudes and behavior.

ETHICS AND SOCIAL RESPONSIBILITY

There are serious ethical issues involved in deliberately attempting to influence the attitudes of other individuals. Before such an attempt is made the value and necessity of such influence attempts must be weighed against the possibility of manipulating, exploiting, or brainwashing others for one's own needs and satisfactions. *Attempting to help another person carries with it a responsibility not to work against the person's best interests and needs*. It should also be noted that the only way to promote ethical standards in helping relationships is for the helpers to enforce their code of ethics on themselves and to use good judgment in what they do. As long as a helper's behavior is based on caring, respect, and regard for the clients, ethical violations will be minimized. Any person engaging in helping activities must, therefore, develop a personal code of ethics to which he holds himself accountable. Hopefully, the following points will generate some thought as to what that personal code of ethics might include.

The first set of issues in using attitude change methods to help another person revolves around the contract between the helper and client. The nature of the contract should be clear to both the helper and the client; the number of experiences, the appropriateness and objectives of the helping activities, the ending point of the relationship, and the helper's intentions and objectives should be clear to both parties. There must be informed consent and mutual agreement as to what is to be done before helping begins.

The second set of issues involves the activities in which the helper engages. First, what the helper does needs to be based upon empirically validated knowledge. Folklore, superstition, common sense, fads and popular gimmicks, and personal experience are not adequate bases for helping other people; thus a thorough knowledge of the social psychology of attitude change is needed before a person represents himself as someone who can help others with attitude change problems. *To attempt to help a person when one is ignorant of how to help is both unethical and irresponsible*. A great deal of damage has been caused by persons with good intentions but no knowledge who just wanted to help other people. A second and related point is that the helper should have the competence, preparation, and training to apply what he knows. *Theoretical knowledge is not enough; there must also be trained skills and competencies*. Third, at any time during the helping relationship, the helper should be able to explain the theory he is operating upon and the way in which current activities relate to the theory. This does not mean that a helper will not use his intuition and impulses when helping others, but after the fact it should be possible to reconstruct the theory behind the intuition.

Fourth, the helper should be aware of his behavior styles and personal needs and deal with them productively in the performance of his role; the helper should be aware of the impact of his needs and style upon the client. Fifth, the personal information disclosed by the client should be held in strict confidence; even if you are helping a child and the parent wants to know what the child is saying, it is important to get the child's permission to reveal the child's disclosures. Any possibility of disclosed information being used in any way to damage the client must be minimized.

Sixth, ideally the helper should be able to recognize symptoms of serious psychological stress and be able to make responsible decisions when such problems arise. The helper should know where emergency services (such as the nearest hospital with psychiatric facilities) are available. Seventh, helping sessions should be evaluated in order to provide the helper with feedback to improve his performance in the future. Hopefully the helper will arrange for more experienced helpers to consult with him about what he is doing as well as ask the client for feelings and reactions. Finally, follow-up on the clients should be possible in order to assess the impact of the helping sessions on the participants and discuss any feelings and reactions clients have at later dates.

Reading this chapter carefully several times and applying the material with intelligence and caution will improve the helping ability of most readers. Readers interested in more specific skill building procedures are referred to Johnson (1972a) and Johnson and Johnson (1975a). You do not have to be a skilled therapist to help a friend problem solve an important issue or correct a set of self-defeating attitudes. But it is important to recognize the difference between being a helpful friend and conducting more formal psychotherapy, and only to do helping within the general range of your trained competencies.

REFERENCES

Blechman, E. Attribution theory and family therapy. Paper presented at the 1973 Convention of the American Psychological Association in Montreal, Quebec.

Chittick, E. V. and Himelstein, P. The manipulation of self-disclosure. *Journal of Psychology*, 1967, **65**, 117–121.

Colson, W. N. Self-disclosure as a function of social approval. Unpublished Master's thesis, Howard University, 1968.

Deutsch, M. Conditions affecting cooperation. Final Technical Report for the Office of Naval Research, Contract NONR-285, 1957.

Deutsch, M. Cooperation and trust: Some theoretical notes. In M. R. Jones (Ed.), *Nebraska symposium on motivation*. Lincoln, Nebraska: University of Nebraska Press, 1962, 275–320.

Deutsch, M. and Krauss, R. Studies of interpersonal bargaining. *Journal of Conflict Resolution*, 1962, **6**, 52–76.

Drag, L. R. Experimenter-subject interaction: A situational determinant of differential levels of self-disclosure. Unpublished Master's thesis, University of Florida, 1968.

Ellis, A. *Reason and emotion in psychotherapy*. New York: Lyle Stuart, 1962.

Festinger, L. *A theory of cognitive dissonance*. Evanston, Ill.: Row, Peterson, 1957.

Frank, J. D. *Persuasion and healing. A comparative study of psychotherapy*. Revised edition. Baltimore: The John Hopkins University Press, 1973.

Friedlander, F. The primacy of trust as a facilitator of further group accomplishment. *Journal of Applied Behavioral Science*, 1970, **6**, 387–400.

Fromm-Reichmann, F. *Principles of intensive psychotherapy*. Chicago: University of Chicago Press, 1950.

Gahagan, J. P. and Tedeschi, J. T. Strategy and the credibility of promises in the Prisoner's Dilemma game. *Journal of Conflict Resolution*, 1968, **12**, 224–234.

Gibb, J. R. Climate for trust formation. In L. P. Bradford, J. R. Gibb, and K. D. Benne (Eds.), *T-group theory and laboratory method*. New York: Wiley, 1964.

Glasser, W. *Reality therapy: A new approach to psychiatry*. New York: Harper, 1965.

Goldstein, A. P., Heller, K., and Sechrest, L. B. *Psychotherapy and the psychology of behavior change*. New York: Wiley, 1966.

Heider, F. *The psychology of interpersonal relations*. New York: Wiley, 1958.

Johnson, D. W. The use of role reversal in intergroup competition. Unpublished Doctoral dissertation, Columbia University, 1966.

Johnson, D. W. The use of role reversal in intergroup competition. *Journal of Personality and Social Psychology*, 1967, 7, 135–141.

Johnson, D. W. The effects upon cooperation of commitment to one's position and engaging in or listening to role reversal. Unpublished research report, University of Minnesota, 1968.

Johnson, D. W. Role reversal: A summary and review of the research. *International Journal of Group Tensions*, 1971, **1**, 318–334. (a)

Johnson, D. W. The effects of warmth of interaction, accuracy of understanding, and the proposal of compromises on the listener's behavior. *Journal of Counseling Psychology*, 1971, **18**, 207–216. (b)

Johnson, D. W. The effectiveness of role reversal: The actor or the listener. *Psychological Reports*, 1971, **28**, 275–282. (c)

Johnson, D. W. The effects of the order of expressing warmth and anger upon the actor and the listener. *Journal of Counseling Psychology*, 1971, **18**, 571–578. (d)

Johnson, D. W. *Reaching out: Interpersonal effectiveness and self-actualization*. Englewood Cliffs, N.J.: Prentice-Hall, 1972. (a)

Johnson, D. W. The effects of role reversal on seeing a conflict from the opponent's frame of reference. Unpublished manuscript, University of Minnesota, 1972. (b)

Johnson, D. W. *Contemporary social psychology*. Philadelphia: Lippincott, 1973. (a)

Johnson, D. W. Communication in conflict situations: A critical review of the research. *International Journal of Group Tensions*, 1973, **3**. (b)

Johnson, D. W. Cooperativeness and social perspective taking. *Journal of Personality and Social Psychology*, 1975, **31**, in press.

Johnson, D. W. and Neale, D. The effects of models, reference groups, and social responsibility norms upon participation in prosocial action activities. *Journal of Social Psychology*, 1970, **81**, 87–92.

Johnson, D. W. and Noonan, M. P. The effects of acceptance and reciprocation of self-disclosures on the development of trust. *Journal of Counseling Psychology*, 1972, **19**, 411–416.

Johnson, D. W. and Johnson, S. The effects of attitude similarity, expectation of goal facilitation, and actual goal facilitation on interpersonal attraction. *Journal of Experimental Social Psychology*, 1972, **8**, 197–206.

Johnson, D. W. and Johnson, R. T. Instructional structure: Cooperative, competitive, or individualistic. *Review of Educational Research*, 1974, **44**, 213–240.

Johnson, D. W. and Johnson, R. T. *Joining together: Group theory and group skills*. Englewood Cliffs, N.J.: Prentice-Hall, 1975. (a)

Johnson, D. W. and Johnson, F. P. *Learning together and alone: Cooperation, competition, and individualization*. Englewood Cliffs, N.J.: Prentice-Hall, 1975. (b)

Johnson, S. and Johnson, D. W. The effects of other's actions, attitude similarity, and race on attraction towards the other. *Human Relations*, 1972, **25**, 121–130.

Jones, E. E., Kanouse, D. E., Kelly, H. H., Nisbett, R. E., Valins, S., and Weiner, B. *Attribution: Perceiving the causes of behavior*. Morristown, N.J.: General Learning Press, 1971.

Jourard, S. M. and Friedman, R. Experimenter-subject distance and self-disclosure. *Journal of Personality and Social Psychology*, 1970, **15**, 278–282.

Katz, D. The functional approach to the study of attitudes. *Public Opinion Quarterly*, 1960, **24**, 163–204.

Katz, D. and Stotland, E. A. A preliminary statement to a theory of attitude structure and change. In S. Koch (Ed.), *Psychology: A study of a science*. Vol. 3. New York: McGraw-Hill, 1959, 423–475.

Kelly, G. A. *The psychology of personal constructs, Vol. 2: Clinical diagnosis and psychotherapy*. New York: Norton, 1955.

Kirtner, W. L. and Cartwright, D. S. Success and failure in client-centered therapy as a function of initial in-therapy behavior. *Journal of Consulting Psychology*, 1958, **22**, 329–333.

Krauss, R. M. and Deutsch, M. Communication in interpersonal bargaining. *Journal of Personality and Social Psychology*, 1966, **4**, 572–577.

Litcher, J. and Johnson, D. W. Changes in attitudes towards Negroes of white elementary school students after use of multi-ethnic readers. *Journal of Educational Psychology*, 1969, **60**, 148–152.

McCroskey, J. C., Larson, C. E., and Knapp, M. L. *Introduction to interpersonal communication*. Englewood Cliffs, N.J.: Prentice-Hall, 1971.

Matross, R. P. Insight and attribution in counseling and psychotherapy. *Office for Student Affairs Research Bulletin*, University of Minnesota, 1974. (a)

Matross, R. P. Socratic methods in counseling and psychotherapy. *Office for Student Affairs Research Bulletin*, University of Minnestoa, 1974. (b)

Mellinger, C. D. Interpersonal trust as a factor in communication. *Journal of Abnormal and Social Psychology*, 1956, **52**, 304–309.

Mischel, W. *Personality and assessment*. New York: Wiley, 1968.

Murdoch, P., Chenowith, R., and Riseman, K. Eligibility and intimacy effects on self-disclosure. Paper presented at the meeting of the Society of Experimental Social Psychology, Madison, Wisconsin, 1969.

Rogers, C. R. *Client-centered therapy*. Boston: Houghton Mifflin, 1951.

Rogers, C. R. Dealing with psychological tensions. *Journal of Applied Behavioral Science*, 1965, **1**, 6–25.

Sarnoff, I. and Katz, D. The motivational basis of attitude change. *Journal of Abnormal and Social Psychology*, 1954, **49**, 115–124.

Schlenker, B. R., Helm, B., and Tedeschi, J. T. The effects of personality and situational variables on behavioral trust. *Journal of Personality and Social Psychology*, 1973, **25**, 419–427.

Schlenker, B. R., Helm, B., Nacci, P., and Tedeschi, J. T. The generalization of credibility across influence modes: Compliance to threats as a function of promise credibility. State University of New York at Albany: Authors, 1972. (mimeo)

Schmidt, L. D. and Strong, S. R. Expert and in-expert counselors. *Journal of Counseling Psychology*, 1970, **17**, 115–118.

Schroeder, P. Client acceptance of responsibility and difficulty of therapy. *Journal of Consulting Psychology*, 1960, **24**, 467–471.

Skilbeck, W. M. Attribution theory and crisis intervention therapy. Paper presented at the 1973 Convention of the American Psychological Association in Montreal, Quebec, Canada.

Strong, S. R. Counseling: An interpersonal influence process. *Journal of Counseling Psychology*, 1968, **15**, 215–224.

Sullivan, H. S. *The interpersonal theory of psychiatry*. New York: Norton, 1953.

Taylor, D. A. The effects of social reinforcement and self-disclosure patterns on interpersonal behavior. Unpublished manuscript, University of Delaware, 1964.

Taylor, D. A., Altman, I., and Sorrentino, R. Interpersonal exchange as a function of rewards and costs and situational factors: Expectancy confirmation-disconfirmation. *Journal of Experimental Social Psychology*, 1969, **5**, 324–339.

Walton, R. E. and McKersie, R. B. Attitude change in intergroup relations. Institute for research in the behavioral, economic, and management sciences. Paper No. 86, Purdue University.

Watson, G. and Johnson, D. W. *Social psychology: Issues and insights*. Philadelphia: Lippincott, 1972.

Wolpe, J. and Lazarus, A. A. *Behavior therapy techniques*. New York: Pergamon Press, 1966.

Worthy, M., Gary, A. L., and Kahn, G. M. Self-disclosure as an exchange process. *Journal of Personality and Social Psychology*, 1969, **13**, 59–63.

CHAPTER 4

Cognitive Change Methods*

MARVIN R. GOLDFRIED AND ANITA P. GOLDFRIED

People don't think . . .
They just think they do.

Behavior therapy met with widespread criticism when it first presented to the mental health profession its approach to helping people change. As initially outlined, the behavioral orientation to clinical work represented a very marked departure from what constituted traditional practice. Among the many points criticized was the striking absence of any reference to the client's cognitive processes. In its "early days"—which is actually not that long ago—behavior therapy was typically defined as the application of learning principles to deviant behavior. Such learning principles were derived from laboratory settings, and were primarily based on research utilizing classical conditioning and operant reinforcement procedures. According to the view at that time, maladaptive human behavior could be modified by the relatively straightforward pairing of certain stimuli or the arrangement of appropriate reinforcement contingencies.

Within the relatively brief time that behavior therapy has become popular, numerous advancements in theory and technique have been made. Among them advancements have included a greater recognition paid to the importance of cognitive variables in the understanding and modification of human behavior. Without necessarily denying the effectiveness of clinical procedures derived from principles of classical and instrumental conditioning, behavior therapists have begun to recognize that techniques based solely on such principles were inadequate in dealing with more complex cases. Thus, Davison and Goldfried (1973) maintain: "Although we clearly acknowledge the importance of classical and operant conditioning procedures as vehicles for behavior change, our conception of behavior modification does not exclude those investigations which stress that cognitive and other mediational processes play a significant role in the changing of human behavior" (p. 82). Other behaviorally oriented clinicians have carried this one step further, such as Kanfer (1970), who suggests: "Without incorporation of these [cognitive] phenomena into the behavioristic model, it is

*Work on this chapter was facilitated by Grant MH24327 from the National Institute of Mental Health.

quite probable that the days of even a methodological behaviorism are numbered" (p. 212).

The early neglect of cognitive variables undoubtedly stemmed in part from an attempt to develop an orientation having a firm "scientific" basis. With some hindsight, it becomes clear that these concerns were unfounded. In fact, some of the most respected authorities in the area of learning and experimental psychology have gone to great lengths to suggest that a narrow conception of the learning process provides a most inadequate frame of reference from which to understand complex human behavior. For example, Hilgard and Bower (1966), in what perhaps is the most widely used text on learning theory, reached the following conclusion:

> There may be several kinds of learning from the simpler to the more complex, not all following the same principles. If so, we have no assurance that the only sharp break comes when "reasoning" appears. Leaving the doubtful processes in simply asserts that a complete theory of learning must have something to say about reasoning, creative imagination, and inventiveness, in addition to what may be said about memorizing and retaining or about the acquisition of skill. (p. 6.)*

Estes (1971), one of the nation's more prominent learning theorists—who, interestingly enough, happens to be a former student of Skinner—has reached a similar conclusion. He notes:

> For the lower animals, for very young children, and to some extent for human beings of all ages who are mentally retarded or subject to severe neurological or behavior disorders, behavior from moment to moment is largely describably and predictably in terms of responses to particular stimuli and the rewarding or punishing outcomes of previous stimulus-response sequences.
>
> In more mature human beings, much instrumental behavior and, more especially, a great part of verbal behavior is organized into higher-order routines and is, in many instances, better understood in terms of the operation of rules, principles, strategies, and the like than in terms of successions of responses to particular stimuli. Thus, in many situations, an individual's behavior from moment to moment may be governed by a relatively broad strategy which, once adopted, dictates response sequences, rather than by anticipated consequences of specific actions. In these situations it is the selection of strategies rather than the selection of particular reactions to stimuli which is modified by past experiences with rewarding or punishing consequences. (p. 23.)†

But the scope of behavior therapy has extended even beyond the greater appreciation of how complex human learning operates. Rather than merely defining the field as the application of learning principles to the modification of deviant human behavior, more and more behavior therapists are following the lead of Goldstein, Heller, and Sechrest (1966) who pointed out the relevance that all principles of psychology might have in the clinical setting. From this vantage point, behavior therapists have become even less constrained in the types of procedures they may legitimately employ.

The net result of the changes that have been occurring over the past several years is that cognitive processes now play a most important role within the

---

*From Hilgard, Ernest R. and Bower, Gordon H. *Theories of learning.* Copyright © 1966, 3rd ed. By permission of Appleton-Century-Crofts.

†From Estes, W. K. Reward in human learning: Theoretical issues and strategic choice points. In R. Glaser (Ed.), *The nature of reinforcement.* New York: Academic Press, 1971. Reprinted by permission.

behavioral orientation to clinical work. One need only to skim through some of the more current books on behavior therapy to see that this is so (e.g., Bandura, 1969; Goldfried and Merbaum, 1973; Kanfer and Phillips, 1970; Lazarus, 1971; Thoreson and Mahoney, 1974).

Our plan for the remainder of the chapter is to describe and illustrate the use of two behavior modification procedures that most strongly emphasize cognitive processes. The section on systematic rational restructuring will focus on procedures whereby an individual may be taught to reduce maladaptive emotional reactions by learning to label situations more accurately. Simply put, the approach involves teaching people how to "think straight." The second procedure, problem solving training, is designed to provide the individual with a general strategy for coping with the complexities of the world around him. English translation: It teaches a person how to "figure things out" and make wise decisions.

One final point should be made before actually describing the therapeutic procedures. In using such concepts as "restructuring" and "coping strategies," we are not inferring any specific processes that may be going on within the individual's head. Rather, our use of such terms are purely descriptive or operational, in that we are referring to the therapeutic instructions given to clients, as well as the client's acknowledgment that they are following the guidelines outlined to them.

SYSTEMATIC RATIONAL RESTRUCTURING

An individual's expectations and assumptions about the world around him can have significant implications for his emotional reactions to, and actual overt behavior in, that world. With regard to any given therapeutic process, for example, individuals' expectancies regarding the likely outcome of treatment have been found to be related to actual success in therapy (Goldstein, 1962). Further, actual therapeutic procedures have been developed on the assumption that behavior change can be brought about by modifying a person's more generalized expectancies (e.g., Beck, 1970; Ellis, 1962; Goldfried, Decenteceo, and Weinberg, 1974; Kelly, 1955; Meichenbaum, 1974; Rotter, 1954; Staats, 1972).

The concepts "expectancy" and "assumption" can readily be translated into what has generally been known experimentally as "set." It has been demonstrated in numerous experimental investigations that varying the set with which a subject approaches an experimental task can greatly influence his emotional reaction to and actual performance in that situation. Based on the findings that a person can be taught to approach specific experimental tasks with one or another set, it may also be assumed that people learn more generalized sets which they carry with them as they approach various real-life situations. Thus, the pessimist will give up early, if he indeed makes an effort at all, based on his belief that "things are not likely to work out anyway." The optimist will persist longer at a task on the assumption he will eventually succeed. Further, the failure or success of one's efforts will clearly tend to reinforce these initial expectations.

In one of the earliest attempts to apply behavioral principles to complex cognitive processes, Dollard and Miller (1950) described the manner in which overt language might play an important role in creating emotional arousal. They reasoned that one's emotional state frequently resulted from the way in which an individual evaluated or labeled a stimulus, and not necessarily from the objective characteristics of the situation itself. For example, if a person labeled a situation as being "dangerous," his upset would be in direct response to the label "dangerous." To the extent that the situation was labeled appropriately—such as if one's car were stuck on the railroad tracks in the path of an on-coming train—the emotional arousal would be deemed as being appropriate, and even adaptive to the situation at hand. If, on the other hand, the person mislabeled a situation as being dangerous—as in the case of the interpersonally anxious individual who is uncomfortable even in friendly settings—then one would judge the reaction to be inappropriate or maladaptive. The important point to recognize in the second instance is that the person's emotional reaction is a reasonable response to the label he applies to the situation; however, it is the label that is inaccurate. In such instances, it would seem appropriate that the therapeutic endeavor be directed toward the modification of the person's distorted perceptions of the world, as any such inappropriate labels are likely to mediate maladaptive emotional arousal and behavior.

The basic assumption that emotional arousal and maladaptive behavior are mediated by one's interpretations of situations has laid the groundwork for Albert Ellis' (1962) rational-emotive therapy. In more recent years, behaviorally oriented clinicians have similarly begun to recognize the importance of Ellis' work, and have attempted to systematize the therapeutic approach within a general behavioral orientation (Goldfried, Decenteceo, and Weinberg, 1974; Meichenbaum, 1974).

Central to Ellis' therapeutic approach is the idea that there are certain irrational beliefs, expectations, or assumptions with which a number of people in our culture tend to approach situations. To the extent that an individual is likely to maintain such irrational beliefs, he increases the likelihood of mislabeling situations.

According to Ellis (1962), typical irrational beliefs consist of the following:

1. The idea that it is a dire necessity for an adult human being to be loved or approved by virtually every significant other person in his community (p. 61).

2. The idea that one should be thoroughly competent, adequate, and achieving in all possible respects, if one is to consider oneself worthwhile (p. 63).

3. The idea that certain people are bad, wicked, or villainous and that they should be severely blamed and punished for their villainy (p. 65).

4. The idea that it is awful and catastrophic when things are not the way one would very much like them to be (p. 69).

5. The idea that human unhappiness is externally caused and that people have little or no ability to control their sorrows and disturbances (p. 72).

6. The idea that if something is or may be dangerous or fearsome one should be terribly concerned about it and should keep dwelling on the possibility of its occurring (p. 75).

7. The idea that it is easier to avoid than to face certain life difficulties and self-responsibilities (p. 78).

8. The idea that one should be dependent on others and needs someone stronger than oneself on whom to rely (p. 80).

9. The idea that one's past history is an all-important determinant of one's present behavior and that because something once strongly affected one's life, it should indefinitely have a similar effect (p. 82).

10. The idea that one should become quite upset over other people's problems and disturbances (p. 85).

11. The idea that there is invariably a right, precise, and perfect solution to human problems and that it is catastrophic if this correct solution is not found. (p. 87.)*

A recent study by Goldfried and Sobocinski (1975) found a positive relationship between the extent to which individuals held such irrational beliefs, and their scores on measures of interpersonal, public speaking, and test anxiety. It was also found that the tendency to view situations irrationally was related to the individual's susceptibility to emotional upset in situations related to such irrational expectations. Specifically, Goldfried and Sobicinski selected individuals who tended to be high or low in their irrational expectation that everyone must love and approve of them. Individuals at the two extremes were then asked to imagine themselves in a series of situations where they might interpret themselves as being rejected by others. A typical situation was as follows:

> It's a Saturday night, and you're sitting in your room by yourself. You have nothing in particular to do tonight; no place to go. You're all by yourself. Everyone you know is busy. It's very quiet, and you're feeling kind of lonely. You would like to be with someone, but nobody seems to be around; everyone else is doing something else. You have something to read, but you're really not too interested in reading; you would rather be with someone. (Goldfried and Sobicinski, unpublished manuscript.)

As a result of their imagining themselves in this and other similar situations, the high irrational group reported feeling more anxious and angry than did individuals who felt less of a need to be approved of by others.

For quite some time, the efficacy of rational-emotive therapy was primarily substantiated by case studies (Ellis, 1962). In more recent years, controlled outcome studies have provided a more scientifically valid confirmation that this general approach to the modification of irrational beliefs can successfully reduce test anxiety (Meichenbaum, 1972), speech anxiety (Meichenbaum, Gilmore, and Fedoravicius, 1971; Trexler and Karst, 1972) and interpersonal anxiety (DiLoreto, 1971).

Goldfried, Decenteceo, and Weinberg (1974) have attempted to place rational-emotive therapy within more of a behavioral framework, providing clearly delineated steps that the therapist might take in training the individual to modify the emotionally arousing set with which he may be approaching various life situations. The material which follows provides the therapeutic guidelines associated with this approach to systematic rational restructuring.

Therapeutic Guidelines

This section deals with the practical application of rational restructuring, using actual examples of the therapist-client interchange. The particular examples will

---

*From Ellis, A. *Reason and emotion in psychotherapy.* New York: Lyle Stuart, 1962. Reprinted by permission.

be within a group therapy setting because (1) it is an economical method of treating large numbers of people, and (2) the technique lends itself to a group setting, where other members can serve as models for successful performance. However, the guidelines which follow can easily be translated into an individual therapy setting. Similarly, while the illustrations will be based on a group whose target problem is test anxiety, one can readily apply the same guidelines to teach clients with other problems to think rationally.

As is the case with most behavior therapy techniques, one typically begins with some therapeutic structuring. In the application of rational restructuring to a group of text anxious clients, the therapist should explain in general terms what the group will be doing, and also give his view of what underlies test anxiety. This is illustrated in the following transcript:

> *Therapist*: Let me describe the rationale underlying the whole notion of anxiety generally, and specifically as it relates to test-taking situations. We can then get into exactly what the program will involve. First of all, we are operating under the assumption that your current anxiety in test-taking situations—and this includes anything related to test-taking, like studying—is undoubtedly related to your past experiences. These may have been direct unpleasant experiences while taking tests, or indirect experiences of seeing or hearing about others having unpleasant test-taking experiences. You have also probably developed an attitude or reaction that tests are terribly important, and that you have to do well on them.
>
> In thinking back on specific experiences each of you may have had which created this problem, you may or may not be able to come up with relevant experiences. My own feeling is that even if you eventually can come up with some ideas as to what may have caused this in the past, it might not be all that useful in helping you to become calmer right now. Instead, the best way to help you to become calmer is to provide you with new learning experiences now—in the here and now.
>
> In essence, the program is based on some notions of learning, or re-learning, which I'll describe to you. The main goal is to reduce anxiety. We're assuming that everyone will study, and that this is not going to be a course in how to take a test or how to study. Rather, it's a therapy program in how to reduce anxiety. If you don't study you have some reason to be anxious. On the other hand, if you do study, you will find that there is little need for you to be anxious.
>
> Another thing that this is not going to be is an encounter group. Somehow, when people sit down in a room together where everyone faces each other nowadays, the stage seems to be set for pouring out emotions. It's a lot of fun, and I really enjoy it, but I don't think it's going to give you what you want. So, instead, what we're going to focus on directly is a new way to cope with anxiety in testing situations. Are there any questions you have or any points you want to make before we move on any further?
>
> *Client*: Will we learn something about studying for tests?
>
> *Therapist*: No, the program will not involve how to study, but it will involve a learning of sorts. It will be learning from actual experiences which we will simulate in therapy and in which you will undoubtedly find yourself in your day-to-day living between our sessions.

The therapist is now ready to proceed with rational restructuring. The four procedural steps to be used are: (1) presentation of rationale; (2) overview of irrational assumptions; (3) analysis of client's problems in rational terms; and (4) teaching the client to modify the statements he makes to himself.

1. Presentation of Rationale

The therapist explains the underlying assumptions of rational restructuring, using various examples to show that what we tell ourselves can affect our feelings.

It may be helpful for the therapist to indicate that we may not literally "tell ourselves" things that cause emotional upset, as these self-statements have been so well-learned that they have become more or less automatic. At this point the therapist wants the client to understand the general significance of self-statements without applying this knowledge to his own particular problems, which is a much more complicated process. With an acceptance of the basic rationale using simple examples, the groundwork is laid for the more complicated application to the client's own problems. This is illustrated in the following transcript:

> *Therapist*: The notion of anxiety can be looked at from the point of view of how you interpret a situation in which you are anxious. For example, if I take this pencil and I point it at you, what's your reaction?
>
> *Client # 1*: Nothing.
>
> *Therapist*: Do you feel nervous?
>
> *Client # 1*: No, why should I?
>
> *Therapist*: If this were a gun, and I was pointing it at each of you, I think I would see a different reaction. Why? Is it because the size and shape of a gun is different from this (holding up pencil)? Why would you be nervous (looking at another client)?
>
> *Client # 2*: Because you know the danger of a gun.
>
> *Therapist*: So what you would do is to size up the situation. You're not reacting to the gun, but what you know about the thing—that it's dangerous. Also, if I pointed the gun at you, you wouldn't sit back and say "let's see, I know that a gun is dangerous." You would react automatically with anxiety.
>
> Probably underlying this reaction would be a very rapid evaluation of the situation where you would "tell yourself" that the situation was dangerous. In essence there is an immediate sizing up of the situation. Now, I really don't mean that you are literally telling yourself something. It's more of a rapid, automatic, overlearned reaction. Let me carry it a little bit further, making it more relevant to anxiety in real-life situations. Two people are getting ready to go to a party. Let's suppose that it's exactly the same party. Neither one of these people know many people at the party, although there are a few people that they do know. One person is very, very nervous. The other person is very calm, and in fact is looking forward to it. It's the same party, they know the same number of people, and it's held in the same place. The person who is nervous may be telling himself: "This is going to be quite a miserable evening. There are going to be a lot of people there that I don't know, and I wonder whether I'll know what to say or how to handle myself. What if I look foolish? What will they think about me? What will the people I know think about me if I look foolish. This is terrible." And he gets all worked up.
>
> The other person is getting ready for the same party and he's thinking: "There are a lot of people I won't know. It should be interesting; I might be able to meet some new friends. What's more, there'll be some people there that I do know, and I'll be able to get together with them." A very different emotional reaction. It's the same situation, but what's going on in their heads makes the difference, and results in the different type of emotional experiences that they have. It's the same principle as the pen and gun, except it's a little closer to a real-life situation; it has more relevance to you and the problems you have in a test-taking situation.

2. Overview of Irrational Assumptions

Before discussing the client's problems in rational terms, it is helpful to get their reaction to the various irrational beliefs stated on pages 92–93. These beliefs may be stated in an even more extreme form, making it more likely for clients to disagree with them and find them untenable (e.g., "If other people do not love me, or approve of everything I say or do, then this is proof that I have little worth as a person"). This is exactly what the therapist is aiming for. The therapist wants the client to distinguish between thinking that "it would be nice" if these expectations (such as perfection and universal love) were met, as opposed to the thought that they "must" or "should" be met, which will only lead to frustration. It is advisable for the therapist to play devil's advocate and let the client himself refute the irrational beliefs, as the social psychological literature indicates that such a method can be more effective in changing attitudes (Brehm and Cohen, 1962).

It is probably unnecessary to review all eleven irrational ideas. The two that seem to be most appropriate in a large number of cases are "Everybody must love me" and "I must be perfect in everything I do." However, there is no hard and fast rule about this, and much depends on the therapist's clinical judgment and the client's particular problems. This is an example of how this step may be implemented in a group therapy setting:

> *Therapist*:   Let's talk about certain attitudes in general, and then try to relate them to anxiety in testing situations. There are certain notions that people have in our culture which tend to be fairly widespread. I would like to get your reactions to these. One is the notion that it is very important to be perfect. Unless you're perfect, and do everything extremely well—meeting a certain very high standard—then essentially you are a failure as a person. In other words, unless you have attained perfection, you are worthless. That's one notion. A second notion I would like to have you consider is that it is imperative to have everyone you know love you, think well of you, and approve of everything you do. And if anyone does not think well of you, that means that you are completely worthless. In other words, you're either perfect or you're worthless. Either everyone must love you, or you're not worth loving at all. What's your reaction? I noticed some smiles and nods.

> *Client #1*:   I don't know if it's widespread, but I know that's the way I think. I've always recognized that it's wrong to think that way, but I still do. I always exaggerate. If I fail a test, I think that I'm really terrible.

> *Therapist*:   You say you know that it's wrong?

> *Client #1*:   I know it intellectually. I know you can't be perfect, you just have to accept yourself as an individual.

> *Therapist*:   Why can't you be perfect?

> *Client #2*:   Well, it's impossible to be perfect. Human beings are just not made that way. However, it's probably good to strive for perfection because in that way we are constantly improving ourselves.

> *Client #3*:   But there's a big difference between trying to do your best and trying to be perfect. You said yourself that you can't possibly be perfect.

> *Therapist*:   Why not? Don't you know people who are perfect?

> *Client #4*:   I find that I compare myself to other people a lot and there's always someone who does something better than me. But, really, I don't think I could call anybody else perfect. I admit that it sometimes seems as if I expect it of myself, though when we talk about it here it doesn't make any sense. I agree that perfection is impossible.

> *Therapist*:   O.K. What about the notion that you must be loved by everyone or you are worthless.

> *Client #1*:   It's just not true. I mean, some people are bound to be wrong.

> *Therapist*:   Is it a question of right or wrong, or a matter of taste? For example, what is the "best" color? Red? No, I think it's green! It's the same as liking somebody or not liking somebody.

> *Client #3*:   O.K., but I may make an attempt to try to find out why someone doesn't like me. I may try to discuss it with him. If I can't get him to like me, I'll have to deal with it the best I can.

Client #2: It would be very boring if everybody liked you. Who would you argue with when you're in an argumentative mood? You have to realize that there are a lot of people around you, and you can't even begin to attempt to have everybody love you.

Therapist: But perhaps you can have everybody love you if you keep changing what you say and do to please others.

Client #3: I know some people who've tried to do that, and as a result everybody hates them. Also striving for perfection is a bad idea because a lot of people can't reach it and then all that happens is that they're constantly anxious and unhappy.

Therapist: A lot of people?

Client #4: Nobody can. Nobody can be perfect.

Client #3: But a lot of people strive for it.

Therapist: But it's probably true that nobody can get to it. It's the same as getting everyone to love you. There are too many people. And in being perfect there are too many things that one has to do.

3. Analysis of Client's Problems in Rational Terms

After the client agrees in principle that self-statements can create emotional upset, and that certain beliefs and expectations are irrational, the therapist can begin to focus more closely on the client's own personal problems.

The client's self-statements can be analyzed from two possible sources of irrationality: (1) how likely is it that the client's interpretation of the situation is in fact realistic, and (2) what are the ultimate implications of the way in which the client has labeled the situation. For example, let's look at a situation where a young woman is excessively upset because a male acquaintance she likes has declined an invitation to a party she is giving. Her readily available and upsetting interpretation might be: "He does not like me." How rational this interpretation is may be looked at from the likelihood of there being other reasonable explanations for his refusal, such as other commitments for that evening. The second source of irrationality, which is actually at a "deeper" level can take the following form: "What if this young man, in fact, really does not like you? Why should this make you so upset? Are there other things you may be implicitly telling yourself about his not liking you?" Further questioning (e.g., "Yes, but why should that upset you?") may help the client to recognize that what she has been telling herself in situations like these stem from a previously disavowed irrational belief (e.g., everyone must love me).

This general phase is illustrated in the following:

Therapist: I think that an important distinction is whether or not you think you must be a certain way, or whether it would be nice to be that way.

Client #2: I don't understand.

Therapist: If you enter a situation with the attitude that "I must be perfect on this test," you will be anxious, because you can't be perfect. You set yourself up for failure right away. "I must do well on my exam, otherwise there are going to be people that will disapprove of me. They will not love me, therefore I will be no good." Yes, it would be nice—it would be very nice—if people would like you. It would be nice if you could do very well in all kinds of things. But there is a difference between "it would be nice" and "must." I think that the problem you may be experiencing when it comes to taking tests, and perhaps other situations as well, is that you may be overly harsh in what you demand of yourself. There is no reason why you cannot evaluate situations logically and intellectually from a more sensible point of view. You can say to yourself: "First of all, the chances are that if I do poorly on this test, people are still going to like me. Second of all, even if they don't like me, what kind of people are not going to like me just because I don't do well on a test? Are these friends? Are these people that are important to me?" So you can analyze the situation in terms of the chances of your worst fears coming to pass. And, if they actually did, would it really be so terrible?

Client #4:   My husband would like me to be perfect in everything that I do. But interestingly enough, he himself doesn't strive for that. When I take tests, I think I try to prove to him that I can do really well.

Therapist: What would happen if you didn't do really well? Would he think less of you as a person?

Client #4:   No, I think the problem is within myself.

Therapist: What would he think of you if you didn't do well? Would he ask for a divorce?

Client #4:   No.

Therapist: Would he say "you have to pack up your bags and leave because you didn't do well on that test?"

Client #4:   No, obviously not.

Client #1:   It sounds almost as if its a parent-child relationship.

Therapist: There is a remnant of child-like thinking if you think you must be perfect, otherwise you're nothing. You must be loved, otherwise you're hated.

Client #4:   This is an extreme, I don't know if I think that way.

Therapist: When we sit here and talk intellectually, we can agree that one shouldn't really think that way.

Client #4:   I didn't say that (laughter).

Therapist: But you did say that you didn't think it was rational.

Client #4:   Yes, that's true.

Client #5:   I think you left out one point. You're talking about perfection, but you're not talking about the way in which the system is set up right now. Most of the people who attend college hope to go on to graduate school, and you have to meet a certain high standard, or else you're not going to get into graduate school. So maybe you're not looking for perfection, but you are trying to meet this standard that has been handed down to you. This is where a lot of anxiety comes from—the external pressure of getting into graduate school.

Therapist: O.K., let's look at that, because that happens to be a particularly important point. What happens if you don't get into graduate school?

Client: It depends. I don't know what I would do.

Therapist: Why is it so important?

Client: Because I want to work at something that I like, preferably the sciences. I don't want to work at something just to make money.

Therapist: In other words, if you don't go into graduate school, you would be wasting the rest of your life.

Client: No, because I would try to get into graduate school a second time. If I were rejected again, I would have to reevaluate my goals, and find other ways to reach them.

Therapist: You know, I admit that there is a difference between feeling nervous about a party and feeling nervous about an exam, particularly an exam that may be very important. However, you can still apply the same reasoning. What are the chances that not doing well on this particular exam will interfere with getting into graduate school? It probably would be relatively small. But even if the chances were great, what would happen if you didn't get into graduate school? Is that the end of the world? You may very well be reacting indiscriminately with your emotions. Even with minor examination situations you may be reacting as if a catastrophe had befallen you—as if you would never again be able to work, or were physically incapacitated, or had lost your family. The purpose of this program is to get you to make some finer discriminations between what is really terrible and what is merely an inconvenience.

4. Teaching the Client to Modify His Internal Sentences

Up until now the therapist has been laying the groundwork for the actual treatment. The objective has been for the client to understand how his internal sentences have been causing his own upset, and once this is achieved, the therapist can begin to help the client to change. Simply understanding the cause of the problem will do little to alleviate it; the client must consciously and deliberately engage in doing something differently when feeling upset. This emotional reaction must now serve as a "cue" for him to stop and think: "What am I telling myself that may be irrational?" He must learn to "break-up" what was before an automatic reaction and replace it with a more realistic appraisal of the situation. At first, this is no easy task, but, with practice, the procedure becomes less and less tedious and deliberate, until the client eventually can totally eliminate the initial upset phase by having made the more realistic appraisal an automatic reaction.

The general procedure involves getting the client to think rationally while in the situation rather than through hindsight. In essence, the client learns to put things in proper perspective while the upsetting event is happening, and this involves practice in rational reevaluation. Because the person must practice coping while in the problematic situation, imagination can be used as a means of controlling the training procedure. In this way the therapist can regulate the length of time the client is exposed to the situation and can control the anxiety-provoking nature of the situation. In addition, each client personalizes the situation by filling in the relevant details by himself. As with systematic desensitization, a hierarchy of least to most upsetting situations is used to enable the client to proceed systematically one step at a time. In this way a client is never faced with an overwhelming situation with which he is incapable of coping at the time. Instead, successful coping at one step determines the progression to a more difficult situation in the sequence.

In the actual procedure, the therapist describes a situation and the client imagines himself in that situation, noting how nervous (or sad, or angry) he feels. If his emotional reaction exceeds a certain predetermined level, he stops and thinks as follows: "What am I telling myself that is making me upset?" He must now determine the irrational thoughts he is telling himself that are making him upset. After evaluating the situation in more rational terms, he then notes the new anxiety (or depression, anger) level.*

---

*In many respects, the technique is very similar to Goldfried's (1971) self-control variation of systematic desensitization, except that rational reevaluation and not relaxation is the coping skill to be learned. Methods of systematic desensitization are described in detail in Chapter 8.

At the very start, the therapist can serve as a model to illustrate the rational restructuring technique. For example:

> I have just arrived at a party where I know very few people. Everyone is clustered in little groups talking, and I don't feel a part of things. I feel myself becoming tense. On a scale of 0–100 percent tension, I classify my tension at about 40. I now stop what I'm doing and think: "What am I telling myself that is creating this feeling of anxiety?" Let's see, now. I'm worried that I won't handle myself well, that people won't like me—that I'll appear inadequate and foolish in their eyes. But, now why should they think that of me? I'm not behaving foolishly. Really, the very worst they can think of me is that I'm kind of quiet and that's not so bad. Actually, whatever they thought of me wouldn't change the way I really am. I'm still me. Well, I don't feel as tense about the party now—maybe I'm now at an anxiety level of about 20.

It should be recognized that the imaginal presentation of situations represents a compromise, albeit a reasonable one, based primarily on practical considerations. One may not be able to realistically "bring into" the consultation room emotionally arousing situations in any manner other than by imagery (e.g., situations involving intimate sexual contact). However, behavior therapists have relied so extensively on the use of imaginal presentations of problematic situations that they have often overlooked the potential for a more realistic simulation during the consultation session. Here we are referring to the utility of behavioral rehearsal, which can frequently enable the client to create a more vivid situation with which he must learn to cope. When rational restructuring is conducted in groups, the setting lends itself particularly well to the use of behavior rehearsal, particularly in instances entailing social-evaluative anxiety. For example, if the group consists of individuals experiencing interpersonal anxiety, a hierarchy of items in order of increasing anxiety can readily be constructed such that it may be simulated in interactions among the various group members. Anxiety in public speaking situations similarly lends itself particularly well to treatment in group settings, where clients can learn to modify their anxiety-arousing expectations while presenting actual practice speeches before fellow group members.

In addition to simulating rational reevaluation in the consultation session—via imagery or behavior rehearsal—the client should be encouraged to utilize the same procedure in upsetting situations which occur on a day-to-day basis. The client should be forewarned, however, that real-life situations will not occur in a hierarchical fashion, and some of the situations may be too stressful for rational reevaluation to be initially successful. Still, even if unsuccessful, the real-life trials will serve the purpose of giving the client a coping set. We have found it useful to provide clients with a homework sheet such as that shown in Fig. 4.1, which we have used in actual in-vivo homework assignments.

Applications

From a theoretical point of view, rational restructuring would seem to be appropriate in the treatment of any maladaptive emotional reaction or behavior pattern that is maintained primarily by the individual's unrealistic attitudes and inappropriate labels. Among the typical problems for which the technique has

Date	Description of Situation	Initial Anxiety Level (0 to 100)	Irrational Thoughts	Rational Evaluation	Subsequent Anxiety Level (0 to 100)

Figure 4.1. Record of attempts to overcome anxiety in daily situations.

been used are various forms of anxiety (e.g. test anxiety, public speaking anxiety, interpersonal anxiety), depression, anger, and excessively perfectionistic standards.

Drawing from our experience in treating various problems with rational restructuring, we have become sensitized to particular issues that may come up in the course of treatment. For example, in utilizing rational restructuring for reduction of test anxiety, one should be aware of some typical problems likely to arise. Although test anxious individuals may tend to distort the significance of any given examination, the therapist should not fail to recognize that performance on tests can at times have far-reaching impact on an individual's future. The central question here is just how far reaching the impact will be. Although a person may justifiably become upset because he may not have been able to get into graduate school, the amount of upset need not be equivalent to that which would be experienced if his entire life were about to come to an end. We had the occasion to see one student who was extremely anxious immediately before an examination. When asked to rate his anxiety on a scale of 1 to 10, he described his anxiety state at the level of "9." When asked how he would feel if he knew for certain he would fail the exam, he said he would be at a level of "10." The therapist then asked a series of additional questions, each reflecting a potentially more disastrous outcome (e.g., How would you feel if you failed the course? Flunked out of school? Were only able to get a poor paying job? Were unable to get any job at all?, etc.). The student's initial response to such questions was "Wait a minute. I think I'm going to have to change my use of the rating scale." What happened was that he became dramatically aware of the fact that he was being indiscriminate in his emotional reaction to the examination situation, and soon realized that its importance more justifiably warranted an anxiety reaction of no more than "2."

A related potential problem using rational restructuring with test anxious students is that they may have difficulty in placing examination situations in a broader perspective. This is certainly understandable, especially if one's entire existence at any particular time consists primarily of school work. In one of our test anxiety groups, there was an older married woman with a family, who had more recently returned to college. Although she was admittedly anxious in testing situations, she very rapidly appreciated the fact that her evaluation of such examination situations was disproportionate to its realistic import. As she put it, she still had her husband, her children, and an active social life. To the extent that one's life is dominated by school work, attempts to put exams into realistic perspective may not so readily be accomplished. Despite these potential problems, rational restructuring would certainly seem to be a method well-suited for treating test anxiety problems.

Another type of anxiety situation where rational restructuring is particularly useful includes such social evaluative anxieties as public speaking and interpersonal anxiety. In such cases, the emotional upset experienced by individuals is presumably mediated by their concern about what others will think of them. However, anxiety in such situations may also be alleviated by means of systematic desensitization. Although there is little evidence to indicate which

(a) the recognition that the problematic situations comprise a normal aspect of living, (b) the assumption that one can actively make attempts to cope with such situations, (c) the readiness to recognize problematic situations as they occur, and (d) the set to inhibit the temptation to act impulsively.

The first two subsets relate directly to what we have discussed within the context of rational restructuring. In fact, one may find the unrealistic counterparts to these attitudes in the list presented on pages 92–93.

The ability to recognize problematic situations as they are occurring may not be straightforward as one might imagine. There are times when we may be "in" problematic situations and still not realize it. Miller, Galanter, and Pribram (1960) have hypothesized that the process of problem recognition proceeds along the following lines:

> In ordinary affairs we usually muddle ahead, doing what is habitual and customary, being slightly puzzled when it sometimes fails to give the intended outcome, but not stopping to worry much about the failures because there are too many other things still to do. Then circumstances conspire against us and we find ourselves caught failing where we must succeed—where we cannot withdraw from the field, or lower our self-imposed standards, or ask for help, or throw a tantrum. Then we may begin to suspect that we face a problem. (p. 171.)*

Thus, we frequently recognize that we are in a problematic situation only by virtue of the fact that we are upset about "something." Upon realizing this, one's task is to refocus attention from the emotional state to the situation creating the upset.

The final subset is axiomatic. If a situation is truly problematic—that is, if an effective solution is not immediately apparent—it is hard to imagine how one could even begin to engage in the actual problem-solving process without first stopping to think.

2. Problem Definition and Formulation

In basic research on problem solving, the subject is typically presented with a relatively well-defined task for which he must arrive at some solution. In real life, problematic situations are not always clearly specified. It is therefore necessary to define the various aspects of the situation in relatively concrete terms. Research by Bloom and Broder (1950) has demonstrated that more effective problem solvers typically translate abstract terms into concrete examples, whereas poor problem solvers typically make no such translation. But one cannot deal directly with an array of facts. By formulating the various issues reflected in the details of the situation, the direction of the problem-solving process becomes more clearly focused.

3. Generation of Alternatives

The research most relevant to this stage of problem solving is based on

---

*From Miller, G. A., Galanter, E., and Pribram, K. H. *Plans and the structure of behavior.* New York: Holt, Rinehart and Winston, 1960. Reprinted by permission.

"brainstorming" techniques (Osborn, 1963; Parnes, 1967). As a kind of a focused free association, the procedure is based on two principles: (1) deferment of judgment, and (2) quantity breeds quality. The deferment of judgment principle states that if an individual can temporarily withhold any evaluation of the quality of his solution, there is a greater likelihood that good solutions will be produced. According to the second principle, the more alternatives produced, the greater the likelihood that good ones will be included within the list. Numerous studies have been carried out on brainstorming, all of which lead to the conclusion that training in this procedure does, in fact, increase the likelihood of producing good quality solutions (D'Zurilla and Goldfried, 1971).

4. Decision Making

Basic research on information processing has employed utility theory in evaluating the "goodness" of any particular course of action (Becker and McClintoch, 1967; Churchman, 1961; Edwards, 1961; Simon, 1955). In essence, utility theory provides one with a functional evaluation of any given alternative. In the area of business and economics, a given course of action can be evaluated in terms of its financial payoff. In using this approach for more personal or interpersonal problem situations, the utility of the alternative may be evaluated according to its likelihood of resolving the issues delineated during the problem definition and formulation phase.

5. Verification

Once the individual has entered the problem-solving task, defined the problem and formulated the issues at hand, generated potential alternatives, and made some decision as to a particular course of action, the problem solver must verify the extent to which his alternative was a good one. This requires that he act on his decision, and then evaluate the extent to which the problem situation has been resolved.

The theoretical model most relevant to the verification stage comes from the work of Miller, Galanter, and Pribram, (1960), who theorized on the interrelationship between an individual's plans and actions. They suggest a "Test-Operate-Test-Exit" (TOTE) model, whereby an individual's activities (overt or covert) are guided by the extent to which the outcome of these activities matches up to a given standard. Thus, one maintains a given standard for adequacy ("Test"), and engages in relevant activities ("Operate"). The results of such activities are matched to a standard ("Test"), and if that standard is achieved, the activity is ended ("Exit"). If performance falls short of this standard, the individual continues to "Operate," until the standard has been reached.

During the verification stage, then, the problem solver, after having actually implemented his preferred course of action, determines for himself whether or not problematic situation has been satisfactorily resolved. If so, he "exits" from the problem-solving process. If not, he returns to problem solving in the hope of generating a more effective solution.

THERAPEUTIC GUIDELINES

To review the five stages involved in training a person to become adept at problem solving: first of all there is a general orientation toward problem situations which the person must develop. This orientation helps one to recognize a problematic situation when it occurs, to have a set that problems can be coped with, and to avoid impulsivity in confronting a problematic situation. The second stage consists of defining the problem situation in concrete terms and examining the relevant issues involved. Next comes the generation of alternatives stage, in which the person tries to accumulate potential solutions to the problem. This is followed by a time of actual decision making when he selects the optimal course of action from the various alternatives available. Finally there is the verification stage when he assesses the effectiveness of the solution he has decided to put into effect.

Clearly, different people will have difficulty at different stages of the problem-solving procedure. Some people will be very vague in their definition of the problem, others will not be able to think up various alternatives to a problem. Others may have a general set of helplessness—a feeling that they cannot cope with things in general. The therapist would naturally place greater emphasis on those aspects of the problem-solving procedure in which the client is weakest.

Training in problem solving may be understood as a behavior modification program, in which the target behavior—problem solving—is treated in progressive steps. The therapist introduces a "problematic situation" and the client must achieve some minimum performance at each stage of the process before going on to the next. The client must pass through all stages before he can be said to have "solved the problem." New and more difficult problem situations are then introduced and once again, all stages must be completed by the client. The repetition is intended so that the various stages in the problem-solving sequence will become more or less automatic and so that each response in the series serves as a cue for the next response and as a reinforcer for the previous response. The entire series is reinforced by the final outcome, i.e., successful solution to the problem.

In the initial phases of training, the therapist models the problem-solving procedures, verbalizing all thoughts, while the client merely observes. As the client becomes more active in the process, the therapist's role changes to that of a consultant, providing guidance in and evaluation of the real-life application.

1. General Orientation

At the start of training in problem solving, the therapist explains the rationale of the treatment and in general aims for the client's understanding that problematic situations are a part of everyone's life. He emphasizes that the client should learn to recognize when these situations occur, and that his response should not be made automatically or impulsively. The client may be presented with examples of common problematic situations and/or asked to identify such situations which have occurred in his own life. Initially, it is a good idea to have the client actually keep a record of problematic situations in which he finds himself, and to note his emotional reactions. These emotions (e.g., confusion, frustration, etc.) can serve as a signal for the client to look at what is happening around him—to look at the situations that are triggering these reactions. In essence the therapist wants to establish a problem-solving "set" before the actual training begins.

2. Problem Definition and Formulation

In the beginning, most clients will record their own problematic situations in rather vague or abstract terms, giving general descriptions of the basic nature of the problem. The client must learn to define problems specifically and to include all related details. Not only external events, but also thoughts and feelings (internal events) are often very important in completely describing a situation. In addition, he must learn to exclude irrelevant information and to focus on those areas of information most likely to assist him in the eventual solution of the problem.

The following transcript illustrates how a vague description of a problematic situation can be spelled out in detail:

> *Client*: I've been feeling very tired and irritable lately, and sometimes I get very depressed.
>
> *Therapist*: How long have you been feeling this way?
>
> *Client*: Oh, for about the past couple of months. I guess it started soon after I moved here and found this new apartment. Actually, I like the apartment very much. It's very convenient to work and restaurants and movies—I mean it's really in a terrific area and fairly safe at night too. The problem is that it's kind of small. The living arrangement is not too good.
>
> *Therapist*: In what way do you feel the size of your apartment is related to your upset?
>
> *Client*: Well, it's really a very large studio apartment, but I can't afford the rent by myself, so I have a roommate. That means we have to use that one room as both bedroom and living room and it gets a bit cramped at times.
>
> *Therapist*: Are you having trouble getting along with your roommate?
>
> *Client*: No, I don't think that's a problem. I like her and she's friendly and easy to get along with. But you're right. There is one problem with her. Well, maybe it's a problem with me. I have this great new job, which is very challenging and demanding, but it takes a lot out of me and I find I have to get a good night's sleep in order to function. My roommate and her friends are "night people" and like to stay up late talking or listening to records. I really envy her—she also has to get up early and go to work, but she seems to manage on much less sleep than me.
>
> *Therapist*: What has been happening?
>
> *Client*: I haven't been getting enough sleep and I feel very tired much of the time. I end up staying up with them and not only do I feel tired, but I'm not too crazy about my roommate's friends. The next morning I'm usually tired and depressed because socializing with people I don't particularly like only points out to me how lonely I am.
>
> *Therapist*: So, it's not only that you'd like some other arrangement about the time of night the apartment is free of guests. You'd also like to have more social contacts yourself.
>
> *Client*: Yes, I think that's also part of it. I had some good friends before I moved to the area, but I haven't been able to find anyone around here.

In the above example the aim was to specify the details of the situation and formulate the problem by identifying the major goals and those issues or conflicts which made the situation problematic. This client's goals included a need for more sleep, the continuation of a good relationship with her roommate, and a desire for more friends. The issues or conflicts in the situation involved: need for sleep vs. other people present in the apartment, wanting more friends vs. being new in town, and not knowing many people.

Learning to specify goals and issues is a critical first step in the treatment program and in some instances may be sufficient to make the client immediately aware of possible solutions. When this is the case, further formal problem solving may not be necessary for that particular problem situation. However, when this is not the case, the client would then move on to the next stage in the process—learning to identify possible response alternatives.

3. Generation of Alternatives

In deciding how to go about solving an operationally defined problem, the client must be able to differentiate "strategies" and "tactics." The strategy outlines a course of action stated in general terms, while the tactic gives the specifics for putting the plan into effect. During this stage the client is instructed to "brainstorm" possible solutions. For example:

Therapist: Now that we have a better idea of what your current problem is, let's investigate some possible solutions. I'd like you to use the brainstorming technique I told you about, where you think of as many possibilities as you can, no matter how silly or impractical they may seem. Let your mind run free.

Client: I'll try.

Therapist: Remember, try to think of as many solutions as possible. You don't really have to carry them all out. And don't worry at this point about being too specific. Later on we'll be concerned about specific solutions to actually carry out. Right now, I'd like you to concentrate on general approaches to the problem.

Client: Could you explain what you mean by a general approach.

Therapist: Well, for example, let's assume that in a particular problematic situation one possible solution was "I would get a better job." That possible solution is described at a very general level, telling what you would do, but not how you would go about doing it. The "how to do it" part might involve reading the want ads in the paper every day, calling friends and asking if they know of any job openings, registering with employment agencies, as well as a host of other specific ways of following through the general approach of "get a better job."

Client: Yes, I understand now.

Therapist: Good, Now I'd like you to tell me as many possible solutions as you can and I'll write them down. Just let the possibilities come—no matter how silly some may seem. But do keep in mind the two major concerns in your situation: The need for more sleep, and the desire for more friends.

Client: Well, I could try and go to sleep even when they're in the room by using earplugs. I could tell her friends to leave at a certain hour. I could ask my roommate to start and end the socializing earlier in the evening. I guess I could just have a good talk with her, explain the problem and work something out together. Maybe we could have people over just on weekends when I could sleep later in the morning. Or we could not have people over at all. Maybe I could find a way to live on less sleep. I know I'll have to find friends of my own so I won't be lonely.

Therapist: Anything else? What about finding another job that paid more, so you could get a different apartment?

Client: Oh no! I like my job.

Therapist: Remember, we're not excluding anything at this point.

Client: O.K. Well, maybe I could get a supplemental job and earn a little more money.

The therapist would then move on to the issue of not having friends, and similarly have the client generate various options. It is up to the therapist to determine when most of the potential solutions have been listed and it is time to move on to the next phase.

4. Decision Making

The client must now estimate which alternatives are worth pursuing, choosing among the number of wide ranging alternatives he has freely enumerated. With each strategy, the client must anticipate the likely consequences and evaluate those in terms of the major issues and conflicts comprising the problematic situation. There may be some obviously unrealistic alternatives which the client will want to eliminate at the outset.

In considering the likely consequences of a particular alternative, the client should keep in mind the following:

(a) The personal consequences, particularly as they relate to the major issues or conflicts of the situation.
(b) The social consequences that the course of action would have, particularly on the significant others in the person's life.
(c) The short-term consequences as they relate to both his own problem and the effects on others.
(d) The long-term consequences that the solution will have on future personal-social functioning, and the possible prevention of a similar problematic situation in the future.

Practically speaking, we are all limited in our ability to forecast the future, and the client cannot realistically consider all possible consequences of an action. In reality, he will be examining only a limited number of "significant" outcomes, and the likelihood of a particular outcome occurring can only be stated in general terms such as "highly likely," "likely," or "unlikely" to occur. The judgments regarding the efficacy of the various alternatives will also be in general terms, e.g., "very good," "good," "neutral," "bad," and "very bad." However, after considering the various alternatives, the client should be able to select the one which seems likely to yield the best results. The following illustrates this:

Therapist: I have here a list of the alternatives you suggested and I'd like you to consider which would be worthwhile pursuing. First of all, are there any not worth bothering with at all?

Client: Frankly, I don't think it would be physically possible for me to live on less sleep and still function well. I've always needed about eight hours of sleep a night and I'm in good health otherwise. I just think it's my constitution, and I doubt that it can be changed.

Therapist: Any others that you want to reject?

Client: No.

Therapist: I'd like you to think about each of these possible solutions in terms of the implications not only for you, but for others around you—friends and family. In addition, think not only of the immediate consequences, but also what the long term results may be. Why don't we think first about your trying to sleep while people are socializing in the room.

Client: I'd probably find the noise more annoying than the light so maybe I could use earplugs, or perhaps one of those machines that have a steady humming sound to blot out the noise. Actually, even if I could get to sleep it seems like a pretty awkward situation and I'm sure it would put a strain on my relationship with my roommate. Maybe I should concentrate on working out an arrangement with my roommate where the apartment is free of guests at my bedtime.

Therapist: O.K. Let's look at that.

Client: One of the things we could do is to have people come over only on weekends. That way I could choose to be home or be out socializing on my own, without worrying about how late it is getting. I'll talk to my roommate and maybe we can come up with something like "house rules." Maybe I'm doing things that she doesn't like and I'd offer to change some of my ways—so it would be a compromise of sorts.

Therapist: How do you think that would affect your relationship with your roommate?

Client: I'm not sure, but she's pretty easygoing, so somehow I think it would be all right. At least it's worth a try.

Therapist: How would you evaluate this alternative?

Client: Good, even very good.

Therapist: O.K., let's go on to some other alternatives.

After choosing a strategy (or strategies) the person must elaborate the tactics, i.e., specific ways in which the strategy will be carried out. The same procedure used for generating strategies should be used for generating tactics. In our case illustration, let us assume that our client has decided that talking to her roommate and working out a solution together is the best strategy for solving her initial conflict. She must now work out the specifics of that action (the tactics she will use) and decide when to best approach her roommate, making sure there is enough time for a long relaxed talk. She must work out how to talk to her, discussing the problem in a conciliatory rather than a hostile attitude, so that the roommate is not put on the defensive. She must also decide what to say, by sorting out the important issues and by recognizing that there may be other elements in the living arrangement that the roommate would want changed as a compromise solution. This still leaves the second conflict of wanting more friends vs. being new in town which, for example, might lead to the strategy of "finding friends." The following specific behaviors could be generated. "Take evening courses," "join clubs," "attend lectures," "go on singles weekends," "seek out interesting people at work." The client has to again engage in decision making regarding which of these behaviors would be the most effective.

While the above example is relatively simple, other more complicated situations might involve many major issues and would necessitate more than one alternative course of action to resolve the problem. Also, it must be kept in mind that there are some problematic situations for which there is really no good solution. Situations involving severe illness, or death of a family member may offer no really satisfactory solution, though the problem-solving method can still enable one to carry through on the best of the available solutions.

5. Verification

While much of the training in problem solving goes on at a cognitive level, the aim of it all is to have the client actually carry out in real life the behavior decided upon as the most effective course of action. In fact, all along, the client is given "homework" wherein he is encouraged to practice problem solving in vivo between sessions. The therapist not only encourages this carrying out of the selected behavior, but also acts as a guide in helping the client verify its efficacy. To verify an outcome one must first learn to observe the consequences of one's actions. If consequences are produced that satisfy the client, then the problem solving sequence is complete. If the solution produces unsatisfactory consequences, then the problem-solving procedure is resumed and another solution tried out.

APPLICATIONS

The problem-solving procedures outlined in the previous section are particularly relevant in assisting individuals who are required to cope with complex and relatively unfamiliar situational demands, for individuals whose previous learning experiences have left them ill-prepared to function at an independent level, and for cases reflecting a combination of these two conditions.

Problem solving may be found to be useful in crisis intervention, where individuals are confronted with problematic situations of the most serious sort. Here we are referring to such stressful life events as divorce, separation, death of a loved one, and other major upheavals in an individual's life style. The primary use of a problem-solving strategy in such instances is not so much to train the person to become a better problem solver; even the most effective of individuals is likely to have difficulty under such conditions. Instead, the major purpose is to assist the person to more intelligently think through what otherwise may appear as an overwhelming situation defying any attempts at resolution. In more extreme form—although not at all atypical of the type of instance one is confronted with on telephone "hot lines" throughout the country—the individual may have reached the point where suicide seems to be the only possible resolution to the dilemma. Although we readily admit that not all of life's problematic situations have conclusive solutions, a systematic approach to problem solving can nonetheless help a person in sorting out the complexities and deriving at least partial resolutions.

Although perhaps not undergoing major crises, students entering college are nonetheless confronted with a highly complex and novel environment, and this life change frequently results in the occurrence of numerous problem situations (Goldfried and D'Zurilla, 1969). For a number of individuals, this may be the first time they have had to function on a completely independent level. It would seem likely, then, that college freshman orientation sessions might include a certain amount of problem solving training, using as a training vehicle numerous hypothetical problematic situations that are likely to confront the student in the months and years to come.

Another use of problem solving has been with ex-drug addicts, and has been included in a behaviorally oriented treatment program for heroin addicts (Copeman, 1973). Once the program participants became free of their drug habit, they were faced with the prospect of returning to the environment containing those very frustrations and temptations that led them to become drug users to begin with. Thus, problem-solving training was used to assist the ex-addict in learning to more effectively cope with this environment, so that he would be able to "make it" without having to revert to drug use. Preliminary findings on the use of problem solving as part of a larger treatment package have thus far been most encouraging (Copeman, 1973).

As in the case of ex-drug addicts who are about to enter a different environment, psychiatric hospital patients and prisoners awaiting discharge are likely to have some difficulties functioning in the outside environment. Even if one assumes that they have been successfully rehabilitated and no longer manifest the problem behaviors that resulted in their original institutionalization—an assumption which may not be entirely warranted—they nonetheless may be expected to have some difficulties in coping. As observed by such writers as Goffman (1961) and Rosenhan (1973), the environment within institutions can be radically different in its demands from the way in which things are in the "real world." For example, in such settings there exists the tendency to discourage independent functioning. To further complicate matters, if a person had been institutionalized for a long time, it is likely that he will be returning to an environment that is markedly different from that which he left. Consequently, training in problem solving could very well represent a crucial phase in the reentry procedure.

A further use of problem solving has been in assisting adolescents and children in handling various conflict situations. For example, Kifer, Lewis, Green, and Phillips (1973) report the use of problem solving in getting predelinquent adolescents and their parents to jointly resolve various conflict situations that had been occurring in their daily lives. Problem-solving procedures have also been employed as part of a leadership training program for adolescents (Almedina and Rubin, 1974), and at the grade school and kindergarten level as a means of fostering peer cooperation (Shaftel and Shaftel, 1967; Spivack and Shure, 1974).

In most uses of problem solving, it is rare that it is employed as the only intervention method. What one frequently finds is that the inability to effectively resolve various problematic situations is accompanied by other problem behaviors as well. For example, certain individuals may be capable of learning to apply a problem-solving strategy, but may nonetheless have difficulty in carrying out the preferred course of action. This may either be due to certain inhibitions or fears of responding in a given way, or to the lack of certain responses within the individual's behavioral repertoire. In such instances, the use of supplementary behavior modification procedures would clearly be in order. For example, a person too fearful to carry out a course of action might first have his fears reduced through the use of systematic desensitization. Similarly, a person too unassertive to carry out certain actions in a social setting would need assertive training.

Although we have presented general guidelines for the use of problem solving as a therapeutic procedure, the precise way in which it would be implemented is likely to vary from instance to instance. As we have noted above, individuals will differ as to the phase of problem solving in which they may be most deficient. As a result, the exact procedures will have to be tailor-made to fit the needs of any given case. Further, the general nature of the training procedures will have to vary as a function of the ability of the client to comprehend the problem-solving procedure. One clearly does not go into the same amount of detail when working with children as when one works with adults, and the training would have to be simplified accordingly.

Finally, we want to emphasize that in providing a set of therapeutic guidelines, we would not want it to be mistaken for a cookbook. We have mentioned this point in connection with rational restructuring, but it is important enough to have it restated: therapeutic guidelines cannot substitute for the clinical sensitivity and ingenuity of the therapist (see Chapters 1 and 2).

CONCLUDING COMMENTS

While it is true that behavior therapists are now beginning to accept the role that cognitive processes play in the behavior change process, and to incorporate such variables in their therapeutic techniques, there are some fundamental differences between the cognitive-behavioral approach to therapy and more psychodynamically oriented techniques. The primary difference is that cognitive techniques used by behavior therapists ultimately have their roots in basic research. Notwithstanding their progressive disillusionment with the notion that all human behavior can readily be translated into principles of classical and operant conditioning, behavior therapists continue to affirm the overriding importance of an operationally and methodologically sound approach to the study of human behavior. Thus, not only do the cognitively based techniques that we have discussed have their origins in research, but the procedures themselves are specific enough to be readily learned by others and their effectiveness can be put to the empirical test.

As behavior therapists become more involved in cognitive factors, the question of how such variables interrelate with emotional reactions and overt behavior will need to be more clearly answered. When one sets out to teach a person to think more rationally or to solve problems more effectively, the primary goal is to have some impact on the person's emotional state and overt behavior. Although we are not certain exactly how changes in thinking affect feelings and behavior, we tend to operate on the assumption that improvement in one area facilitates change in others.

The therapist also has another important goal in teaching a person to think rationally or solve problems effectively. The goal is to teach the client a general coping strategy so that he can more effectively control his own life. Consequently, both rational restructuring and problem-solving techniques may be viewed within the broad context of self-control, where the ultimate objective is to provide individuals with skills for regulating their own behavior (Goldfried, 1971;

Goldfried and Merbaum, 1973; Thoresen and Mahoney, 1974). Clients frequently leave a given therapeutic session with the feeling that the therapist's support and encouragement have enabled them to put a particular problem into better perspective. The goal of systematic rational restructuring is to teach this technique to the client himself, so that once he terminates treatment, he can cope with upsetting situations on his own. Problem-solving techniques have been used in industry for years, particularly as a way of providing executives with the skills to manage their corporations. From a more personal standpoint, problem-solving training may be used toward the goal of providing the individual with a greater capacity to manage his own life. One can scarcely think of individuals who cannot benefit from such self-help skills.

REFERENCES

Almedina, J. and Rubin, A. Environmental design. Unpublished manuscript, State University of New York at Stony Brook, 1974.

Bandura, A. *Principles of behavior modification*. New York: Holt, Rinehart and Winston, 1969.

Beck, A. Cognitive therapy: Nature and relation to behavior therapy. *Behavior Therapy*, 1970, **1**, 184–200.

Becker, G. M. and McClintock, C. G. Value: Behavioral decision theory. *Annual Review of Psychology*, 1967, **18**, 239–286.

Bloom, B. S. and Broder, L. J. *Problem-solving processes of college students*. Chicago: University of Chicago Press, 1950.

Brehm, J. W. and Cohen, A. R. *Explorations in cognitive dissonance*. New York: Wiley, 1962.

Churchman, C. W. *Prediction and optimal decision*. Englewood Cliffs, N.J.: Prentice-Hall, 1961.

Copeman, C. D. Aversive counterconditioning and social restraining: A learning theory approach to drug rehabilitation. Unpublished doctoral dissertation, State University of New York at Stony Brook, 1973.

Davison, G. C. and Goldfried, M. R. Postdoctoral training in clinical behavior therapy. In I. B. Weiner (Ed.), *Postdoctoral education in clinical psychology*. Topeka, Kansas: Menninger Foundation, 1973.

DiLoreto, A. O. *Comparative psychotherapy: An experimental analysis*. Chicago: Aldine-Atherton, 1971.

Dollard, J. and Miller, N. E. *Personality and psychotherapy*. New York: McGraw-Hill, 1950.

D'Zurilla, T. J. and Goldfried, M. R. Problem solving and behavior modification. *Journal of Abnormal Psychology*, 1971, **78**, 107–126.

Edwards, W. Behavioral decision theory. *Annual Review of Psychology*, 1961, **12**, 473–498.

Ellis, A. *Reason and emotion in psychotherapy*. New York: Lyle Stuart, 1962.

Estes, W. K. Reward in human learning: Theoretical issues and strategic choice points. In R. Glaser (Ed.), *The nature of reinforcement*. New York: Academic Press, 1971.

Goffman, E. *Asylums*. Garden City, N.Y.: Doubleday, 1961.

Goldfried, M. R. Systematic desensitization as training in self-control. *Journal of Consulting and Clinical Psychology*, 1971, **37**, 228–234.

Goldfried, M. R. and D'Zurilla, T. J. A behavioral-analytic model for assessment competence. In C. D. Spielberger (Ed.), *Current topics in clinical and community psychology*. New York: Academic Press, 1969.

Goldfried, M. R. and Merbaum, M. (Eds.), *Behavior change through self-control*. New York: Holt, Rinehart and Winston, 1973.

Goldfried, M. R., Decenteceo, E. T., and Weinberg, L. Systematic rational restructuring as a self-control technique. *Behavior Therapy*, 1974, **5**, 247–254.

Goldfried, M. R. and Sobicinski, D. The effect of irrational beliefs on emotional arousal. *Journal of Consulting and Clinical Psychology*, 1975, in press.

Goldstein, A. P. *Therapist-patient expectancies in psychotherapy*. New York: Pergamon Press, 1962.

Goldstein, A. P., Heller, K., and Sechrest, L. B. *Psychotherapy and the psychology of behavior change*. New York: Wiley, 1966.

Hilgard, E. R. and Bower, G. H. *Theories of learning* (3rd ed.). New York: Appleton-Century-Crofts, 1966.

Kanfer, F. H. Self-regulation: Research and speculations. In C. Neuringer and J. L. Michael (Eds.), *Behavior modification in clinical psychology*. New York: Appleton-Century-Crofts, 1970.

Kanfer, F. H. and Phillips, J. S. *Learning foundations of behavior therapy*. New York: Wiley, 1970.

Kelly, G. A. *The psychology of personal constructs*. New York: Norton, 1955.

Kifer, R. E., Lewis, M. A., Green, D. R., and Phillips, E. L. The S.O.C.S. model: Training pre-delinquent youths and their parents in negotiation responses to conflict situations. Paper presented at the annual convention of the American Psychological Association, Montreal, Quebec, Canada, August, 1973.

Lazarus, A. A. *Behavior therapy and beyond*. New York: McGraw-Hill, 1971.

Meichenbaum, D. H. Cognitive modification of test anxious college students. *Journal of Consulting and Clinical Psychology*, 1972, **39**, 370–380.

Meichenbaum, D. H. *Cognitive behavior modification*. Morristown, N.J.: General Learning Press, 1974.

Meichenbaum, D. H., Gilmore, J. B., and Fedoravicius, A. Group insight versus desensitization in treating speech anxiety. *Journal of Consulting and Clinical Psychology*, 1971, **36**, 410–421.

Miller, G. A., Galanter, E., and Pribram, K. H. *Plans and the structure of behavior*. New York: Holt, Rinehart and Winston, 1960.

Osborn, A. F. *Applied imagination: Principles and procedures of creative problem-solving* (3rd ed.). New York: Scribner's, 1963.

Parnes, S. J. *Creative behavior guidebook*. New York: Scribner's, 1967.

Rosenhan, D. L. On being sane in insane places. *Science*, 1973, **179**, 250–258.

Rotter, J. B. *Social learning and clinical psychology*. Englewood Cliffs, N.J.: Prentice-Hall, 1954.

Shaftel, F. R. and Shaftel, G. *Role-playing for social values: Decision-making in the social studies*. Englewood Cliffs, N.J.: Prentice-Hall, 1967.

Simon, H. A. A behavioral model of rational choice. *Quarterly Journal of Economics*, 1955, **69**, 99–118.

Spivack, G. and Shure, M. B. *Social adjustment of young children*. San Francisco, Calif.: Jossey-Bass, 1974.

Staats, A. W. Language behavior therapy: A derivative of social behaviorism. *Behavior Therapy*, 1972, **3**, 165–192.

Thoresen, C. E. and Mahoney, M. J. *Behavioral self-control*. New York: Holt, Rinehart and Winston, 1974.

Trexler, L. D. and Karst, T. O. Rational-emotive therapy, placebo, and no-treatment effects on public-speaking anxiety. *Journal of Abnormal Psychology*, 1972, **79**, 60–67.

CHAPTER 5

Modeling Methods

G. Alan Marlatt and Martha A. Perry

I. INTRODUCTION

Imagine the following series of events. A boy about to try walking on the ice of a newly frozen pond suddenly notices that another boy walking on the ice has caused it to crack, and so he decides to go bike riding instead. Back at home, his little sister dresses up in her mother's clothes and tries to walk in high-heel shoes. His older brother is out in the family car for a driving lesson with the father, who is demonstrating the use of the clutch in changing gears. The evening newspaper reports another in a long chain of commercial airliner hi-jackings. At home, the mother prepares a fancy dinner using a recipe she saw the Galloping Gourmet prepare on television. Taking a short cut home on his bike, the boy pauses at the top of a hill wondering whether it is too steep to ride down safely. He waits until he sees two other children on bicycles make the descent with no apparent difficulty and then begins to coast downhill himself.

What do these events have in common? In each instance, the actions or behavior of one individual or group influenced the behavior of another. Many different terms have been offered to account for this process, including imitation, copying, mimicry, identification, and modeling. In this chapter, we will use the term modeling to refer to the process of observational learning in which the behavior of one individual or group, the model, acts as a stimulus for the thoughts, attitudes, or behavior of another individual who observes the model's performance.

While the role of imitation learning has been discussed at least since the time of Aristotle, only in recent years have investigators turned their full attention to this topic. In psychology, the study of imitation was almost totally neglected until the pioneering work by Miller and Dollard (1941). These authors reviewed the theories existing at the time and formulated their own analysis of imitation using a behavioristic framework. Over twenty years passed before the importance of imitative learning for social learning and personality development was highlighted in an important book authored by Bandura and Walters (1963). Since that time, the name of Bandura has become almost synonymous with the study of observational learning and its effects upon social behavior. The term modeling has come to replace imitation as a catch-all label for a variety of observational learning processes.

While there are a number of conflicting theories concerning the nature and operation of the modeling process, the position adopted by Bandura seems to be the most widely accepted. The interested reader may wish to refer to the introductory chapter of a recent book edited by Bandura (1971a), in which most of these theoretical controversies are outlined in detail. Other reviews of the extensive experimental and theoretical literature on modeling can be found in the basic behavior modification texts authored by Bandura (1969) and Kanfer and Phillips (1970).

Stated in simple terms, Bandura's account of the modeling process is as follows. In the first stage of the process, a model's behavior is attended to by an observer. This is called the *acquisition* phase, in which the actions of the model are initially acquired by the onlooker observing the model. It is not necessary that the observer be reinforced during the acquisition phase or engage in any overt practice in order for observational learning to occur. Rather, it is assumed that during the process of observation the observer acquires images and verbal representations of the model's behavior which are then "stored" in memory.

The second stage of the process concerns the *performance* of the modeled behavior by the observer. The distinction between the acquisition and performance of a modeled response is an important one, for it is often the case that a response acquired through observation is never actually performed by the observer. For example, you may have observed the behavior of a sky-diver by watching detailed films of his jumps to the extent that you have *learned* what steps are involved in this activity (acquisition phase), even though you have yet to jump out of a plane in an attempt to *perform* this behavior yourself.

Bandura states that it is primarily in the observer's performance of modeled behaviors that the role of reinforcement and punishment is of greatest importance. Whether or not a modeled response will increase or decrease in terms of the probability of subsequent performance will be determined by the action or reinforcement which follows the response at this point. There are a variety of factors which may determine whether a behavior which has been acquired through observational learning is subsequently performed by the observer. Many of these factors will be described in the discussion of the practical application of modeling principles which follows.

Before beginning the discussion of how modeling methods may be applied in the clinical setting, it would be helpful at this point to briefly review the major *effects* of observational learning. Bandura (1969) outlines three major effects of modeling, each of which has an important counterpart in clinical application. First, an observer may acquire behaviors which he or she may never have performed before observing the model's performance. The learning of new or novel discrete behaviors or newly integrated patterns of behavior is termed the *observational learning effect*. The description given earlier of the brother who is learning how to operate the clutch and change gears by watching his father demonstrate this skill is an example of the observational learning effect. This effect of modeling lends itself to a variety of applications such as teaching basic social skills to withdrawn or socially inept clients, training autistic or retarded children in the basic fundamentals of speech, and instructing hospitalized psychotic patients how to perform in a variety of new social situations they are likely to encounter upon their return to the community.

The second function of modeling concerns its effect on behaviors which are under some form of existing inhibition or restraint for the observer. Here, the observer already has learned how to perform the behaviors in question prior to exposure to the model, but the effect of the model is to either increase or decrease the rate of performance of this behavior by the observer. In most cases, observation of the consequences or reinforcement experienced by the model following his behavior is of paramount importance. Behaviors exhibited by the model which are followed by positive reinforcement are likely to produce an increase in the performance of these behaviors by the observer. If this increased performance involves behavior which was previously under inhibition or restraint on the part of the observer, a *disinhibitory effect* is said to occur. In the case of the boy who was uncertain as to whether he should ride his bike down the steep hill, the effect of observing someone else coast down the hill safely served to disinhibit his own behavior in this setting. On the other hand, if another bike rider was observed to fall off his bike after skidding on the gravel in an unsuccessful attempt to slow down while coasting down the hill, such a consequence might lead the boy to seek a safer route home. In this latter case, an *inhibitory effect* is involved. The case of the boy who was unsure about walking out on the ice on the pond is another example of the inhibitory effect. If he were to see someone else fall through the ice, he would probably be inhibited from walking on the ice, afraid that he might experience the same adverse consequences as the model.

Many of the clinical applications of modeling principles which have been described to date (Bandura, 1971b; Rachman, 1972) fall within the category of disinhibition effects. Behaviors which have been inhibited by the presence of strong fears or anxiety, as in phobic disorders, have been successfully treated by having phobic individuals witness models who engage in these feared behaviors and experience positive or safe consequences. Some attention has also been paid to the use of inhibitory effects in the clinical setting. Clients who engage in unrestrained behaviors which are socially disapproved (e.g., alcoholics or delinquents who have difficulty in controlling their own impulsive behavior) may be able to strengthen their own inhibitions against such behaviors by observing a model experience negative consequences for performing those same actions.

The third effect of modeling is termed the *response facilitation effect*. In this case, the effect of modeling is an increase in behaviors which the observer has already learned and for which there are no existing constraints or inhibitions. Here the effect of the model is simply to provide an informational "cue" which triggers similar behavior on the part of the observer. During a recent concert tour given by Bob Dylan, an example of the response facilitation effect was seen. Toward the end of the concert, a few individuals in the audience lit matches as a token of their esteem for Dylan—in a matter of seconds, thousands of others in the audience were also holding up lit matches. Assuming that almost everyone has learned how to light a match, and that there are few if any inhibitions constraining this behavior, the effect of the first members of the audience who lit matches was simply to facilitate this response in others. Few clinical applications of modeling involve the response facilitation effect—except perhaps for the use of modeling in increasing the frequency of normally occurring social behaviors. In this chapter we will focus primarily upon the use of observational learning effects and disinhibitory/inhibitory effects as practical methods of changing behavior.

The plan for the remainder of this chapter is as follows. In Part II, which follows, the general principles of modeling as a method for changing behavior in the clinical setting are discussed with regard to three classes of behavior. In the first section, we review the use of modeling methods in the modification of problems which are characterized by the presence of fears or anxiety, such as phobias. The treatment of one such problem, snake phobia, is outlined in detail in order to present the reader with a variety of practical concerns, many of which should be considered in any treatment application of modeling procedures. In this second section, the use of modeling as a technique to alter verbal behavior is described. Highlighted in this section are the disinhibitory effects of modeling upon verbal self-disclosure. The third section discusses modeling applications with individuals who frequently engage in inappropriate social behavior. Observational learning programs which attempt to teach new social behaviors to juvenile delinquents and alcoholics are described to illustrate these procedures. Because the behaviors selected for study in Part II are common to a variety of clinical populations, the discussion focuses upon a number of general principles which are important in any application of modeling methods.

In Part III, we provide a number of detailed examples of modeling as applied to specific client populations. The use of modeling in the classroom setting is described in the first section. In the following sections of Part III, modeling programs are described which have been used with the following clinical populations: autistic children, retarded individuals, and psychotic adults. A discussion of modeling as a training method for psychotherapists and paraprofessionals is given in the final section. The chapter concludes with some comments concerning the incidental effects of modeling which are likely to occur in any treatment setting.

II. PRINCIPLES OF MODELING METHODS IN
THE CLINICAL SETTING

Treatment of Fear-Related Behaviors

The most common use of modeling in the clinical setting to date has been in the treatment of behaviors which are under the inhibition of fear or anxiety, such as phobias. Here the client presumably already knows how to perform the appropriate behaviors but is constrained from performing them because of the feared consequences which may ensue. A model who is able to perform adequately and safely in the feared situation may disinhibit these responses in an observer. The technical term used to describe such effects is called *vicarious extinction*. If a snake phobic observes a model safely handle a snake, it is assumed that the observer's anxiety will extinguish because the model's actions (vicariously perceived and experienced by the observer) are not met with aversive consequences such as being bitten by the snake. As a result, the usual avoidant behavior which keeps the phobic from directly experiencing such safe consequences should also extinguish to the extent that the anxiety is diminished.

A successful application of modeling techniques for the treatment of snake phobia is reported in a classic study by Bandura, Blanchard, and Ritter (1969). We will examine the procedures used in this study in some detail in order to highlight the importance of a number of practical issues. The subjects in this study consisted of individuals who responded to a newspaper ad recruiting people who had an intense fear of snakes. All subjects were screened prior to treatment by means of a behavioral avoidance test in which they were asked to perform a number of approach behaviors in the presence of a live snake; only subjects who refused to lift the snake out of the cage with a gloved hand were included in the final treatment sample. These 48 subjects were divided into four groups: one of two modeling groups, a no-treatment control condition, and a final control group which received standard desensitization treatment (see Chapter 8). What are some of the general questions which must be answered before this form of treatment can be applied?

Choice of the Model

There are two forms of model presentation to choose from. The first form involves the use of a real-life or *live model* who actually performs the behavior in the presence of the observer. In many cases, the use of a live model is preferable because the observer is more likely to attend to and become involved in the naturalistic portrayal of real human beings in live situations. The use of live models does carry certain risks, however, in that the model's behavior cannot be exactly predicted or controlled. It would be disastrous, for example, if the model in a snake phobia treatment procedure began to exhibit increasing anxiety (or even worse, was bitten by the snake) in the presence of the observer. If this were to happen, the treatment would "backfire" and the client would likely show an increase in sensitivity and fear of snakes—an inhibition effect instead of a disinhibition effect.

In many other applications of modeling, the therapist may prefer to use a *symbolic model*, consisting of representations of the model's behavior in the form of films, videotapes, audiotapes, or even written scripts. The particular medium chosen for presentation of a symbolic model depends on the behavior to be changed and on other practical considerations. The bulk of the evidence (Bandura, 1969) reveals that modeling effects can be successfully obtained in most circumstances through the use of symbolic models. Symbolic models offer several advantages over live models. The model's recorded behavior can be controlled and edited, if necessary, to highlight the relevant portions of the model's behavior. Modeling tapes or films can also be kept on hand for repeated use in a clinic setting. Dubbed-in comments of a narrator can be used to distinguish the outstanding features or components of the model's performance, as in the case of training films which instruct viewers how to perform complicated motor acts. Symbolic models are also more likely to be useful in a group treatment situation, where the intent is to modify the behavior of a number of observers at the same time.

Who should play the role of the model? What characteristics of a model are most likely to produce imitative effects? A great deal of research has been conducted on this question, much of which is reviewed by Bandura and others (e.g., Bandura, 1969; Bandura and Walters, 1963; Flanders, 1968). An exact answer to this question again depends on the nature of the problem to be treated, but the following guidelines may be helpful in selecting models in a variety of treatment applications. Models who are competent, and who possess prestige in the eyes of the observer, are generally more likely to be emulated than low prestige models. Similarly, models who are regarded as warm and nurturant by the observer are more likely to facilitate modeling effects. These effects may be augmented by the fact that the observer associates rewarding qualities to the model's behavior, and thus is more motivated to match the behaviors.

Other considerations must be taken into account when selecting an appropriate model. A model who is too dissimilar to the observer, or whose behavior is on a level far superior or technically advanced relative to the observer's own capacity, may be rejected by the observer. The observer may discard the model's influence because he attributes "magical powers" to the performer or because he feels totally incompetent to match the model's superior performance. Probably the best choice of a model in this regard is someone who is just "one or two steps" advanced from the position of the observer, or who proceeds from a position of relative similarity to the observer to one of greater competence in graduated steps. A model who demonstrates progressively more difficult stages of performance is sometimes referred to as a "slider" model in the literature. A model who verbalizes his own initial uncertainty and subsequent problem-solving or coping strategies as he continues in the modeling sequence may be extremely helpful in this regard, as discussed by Meichenbaum elsewhere in this volume (Chapter 11).

Additional advantages in the modeling procedure are often obtained through the use of *multiple models*. The problems inherent with the use of one particular model in terms of the considerations discussed above can be partially overcome by the use of several different models who vary from the observer in terms of age, sex, socio-economic level, and other factors. Increases in the generalization of treatment effects are much more likely when the observer witnesses a variety of models engage in the desired behavior. The situational factors present in the modeling sequence can also be varied in the same manner. In the case of the snake phobic treatment, for example, the observer could be presented with a number of models of different ages and of both sexes who safely interact with a variety of snakes of different colors and lengths in order to maximize generalization effects.

With these considerations in mind, note the following description of the modeling sequence adopted by Bandura, Blanchard, and Ritter (1969, p. 178).

Subjects participated in self-administered symbolic modeling treatment in which they observed a graduated film depicting young children, adolescents, and adults engaging in progressively more threatening interactions with a snake. The colored film, which was approximately 35 minutes long, began with scenes showing the fearless models handling plastic snakes and proceeded through displays in which they touched and held a large king snake, draped it around their necks, and let it crawl freely over their bodies.

This model presentation incorporates the following features: the presentation of a symbolic model, the use of multiple models, and a series of activities which gradually increase in difficulty. These considerations are particularly important in modeling treatments applied to behaviors inhibited by anxiety.

Attending to the Model

In order for the modeling treatment to be effective during the acquisition phase of observational learning, the observer must pay close attention to the model's behavior. Attention may be focused in a number of ways. In addition to the careful selection of the model, as described above, the salient aspects of the model's behavior may be highlighted in the procedure. The instructions presented to the observer may "prime" him to watch for particular aspects of the model's performance, thus establishing an appropriate attentional set. The model should also be presented in such a way that the observer is free from other distracting stimuli; the use of a symbolic model is preferable in this regard, as the observer's attention can more easily be directed to watching a film or television monitor in a darkened, quiet room. An audiotape model can be highlighted by presenting it to the observer through earphones. When live models are used, particularly in the naturalistic setting, every attempt should be made to reduce or minimize the distracting influence of other individuals or ongoing situations.

Models provide a source of information to the observer. They often tell people what to do, how to do it, and when to do it. As such, the observer is most likely to attend to the behavior of a model when he is in a state of uncertainty about his own behavior (Heller and Marlatt, 1969; Marlatt, 1972). When an individual is faced with a choice among several behavioral alternatives and the situation itself is ambiguous, a model's behavior and its consequences can serve as directional signposts for the observer. At a formal dinner party, for example, several uncertain guests may wait until the host uses the fingerbowl in order to learn the proper use of this procedure. Attention to the model's behavior can be increased if the observer is in a state of uncertainty and is seeking information about what to do next.

Additional factors concerning the observer's attention must be taken into consideration in the treatment of anxiety disorders. If the model's behavior in the feared situation elicits too much anxiety for the observer, he may avoid watching the model or otherwise ignore the procedure. Here, the careful use of a graduated "slider" model may keep anxiety at a minimum. Another possibility is to train the observer in relaxation techniques prior to the model's presentation and instruct him to relax during the model's actual performance. This procedure is similar to the use of relaxation in desensitization therapy, where it is assumed that relaxation will counter the anxiety responses. The use of a symbolic model can be combined with relaxation procedures so that the observer can actually control the scenes presented to him at his own pace. This procedure was adopted by Bandura and his co-workers in the symbolic modeling condition used in the treatment of snake phobics:

> To further increase the efficacy of this method, two other features were added: first, subjects were taught to induce and maintain anxiety-neutralizing relaxation throughout the period of exposure. The second factor concerned the control of stimulus presentation. A self-regulated modeling treatment would be expected to permit greater control over extinction outcomes than one in which subjects were exposed to a sequence of aversive modeling stimuli without regard to their anxiety responses. Therefore, the rate of presentation of modeling stimuli was regulated by subjects through a Kodak analyst projector equipped with remote control starting and reversing devices. Subjects were instructed to stop the film whenever a particular model performance was anxiety-provoking, to reverse the film to the beginning of the aversive sequence, and to reinduce deep relaxation. They then reviewed the threatening scene repeatedly in this manner until it was completely neutralized before proceeding to the next item in the graduated sequence. After subjects became skillful in handling the projector controls and the self-induction of relaxation, the experimenter absented himself from the situation so that the subjects themselves conducted their own treatment until their anxieties to the depicted scenes were thoroughly extinguished. Treatment was terminated when they could view the entire film without experiencing any emotional arousal. (p. 178.)*

While the effectiveness of relaxation training in modeling treatment programs has yet to be fully determined (cf. Rimm and Medeiros, 1970), its use may prove very helpful for observers who are unusually apprehensive about viewing the model's behavior in the feared situation.

Presentation of the Model

In addition to focusing the observer's attention prior to the presentation of the model, the therapist should make every attempt to ensure that the model's performance is both attended to, and retained by, the observer during the process of observation itself. Unless the observer is able to retain the essential characteristics of the model's behavior, the treatment will be of no avail. In cases in which the modeled behavior is particularly complicated or abstract, retention may be facilitated by having either the model or a narrator comment verbally both on the important features of the modeled behavior and on the general principle or rule which governs the model's performance. As an example, suppose a model were demonstrating socially assertive behavior to a withdrawn, socially inept observer. The scene involves ordering a dinner in a restaurant and finding that the steak is too tough to eat. The model demonstrates an assertive response in this situation by requesting the waitress to bring him another steak. The model or other narrator could comment at this point: "This is an example of an assertive response. I was

---

*From Bandura, A., Blanchard, E. B., and Ritter, B. Relative efficiency of desensitization and modeling approaches for inducing behavioral, affective and attitudinal changes. *Journal of Personality and Social Psychology*, 1969, **13**, 173–199. Reprinted by permission.

entitled to a good steak and was willing to pay for it, yet I was given an unacceptable piece of meat. I explained the difficulty in an open and friendly manner to the waitress, and asked her to bring me another steak. Afterwards, I felt good about myself and enjoyed my meal." By listening to the model highlight the essential characteristics of an assertive response, the observer is more likely to remember the rules or principles governing this behavior, and is in a better position to apply this form of response in a variety of different situations. As an additional aid to retention, the observer could be asked by the therapist to summarize the main features and general rules associated with the model's behavior following the model's performance. Several studies (e.g., Bandura, Grusec, and Menlove, 1966) demonstrate the finding that observers who actively summarize or code the model's behavior are better able to learn and retain this information.

Retention is also aided by having the observer actively rehearse and practice the modeled behavior either during the modeling presentation itself or at periods following the demonstration. Rehearsal and practice serve both as aids for coding the modeled behavior and for developing the necessary motor or verbal skills required to perform the behavior smoothly and efficiently. For teaching very complex motor behaviors, such as learning to drive an automobile or play a musical instrument, it is advisable to break down the sequence into simple components and present the most basic step in the procedure before demonstrating the entire chain of responses. Similarly, for those individuals who lack the necessary motor skills to perform the modeled behavior (e.g., the physically handicapped or brain damaged patient), a step-by-step modeling sequence, interspersed with rehearsal and practice trials, is recommended. The therapist may also wish to make use of verbal prompts or "coaching" if the observer fails to respond or responds incorrectly during rehearsal and practice trials. The therapist may say, for example, "Well, that was a good try, but you didn't get it exactly right that time, for the following reasons.... Okay, let's try it once more, and see if you can do it the way I suggested."

A procedure closely related to rehearsal and practice is the process of *participant modeling*. Originally developed by Ritter (1968, 1969) as a treatment method for phobic disorders, this procedure involves direct interaction between the model and the observer. After demonstrating the desired behavior, the model guides the observer personally through the steps involved, manually assisting him if necessary. The essential features of participant modeling as applied to the treatment of phobias is illustrated by the third modeling group in Bandura, Blanchard, and Ritter's study (1969, p. 180):

> Subjects assigned to the third group received the treatment combining graduated live modeling with guided participation. After observing intimate snake-interaction behavior repeatedly modeled by the experimenter, subjects were aided through demonstration and joint participation to perform progressively more threatening approach responses toward the king snake. In the initial procedure, subjects observed through a one-way mirror the experimenter perform a series of threatening activities with the king snake that provided striking demonstrations that close interaction with the snake does not have harmful consequences. During this period, which lasted approximately 15 minutes, the experimenter held the snake close to his face, allowed it to crawl over his body at will, and let it loose to slither about the room. After returning the snake to its glass cage, the experimenter

invited the subject to join him in the room and to be seated in one of four chairs placed at varying distances from the experimenter's chair. The experimenter then removed the snake from the cage and commenced the treatment, beginning with relatively nonthreatening performance tasks and proceeding through increasingly fear-provoking activities. This treatment was conducted without the use of relaxation procedures.

At each step the experimenter himself performed fearless behavior and gradually led subjects into touching, stroking, and then holding the midsection of the snake's body with gloved and then bare hands while the experimenter held the snake securely by the head and tail. Whenever a subject was unable to perform the behavior upon demonstration alone, she was asked to place her hand on the experimenter's and to move her hand down gradually until it touched the snake's body. After subjects no longer felt any apprehension about touching the snake under these secure conditions, anxieties about contact with the snake's head area and entwining tail were extinguished. The experimenter again performed the tasks fearlessly, and then he and the subject enacted the responses jointly; as subjects became less fearful the experimenter gradually reduced his participation and control over the snake until eventually subjects were able to hold the snake to their laps without assistance, to let the snake loose in the room and to retrieve it, and to let it crawl freely over their bodies. Progress through the graded approach tasks was paced according to the subjects' apprehensiveness. The threat value of the activities for each subject determined the particular order in which they were performed. When they reported being able to perform one activity with little or no fear, they were eased into a more difficult interaction. Treatment was terminated when subjects were able to execute all the snake interaction tasks independently.*

Participant modeling has been shown to be an extremely effective modeling treatment for fear-related problems in several controlled outcome studies. In Bandura's study, described above, this treatment method led to the virtual elimination of the snake phobia in 92 percent of the subjects tested, as assessed by a battery of behavioral and attitudinal measures. The method was more successful than the symbolic modeling condition, and both modeling groups proved superior to the standard desensitization treatment group. There is little doubt that participant modeling is one of the most powerful treatment techniques available for phobic problems.

Incentives to Perform Modeled Behaviors

In addition to the considerations described above concerning the observer's attention to the model and methods designed to increase retention of this material (rehearsal, practice, and participant modeling), there is the question of motivating the observer to perform these newly acquired behaviors after the treatment itself is completed. How can the therapist build in *incentives* during the modeling presentation which may motivate the observer to perform these same responses? A variety of experimental studies reveals that when a model's behavior is rewarded, or when the consequences of his actions are not aversive, the probability that the observer will match these behaviors is significantly increased. Observation of a model who is punished for his performance, on the other hand, usually produces a decrease in imitation on the part of the observer.

Observation of the reinforcing consequences of the model's behavior by the observer involves the process of *vicarious reinforcement*, as distinguished from

---

*Reprinted by permission from *Journal of Personality and Social Psychology*, 1969, **13**, 173–199.

direct reinforcement in which the observer is reinforced for the performance of an imitative response. Vicarious positive reinforcement has two main effects. It both provides the observer with *information* concerning the relevant features of the model's performance, and it provides the observer with an *incentive* or inducement to copy the model's behavior. As an example, suppose a model is shown engaging in a series of trial-and-error behaviors as he tries to solve a difficult puzzle. Suddenly he chances upon the key response which leads to a correct solution. At this point, he is rewarded by an onlooker who says, "Good! You have solved the puzzle by that last move!" By seeing the model obtain a social reward at that particular moment, the observer gains both information concerning the most effective response in that situation (as the reinforcement "cues in" the correct response), and an incentive to match that behavior to receive the rewarding consequences himself. In the absence of an extrinsic source of reinforcement, similar effects may be obtained by having the model reward himself for the desired behavior. An example of verbal self-reinforcement might include the model's saying, "Wow! I solved the puzzle myself—good for me!" The use of self-reinforcement by the model has an additional advantage in that the observer can begin to learn methods of controlling his own behavior by the use of self-reward. Here the model not only demonstrates the desired behavior, but he also models a pattern of built-in incentives in the form of self-reinforcement techniques which can be learned by the observer (also see Chapters 10 and 11).

In the treatment of fear-related behaviors, the very fact that the model experiences no negative consequences for his behavior operates in a similar manner to positive vicarious reinforcement for the observer. A model who safely engages in the feared behavior is much more likely to produce the desired modeling effect than a model who experiences pain or extreme anxiety as a result of his actions.

Direct reinforcement of the observer for performing the modeled behavior also increases the probability that this behavior will be repeated. During practice or rehearsal sessions, the therapist can greatly augment the effects of treatment by encouraging and actively rewarding the observer for the successful performance of his modeled responses. The direct experience of reinforcement in this manner operates on the same principles as *vicarious reinforcement* and is likely to be equally or even more effective. In participant modeling programs, the model may also provide direct reward to the observer during the actual modeling sequence. The principles of vicarious and direct reinforcement in the modeling process have been well documented in the literature (Bandura, 1971c; Kanfer, 1965).

This completes the discussion of the fundamental techniques of applying modeling methods in the treatment of fear-related problems. Many of the basic procedures discussed apply to other clinical uses of modeling as well, and the reader is advised to keep these principles in mind when planning and developing modeling treatments for use with any clinical problem. Further details of modeling procedures in the treatment of fears and phobias can be found in recent articles by Bandura and Barab (1973); Bandura, Jeffery, and Wright (1974); Bandura and Menlove (1968); Blanchard (1970); Geer and Turtletaub (1967); Kazdin (1973); and

Meichenbaum (1971). A critical review article by Rachman (1972) also summarizes the pertinent literature in this area.

Modification of Verbal Behavior

The principles of modeling described above also apply to the modification of verbal behavior. There is no doubt that the verbalizations of others, either in spoken or written form, exert a profound influence on our words and actions. In this section, we will discuss verbal modeling procedures which can be applied in the clinical setting. In the context of psychotherapy and behavior change, words are the basic token of information exchange between the client and the therapist. The client must first use words in order to express the nature of his problem to the therapist, often during an initial intake or assessment interview. The therapist and client also interact through the course of treatment, interchanging feelings and information through the medium of verbal expression.

In the initial discussion of a presenting complaint, many clients experience considerable difficulty putting their problems into words which are useful or acceptable to the therapist. For one thing, the client may experience anxiety, embarrassment, or extreme self-consciousness when faced with the prospect of revealing his or her deepest secrets and personal concerns to a relative stranger. These verbal behaviors are subject to inhibitions not unlike the fear-related behaviors described in the previous section. As a second factor, many clients who appear reticent or reluctant to discuss their problems to the therapist may lack the necessary verbal skills to communicate this information—modeling may help these clients learn a general set or verbal style which will help them be more self-disclosing.

We may ask why direct instructions to the client could not be used to bring about desired changes in verbal behavior. It is often the case, however, that instructions alone are insufficient sources of information (Marlatt, 1972). Instructions usually contain rules of the "do" and "don't do" variety, from which the listener must deduce specific examples which conform to the general rule. For example, if a therapist tells his client to "just tell me about your feelings in this regard," the client may have some difficulty in interpreting the rule to limit his discussion to feelings. How are feelings defined? What makes the difference between an opinion and a feeling? In such a case, the presentation of a model who illustrates the meaning of this rule by elaborating on specific examples of his own feelings may provide the needed information. In addition, if the model sequence involves an interview between a client and a therapist or interviewer, the interviewer can reinforce the model's self-disclosure, thus providing a source of positive vicarious reinforcement for the observer. Fears of being ridiculed or scorned for admitting certain feelings, personal problems, or weaknesses may be disinhibited as a result.

The first visit to a therapist or clinic by someone who is troubled with personal or behavioral problems is often a threatening experience for many prospective clients. At this early stage in the treatment process, clients may benefit from any information which tells them what to expect about the course of treatment. Written pamphlets or books which describe the process of therapy (e.g., Duke and Frankel, 1971) may serve as symbolic models which clients may use to direct their own behavior. The use of live or tape-recorded models may prove especially useful in this regard.

In one study on verbal modeling effects (Marlatt, Jacobson, Johnson, and Morrice, 1970), for example, subjects were exposed to a brief waiting room conversation between a model (thought by the subject to be another subject in the experiment) and the experimenter, in which the model described a series of personal problems. The exposure to this dialogue significantly increased the observer's own problem-admitting behavior in a subsequent quasi-clinical interview, particularly when the experimenter had encouraged or passively accepted the model's self-disclosure. Other studies in this series found that the modeling effect increased when the observer was uncertain of what was expected of him in the disclosure task (Marlatt, 1971), and that vicarious and direct reinforcement were of considerable importance in the modification of verbal behavior (Marlatt, 1970).

As an example of how these modeling procedures might be applied in a clinical setting, a study conducted by Kaplan (1971) is described. The investigator was interested in determining whether verbal models could be used to increase the disclosure of personal problems among a hospitalized group of veterans in a psychiatric service of a V.A. hospital. The patients, ranging in age from 17 to 64, represented a variety of nonpsychotic disorders including depression, alcoholism, and neurotic anxiety reactions. Many of these individuals had considerable difficulty in expressing their problems to members of the professional staff. Those who volunteered to participate in the study were told by the experimenter:

> This is a research project studying Veterans Administration patients. We are interested in getting an idea of the reasons which bring veterans to the hospital, and how veterans think and feel about themselves. Your instructions are to discuss the reasons that led you to seek admission to the hospital, to describe the problems that you've been having, and to tell us about yourself as a person. You will have 15 minutes to talk into the microphone which is in front of you. (Kaplan, 1971.)

These "minimal" instructions are similar to the instructions an interviewer might give a client at the beginning of the first intake session: "I wonder if you could tell me something about yourself and why you came to the clinic at this time." In this particular experiment, although these minimal instructions were compared with a set of more detailed instructions, the use of a model was superior to either set of instructions in increasing the number of problem statements given by most of the patients. Patients hearing the model were also told:

> You are probably wondering now what you will say. In order for you to get some idea of the things we are interested in, we will first let you listen to part of a tape-recording made by another patient who, like yourself, took part in this study. He has given us permission to use his tape in this way. (Kaplan, 1971.)

The reference to "another patient" was made in order to increase the observer's perception of similarity between himself and the model. The entire tape-recorded segment lasted less than four minutes. In the beginning section of the tape, the model speaks:

> Well, lately I've been having trouble with my nerves. Three weeks ago I was fired from my job. I've been working at a brewery here in town for the past three years. But a few weeks ago I had an argument with my foreman. He bawled me out for letting some defective bottles pass and I guess because I knew that he was probably right I couldn't control my temper and I really told him off. Well, he put me on third shift, which I put up with for awhile, but I finally complained to the union which backed up the foreman and I was fired. I feel ashamed now about how I handled the situation. My pride was hurt, I guess, and I didn't have the patience to just keep quiet and let the whole thing straighten itself out. Of course, getting fired didn't help the way things had been going at home. We have three children and just bought a house two years ago, and ever since we moved into this place things have gotten worse. It has always bothered me not being able to afford our own home, and then when I got this job with the brewery, we bought the house and have had a hard time keeping up with the payments. And I haven't looked for a new job because it bothers me to admit to the personnel directors that I was fired from the brewery. At my age, it's pretty hard to think that I'm out of work, and then when I think about all the bills that're piling up I get depressed.*

A second application of verbal modeling procedures which has received some attention is the use of models to influence the verbal behavior of participants in group psychotherapy. Two examples of this method are described. In one approach (Whalen, 1969), prospective group members (male undergraduate volunteers) saw a 12-minute film of a four-member group prior to participating in their own group sessions:

> In the experimental film a group of four male undergraduates conversed after implying that they had just met. Two of the film participants spent a few seconds conveying biographical information, and then a third member, interrupting these interchanges, maintained that the group members were not using the best method of getting to know each other. For the remainder of the time the participants talked on a more personal level, describing their anxieties and other feelings, and feeding back their impressions—whether positive, negative, or neutral—to the other group members. (Whalen, 1969, p. 510.)

The results of this manipulation showed that the model film, combined with detailed instructions to the observers, led to the greatest level of interpersonal openness in the observers' own groups compared to the other conditions tested. The use of detailed, explicit instructions describing the desired behavior in conjunction with the modeling presentation seems to lead to the best results in studies of this kind. (cf. Green and Marlatt, 1972.)

A related approach involves the use of a model who is "planted" as a member of the group, and who engages in self-disclosing behavior in the presence of the observers (e.g., Schwartz and Hawkins, 1965). In a more recent example of this approach, Hall (1973) investigated the influence of a planted model in four-person groups, consisting of undergraduate students. In some of the groups, the model led off the discussion with the following comments (excerpted from the first part of the model script):

> Well, let's see . . . I'm twenty years old; I'm a sophomore from [a nearby town]. Let's see, what

---

*This and two quotes above from Kaplan, S. J. The effects of a model and instructions upon problem admission in two types of psychiatric patients. Unpublished Master's thesis, University of Wisconsin, 1971. Reprinted by permission.

can I tell you about myself that would help you to get to know me better? Well, I guess I'd say that inside I'm basically kind of a shy person. At least I used to be really uncomfortable with other people and afraid to say much of anything, but I guess I've changed a lot the last couple of years, gained some self-confidence and poise so that even though I feel scared inside, I can talk to people and make friends and communicate how I feel and all that. Like right now, I feel a little awkward sitting here talking to three strangers, and yet I'm talking to you, and it feels okay. That used to be my worst problem, talking to people I didn't know. I guess I've really changed a lot since I got to Madison.*

Subjects who were exposed to this personal model engaged in significantly more disclosure of a personal nature than did control subjects who were exposed to a model who described himself in more factual, impersonal terms.

The use of verbal models is not limited to use with personal self-disclosure or interpersonal communication in groups. In the following section, verbal models are also utilized to teach social behavior and problem-solving skills.

Modification of Social Behavior

In the previous two sections, the disinhibiting effect of modeling was discussed in the treatment of fear-related behaviors and in the modification of verbal self-disclosure. The importance of the reinforcement consequences of the model's behaviors was stressed in the discussion of the disinhibition process. For many clinical problems, however, the lifting of inhibitions or constraints alone is not enough. Many behaviors appear to be "inhibited" or absent simply because the individual does not possess the requisite skills or behaviors necessary to engage in the desired behavior. In many cases, both an *anxiety* component and a *learning deficiency* component are involved in the same problem, and the therapist must devise a treatment program which is designed to modify both these elements. In the present section, observational learning procedures are described which are designed to teach new behaviors or skills. In addition, the use of vicarious processes to modify emotional or affective responses is briefly discussed.

Acquisition of Social Skills

The following is an example which highlights some of the above issues. In a recent evaluation of the effectiveness of a treatment program with male alcoholics (Marlatt, 1973), each patient who resumed drinking following his discharge from an alcoholism treatment hospital was interviewed in depth concerning the exact situation and circumstances in which he took his first relapse drink. An analysis of these relapse situations reported by 48 patients revealed that over half of the sample took their first drink in one of the following two situations. The first type of situation, accounting for 29 percent of the relapses, was characterized by these features: the patient was frustrated in some goal-directed activity and reported experiencing anger and resentment. Rather than expressing this anger in a

---

*From Hall, H. L. The effect of personal and impersonal participant models on interpersonal openness in same and mixed sex groups. Unpublished Doctoral dissertation, University of Wisconsin 1973. Reprinted by permission.

constructive manner, he began to drink. For example, one patient tried to call his estranged wife shortly after leaving the hospital in order to make arrangements to see his children. As soon as his wife heard his voice on the phone, she hung up on him. When asked about his feelings at that moment, he replied, "The bitch! I could kill her for doing that!" What did he actually do? "I went down to the corner bar for a drink."

The second type of situation involved social pressure (23 percent of all relapses), in which the patient was unable to resist the social pressure from other individuals to resume drinking. In one case, the patient had just completed his first week of work on a new job. It was a Friday afternoon, and his new co-workers invited him down to the corner bar for a well-deserved drink. He made a few meek attempts to resist but soon gave up and joined the insistent crowd. By closing time that evening, he had consumed over 30 glasses of beer.

How can modeling be used to help individuals resist the temptation to drink in these "high-risk" situations? One approach is to use modeling and role-playing procedures in a program designed to teach new, constructive alternative behaviors. Such a program can be administered while the patient is still in treatment in order to build up his behavioral repetoire before he is actually confronted with troublesome situations in the outside world.

One program of this type has been developed by Sarason (Sarason, 1968; Sarason and Ganzer, 1973) for use with juvenile delinquents. In this study, Sarason and his affiliates investigated the effectiveness of modeling procedures, compared to traditional group discussion approaches, with institutionalized male delinquents. The groups met four times a week for a one-month period, with each session devoted to a particular adjustment problem. Sessions included such topics as: how to apply for a new job, how to resist social pressure from peers to engage in antisocial behaviors, and how to delay immediate sources of gratification in order to obtain more valued goals in the future. In the modeling groups, consisting of four or five youths, two models (graduate students in psychology) acted out a script which demonstrated appropriate behavior in these problem situations. Following the modeling sequence, the observers were called upon to summarize and explain the main points of what they had just observed. Each youth then enacted the same scene with either another boy or a model as a partner. In the example which follows, the problem situation is very similar to that described above in the discussion of alcoholic relapses. Here, the boys are exposed to a modeled interaction in which Tom, a newly paroled youth, is pressured to go out drinking (Sarason and Ganzer, 1971).

(George knocks on the door and Tom answers)

Tom: Hi, George, how're you doing?

George: Hey, Man, we're glad to see you back. Gotta celebrate your return. We got a couple cases of beer out in the car. Come on, we're gonna have a party.

Tom: Oh, you know I got to stay clean.

George: What do you mean, you gotta stay clean? Come on, this party was planned just for you. We even got a date with Debbie lined up for you. It won't hurt just this once.

Tom: Well, you know I'm on parole. I can't go drinking . . . I might get caught and if I get caught now, I'll really get screwed.

George: Oh, Man, we won't get caught. We never get caught doing anything like that.

Tom: Well, maybe you guys have never gotten caught, but the night I got in trouble I was out drinking and ended up stealing a car. (pause) You know, I just got back.

George: Look, Man, you don't have to drink. Just come to the party and have a little fun. What are we gonna tell Debbie anyway?

Tom: You know being there is the same as drinking to the fuzz. And Debbie won't have any trouble finding someone else.

George: You mean you don't want to go out with Debbie?

Tom: Not to this party. Maybe to a show sometime or something like that.

George: Boy, I sure don't understand you. You have sure changed since you got back from that place. You trying to kiss us off?

Tom: No, that's not it, Man. If you want to do something else where we wouldn't get into trouble, (pause) like go to a show, the dance or something, that would be okay but . . . well . . . I know some guys who were in there for a second or third time and they don't get the breaks anymore. You know what it is to be on parole.

George: Okay, look, let's just have one quick beer now out in the car, okay? For old times sake.

Tom: No, Man, I know where that leads. Then it would be just one more and then pretty soon we'll be drunk. I can't do it, Man.

George: Jeez! What is the matter with you, Man? Just one beer?

Tom: Maybe another night. My old man expects me to help him work on the boat tonight anyway. I'll be in trouble with him if I take off. Look, I'm sorry, maybe some other time, okay?

George: Okay. Can't be helped, I guess. Look, we'll be at John's place. Come on over later if you can.

Tom: Sure. See you tomorrow, anyway. (p. 139.)*

The treatment method which Sarason described was found to be highly effective as assessed by a variety of attitudinal and behavioral adjustment measures. This method can be applied to a variety of cases in which the therapist desires to train clients to perform new behaviors or acquire new social skills.

Another use of this procedure is the training of observers to engage in assertive, independent behaviors when faced with an unreasonable request from others. Many passive, socially withdrawn individuals can be taught to be more outgoing and aggressive through the use of modeling techniques. The work of McFall and his associates is illustrative of this approach. In one study (McFall and Lillesand, 1971), patterned after procedures developed in an earlier experiment (McFall and Marston, 1970), nonassertive college students were trained in assertive behaviors in a program which included the components of symbolic verbal modeling, practice or rehearsal sessions, and informational "coaching" by the therapist. Observers were exposed to ten situations which called for appropriate refusal responses to unreasonable requests. Each situation was presented to observers on audiotape, as the following example† illustrates:

> The training sequence for each situation was as follows: (a) the narrator described the situation; (b) S responded overtly or covertly; (c) S heard the responses of one male and one female assertive

---

*Reprinted by permission from Sarason, I. G. and Ganzer, V. J. Modeling: An approach to the rehabilitation of juvenile offenders. *HEW*, 1971.

†From McFall, R. M. and Lillesand, D. B. Behavior rehearsal with modeling and coaching in assertion training. *Journal of Abnormal Psychology*, 1971, **77**, 313–323. Reprinted by permission.

model; (d) the narrator coached S regarding what makes a good assertive response in the situation; (e) S either heard his response replayed or reflected on it; (f) the situation was repeated; and (g) S responded overtly or covertly again.

The following segment of a transcript of the training tape illustrates the training procedure and material:

Narrator: A person in one of your classes, someone whom you do not know very well, borrowed your class notes weeks ago, then failed to return them at the next class, thus forcing you to take notes on scrap paper. Now this person comes up to you again and says, "Hey, mind if I borrow your class notes again?" What do you say? (Subject practices responding, either overtly or covertly.)

Narrator: Now, listen to the responses of two assertive subjects to this same situation.

Male Model: You didn't return my notes last time, so I'm not going to lend them to you this time.

Female Model: No, I just can't be sure you're going to have them back in time.

Narrator (coaching):   Notice that both of these assertive subjects let the person know that their refusal was based on his past behavior. Their responses were brief and without any ambiguity. Their voices express some irritation over the past behavior of this person, but in general their responses were well controlled. Now, (listen to/think back to) your response to this situation and compare it to the responses of the models you have just heard. (playback or 10-second pause)

Narrator: Now you will hear the same situation again. This time try to make your response more assertive. (Repeat situation. Subject practices responding.) (pp. 315–316.)

McFall's research demonstrates the effectiveness of modeling procedures for assertive training programs. A number of other applications of similar techniques have been reported in which social skills and behaviors have been modified through the use of modeling. The reader may wish to consult the work of Goldstein (1973); Krumboltz and Thoreson (1969); and O'Connor (1972) for examples of additional procedures.

Acquisition of Emotional Responses

There is a body of experimental evidence which shows that emotional responses can be acquired vicariously by exposure to the emotional reactions of models. While much of this research has dealt with the acquisition of aversive emotional responses such as anxiety or pain, similar principles may apply to the modeling of positive emotional reactions, including joy, humor, or even sexual arousal. In many recent experiments (Bandura and Rosenthal, 1966; Berger, 1962; Craig and Lowery, 1969), the procedure is as follows. The observer is exposed to a model who ostensibly receives punishment, often in the form of electric shock, following the presentation of a stimulus such as a light or tone. When the observer is subsequently presented with this same stimulus, the results show that he also responds with increased arousal or anxiety, as indicated by a number of behavioral and psychophysiological measures. This procedure has been called *vicarious classical conditioning*.

While this method has not often been applied in the clinical setting, it is not difficult to speculate on possible applications. Vicarious conditioning may prove to be an effective method of training emotional responsiveness in those individuals who, when compared to the normal population, seem to show little or no affective response to stressful situations. The so-called "sociopathic personality" may be of this type. The possibility exists that *inhibitory* mechanisms may be acquired by individuals who show little ability to otherwise control their impulsive, antisocial behavior by being exposed to models who both receive aversive consequences for engaging in this same behavior and who demonstrate clear emotional reactions to this punishment. Because of the limited data currently available, and because of the ethical issues involved, the use of aversive control in this manner should await further laboratory tests before it is applied as a treatment method.

Several additional lines of inquiry also remain to be investigated. What is the effectiveness of vicarious aversion therapy, in which patients observe another individual receive aversive consequences (e.g., shock or nausea) for engaging in maladaptive behaviors such as alcohol or drug abuse, or sexual deviations? If vicarious exposure to this treatment method proves to be as effective as the direct experience of noxious consequences, the method could provide a safer, more acceptable substitute for aversion therapy (see Chapter 9). Another possible use of vicarious aversion is the exposure of the client to a video-taped playback of his own maladaptive behavior and associated consequences. For example, Sobell and Sobell (1973) have described a treatment method for alcoholics which includes a procedure in which patients view their own "drunk" behavior (video-taped earlier) while in the sober state. This experience seems to be an effective one and deserves further study.

III. APPLICATIONS OF MODELING METHODS WITH SPECIFIC SUBJECT POPULATIONS

Modification of Classroom Behaviors

The planned use of modeling in classroom settings gives schools flexible opportunities for affecting the academic and classroom behaviors of the students. What are some of the possibilities?

Typically, the teacher is the major *planned* model in the classroom, showing the academic skills that students are expected to perform. For example, $2 \times 2 = 4$ is written on the board; "Now, class, you do the problems on your worksheets like this one I've shown you.", or:

Johnny (reading aloud):   Bob and his brother looked in the . . uh . . the . .
Teacher: . . . window . . .
Johnny: . . the window of the pet shop.

Other models are or could be available in the classroom, however, to demonstrate and elicit both academic performance and appropriate classroom behaviors. Several examples show how peers, paraprofessionals, and filmed models could be effectively used in schools.

Csapo (1972) solicited the help of six normal primary school children to be models of appropriate classroom behavior to six emotionally disturbed classmates. Six other normal children participated in the program as behavioral observers and recorders. She reports:

> I was introduced to the students as a teacher interested in children's classroom behavior and in helping children find ways to get along better in school. I explained to the peer model that the teacher had selected him because she considered him a pupil who knew the right way to behave in the classroom. I asked the peer models to participate in an experiment designed to help the emotionally disturbed peer learn and exhibit better classroom behavior. I explained that the task of the peer model was to sit together with the emotionally disturbed peer, side by side at adjoining desks, for 15 consecutive school days, and that he would be expected to show the right kinds of behavior required by the given classroom situation. The peer model was asked to sit beside the emotionally disturbed peer all day except for 30 minutes in the afternoon.
>
> To the emotionally disturbed children, I stated that some behaviors had been observed in the classroom which appeared to interfere with all the students' chances to learn and get along well in school. I proposed a small experiment which could help the emotionally disturbed peer learn better ways to act in the classroom. The emotionally disturbed student was told that in order to help him learn these new things, his peers had offered to help him. This fellow student would sit beside him and serve as a model. All he had to do was to look at the peer model and try to do what he was doing. If he followed this procedure for a few weeks, it was expected that he would learn and be able to exhibit the same behaviors by himself.
>
> To let him know that he was doing things right, the peer model would give him a token whenever his behavior was appropriate. He was to record on a sheet, showing the date and a column for daily totals, each time he received a token. The number of tokens received each day would show him his progress. (pp. 20–21.)*

The target behaviors for each child were defined. Inappropriate behaviors to be modified included such things as speaking out of turn, thumb sucking, and poking others. Each emotionally disturbed child exhibited fewer inappropriate behaviors and more appropriate behaviors over the course of the program. In addition, it is reported anecdotally that peer models developed more positive attitudes toward their partners and that peer relationships in general improved.

What is important to note here? First, once intervention procedures are initiated, the teacher can proceed with the regular academic program for all children. She need not interrupt the entire class to attend to misbehavior. Second, not only do target students gain, but the models may show important gains as well. And third, that such young children can successfully participate in this type of program suggests that almost any mature-for-his-age child could serve as an effective peer model. Variations of this plan would permit simultaneous modeling to a number of children by one model or one-to-one peer modeling to just one child in a classroom who might need special help. Several children could be selected to all model a single behavior for one child or to model different behaviors to the same child.

Sometimes, however, a variety of circumstances make peer or teacher modeling an inappropriate choice for treatment. Ross, Ross, and Evans (1971) have reported the modification of behaviors by modeling and guided participation of an extremely withdrawn six-year-old child. In this case, because of the severity of the child's

---

*From Csapo, M. Peer models reverse the "one bad apple spoils the barrel" theory. *Teaching Exceptional Children*, 1972, **4**, 20–24. Reprinted by permission.

problem, teacher as therapist was not possible. This child needed so much attention that the teacher would have had to ignore the rest of the class to attend to him. And since the child avoided his peers, they could not serve as models for him.

In this study, an experimenter (psychologist) and a model (undergraduate student) conducted a seven week treatment program in the preschool. While such personnel may not be routinely available, a program could be conducted by trained paraprofessionals such as willing mothers or other volunteers. This program was designed first to establish generalized imitation of the model, that is, to get the child to copy or imitate any model behaviors. Second, the program used modeling to eliminate fear and avoidance behaviors and to teach social interaction, motor, and game skills.

> In the first phase, lasting four sessions, M [model] was paired with a variety of tangible and social rewards; was positive and demonstrative to S [subject] and rewarded him for imitative responses; and was immediately responsive to S's bids for attention, help, and approval. When M was absent, E [experimenter] encouraged S to reproduce M's behaviors and rewarded him for imitative responses. By the end of this phase, the facilitating effect of nurturance on imitation was confirmed, S was strongly attached to M: he talked constantly about M to E, reproduced many of M's verbal and nonverbal behaviors, and waited eagerly at the door of the preschool for M to come.* (p. 275.)

Now that the model had become valued to the child and was imitated by him, the second phase of the program was initiated. This phase had several steps:

1. The model demonstrated social interactions with other children. These were graduated in degree of approach and interaction. If the child did not watch, as sometimes happened, a commentary by either the experimenter or the model was given.
2. Pictures, stories, and movies were shown to the child and discussed with him by the model or the experimenter (symbolic modeling).
3. Reluctant peer interactions were modeled, and the model received reassurance and encouragement from the experimenter. This step was taken to create similarity between the child and the model and to show progression in social interaction.
4. The model and/or experimenter modeled appropriate social behaviors in humorous situations. The child was drawn into these sessions.
5. The model and the child together participated in a graduated series of social interactions.
6. The model demonstrated and helped the child practice game and other preschool appropriate skills.
7. The child was tested outside of the school setting (e.g., sent into a group of strange children in a park). He received encouragement and reward from the model or the experimenter for his performance on these occasions. In addition, these situations provided material for additional role playing.

---

*From Ross, D. M., Ross, S. A., and Evans, T. A. The modification of extreme social withdrawal by modeling with guided participation. *Journal of Behavior Therapy and Experimental Psychiatry*, 1971, **2**, 273–279. Reprinted by permission.

After treatment, according to the measurements used in this study, the child's behaviors were very similar to those of the socially competent children in the classroom. Thus, through the help of outside personnel, major changes can be brought about within the naturalistic school setting using models and guided participation. Note that this program made use of both live and symbolic models, guided participation, prompting, and direct reinforcement.

On the other end of the spectrum, we can consider a treatment approach that is directed toward many children at one time. Because observation of filmed models is as effective in many cases as observation of live models, schools can make use of prepared film materials that apply to problems experienced by many school-aged children. Hosford and Sorenson (1969) took this approach to help shy students participate more readily in classroom discussions. These authors estimated from a survey of fourth, fifth, and sixth graders that inability to participate in class discussions is a problem for about 25 percent of the children.

Hosford and Sorenson explain their procedures:*

> We began with a student, Steve, who was identified by his teachers and parents as being unable to speak up in class and who had indicated that he would like help with his problem. The counselor made a tape recording of the interview with Steve, the "model student." Basically the counseling session consisted of verbal interchanges between Steve and the counselor in which Steve responded to cues and questions as to what he might do to begin speaking up in class. Often the cues were such that Steve had little difficulty responding with a "good" question. Whenever he suggested, for example, "I would begin by asking a question," he was reinforced with, "That's an excellent way in which to begin." The interview was terminated after Steve had made several suggestions of things he might do. (p. 203.)

Here is an excerpt from the final eight-minute videotape:

> *Counselor*:   Good, Good. Now that's one way to start, isn't it?
>
> *Steve*:   Yeah.
>
> *Counselor*:   You know—would you like to practice this now so that tomorrow you'll know what you're going to do?
>
> *Steve*:   Uh huh. Okay.
>
> *Counselor*:   Now, why don't I pretend that I'm your teacher? Now that's Mrs. Jones, isn't it?
>
> *Steve*:   Uh huh.
>
> *Counselor*:   Okay, class, it's time for science and we've been studying the stars. Now is there anyone in here who has read anything about the stars?
>
> *Steve*:   I have.
>
> *Counselor*:   Oh you have, Steve, good. What have you read about the stars that you would like to tell us?
>
> *Steve*:   Well . . . the earth circles the sun every year.
>
> *Counselor*:   Right! Now is the sun a star?
>
> *Steve*:   Uh huh.

---

*From Hosford, R. E. and Sorenson, D. L. Participating in classroom discussions. In J. D. Krumboltz and C. E. Thoresen (Eds.), *Behavioral counseling: Cases and techniques.* New York: Holt, Rinehart and Winston, 1969. Reprinted by permission.

Counselor: Good. Now do you think maybe you could try this tomorrow in Mrs. Jones class?

Steve: Uh huh. Okay. Suppose so. (pp. 203–204.)

Although the critical question of whether the observers of the film actually participated more in class discussions was not asked in this study, the students indicated in a questionnaire that they learned something from watching Steve and that they would use some of the ideas they observed Steve using.

Certainly some of the advantages of planned use of modeling in school settings have been demonstrated in these examples: there are many models available in a school; flexibility in planning a program is maximal; disruption to regular classroom procedures can be held to a minimum; and programs can be planned for one child or for many using a model or multiple models. Academic skills, appropriate classroom behaviors, and social interaction skills are the usual target of school programs. Additional ideas for school applications of modeling can be found in Sarason and Sarason (1973).

Modeling in the Training of the Mentally Retarded

Modeling can be a valuable training aid in work with the mentally retarded. Workers often resort to modeling a skill when verbal instructions fail. It is natural to say, "Look, Johnny, do it like this," while demonstrating what it is you want the child to do. Is this approach effective with mentally retarded persons? It depends.

Zigler and his associates (Turnure and Zigler, 1964; Yando and Zigler, 1971) have found that familial retardates, those with no identifiable damage or genetic abnormality, are more outerdirected than children of average intelligence. That is, they look to others for cues of how to solve problems that face them. This suggests that modeling would be an effective training technique for this group of retarded individuals. A number of laboratory studies support this. However, let us examine studies in more naturalistic settings which can provide us with models for possible training programs.

Survival skill training, in particular the adequate use of the telephone, was the focus of a study by Stephen, Stephano, and Talkington (1973). Retarded girls of ages 16 to 22 years (mean age 19) and IQs of 55–85 (mean IQ 64.9) participated in the training. Of interest to these experimenters was the comparison of training by a live model with training through the use of videotapes.

Procedures for training programs such as this can be quite simple. In this case, some of the girls were introduced to a model (female college student) and told: "This lady is going to show you how to use the telephone. Watch closely as you will have to use the telephone in the same way as shown" (p. 65). Other girls were asked to watch a videotape on the use of the telephone. They were told: "The girl on the videotape is going to show you how to use the telephone. Watch closely as you will have to use the telephone in the same way as the girl on the videotape" (p. 65). In both cases, the model then identified six parts of the telephone, demonstrated how to make a phone call to the police, and demonstrated how to answer the phone and take a message for a person who is not at home. Girls were then asked to perform the tasks. The demonstration-test sequence was presented three times.

Findings encourage pursuit of modeling training with retarded persons. The two modeling groups just described performed significantly better than a control group which saw no model, though the group which had a live model was not significantly different in performance from the group which watched the videotape. We suggest then that the use of a series of training videotapes could be an effective time saving method of training moderately retarded individuals to perform certain basic skills.

We might ask how much repetition of the modeling displays would be needed in a film modeling program. Stephan, Stephano, and Talkington (1973) found that the greatest gain in behavior occurred between the first and second modeling trials. However, the amount of repetition needed would probably vary depending upon the task and its complexity. Thus, any individual training program would need to determine for itself the amount of repetition of modeling needed.

Dorothea Ross (1970) demonstrated that learning from audio-visual presentation can be facilitated by the prior association of the model with rewards to the child. The subjects in her study were educable mentally retarded boys and girls ranging in age from three years four months to 10 years eight months (mean age six years 10 months) and in IQ from 50 to 82 (mean IQ 64.24). The peer model–child relationship was established in the following way:

> The following procedure was used to teach each subject to attach reward value to a same-age, film-mediated model. The experimenter, who was well known to the subjects, invited a subject or a group of three subjects to come to the experimental room to play with some toys. As soon as they entered the room, the subject was shown colored slides of the model figure. In subsequent sessions, the slide projector was always turned on when the subject first entered the room. The subject was also shown how to work the slide projector and was allowed to use it whenever he wished to do so. The experimenter made no comment if the subject turned off the projector.
>
> For experimental reasons, some children saw Polly as the model and some saw Susan. "Polly was a child of elementary school age with dark brown hair and a distinctive red dress, while Susan had blond hair and a pale pink dress."
>
> In introducing the subject to the model figure, the experimenter said, "This is a picture of Polly (or Susan). She goes to another school. She has sent all the toys and games in this room for you to play with. Do you want to see some pictures of her? Look, you can show the pictures yourself. It's easy, I'll help you. You can play with these toys now if you want to."
>
> The experimenter then sat down well to one side of the room. She made frequent comments designed to focus the subject's attention on the model figure, e.g., "I'll bet Polly will think you're really good at that game when I tell her you hit the target almost every time," and to remind the subject that the model (not the experimenter) owned the toys, games, and edibles available to the subject. The experimenter always acted as an *agent* of the model figure, a person with no authority except the right to tell the subject when he had had his turn and must leave the room.* (pp. 702–703.)

Later Polly modeled, by way of videotape, some learning tasks for the subjects by saying, "Hello, everybody, this is your friend Polly. Today I . . ," and went on to explain the task.

A similar preliminary preparation for enhancing the effectiveness of a model could be easily used with an individual or with groups. This technique would be

---

*From Ross, D. M. Effect on learning of psychological attachment to a film model. *American Journal of Mental Deficiency*, 1970, **74**, 701–707. Reprinted by permission.

particularly effective with institutionalized retarded persons whose rewarding interactions with peers are generally quite limited.

We have seen from these two examples that modeling techniques can be effective tools in training at least one class of retarded individuals, moderate or educable retardates. What about those who have more severe deficits? Here the evidence is not so encouraging. Altman, Talkington, and Cleland (1972) found no spontaneous modeling of motor skills and no following of motor instructions by boys of ages 6.3 to 15.8 years and IQ of 10 to 50 (mean IQ 17.5). However, modeling combined with reinforcement has led to acquisition of generalized imitative repertoires in severely and profoundly retarded subjects who before training do not imitate (Baer, Peterson, and Sherman, 1967). One program of modeling treatment to institutionalized severely retarded persons is described below.

Whalen and Henker (1969, 1971) have made use of both modeling and reinforcement as training procedures for a "therapeutic pyramid" program in an institution for the mentally retarded. In their program, teenagers with IQs in the 40's to high 60's were first trained in behavior modification techniques by the experimenters. Modeling was a major component of this training of assistants or tutors as shown in the following excerpts:*

> During the initial session, the tutor received a brief orientation to the goals and procedures of the project. He was told he had been selected to be a "special teacher" for a younger child. He then observed an experienced behavior therapist begin to teach a trainee to imitate a particular response. Following this brief observation, the beginning tutor practiced the technique with the same trainee. The experimenter remained in the room with the dyad and closely supervised all interactions. In his supervising role, the experimenter provided the tutor with frequent verbal evaluations (feedback) regarding his performance and suggestions for improvement. In addition to verbal feedback, further demonstrations were provided when the tutor failed to understand or remember the technique and when each new phase of the program (e.g., gaining attention, extinguishing tantrums, shaping imitative speech and action) was introduced.
>
> The experimenter's use of modeling and feedback was gradually decreased as the tutor became increasingly confident and adept. The goal was to withdraw supervision progressively so that the tutor would learn to assume increasing responsibility for the training of his child. The tutors also began to teach each other, spontaneously modeling for and providing feedback to their "colleagues." (p. 332.)

When their training was completed, the tutors began to work with their charges. Again modeling and reinforcement techniques were used.

> The initial focus of training was on extinguishing tantrums and establishing eye contact. The next phase consisted of teaching the trainees to imitate simple sounds and gestures. The tutor first demonstrated the behavior he was attempting to teach the trainee. If the trainees failed to imitate, attention getting prompts were employed to elicit the desired responses. For example, in verbal imitation training the tutor would hold the reward (food) next to his mouth as he pronounced the stimulus word so that the trainee, whose attention had been focused by the reward, would see how the word was formed on the tutor's lips. When necessary, sounds were prompted by manipulating the child's mouth and lips. Analogously, the tutor prompted gestures by moving the trainee's limbs.

---

*From Whalen, C. K. and Henker, B. A. Creating therapeutic pyramids using mentally retarded patients. *American Journal of Mental Deficiency*, 1969, **74**, 331–337. Reprinted by permission.

> The prompts were "faded" as rapidly as the trainee's performance allowed ... After the trainee
> performed an accurate imitative response or an adequate approximation, the tutor rewarded him
> with food, praise, and physical affection. (p. 333.)

How successful was this program? After 25 sessions, Joey "now has an imitative vocabulary of about 40 words and can understand and follow several directions, such as 'turn off the light' and 'touch your nose'" (p. 334). His tutor, Jud, "has demonstrated his ability to function relatively independently as a tutor. Moreover, he is quite adept at prompting and evaluating the performance of his fellow tutors" (p. 334).

From the above material, it can be seen that modeling is an important and valuable part of the training battery to be used with the mentally retarded. Models and trainers may be other retarded persons, or, if available, other nonprofessional helpers could be trained as tutors. Prompting and reinforcement in combination with modeling also facilitate learning with severely retarded subjects. These findings are important in this field which has few effective training techniques. So many retarded individuals, particularly those in institutions, have not had the benefit of training programs because of limited staff and resources. However, if nonprofessionals can be trained as tutors and if presentation of filmed models is effective in teaching new skills, training can be programmed to proceed even without additions of large numbers of staff and without overburdening those who are already working with the retarded. Continued development of programs using modeling alone and in combination with other training techniques is needed.

Modeling in the Training of Autistic Children

Autistic children are characterized by their lack of social responsiveness and by their general failure to imitate other people. Since much human learning is facilitated by the use of models and imitation, this deficit is extremely limiting. In this respect, autistic children behave much like severely retarded children who demonstrate no spontaneous imitation, and training programs for imitation in autistic children are very similar to the programs described in the previous section. These programs use demonstration, prompting, and reinforcement to establish imitative behavioral repertoires.

Hingtgen, Coulter, and Churchill (1967) have provided a detailed description of an intensive short-term (three-week) training program with Sonny, a six-and-one-half-year-old who spent most of his day ritualistically manipulating objects or playing with his fingers and spitting, and Becky, a five-and-a-half-year-old girl who spent most of the day rocking. Both children were mute. The program proceeded as follows:*

> ... the child was isolated in an 8 × 15 foot room, 24 hours per day, for 21 consecutive days.
> Throughout this time the child received all food, water, and social contact from adults (two in the
> case of Sonny, six in the case of Becky) contingent upon the emission of specific behaviors. During
> an average of six hours of daily training sessions spread over a 12-hour period, food, water, and

---

*From Hingtgen, J. N., Coulter, S. K., and Churchill, D. W. Intensive reinforcement of imitative behavior in mute autistic children. *Archives of General Psychiatry*, 1967, **17**, 36–43. Copyright 1967 American Medical Association. Reprinted by permission.

release from physical restraint (all paired with verbal approval) were used to reinforce *three* types of imitative responses (p. 37).

    1. Individual and combinational uses of body parts—e.g., holding up one finger, clapping hands, touching parts of the body, various hand, tongue, and mouth positions, running, jumping, etc . . . (p. 37).

    2. Simple and complex uses of objects—e.g., dropping a ball in a bucket, hooking a toy train together, buttoning, line drawing, brushing teeth, playing appropriately with toys, cutting with scissors, etc . . . (p. 38.)

    3. Vocal responses—e.g., the imitation of vowel and consonant sounds with a gradual progression to words. (p. 38.)

Some examples give a flavor of the procedures of the training sessions:

    Imitation of vocal responses—blowing. During an 80-minute session on the third day of Sonny's isolation, he was placed on a chair sitting directly in front of and facing E-1 (the first experimenter), and was physically restrained from getting off the chair. During this session a blowing response was to be imitated in preparation for the later imitation of forcing air for the "puh" sound. Sonny had been observed making a blowing sound spontaneously during rituals, but never in imitation of an adult model. Since Sonny did blow on a harmonica in imitation of an adult during the use of objects session, E-1 started the session by blowing on a large toy harmonica, which Sonny imitated very consistently. With each imitative response, E-1 pulled the harmonica slightly away from Sonny's mouth, so that Sonny was required to blow harder to get the musical tone. Then E-1 took Sonny's hand and blew on it and asked Sonny to imitate that response. After presenting over 30 models, Sonny had not attempted to blow on his own hand, and after 15 minutes, E-1 left the room and E-2 (the second experimenter) entered. E-2 then attempted to have Sonny imitate blowing on a pinwheel, although no response was emitted during 15 minutes of continuous models. In the next 30 minutes, E-2 alternated between presenting models of blowing on the harmonica and blowing on the pinwheel. Sonny became very agitated during this period and emitted much of the avoidance behavior that was typical during the first few days of intensive training. He cried, pinched, hit, hugged, laughed, giggled, and teased in attempting to avoid making the blowing response. As his avoidance behavior increased in intensity, E-2 increased the amount of physical restraint used. Finally, Sonny made an excellent blowing response, and was rewarded by E-2 with a partial release from physical restraint and lavish praise. E-1 then entered the room again, replacing E-2, and tried to get a consistent blowing response. After ten minutes of crying and squirming by Sonny, which necessitated E-1 reinstating the physical restraint, Sonny made another excellent blowing response. E-1 rewarded Sonny by releasing the physical restraint and swinging him up in the air. During the last five minutes of this period Sonny made 33 blowing responses in imitation of E-1. Then E-2 came in for five minutes more and obtained 32 blowing responses from Sonny. No food was used as a reward during this session, and all imitative responses were rewarded by the release of physical restraint and the presentation of social reinforcers. (pp. 38–39.)

    Imitation of use of objects—scissors. During one session in Becky's third day in the room, a pair of children's scissors were taped to the thumb and middle finger of Becky's hand. Holding scissors in her own hand, E then presented a model of opening and closing of the hand. With some help Becky was able to imitate the response. By the end of the 45-minute session Becky was beginning to make small cuts in a thick piece of paper in imitation of E. (p. 39.)

Obviously the treatment of Sonny and Becky was an intensive and time-consuming one-to-one approach. Because of the degree of deficit in the functioning of an autistic child, it is perhaps inevitable that such must be the case. However, Stilwell (1969) reports a case which made effective use of peer models to aid in the treatment of a socially isolated and self-destructive hospitalized autistic child.

Stilwell points out very clearly the steps in setting up the training program used with Curt, an autistic boy. These included: (1) Assessing the problem, or determining the current patterns of behavior. Curt demonstrated a behavioral chain consisting of isolated walking and crying, and when approached, gnawing on his hand. (2) Selecting behavioral goals. For Curt, the goal was to modify the first element of the chain, the isolated walking. (3) Analyzing the contingencies or determining the most effective reinforcers. M & M's as well as strong social reinforcers were used for Curt. (4) Establishing control or developing attention to the counselor; and (5) Developing a sequence. The sequence depends on what has been determined in the previous four steps. The sequence is set up in a stepwise manner of graduated difficulty.

Curt's sequence was designed to establish "playing on the slide." Though he had the skills to do this activity, he did not spontaneously engage in it. In a series of steps he did perform the activity and was rewarded for it. Then the assistance of a peer as model was solicited.

> *Counselor*:   I will hire you to work for me, Mark. We can have a contract and shake hands and you can get paid.
>
> *Mark*:   Silence.
>
> *Counselor*:   I want Curt to slide down the slide. Will you help me?
>
> *Mark*:   Alright.
>
> *Counselor*:   For every trip down the slide that Curt makes after you, I will give you one M & M. (p. 197.)

After some haggling, Mark agreed to be a model, and later other children made similar contracts to help Curt.

Though modeling in this case did not reduce the amount of counselor contact required for Curt's training (the counselor continued verbal and nonverbal reinforcement while models were sliding), the modeling provided an important stimulus for Curt's playing on the slide. Unfortunately, when the counselor was absent, Curt's behavior did not continue, as the peers, while good models, were not rewarding to him.

We can note in these examples that the model is made very salient to the child so that attention is assured, complex behaviors are presented in small segments first and gradually elaborated, and immediate reinforcement is given to the child for imitation. It is apparent from the work cited here and from other programs for autistic children (Lovaas, Freitag, Nelson, and Whalen, 1967) that modeling is a useful aid for teaching both verbal and nonverbal behaviors to autistic children.

Modeling in the Treatment of Psychotic Adults

In many ways, the deficits of some psychotic adults resemble the deficits found in autistic children. In some more severely disturbed schizophrenic patients, behavioral repertoires are severely limited, and are often characterized by lack of speech and social withdrawal. It is not surprising that applications of modeling to the treatment of psychotic adults are very similar to programs discussed in the previous section. One difference, however, is that in training autistic children we are usually concerned with the observational learning of new skills, since the child often has never previously learned or performed the target skills. With psychotic adults, on the other hand, the intent may be to reinstate the use of skills which have been in the patient's behavioral repertoire at some time in the past.

Sherman (1965) and Wilson and Walters (1966) have demonstrated the usefulness of a modeling-reinforcement combination in stimulating speech in mute or near-mute schizophrenic patients. Note how the Wilson and Walters work differs from Hingtgen, Coulter, and Churchill's training of Sonny and Becky for speech.

The study of Wilson and Walters examined the effects on speech output of modeling-plus-reinforcement, modeling only, and neither modeling nor reinforcement (control). Since model-plus-reinforcement was the most powerful treatment, only the procedures for that condition will be presented.

Repeated sessions of watching colored slides were given to subjects individually in a testing room. During training sessions (as opposed to testing), subjects were first presented with a verbalizing model. "The experimenter, who served as a model, commenced the session by taking the seat in front of the rear-projection screen and speaking rapidly and continuously in response to each slide as one of the sets was projected on the screen. The subject, whose view of the slides was obstructed by the baffle, meanwhile listened to the experimenter talk" (p. 63). Each subject, during his turn with a second set of slides, was reinforced on a fixed-ratio schedule with pennies for either specific or nonspecific verbal imitation. Prompts such as "What do you see in this picture?" and "Tell me about this one" were given to five of the 20 slides if the subject had not responded after 15 seconds of exposure to a slide. Note that this study, instead of requiring an exact match of the model's behavior, reinforced *any* verbalization.

As is frequently the case with treatment procedures which occur outside of a patient's normal setting, Wilson and Walters found that while verbal behaviors changed in the laboratory in response to slides, ratings of verbal output on the patients' ward showed no change. Thus, while the methods just presented offer some suggestions for treatment, future programs should train behaviors which are needed both in and out of the hospital in order to increase generalization of treatment effects.

Gutride, Goldstein, and Hunter (1973, 1974), in two studies with hospitalized schizophrenic patients, attempted to respond to the questions raised above. They trained patients in skills useful in the hospital and out, and they tried to promote generalization of treatment effects. In the first of the studies (1973), four modeling videotapes were used for training.

> ... the first tape contained enactments indicating how one individual (the model) can interact with another individual who approaches him. The second, how an individual (the model) can initiate interaction with a second person. The third, how an individual (the model) can initiate interaction with a group of people. Finally continuing this progression reflecting increasing complexity of social interaction, the fourth tape depicted how an individual (the model) can resume relationships with relatives, friends and co-workers from outside the hospital. In several respects, in both the development and experimental usage of these modeling displays, we again sought to be responsive to laboratory research findings that have identified characteristics of the

observer, the model, and the modeling display that function to enhance the level of vicarious learning which occurs. This included our portrayal of several heterogeneous models; the introduction and summarization of each tape by a high status narrator (hospital superintendent and clinic director), who sought by his introduction to maximize observer attention and by his summary to re-emphasize the nature of the specific, concrete social interaction behaviors; portrayal of the model's characteristics as similar to that of most participating study patients (age, sex, patient status); and frequent and readily observable reward provided the model contingent upon his social interaction behavior. (p. 410.)

Note in the following excerpts* from the modeling tapes the attention given to the modeling enhancement variables.

Tape 1

Narrator's introduction

Hello, I'm Dr. Turner from Denver State Hospital. You are now going to see some very important movies which will show you how some patients at another hospital were able to get to know and talk to another person who came over to them. I want you to pay close attention to these movies and notice what these patients did in order to get to know the person who came over to them.

The narrator went on to give a reason (to feel better and be happier) for people to know and to talk with others. He stated four important points to be noticed about how the model would respond. He reviewed the points made and the reasons for interacting. And finally, he directed the viewer's attention to the task.

Since we want you to feel better and since we also want you to be happier, we want you to do all these things, just like the patients in the movies. So pay close attention and learn what to do. Thank you.

Scene 1

M (model) is seated by himself, doing nothing.
P (patient): Hello, my name is Tom. What's your name? (extends hand)
M: I'm Steve. (shakes his hand and looks at P)
P: How are you today?
M: Fine thanks, and you?

Conversation continued for a few more interchanges with M being reinforced for his friendly behaviors.

P: ...I'm really happy to meet you. It's always nice to meet new people and to have new friends to talk to too.

Other scenes continued to model both verbal and nonverbal interaction patterns and provide reinforcement to the model for his efforts.

---

*From Gutride, M. E., Goldstein, A. P., and Hunter, G. F. The use of modeling and role playing to increase social interaction among asocial psychiatric patients. *Journal of Consulting and Clinical Psychology*, 1973, **40**, 408–415. Reprinted by permission.

Scene 3

The model is seated alone, reading newspaper.

P: Can I see a section of the newspaper?

M: Sure, which section would you like? (looks at P)

P: The sports page if you've finished it already. Do you read the sports page?

M: Yes I do. I like reading about football and hockey. I've finished that section so here it is. (looks at and leans toward P)

P: Thanks a lot. That's nice of you to share your newspaper. I also like to follow the football and hockey scores.

M: Good ... Maybe then we can talk about our favorite teams after you read the sports news. Who do you think will go to the superbowl this year?

P: I don't know but I think it'll be Dallas again. Say, y'know, I really like talking to you about sports.

After ten scenes, the narrator returned to sum up the films just seen:

You just saw some very important movies which showed you how some patients were able to get to know and talk to another person who came over to them.

The narrator again reviewed the material stated in the introduction. Then:

Because these patients were able to get to know and talk with the person who came over to them they felt much better and they were happier. When we talk with people, we are healthier and we have more fun. We want you to feel better and be happier too, so now we want you to do all the things you saw the patients in the movies do, right here with the other people in your group. Thank you.

As is suggested in the narrator's last statement, the training did not end with the presentation of the models. The patient group then discussed and role-played the scenes they had seen. They received feedback and reinforcement for their own efforts at successful imitation of the roles played by the model.

The second study (1974) focused on training in specific skill deficit areas. For example:*

Narrator's introduction
  Hello, I'm Dr. K ....
  This week we are starting with the absolute basics of social interaction—simple eating behavior ... Watch this tape carefully as it demonstrates eating behaviors that can really affect your sociability.

Scene 1

Narrator: Put your napkin on your lap.

Patient A sits down at dining hall table, takes his napkin off the table, unfolds it, puts it on his lap.

Narrator: Good.

Patient A smiles.

---

*From Gutride, M. E., Goldstein, A. P. and Hunter, G. F. The use of structured learning therapy and transfer training in the treatment of chronic psychiatric inpatients. *Journal of Clinical Psychology*, July 1974, 277–280. Reproduced by permission.

Patient B sits down at dining hall table, takes his napkin off the table, unfolds it, puts it in his lap.

Narrator: Good.

Patient B smiles.

Narrator continues with patient C.

Narrator: Also use your napkin during the meal when you need it.

Patients A and B perform.

Patient C, eating, takes napkin off his lap, wipes his mouth, puts napkin back in his lap.

Narrator: Very good.

Patient C smiles.

Narrator: That was good, that's how to use your napkin.

After other scenes, the narrator summed up the action:

Now that you've seen the actors demonstrate the importance of good eating posture and using your napkin, fork, and knife properly, you will have a chance to do it yourselves, and by seeing yourselves on television learn just how sociable you can look through good eating habits. Sit up straight, use your napkin, hold your knife and fork properly, and I guarantee that you will not only look good, but feel good as well. "Try it, you'll like it."

Results from these two studies are encouraging for the use of the described techniques in training hospitalized schizophrenics. Results were better for simple than for complex skills, and they were better for acute patients than for chronic patients. As in other studies, having patients use these newly practiced skills in ongoing hospital situations and interactions remains a problem. Training of hospital personnel to prompt and reinforce the same behaviors on the ward and in the general hospital environment might be a good supplement to the program described above.

The examples cited above show that procedures which incorporate modeling as a major part of training have some effectiveness in the treatment of psychotic adults. The models are used to elicit behaviors which have at some time been in the patients' repertoires or to teach new behavior. Attention must still be given, however, to maintenance of patient motivation to perform the behaviors outside of the treatment setting.

Modeling in the Training of Helpers

Modeling is an effective technique for behavior modification of persons of all ages (children, adolescents, adults), of many classifications (normal, delinquent, mentally retarded, psychotic), and with many different problems (fears, behavior deficits, behavior excesses). For the readers of this book, the professionals and nonprofessionals whose concerns are with behavior change, we can expect it to be equally effective. Professional training has often used examples of desired behavior (symbolic modeling) and demonstrations of the behavior (behavioral modeling), but the systematic application and evaluation of these techniques is a relatively new development. We turn now to a consideration of some recent applications of modeling to the training of helping personnel.

The training of ministers to be more empathic in their responses to a counselee was the focus of a study by Perry (1970). An empathic model was presented to the ministers on an audiotape. Subjects were told that the counselor they would hear was a "minister who has been doing a great deal of therapeutic counseling in his ministry for the past four years and is highly thought of by his colleagues for the quality of his counseling" (same sex and occupation as subjects, high status, experienced). In the modeled interactions between the minister (model) and client, the client periodically rewarded the minister (as indicated by the italicized statements).

> *Patient*:   Well—I've been drinking quite a few years I guess. I think—I can't figure out the exact time.—It just happens you know, you—you don't really know when you start, when you—start drinking—there's no big change in your life. You know I—I really don't drink that much I—have a few drinks now and then—but not that many.
>
> *Therapist*:   You don't think that drinking's the big problem.
>
> *Patient*:   Probably every guy I know drinks more than I do. My wife thinks I drink a lot though—she's—boy, you talk to her you'd think I was the biggest bum on skid row. *My wife doesn't understand me the way you do.*
>
> *Therapist*:   Sounds like she nags you about drinking as well as money.
>
> *Patient*:   *You do—do understand* . . . (p. 90.)*

And later:

> *Patient*:   . . . People just don't care anymore—they don't seem to care about anything—care about other people. But you seem to care about me. *You remind me of an uncle I had that I liked a lot* . . . (p. 93.)*

And:

> *Patient*:   . . . I'm no superman—I just—do the work I'm supposed to do. Or try to do it any-way. You seem to understand that. I wish everybody understood me the way you do. *I really like you.* But . . . (p. 96.)*

Subjects heard 12 scenes between the minister and his client during which the minister made a total of 44 responses to the client. At the end of each scene, the subject was requested to respond empathically to the client as he would if he were counseling. For example:

> *Patient*:   It seems that way. Before we had the kids we didn't have these problems. Now it—it's just not the same. Now it seems like I'm either ignored or it's nag, nag, nag—all the time.
>
> *Other voice*:   What would you say? (p. 88.)*

Subjects who heard a high empathy model, as in the examples above, gave responses that were significantly higher in empathy than subjects who heard no model or heard a model low in empathy. Unfortunately this study, like much of the previously discussed research, suffered from the lack of carryover or generalization effects. When the minister subjects were asked to conduct an actual interview with an alcoholic client (actor), the results were much weaker.

---

*From Perry, M. Didactic instructions for and modeling of empathy. Unpublished Doctoral dissertation, Syracuse University, 1970. Reprinted by permission.

Apparently, while a good start was made in modeling appropriate counseling behaviors, a much more powerful training procedure is needed. What can one do to make it more powerful? While instructions which explained empathy and its importance in counseling had some effect, it was very weak. Perhaps instructions should be expanded not only to explain empathy but to also give examples of such responses and to point out what makes them empathic. Training might be also enhanced by giving feedback and reinforcement to the trainee for each response that he makes. In the following study, note that procedures have been expanded in this manner in an attempt to obtain lasting effects from a training program.

Goldstein and Goedhart (1973) offered a two-day, 10-hour training course to nurses in a psychiatric hospital. Their training program consisted of the following:

1. A presentation and discussion of the meaning and nature of empathy and its importance for patient change, nurse skill development, and hospital climate.

2. Distribution and discussion of the Carkhuff empathy scale (Carkhuff, 1969) highlighting with concrete examples the five levels represented.

3. Discussion of such supporting topics as (a) means for identifying patient feelings, (b) means for communicating to patients that their feelings are understood, (c) empathy versus sympathy, (d) empathy versus diagnosis or evaluation, (e) empathy versus directiveness or questioning, and so forth.

Following the introductory group discussion, the modeling and role playing phases of the training were initiated:

4. Initial modeling. All 30 situations from the Hospital Training Questionnaire (developed by these authors) were enacted by the two group leaders. One served as patient and the other as nurse (model), the latter offering a level 3, 4, or 5 response on the empathy scale to each patient statement. Examples of such situation enactment include:

(a) *Nurse*:   Here is your medicine, Mr. _____.

Patient: I don't want it. People here are always telling me to do this, do that, do the other thing. I'll take the medicine when *I* want to.

Nurse: So it's not so much the medicine itself, but you feel you're bossed around all the time. You're tired of people giving you orders.

(b) *Patient*:   My husband was in his own world. He didn't care about anything I did or said. He just didn't care about me. There's nothing there anymore.

Nurse: It sounds really kind of sad and lonely, like he turned his back on you and walked away.

During each situation enactment, group members were requested to refer to the empathy scale after each patient statement and silently role play their own response prior to hearing the model's.

5. Initial role playing. Using the same 30 situations, one group leader then read each patient statement aloud and asked group members, first on a volunteer basis and then in turn, to offer a response. Non-empathic responses (levels 1 and 2) by the participants were responded to by the group leader with further modeling or empathic responses (levels 3, 4, and 5) for that situation.

6. Further modeling–role playing. This sequence of empathy modeling by the group leaders and role play responding by the group members was repeated two additional times, thus providing each member the opportunity to respond to several patient statements and receive feedback thereon. Following this procedure, each member engaged in one or more extended role play sequences, in which one group leader was the patient and the member the nurse. These sequences began with one of our standard situations, but led wherever the enactors took it. Again, both the group leaders and other members provided corrective feedback when necessary, in the form of additional high empathy modeling. This same modeling–role playing feedback sequence was

then implemented again, this time in response to new problematic situations volunteered by each group member. Finally, the two group leaders once again modeled and role played across all 30 situations.* (pp. 169–170.)

When the nurses were asked after training to respond to situation items, they did indeed respond with higher empathy statements than before training, and one month later they still gave higher empathy statements to situation test items. As an added bonus in this study, head nurses who were participant members and observers in the original training groups became trainers for a second group. Their nurse trainees also increased in empathy after their training program. Thus, not only were intensive modeling and role playing techniques effective in altering the nurses' verbal behavior, but they were effective in teaching trainers who also were able to produce changes in their trainees. In an extension and replication of the above study, Goldstein added on-the-ward feedback and training for the psychiatric hospital personnel. In addition to replicating the previous findings, results showed that the trainees used their new skills on the ward.

Modeling of quite a different sort was used by Wallace, Davis, Liberman, and Baker (1973) to change staff behavior in a hospital setting. This was not a training program, but rather the intent of the investigators was to encourage the psychiatric nurses and technicians to continue offering a "social interaction" hour in the unit. Often treatment staff are initially excited by a new program such as a social interaction hour, but when the newness wears off, getting them to maintain the program is difficult. In a series of phases of treatments and reversals, this study tried to determine how staff behavior might best be maintained. The first phase involved modeling by the professional staff:

> 1. They (clinical psychologist and research assistant) ... modeled the target behavior by (a) appearing on the Clinical Research Unit at 1:15; (b) announcing to the patients that the social interaction hour was beginning; (c) proceeding to the dining areas; (d) setting up the various games; (e) participating with the patients in these activities. No mention was made to the staff that it was the appropriate time for the social interaction hour nor that they should participate in the activities.

This was an effective procedure. Staff participation averaged approximately 40 percent during this phase. When the models quit, however, the participation of both staff and patients declined. Another phase, a memorandum to the staff, failed to improve the situation (no staff attendence). However, a still later procedure did again increase staff participation in the activities. In phase 6, the nursing supervisor repeated the modeling of phase 1. This time participation jumped to a mean of about 67 percent. Those in charge of treatment programs such as this must be aware that their own behavior is an effective tool in establishing and maintaining staff behaviors.

---

*From Goldstein, A. P. and Goedhart, A. The use of structured learning for empathy enhancement in paraprofessional psychotherapist training, *Journal of Community Psychology*, Vol. 1, No. 2, April 1973, 168–173. Reproduced by permission.

Incidental Modeling in Treatment Settings

While the study described in the previous section demonstrates a planned program of modeling, it also suggests that we must concern ourselves with the modeling effects that treatment personnel, in positions of status and authority have on the behavior of patients when neither staff nor patients are directly aware of such influences. In other words, what is the incidental modeling that occurs in treatment settings? The following sampling of studies suggests that incidental modeling effects might be quite pervasive:

1. If the nurses and aides in the psychiatric unit model the head nurse's behaviors during the social intersection hour (Wallace *et al.*, 1973), we would expect that they would also model them during her other seven hours on duty.
2. Emotionally disturbed children have been shown to model child care workers more than they do therapists and they model both of these more than they do a neutral person (Portnoy, 1973). Child care workers spend many hours with those children and could have a powerful influence on them.
3. Some psychotherapy research suggests that therapists, without intention, may be models for their clients in a variety of areas. Rosenthal's finding (1955) that moral values of improved patients come to be more like the values of their therapists might be explained, in part, by modeling.
4. In a very different domain, Yando and Kagan (1968) found that teacher tempo (reflective or impulsive) had an effect, over a school year, on the behavioral tempo of the children in the classroom.

While other explanations than modeling could be put forward as alternatives in all these studies, the strong possibility of the modeling of status persons by their charges should lead us to examine our behaviors and be aware of the influence we might have on others.

IV. SUMMARY

This chapter describes the use of modeling as a technique which can be used to modify behavior in a wide variety of clinical settings. The term *modeling* refers to the process by which the behavior of one individual or group, the model, acts as a stimulus for the thoughts, attitudes, and/or behaviors of another individual, the observer. Some of the basic concepts which apply to modeling are discussed in Part I of the chapter. An important distinction is drawn between the *acquisition phase* of modeling, in which the model's behaviors are first acquired or learned by the observer, and the *performance phase*, in which the observer subsequently performs the behavior demonstrated by the model. Three effects of modeling on behavior are described:

1. the observational learning effect, in which observers learn new or novel responses;

2. the disinhibitory/inhibitory effect, in which performance of previously learned behaviors is increased (disinhibited) or decreased (inhibited); and
3. the response facilitation effect, in which the performance of an already learned behavior, which is not under an existing restraint or inhibition, is increased.

The basic principles to be considered in the clinical application of modeling methods are described in Part II. Many of these issues are discussed in relation to the treatment of a fear-related behavior, a snake phobia. The highlights of this discussion serve as an important "check-list" of items to be considered in the application of modeling procedures:

Choice of a model. One can use either a *live* ("real-life") *model* or a *symbolic model* (written materials, films, audio-, or videotaped model presentations) to present the desired or target behavior. While live models may increase the involvement and motivation of the observer, symbolic models offer the advantage of increased therapist control over presentation; tapes may be edited, narrated, and used on repeated occasions. Symbolic modeling may be the only practical method to use in many applied situations, and it has often been found to be as effective as live modeling. Model characteristics are also an important consideration: such factors as the model's prestige and personal "warmth" will usually increase the modeling effect. Models who are competent in the performance of the target behavior are the best choice, although if a model is *too* competent relative to the observer, the observer may fail to attend to the presentation ("I give up—I could never be as good as he is!"). The use of a "slider" model who gradually improves upon his performance during the modeling sequence may help overcome this limitation. In many cases, the use of *multiple models* will increase the generalizability and strength of the modeling treatment.

Presentation of the model. The model should be presented so as to maximize the observer's *attention* to and *retention* of the model's behavior. Attention may be aided by choosing an appropriate context free from distraction, and by highlighting the model's behavior through the use of preliminary instructions and narration of the key features of the model's performance. If the model is engaging in behaviors which are likely to make the observer anxious, supplementary instructions in relaxation may enhance attention to the model. The observer is also more likely to attend to the model if he is *uncertain* about how to perform the behavior himself and needs information in order to respond appropriately. Retention of the model's behavior is aided by giving the observer the opportunity to *practice* or *rehearse* the target behavior either during or immediately following the model's performance. A particularly effective modeling procedure is *participant modeling*, in which the model interacts directly with the observer in *guided demonstrations* of the desired behavior.

Incentives to perform the modeled behaviors. The initial learning or acquisition of the modeled behavior by the observer may be insufficient to insure performance of the behavior. Thus, attention must be paid to factors which will increase the probability that the observer will *perform* the behaviors he has learned. Reinforcement to the model (*vicarious reinforcement*) is one such factor; positive reinforcement to the model both informs the observer which particular behavioral components are essential to the "successful" outcome of the behavior and provides the observer with a motivational incentive to perform the same behaviors. Similarly, the use of *direct reinforcement* to the observer for his performance of the modeled behavior will increase the likelihood that he will continue to perform this behavior. Performance by the observer may also be facilitated by using verbal directives or *"prompts"* to perform, and by giving the observer feedback or *"coaching"* following his performance.

Many of the above principles are examined in detail in the presentation of a case study in which *snake-phobic* behavior was successfully treated by a method of participant modeling. Part II also describes the use of modeling methods to modify *verbal behavior*. The use of verbal models to increase self-disclosure or problem-admission in clinical intake or assessment interviews is described. Noted in this section is the use of symbolic models (written materials) to *pre-structure* the expectations of clients and provide an overview of behaviors which will facilitate their treatment program. The use of models in *group therapy* is also discussed in this section. Examples include the use of filmed model presentations and "planted" live models to increase participation and self-disclosure in the group setting.

Part II concludes with a description of the use of modeling to modify social behavior. In addition to inhibition due to anxiety, many problems experienced by a client may be the result of the client's lack of essential skills or "know-how" to successfully perform adequate social coping responses. Examples are provided which demonstrate the use of modeling procedures to teach appropriate social behaviors to alcoholics and juvenile delinquents. These procedures show the combined effects of disinhibition and observational learning which are possible within the same modeling treatment program. Part II also concludes with a brief discussion of how emotional reactions may be fostered or inhibited in certain clinical populations through the use of either positive or aversive classical conditioning.

Part III of the chapter describes the use of modeling methods with a variety of special populations. Several examples are presented in which the teacher, peers, and nonprofessionals act as models teaching new behaviors to socially disturbed and withdrawn children in the classroom. Filmed models are presented as a method of facilitating classroom discussion. Modeling has also proven effective in the treatment of *mentally retarded* persons. Teaching basic *survival skills* such as using a telephone can be presented to retarded individuals by the use of live or video-taped models. In one study reported in this section, the modeling effect was enhanced by associating rewarding characteristics with the model's performance. Success has also been reported in training more intellectually competent retarded youths to serve as models for the less able. The combined use of modeling and reinforcement procedures is illustrated in the treatment of *autistic children*. Basic verbal and motor skills can be acquired by autistic children who observe adult or peer models and then receive rewards for their performance of the modeled behaviors.

Modeling has also been used successfully in the treatment of *psychotic adults*. In contrast to the treatment of autistic children where the aim of treatment is to develop new or novel behaviors, the goal of modeling treatment methods with psychotic patients often is to re-establish previously learned ·but no longer performed responses (e.g., reinstating speech patterns in a mute patient). Other examples presented in this section show how modeling can be introduced as a method of teaching psychotic adults appropriate interpersonal behaviors to use upon their return to the community.

Modeling can also be used effectively to teach counseling and therapeutic skills to the *staff* members in any clinical setting. Examples are presented which show how the modeling of empathy can lead to an improvement in therapist-client interaction. In one study, a combination of methods (instructions, modeling, feedback, reinforcement, and role playing) was used successfully to train nurses to increase their empathic level of responding when working with their patients. Such "package" treatment programs which combine several modification methods are likely to increase the generalization of treatment effects. The chapter concludes with a brief discussion of the *incidental modeling effects* which occur in any treatment situation. Staff members who serve as "role models" for their clients need to be aware of their possible therapeutic impact in this regard. Hopefully, this chapter will serve as a symbolic model to the reader who plans to employ modeling methods in the treatment setting.

REFERENCES

Altman, R., Talkington, L. W., and Cleland, C. C. Relative effectiveness of modeling and verbal instructions on severe retardates' gross motor performance. *Psychological Reports*, 1972, **31**, 695–698.

Baer, D. M., Peterson, R. F., and Sherman, J. A. The development of imitation by reinforcing behavioral similarity to a model. *Journal of the Experimental Analysis of Behavior*, 1967, **10**, 405–416.

Bandura, A. *Principles of behavior modification*. New York: Holt, Rinehart and Winston, 1969.

Bandura, A. (Ed.), *Psychological modeling: Conflicting theories*. Chicago: Aldine-Atherton, 1971. (a)

Bandura, A. Psychotherapy based upon modeling principles. In A. E. Bergin and S. L. Garfield (Eds.), *Handbook of psychotherapy and behavior change*. New York: Wiley, 1971. (b)

Bandura, A. Vicarious and self-reinforcement processes. In R. Glaser (Ed.), *The nature of reinforcement*. Columbus, Ohio: Merrill, 1971. (c)

Bandura, A. and Barab, P. G. Processes governing disinhibitory effects through symbolic modeling. *Journal of Abnormal Psychology*, 1973, **82**, 1–9.

Bandura, A. and Menlove, F. L., Factors determining vicarious extinction of avoidance behavior through symbolic modeling. *Journal of Personality and Social Psychology*, 1968, **8**, 99–108.

Bandura, A. and Rosenthal, T. L., Vicarious classical conditioning as a function of arousal level. *Journal of Personality and Social Psychology*, 1966, **3**, 54–62.

Bandura, A. and Walters, R. H. *Social learning and personality development*. New York: Holt, Rinehart and Winston, 1963.

Bandura, A., Blanchard, E. B., and Ritter, B. Relative efficacy of desensitization and modeling approaches for inducing behavioral, affective, and attitudinal changes. *Journal of Personality and Social Psychology*, 1969, **13**, 173–199.

Bandura, A., Grusec, J. E., and Menlove, F. L. Observational learning as a function of symbolization and incentive set. *Child Development*, 1966, **37**, 499–506.

Bandura, A., Jeffery, R. W., and Wright, C. L. Efficacy of participant modeling as a function of response induction aids. *Journal of Abnormal Psychology*, 1974, **83**, 56–61.

Berger, S. M. Conditioning through vicarious instigation. *Psychological Review*, 1962, **69**, 450–466.

Blanchard, E. B. Relative contributions of modeling, informational influences, and physical contact in extinction of phobic behaviors. *Journal of Abnormal Psychology*, 1970, **76**, 55–61.

Carkhuff, R. F. *Helping and human relations*. New York: Holt, Rinehart and Winston, 1969.

Craig, K. D. and Lowery, H. J. Heart-rate components of conditioned vicarious autonomic responses. *Journal of Personality and Social Psychology*, 1969, **11**, 381–387.

Csapo, M. Peer models reverse the "one bad apple spoils the barrel" theory. *Teaching Exceptional Children*, 1972, **4**, 20–24.

Duke, M. P. and Frankel, A. S. *Inside psychotherapy*. Chicago, Ill.: Markham, 1971.

Flanders, J. P. A review of research on imitative behavior. *Psychological Bulletin*, 1968, **69**, 316–337.

Geer, J. and Turtletaub, G. Fear reduction following observation of the model. *Journal of Personality and Social Psychology*, 1967, **6**, 327–335.

Goldstein, A. P. *Structured learning therapy: Toward a psychotherapy for the poor*. New York: Academic Press, 1973.

Goldstein, A. P. and Goedhart, A. The use of structured learning for empathy enhancement in paraprofessional psychotherapist training. *Journal of Community Psychology*, 1973, **1**, 168–173.

Green, A. H. and Marlatt, G. A. Effects of instructions and modeling upon affective and descriptive verbalization. *Journal of Abnormal Psychology*, 1972, **80**, 189–196.

Gutride, M. E., Goldstein, A. P., and Hunter, G. F. The use of modeling and role playing to increase social interaction among asocial psychiatric patients. *Journal of Consulting and Clinical Psychology*, 1973, **40**, 408–415.

Gutride, M. E., Goldstein, A. P., and Hunter, G. F. The use of structured learning therapy and transfer training in the treatment of chronic psychiatric inpatients. *Journal of Clinical Psychology*, July 1974, 277–280.

Hall, H. L. The effect of personal and impersonal participant models on interpersonal openness in same and mixed sex groups. Unpublished Doctoral dissertation, University of Wisconsin, 1973.

Heller, K. and Marlatt, G. A. Verbal conditioning, behavior therapy and behavior change: Some problems in extrapolation. In C. M. Franks (Ed.), *Behavior therapy: Appraisal and status*. New York: McGraw-Hill, 1969.

Hingtgen, J. N., Coulter, S. K., and Churchill, D. W. Intensive reinforcement of imitative behavior in mute autistic children. *Archives of General Psychiatry*, 1967, **17**, 36–43.

Hosford, R. E. and Sorenson, D. L. Participating in classroom discussions. In J. D. Krumboltz and C. E. Thoresen (Eds.), *Behavioral counseling: Cases and techniques*. New York: Holt, Rinehart and Winston, 1969.

Kanfer, F. H. Vicarious human reinforcement: A glimpse into the black box. In L. Krasner and L. P. Ullmann (Eds.), *Research in behavior modification*. New York: Holt, Rinehart and Winston, 1965.

Kanfer, F. H. and Phillips, J. S. *Learning foundations of behavior therapy*. New York: Wiley, 1970.

Kaplan, S. J. The effects of a model and instructions upon problem admission in two types of psychiatric patients. Unpublished Master's thesis, University of Wisconsin, 1971.

Kazdin, A. E. Covert modeling and the reduction of avoidance behavior. *Journal of Abnormal Psychology*, 1973, **81**, 87–95.

Krumboltz, J. D. and Thoresen, C. E. (Eds.), *Behavioral counseling: Cases and techniques*. New York: Holt, Rinehart and Winston, 1969.

Lovaas, O. I., Freitag, L., Nelson, K., and Whalen, C. The establishment of imitation and its use for the development of complex behavior in schizophrenic children. *Behaviour Research and Therapy*, 1967, **5**, 171–181.

McFall, R. M. and Lillesand, D. B. Behavior rehearsal with modeling and coaching in assertion training. *Journal of Abnormal Psychology*, 1971, **77**, 313–323.

McFall, R. M. and Marston, A. R. An experimental investigation of behavior rehearsal in assertive training. *Journal of Abnormal Psychology*, 1970, **76**, 295–303.

Marlatt, G. A. Comparison of vicarious and direct reinforcement control of verbal behavior in an interview setting. *Journal of Personality and Social Psychology*, 1970, **16**, 268–276.

Marlatt, G. A. Exposure to a model and task ambiguity as determinants of verbal behavior in an interview. *Journal of Consulting and Clinical Psychology*, 1971, **36**, 268–276.

Marlatt, G. A. Task structure and the experimental modification of verbal behavior. *Psychological Bulletin*, 1972, **78**, 335–350.

Marlatt, G. A. A comparison of aversive conditioning procedures in the treatment of alcoholism. Paper presented at the annual meeting of the Western Psychological Association, Anaheim, California, April, 1973.

Marlatt, G. A., Jacobson, E. A., Johnson, D. L., and Morrice, D. J. Effect of exposure to a model receiving evaluative feedback upon subsequent behavior in an interview. *Journal of Consulting and Clinical Psychology*, 1970, **34**, 104–112.

Meichenbaum, D. H. Examination of model characteristics in reducing avoidance behavior. *Journal of Personality and Social Psychology*, 1971, **17**, 298–307.

Miller, N. E. and Dollard, J. *Social learning and imitation*. New Haven: Yale University Press, 1941.

O'Connor, R. D. Relative efficacy of modeling, shaping, and the combined procedures for modification of social withdrawal. *Journal of Abnormal Psychology*, 1972, **79**, 327–334.

Perry, M. A. Didactic instructions for and modeling of empathy. Unpublished Doctoral dissertation, Syracuse University, 1970.

Portnoy, S. M. Power of child care worker and therapist figures and their effectiveness as models for emotionally disturbed children in residential treatment. *Journal of Consulting and Clinical Psychology*, 1973, **40**, 15–19.

Rachman, S. Clinical applications of observational learning, imitation and modeling. *Behavior Therapy*, 1972, **3**, 379–397.

Rimm, D. C. and Medeiros, D. C. The role of muscle relaxation in participant modeling. *Behaviour Research and Therapy*, 1970, **8**, 127–132.

Ritter, B. The group treatment of children's snake phobias using vicarious and contact desensitization procedures. *Behaviour Research and Therapy*, 1968, **6**, 1–6.

Ritter, B. Treatment of acrophobia with contact desensitization. *Behaviour Research and Therapy*, 1969, **7**, 41–45.

Rosenthal, D. Changes in some moral values following psychotherapy. *Journal of Consulting Psychology*, 1955, **19**, 431–436.

Ross, D. M. Effect on learning of psychological attachment to a film model. *American Journal of Mental Deficiency*, 1970, **74**, 701–707.

Ross, D. M., Ross, S. A., and Evans, T. A. The modification of extreme social withdrawal by modeling with guided participation. *Journal of Behavior Therapy and Experimental Psychiatry*, 1971, **2**, 273–279.

Sarason, I. G. Verbal learning, modeling, and juvenile delinquency. *American Psychologist*, 1968, **23**, 254–266.

Sarason, I. G. and Ganzer, V. J. Modeling: An approach to the rehabilitation of juvenile offenders. Final report to the Social and Rehabilitation Service of the Department of Health, Education and Welfare, June, 1971.

Sarason, I. G. and Ganzer, V. J. Modeling and group discussion in the rehabilitation of juvenile delinquents. *Journal of Counseling Psychology*, 1973, **20**, 442–449.

Sarason, I. G. and Sarason, B. R. *Modeling and role-playing in the schools: A manual with special reference to the disadvantaged student*. Los Angeles, Calif.: Human Interaction Research Institute, 1973.

Schwartz, A. N. and Hawkins, H. L. Patient models and affect statements in group therapy. In *Proceedings of the 73rd Annual Convention of the American Psychological Association*, 1965.

Sherman, J. A. Use of reinforcement and imitation to reinstate verbal behavior in mute psychotics. *Journal of Abnormal and Social Psychology*, 1965, **70**, 155–164.

Sobell, M. B. and Sobell, L. C. Individualized behavior therapy for alcoholics. *Behavior Therapy*, 1973, **4**, 49–72.

Stephan, C., Stephano, S., and Talkington, L. W. Use of modeling in survival social training with educable mentally retarded. *Training School Bulletin*, 1973, **70**, 63–68.

Stilwell, W. E. Using behavioral techniques with autistic children. In J. D. Krumboltz and C. E. Thoresen (Eds.), *Behavioral counseling: Cases and techniques*. New York: Holt, Rinehart and Winston, 1969.

Turnure, J. and Zigler, E. Outer-directedness in the problem solving of normal and retarded children. *Journal of Abnormal and Social Psychology*, 1964, **69**, 427–436.

Wallace, C. J., Davis, J. R., Liberman, R. P., and Baker, V. Modeling and staff behavior. *Journal of Consulting and Clinical Psychology*, 1973, **41**, 422–425.

Whalen, C. Effects of a model and instructions on group verbal behaviors. *Journal of Consulting and Clinical Psychology*, 1969, **33**, 509–521.

Whalen, C. K. and Henker, B. A. Creating therapeutic pyramids using mentally retarded patients. *American Journal of Mental Deficiency*, 1969, **74**, 331–337.

Whalen, C. K. and Henker, B. A. Pyramid therapy in a hospital for the retarded: Methods, program evaluation, and long-term effects. *American Journal of Mental Deficiency*, 1971, **75**, 414–434.

Wilson, F. S. and Walters, R. H. Modification of speech output of near-mute schizophrenics through social learning procedures. *Behaviour Research and Therapy*, 1966, **4**, 59–67.

Yando, R. M. and Kagan, J. The effect of teacher tempo on the child. *Child Development*, 1968, **39**, 27–34.

Yando, R. and Zigler, E. Outer-directedness in the problem-solving of institutionalized and non-institutionalized normal and retarded children. *Developmental Psychology*, 1971, **4**, 277–288.

CHAPTER 6

Simulation and Role Playing Methods

JOHN V. FLOWERS*

INTRODUCTION

The major difficulty in writing about simulation and role playing in psychotherapy and related helping endeavors is that almost all therapy can be viewed as a simulation of the client's real life. To simulate means to imitate or to assume the form of something or someone else without assuming the reality. Therapies vary in the way they simulate real life along a number of dimensions. These dimensions include: time reference, covert or private versus overt or public behavior, real versus exaggerated enactments, and the choice of content area. The present chapter will deal primarily with simulations that are realistic, overt, and aimed at extratherapeutic behavior change.

With respect to the time reference dimension, the basic concept of transference in psychodynamic therapy describes a process in which the client simulates earlier important relationships in the present therapeutic situation. This simulation allows the client to work through previously unresolvable conflicts by re-experiencing them in an environment where the therapist is present to help the client with the earlier difficulty. Psychoanalysis is a simulation in which historical conflicts are brought into the present so that they can be dealt with in a real relationship rather than in an imagined or remembered one. Interestingly, the most common form of role playing in analytic therapy, psychodrama, was originated by Moreno (1953) not primarily as a method of resolving conflicts but as a skill development program for delinquent girls living in institutions. Moreno felt that the girls with whom he was working were living in a limited social world that did not prepare them for the problems they would face outside the institution. Despite this origin, psychodrama has been more widely used to resolve presumed intrapsychic difficulties than to help clients with behavioral deficits. Since analytic

*The author wishes to express his gratitude to Dr. Albert R. Marston, Dr. Frederick H. Kanfer, and Dr. Arnold P. Goldstein for their helpful comments during this chapter's preparation.

therapy is in a sense a simulation, the use of psychodrama in psychoanalytic therapy is a role playing simulation within a larger simulation.

Somewhat differently, client centered therapies (Rogers, 1951) attempt to create an atmosphere of "unconditional positive regard" as a simulation of what a person with greater self-esteem would have experienced in a more healthy childhood. Thus, the simulations involved in analytic and client centered-type therapies are not identical. The analytic use of simulation places more emphasis on the historical conflict, while the client centered therapy places more emphasis on creating a present therapeutic atmosphere which fosters personal growth.

This chapter will deal with neither of these types of therapeutic simulation, but will deal with simulation and role playing with a distinct future orientation. In a future oriented simulation, which was Moreno's original conception of psychodrama, the client is systematically taught skills for use in the extratherapeutic or natural environment. Such simulation uses a step by step learning procedure that is clearly aimed at improving what the client does outside the therapy session in his life.

On another dimension, therapists vary as to whether the simulation is overt and deals with observable behavior, or whether it is covert and deals with non-observable behavior such as thoughts or imagination. On the overt side of the dimension the therapist may choose to have the client simulate his life difficulty in terms of observable behavior, such as role playing assertive behavior, or in terms of covert behavior, such as imagining a feared object in desensitization. For example, hypnotherapy focuses on the covert end of this dimension. This chapter will deal with overt simulation.

On the exaggerated-real dimension, one can contrast behaviorally rehearsing how to act in a job interview situation as an example of realistic simulation, with a psychodrama session in which the client deliberately overacts a fawning dependency for purposes of gaining insight, as an example of an exaggerated simulation. This chapter will deal with realistic as opposed to exaggerated forms of simulation.

Finally, there is the content of the simulation. One can use simulation exercises as a behavior change device in business, education, psychotherapy, or, for that matter, in any area where behavior change is appropriate. By and large, this chapter will deal with the use of simulation and role playing in the therapeutic context, although business and educational uses will be briefly inspected. To summarize, we will be dealing with therapeutic, overt, realistic systematic simulation exercises.

Why use simulations at all? In so far as you are not dealing with the client in his actual life situation, you are automatically dealing with a simulation of his life. Even when the behavior change agent is present in the client's real-life situation, the agent's presence has changed the situation into a simulation of what it would be without the agent present. However, the reason for the increase in the use of simulation strategies over the past few years is not merely that they are unavoidable. Simulation exercises possess distinct therapeutic advantages. Simulation exercises are fun and highly engaging; many therapists using role playing and simulation report lower dropout rates when the exercises are being used, as contrasted to when they are not. Systematic simulation also allows the therapist to structure the behavior engaged in by the client, at least in the therapeutic setting. This structuring allows the therapist to deal effectively with two major therapeutic problems, anxiety and behavioral deficits.

Many clients are highly anxious when they are asked to change their behavior. If you ask a timid Casper Milquetoast to send back an incorrectly cooked steak in a restaurant, he will probably tremble at the thought of sending it back. In the real situation, he will most probably eat the steak, and, if he even remembers your therapeutic instruction, he will eat it in the fear that the terrifying waiter has read his mind. By using systematic simulation, the therapist can help the client to engage in behavior that is not as anxiety-provoking with more chance of success. The therapist continues to change the simulation exercises, literally working up a hierarchy of situations of increasing capacity potential as the client is ready for more difficult tasks. Technically, simulation allows the therapist to systematically design successive approximations toward the treatment objectives.

Secondly, many clients simply don't know how to change their behavior. We often presume that the behaviors that most of us execute with ease have been universally taught and learned, and that anyone not performing them must be incapable because of some intrapsychic difficulty. If the behavior is a rare one, such as programming a computer, we are more willing to view someone's inability to carry it out as due to a simple lack of training in the necessary skills. If the behavior is common, such as asking another person for a date, we usually presume that any difficulty in its execution must be intrapsychic. In fact, many people don't know and have never been taught how to start conversations. Such a person may be acutely anxious in a situation where he wishes to meet someone, but we may be premature in our presumption that it is anxiety that prevents him from starting the conversation. He actually may not know what kinds of questions to ask, or what to do with a certain type of response. Simulations have the therapeutic advantage of breaking behaviors down into discrete steps which can be easily learned. Any school teacher knows that for most students you teach division by one number before you teach division by two numbers, i.e., most skills are best learned in small, easily manageable steps. Simulation allows this same model to be applied to the therapy situation. One might describe it as participatory programmed interaction. As will be pointed out later in the chapter, the fact that simulations can lead to generalized learning presents a complex phenomenon, one which may be explained on the basis of a number of important factors, of which role playing is only one.

While this chapter distinguishes role playing and simulation in the title, this distinction is made for convenience and is not meant to point out a general or essential theoretical distinction. As stated before, to simulate means to imitate, or to assume the form of something or someone else without assuming the reality. In this sense, role playing, which means to play a role not normally one's own, is a specific example of simulation and is a form of what Kanfer and Phillips (1970) call replication therapy. When we use role playing therapeutically, we often ask the client to enact a set of behaviors different from his usual behaviors in the world, but which we as therapists presume to be possible and useful for him in the outside world. Even more specifically we ask the client to replicate a situation in his life that has really happened or is likely to happen, and have him practice behaving differently than he would or thinks he would behave. We call it "playing" both as a propaganda device to reduce potential anxiety, and with the understanding that, at least at first, the behaviors are feigned.

Simulation generally is often presented lightly and called a game. The distinction between simulation and role playing is usually that simulation operates under more rules than role playing and represents less of an attempt to replicate the client's actual life situations. Instead of replicating the client's actual problems in the therapy situation, simulation usually attempts to teach the client a more general problem solving repertoire. For this reason, the same simulation game is often used with many different clients. While this distinction between role playing and simulation is useful, it should not be taken too seriously. As we will find, many role playing exercises are used with different clients, and many simulation games are individually tailored to individual situations.

ROLE PLAYING

Assertion Training

Many people, clients and professionals alike, encountering assertion training for the first time, simply do not believe that it is a form of behavior therapy. It is too human, too complex, and resembles traditional therapy too much. This confusion occurs because behavior therapy is often misunderstood as being simplistic instead of as simple as possible, as being mechanistic instead of systematic.

1. Initial Assessment

As in almost all behavior therapy, assertion training begins with an assessment of the client's need for, and the appropriateness of, this form of therapy. Sometimes, the appropriateness of assertion training is evident from the referral or from previous acquaintance with the client. However, it should not be presumed that assertion training is the treatment of choice simply because the client appears passive or reports some difficulties that might be dealt with by assertion training. If the initial interview leads the therapist to believe that assertion training may be appropriate, he may wish to give an assertion test. The most reliable and valid is the one designed by Rathus (1973). However, rather than relying on general self reports or on paper and pencil tests, the therapist should instruct the client to record for a period of several days, all interactions where he wished he had behaved differently and to specify how he wished he had behaved.

2. Stage One, the Therapist as an Assertive Model

Given that the therapist considers assertion training appropriate, the therapy begins, as does a great deal of effective behavior therapy, with an explanation of the therapy and its rationale. The therapist should be assertive and confident about the use of assertion training in this case. The client should be told exactly what is going to happen and why, and should be told that this has worked in the past with similar cases. Two points seem to be critical in this introduction to assertion training. One is that the client be repeatedly told he has the right to ask for what he wants and the right to refuse what he doesn't. If he doesn't exercise these rights and acts like a rug, people (even good people) will walk on him. If he looks like a loser and acts like a loser, people will treat him like a loser and he will lose. Secondly, assertion should be clearly differentiated from aggression. Clients seem to understand this distinction if behavior is placed on a continuum

Passive————Assertive————Aggressive

in which assertion is the right to ask and the right to refuse, without involving the deliberate violation of another person's rights. Aggression, on the other hand, does involve the violation of another's rights and often involves the use of a more imperative request, i.e., a demand. When one person asks, the other person can refuse, but when a demand is made, the other person is presumed not to have the right to refuse. Passive behavior is the stance that one does not have the right to ask or refuse. While the client's behavior will usually not be changed by such "insight," a number of assertion trainers have found that such an introduction facilitates the actual therapy and role playing that follows.

3. Review Life Situation

When possible, the client should be seen in an assertion training group. While there is as yet no empirical comparison of individual and group assertion training, many of the procedures outlined below are more difficult or actually impossible to do in individual sessions. Whether in individual sessions, or in a group, the therapy begins with a thorough assessment of the individual's life situation. This may seem like a repetition of what was done to assess if assertion training is appropriate for the client, but the purpose is quite different, namely, to find out what situations to deal with in the therapy and to continually assess if the therapy is effective. It is critical that after the initial assessment clients not only record assertion problems, but also record situations in which they behaved assertively, that they record every situation in which they wished to behave differently, and that they answer four questions: (1) what happened, (2) with whom, (3) when and (4) where. In this regard, good record keeping is like good journalism. Just as answers to the question why are left to the editorial section of a newspaper and are not found in the story section, the client's answer to the question "why?" should not be encouraged in the client's weekly report. Therapeutically, encouraging the question "why?" and its answers may cause the client to feel defeated because he cannot answer, or it may encourage him to write long essays and make the problem seem unsolvable. On a purely pragmatic level, writing a lot about "why" may often make the client very tired of record keeping. When this happens, the therapist finds himself using the therapy time to design programs to get a change in data keeping behavior rather than in assertive behavior.

One strategy that has been found useful in helping the client keep records and conceptualize assertive behavior is to break assertive behavior into requests and refusals of objects and interactions: (1) refusing of objects refers to refusing to give an object when one does not want to; for instance, refusing to loan one's car to a friend who is a bad driver. The caution here is that in the first blush of assertion training success, some clients begin to sense their power and say no before assessing if the answer really should be no, i.e. before looking at the consequences of the refusal. (2) Requesting an object is the right to ask for things, such as for a glass of water in a restaurant without having to buy something. (3) *Refusing an interaction* is the right to terminate an interaction that is aversive, such as telling to a salesman that you are through with interaction and closing the door or hanging up the phone. (4) *Requesting an interaction* means asking for some form of relationship and is usually the most difficult class of assertive behaviors for a non-assertive person to perform. This breakdown of categories of assertive behavior helps the client and therapist assess the client's strengths and deficits. One final recommendation for reviewing the client's life situation is always to assess both strengths and weaknesses. This is important not only for planning the session content, but also for reinforcing the client's present level of competence and for later reinforcing the client's gains.

4. Role Playing in Structured Situations

After the daily record keeping has been explained and the client(s) have clearly understood the types of situations, the therapy should proceed with role playing of structured situations supplied by the therapist. Since the rehearsal is done in successive order with those situations that are least difficult being practiced first, the early role play situations are supplied by the therapist and are not taken from the client's life situation. The therapist can create these standard situations before the session or can have the group or the individual help create them in the session. For example, a standard practice hierarchy would be

(a) Refusing to lend $10 to an acquaintance when you don't have it.
(b) Refusing to lend $10 to a friend when you don't have it.
(c) Refusing to lend $10 to an acquaintance when you do have it.
(d) Refusing to lend $10 to a friend when you do have it.

It is always wise to check with each client to find if the hierarchy as constructed is in fact in increasing order of difficulty. Sometimes, to make a situation harder, the therapist may have to make the issue smaller—e.g., refusing a request for *less* money; or a request in the future, whereas to make an item easier, the therapist can make the issue bigger, in this case refusing a request for more money.

In a group, such role playing is done in triads, with one client being the asserter and one the recipient. At first, the therapist is the coach and keeps the interaction going by suggesting words and strategies to either party. When coaching suggestions are made, it is important that the client carry them out, or at least carry out his version of them, i.e. actively practice and not merely listen. As the group progresses, the coaching position should be taken by other clients, since it has been demonstrated that the clients who have coached others are better in later assertive performance than clients who have not coached (Flowers and Guerra, 1974). Such standard scenes should be role played until the client is comfortable with his performance. If any scene continues to cause discomfort, an easier scene should be chosen or created. Always try to end a session with a success for the client.

5. The SUDS Scale

An assessment device which has been found useful in such role playing, is SUDS (Wolpe and Lazarus, 1966), or "Subjective Units of Discomfort Scale" that the client is taught to use in both the role playing and in his daily records. This scale is totally subjective with 0 standing for the most comfortable the client can remember ever having been and 100 being the most uncomfortable. By and large, discomfort as used in this scale's description means anxiety, although there seems to be therapeutic value in calling it discomfort instead of anxiety. The client is given a homework assignment of constructing a hierarchy of situations no more than 10 units apart to get a feeling for the use of the scale. In a session, it is helpful to have the client report his present SUDS level and then question him strongly as to whether he is sure he is correct. Usually this mild attack will cause him to feel more discomfort and he will get an immediate feeling for the scale's being similar to a temperature gauge which goes up and down in various situations. After the scale has been learned reasonably well, usually by the end of the second session, the client's SUDS level should be reported on every critical incident in his daily record and after each role playing situation.

6. Role Playing Life Situations

After the client has learned how to keep life situation records, how to play roles, how to use the SUDS scale, and learned how to coach if in group training, the next stage of treatment can proceed with real-life situations from the client's records being chosen for the role playing situations. The situations producing the least discomfort should be used first. Furthermore, the client in a group should be able to choose the recipient who also causes the least discomfort. Again, as the client becomes comfortable in the role, he should move to both more difficult situations and more difficult (for him) recipients. A client who is chosen as a difficult recipient should be reminded that this means that he is either like someone difficult for the client to deal with in the real world, or that he is being perceived as assertive. But being chosen for this role does not mean he is a "bad" person.

Recently, it has been demonstrated (Booream, 1974), that the therapist sometimes terminates the role playing with too few trials, i.e., before the skill has been learned well enough, or before the client is comfortable enough, to perform it in the outside world. It is important that the therapist remember that the role playing is used for practice and not for insight. The therapist, with his own relatively higher levels of assertive skill, will often become bored and may assume that the client is ready to perform the behavior in the world before the client is actually ready.

7. Playing the Role in the World, Mini Exercises

Mini exercises are much like structured "canned" situations except that they are homework assignments to be attempted in the real-life situation of the client. They involve such tasks as:

(a) Going into a drycleaning store and asking for a hanger because one has locked oneself out of one's car.
(b) Going into a drycleaning store and asking for a hanger with no explanation.
(c) Going into a market, buying one item and asking a person with a full basket if you can go ahead in the checkout line.
(d) Sending back food in a restaurant.
(e) Interrupting and hanging up on a telephone salesman within 20 seconds.

The task should be role played in a group, should not be a regular problem in the client's life situation, and should only be assigned with the client's willing acceptance and with the therapist's judgment that the client has a good chance of success. The results of such exercises should be reviewed in the next group or individual session. If the client has not succeeded, the therapist should point out that he was not ready (not that he failed) and either find an easier exercise or role play the assigned one again until both the client and the therapist think it can be accomplished.

8. "Playing" the Assertive Role in Life

When a client is ready to try assertive behavior in a real-life situation that he has reported as difficult, the whole group should review his strategy and his goal. This is because there is evidence that non-assertive people have less clear goals than assertive people. If the goal of an assertive interaction is unclear, the client will fail more often than if the goal is clear. A rule of thumb is that if the goal cannot be stated in one sentence, it is usually two goals.

A second rule is that if the goal puts the power in the recipient's hands (Rehm and Marston, 1968), it is a poor goal. For example, if a client wishes to call another person for a date, he should judge his assertive performance on how well he does this and not on whether the other person accepts or not. Just as the client has the right to request, the other person has the right to refuse. Assertion training uses role playing to teach the client how to request clearly and sometimes repeatedly, with the understanding that people who don't request get very little. The success of the request is not guaranteed, only its chances are improved. In rare cases (cf. Davidson, 1969) the therapist will realize that the client's life situation is such that assertive behavior will usually be punished. In such cases, the therapist should discontinue assertion training and try to change the environment or move the client from that environment. However, the therapist should not jump to the conclusion that he has one of these rare cases simply because the client gets punished for his first assertive attempt.

The group, or the therapist in individual sessions, should also review the consequences of an assertive behavior that the client is going to attempt. For instance, while the client has the right to refuse to do what his employer tells him to do, the consequences of such a refusal may be highly unpleasant to the client. The client's daily records, which are kept throughout the therapy, should be reviewed in terms of the appropriateness of the goal and the consequences of the desired assertive behavior.

9. Special Issues in Group Training

If the client is in an assertion group and has outside exercises, either "mini" or real-life ones, he should report the results of his attempt to the group before role playing starts. The group should not be allowed to attack failure, but should be encouraged to cheer success. A single report of success can carry over through the entire group session. Assertion training groups seem to function best when they consist of from eight to ten members and two therapists. After the group has been going for a while (three weeks), more than one triad can practice at a time, with the therapist acting as a consultant. Groups can be time limited, from six to twelve sessions, or can be open ended with new members replacing those who graduate. Both homogeneous and heterogeneous groups have been conducted with good results. Assertion training has been used with inpatients, outpatients, delinquents, normal therapy clients, and students. The major issue in the use of assertion training is not how a person is labeled, but whether or not he can behave more adaptively when he behaves more assertively. If videotape is available, it should be used. Videotape feedback allows the client to view both the verbal and nonverbal (eye contact, posture, or nervous habits) components of his assertive role playing and improves his performance more quickly than merely having the group tell him about these components. Eisler, Miller, and Hersen (1973) have demonstrated that the most important component in having someone else judge a client as assertive is his display of affect, and this display is more easily taught with videotape than without it.

A simulation that this author has recently used within the role playing situations is to have the clients who are not role playing give tokens to the active participants for the purpose of feedback. Thus, the "silent" clients give a blue token for what they consider a passive response, a red token for what they consider an aggressive response, and a white token for what they consider an assertive response. The token giving simulates verbal feedback, but has the advantage of not interrupting the role playing exercise. While this simulation within the role playing situation is still being investigated, it has already shown two distinct results. First, it keeps the "silent" members more involved by significantly increasing their visual contact with the participants. Secondly, there are a number of clients who enter assertion training with the idea that assertive responses are unreasonable and aggressive. Clients who use the tokens in group, i.e., see their evaluation of a response as compared with that of other "silent" members, more quickly rate their own assertive behavior as reasonable as opposed to unreasonable, and assertive as opposed to aggressive, than do clients not using the tokens.

A modification of this token system using only two colors, one for assertive and one for passive behaviors, has also been employed for having the client rate his own behavior in the role playing situation. Comparing clients who evaluate themselves versus those who are evaluated by the therapist, it has been found that clients who self-evaluate their role playing as assertive are more likely to engage in assertive behavior outside of the therapy session than those who are similarly evaluated by the therapist. While this simulation and a similar one for use in group therapy will be considered again in the section on simulation games, it is included here to demonstrate a technique that has both clinical and research applications for assertion training.

10. Other Issues

While assertion training makes use of role playing, it should be noted that such training involves instruction, modeling and feedback, and reinforcement components as well. In one sense the role playing provides the situation in which the other treatment components can be implemented. For experimental purposes it is necessary to separate and test the components to assess their impact and interaction. However, when helping people change in clinical situations, the counselor will seldom use role playing that does not involve other components such as instructions, modeling, feedback, reinforcement and, perhaps most importantly, self-observation, and self-evaluation.

Other Role Playing

While the most extensive use of role playing has been in the area of assertion training, it should be clear that role playing can be used as a behavior change technique whenever the client can benefit by learning a new way of behaving, especially in social situations. Aside from its use in teaching assertive behavior, role playing has been used to develop appropriate social behavior in delinquents (Sarason, 1968), to teach job interview skills (Prazak, 1969), to help control overt aggressive behavior (Kaufmann and Wagner, 1972) and to change the social behavior of minimally dating males (Melnick, 1973). Each of these uses of role playing bears some resemblance to assertion training, yet each extends either what is being taught in the role playing situation, or how it is being thought.

In Sarason's use of role playing to develop appropriate social behavior in delinquents, complete scripts are preconstructed dealing with how to behave outside the institution where the youths were held. These scenes were first role played by graduate students with the youths watching. The scripts were then role played by the youths in pairs. Some of the youths also got audio or video feedback so that they could review their own performance in the scene. Some groups discussed their performance and some did not. Fifteen scenes, one per session, were used and the youths were encouraged to personalize each scene when they played it. Generally, the scenes fell into four categories: (1) coping with authority figures such as police, school principals, etc., (2) resisting negative peer pressure such as showing off or skipping school, (3) self-control such as planning ahead or handling anger and, (4) making a good impression such as how to join a new group or function in a job interview.

An example of a scene* used by Sarason is one that demonstrates how to avoid a fight. In this scene, two boys are walking home from school and talking. The scene is first played the wrong way and then played correctly. For example:

WRONG WAY

Bill: "What's the matter, George, trying to make it through the easy way?"

George: "What do you mean?"
(a little angry)

Bill: "Trying to convince the teacher you're not as stupid as you look, huh?"

George: "Just what the hell are you getting at?"

Bill: "Now don't start playing innocent, we all saw you brown-nosing the teacher after class."

George: "I don't kiss up to nobody. I was just trying to get something clear."

Bill: "Sure you were. That's the third time this week. Man, have you turned into a fink."

George: "What the hell's bugging you? Sheila turn you down again?"

Bill: "Nothing's bugging me and leave Sheila out of it. I just wanted to tell you you look like a real ass trotting up to the teacher like that. And we don't need any punks like you trying to cut our throats."

George: "Talking about asses, you sure made a fool out of yourself in class today. We haven't had such a good laugh in a long time. You're almost as stupid as your fat sister."

Bill: "Shut up."

George: "That was the dumbest comment I ever heard."

Bill: "Just one more peep out of you, and..."

George: "The teacher says, 'What's an equilateral triangle?' and you said..."

Bill: "You bastard."
(hits him)

RIGHT WAY

Bill: "What's the matter, George, trying to make it through the easy way?"

George: "What do you mean?"

Bill: "Trying to convince the teacher you're not as stupid as you look, huh?"

---

*From Sarason, I. G. Verbal learning, modeling and juvenile delinquency. *American Psychologist*, 1968, **23**, 254–256. Reprinted by permission.

George: "What's bothering you? So far, you aren't getting through."

Bill: "Now don't play innocent. Today was the third time this week you talked to the teacher after class, if that isn't brown-nosing, I don't know what is."

George: "Oh, that, well, you know, I've been having a lot of trouble in geometry. So I went up and asked the teacher a couple questions about last night's assignment."

Bill: "And at the same time, you were trying to get a little pull with him."

George: "You know damn well I don't brown-nose anyone. As it is, I'll be lucky to make a C in that class. Look, if you were having trouble in that class, wouldn't you do the same thing?"

Bill: "Are you nuts? I'd never do anything like that."

George: "Well, it's sure better than flunking the course. An if people don't like it, that's just tough."

Bill: "I still think it looks real funny."

George: "Yeah, but what can you do?"

Bill: "I don't know, but I don't think I'd do that."

George: "Well, maybe you don't mind flunking. I gotta get home. See you."

Bill: "Yeah, see you around."

Sarason's scenes were constructed by having the graduate students meet informally with the youths and find out the youths' perceptions of the problem areas in living that they would have outside the institution. The youths were asked to spontaneously role play their difficulties and these sessions were tape recorded and edited into the scripts for use. The issue of which the therapist should be aware is that the source for such scripts does not have to be the therapist's imagination. It is both easier and probably more relevant to use the client as the source of the content of the role playing situations.

Role playing can be used to teach any behavior in which the client shows deficiency. Of course, to be sure the behavior is in fact taught and can be performed appropriately, outcome in the client's out of therapy behavior must be assessed. In the Sarason example, delinquents were trained in the general class of responses that might be labeled social skills. Some of the situations used closely resemble those used in assertion training; however, Sarason's use of role playing extends the use of role playing from assertive behaviors to other areas of social skills. Again, there is more involved in this treatment than merely role playing. There is modeling, instructions, and for some groups there is feedback and a special kind of feedback that can be labeled self-observation. How much each component contributes to the change effort is still being investigated. For the practicing therapist, the key point is that role playing provides another tool for use in trying to help people change.

Another use of role playing that somewhat resembles assertion training, but is designed to change behavior in only one specific situation is Prazak's use of role playing to teach clients job interview skills. Prazak (1969) points out the rehabilitation services have the same problems that mental health agencies have; namely that many clients return again and again for treatment in what has been called the "revolving door." The rehabilitation service gets the clients jobs which they often promptly lose. Since the clientele has a job turnover rate twice that of the national average, Prazak decided that directly placing the clients in jobs was a losing cause. She decided instead to teach the clients the skills necessary to seek their own jobs.

The skills that this program attempts to teach are:

(a) The ability to explain one's skills.
(b) The ability to answer problem questions.
(c) Appropriate appearance and mannerisms.
(d) The appearance of enthusiasm.
(e) The call back techniques of how to terminate the interview.

In this, as in any role playing situation, the behaviors that the therapist wants to teach have to be clearly defined. The rule is generally that if you don't know what you want the client to be able to do, he generally won't do it. In this use of role playing, Prazak first showed the clients a videotape of a good interview. In any modeling situation such as this, the therapist should be aware that the tape or demonstration should not be too good at the beginning since there is evidence that modeling occurs more readily if the modeled behavior is not too different from what the client can actually perform or at least imagine himself performing. Next, the clients role played mock interviews which were videotaped for feedback. Instead of confronting the clients when they fell short of the model's performance, the therapist praised them for those behaviors that were like the model's performance. The staff also used these tapes of the initial role played situations to assess the clients' strengths and weaknesses in the interview situation. It is critical that both strong and weak points be explored, since there is a widespread and distructive tendency to explore only deficits when dealing with people in need of help.

The first behavior that is necessary in the job interview is to explain one's skills. Each client explores his assets and records them in a notebook so that he can memorize them. Few clients are aware of their skills until the staff help them explore their past history in detail including hobbies, military service, or high school.

The next behavior to be taught is how to deal with problem questions. Most people in rehabilitation have more problems than the average interviewee, e.g., intermittent employment history, jail sentences, hospitalizations, physical problems, etc. Role playing is used to teach them how to handle these issues in the interview. The reason why role playing is critical is that the knowledge is not enough to insure success, the client must practice until he is skilled enough and/or comfortable enough to perform the behaviors in the real situation. Again, the behaviors are specified:

(a) Keep the answer short and end on a positive note.
(b) If the problem is obvious to the employer, bring it up before the interviewer asks.
(c) Never use psychiatric or medical labels and never say you were sent to the hospital, say you went.

The client is also taught whatever grooming and postural skills necessary for presenting himself for and during the interview. Prazak takes Polaroid pictures before and after the training to show the clients how much better they look. During the role playing, the clients are taught to display enthusiasm and are reinforced for its display. The clients are taught to maintain eye contact, to shake hands firmly, and are taught to terminate the interview by asking if they can call back to see if they got the job.

This use of role playing demonstrates that the role playing technique can be adapted to very specific problem areas. The reader should be aware that this particular use of role playing has not yet been accurately assessed in terms of its success. In any use of role playing, but especially in essentially untested ones, it is the therapist's responsibility to assess the outcome and determine if the treatment in fact helps his own clients change.

Another intriguing role playing technique is one labeled "Barb" by Kaufmann and Wagner (1972). With the possible exception of Sarason's use of scripts with delinquents, most role playing techniques deal with "passive" people and are used to train the client in adaptive responses. "Barb," on the other hand, is used with very aggressive people and used to teach them alternatives to aggressive behavior. Cues that elicit aggression can be either verbal (such as "Why didn't you clean your room?") or physical, such as having one's pencil taken out of one's hand forcibly. To stop such situations from escalating into either a verbal or physical confrontation, the client in "barb" training role plays

(a) maintaining eye contact when responding,
(b) maintaining an assertive, but non-aggressive posture,
(c) maintaining a moderate, not loud or soft tone of voice,
(d) responding verbally to avoid problems, but to try to get positive consequences (i.e. assertive verbal responses).

One of the assertive techniques that this author has found to be useful in step *d* is entitled "negative assertion." In it the client, if he is wrong, says generally "I was wrong, but I am not a bad person." If the client, is, in fact, somewhere he shouldn't be, he may be coached to role play the response "You're right, I shouldn't be here and I'll try to not let it happen again." Or "My mistake, I'll do better next time." The reason that techniques like this are given titles like "negative assertion" is that they are easier for the client to call to mind when they are appropriate strategies with which to respond. An appendix of assertion techniques for use in "barb" and in assertion training in general will be found at the end of the chapter.

The "Barb" program was first used with delinquents on an inpatient basis, but has been used by this author on an outpatient basis as well. A barb is any stimulus which has or would, by the client's own admission, lead to a fight. In the first stage, the counselor explains that he is going to deliberately "barb" the client, but that he will clearly warn the client by saying "this is going to be a barb." The counselor then coaches the client in how to respond. In a group inpatient population, the counselor increases the number of people barbing and the severity of the barbs while fading the cue that what is being said or done is a barb. On an outpatient basis, this author has the client keep records of naturally occurring barbs and how he handled them. Besides providing the opportunity to reward the client when he succeeds, these records provide material to be role played in the therapy session. While this specific role playing technique is presently being investigated with children, delinquents and adult offenders, the therapist using it should remember that it is still experimental and should closely monitor the treatment results at all stages of therapy.

Most of the role playing literature mentioned above concerns primarily clinical applications of the technique. Two other uses, while having clear clinical applications, are primarily experimental in nature. Melnick (1973) compared six methods of changing the social behavior of minimally dating males who were uncomfortable about their behavior. Three of the groups (the control, traditional therapy and modeling) had no role playing involvement, while three of the groups, (modeling plus role playing, modeling plus role playing plus self-observation, and modeling plus role playing plus self-observation plus reinforcement) did role play interactions with females. Before and after treatment, these clients were rated in a simulated dating interaction and in a structured test in which the clients responded to 10 videotape simulated situations. Melnick's results demonstrate that neither traditional therapy, nor modeling, nor modeling plus role playing alone caused significant changes. However, when self-observation via videotape feedback was added to the modeling plus role playing, the clients significantly changed their behavior in the test situations. In terms of this chapter, Melnick's findings about the modeling plus role playing group are important. The participant modeling clients were shown a model, did role play how to interact with a female and did get a minimum level of feedback (three suggestions), but did not improve in their after treatment interactions with either a live female, or in their responses to videotaped sequences. This strongly suggests that when the client is attempting to change a complex behavior, such as a social interaction, modeling, role playing and minimum feedback are not enough. In the successful uses of role playing cited above, there has either been much more extensive feedback, such as an entire group helping the client, or there has been videotape feedback for self-observation, or there has been both. While Melnick's study does not address the issue of more feedback, it clearly shows that videotape feedback increases the effects of the treatment.

Thus, role playing, in so far as it is merely the practice of a response, may not be the most effective method of changing behavior. However, while Melnick's study suggests that neither modeling nor participant modeling alone are sufficient for behavior change, this should not be taken to mean that they are not necessary for changing behavior. Freedman (1971, 1972) has demonstrated that modeling plus role playing is more effective than role playing alone. If one thinks of the therapeutic process as one that involves instructions, modeling, role playing, feedback, external reinforcement, self-observation, and self-reinforcement, role playing may simply be a behavior that increases the effects of instructions and modeling, and may be an event which provides an easily instituted opportunity for various types of feedback and reinforcement. Clinically, the therapist should be aware that when he employs role playing, he is employing a technique that is almost surely made less effective without modeling and self-evaluation, and may be made less effective without clear instructions, external feedback and both external and self-reinforcement. Actually, it would be very difficult to use role playing without other components in a clinical setting. However, the key issue for the therapist is not that role playing almost always involves more than merely practicing a behavior simply by virtue of the situation created. He should consciously employ the other components in as effective a way as possible.

SIMULATION GAMES

As pointed out earlier, the distinction between role playing and simulation is actually one of convenience. The simulation exercises that are presented in this chapter differ from the role playing examples in that the simulations are less specific to a single client's life problems and are predesigned to teach a set of skills to a broad range of clients. This section will concentrate on simulation exercises that a therapist or behavior change agent would use to help people change and will deal only briefly with the extensive literature of simulations designed for business and academic uses. Simulation exercises are often called simulation games and while they have been shown to have high motivational value, i.e., people tend to like to play them, the actual research on the effectiveness of simulation games on behavior change is less extensive than the research in role playing. For this reason, many of the simulation games presented below are chosen on the basis of clinical rather than experimental evidence. The counselor should keep this in mind when using simulation games to help people change and should continually monitor the results to determine that the simulation is accomplishing what he has in mind.

Simulation Exercises in Business

Most simulators used in business have the specific aim of teaching the players some aspects of effective management. Simulation games in this area are among the most complex presently in use and often require computers in the running of the game. The Carnegie-Tech Management Game and its most recent revision, The Management Game, (Uretsky, 1973) is a widely used example of such a game. This simulation requires an entire college semester to play and simulates up to 10 years in the history of the detergent industry. The complexity is such that over 300 decisions based on over 2000 pieces of information are made each planning period. In such a game, three companies, all producing the same product, compete over the semester. Each company is run by a team of students who act as the top management. The decisions of these students in areas such as marketing, advertising, and research are fed into the computer and the financial results of the students decisions are based on actuarial data of the results of similar decisions in the past. The most recent revision of the game requires the students to use outside community experts in such areas as law, internal revenue, banking, and accounting. Such management games have been shown to improve student test performance in school, but assessment in the actual business world has generally been impossible to conduct. The problem of testing simulations used in education settings is a complex one. The business school itself is a simulation of the real business world, hence an educational simulation is a simulator within a simulation. The skills taught the student will not be applied for years, and then only within a complex organization that includes many other people not taught by the simulation exercise. Like most education, business schools use simulations on the basis of faith that academic progress relates to extra-academic success.

Simulation Games in Education

While simulation games in business and business schools are usually very complex, those in education are usually less complicated. Most of the academic simulators in education involve the general area called social studies. Games in this area have been designed for all age students from kindergarten to graduate school. Behavior change agents interested in these or in the business games should review the journal titled *"Simulation and Games: an international journal of theory, design and research,"* in which such games are researched, reviewed, and annotated.

Of the many such games, one, *The Life Career Game* (Boocock, 1968), has been used by school counselors to help people change in a more therapeutic sense. This game is designed to show students how to plan the daily activities of a fictitious person to maximize that person's life satisfaction over an eight year period. Scoring is based on probability data from national statistics and does not require the use of a computer. Teams of students take the fictitious person through life with future options based on past decisions. Thus, a team cannot get their person a job requiring a college education without planning a daily high school schedule which will qualify the person for college. If the character is presented in such a way to make college questionable, and if the team makes the decisions to get the fictitious character through college, the character will ultimately lose satisfaction points when his college education gets him a job he will not like. There are decisions to be made in terms of education, employment, marriage, and family, and there are unexpected event cards such as being laid off, being promoted, being drafted, having an unexpected child, etc., which add reality to the game. At various times, the team stops and discusses the life they are planning. In the original study, Boocock found that the game taught career information, especially to females. While this game has not been experimentally demonstrated to be effective in helping students with their own decisions, Varenhorst (1969) cites clinical examples of students helped with their own life by virtue of having played the game. She uses the game as an adjunct to career counseling.

In this author's experience, the major problem with complex games such as this is that counselors and teachers who read of them will seldom order them. Of those who do order them, few will use them. Of the few who use them, most will not use them to completion or followup. Since professionals who help people change are busy people, simpler simulation games that do not require purchase or complicated scoring systems seem more useful, or at least more likely to be used.

The *Honesty Game* (Flowers, 1972) is an example of a simple game that can be applied in a classroom without extensive commitment of time or money. This game is designed to be used with a student or students who cheat extensively in class. The behavior change agent selects the subject areas in which the game is to be used and informs the student that on four days a week, the student will grade his or her own work. The student is told that the purpose of these scores is to tell the student what he does and does not know, i.e., what to study. These scores are entered by the student on a personal chart with a special pen. On one day a week, the teacher gives the student a closely supervised test over the same material and enters the score on the chart with a different colored pen. The student's weekly grade is based on the match of the student's self evaluations and the teacher assessed score. If the student's score on the teacher proctored test is below his weekly average, he loses one grade for every 10 points of difference. Thus, if the student got four 100 scores when he evaluated his daily work and got 80 on the test, he would receive a C. On the other hand, if his self evaluation average was 75 for four days and he received 80 on the closely monitored test, he would receive an A.

Since the game itself offers an opportunity for cheating, the author originally included rules to prevent a student from deliberately lowering his self-evaluation scores so that the proctored tests could not fall below his average self-evaluation. First the teacher was told to assign a minimum below which the weekly work would have to be done again. Thus a student could not evaluate his own work at 40 for his four days and receive a 70 on the monitored test and thereby get an automatic A. Interestingly, this rule has never had to be applied. Apparently a cheating student finds it difficult to lower his self-evaluation, even if it would appear to offer the desired payoff.

This game can be used for one or more students and can be modified to fit almost any classroom schedule, for instance the self-evaluation can be done every other day and the test given every two weeks. In the original use, the game was applied for six weeks with the student's cheating ceasing not only in the subject areas involved in the game, but in all other subject areas as well, even after the game was discontinued. In that case and in subsequent uses of the game, the students' grades in the classroom actually increase after the game is discontinued.

This game demonstrates a principle common to simulation games: If the behavior change agent can clearly define what is to be changed, the design of the simulation game becomes much easier. In this case, the definition of the desired behavior is not that the child be "honest." Such a definition does little to help us change the behavior. The desired behavior is that the child's self-evaluation of his performance when cheating is possible closely match an external evaluation when cheating is not possible. Obviously, if the student changes answers on his work after seeing the correct ones, his self-recorded score will not match the score from a test in which answers are not changed. However, there is another issue which may be even more important. If the child changes answers to get a better score, he is not using the test as a feedback device to tell him what he needs to study, i.e., he has been taught that the purpose of evaluation is absolute scores, not feedback. It seems to this author that this is actually more maladaptive in an educational sense than the case of a child taking credit for a performance which he did not achieve. Simulation games are very useful in behavior change areas such as this in that they can present the player with rules that do more than specify the behaviors and the rewards; simulation games can specifiy the tactics or process the player should use and reward him for a strategy as well as for a specific behavior.

Take for example the common classroom problem that some children ask more questions of the teacher than other children, and that some of these high frequency question asking students ask many questions that are unwarranted. An example of an unwarranted question would be a student asking what page to turn to immediately after the teacher had said to turn to page 21, or a student asking where the paper is when the paper has been in the same place throughout the year and the whole class has been repeatedly told where it is. The behavior change desired is not that these students stop asking questions or to put it more prosaically to "shut up." Such students have legitimate needs for real assistance and for the teacher's attention. The behavior change that is desired is that the students ask warranted questions, but refrain from asking unwarranted ones. While such a discrimination would be difficult to teach *per se*, simulation game rules can be designed to make warranted questions more reinforcing than unwarranted questions, i.e., to teach the student a question asking strategy as well as a question asking behavior. To design such a game (Flowers, 1974) we have only to look at how people in general are shaped to limit their responses to those defined as valuable. When someone shops at a market on a budget, the buying is shaped by need and resources. The budget in a classroom is determined by the fact that the teacher does not have infinite resources, i.e., time to interact continually with each individual student. To make this budget clear to the consumer, in this case the child, he, too, must be put on a budget.

In this simulation, the purpose is to make questions and interactions with the teacher valuable so that they will be wisely used. Each student asking a high frequency of unwarranted questions is given five certificates each morning, each of which is good for one question of the teacher. Each question requires the expenditure of one certificate, and after five have been spent, no more questions will be answered by the teacher. This simulation is presented to the students as a game, and the teacher is told to play it as a game, dramatically holding out her hand for a certificate before answering a question, and dramatically turning away holding her lips together with her fingers when the student is out of certificates. This game has elements of response cost and extinction in its playing. Each response costs a certificate, and after the certificates are spent, the student is ignored. By the end of the game period, usually three to four weeks, the students who previously asked well above 10 questions a day had "saved" at the end of the day and came up to show the teacher their "savings" or to spend them at that time on interpersonal or problem solving situations such as: "I'm getting teased because I have a boy friend, what can I do about it?"

Experimental results from this game clearly demonstrate that the students involved learn to ask warranted questions as they play it. This is not surprising. An unwarranted question from the student gets the teacher's attention; while a warranted question gets both attention and information that the student needs, i.e., it has a double payoff. Teachers who use the game maintain that warranted questions actually get more attention than unwarranted ones, i.e., there may be a triple payoff. Not only do the behavior changes continue after the game has been discontinued, the other students in the classroom also begin to ask more warranted questions, probably because the teacher now is more available to the less assertive students. This last finding brings up a critical point for behavior change agents who use simulation games in a classroom. The classroom is a closed ecology in which a change in any one part will probably cause changes in other non-treated parts. In this game, decreasing the frequency and increasing the percentage of warranted questions by the high frequency question askers also increased the frequency of warranted questions by the previously quiet children. Both changes were desired; however, it would be possible for a simulation to change the treated subjects for the better while changing some other part of the system for the worse. In any ecological system such as a classroom or a family, the results of the simulation should not only be assessed insofar as the target subjects are concerned. The entire system should be measured for change even if only one part is being treated.

With the exception of the *Life Career Game*, the simulation games above are quite simple and easy to implement. An example of a more complicated game that can still be used in a regular classroom to help people change is the *Self-Confidence Game* (Flowers and Marston, 1972; Flowers, 1972). This game is designed to change the self-confident behavior of upper elementary of junior high school students in the classroom. Again, as with all simulation games, the behavior to be changed must be clearly defined. On the basis of a suggestion by Marston (1968), self-confidence in a classroom can be simply defined as a student raising his hand to answer a question posed to a group of students in the classroom. School personnel are well aware that many students get through early school years by being "good, quiet" students. This generally means they don't move their bodies or mouths, much. While such behavior may indeed keep a classroom in control, it is highly questionable if such behavior is adaptive in terms of later educational and vocational performance. In college, there are many students who will not go to a professor for help with a subject, to become involved in research in which they are interested, or to legitimately bargain how to make up incompleted work, etc. In business there are even books and courses that sell confidence as a major element of vocational success.

Unlike the honest game or the questions game, the *Self-Confidence Game* requires that classroom time be spent solely in the performance of the game. The game is played as follows:

Instructions for the Self-Confidence Game

1. Have questions made up by the students on any and all classroom subjects. The questions should be from material to which all students have been exposed. The question, answer and the name of the originating student should be put on similar size cards (three by five inches are good) and filed in a question box. The teacher or good students should exclude inappropriate questions. Generally, the students should be allowed five minutes, twice a week, to make up new questions so that recent material and new questions are in use. This assignment should be voluntary and no student should ever be forced to make up questions or to perform in the game against his will.

2. Randomly compose teams of three students each. This can be done by drawing names from a hat.

3. The game, as explained below, should be played from two to three times a week for 20 to 30 minutes each time. Randomly select which teams will play with the understanding that all teams will play at least three times and no more than four in this phase. If a team member is absent when a team is drawn to play, either replace him with an alternate member or draw another team to play.

4. Besides the six players, three from each team, the following students are involved in running the game:

(a) Moderator
(b) Blackboard scorer
(c) Hand-raising judge
(d) Score keepers (2)
(e) Timer

5. The two teams sit in front of the class and the moderator reads a question from the question box to the two competing teams. The first person on either team who raises his hand gets the first opportunity to answer the question. This is judged by the hand-raising judge whose decision is final. The moderator announces whether the answer is right or wrong. If it is right, the blackboard scorer scores a point for that team. The scorers keep track of who answers each question and whether the answer is right or wrong. If the question is answered incorrectly, the first person on the other team to raise his hand gets the next and final opportunity to answer the question. The timer calls time if 20 seconds elapse between a question and either the first or second attempt to answer it. The timer does not interrupt an answer in progress. If time is called, the next question is read. If a question is answered correctly, the next question is read.

6. At the end of the game, the scorers turn in their score cards to the teacher.

7. The questions in the box should be shuffled prior to each game. In the game, the moderator should not use a question made up by one of the game-playing students.

Phase one of the game simply consists of the players playing at least three times. This is a "baseline" phase and students who answer less than 10 percent of the questions asked are considered low in self-confidence in the game. Research has demonstrated that such students are rated low in general self-confidence by the teacher and by other students prior to the game.

Phase two consists of what has been called forced response and its purpose is similar to that of junior varsity teams in athletics. All students who answered less than 10 percent of the questions posed in phase one are randomly placed on teams with other such students. All students who answered more than 10 percent of the questions in phase one are likewise placed on teams together. In phase two, the low self-confident teams only play the other low self-confident teams and the high self-confident teams only play the other high self-confident teams. Just as junior varsity athletics give the lesser athlete a chance to play without having to compete with the better athlete, this gives the low self-confident child a chance to raise his hand to answer questions without the competition from the quicker students.

Phase three is the same as phase one with the teams being composed totally at random and with students playing against all students. The results of this phase determine if the treatment in phase two is effective in increasing the child's hand raising in the regular competition of the classroom.

Results from the extensive use of this simulator demonstrate the motivational properties of such games. In over 5000 team trials, no student has ever willingly missed a trial. However, the behavior change agent should not confuse the motivational properties of simulation games, which have been cited often, with the more important result of behavior change. A simulator could be highly motivating and not change anything. About half the students in an elementary school classroom will answer less than 10 percent of the questions in phase one with over 80 percent of these students answering less than five percent. The distribution tends to be bimodal since about 70 percent of the high self-confident students will answer more than 20 percent of the questions posed in phase one. After the treatment phase, the previously low self-confident students will answer two to three times the number of questions they answered in phase one and will answer significantly more of those correctly. In terms of generalization, these same students will answer significantly more questions in the open class situation where the teacher asks a question of the whole class than before treatment. Beyond this question-answer response, these previously low self-confident students will demonstrate a significant increase in their grades, will volunteer more often for public speaking assignments in the class and will volunteer more often to be class officers.

Again, the behavior change agent should be aware that he is dealing with an entire ecology in the classroom, and should be aware that this ecology includes the teacher. If the teacher attempts to create a quiet nonquestioning student population, the game may be inappropriate for the classroom. Twice in this author's experience, the game has been instituted in classrooms where the teacher did not like the results and wished to discontinue the game. In both cases, the phase two treatment was already well in progress and the students strongly questioned why the game should be discontinued, and in both cases, the students, especially the ones low in self-confidence, were successful in continuing the game. While this may demonstrate that the results of this simulation game generalize to other classroom interactions, it should be remembered that this change in the students' behavior made the rest of the year difficult for the teachers involved. Both teachers had been informed of the purpose of the game and both had said they approved of increased self-confidence in the nonconfident children; however, debriefing clearly showed that neither teacher understood that self-confidence needed to be more than an abstract concept. It is not enough that the behavior change agent explain the simulation to be used in general terms. The changes that the simulation attempts to accomplish should be explained in terms of likely behavior changes to the involved parties before the simulation is used. So far, about 20 percent of the teachers who have used this simulation don't like its results, about 20 percent like it but discontinue it after the experimenter is gone, and about 60 percent continue it on their own.

Thus, there are really two issues involved in the use of simulation games in education. One is whether or not the simulation change behavior in the desired manner? The second is whether the simulation is used again. Many simulation games instituted by outsiders fail; not because they don't achieve the behavior change, but because they are no longer used when the outsider's involvement ends. The more the outside behavior change agent can involve the indigenous professional as a behavior change agent in the simulation, in its application, assessment, and revision, the greater the chance that the indigenous professional will continue as the behavior change agent after the outsider is gone. If the simulation games are presented as research, there is a decreased probability that they will be used again. Sadly, many indigenous professionals are used to research being done in their environment and published without it ever being explained to them. Often they are not actively involved except to supply subject populations, and they have little or no understanding how the research might be useful for them. Since this is a common experience, if the change agent presents himself as an outsider bouncing in and collecting data for a Ph.D. or his personal use, and bouncing out, the simulation game will meet the same fate that other relevant research now meets.

Those who wish to help people change can use existing simulators; however, even more significant is the fact that behavior change agents can design their own simulations for their specific needs. To construct a game, the behavior change agent must clearly specify the change and make game rules that encourage the behavior in question. Often the behavior change agent can look to the natural environment of athletics, business, or life in general, to see how natural rules shape behavior and construct the game accordingly. Results from trying a game will help the designer improve that game and others. For instance, results from the self-confidence game indicate that low self-confident students who only watched high self-confident students play together in the treatment phase do not model the question-asking behavior. However, low self-confident students who watched other low self-confident students being forced to respond more during the treatment phase did model the question-asking behavior. This result recalls a point made earlier, namely, that the model should not be too different from the modeler if the modeler's behavior is to be changed. While such a result is not unexpected, it suggests a way to improve the game effectiveness, i.e., to have low self-confident students run the game when other low self-confident students are playing it in the treatment phase. Thus, the issue of assessment bears not only on the utility of the simulator, but on its continued improvement as well. As in the acquisition of any skill, once the behavior change agent has designed and tried one simulation game, he will find that the next one is easier to construct and usually better. Since the hardest step is the first one, you may wish to try successive approximation and use an existing simulation game, then revise it to make it better for your needs. Then design one for yourself.

Simulation in Psychotherapy

While role playing has been investigated and used extensively in psychotherapy, other forms of simulation have been used less frequently. One reason for this involves the individual nature of psychotherapy. While role playing can be tailored to an individual's unique problem, simulation games tend to be more general and are used when the same behavior change is desired from a group of people. For this reason simulation games tend to be used more frequently in group therapy and by therapists who deal with a group of persons who have similar problems.

One form of well known simulation that has been extensively employed with groups other than traditional psychotherapy or training groups is the ward wide token economy (see Chapter 7). While many readers may not initially perceive a token economy as a simulation game, the work of Winkler (1971) demonstrates that token economy programs function in the same manner as national economies, perhaps the most extensive simulation game known. The token economy program attempts to roughly simulate the more subtle (often meaning more delayed) payoff system that operates for prosocial behavior in the outside world. In the token economy program as in many simulation games, what we essentially have is an attempt to adjust the psychoeconomy of the individual, i.e., what behaviors are payed off or what behaviors the individual has in his repertoire to use to get payoff. The most successful simulation games are probably those which simulate both the behavior and the payoff expected in the outside world.

However, most psychotherapeutic simulation games foster the expected behavior and merely hope for the payoff, both in and out of the group.

An example of the use of such a simulation for a group of people who are presumed to have similar problems is the fight training exercises of Bach and Bernhard (1971). In this form of therapy the clients are trained to fight with each other, first verbally and then physically with a foam rubber bat called a bataca. Some of the simulation exercises are more like role playing than simulation games in that the participants, especially if they are couples, fight about real life problems. Other exercises, such as trying to break into a circle of people whose arms are interlocked to prevent entry, is more like a simulation game in that the rules are specified for all the participants.

Such simulation exercises as used by Bach or by the Gestalt Therapists (Perls,

Hafferline, and Goodman, 1951) are not as systematically structured as the simulation games described above. They require less time than most simulation games and are usually designed to make the participant aware of an emotional state when attempting a certain task. This is not to say that Gestalt and fight training exercises do not produce behavior change. We simply do not know to what extent such simulations help people change. Like other simulation games, those described above are highly motivating for a number of clients. The counselor using such exercises should not confuse the motivational properties and the clients' obvious involvement in the exercises with behavior change. Like any simulation game, these exercises should be assessed in terms of their outcome, i.e., does the client function better not only in the therapeutic environment but more importantly in the extratherapeutic environment as well.

A handbook of such exercises is available (Pfeiffer and Jones, 1970). While most of the games in this four volume set are more applicable to educational settings such as management or teacher training, a number of the games are directly applicable to therapy groups, especially during the warm up phase; and others could be easily adapted to therapeutic use to have clients actively engage in new behavior.

The handbook lists over 100 games ranging from very simple to highly complex games with scoring sheets. Included are verbal techniques such as "active listening" wherein a group participant makes a declaratory statement and the responder acknowledges the message by saying "you feel (somehow) about (something)." The sender simply says yes or no and the responder then makes a declaratory statement to which the first sender responds. This is continued until the pair agree that they understand each other. The handbook also includes nonverbal techniques such as having a group member express his feelings toward another group member in pantomime without use of words. While still untested, such exercises may prove useful and testable in terms of helping people change.

A more complete simulation game that includes many of these Gestalt exercises and also structures verbal communication is a game by the Bell and Howell Corporation titled *Intimacy* (1969). Actually this Bell and Howell game, as well as others by the same company, are not specifically designed to be used as part of therapy, but are simulations of therapy itself. In this particular game married couples participate in structured interactions controlled by tape recorded and written instructions. These include instructions that ask the couples to describe themselves and their partner in terms of self-disclosure and standard roles in the relationship. The parties are then guided through practice in self-disclosure and active listening. The program also has the couples practice changing "you" statements into "I" statements, practice unusual roles with each other, and practice use of the body to send nonverbal messages. In each session a separate tape and set of written instructions is offered to the couple for listening and practice. This and other games by the same corporation, such as Group Therapy, Fighting, Child-Parent Relationships, and Sexual Inadequacy, are essentially simulations of certain traditional therapy programs in those problem areas. Obviously, such simulation games can be used by counselors as simulations within ongoing therapy programs. However, a counselor who chooses to use such simulators to help people change should realize that these games, like most in present use, are essentially untested in terms of the actual benefit to the client.

One reason why the simulation games in use in therapy have been less extensively researched than some other therapy interventions, is that the behavior to be changed is often not defined clearly. When the behavior to be changed is not clearly specified, it is difficult to know whether the simulation has worked or not. For example if a client tries to break into a circle of people with arms locked, the counselor using this simulation exercise usually does not specify what change he wants in the client's behavior after the exercise. When the client changes are specified, they are usually changes that the therapist defines in terms of the therapy session itself and not in terms of desired changes in the client's daily living.

However, there is nothing in the nature of simulation games that prevents clear definitions of the behavior to be changed. Of course, clear specification of the behavior to be changed still does not guarantee that the simulation game actually helps actualize that change, but at least a clearly defined change is a therapeutic goal that can be assessed.

One simulation game that this author has found useful in marital and family therapy is a communication game. Many couples or families coming into therapy demonstrate a communication pattern that reveals that they disagree with each other even before the issue under discussion is made clear. Often one or more parties are phrasing their response before the other person has stopped talking; hence they do not listen to the last part of the other person's message. In such cases the communication of one or more of the parties often becomes faster, i.e., more words per minute are spoken and disagreement increases. The communication game is structured to discourage early disagreements, to decrease the number of words per minute in the debate, and to create longer pauses between the time one person finishes speaking and the start of the next communication. The couple, or a parent and older child set up the game board as shown in Fig. 6.1.

The discussion card is a 3×5 card on which the issue to be discussed is written. The pointer is rotated to the first speaker who says what he or she wishes. The therapist hands him a penalty token if he says more than two or three sentences and explains that long messages are hard to respond to because they contain too much information. The therapist assures the client that he will get another chance to talk. When the first speaker has finished the message, he placed a chip on the board assessing whether his own communication is absolutely clear, fairly clear, or somewhat unclear, and he rotates the pointer to the other party. Before starting to speak, the second player indicates with a chip whether she assesses the message to be absolutely clear, fairly clear, or somewhat unclear and indicates whether he agrees, is uncertain, or disagrees. The therapist gives a penalty token if there is an agreement or disagreement with any message that is not rated clear by both the sender and receiver. The therapist also coaches the clients when to place a chip in the six penalty squares. The I square indicates that a speaker has been interrupted without turning the pointer. If true, the therapist

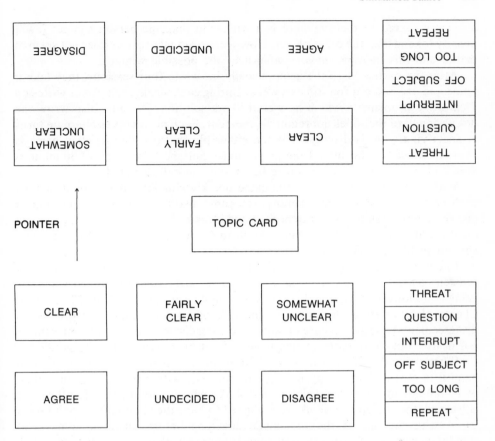

Fig. 6.1. Communication game board.

gives the interrupter a penalty chip. The *T* square means the listener perceived an implied or open threat. When this square is used, the pointer is turned back to the speaker without reply. The therapist asks if the speaker meant a threat. If he did, he gets a penalty chip, if he did not, he does not get a chip, but he is asked to try to communicate his message so that the other party will not perceive a threat. The *Q* square means the listener perceived a rhetorical question, i.e., a question that did not ask for information. The rules for the use of this square are the same as for the *T* square. The *S* square means the listener thinks the speaker has strayed from the subject. The rules for this square are the same as for the *T* square except that any speaker can ask for a subject change and if the other party agrees, the topic card is re-written. The *R* square is used by the listener when he thinks his last message was misunderstood. A chip in this square asks for a repeat of the last message sent by the person putting the chip in the square. Penalty chips are not given with this square. The *L* square is used when the listener perceives a message that is too long or one that has two parts, one of which he may agree with and one of which he may disagree with. If the therapist has sensed this he should have already given a penalty token. In theory, there is a winner in that one person can get fewer penalty tokens than the other player. However, in actual use, this does not seem to matter and this therapist never emphasizes the possible winning.

After the parties learn the game, usually in two to four sessions, they take it home and use it about four times a week. During each week, each player writes on a card one problem to which he would like a solution. He must also write one discussion card that does not require agreement. Each player takes alternate turns at specifying what is discussed. When either player says "finish," that game is over. In week two (at home) the player must call one "time out" of 30 minutes then and return to the game before he or she can call "finish."

Within the therapy session, the game quickly equalizes the amount of time each party talks. Within the therapy, the game also quickly stops agreement or disagreement when the message is not rated clear by both parties. The agreement on the clarity ratings usually starts at 40 to 60 percent and rises to 90 percent agreement by session three.

Client data recorded at home indicate that the game increases the amount of time the parties talk to each other, and equalizes the talk time (even when the game is no longer played) and reduces the number of unresolved disagreements. Clients also report a slowdown in the rate of communication, (especially in disagreements) and an increase of laughter during disagreements when the game is not in use; but these latter results have not yet been experimentally verified.

When using this game with older children and parents, the author has found it helpful to teach the game by having children play with parents other than their own; and having the parents play with children who are not theirs. After the game is learned, the therapy sessions are realigned to have the children and their family try it with the aid of the therapist's coaching before taking it home. This simulation game obviously attempts to institute many changes in behavior, not all of which have been demonstrated in experiments. The counselor using the game in cases where outcomes not yet tested are required or expected should carefully assess the results of the use of this simulation game. One advantage of simulations such as this is that they can be used after counseling is terminated. The author has been told by previous clients that after not using the game for up to four months, they would get it our during particularly stressful problem situations and use it to resolve the problem.

Group Therapy as a Simulation Game

For many therapists, group therapy is a simulation of interactions that the client should attempt to carry out in the extratherapeutic environment. While group therapy obviously can focus on the content of the clients' problems, it can also be used as a laboratory in which clients are encouraged to experiment with new ways of interacting. From the point of view of this chapter, the difficulty with such a simulation is that the specific behavior change being taught is usually only vaguely defined.

In an attempt to specify more clearly the communication process that a therapy group might help the client to change, this author and others (Flowers, Booraem, Brown, and Harris, 1974; Flowers and Booraem, 1975) have devised a simulation game used within group therapy that aims to specify clearly and help change communication behavior. Much like the token simulation described in the section on assertion training, the clients or therapists hand out a blue token with positive verbal evaluation and a red token with negative verbal evaluation for any behavior occurring in the group session. This practice differs from the use of tokens described in the assertion training section in that in assertion training, the tokens can be used without interrupting the group process. In the present use of tokens, the token must accompany a verbal evaluation. Clinically, this simulation seems to allow the quick identification of verbal statements with discrepant affect and content, such as handing a blue (positive) token and saying, "Damn it, you're right" with negative nonverbal cues. The ease of identifying evaluations to which response is difficult, (i.e., the receiver perceives the evaluation as both positive and negative) is probably increased because of the added source of feedback (i.e., the color of the token given). Experimentally, when this simulation game was used in a therapy group, there was a significant increase in the frequency of both positive and negative verbal evaluations and a significant increase in the proportion of patient to patient (as opposed to therapist to patient or patient to therapist) interactions. Furthermore, the clients in such a token group engaged in significantly more desirable behaviors outside of therapy such as getting a job, engaging in social interactions, and going back to school, than similar clients from a traditional therapy control group.

In a second study (Flowers, Booraem, and Seacat, 1975) the same simulation was used to help train group therapists. In this study, it was first demonstrated that the count of tokens given and received during the therapy session accurately reflected the number of positive and negative statements rated from an audio tape. Thus, a count of the tokens used in a therapy group gives the trainer an objective measure of the behaviors in which each participant engaged. Each participant can therefore be classified as high, medium, or low in terms of the frequency of evaluations in which he was involved. Each participant could be classified along the dimension of giving versus getting evaluation. In terms of the evaluations that each participant got or gave, he could be classified along the positive-negative dimension. By asking each trainee to rate the behavior of every other participant prior to counting the tokens, their subjective "sensitivity" as to who did what to whom could be matched to an objective count. Experimentally, it has been demonstrated that this procedure increased the trainee's sensitivity, even in later groups that did not use tokens. It has also been shown that trainees who were independently rated higher in terms of therapeutic ability, changed their behavior more from session to session than trainees who were rated lower.

This last finding suggests an intriguing use of the token data, namely to see if a client can change his evaluation behavior in different therapy sessions and in different situations. Such a change of evaluation behavior might be considered one sign of behavioral flexibility. Pilot data by this author indicates that a number of clients have something like a standard role, or set of evaluation behaviors, session after session regardless of what happens during the session. Thus, a client who is high in evaluation interactions, who tends to give more than he receives, and tends to give a high proportion of negative evaluations in a session, may continue that behavior in the group session after session. One obvious question is whether or not such an in group behavior reflects the client's behavior out of group, and whether change in this in group behavior would produce similar change out of group. While this is admittedly a complex question, the token simulation can help to provide data for answering this question.

The token simulation can be used in still other ways. The behavior specified depends on the rules used in the simulation. The tokens can be used, as they are in assertion training, to give feedback without verbal interaction, thereby not interrupting the on-going group process. This author has found it very useful to employ tokens as a first step in group with severely withdrawn clients who seldom make verbal judgments. At first, the client is allowed to simulate evaluation with tokens alone. Later, the client is prompted to speak after giving a token. Finally, the client is encouraged to speak while giving a token. While it is not yet known if such training increases the client's out of group evaluation behaviors, this author has evidence that the training increases the frequency and duration of the client's social interactions outside of the group.

A final way in which the token simulation games have been used in group therapy is still totally experimental, but is included here as a technique that the counselor may wish to test for himself. The rules can be changed so that the client has to self-administer evaluations in the group session rather than to receive them from others. The frequency of such self-administered evaluations can be changed by having alternate sessions where tokens can be administered when any other group member thinks the client should have self-administered an evaluation but did not. Preliminary data indicates that an increase in positive self-administered tokens relates to increases in daily mood ratings and to increases in the reinforcement ratings of pleasant events in which the client engages out of group. However, it should be remembered that such training can potentially also increase the frequency of negative self-administered token game, the counselor should proceed with caution and with continual assessment of exactly what is being changed, and is this change helping the client. The possibilities are intriguing; however, the possibilities are only just that until the counselor finds that such simulations work for him, that is, they are helpful for his clients.

Future Trends in Simulation

The counselor who is interested in the use of simulation and role playing should be aware that there are two other complete bodies of literature which bear upon the issues discussed in this chapter. There is a large literature in the use of games, such as *Prisoner's Dilemma*, as assessment devices (see Harris, 1971 for a review). *Prisoner's Dilemma* generally involves a game structured after the anecdote in which two collaborators in crime are questioned separately by the police. The police explain to each prisoner (who must choose in isolation from his partner) that if neither confesses they will both receive a one year sentence for a minor crime in which they were both caught. If both confess, they will receive the standard sentence of five years each for the major crime of which they both are suspected. If one of them turns "state's evidence" while the other holds out, the person who confesses will get off with a reprimand from the judge while the holdout will get the maximum sentence of 20 years. In this type game confessing is called noncooperative behavior while holding out is called cooperative. For the individual, noncooperative behavior is the best bet since if he confesses when the partner does not he gets off with a reprimand instead of a year prison sentence, while if he confesses and the partner also does he gets a 5 versus a 20 year sentence. However, for the team, cooperative behavior is best since each only gets a one year sentence if they both hold to their innocence. This game and others of similar design, have generally been used to look at differing rates of cooperative and noncooperative behavior with respect to differing populations and situations, such as male versus female participants and normals versus hospitalized patients. However, the game could also be used to teach people how to respond to differing situations of gain and loss and differing partners. Such games can be used by the counselor to provide simulations that may have some effectiveness in helping produce behavior change.

Another related literature area is that of microteaching (see McAleese and Unwin, 1973 for an annotated bibliography) in which simulation games and role playing is used to teach teachers and counselors.

The process of microteaching usually involves an abbreviated (5 to 10 minute) teaching or counseling session. This microsession is often preceded by a videotape presentation of a desired behavior or set of behaviors, and is followed by immediate feedback, usually using videotape, concerning the trainee's performance. The behavior change desired depends on the trainer. Wagner (1973), for example, has used microteaching to increase the percentage of student as opposed to teacher talk time in lessons given by student teachers. In the area of counseling, Ivey (1971) has used the microteaching technique to increase counseling students' rates of attending, reflecting the client's feeling, and summarizing the client's feelings. This miniaturized practice and feedback prior to the trainee's actual exposure to a live classroom or counseling session, provides a training method that reduces risk, for clients or students, and potential anxiety for the trainee. Again, this literature, while not precisely relevant for the present chapter, can provide the counselor with valuable material.

Simulation games and their applications in therapy, in research, and in training are exciting, too exciting. Up to now, this excitement has led many behavior change agents to use simulations in a wholesale manner without finding out what they do or for what problems they are best suited. Like any therapy intervention, simulations are only a tool, one of many. The question the behavior change agent should ask is not which tool is best, but which tool is best for which job. In so far as simulations help people change their behavior so that their lives are more satisfying, these simulations have a future in therapy. In so far as simulations are merely novel, exciting ways to spend time, they will be relegated to the class of other games and become recreation; whether called therapy or not.

Table 6.1. Summary of Simulation Games and Role Playing Exercises.

Type of Simulation	Type of Problem	Technique Reference	Research Reference
Psychodrama	Conflict Resolution	Moreno (1953)	Boies (1972)
Client Centered Active Listening	Low Self-Esteem	Pfeiffer and Jones (1970)	Truax and Mitchell (1971)
Assertion Training	Passive or Aggressive Behavior	Alberti and Emmons (1970)	see below
(a) Behavior Rehearsal		Casey (1973)	Lazarus (1966)
(b) Coaching			McFall and Marston (1970)
(c) Feedback		McFall and Lillesand (1971)	Flowers and Guerra (1974)
(d) Modeling		Rathus (1972)	Melnick (1973)
Socialization Training	Low Social Skill Development	Freedman (1972)	same
Job Interview Training	Unemployment	Sarason (1969)	Sarason (1968)
Barb	Low Impulse Control	Prazak (1969)	none
Management Game	Training Business Administration	Kaufmann and Wagner (1972)	none
Life Career Game	High School Students Life Decisions	Uretsky (1973)	same
Honesty Game	School Students Cheating	Varenhorst (1969)	Boocock (1968)
Reducing Unwarranted Questions	School Children Gaining Maladaptive Teacher Attention	Flowers (1972)	same
Self-Confidence Game	Low Student Self-Confidence	Flowers (in press)	same
Fight Training	Fear of Verbal Fighting	Flowers and Marston (1972)	same
Group Warmup	Starting Group Process in Therapy or Training Groups	Bach and Bernhard (1971)	none
Marriage Communication Game	Marital Discord and Poor Partner Communication	Pfeiffer and Jones (1970)	none
Group Therapy Token Game	Unclear or Low Verbal Reinforcement and Punishment Levels, Low Self-Reinforcement Level	This chapter 186 to 188 This chapter 186 to 188	none Flowers, Booraem, Brown, and Harris (1974); Flowers, Booraem, and Seacat (1975)
Microteaching	Training Teaching or Counseling Skills	McAleese and Unwin (1973)	same
Personality Games	Decision Making	Harris (1971)	same

APPENDIX—ASSERTION TECHNIQUES*

The reader should be aware that these techniques involve standard types of interaction that the client should only use in appropriate situations. The interactions are not novel, but require practice to be used in stressful situations. The therapeutic issue in the acquisition of these skills is not insight, it is practice: however, considerable discrimination is required in learning when to use them.

Broken Record. The Broken Record technique involves having the client ignore any extraneous issues brought up by the other person and return to his original point. The standard phrase taught is "but the point is . . .."

Disarming Anger. The Disarming Anger Technique involves having the client ignore the content of the angry message and focus his attention and conversation on the fact that the other person is angry. The client must openly promise to take up the content as soon as the other person calms down but must politely refuse to address the content until the other person has cooled off. The client must attempt to maintain eye contact and must use a moderate, not loud or soft tone of voice.

Fog. The Fog technique is only used when the client is being repeatedly nagged. The fog involves agreeing with any charges made and conditionally agreeing with any requests for action, i.e. "I probably should . . .." This technique often causes the nagger to ask, "What are you doing?," at which time the asserter must tell the nagger that he is using a technique titled the fog and explain it to the nagger. He must then say he is willing to respond differently if the nagger is willing to try another mode of response.

Content-Process-Shift. The Content-Process-Shift involves shifting the focus of the conversation from the content to some process observed in the speaker such as an emotion they are "displaying" or something like the speed of their speech. Disarming anger is a specific example of process-content shift but also involves a clear promise to shift back to the content after the anger has subsided.

Negative Assertion. Negative Assertion is only used when the client has in fact made a mistake. Negative assertion involves a clear admission of the mistake but also clearly separates the fact that an error has been made from any implication that the client is a bad person or incompetent, etc. It can involve direct confrontation such as, "Are you saying because I forgot to deliver the one paper, which I did forget, that I am not a good paperboy?," or can involve, "I did do it, damn, I'm usually better than that."

Shelter. This assertion technique is used primarily with severely disturbed clients. It involves having the client respond with only yes, no, or straight facts (such as his name) in stressful situations. The client counts to five slowly, and if not asked another question he leaves the interaction.

---

*The author is indebted to Dr. Julio Guerra for the labels for many of the assertion techniques.

Negative Inquiry. This technique is used to terminate an aversive relationship. The client responds to any criticism by asking the other person what else the client has done that displeases the other. He assures the other that he wishes to know so that he can do better in the future and when the person runs out of initial criticisms the asserter summarizes the list and says, "Then of all the things I do, this, this and this displease you." The client asks again if that is all. If it is not, the client resummarizes, and when the other person has finally run out of criticisms, the client thanks him and tells him to be sure to tell the client of anything else he can think of in the future.

Clipping. Clipping is a technique that is used when a criticism is delivered that the asserter thinks is true but not really a criticism. For instance, having the other person say, "This report looks like it was written by four different people," when in fact it was. The asserter says yes or no as appropriate and then remains silent.

Free Information. Free information is a technique designed to train an individual in how to start and maintain verbal interactions and in how to move the conversation to areas of content where maximum contact is made.

The first step in free information involves asking open as opposed to closed questions. A closed question can be answered "yes" or "no" or can be answered by a single piece of information. Questions involving "where, when and who" are usually closed.

An open question is a question that seeks additional information; i.e., information beyond the specific content of the question. Questions stressing "what, how" and especially "why" are usually open.

If free information is given, the second step involves following up that information where your level of expertise is greatest or further questions in the area where the other person's expertise seems to be greatest.

Since free information is information not specifically asked for by the question, it can usually be presumed that such information is in a high interest area for the speaker. The asserter's task is to find and follow-up free information about which he can converse or interrogate.

The third, and critical step, is to offer free information about oneself. If the recipient follows up any of the asserter's free information the conversation has truly become communication, and no further systematized steps are necessary for deepening social contact.

REFERENCES

Alberti, R. E. and Emmons, M. L. *Your perfect right*. San Luis Obispo: Impact, 1970. (P.O. Box 1094, San Luis Obispo, CA 93401).

Bach, G. and Bernhard, Y. *Aggression lab*. Dubuque, Iowa: Kendall/Hunt, 1971.

Boies, K. G. Role playing as a behavior change technique: Review of the empirical literature. *Psychotherapy: Theory, Research and Practice*, 1972, **9**, 2, 185–192.

Boocock, S. S. An experimental study of the learning effects of two games with simulated environments. In S. S. Boocock and E. O. Schild (Eds.), *Simulation games in learning*. Beverly Hills, Calif.: Sage, 1968, pp. 107–133.

Booraem, C. D. Differential effectiveness of external versus self reinforcement in the acquisition of assertive responses. Unpublished Doctoral dissertation. University of Southern California, 1974.

Casey, G. A. Behavioral rehearsal: Principles and procedures. *Psychotherapy: Theory, Research and Practice*, 1973, **10**, 4, 331–333.

Corsini, R. *Roleplaying in psychotherapy*. Chicago, Ill.: Aldine, 1966.

Davidson, G. C. Self-control through "imaginal aversive contingency" and "one downsmanship": Enabling the powerless to accommodate unreasonableness. In J. D. Krumboltz and C. E. Thorsen Eds.), *Behavioral counseling: Cases and techniques*. New York: Holt, Rinehart and Winston, 1969, pp. 319–328.

Eisler, R. M., Miller, P. M., and Hersen, M. Components of assertive behavior. *Journal of Clinical Psychology*, 1973, **29**, 3, 295–299.

Flowers, J. V. Modification of low self-confidence in elementary school children by reinforcement and modeling. Unpublished Doctoral dissertation. University of Southern California, 1972.

Flowers, J. V. Behavior modification of cheating in an elementary school student: A brief note. *Behavior Therapy*, 1972, **3**, 311–312.

Flowers, J. V. A behavior modification technique to reduce the frequency of unwarranted questions by target students in an elementary school classroom. *Behavior Therapy*, in press.

Flowers, J. V. and Guerra, J. The use of client-coaching in assertion training with large groups. *Journal of Community Mental Health*, 1974, **10**, 414–417.

Flowers, J. V. and Booraem, C. D. The use of tokens to facilitate outcome and monitor process in group therapy. *International Journal of Group Psychotherapy*. in press. (1975).

Flowers, J. V. and Marston, A. R. Modification of low self confidence in elementary school children. *Journal of Education Research*, 1972, **66**, 1, 30–34.

Flowers, J. V., Booraem, C. D., Brown, T. R., and Harris, D. E. An investigation of a technique for facilitating patient to patient interactions in group therapy. *Journal of Community Psychology*, 1974, **2**, 1, 39–42.

Flowers, J. V., Booraem, C. D., and Seacat, G. F. The effect of positive and negative feedback on group members' sensitivity to the roles of other members in group therapy. *Psychotherapy: Theory, Research and Practice*, 1975.

Freedman, P. H. The effects of modeling and role playing on assertive behavior. In R. D. Rubin, H. Fensterheim, A. A. Lazarus, and C. M. Franks (Eds.), *Advances in behavior therapy 1969*. New York: Academic Press, 1971, pp. 149–169.

Freedman, P. H. The effects of modeling, role playing and participation on behavior change. In B. A. Maher (Ed.), *Progress in experimental personality research, Vol. 6*. New York: Academic Press, 1972, pp. 42–81.

Harris, R. J. Experimental games as tools for personality research. In P. McReynolds (Ed.), *Advances in psychological assessment, Vol. II*. Palo Alto, Calif.: Science and Behavior Books, 1971, pp. 236–259.

"Intimacy, an encounter program for couples," Human Development Institute, Atlanta, Georgia, 1969.

Ivey, A. E. *Microcounseling: Innovations in interview training*. Springfield, Ill.: Thomas, 1971.

Kagen, S. and Madsen, M. C. Experimental analyses of cooperation and competition of Anglo-American and Mexican children. *Developmental Psychology*, 1972, **6**, 49–59.

Kanfer, F. H. and Phillips, J. S. *Learning foundations of behavior therapy*. New York: Wiley, 1970.

Kaufmann, L. M. and Wagner, B. R. Barb: A systematic treatment technology for temper control disorders. *Behavior Therapy*, 1972, **3**, 84–90.

Lazarus, A. A. Behavioral rehearsal vs. non-directive therapy vs. advice in effecting behavior change. *Behaviour Research and Therapy*, 1966, **4**, 209–212.

Marston, A. R. Dealing with low self-confidence. *Educational Research*, 1968, **10**, 134–138.

McAleese, W. R. and Unwin, D. A bibliography of microteaching. *Programmed Learning and Educational Technology*, 1973, **10**, 1, 40–54.

McFall, R. M. and Lillesand, D. B. Behavioral rehearsal with modeling and coaching in assertion training. *Journal of Abnormal Psychology*, 1971, **77**, 313–323.

McFall, R. M. and Marston, A. R. An experimental investigation of behavior rehearsal in assertive training. *Journal of Abnormal Psychology*, 1970, **76**, 295–303.

Melnick, J. A comparison of replication techniques in the modification of minimal dating behavior. *Journal of Abnormal Psychology*, 1973, **81**, 1, 51–59.

Moreno, J. L. *Who shall survive?* Beacon, New York: Beacon House, 1953.

Perls, F. S., Hefferline, R. F., and Goodman, P. *Gestalt therapy.* New York: Julian Press, 1951.

Pfeiffer, J. W. and Jones, J. E. *A handbook of structured experiences for human relations training.* Iowa City, Iowa: University Associates Press, 1970. (4 volumes.)

Prazak, J. A. Learning job-seeking interview skills. In J. D. Krumboltz and C. E. Thorsen (Eds.), *Behavioral counseling: Cases and techniques.* New York: Holt, Rinehart and Winston, 1969, pp. 414–428.

Rathus, S. A. An experimental investigation of assertive training in a group setting. *Journal of Behavior Therapy and Experimental Psychiatry*, 1972, **3**, 81–86.

Rathus, S. A. A thirty-item schedule for assessing assertive behavior. *Behavior Therapy*, 1973, **4**, 398–406.

Rehm, L. P. and Marston, A. R. Reduction of social anxiety through modifications of self-reinforcement: An instigation therapy technique. *Journal of Consulting and Clinical Psychology*, 1968, **32**, 565–574.

Rogers, C. R. *Client centered therapy.* New York: Houghton Mifflin, 1951.

Sarason, I. G. Verbal learning, modeling and juvenile delinquency. *American Psychologist*, 1968, **23**, 254–266.

Sarason, I. G. and Ganzer, V. J. Developing appropriate social behaviors of juvenile delinquents. In J. D. Krumboltz and C. E. Thorsen (Eds.), *Behavioral counseling: Cases and techniques.* New York: Holt, Rinehart and Winston, 1969, pp. 178–192.

Truax, C. B. and Mitchell, K. N. Research on certain therapist interpersonal skills in relation to process and outcome. In A. E. Bergin and S. L. Garfield (Eds.), *Handbook of psychotherapy and behavior chance.* New York: Wiley, 1971, pp. 299–344.

Uretsky, M. The management game: An experiment in reality. *Simulation and Games*, 1973, **4**, 2, 221–240.

Varenhorst, B. B. Learning the consequences of life's decisions. In J. D. Krumboltz and C. E. Thorsen (Eds.), *Behavioral counseling: Cases and techniques.* New York: Holt, Rinehart and Winston, 1969, pp. 306–318.

Varenhorst, B. B. Game theory, simulations and group counseling. *Educational Technology*, 1973, 40–43.

Wagner, A. C. Changing teaching behavior: A comparison of microteaching and cognitive discrimination training. *Journal of Educational Psychology*, 1973, **64**, 3, 299–305.

Winkler, R. C. The relevance of economic theory and technology to token reinforcement systems. *Behaviour Research and Therapy*, 1971, **9**, 81–88.

Wolpe, J. and Lazarus, A. A. *Behavior therapy techniques.* New York: Pergamon Press, 1966.

CHAPTER 7

Operant Methods

PAUL KAROLY

I. INTRODUCTION

Few human motives seem more pervasive than the desire to influence the behaviors and attitudes of others. Psychotherapists and advertising executives are among those in "the business" of behavior influence, while countless millions are continuously involved in behavior change efforts that fall under the headings of child-rearing, civic affairs, and everyday social interaction. The search for a clear conceptualization of the why's and how's of social influence has been carried on at various levels, for various reasons, and with varying degrees of success since before the dawn of recorded history. The present chapter will introduce the reader to a modern "self-examining, self-evaluating, discovery-oriented research proce- dure for studying behavior" (Baer, Wolf, and Risley, 1968, p. 91), based on the experimental programs of B. F. Skinner and his colleagues, which has been successfully extended (especially in the last twenty-five years) to the study and therapeutic modification of human behavior disorders. The applied science of operant conditioning, known as *the experimental analysis of behavior*, is unique in that it provides both an objective view of the "causes and cures" of nonfunctional or abnormal behavior, and a relatively simple and systematic technology for behavior measurement and change.

The Psychology of Behavior Influence

The operant approach is based upon the assumption that a great many complex human activities are learned. A useful working definition of learning is:

> the process by which an activity originates or is changed through reacting to an encountered situation, provided that the characteristics of the change in activity cannot be explained on the basis of native response tendencies, maturation, or temporary states of the organism (e.g., fatigue, drugs, etc). (Hilgard and Bower, 1966, p. 2.)

This general definition illustrates the learning-oriented psychologist's concern with (a) the person-environment relationship, (b) the questions of how behavior

195

originates and how it changes as a result of the person-environment interaction, (c) the necessity for specifying "reactions" as observable behaviors, (d) the necessity for representing measurable aspects of situations, and (e) the necessity of a reliable system for detecting change (Levy, 1970).

Such a view can be contrasted with the traditional conceptual approach of descriptive psychiatry whose adherents have attempted to unravel the mysteries of human action first, by positing an analogy between physical illness and "mental illness," and then by employing specialized interview and "psychological testing" procedures to identify the nature of a given patient's inner disturbance. Typically, any odd, personally disruptive, emotionally unpleasant, or socially unacceptable behavior could be labelled a "symptom" of inner conflicts whose roots would be expected to go deep into the individual's past, and with current pathways likewise deeply embedded in hidden "regions" of the mind. To effect a "cure," various forms of verbal exchange between therapist and patient might be used (depending upon the theoretical preference of the therapist).

Among the serious challenges to the traditional conceptualizations of dysfunctional behavior ("psychopathology"), its assessment, and its modification are: the unreliability of diagnostic categories, the potential for personal bias in clinical evaluation, the absence of clear and specific treatment implications associated with diagnostic findings, the restricted availability of psychotherapy (a largely white, middle-class endeavor), and the limited demonstrable effectiveness of treatment (be it strict Freudian psychoanalysis or its many variants and offshoots). Although talking over one's problems with a sensitive and insightful therapist can sometimes produce emotional release, renewed confidence, and a new perspective on one's personal makeup, lasting changes in the effectiveness of *behavior* have not generally been achieved. As Schwitzgebel and Kolb (1974) put it: "traditional psychotherapy seems to produce changes localized within the region of the lips without affecting the hands or feet" (p. 8).

The behavioral psychologist, on the other hand, may be characterized by objectivity in the definition of behavior (dealing typically with small, observable units), practicality in the choice of behavior to be changed (i.e., Can "target" behaviors be easily recorded; and will their alteration produce the greatest short- or long-term benefits to the client?), and responsivity to the flow of information in the system (modifying or correcting his interventions to insure maximum learning and development of the client). Unlike the traditional psychotherapist, who searches "inside the head" of his client, the behavior psychologist's domain of investigation includes both the person and his social and physical surroundings.

Throughout the course of his life, the individual is said to be adapting—learning (and unlearning) various ways of behaving and perceiving in accordance with the demands of the situation and self-set standards. Problems can occur, for example, when learning is incomplete, when behavior that is learned in one setting is inappropriately employed in another, when a set of behaviors are personally satisfying but disruptive of others' attempts at adaptation (and eventually troublesome to the individual), or when adaptive skills have never been acquired. The psychologist who relies on the operant-experimental framework has the vast literature on animal and human learning from which to draw for conceptual and technical direction in the pursuit of therapeutic goals. From a basic view that stresses learning, behaving, and adaptation, other distinctive features of the experimental analysis of behavior flow quite naturally. These include: (1) a primary concern with the "here-and-now," (2) the disavowal of summary labels (psychiatric categories), and (3) the use of nonprofessionals (community resources, relatives and friends of the client, the client himself) as implementers of change programs.

Historically, one can trace the study of learning (the organism-environment relationship) to the work of the Russian psychologist Ivan Pavlov, and to the American investigator Edward L. Thorndike, both working at around the turn of the century. Pavlov's *classical conditioning* view represents an approach to the question of how behavior originates and changes which places heavy emphasis on how new or *neutral stimuli* (usually external events) come to elicit *innate responses* by virtue of their having been temporally paired with *eliciting stimuli* (events which automatically lead to innate responding). Pavlov, studying the digestive system of dogs, noticed that while the presence of food (the eliciting stimulus) in the animal's mouth could reliably predict the flow of saliva (the innate response), the sight of the experimenter who brought the food (who was *paired* with the food) soon came to elicit salivation. Learning had occurred (following the above definition). In his laboratory, Pavlov and his co-workers set out to verify, quantify, and systematize their "casual" observations, thus, giving a major impetus to the study of animal and human learning. Today, several widely-used behavior-change techniques can be termed "derivatives" of the Pavlovian experimental perspective (e.g., systematic desensitization and aversive conditioning).

The operations and measurements of the typical Pavlovian experiment can be distinguished from those associated with the *instrumental conditioning*, and *operant conditioning* paradigms developed in America by E. L. Thorndike (1898) and B. F. Skinner (1938).

Thorndike's experiments with dogs, cats, and chicks, for example, differed in at least one very basic way from those of Pavlov; namely, Thorndike's animals were *active* in their engagement of the environment. Thorndike placed his experimental subjects in an enclosed "puzzle box" from which they were required to escape, by the manipulation of the correct lever or pulley, in order to obtain a bit of food reward. Through the process of "trial-and-error," Thorndike's subjects eventually "learned" (i.e., their behavior changed as a result of a situational encounter). Since the animal's behaviors were instrumental in affecting escape from the box and in obtaining food, the paradigm was labelled *instrumental* conditioning. Thorndike viewed the animal as learning through "selecting and connecting." That is, the animal in the puzzle box selected a response from the variety of responses available to it, tried it out, and continued to sample response options until the "solution" (escape from the box) was discovered. The animal would eventually connect the correct response to a particular puzzle box arrangement (stimulus). Learning came to be understood as obeying several basic laws of stimulus-response connectionism, the most important of which was articulated as the *law of effect*. Simply put, this law states that *behavior is controlled by its consequences*. Specifically, behavior that is followed by a "satisfying state of affairs" is *stamped in* (strengthened), and behavior followed by an "annoying state of affairs" is *stamped out* (weakened). Annoyers and satisfiers correspond to the more familiar terms *punishment* and *reward*.

Compare the law of effect with the following statement of the basic law of Pavlovian conditioning:

> A neutral stimulus event (CS), when paired with a stimulus (UCS) that reflexively elicits a response (UCR), soon becomes capable of eliciting the same (or nearly the same) reaction (CR).

Two important differences should be underscored. First, Pavlovian conditioning requires the repeated pairing of a new stimulus with a specific eliciting stimulus that triggers an innate (unlearned) response. The process is one in which the experimenter controls the learning. In the case of Thorndike's animals, pairing of old and new behavior patterns is not a requirement, and the animal is an initiator of activity. Secondly, the innate behavior which is central to learning for Pavlov is under the control of the preceding (eliciting) stimulus, while Thorndikean instrumental responses are influenced by their outcomes (cf., Reynolds, 1968). How much of the complex behavior of higher animals and man can be learned in the Pavlovian fashion? Thorndike and many theorists who followed tended to attribute the lion's share of the learning burden to the more active process of instrumental learning.

Skinner (1937) referred to the Pavlovian model, built upon pairing of two stimuli, as Type *S* conditioning, and to the Thorndikean operation of having a reward follow contingent upon the emission of a response as Type *R* conditioning. Skinner is credited with ushering in a science and technology built upon Type *R* or, as it is now called, *operant conditioning*. It is Skinner's basic position and the experimental elaborations of it that form the nucleus of the present chapter.

Influencing Behavior by Controlling its Consequences

Skinner's break with the traditions of learning and of abnormal psychology was sharp and radical. Whereas many learning theorists had stressed the importance of the immediately preceding stimulus, and clinical theorists (e.g., Freud) had stressed the distant past as a critical antecedent of learning, Skinner (1938) sought to mount a research program in which the stimulus would occupy "no special place among the independent variables." He concentrated his studies on *operants*, behaviors freely emitted which operate upon the environment and which are, in turn, controlled by their environmental consequences (i.e., their future probability of occurrence is either increased or decreased by the events that follow their emission).

Operants are learned behaviors, and can be distinguished from "respondents" in that a respondent is a behavior under the control of prior eliciting stimuli, and is a part of the individual's biological equipment (either at birth or as a result of maturation). The knee jerk reflex is an example of a respondent. Although the term "free operant" is often used to fully describe the absence of constraints on the organism's responding, most contexts actually include limiting features that set "natural boundaries" on the quality and quantity of behaviors emitted. Even the pigeon in the familiar Skinner box could not peck on the response key and gain a food pellet if that key were withdrawn or absent. Similarly, the youngster whose tantrum behavior may be considered an operant (rewarded by parental attention) can only throw his toys about the room when those toys are available to him. These examples simply underscore the *interdependence* of the individual and his context—a recognition that is central to the Skinnerian perspective.

A key concept in operant analysis is the *contingency* relationship between an operant and the environmental events which follow it. The term contingency refers to the nature of the relationship between a response and subsequent environmental events. To exist in a contingent relationship, event *B*, in fact, follows event *A* —but *need not* do so. In contrast, event *B* is in a *dependent* (not contingent) relationship to event *A*, if *B must* follow upon *A* by its very nature. The relationship between walking in the rain and getting wet represents a dependency. However, the relationship between a student's hand raising in a classroom and the teacher's calling upon that student is typically a contingent one. That is, the teacher selectively recognizes the child; she isn't forced to do so. Hand raising can be considered an operant, under the control of contingent environmental events (including, not only the teacher's response, but the reactions of the other students, and of the hand-raiser himself).

Reinforcement, Punishment, and Extinction

Having set the stage for a learning-based understanding of how behavior originates and is changed, it is now time to introduce the leading players. As we shall see later in this chapter, the majority of the therapeutic uses of operant conditioning have been aimed at some combination of the following objectives: (a) the development or establishment of a behavior (e.g., reading in a non-reading child; social interaction in a withdrawn "psychotic" adult), (b) the acceleration or strengthening of a behavior (e.g., cooperative play in a group of nursery school children; the exchange of approving statements in a married couple), or (c) the elimination or weakening of a response (e.g., reduction in the amount of alcohol ingested by the chronic drinker; elimination of self-injurious behavior in developmentally-handicapped children). The operations of *reinforcement*, *extinction*, and *punishment* represent specialized response-environment relationships which produce changes in the probability of emission of operant behavior. In other words, these factors are generally responsible for learning—in humans as well as lower animals. Before discussing how these basic procedures may be employed to modify problem behavior, let us examine each in more detail.

A *reinforcer* is a stimulus which, if it occurs contingent upon the emission of an operant response, will tend to maintain or increase the probability of that response in the future. Reinforcement is a term that refers to the operations involved in using reinforcers to maintain or increase the likelihood of a particular response. Skinner (1938) has distinguished between two kinds of reinforcing stimuli: *positive* reinforcers and *negative* reinforcers. A positive reinforcer is a stimulus which produces a reinforcing effect (response maintenance or acceleration) *when presented*, while a negative reinforcer is a stimulus which strengthens a response (increases its probability or rate of emission) when contingently *removed*. Upon first encounter, the term *negative reinforcement* seems a bit odd—since the word *reinforcement* connotes response strengthening, while *negative* suggests weakening. However, all we need remember is that the process of reinforcement always defines a response-strengthening operation; and that the adjectives positive and negative refer to the response-contingent delivery and withdrawal of stimuli. A little thought will tell you that, if a stimulus is reinforcing when removed, it must possess unpleasant or aversive qualities. Negative reinforcers range from malodorous substances, "dirty looks," and verbal attacks to minor physical discomforts, pain, and severe psychological or physiological shock.*

Thousands of experiments have been conducted over the years to identify factors that influence the effectiveness of reinforcement operations. We can state with a large degree of confidence that, in general, reinforcers exert their greatest effect on response acquisition and strengthening when they are delivered *contingently*, *consistently*, and with *minimal delay*. The number of times a response is reinforced and the quantity of reinforcers per response are related to the strength of the behavior in a negatively accelerated function. That is, small increases in number or magnitude of reinforcers will result in large increases in response strength (rate, speed, probability of occurrence), until the response reaches a plateau (also called an *asymptotic level*), after which the net addition to response strength declines (Deese and Hulse, 1967).

Reinforcers can also be categorized as either *primary* or *conditioned*. A primary reinforcer is a stimulus whose reinforcing properties do not derive from a history of prior conditioning. Primary reinforcers can be viewed as "biological givens." Food, water, air, etc. are examples of potential primary reinforcing stimuli. A neutral stimulus (one that does not serve a reinforcing function prior to conditioning) can be closely associated in time with a primary reinforcer and eventually acquire the power to increase or maintain responding. A neutral stimulus with reinforcing properties acquired in this Pavlovian fashion (i.e., through previous pairing with a primary reinforcer) is called a conditioned reinforcer. The term *generalized reinforcer* is used to describe conditioned reinforcers that have been paired with more than one primary reinforcer. Much of human behavior is established and maintained through the action of generalized reinforcers such as affection, attention, praise, and money (not necessarily in that order!).

A behavior can be contingently reinforced every time it occurs; and common sense might tell us that such a practice would maximize learning. Yet, a little further thought will surely prompt us to reconsider, on the grounds that very few important human (or animal) activities are or can be reliably reinforced after every occurrence. Skinner and his colleagues (e.g., Ferster and Skinner, 1957) have pioneered the study of reinforcement *schedules*, the specification of contingencies

---

*Good examples of negative reinforcement in everyday life are difficult to find. Perhaps the best illustration is the behavior of coming in and out of the rain (assuming that getting wet is aversive).

in terms of responses emitted (*ratio schedules*) and in terms of elapsed time (*interval schedules*). In his *Primer of Operant Conditioning*, Reynolds (1968) explains that:

> Schedules of reinforcement have regular, and profound effects on the organism's rate of responding. The importance of schedules of reinforcement cannot be overestimated. No description, account, or explanation of any operant behavior of any organism is complete unless the schedule of reinforcement is specified. (p. 60.)

Four simple schedules of intermittent (in contrast to continuous) reinforcement are the *fixed interval*, *fixed ratio*, *variable interval*, and *variable ratio* types. In a fixed interval schedule (FI), a reinforcer is presented after the first response emitted in a constant (fixed) interval of time. The timing interval begins from the moment the last reinforcer is delivered. When a laboratory animal is exposed to an FI schedule, its rate of responding eventually forms a recurring pattern: responding is slow at first (as though the animal were pausing), but suddenly speeds up as the time for potential delivery of the reinforcer draws near. A crude human analogy may be found in the work habits of people at dull, repetitive jobs as quitting time approaches. A fixed-ratio (FR) schedule, wherein reinforcement is made contingent upon a fixed number of responses, tends to produce high, stable rates of responding. An everyday example is the piece-work system used in some industries. The more a worker produces, the more he earns. In the variable-interval schedule (VI), reinforcement is made available sometimes after long intervals, and sometimes after shorter ones, in a pattern that continuously varies. Generally, individuals work faster on VI schedules when the intervals are shorter *on the average*. Finally, in variable ratio (VR) schedules, the number of responses necessary for a reward to occur varies from reward to reward, in an irregular but repeating fashion. The VR schedule produces very high and almost constant rates of responding. The best example of behavioral persistence established by a VR schedule is that of the gambler working at a slot machine. When teaching people new forms of behavior, we often desire that they show persistently high rates of responding. Consequently, we employ the most powerful schedules at our disposal (usually variable schedules). The reader is referred to Reynolds (1968), Rachlin (1970), or Williams (1973) for further details on the operation of reinforcement schedules, the nature of reinforcement, and the influence of training conditions (delay, number of reinforcements, etc.) on response acquisition and maintenance.

Thus far, we have considered only reinforcement operations. However, applied behavioral psychologists are also interested in procedures that weaken or eliminate the tendency to respond (when responding is dangerous, inappropriate, or excessive). Punishment refers to a class of operations resulting in the decline, deceleration, suppression (a temporary reduction), or termination of the behavior upon which they are contingent. Operant χ may be weakened in any of three ways: (1) by making a negative reinforcer (aversive or noxious stimulus) contingent upon it; (2) by causing a positive reinforcer to be lost or removed contingent upon its emission; or (3) by presenting a neutral stimulus contingently and consistently after each instance of χ.

The first method is termed punishment, or sometimes *positive punishment* (positive because the event is added; punishment because the result is response reduction). The second type of procedure involves the manipulation of positive reinforcers for the purpose of reducing the frequency of responding. There exist several ways of producing a punishing outcome without having to apply aversive stimuli. *Time-out* is the name given to the practice of cutting off access to any and all pleasant events that may be available in a given setting for a limited period of time, contingent upon the emission of a to-be-changed behavior. Sending a disobedient or disruptive child to his room is an oft-cited example of the use of time-out in everyday life. In most cases, however, the example is a poor one—bordering on the ridiculous, in fact, depending upon the opulence of the child's room! A related operation is the loss of previously held items of value (like money earned or points won) contingent upon a response. Such a procedure, called *response cost*, is involved in a parent's taking back part of a child's allowance when the youngster misbehaves. Finally, the complete withdrawal or discontinuation of the positive events that had previously followed a behavior is called *extinction*. This procedure is equivalent to presenting neutral events, where positive outcomes used to occur. Everyday examples of extinction are common. Parents will ignore a whining child whose cries formerly elicited attention. A jealous lover will ignore the amorous advances of the wayward partner. Or a therapist might ignore the promises of a client to "go on the wagon, once and for all," and pay attention only to "documented" signs of progress.

Later in this chapter, the therapeutic uses and potential misuses of punishment procedures will be addressed. For now, the reader is advised to remember two basic facts about behavior modification via the control of reinforcement contingencies: (1) consequences can either be added or taken away, and (2) *both* pleasant and unpleasant consequences can be used for the purpose of increasing behavior *and* for the purpose of decreasing behavior. Therefore:

- Positive reinforcement = *adding* a pleasant consequence resulting in *increased* responding.
- Negative reinforcement = *taking away* an unpleasant consequence, resulting in *increased* responding.
- (Positive) Punishment = *adding* an unpleasant consequence resulting in *decreased* responding.
- Extinction, Response Cost, Time-Out (Negative Punishment)* = *removing* a pleasant consequence resulting in *decreased* responding.

---

*When the reader is clear on the above definitions, he or she will have succeeded where many professionals and textbook writers appear to have failed. Here's a simple memory aid. If asked the definition of "negative reinforcement," for example, think of negative = taking away (consequences) and reinforcement = increased responding. Negative reinforcement involves taking something away resulting in behavioral increase. Common sense will next tell you that what must be removed is something unpleasant. A little practice here should suffice to forestall future confusion.

Stimulus Control, Generalization, and Discrimination

In the Skinnerian analysis of behavior, stimuli do not act as "goads" to action, as in the case of a reflex. Yet, prior stimulation does influence subsequent behavior. Antecedent conditions act as signals, cues, or more correctly as *discriminative stimuli* (S^Ds) identifying the upcoming conditions as those in which a specific action will be reinforced. Animals as well as humans learn that responses are rewarded *in context*, and that the recurrence of context is likely to signal the re-introduction of response-contingent reward (or punishment). In many cases, as we shall see, the most efficient way to influence behavior is via the manipulation of antecedent cueing stimuli. The discriminative control of behavior is termed *stimulus control*. Including the discriminative stimulus in a behavioral formula, along with the operant response and its contingent reinforcement, yields the basic Skinnerian "three-term contingency," the fundamental explanatory road map of operant psychology:

$$S^D \longrightarrow R \longrightarrow S^R$$

| (1) discriminative stimulus | (2) response | (3) reinforcing stimulus |

Contingency management refers to the manipulation of (3) relative to (2). Stimulus control refers to the control of (1) and its effects on (2). Behavioral engineering is a term used to describe the combined technologies of stimulus control and contingency management (Homme, deBaca, Cottingham, and Homme, 1968).

In nature, and in the laboratory, we may observe some fascinating characteristics of stimulus control. We discover, for example, that the reinforcement of a response in the presence of a particular stimulus results in the ability of *other similar cues* to evoke the same operant. This spread of effect is called *stimulus generalization*; and it accounts for considerable savings in an individual's time and energy. Happily, one doesn't have to relearn each response in every new situation.

Related to generalization is the concept of *discrimination*. In fact, some theorists consider discrimination to be the psychological opposite of generalization. An individual learns to discriminate when he responds differently to various stimuli, even when the stimuli are very similar. As we shall see, many behavioral problems can be traced to a failure to learn appropriate discriminations and generalizations.

II. BEHAVIORAL ASSESSMENT: THE DEFINITION AND MEASUREMENT OF PROBLEM BEHAVIOR

The operant psychologist does not attempt a "diagnosis" in the traditional sense of trying to infer a client's inner dispositions or traits (tendencies to act, think, or feel) as they relate to "universal" childhood crises (e.g., the Oedipal situation emphasized by Freudian theorists). Rather, an experimental analytic approach focuses on what the individual does, and the context in which he does it. A direct sampling of problem behavior may be accomplished via direct observation in the client's home or place of business, through physiological recordings of his internal responses (heart rate, blood pressure, etc.), in a structured interview or role-playing session in the therapist's office, or by asking the client to observe himself over a period of time and provide a detailed report of the specific instances of problem behavior and the environmental conditions that evoke and maintain (reinforce) it.

It is incorrect to assume, however, that the conduct of a behavioral interview is equivalent to placing the client under a "psychological microscope" that focuses in on all of the smallest details of his or her life. Likewise, an equally erroneous conclusion is that a traditional psychiatric interview represents nothing more than an exercise in magical thinking on the interviewer's part. In a standard psychiatric textbook, parts of the description of the process of "examining the patient" are not at all contrary to operant principles:

> One seeks ... a clear psychological picture of the living person as a specific human being with his individual problems .... This requires ... fullest information possible concerning physical, anatomical, physiological, pathological, social, psychological, and educational factors and influences. (Kolb, 1973, p. 146.)

Where, then, is the uniqueness of behavioral assessment to be found? Clearly, it is a question of what the assessor does with the information collected that is most important in distinguishing the traditional from the operant approach. The psychiatric examiner is advised to "reformulate the patient's particular difficulties and behavior and reconstruct his inner life history" (Kolb, 1973, p. 146). The operant or social-learning psychologist is advised, on the other hand, to consider that "a description of the problematic behavior, its controlling factors, and the means by which it can be changed are the most appropriate 'explanations' for the patient's actions" (Kanfer and Saslow, 1969, p. 426). The goal is a *functional analysis*, the complete listing of all the relevant environmental events subsequent and antecedent to an identified problem behavior. An event is relevant if it serves as an effective cue (discriminative stimulus) or reinforcer for the behavior in question. And controlling conditions are not confined exclusively to the external environment. Such covert behaviors as self-instructions, images, or self-reinforcements may also play a critical role (see Chapters 10 and 11 in this volume).

To pinpoint the factors that cue and reinforce the "problem behavior-in-a-situation-unit," it is helpful to think of five rudimentary components in the behavioral analysis: the prior environmental stimulation (S), the biological state of the organism (O), the problem response or responses (R), the contingency relationship of the behavior and subsequent events (K), and the nature of the consequences themselves (C). This formula, $S \longrightarrow O \longrightarrow R \longrightarrow K \longrightarrow C$ provides a crude guideline for areas of investigation. The reader is referred to Ferster and Perrott (1968), Gottman and Leiblum (1974), Holland (1970), Kanfer and Saslow (1969), Lazarus (1971), Wahler and Cormier (1970), and Wolpe (1973) for illustrations of and further suggestions on the conduct of a functional analysis.

But just how does one decide on the correct target for change in a behavioral analysis? Since we don't deal in "psychotic symptoms," "neurotic patterns," or "character disorders" as defined in the diagnostic manual of the American

Psychiatric Association (1968), how then do we define a proper target for clinical intervention? To this deceptively simple question, I will offer a necessarily terse reply: One begins with the client's complaint, and uses the functional analysis to sharpen the focus. If a behavior produces consequences that are harmful to the individual's physical safety, disruptive of his emotions, or damaging to his effectiveness in any of his social roles and it prompts him to seek help, then the behavior is a likely target for behavioral treatment. If several different behaviors are troublesome, the focus may *initially* be placed on the response which, according to the functional analysis, is most disruptive and has the best chance of being altered through available methods. It is important to remember that assessment is a continuous process. From the *baseline* phase (i.e., when a predictable or consistent picture is available of the problem response prior to the introduction of treatment) to *post-baseline*, when treatment contingencies are withdrawn, the behavioral assessor keeps careful records of the course of his client's activities. Thus, revisions in treatment plans are possible, and when instituted, they are based on the "hard facts" of the case—rather than "clinical intuition." At all times, assessment information is used as the foundation of one's treatment strategy; not to "reconstruct the client's personality."

III. METHODS OF BEHAVIOR CHANGE

Although many techniques exist for the alteration of behavior, our focus rests exclusively with those that derive from the operant experimental perspective. Presentation of behavior influence methods has been segmented into four sections to mirror the four interdependent functions of operant intervention: (1) the establishment of effective behavior, (2) the acceleration of desirable activities, (3) the elimination of maladaptive responding, and (4) the maintenance of therapeutic gain. Virtually all programmatic efforts to help people change will include all four elements. Why? Beginning with the propositions (a) that both adaptive and maladaptive behavior must be learned, and (b) that the proper study of behavior is the study of relationships, the behavioral practitioner *never deals with problem behavior in isolation*. Every intervention is (or should be) a *three-pronged* attack: first, increasing (or establishing) desirable responses, second, eliminating the undesirable behaviors that compete with the acquisition or use of acceptable responses, and finally arranging for the stimulus control or eventual generalization of the newly-acquired habits. And, of course, after successful intervention will come programs to insure maintenance. The three-pronged attack is suggested, therefore, regardless of the apparent "singularity" of the target (e.g., "All I want to do is get Johnny to *stop* soiling his pants"; "If Mary would only *start* paying attention in class . . ."). While some of the techniques will be illustrated individually, the reader should keep in mind the complementary nature of operant procedures.

(1) BUILDING BEHAVIORAL CAPABILITIES

(A) Shaping (Differentiation Plus Extinction)

Rationale. If a response must occur to be reinforced (strengthened), how can new behaviors be acquired? A procedure known as *response differentiation* provides the answer. Simply put, the behavioral psychologist relies on already existing forms of behavior to establish new forms. Every action or movement, verbal or motoric, varies along qualitative and quantitative dimensions. A verbal utterance varies in pitch and loudness; a movement in direction, form, force, or duration. We can produce a new behavior by picking one level or variant of an existing response and reinforcing it, while we withdraw all reward from other levels. Soon, new variations will appear. If we apply the procedure of response differentiation progressively and gradually, we may move the behavior in a planned direction. Each new form is an approximation of the desired terminal behavior. This selective reward and extinction process is called *successive approximation* or *shaping* (see Millenson, 1967, Chapter 8 for a more detailed analysis). While the early laboratory demonstrations of shaping were interesting and amusing (Skinner taught pigeons to play ping pong, for example), the procedure can be used to program academic (reading), social (approaching, speaking, cooperation) and complex motor behaviors in normal and biologically deficient children and adults. Shaping is typically used to establish single behaviors. When the goal is the establishment of behavior sequences (e.g., getting dressed; toileting, etc.) shaping is used in conjunction with *chaining* (see below).

Illustration. Hingtgen and Trost (1966) sought to establish cooperative and vocal responses in a group of young children diagnosed as "schizophrenic." It was expected that the acquisition of these responses would lead to increased freedom of action and to greater acceptance of these children in the "natural" environment. The investigators worked with four children, who were trained in pairs and alone. Vocal responses were shaped in a morning session (child alone) and cooperative responses in an afternoon session. Vocal shaping proceeded as follows: the child was taken to a room containing a coin machine and food vendor (with various items such as crackers and M & M's visible through a plastic cover), and was rewarded with a coin for making any sound. Sounds were rewarded on a continuous schedule until the child responded at a steady rate. Next, differential extinction and reinforcement were put into effect. Coughing, giggling, and humming sounds were ignored. Reinforcement was given only for such recognizable sounds as 'ba,' 'ta,' 'da,' 'ma,' 'loo,' etc.

Cooperative responses were shaped using four steps. First, touching was reinforced using the method of successive approximation (moving close, brushing each other accidentally, sustained hand to body contact). Second, only physical contact plus vocalizations were rewarded. Next, touching with both hands plus vocalization was required. And, finally, reinforcement was given only if both children touched each other with both hands and made a vocal response. The results of this demonstration were gratifying in that children who initially showed no tendency toward recognizable speech nor toward peer interaction, and whose psychiatric labels would have been accompanied by a "poor prognosis" and custodial treatment, learned the rudiments of interpersonal behavior. Today, in hospitals, schools, and clinics in the U.S.A. and in many parts of the world, children ("retarded," "brain-injured," "hyperactive," "schizophrenic," etc.) are being taken beyond the rudiments by shaping methods.

Recommendations. The steps in behavior shaping are as follows:

* Begin by observing the individual whose behavioral repertoire is considered deficient. What responses occur at high frequency? Identify the antecedent and consequent (reinforcing) environmental stimuli associated with these high frequency behaviors. Note the variability in topography (form, force, or duration) of the available responses.
* Based upon the observational data, decide (1) whether a desired terminal response can be differentiated out of existing behaviors and if so, (2) what a *first approximation* to the end goal should be.
* Establish the criterion for the first approximation. As Blackwood (1971) points out: "In setting the criterion, we are dividing the responses into two classes; responses most like those we want and responses least like those we want. Notice here that the criterion must be set low or all responding will be extinguished" (Chapter 7, p. 6).
* Arrange the setting for maximum likelihood of response emission. If the desired response involves other people or particular stimuli, then arrange to have them present during shaping.
* Differentially reinforce (with the most powerful reinforcers at your disposal—food, praise, physical affection, etc.) variants of ongoing behavior that may be crude first approximations of the desired response. Withdraw reinforcement from variants that are incompatible with the desired end goal. For example in shaping her son to pay attention to her demonstrations of proper dressing behavior, a mother will talk to her child affectionately when he looks in her direction, but will be silent when the child turns away, closes his eyes, screams, etc.
* Observe the shift in the direction of the goal behavior, and shift the criterion accordingly. If repeated reinforcement fails to reliably establish a response, the criterion may need to be lowered. When a behavior is established at a high, stable rate (little fluctuation) (e.g., a child's verbalization of "da" occurs to the cue "Say da," 95 percent of the time), the criterion may be shifted in the direction of the desired response (reinforce only two consecutive "da" responses; reinforce two consecutive "da" responses separated by a maximum of two seconds of silence; then one second, etc.).
* Use verbal or gestural cues or instructions at all stages of the process, even though the cues do not *at first* reliably elicit the behavior being shaped. At the outset of the shaping procedure the child's behavior will determine what cues the shaper will use (Step 1). That is, if the child spontaneously says "Goo," the shaper will reinforce the sound and then attempt to establish stimulus control by instructing the child, "Say Goo," and rewarding compliance.

(B) Chaining

Rationale. Complex human behaviors are composed of chains of simpler responses. The response units of a behavior chain are joined by stimuli that act as cues (discriminative stimuli) and as reinforcers. For example, the chain of actions that is initiated by the ring of one's alarm clock and that terminates (for the sake of this example) in the eating of one's breakfast is a sequence of operations upon the environment, with reinforcing consequences that likewise set the occasion for (cue) subsequent operations—culminating in the satisfying state of hunger reduction. The overt responses (referred to as *members*) of the chain just described are numerous (e.g., sitting up in bed, putting on slippers, walking to bathroom, washing, brushing teeth, walking to kitchen, sitting down at table, etc.) as are the environmental connectors (called *links*) that tie the chain members together (e.g., the slippers that cue walking and make walking more comfortable, the toothpaste tube which cues brushing and whose release of toothpaste reinforces its squeezing, etc.).

The technology of establishing (teaching) adaptive behavior chains with individuals (adults as well as children) whose performance is judged deficient is built solely upon the principles of shaping, stimulus control, and reinforcement. Precision and common sense in the use of these basic behavioral procedures can produce long, intricate, and socially relevant chains of behavior, the smooth flow of which belies their "premeditated" origin (cf., also Findley, 1962, for a discussion of the complex topic of "branching" chains).

Illustration. Watson (1973) and his colleagues make use of behavioral techniques in their "psychoeducational" treatment of retarded and autistic children. Chaining procedures are typically employed to establish age-appropriate behavior sequences such as those involved in dressing. The act of getting dressed is first conceptually divided into five components: putting on underpants; putting on pants; putting on a shirt; putting on socks; and putting on shoes. A shaping procedure is employed initially to establish each of the five members of the "dressing chain." Then, members are connected by building a chain from the terminal member (the last behavior in the sequence) *backward* to the first. Since the last response in the chain is typically closest to the naturally-occurring reinforcer (i.e., parents usually reward the child for appearing at the breakfast table fully and appropriately dressed), chains are built backwards from the final, most immediately reinforced member. So, starting with a child who has been helped with his dressing through the fourth component, the behavior builder will say to the child, "Get dressed." The child will then be helped on with his shoes and reinforced with candy, Kool-aid or some other preferred reinforcer plus verbal praise, a hug, or a smile. Once the "shoes member" of the chain is brought under verbal control (that is, once the cue "Get dressed" reliably elicits putting on of shoes), the "socks member" can be added, with the primary reinforcement still coming after the last response in the chain (putting on of shoes). Verbal cues are used, along with verbal praise, to add each member to the chain until the child, completely nude, can put on all his clothes, on the signal "Get dressed."

Recommendations: The basic rules for teaching behavior chains are:

• Divide the desired behavior sequence into component units. Size of units should be determined by the demands of the individual case.

• Determine which members of the to-be-conditioned chain already exist and which will need to be individually shaped.

• Shape the chain members which are at low strength (low probability of emission) or at zero strength.

• Begin the chaining procedure by strengthening the final member. Do so in a distraction-free environment.

• Bring the final member under reliable stimulus control. The accomplishment of this and the preceding step is aided by the use of strong reinforcers (determined by observing the client and asking him what he likes), consistently, immediately, and frequently given, contingent upon emission of the desired response. Social reinforcers should also be used (e.g., smiles, praise, etc.).

• Add the next-to-last member to the behavior already acquired. Add each remaining member working backwards to the first response in the chain. For example, a three-member chain can be diagrammed as follows:

$$S_1^D \longrightarrow R_1 \longrightarrow S_1^R$$
$$S_2^D \longrightarrow R_2 \longrightarrow S_2^R$$
$$S_3^D \longrightarrow R_3 \longrightarrow S_3^R$$
$$\text{(Start here)}$$

Let us assume that we are dealing here with the last three members of a toothbrushing chain. R_3 is brushing reinforced by (S_3^R) the delightful tasting toothpaste. The cue for brushing (S_3^D) is the toothbrush in one's hand. Holding the toothbrush will eventually take on reinforcing power. When holding the toothbrush reliably predicts brushing, we can expect toothbrush holding (S_3^D is also S_2^R) to reinforce (S_2^D) toothbrush lifting (R_2). The cue for toothbrush lifting (S_2^D) may be the sight of the toothbrush. Eventually seeing the toothbrush will reinforce (S_1^R) the first response in our mini-chain (R_1) which is switching on the light in the bathroom.

• When an error occurs during performance of a chained sequence correct the error as soon as possible, and require the performer to go back as far as possible in the chain and start over.

• When errors occur in a learned sequence, it may be necessary to punish them. One may need to punish errors that occur early in the chain, since disruption of the initial behaviors undercuts acquisition, and may have adverse effects on the learner's motivation (desire to try).

• In teaching chained sequences (such as proper dressing, toileting, bathing, eating behavior, etc.) it is often helpful and necessary to physically guide the performer through the sequence. The teacher may also demonstrate (model) appropriate behavior.

• Fading and prompting techniques may also be useful in establishing effective chains (see below).

(C) Fading and Prompting

Rationale. Thus far, we have concentrated largely on behavior building by the manipulation of consequences; but we are now ready to consider, more specifically, methods of placing newly established responses under discriminative stimulus control.

Adequate adjustment to an ever-changing environment calls for quick and accurate "tuning into" the cues (stimuli) that signal the expected forms of behavior. Examples are: stop at the red; take off your hat in church (or put it on in synagogue); stand when the National Anthem is played; talk softly in the library. And, there are the subtler social signals which dictate how we approach, converse with and relate to members of the opposite sex, to persons older or younger than ourselves, to authorities, to strangers, to friends, and to enemies. Maladaptive behavior is often the result of responding to an inappropriate stimulus (i.e., the form of the behavior is correct, but it is emitted at the wrong time or place) or a failure to respond to the appropriate cue. If we can bring the responses of others (or of ourselves) under the influence of verbal or nonverbal signals (hints, cues, prompts, directions, advice, requests, or instructions), we can often achieve more efficient management, and set the stage for generalization (extension) and maintenance of change.

Prompts are behavioral interventions which direct the learner's attention to the to-be-learned task and its requirements. In shaping dressing behavior, for example, the teacher may physically guide the child through a series of movements and administer reinforcement at appropriate intervals. In shaping speech behavior, the teacher may utter the required sound first and direct the learner to repeat it. A close approximation of the sound will then be rewarded. *Fading* refers to the gradual elimination of aspects of the cueing stimulus, so that the learner is responding to the minimal cues that exist in the natural environment. Fading refers also to the gradual removal of cues that are artificially established for purposes of aiding acquisition (e.g., writing numbers on the keys of a piano, then, literally "fading them out"). In combination, prompting and fading procedures are used to develop discriminative control of behavior.

Illustrations. Oral reading can be considered an operant under the control of a printed stimulus. The sight method for the teaching of reading, which involves the combination of words and pictures is a commonly used tactic which makes *nonsystematic* use of one aspect of the fading procedure. In a study involving four to six year old non-reading nursery school children, Corey and Shamow (1972) compared a fading technique with a method that involved superimposing words over pictures "without a systematic program for the transfer of the response to the printed stimuli alone." Using a specially constructed slide projection system, the authors could present picture-word combinations wherein both were equally visible (sight method), or wherein the light transmission for pictures could gradually be reduced (fading method). Children in both the superimposition and fading groups were required simply to say the word to a toy clown, whose nose lit up after every correct identification. Verbal prompts, other than initial instructions, were not employed. A six-step fading procedure was found to be effective in facilitating oral reading, and was much more effective than was the superimposition technique. A second experiment demonstrated that the fading technique lead to greater retention of learning (on one to two month follow-up test).

In quite a different type of problem, Barlow and Agras (1973) used a fading procedure to alter the stimulus control of sexual arousal in three homosexual men. The clients sought treatment voluntarily for a problem which the investigators considered to be an example of inappropriate stimulus control. Barlow and Agras employed a procedure much like that used by Corey and Shamow in the teaching of reading. Each subject was seated before a screen on which slides of nude men and/or nude females could be shown. A device that measured expansion of the penis in response to the slides was worn by the subject. Degree of arousal was measured as a percentage of full erection. Prior to the fading treatment, each homosexual subject showed a marked penile response to slides of male nudes and relatively little response to the females slides. The fading procedure operated as follows: An attractive male slide and "the least unattractive" female slide were placed in two synchronized slide projectors. The slide projectors displayed the images superimposed over each other including the genital area. The projector controls were rigged so that increasing the brightness of one image resulted in a simultaneous decrease in the brightness of the other. The subjects began by viewing a 0 percent female, 100 percent male image. If they showed at least 75 percent of full erection during the two-minute presentation, the next step (in a 16-step process) was initiated (six percent female, 94 percent male). This stepwise process continued until the subject was making the criterion response (75 percent of full erection) to the 100 percent female, 0 percent male presentation. Stimulus control was successfully altered in all three subjects (responding in the presence of the female slide alone took 16, 29, and 105 trials for the three clients, respectively). Two of the three subjects were able to successfully approach females and engage in heterosexual intercourse subsequent to treatment. Obviously, the alteration of arousal cues is not sufficient to change behavior. Barlow and Agras pointed out that "an additional important step in the treatment of sexual deviation is to teach the client the necessary social behavior needed to implement newly acquired arousal and thus insure the presence of positive environmental contingencies" (p. 365).

Recommendations.

• Use fading and prompting in combination with reinforcement for desired behavior or successive approximation procedures (as in the Hingtgen and Trost example).

• Use prompts that are as close as possible to those which the learner will encounter in the "real life" situation for which he is being groomed.

• Prompts must be distinctive to snare the attention of young, active learners. In noisy classrooms, only a noisier (louder) prompt can be expected to signal children of a change in the contingencies.

• Gradually fade out the use of artificial prompts (i.e., those not found in the natural environment).

• Establish a criterion for fading (as in Barlow and Agras' example) when the objective is the switching of control from one stimulus to another. The reader is referred to the section on Stimulus Control for further examples and recommendations relevant to the topics of fading and prompting.

(2) INCREASING THE LIKELIHOOD OF DESIRABLE BEHAVIOR

(A) Positive Reinforcement

Rationale. We have seen how the systematic application of response-contingent positive reinforcement can aid in the development of new behaviors. With response strengthening or maintenance as the objective, positive reinforcement again plays a major (if not a starring) role. Whether the target be simple motor acts or "higher level" responses such as attitudes or opinions, the contingent application of reinforcing outcomes is likely to affect the desired acceleration in rate. Positive contingency control may well be the most versatile tool in the realm of behavior change!

Illustrations. The varied role of positive reinforcements in the formation, maintenance and change of marriage relationships is illustrated in the work of Azrin, Naster, and Jones (1973). These authors suggest that the expectation of reinforcement from marriage (sex, companionship, financial gain, social approval, etc.) is a key factor in its initiation, but that in a marriage new sources of positive and negative reinforcers are created and existing sources are rearranged. "The nature and degree of the positive and negative reinforcers for each marital partner will, therefore, be in a constant state of flux. As such no fixed contract or agreement prior to or during marriage can assure maximum happiness and minimal annoyance in the future" (p. 367). Generally, the absence of reciprocity in reinforcer exchange is a major source of marital discord. Specifically, reinforcers received by each spouse may be too infrequent, too restricted, and bought at too great a price, such as the loss of new sources of satisfaction and of personal independence. Reciprocity counseling is designed to maximize the success of marital exchange by focusing on the presence of reinforcers in the current (problematic) situation, by discovering new sources of mutual satisfaction within marriage, and by establishing a contract system that ensures "reciprocity as a general relation." As the authors state: "The overall feeling induced in a partner should be that the spouse is continuously striving to please him(her) and he(she) in turn will strive equally to please the spouse . . ." (p. 368). Azrin and his colleagues use a "package" approach in that they concentrate their training in nine marital problem areas, involving broad response classes and rather indirect measures of personal satisfaction. Yet the procedures are theory-derived, systematic, internally consistent, and apparently quite effective.

The application of reward techniques in classroom and other remediation-training-rehabilitative settings have been growing in popularity and sophistication since Dr. Arthur Staats' demonstrations in the late fifties of the efficacy of token reinforcers in the treatment of reading problems of children. Ward and Baker

(1968), for example, taught first grade teachers how to switch their payoffs to correct the disruptive classroom behavior of selected children. Following a five week baseline phase, during which eight categories of behavior were observed by trained college undergraduates employing an interval recording system, a seven week treatment phase was introduced. Teachers ignored (extinguished) deviant behaviors such as crying, screaming, running, and thumb sucking, and reinforced with *attention* and *praise* (conditioned reinforcers) task relevant "productive" behaviors. Teachers were taught to follow the rule of giving reinforcers *contingently*, *consistently*, and *immediately*. The use of this rather restricted intervention with minimal training of teachers resulted in an almost 20 percent decline in deviant behavior. O'Leary and Becker (1967) employed conditioned reinforcers (tokens), backed up by candy and toys, in a class for highly disruptive children. The mean daily percentage of disruptive behavior fell from a range of 66 to 91 percent in baseline to a range of 3 to 32 percent during the phase involving token reinforcement of appropriate behavior.

Recommendations.

• Identify reinforcers by observing their functional effects on behavior rather than assuming that what is a reward for one individual will serve the same function for another.
• Identify activity reinforcers after systematic observation of the individual across and within a variety of natural settings.
• Deliver reinforcers immediately, contingently, and consistently to maximize response strengthening.
• Reinforce behavior often while bringing it to optimal frequency; then, "thin out" reinforcement to maximize resistance-to-extinction.
• Use a variety of reinforcers to minimize loss of potency due to repeated presentation of a single reinforcing stimulus or event.
• Use social reinforcement (the verbal and nonverbal behavior of people) whenever feasible to permit the developing behavior to be maintained across settings. If necessary develop social reinforcer effectiveness by fading the use of primary reinforcers.

(B) Negative Reinforcement

Rationale. If an individual is subjected to aversive (unpleasant or painful) stimulation, any action which results in the withdrawal of that stimulation is reinforced. In nature, learning to escape or avoid harm or fear of harm is strengthened by a process of negative reinforcement. The reader will note that, in terms of operations and effects, negative reinforcement is the mirrored reverse of punishment—noxious stimuli are terminated (rather than presented) for the purpose of increasing (rather than decreasing) response frequency. Negative reinforcement is most often used for strengthening adaptive avoidance responses (e.g., learning to give up smoking, drinking, or fattening foods). It should be clear, however, that the use of negative reinforcement in a controlled setting (the animal laboratory or a therapist's óffice) constitutes an aversive approach to behavior change, with many of the potential drawbacks associated with punishment procedures (see the present discussion of punishment and also Chapter 9 in this volume).

Illustrations. Negative reinforcement (escape-avoidance conditioning) procedures have been applied to the treatment of homosexuality by Feldman and MacCulloch (1971) and their associates. They call their procedure Anticipatory Avoidance (AA). Male homosexual patients are taught to associate slides of attractive males with electric shock. The pictorial stimuli that cue the onset of the shock soon come to elicit anticipatory fear. The patients learn to avoid the aversive consequences (and the fear) by removing the male stimuli from the screen within eight seconds of their presentation. Hence, in AA, avoidance of homosexual stimuli is reinforced by its production of *relief* from anxiety.

Penick, Filion, Fox, and Stunkard (1971) employed a "symbolic" aversive stimulus in a negative self-reinforcement program for weight control. The behaviors to be accelerated were associated with dieting. While weight reduction can be thought of as resulting in the positive consequence of looking and feeling better, the subjects also arranged for a negatively reinforcing event to occur contingent upon weight loss. The dieter stored large pieces of pork fat in his refrigerator equal in amount to the excess weight to be lost. The investigators simply instructed their subjects to remove the bags of fat contingent upon proportional weight loss. This technique, in combination with others, seemed very effective. Of course the nature of the aversive stimulus, the delay of removal, its "self-mediation," and the absence of any warning stimulus make the weight control program quite unlike most of the laboratory-derived techniques currently in use. However, in general, negative reinforcement can be effective for the treatment of such problems as drug addiction, alcoholism, smoking, and obesity *for which the acquisition of avoidance responses seems clinically desirable and is an expressed goal of the client*.

Recommendations.

• When using negative reinforcement to teach avoidance, provide an incompatible, alternate approach response. In treating an alcoholic, for example, one might arrange for shock during alcohol consumption to be terminated by a response which causes some other beverage to be delivered.

• The termination of the aversive stimulus should be contingent, immediate, and consistent.

• Remember that in avoidance conditioning two events are connected: (1) the aversive stimulus, and (2) the cue to the onset of the aversive stimulus (called the *conditioned aversive stimulus* or CAS). The individual who learns to avoid or remove himself from a situation containing the CAS also causes the association of the CAS and the aversive event to be weakened. Thus, avoidance may also start to weaken. As conditioning proceeds, it is advisable to pair the CAS and the aversive stimulus on an intermittent basis with decreasing frequency.

- The time between escape or avoidance trials must not be too brief. The aversive stimulus should be off long enough to make the "relief" enjoyable.
- If, over time, the individual is not making reliable avoidance or escape responses bring the training to a halt and determine (1) if unknown contingencies (outside of therapy) are interfering with the program or (2) if the aversive consequences are, indeed, functionally aversive.

(C) Stimulus Control

Rationale. Systematically observing the variations in individual behavior across situations will reveal that certain stimuli reliably predict responding more than others. By controlling the antecedent conditions that set the occasion for reinforced behavior, one can produce an increase in the likelihood of response emission. Four classes of antecedent events can be identified: (1) discriminative stimuli that have been linked to response-contingent reinforcement in the past, (2) verbal cues or "rules," the adherence to which have previously resulted in reinforcement, (3) facilitating stimuli, the provision of which makes responding easier (e.g., new clothes facilitate social interaction), and (4) motivational operations that heighten the effectiveness of reinforcement (such as prior deprivation).

In many therapeutic situations, it is easier, cheaper, or faster to program antecedent stimuli for appropriate responding than to try to identify and alter the contingencies. And, as we have already seen, not all clinical problems require behavior acceleration or deceleration—but rather responding in the right place and at the right time (stimulus control development).

Illustrations. Schutte and Hopkins (1970) developed adult verbal control in a kindergarten classroom by training the teacher in the differential use of contingent attention (reinforcement). A list of ten instructions was drawn up (e.g., "Pick up the toys," "Come and get a pencil and paper,") and presented to a group of five girls between 4.8 and 6 years old. The teacher, equipped with stopwatch and score sheet recorded whether her instructions were followed (within 15 seconds). The teacher waited two minutes between instructions. During the first baseline the children had a mean daily instruction-following rate of 60 percent. However, when the teacher made a "natural verbal response" contingent on compliance to instructions (such as "That's nice," or "Thank you for doing what I asked"), the children followed the instructions 78 percent of the time. Removal of the contingencies led to a decline to 68.7 percent; and a second reinforcement phase produced instruction following between 80 and 90 percent (average = 83.7 percent). These results were accomplished in just 20 daily sessions of 20 minutes each.

We might ask if stimulus control procedures can work in more complex settings with adults, involving more resistant problems—such as weight control. As one component in their successful behavioral program for weight control, Stuart and his colleagues (Stuart and Davis, 1972) teach their clients to strengthen the antecedents of appropriate eating. For example, dieters are urged to provide themselves an assortment of acceptable (prescribed) foods and to monitor their cumulative consumption (on handy pocket record sheets). In essence, the dieter restricts or "programs" his environment to maximize success. Fussy eaters can pick and choose—but only from among appropriate food stimuli. Since eating is often cued by the physical characteristics (size, texture, color, etc.) of food, the dieter is also taught to employ low-calorie "garnishments" and "embellishments" (such as parsley and paprika).

Another method of stimulus control, usually employed in conjunction with provision of cues for appropriate behavior, is the weakening of cues for inappropriate behavior. This simultaneous strengthening-weakening tactic employing antecedent stimuli parallels the tandem application of positive reinforcement and extinction in contingency management. In the case of Stuart's dieters, the stimulus control program included such suggestions as eating in only one room, not engaging in any other behaviors while eating (such as talking or watching television), and clearing one's plate directly into the garbage. These "elimination steps" were designed to narrow or reduce the range of cues precipitating overeating.

Recommendations.

• To use stimulus control effectively, identify by observation (not deduction) the functional links between antecedent cues and behaviors to be accelerated.
• Identify the cues for inappropriate behavior.
• Remove cues for inappropriate behavior.
• Make cues for appropriate responding more conspicuous. If certain individuals serve as S^Ds for the appropriate behavior of others, then arrange to have the facilitating persons occupy a more "central" place in the environment.
• Do not overwork stimulus control. Remember, each nonreinforced presentation of a stimulus will weaken its power to evoke responding.
• If an arbitrary cue has been established as a discriminative stimulus, gradually fade in "natural" antecedents.
• Train the individual to take over the cue control of his own behavior (see Chapters 10 and 11).

(3) REDUCING THE LIKELIHOOD OF EXCESSIVE BEHAVIOR

(A) Punishment

Rationale. Aside from legal and ethical considerations, punishment as a method of behavior influence is an "aversive" topic for psychologists because of technical complexities. Reese (1966) succinctly points out that punishment is a complex process:

> It can affect emotional respondent behavior . . . it can affect operants other than the one punished; and its effects on the punished operant itself are a function of several variables, including the subjects' motivation, the severity of the aversive stimulus, the schedule on which punishment is delivered, and many more. (p. 31.)

Punishment procedures can be effective when *properly applied* to behaviors that (a) involve immediate physical danger to the actor or to others in his environment or that (b) cannot be prevented through the control of antecedent cues or reinforcing consequences. When using punishment, one should be prepared to deal with the client's frequent efforts to avoid or escape the "treatment," and, in so doing, to engage in behaviors that are more detrimental than those that are supposedly being "treated." Undesirable outcomes are also likely to occur when punishment is used "as a last resort." Indeed, any procedure that is instituted by an individual or a "system" (a hospital, a school, a prison, etc.) "when all else has failed" has a good chance of being misapplied. Anger, frustration, resentment, desperation, and/or over-commitment can all too easily undermine the goal of therapeutic behavior change.

Illustration. Bucher and King (1971) worked with an 11-year old boy, John, diagnosed as retarded and schizophrenic, whose penchant for playing with electrical devices (TV sets, radios, record players) was both dangerous and costly. The problem had persisted for the five years of John's hospitalization. The therapists wanted to suppress the undesirable behavior across a variety of situations, including those where John would be completely alone.

A chalk circle (3-foot radius) was drawn around a nonfunctional electrical appliance in the treatment room. Baseline measures, taken of how often John touched the appliance or went within the chalk circle, indicated that he did so under a variety of conditions: with a volunteer present or absent, ignoring or playing with John, or restraining John then ignoring him. Thereafter an electric shock was applied to John's arm (producing a "sharp, stinging sensation") whenever he touched the appliance. Over 36 shock sessions, conducted with 16 different setting variations (number of appliances present, different rooms, etc.) the frequency of undesirable responses (and shocks) declined. In general, John learned quickly. He never received more than three shocks in a 10 minute session and showed discrimination among settings. The therapist (a volunteer) was careful not to use verbal prompts, lest John learn to suppress *only* under the therapist's verbal direction.

According to Bucher and King, the child's behavior improved at home and in the hospital school.

Recommendations. Where positive control and nonphysical forms of punishment are ineffective in changing behavior, the use of response-contingent aversive stimulation (RCAS) is best carried out in keeping with the following guidelines:

• Use RCAS in conjunction with positive reinforcement of appropriate behavior.
• Deliver RCAS as soon as possible after a misbehavior.
• The duration of RCAS need not be very long (with moderate electric shocks, a duration of 0.1 second has proven effective).
• Deliver RCAS on a continuous schedule until the response is suppressed or eliminated.

- The intensity level of RCAS should be as high as is ethically permissible.
- Avoid extended periods of RCAS.
- The individual who delivers RCAS should do so only if he is in agreement with the clinical decision that dictates its use.
- Effective and acceptable alternatives to shock and intense auditory stimulation should be sought. For example, pinching, hand-slapping, and even tickling can suppress behavior in youngsters for whom shock would appear to caretakers as unduly harsh or untenable.
- Use fading techniques to bring punished responses under discriminative control.

(B) Extinction

Rationale. Many deviant or maladaptive behaviors are strengthened by the reinforcing effects of attention. Parents and teachers turn to look at, stare down, speak to, or scream at children who are acting in a disorderly or inappropriate fashion in an effort to eliminate the behavior. When these tactics produce the opposite effect, namely, an increase in disruptive behavior, caretakers and educators tend to lapse into mentalistic explanations: "Billy is unmanageable because he has his father's temper"; "Jackie is high strung and temperamental"; "Frank cannot be treated owing to an inadequately-formed superego"; "Regan just hasn't been herself lately ...." One of the most compelling arguments for the psychological approach to the alleviation of problem behavior is in the demonstrated effect of extinction—the "mere" withdrawal of reinforcement from high probability responding. One of the early accounts of successful behavior modification using operant principles was Williams' (1959) study of tantrum elimination through extinction. Since that time, extinction combined with reinforcement of incompatible, desirable behavior has been employed in literally thousands of cases—in classrooms, hospitals, nursery schools, and homes.

Extinction by itself does *not* produce immediate and consistent response reduction as is often the case in the application of aversive stimulation. In fact, when extinction is first introduced, the frequency of a response may *increase*. The clinician using extinction procedures is, therefore, advised to prepare himself, the client, and/or the nonprofessionals working on a behavior problem for the initial extinction-induced "worsening" of the target response. However, extinction will produce a gradual reduction in responding over time. The rate at which a behavior is extinguished has been shown to be a function of the reinforcement schedule under which it was acquired or maintained. Generally speaking, extinction takes longer when the response was acquired under an intermittent or irregular schedule of reinforcement (recall our slot-machine example). Resistance to extinction is a characteristic of a behavior which is troublesome only when the goal is the elimination of excessive responding. On the other hand, when establishing newly-acquired, desirable behaviors, the clinician will try to make them resistant to extinction.

Illustration. Ayllon and Michael (1959) provided one of the first demonstrations of the efficacy of extinction in the treatment of hospitalized psychotic patients. Prior to the enactment of behavioral interventions, the ward nurses conducted systematic observations of patient behavior. Data were collected on the frequency of problem behavior, on the kind of frequency of "naturally occurring" reinforcement, and (a step often neglected by untutored "behavior modifiers") on the frequency of incompatible behavior that could be used to displace the deviant responding. The results indicated that much of the undesirable patient behavior was being maintained by the contingent social approval and attention of the nursing staff. Subsequently, the nurses, who served as the "behavioral engineers" or change agents, were instructed in the use of extinction (being asked, for example, to "ignore the behavior and act deaf and blind whenever it occurs").

The goal for Helen, a patient described as delusional, was the extinction of her "psychotic talk." More than 90 percent of Helen's conversation focussed on her illegitimate child and the men who were after her. After the nurses were instructed to use extinction plus reinforcement of other conversational topics, the sick talk dropped steadily—to a low of less than 25 percent relative frequency on the tenth week (the delusional talk had persisted for three years previously). When the psychotic talk appeared again at higher frequency, it was discovered that Helen was obtaining "bootleg" reinforcement from individuals unfamiliar with the extinction program. The power of extinction was, nonetheless, clearly demonstrated. The reader is referred to Ayllon and Azrin (1968) for further illustrations of the use of extinction with hospitalized patients, and to O'Leary and O'Leary (1972) for examples of classroom applications.

Recommendations.

• Use extinction of inappropriate responding in conjunction with positive reinforcement for incompatible or appropriate behavior.

• Extinction is effective only if the behavioral engineer has correctly identified the reinforcing stimulus to be withheld. Difficulties and failures in the use of extinction can be minimized (1) by careful and reliable observation of the problem situation, with an eye toward identifying *all possible reinforcers* contingent upon undesirable behavior, (2) by interviewing the target person to ascertain (e.g., through the use of a reinforcer survey) the current effective reinforcers in his or her life.

• Extinction works best if all those who are potential reinforcers of inappropriate behavior work toward withholding the payoff. Thus teachers may need to work with parents, hospital personnel will need to be coordinated, and in general every available resource person will need to become involved in the extinction program. Failing this, the deviant response will be intermittently reinforced, making it resistant to extinction.

• Prepare those involved with the client, especially program implementers, for the initial *increase* in the frequency of the undesirable response when extinction begins.

• Extinction, as the exclusive change method, is inappropriate (a) when the behavior must be stopped at once because it is physically harmful to the client or to others (as in the self-mutilation of children, assaultive behavior, or fire-setting), (b) when the "frustrating effects" produced by reward removal cue other behaviors which are dangerous and potentially uncontrollable (i.e., behaviors for which the cues and reinforcement contingencies are unknown or unmanageable), and (c) when the withholding of rewards for inappropriate behavior requires the withholding of rewards for desirable responses.

(C) Response Cost

Rationale. Response cost (RC) represents a form of punishment in which previously acquired primary reinforcers (such as food) or conditioned reinforcers are forfeited contingent upon an undesirable response. RC has been used in institutional settings to suppress the maladaptive behavior of psychiatric patients and retarded individuals, and in "outpatient" settings wherein clients negotiate therapeutic contracts that include RC contingencies (or the "threat" of RC). In most applied settings RC is combined with positive reinforcement for appropriate responding. Occasionally, other punishment techniques (such as time-out or aversive stimulation) are used in conjunction with RC and positive control. In a recent review of research findings, it was tentatively concluded that RC does not evoke the undesirable side-effects attributed to punishment, nor do RC-suppressed behaviors return when the RC contingency is removed (Kazdin, 1972).

Illustrations. A twenty-year old, hospitalized woman who had been labelled an anxiety-depressive, hysterical, and borderline psychotic was treated in a Behavior Modification Unit by response cost and positive reinforcement methods (Reisinger, 1972). The patient's "depressed" behavior (low rate of smiling; high rate of unprovoked crying) was the target of a change program implemented by aides trained in the use of behavior modification procedures. A baseline (nonintervention) period, where target responses were observed three times per day (for a maximum of two hours per observation), showed smiling to be at zero frequency and crying ("inarticulate" sounds accompanied by tears from the patient's eyes ... from five to 30 minutes duration ...) at approximately 29 episodes per week. After baseline, the patient was informed of two new contingencies: that crying would result in loss of tokens (poker chips redeemable for privileges), while smiling would result in receipt of tokens. Thereafter, the aide either presented a token to the patient if she was observed to engage in a smile ("a slight opening of the lips, an upward turn of the corners of the mouth, and an increase in the protrusion of the skin covering the cheek bones"), or he would approach when she cried, and simply say "You will be fined one token for crying." Over a seven week period, the rates for crying and smiling were practically reversed (27 smiles and two crying episodes in the final week of the treatment phase). A three week extinction and three week reversal phase brought crying up and smiling down (thus demonstrating the power of the contingencies). The RC contingency was then reinstated along with social (praise) and token reinforcement. Finally, the RC contingency was dropped and crying was simply ignored. The token reinforcement for smiling was discontinued but social praise was continued. A 14-month follow-up after discharge showed the patient functioning well in the community (for the first time in six years).

Boudin (1972) reported the use of a response cost contract in the outpatient treatment of amphetamine abuse. His patient, a female graduate student, had been using amphetamines for three years prior to treatment. She had resorted to lying and stealing in order to obtain drugs, and was panic-stricken at the thought that she had become an addict. Although the treatment plan involved many elements (including stimulus control, verbal encouragement, and aversive techniques) it included a "stiff" response cost arrangement wherein the client established a joint bank account with her therapist which included all of her capital ($500). The client signed ten $50 checks, which needed only the therapists' signature to be valid. It was agreed that each drug use or suspected drug use would result in the loss of one check. The RC contingency was used only once during the three month contract violation. The client (who was Black) was told that valid checks would be sent to the Ku Klux Klan.

Recommendations.

- Use response-cost (RC) procedures in conjunction with positive reinforcement for appropriate and incompatible behaviors.
- Before establishing an RC system, determine if the reinforcers potentially lost are indeed valued. They must be genuine "reinforcers" in the sense that individuals will work to earn them and will spend them on items not otherwise available.
- Arrange the overall earnings-cost program so that items lost or forfeited cannot be easily or rapidly replaced.
- Arrange the overall earnings-cost program in such a manner that "fines" are realistic (neither bankrupting the individual in a single trial, nor making so little dent in his savings that the loss goes unnoticed).
- Institute the fine as soon as possible after a misbehavior.
- For individuals who have not earned them, it may be necessary to supply reinforcers noncontingently at first. RC procedures can then be applied.
- If RC is paired with verbal criticism, it is possible to fade out the punishment contingency and bring disruptive behavior under the verbal control of change agents (therapists, teachers, parents, aides, etc.).
- With highly motivated clients, it is conceivable that imagined rather than actual reinforcer loss can be used as a punishment procedure (Kazdin, 1972; Weiner, 1965).

(D) Time-Out

Rationale. Behavior reduction can be accomplished through the withdrawal of opportunities to obtain positive reinforcers. Time-out (from reinforcement), although an unpleasant outcome (Leitenberg, 1965), does not evoke the fear and avoidant tendencies that often undermine the effects of aversive control programs. Time-out has proven useful in the management of high frequency disruptive (aggressive, assaultive, destructive) or self-defeating behaviors that appear to be cued and reinforced by the actions of observers and co-performers. When it is not feasible to identify and remove all the reinforcers for deviant behavior, the person emitting the inappropriate responses may be excluded from the problem-enhancing setting. Thus, time-out is useful in classrooms and in institutional settings where it is sometimes simpler to deal with disruptive individuals than with the entire group. If an inappropriate behavior is evidenced across diverse situations, time-out contingencies must be consistently used by controlling agents in each setting (cf., Chapman, 1962).

Illustration. Tyler and Brown (1967), reported the successful application of a time-out program with a group of institutionalized delinquent boys (ages 13–15), whose disruptive behavior in their cottage recreation room was of serious concern to staff. After deciding on target behaviors (throwing or hitting with a pool cue, fighting around the pool table, breaking the rules of the game, and others), the investigators initiated a procedure wherein misbehavior resulted in isolation in a time-out room for 15 minutes. "There were no warnings, no discussions, no arguments, and no second chances. When an S misbehaved, he was simply taken in a very matter-of-fact way to the time-out room. Staff might explain to the point of saying 'You fouled up,' but no more" (p. 2). The 4×8 ft. isolation room was constructed in one corner of the cottage, permitting rapid removal and return of each youngster. Misbehaviors declined under the time-out contingency, increased during reinstatement of the original conditions, and declined once again with reintroduction of time-out.

The success of the cottage time-out program is quite remarkable, considering that the investigators were working with a small staff which was not thoroughly trained in defining target behavior, with a turn-over in the number of delinquent youngsters in the cottage, and with no opportunity to collect information on the peer group reaction to each offense and its consequences. Either group support or group criticism directed at "offenders" might have reinforced the misbehavior and undermined the program. Tyler and Brown speculate that the mildness of the time-out procedure was critical in its success.

> The cottage staff became quite skilled in confining youngsters in a perfunctory non-emotional way which probably minimized the possibility of the group "rallying" and "making a martyr" of the offending S. It is speculated that the mild punishment made it less likely that the staff would evidence feelings of guilt or revenge (p. 6).

No provision was made, in this case, for the systematic reinforcement of alternative desirable behavior, as operant technology dictates. Indeed, the authors suggested that such a procedure might have added to the effectiveness of their program.

Recommendations.

* Use time-out (TO) in conjunction with positive reinforcement of desirable and incompatible behaviors.
* Arrange the time-out area to be free of attractive or distracting activities. It should be small, but well ventilated. Arrange the area in which appropriate behavior is desired in as attractive a manner as possible (with reinforcing activities and

objects immediately available for appropriate behavior). Absence of effects for TO are often attributable to the relatively low magnitude of payoff for correct responding.

* The majority of successful programs with children employ TO durations of between five and 20 minutes. Long durations are undesirable because the individual is removed from opportunities to learn more adaptive responses. One should experiment with short durations of TO first and, if need be, work up to longer durations. Starting out with long durations and subsequently shortening them is *not* recommended (cf., White, Nielsen, and Johnson, 1972).

* In keeping with the TO duration requirements, the distance and travel time to the TO area should be short.

* If possible, monitor the individual's behavior while in TO. The child who can make a "game" out of TO, will not benefit from it.

* Try not to reinforce any behaviors (either with positive attention or with a display of anger or disappointment) while going to or returning from the TO area.

* Use verbal and/or nonverbal signals before initiating a TO. The chain of behaviors leading up to the TO signal should include a "stop cue" which, if noticed, may come to suppress the disruptive behavior at lower magnitudes.

* Never use TO if the situation from which the individual is being removed is primarily an unpleasant one. The child will simply turn TO into an escape or avoidance opportunity, and the behavior upon which TO is contingent will increase in frequency!

(E) Satiation and Restraint

A response that is continuously emitted and reinforced over a brief time span may show a temporary decline in frequency. The individual may tire of responding, and the reinforcer will lose its power to motivate and to inform. Indeed, the requirement of continued performance may turn a once pleasant activity into an aversive one. Perhaps the most well known clinical example of satiation is provided in Ayllon's (1963) famous towel hoarding case. A hospital patient who collected towels in her room (averaging about 20) was, after a baseline period, presented with free towels on a noncontingent basis (reaching 60 a day by the third treatment week). The patient started removing the towels after she had upwards of 625 of them in her room. Following satiation treatment the patient permanently gave up towel hoarding.

Although a "classic," Ayllon's is not a pure case of satiation treatment since the "reinforcer" was delivered noncontingently. The satiation approach to the treatment of habitual cigarette smoking, however, requires that smoker engage in the response continuously (on command) and experience the outcome until the process becomes intolerable. Schmahl, Lichtenstein, and Harris (1972) have reported that stimulus satiation combined with having to inhale either warm smoky air or mentholated air rapidly reduced smoking behavior to zero, with approximately 60 percent of the subjects still abstaining after six months.

Response reduction can also be accomplished via physical restraint. In severe or extreme cases involving dangerous or life-threatening behavior, the individual may need to be confined and physically restricted. This is a practical method which only temporarily reduces disruptive responding. However, the risks are so great that the theoretically low long-range efficiency is not important.

(4) MAINTAINING BEHAVIORAL PROGRESS

The *adaptational-learning* model outlined in this chapter is built upon the proposition that human adjustment is a fluid process, that shifts in what is considered the "appropriate" direction or form of behavior represent the challenge and excitement as well as the stress and upheaval of modern life. As therapists or change agents we want our interventions to have durable effects in the face of ever-changing environmental demands. Yet, we do not want to produce an "improved" behavior which, in time, may itself be in need of alteration. Let's briefly examine the problems of *persistence* and *obsolescence* of learning.

(A) Persistence of Treatment Effects

The paradox of operant technology is that its power to affect change may be bought at the expense of generalization or persistence of treatment gains. Evidence is now accumulating which suggests that changes brought about in hospitals, clinics, residential facilities, or in the therapist's office often fail to extend to the other relevant behavior settings in a client's life. One reason for the failure of persistence is the dissimilarity of treatment environments from the "real life" settings in which clients are expected to function. Obviously, when discriminative stimuli and reinforcement contingencies change, so does behavior.

However, our knowledge about stimulus control procedures, schedule effects, and the creation of conditioned reinforcers provides some possible remedies to persistence and generalization problems, as do newer developments in the area of environmental control. Data bearing on the comparative effectiveness of the various techniques for maintenance-induction are, unfortunately, not yet available.

First, the most obvious way to ensure resistance to extinction of a newly acquired operant is to reinforce it on an intermittent schedule. While a continuous schedule of reward may be necessary in developing a response, durability in the absence of programmed contingencies is made possible by schedule "thinning," i.e., gradual shifting from a variable ratio to a variable interval and from an immediate to a more delayed format. Sudden transitions are to be avoided. Kanfer and Phillips (1970), in fact, suggest training a client in the ability to "tolerate" changing schedules might be an explicit goal of treatment.

We have discussed fading in some detail as a response building technique. However, fading can be employed to introduce into a client's repertoire discriminated operants with genuine "survival" value. For example, it is necessary for a chronically hospitalized patient to learn to smile and say "Good morning," not only to the ward nurses, but to others who might appropriately elicit such a response (friends, relatives, hospital staff and patients who live on the same ward). The motto of stimulus generalization might be "Fade out the artificial, Fade in the natural."

Responsiveness to various cues is a necessity for generalization, as is responsiveness to increasing varieties and more natural kinds of reinforcers. In a halfway house for delinquent girls, where the writer serves as consultant, the practice of coaxing girls into new (ordinarily low probability) activities—such as playing baseball together, going to concerts, or to "fancy" restaurants—is being tried to make the girls aware of alternate environments and ways of obtaining satisfaction within them.

Though usually considered impractical, re-programming of the natural social environment has also been suggested as a maintenance measure (cf., Atthowe, 1973; Patterson, McNeal, Hawkins, and Phelps, 1967). Often it is the reluctance of mental-health professionals to leave their offices, to "mix it up" with members of a client's family or peer group, to learn new skills, to consult with those whose skills might be helpful, that dictates the "impracticality" of environmental manipulation. Today, psychologists are being urged to become social planners—and some are taking up the challenge. The recognition that nonprofessionals—parents, siblings, friends, teachers, employers, etc.—can and do perform the job of behavioral engineer has contributed greatly to a new look in psychotherapy and to a new kind of "team approach." It will require a special team, however, to help redesign environments for individuals with a long history of marginal performance. For these individuals, Atthowe (1973) suggests that:

> Rehabilitation mediators can be of three types: (a) the indigenous leader who is a social reinforcing agent in the community to whom others turn for help and advice; (b) the political influencer who knows how to deal with the relevant power structure, the Ralph Nader of mental health; and (c) the trained rehabilitation worker and specialist. (p. 37.)

It is important to note that only rarely should a target operant be maintained in its original form over time and across a variety of settings. Response generalization (the increase in frequency of responses similar to the target operant but not explicitly reinforced in training) is usually a necessity, as the individual will be exposed to persons and situations that require alternate "versions" of the newly acquired behavior. Obviously, then, planning for response generalization is another prerequisite for complete behavioral training. Thus, in addition to changing the cues and reinforcers, within and outside of the training environment, it will be necessary to change response requirements as well, building flexibility into the learner's repertoire. For further discussion and illustration of the programmed maintenance of behavior the reader is referred to Rubin and Stolz (1974), Walker and Buckley (1972), and O'Leary, Poulos, and Devine (1972).

(B) Obsolescence

The requirement of building the potential for flexibility into our training involves a recognition of the nonmechanical nature of people and of programs. Although still a controversial issue, the question of *what is learned* in behavioral training is being answered by some in terms of "learning sets," "self-regulatory skills," "expectancies," "problem-solving abilities," and "rules of the game." Obsolescence (the long-range limiting effects) of training is certainly mitigated to the extent that recognition is given to the active role of the learner in the process of behavior change. The available data on the ability of individuals to maintain their own behavior by self-generated stimuli and reinforcement and to show even unprogrammed stimulus and response generalization indicates that changing a human being's behavioral repertoire is in no way analogous to changing a light bulb. Obsolescence need only be a problem to the unsophisticated user of general behavioral techniques.

SUMMARY

This chapter has provided a broad overview of the applied science of operant conditioning, known as *the experimental analysis of behavior*. The defining characteristics of this approach include: (1) a focus on precise definition and measurement of observable behaviors, (2) the functional analysis of environmental antecedents and consequences that control maladaptive responding, (3) the use of principles derived from experimental studies of learning in the design of treatment interventions, and (4) the continuous evaluation of behavior change.

But it is not just technology that sets an operant approach apart from the traditional insight-oriented systems of psychotherapy. The techniques described here for establishing new behaviors, accelerating personally and interpersonally desirable behaviors, decelerating maladaptive modes of responding, and maintaining treatment-induced learning are all applied in the context of an objective and nonjudgmental view of human action. A behavior is not selected for change because it is unconventional, contrary to someone's view of "human nature," or listed in a catalogue of symptoms. Rather, when the relationship between an individual's behavior, or pattern of behaviors, and the effective environment is reliably disruptive of that individual's pursuit of personal objectives, his ability to adjust to his life circumstances, or his sense of comfort, satisfaction, or freedom *and* when the behavioral clinician is technically and ethically able to intervene, then the two will embark jointly on a venture in behavior modification. In the case of behavior modification with "problem children," the negotiating client may be the parents or the teacher; but their behavior change objective must, in fact, be in the "adaptive" interests of the child.

The task of behavior change is, in a sense, secondary to the complete functional analysis of a specific problem and its social and environmental determinants. Following a behavioral assessment, therapeutic goals can be established, subject to continued revision. Treatment consists, essentially, of the systematic use of four procedures: reinforcement, punishment, extinction, and stimulus control—singly, and in various combinations.

REFERENCES

American Psychiatric Association. *Diagnostic and statistical manual of mental disorders*. Second Ed., Washington, D.C.: APA, 1968.

Atthowe, J. M. Behavior innovation and persistence. *American Psychologist*, 1973, **28**, 34–41.

Ayllon, T. Intensive treatment of psychotic behavior by stimulus satiation and food reinforcement. *Behaviour Research and Therapy*, 1963, **1**, 53–61.

Ayllon, T. and Azrin, N. H. *The token economy: A motivational system for therapy and rehabilitation*. New York: Appleton-Century-Crofts, 1968.

Ayllon, T. and Michael, J. The psychiatric nurse as a behavioral engineer. *Journal of the Experimental Analysis of Behavior*, 1959, **2**, 323–334.

Azrin, N. H., Naster, B. J., and Jones, R. Reciprocity counseling: A rapid learning based procedure for marital counseling. *Behaviour Research and Therapy*, 1973, **11**, 365–382.

Baer, D. M., Wolf, M. M., and Risley, T. R. Some current dimensions of applied behavior analysis. *Journal of Applied Behavior Analysis*, 1968, **1**, 91–97.

Barlow, D. H. and Agras, W. S. Fading to increase heterosexual responsiveness in homosexuals. *Journal of Applied Behavior Analysis*, 1973, **6**, 355–366.

Blackwood, R. O. *Operant control of behavior*. Akron, Ohio: Exordium Press, 1971.

Boudin, H. M. Contingency contracting as a therapeutic tool in the deceleration of amphetamine use. *Behavior Therapy*, 1972, **3**, 604–608.

Bucher, B. and King, L. W. Generalization of punishment effects in the deviant behavior of a psychotic child. *Behavior Therapy*, 1971, **2**, 68–77.

Chapman, R. W. School suspension as therapy. *Personnel and Guidance Journal*, 1962, **40**, 731–732.

Corey, J. R. and Shamow, J. The effects of fading on the acquisition and retention of oral reading. *Journal of Applied Behavior Analysis*, 1972, **5**, 311–315.

Deese, J. and Hulse, S. H. *The psychology of learning*. New York: McGraw-Hill, 1967.

Feldman, M. P. and MacCulloch, M. J. *Homosexual behavior: Therapy and assessment*. Oxford: Pergamon Press, 1971.

Ferster, C. B. and Perrott, M. C. *Behavior principles*. New York: Appleton-Century-Crofts, 1968.

Ferster, C. B. and Skinner, B. F. *Schedules of reinforcement*. New York: Appleton-Century-Crofts, 1957.

Findley, J. D. An experimental outline for building and exploring multi-operant behavior repertoires. *Journal of the Experimental Analysis of Behavior*, 1962, **5**, 113–166.

Gottman, J. M. and Leiblum, S. R. *How to do psychotherapy and how to evaluate it*. New York: Holt, Rinehart and Winston, 1974.

Hilgard, E. R. and Bower, G. H. *Theories of learning*. New York: Appleton-Century-Crofts, 1966.

Hingtgen, J. N. and Trost, F. C. Shaping cooperative responses in early childhood schizophrenics: II. Reinforcement of mutual physical contact and vocal responses. In R. Ulrich, T. Stachnik, and J. Mabry (Eds.), *Control of human behavior*. Glenview, Illinois: Scott, Foresman, 1966.

Holland, C. J. An interview guide for behavioral counseling with parents. *Behavior Therapy*, 1970, **1**, 70–79.

Homme, L., deBaca, P., Cottingham, L., and Homme, A. What behavioral engineering is. *The Psychological Record*, 1968, **18**, 425–434.

Kanfer, F. H. and Phillips, J. S. *Learning foundations of behavior therapy*. New York: Wiley, 1970.

Kanfer, F. H. and Saslow, G. Behavioral diagnosis. In C. M. Franks (Ed.), *Behavior therapy; Appraisal and status*. New York: McGraw-Hill, 1969, 417–444.

Kazdin, A. E. Response cost: The removal of conditioned reinforcers for therapeutic change. *Behavior Therapy*, 1972, **3**, 533–546.

Kolb, L. C. *Modern clinical psychiatry*. Philadelphia, Pa.: Saunders, 1973.

Lazarus, A. A. *Behavior therapy and beyond*. New York: McGraw-Hill, 1971.

Leitenberg, H. Is time-out from positive reinforcement an aversive event? A review of experimental evidence. *Psychological Bulletin*, 1965, **64**, 428–441.

Levy, L. H. *Conceptions of personality*. New York: Random House, 1970.

Millenson, J. R. *Principles of behavioral analysis*. New York: Macmillan, 1967.

O'Leary, K. D. and Becker, W. C. Behavior modification of an adjustment class. *Exceptional Children*, 1967, **33**, 637–642.

O'Leary, K. D. and O'Leary, S. G. (Eds.) *Classroom management*. New York: Pergamon Press, 1972.

O'Leary, K. D., Poulos, R. W., and Devine, V. T. Tangible reinforcers: Bonuses or bribes. *Journal of Consulting and Clinical Psychology*, 1972, **38**, 1–8.

Patterson, G. R., McNeal, S., Hawkins, N., and Phelps, R. Reprogramming the social environment. *Journal of Child Psychology and Psychiatry*, 1967, **8**, 181–195.

Penick, S. B., Filion, R., Fox, S., and Stunkard, A. J. Behavior modification in the treatment of obesity. *Psychosomatic Medicine*, 1971, **33**, 49–55.

Rachlin, H. *Introduction to modern behaviorism*. San Francisco, Calif.: Freeman, 1970.

Reese, E. P. *The analysis of human operant behavior*. Dubuque, Iowa: Brown, 1966.

Reisinger, J. J. The treatment of "anxiety-depression" via positive reinforcement and response cost. *Journal of Applied Behavior Analysis*, 1972, **5**, 125–130.

Reynolds, G. S. *A primer of operant conditioning*. Glenview, Ill.: Scott, Foresman, 1968.

Rubin, B. K. and Stolz, S. B. Generalization of self-referent speech established in a retarded adolescent by operant procedures. *Behavior Therapy*, 1974, **5**, 93–106.

Schmahl, D. P., Lichtenstein, E., and Harris, D. E. Successful treatment of habitual smokers with warm, smoky air and rapid smoking. *Journal of Consulting and Clinical Psychology*, 1972, **38**, 105–111.

Schutte, R. C. and Hopkins, B. L. The effects of teacher attention of following instructions in a kindergarten class. *Journal of Applied Behavior Analysis*, 1970, **3**, 117–122.

Schwitzgebel, R. K. and Kolb, D. A. *Changing human behavior: Principles of planned intervention*. New York: McGraw-Hill, 1974.

Skinner, B. F. Two types of conditioned reflex: A reply to Konorski and Miller. *Journal of General Psychology*, 1937, **16**, 272–279.

Skinner, B. F. *The behavior of organisms: An experimental analysis*. New York: Appleton-Century-Crofts, 1938.

Stuart, R. B. and Davis, B. *Slim chance in a fat world*. Champaign, Ill.: Research Press, 1972.

Thorndike, E. L. Animal intelligence: An experimental study of associative processes in animals. *Psychological Monographs*, 1898, **2**, (No. 2).

Tyler, V. O. and Brown, G. D. The use of swift, brief isolation as a group control device for institutionalized delinquents. *Behaviour Research and Therapy*, 1967, **5**, 1–9.

Wahler, R. G. and Cormier, W. The ecological interview: A first step in out-patient child behavior therapy. *Journal of Behavior Therapy and Experimental Psychiatry*, 1970, **1**, 279–289.

Walker, H. M. and Buckley, N. K. Programming generalization and maintenance of treatment effects across time and across settings. *Journal of Applied Behavior Analysis*, 1972, **5**, 209–224.

Ward, M. H. and Baker, B. L. Reinforcement therapy in the classroom. *Journal of Applied Behavior Analysis*, 1968, **1**, 323–328.

Watson, L. S. *Child behavior modification: A manual for teachers, nurses, and parents*. New York: Pergamon Press, 1973.

Weiner, H. Real and imagined cost effects upon human fixed-interval responding. *Psychological Reports*, 1965, **17**, 659–662.

White, G. D., Nielsen, G., and Johnson, S. M. Time-out duration and the suppression of deviant behavior in children. *Journal of Applied Behavior Analysis*, 1972, **5**, 111–120.

Williams, C. D. The elimination of tantrum behavior by extinction procedures: A case report. *Journal of Abnormal and Social Psychology*, 1959, **59**, 269.

Williams, J. L. *Operant learning: Procedures for changing behavior*. Monterey, California: Brooks/Cole, 1973.

Wolpe, J. *The practice of behavior therapy*, 2nd Ed. New York: Pergamon Press, 1973.

CHAPTER 8

Fear Reduction Methods

RICHARD J. MORRIS*

Much of the effort of psychotherapists is directed toward helping people overcome their fears of situations, other people, animals, and/or objects. Fear is a very strong emotion and is associated with many signs of anxiety—for example, rapid pulse rate and a pounding heart, very tense muscles, perspiring in a room of average temperature and humidity, "butterflies" in the stomach, irritability, inability to concentrate, dizziness, and headaches. When someone experiences fear in a situation where there is no obvious external danger, his fear is irrational and is called a *phobia*. Table 8.1 lists a number of common phobias which people experience. When a person begins to avoid a non-dangerous feared situation—even though he realizes that such behavior is foolish or irrational—his fear then turns into a *phobic reaction*.

Table 8.1. Selected Phobias Which People Experience.

Technical Name	Fear
Acrophobia	Heights
Agoraphobia	Open places
Aichmophobia	Sharp and pointed objects
Claustrophobia	Enclosed places
Menophobia	Being alone
Nyctophobia	Darkness
Ochlophobia	Crowds
Pyrophobia	Fires
Xenophobia	Strangers
Zoophobia	Animals

*The author wishes to express his gratitude to Vinnie Morris, Mark Sherman, Kenneth Suckerman, Elaine Morisano, John O'Neill, and Marcie Berman, for critically reading various preliminary drafts of this chapter.

Phobic reactions are among the most common forms of maladaptive behavior in people. They occur in both children and adults. Some phobias, because of their high incidence, are considered "normal" in children, while others are viewed as "normal" in adults. For example, fear of dogs and other animals, fear of the dark, ghosts, and being alone are among the more common childhood phobias, while fear of heights, bugs, and snakes frequently occurs in adults. Some irrational fears are fleeting while others persist over a long time.

When fears become intolerable to an individual, professional help is sought. Over the past 75 years, various procedures have been used in the treatment of fears. Psychoanalysis and other forms of "verbal therapy" have been utilized, as well as drugs, hypnosis, electro-convulsive shock treatment, and certain forms of brain surgery (e.g., leucotomy). In general, these methods have been found to be only moderately successful.

Some therapy procedures, however, have been found to be much more effective. These procedures are based on the learning theory positions of, for example, Skinner (1938, 1953), Pavlov (1927), Hull (1943), and Mowrer (1950). Though the specifics of each method differ, they do share certain general underlying assumptions: (1) phobias and the avoidance reactions which accompany them are learned by the individual, (2) phobias do not occur as a result of innate factors, and (3) phobias are not the *result* of an underlying psychic or psychological disturbance. Specifically, three procedures which have been found to be effective in the treatment of phobic reactions and fears are: *systematic desensitization, assertive training*, and *implosive therapy*. In the present chapter, we plan to describe each of these methods in detail, as well as present case examples that demonstrate their use.

SYSTEMATIC DESENSITIZATION

Systematic desensitization was developed in the early 1950's by Joseph Wolpe, a psychiatrist. The basic assumption of this technique is that a fear response (for example, a fear response to heights) can be inhibited by substituting an activity which is antagonistic to the fear response. The response which is most typically inhibited by this treatment process is anxiety, and the response frequently substituted for the anxiety is relaxation and calmness. For example, if a person has a fear of heights and feels very anxious and uncomfortable each time he has to go into a tall office building and take an elevator higher than the third floor, we would help him inhibit his anxiety in this situation by teaching him to relax and feel calm. Thus, we would *desensitize* him or *counter-condition* his fear of heights.

Desensitization is accomplished by gradually exposing an individual in small steps to the feared situation while he is performing the activity that is antagonistic to anxiety. The gradual exposure to the fear can take place either in the person's fantasy—where he is asked to imagine himself in various fear-related situations—or it can occur in real life. The principle which underlies the desensitization process is called reciprocal inhibition by Wolpe. He describes this principle in the following way: "If a response inhibitory to anxiety can be made to occur in the presence of anxiety-evoking stimuli, it will weaken the connection between these stimuli and the anxiety responses" (Wolpe, 1962, p. 562).

The Initial Interview

Before initiating the desensitization procedure, or any of the other fear reduction methods discussed in this chapter, the therapist must first identify the client's fear(s) as well as the circumstances under which his fear(s) occurs. This is not an easy assignment. The interview must be conducted within a therapeutic atmosphere of respect for the client, sensitivity to and understanding of the client's difficulties, and genuine concern for his overall well-being. The therapist has to probe *thoroughly* into the client's life history to make sure that both of them have a clear understanding of all aspects of the client's fear, as well as to those factors which have contributed (and are contributing) to his fear. Such information is also useful in helping the therapist support or refute various hypotheses about the development and maintenance of the client's problem, and in determining which fear reduction method is most appropriate for the client. It is therefore quite likely that the initial interview will last over a number of sessions.

Though there is neither a standardized approach nor a standard set of questions used in the initial interview, most therapists explore the following topic areas with clients.

Identification of the Target Behavior

This involves not only helping the client identify what is specifically troubling him, but also trying to determine the types of situations and circumstances in which his fear occurs. In addition, the therapist inquires about how long the client has had his fear, whether it has gotten better or worse with the passage of time, and the types of situations in which it seems to be better/worse than "usual." It is also desirable to ask the client about his thoughts and feelings concerning his fear.

General Background Information

Here, discussion is centered around the date and place of the client's birth, number and age of siblings, where the client stands in the family birth order, and the types of interactions he has had with his siblings while growing up. Inquiry is also made into which of the children was favored in the family, as well as how the client was treated by each of the parents relative to the other children. The therapist should also discuss other aspects regarding the parents, e.g., the client's perception of each of his parents during childhood and adolescence, how he was punished and by whom, characteristics that he liked/disliked in each parent, etc. It is also important to know the manner in which the parents interacted with each other, and to determine what type of role models they provided for the client. For example, did they generally like one another, did they fight, and, if so, was it usually in front of the children, did they ever talk about divorce or separation, and did they try to use one or all of the children against the other parent.

For many clients during their childhood there are people who are as (or more) important than their parents, e.g., favorite aunts, uncles, grandparents, etc. These "significant others" should also be discussed—making it a point to determine the unique contribution of such people to the client's life.

One additional aspect of the individual's background involves the fears which he experienced during childhood. The therapist should not only determine the particular childhood fears, but also when they occurred, when they ended, or whether they are still present.

School and Job

For this category, inquiry should be made into the client's likes and dislikes in elementary and high school and college, his best/least liked subjects, what he did after school, and what his extracurricular activities were, etc. Moreover, the therapist should discuss the client's friendships in and out of school, e.g., whether he had any close friends and if these friendships have been maintained over the years.

The client's work experience should also be brought into this discussion—asking how far he went in school and, if appropriate, why he did not continue. Particular attention should be paid to the client's work history, his likes and dislikes about his job, his ability to advance, and whether his present job is consistent with his own goals and desires.

Dating and Marriage

Here, the therapist explores the client's dating pattern during his teenage and adult years. In addition, the client's sexual experiences before and after marriage are discussed. Difficulties in the marriage are also discussed, as well as relationships with in-laws, children, and the environment in which the client lives. Since these are very sensitive topics for some people, they should be explored within a framework of understanding acceptance of the client.

A summary of a suggested guide for the initial interview is presented in Table 8.2. As the reader has no doubt already determined, the information gained in the initial interview is quite extensive. Some therapists use tape recorders to record this information, while others take notes on the client's answers. Still others have asked their clients to fill out a standard background information packet which contains many of the same types of questions as those outlined in Table 8.2.

An excerpt from part of the first session of an initial interview with a 35-year-old woman who had been recently divorced illustrates the manner in which the interview is conducted.*

---

*Throughout this chapter the case transcripts, case descriptions, and hierarchies have been changed slightly to protect the anonymity of the clients involved.

Table 8.2. Suggested Guide For The Conduct Of The Initial Interview.*

A. *What is the problem behavior? ... What seems to be troubling you?*
   1. How long have you had this problem?
   2. When does this fear or thought usually come into your mind? When does this problem seem to occur the most? In what types of situations or circumstances does the problem occur? Are there any reasons you can think of for its occurrence?
      (a) When doesn't the problem bother you?
   3. Has the problem been the same all along—or has it gotten better or worse?
      (a) Is there any situation that you can associate with it getting better or worse?
B. *General Background*
   1. When born? Where?
   2. How many brothers and sisters do you have?
      (a) Where are you in the birth order?
      (b) How much older is your eldest or youngest same sex sibling?
      (c) How did (do) you get along with him (her)?
   3. Parents—are they still alive? When did each die?
C. *Father*
   1. What kind of person was (is) he—especially during your childhood?
   2. Was he interested in you? Were you interested in what he had to say?
   3. Did he ever punish you?
   4. Did he play favorites with the children? How did you feel about this?
D. *Mother*
   Same questions asked about the father
E. *Parents*
   1. Did they like each other? Did they like you?
   2. Did they behave toward you as though they liked you?
   3. Did they get along together?
      (a) Fight much? ... Divorce threats? etc.
      (b) Did they fight in front of children or in privacy?
F. *Significant others*
   1. Were there any other adults who played an important part in your life?
   2. Describe what they were like and how they played an important role in your life.
G. *Fears during childhood*
   1. Any particular fears?
   2. When did they occur?
   3. Do you still have some of these?
H. *School*
   1. Like school?
   2. Best liked subjects: Worse liked subjects?
   3. Sports.—Did you participate in them or watch them?
      (a) How were you in them?
   4. Friends
      (a) Did you make any friends at school (college)?
      (b) Any close ones?
      (c) Do you maintain any of those friendships today?
      (d) Anyone at school (college) that you were afraid of? Was the person the same sex as you? Were you afraid of any teachers? Why?
      (e) How far did you go in school? Why did you stop your education?
   5. What did you do after you stopped school?

*Adapted from Wolpe and Lazarus (1966).

Table 8.2.   (Continued).

I. *Job*
1. What kind of work do you do?
2. Do you like your job? What do you like the best/least about your job?
3. Any thoughts about quitting?
4. What other types of jobs have you had? Why did you leave them?
5. If a client is a housewife, ask: How do you like being a housewife?
     What do you specifically like about it?
     What don't you specifically like about it?

J. *Sex*
1. At what age did you begin to have any kind of sexual feelings?
   (a) If client has problem in answering, ask: Well, roughly, were you 10, 15, 20 . . . more or less
   (b) or go to the following: Before 10? . . . Before 15? . . . Before 20? . . .
2. In what kind of situation did you have your first sexual feelings?
   For example, was it out with boys? . . . (girls?) . . . At a movie house? or what?
3. At this stage, did you date several boys (girls) or just one at a time?
   (a) Did you go to parties?
   (b) What was the pattern of your dating? . . . Always movies? . . . Dinners?
4. When did you especially become interested in anybody?
5. Was there anyone else whom you became interested in?
6. When did you become really serious? (implying going steady, become engaged, etc.) or, have you ever become serious with anyone?
   (a) What did you like about him (her)
7. Have you ever petted (made-out) with anyone? Did you ever masturbate? Any feelings of guilt or fear about doing (not doing) either of these?
8. Have you ever had intercourse? Have you ever wanted to? What stopped you?
9. (If married, ask: Did you ever have intercourse before you were married?)

K. *Marriage*
1. When did you meet your husband (wife)?
   (a) What did you like about him (her)?
2. When did you feel that you were ready to marry him (her)?
3. Was he (she) interested in marrying you?
4. Since (or while) you were married, did you ever become interested in other men (women)?
5. Is (was) your marriage satisfying? What about it makes it satisfying? What about it doesn't make it satisfying? In what way would you like to change your marriage?
6. If divorced and remarried, how about with your second husband (wife)? Is this marriage satisfying?
   (a) How is he (she) different from your first husband (wife)?
   (b) How soon after the divorce did you remarry?
   (c) Was he (she) married before?

L. *Sex and Marriage*
1. How is the sexual side of your marriage (dating)? How about the sexual side of your second marriage?
2. Do you have orgasms?
   (a) How often?
3. Are you happy with your marriage (the person you are dating)?
   (a) Any complaints?
4. Do the two of you fight with each other? That is, are there arguments?
   (a) What do you usually fight about?
   (b) How long do they usually last?
   (c) How are your fights usually resolved?
5. Any plans for marriage (thoughts of divorce)?

Table 8.2. (Continued).

M. *Children*
 1. How many children do you have? (Do you plan to have children? How many?)
 2. Do you like all of your children? Any favorites?
    (a) Are they all well?
 3. How old is each?
 4. Were they each planned?
N. *Environment*:
 1. Do you like where you are now living?
 2. Anything that you are not satisfied with?
 3. What's your religion?
    (a) Is it important to you? In what way?
    (b) How religious are you?... not at all, mildly, moderately, or extremely?
    (c) Do you spend a lot of time in church activities?

Therapist: ...What is the difficulty that you are having?

Client: I can't fly in airplanes or go up in elevators... at least not higher than the third floor, though I am still nervous even then.

Therapist: Let's talk about the airplane difficulty first. What about flying makes you feel uncomfortable?

Client: Well, watching a plane take off is fearful, though as a child I did take lessons in flying and was not afraid. (Pause). It's the feeling of being suspended in air and immobile, and of being trapped and feeling that I can't get out.

Therapist: When do you remember this fear beginning?

Client: It started about 10 years ago. My husband had to fly as part of his job with his company and I would go with him on a number of occasions. Then the fear began getting worse as I would fly more, and about five years ago I began having difficulty looking down (out the window). Now I can't look down at all or even out the window—even if I got up enough nerve to fly in a plane.

Therapist: Can you think of any situation regarding flying that doesn't make you feel uneasy?

Client: Yes (laughs), if I don't think about it, it doesn't bother me.

Therapist: Let's be a little more specific. If we could rate your level of fear about airplanes on a 10 point scale, what about flying would be most anxiety provoking for you; that is, a 10 for you.

Client: Flying over the ocean.

Therapist: What would be a zero?

Client: ...Being at the airport to pick someone up.

Therapist: What would be a five?

Client: The plane taking off.

Therapist: So, your fear is related to all aspects of you actually flying in a plane. What about seeing a plane on television, or in a movie, for example, seeing one in the air?

Client: That bothers me, too... especially watching a movie of a plane which was filmed from another plane, and especially when the plane banks.

Therapist: What number would this be on the rating scale?

Client: A five or six.

Therapist: Are there any reasons that you can think of, or ideas that you might have, concerning the development of your fear?

Client: Not really, except that around the time my nervousness began my husband was seeing another woman, and sometime during that period the fear developed . . . I guess I was feeling very threatened that we would break up.

Therapist: What was your relationship with your husband like during this time.

Client: Very poor . . . a lot of fighting and yelling.

Therapist: Any talk of divorce at that time.

Client: No, not really. I guess we both knew that the marriage was shaky, but that we would stay together at least until the children got older.

Therapist: And what about your fear of elevators. When did it begin?

Client: (Pause). I think it goes back almost 20 years ago. I remember being in a tall building in Chicago . . . don't remember why . . . and getting a feeling of fright in an express elevator. But I guess you can say I became really scared about five years ago. And, it became very bad three years ago, right after I took an express elevator to the 20th floor of the Acme building and threw-up as I came out after feeling so nervous and nauseous while going up.

Therapist: Is there anything about riding in an elevator or about elevators in general that doesn't make you feel uncomfortable?

Client: Walking past an elevator with someone and knowing that I don't have to go in.

Therapist: What about going past it, and you're by yourself.

Client: It bothers me a bit. It's at the point now where just walking by one by myself makes me feel uncomfortable.

Therapist: How much . . . using for a moment our 10 point rating scale?

Client: About one.

Therapist: What would be zero?

Client: Walking past it with someone and knowing I don't have to take it.

Therapist: What would be a 10?

Client: (Laughs and then a pause). Being stuck in the elevator and alone by myself.

Therapist: Any thoughts about what events contributed to this fear.

Client: None. I can't figure it out, unless it's related to my airplane fear. But I don't know how.

Therapist: Let's hold on that for a bit and talk a little more about your background. Where were you born and in what year?

Client: In Chicago, . . .

At the end of the first or second session, the therapist often gives the client some questionnaires to fill out at home for the next session. They are used to help the therapist gain any additional information about the client which was or could have been missed during the initial interview. In addition, it is a good idea for the therapist to ask the client to write-out a paragraph or two about his fears—describing each of them and any reasons why he feels they occur, as well as his thoughts about them. The three most commonly used questionnaires are presented in the Appendixes (pp. 265–270). They are the following:

The Fear Survey Schedule

This is a five point rating scale which asks the client to rate the amount of fear or discomfort caused by each of the things and events listed in the questionnaire from "Not At All" to "Very Much."

The Willoughby Questionnaire

This questionnaire is also a five point rating scale. It contains questions about how the client reacts in various situations. The client is to respond with an answer ranging from "Never" ("Not At All;" "No") to "Practically Always" ("Entirely").

The Bernreuter Self-Sufficiency Inventory

The Bernreuter lists a number of questions regarding self-sufficiency. The client is asked to circle "Yes" if the question applies to him, "No" if it does not apply to him, or to circle the question mark (?) if he is not sure whether it applies to him.

The purpose behind the use of the extensive interview and questionnaires is not necessarily to determine the etiology of the client's problem, but rather to provide the therapist with a thorough comprehensive picture of who the client is, what kind of environment he came from, and how he came to be what he is. Though this information is important in helping the therapist gain a general understanding of client and his life, what is *primarily* important in the interview is a determination of (1) the circumstances and situations under which the fear occurs, and (2) the relative intensity in various situations of the feelings associated with the fear. The general assumption is that an individual's fear is learned and that it can be unlearned by applying principles based on theories of learning.

Specific questions are also asked in the initial interview, and extensive discussion occurs because the goal of the therapy is very specific, namely, the reduction of the individual's fear(s). No attempt is made at reorganizing the client's personality, nor is there any general goal of helping the client achieve a higher level of emotional and psychological functioning. The only goal is to reduce the client's fear or phobic reaction to that point where he can carry-on his daily activities without being bothered by his fear.

If the therapist has even the slightest belief that the client may be suffering from a physical disorder which could be causing the problem or possibly interfere with treatment, he should refer the client to a physician for a thorough examination before proceeding further.

THE DESENSITIZATION PROCEDURE

After obtaining all of the relevant information about the client, the therapist then decides on the treatment procedure and discusses with the client what will take place next. If systematic desensitization is used the therapist briefly explains the rationale behind the treatment procedure, and describes the various stages in the treatment process. For example, the therapist might say the following:

The emotional reactions that you experience are a result of your previous experiences with people and situations; these reactions oftentimes lead to feelings of anxiety or tenseness which are really inappropriate. Since perceptions of situations occur within ourselves, it is possible to work with your reactions right here in the office by having you . . . [imagine] or visualize those situations. (Paul, 1966, p. 116.)

The therapist would then mention that a technique called systematic desensitization is going to be used with the client, and that it consists of two primary stages.

> The first stage consists of relaxation training where I am going to teach you how to become very relaxed—more relaxed than you have probably felt in a very long time. Once you have learned to relax, we will then use this relaxed state to counter the anxiety and tenseness that you feel whenever you are in the feared situation(s). We will do this by having you imagine—while you are still very relaxed—a series of progressively more tension-provoking scenes which you and I will develop . . . and which are directly related to your fear. We will thus countercondition your fear or desensitize your tenseness to the feared situation(s).
> This procedure has been found to be very effective in the treatment of many types of fears, and we have used it successfully in the past with people who have fears like yours. We will start the procedure by first teaching you how to become more relaxed and then asking you to practice the procedure at home.
> Do you have any questions?*

Before proceeding further, any questions that the client has regarding the procedure should be answered fully.

Throughout this initial period, as well as during the remainder of therapy, the therapist should make sure that he has established a good relationship with the client and that he behaves in a way that conveys warmth and acceptance of him. In fact, therapist warmth was found by Morris and Suckerman (1974a, 1974b) to be a significant factor in the outcome of desensitization with snake phobic college students. (The reader should review Cnapter 2 by Goldstein for a detailed discussion concerning methods of enhancing the therapeutic relationship).

There are essentially three steps in the use of systematic desensitization: (1) relaxation training, (2) development of the anxiety hierarchy, and (3) systematic desensitization proper. Since therapists differ from one another in regard to some of the details of systematic desensitization, what is described here is the manner in which the present author conducts this therapy.

Relaxation Training

The therapist begins desensitization by first training the client to relax. This training should take place in a quiet, softly lighted room located in a building where there is a negligible amount of outside noise. (Where possible, the therapist should use the same room as the one in which the initial interview took place). Besides comfortable office furniture, the therapist should have either a couch or recliner chair in the room so that relaxation can be facilitated by having the client lie on his back.

---

*Adapted from Paul, G. L. *Insight vs. desensitization in psychotherapy.* Stanford, Calif.: Stanford University Press, 1966.

The first step in the procedure is to have the client lean back in the chair (lie down on the couch) and close his eyes. The therapist then says the following:

> I am going to teach you how to become very relaxed. In doing this I am going to ask you to tense up and relax opposing sets of muscles—proceeding through a series of these. That is, I am going to ask you to tense up and relax different sets of muscles so that there is a cumulative effect of relaxation over your whole body. (Pause) Okay, now I would like you to . . .

The relaxation steps presented in Table 8.3 are then initiated. These steps represent a modified version of a technique developed by Jacobson (1938) for inducing deep muscular relaxation. The procedure should be presented in a very quiet, soft, and pleasant tone of voice. Each step should take about 10 seconds, with a 10–15 second pause between each step. The whole procedure should take 20–25 minutes.*

During the first relaxation training session, it is often helpful for the therapist to practice the relaxation procedure with the client—so that the client can observe (whenever necessary) how to perform a particular step. It is also advisable for the therapist to pace the presentation of each step to the client's ease of performing the steps.

It is not uncommon for clients to feel uncomfortable during the first relaxation session and not achieve a very deep relaxation level. But over a few sessions, the client will become more comfortable and will be able to reach deep relaxation more easily. The client should also be encouraged to practice the relaxation at home alone, preferably twice a day for 10–15 minutes. In order to enhance the client's practice at home, some therapists record the relaxation procedure on cassette tapes and have the client play the tape while practicing each day. Others give the client an outline of the muscle groups to be relaxed. Both could be done. The most important goal is to teach the client how to relax by himself with a fair degree of ease.

In most cases, relaxation training will last for about two or three sessions and will usually overlap with part of the initial interview. Throughout this training, it is a good idea to repeat such phrases as: "Breathe normally."; "Smooth, even breathing."; "Keep your   muscle groups) relaxed."; "Remember to keep the rest of your body relaxed."; "Just let your body relax . . . and become more and more relaxed."

It is also helpful throughout relaxation training to point out to the client the changes he will be experiencing in his bodily sensations. For example, the therapist might say some of the following phrases: "Notice the difference between tensing and relaxing your muscles."; "Notice the warm, soft feeling of relaxation."; "Notice how your _____ (particular muscle group) now feels . . . they are

---

*Before initiating the relaxation procedure, it is often helpful, as a precaution, to ask the client if he has any physical problem which might interfere with the tensing and relaxing of various muscles. If the client mentions a problem area, the therapist should omit this muscle grouping from the procedure or not request the client to strongly tense this set of muscles.

Table 8.3.   An Introduction To The Relaxation Training Steps Of Systematic Desensitization.

Steps in Relaxation

 1. Take a deep breath and hold it (for about ten seconds). Hold it. Okay, let it out.

 2. Raise both of your hands about half way above the couch (or, arms of the chair), and breathe normally. Now, drop your hands to the couch (or, down).

 3. Now, hold your arms out and make a tight fist. Really tight. Feel the tension in your hands. I am going to count to three and when I say "three," I want you to drop your hands. One ... Two ... Three.

 4. Raise your arms again, and bend your fingers back the other way (toward your body). Now drop your hands and relax.

 5. Raise your arms. Now drop them and relax.

 6. Now, raise your arms again, but this time "flap" your hands around. Okay, relax again.

 7. Raise your arms again. Now, relax.

 8. Raise your arms above the couch (chair) again and tense your biceps until they shake. Breathe normally, and keep your hands loose. Relax your hands.
    (Notice how you have a warm feeling of relaxation).

 9. Now hold your arms out to your side and tense your biceps. Make sure that you breathe normally. Relax your arms.

10. Now arch your shoulders back. Hold it. Make sure that your arms are relaxed. Now relax.

11. Hunch your shoulders forward. Hold it, and make sure that you breathe normally and keep your arms relaxed. Okay, relax.
    (Notice the feeling of relief from tensing and relaxing your muscles).

12. Now, turn your head to the right and tense your neck. Hold it. Okay, relax and allow your head to come back to its natural position.

13. Turn your head to the left and tense your neck. Relax and bring your head back again to its natural position.

14. Now, bend your head back slightly towards the chair. Hold it. Okay, now bring your head back slowly to its natural position.*

15. This time bring your head down almost to your chest. Hold it. Now relax and let your head come back to its natural resting position.*

16. Now, open your mouth as much as possible. A little wider, okay, relax. (Mouth must be partly open at end).

17. Now tense your lips by closing your mouth. O.K., relax.
    (Notice the feeling of relaxation).

18. Put your tongue at the roof of your mouth. Press hard. (Pause) Relax and allow your tongue to come to a comfortable position in your mouth.

19. Now put your tongue at the bottom of your mouth. Press down hard. Relax and let your tongue come to a comfortable position in your mouth.

20. Now just lay (sit) there and relax. Try not to think of anything.

21. To control self-verbalizations, I want you to go through the motions of singing a high note—Not aloud! Okay, start singing to yourself. Hold that note, and now relax.

22. Now sing a medium note and make your vocal cords tense again. Relax.

23. Now sing a low note and make your vocal cords tense again. Relax.
    (Your vocal apparatus should be relaxed now. Relax your mouth).

*The client should not be encouraged to bend his neck either all the way back or forward.

Table 8.3.   (Continued).

24. Now, close your eyes. Squeeze them tight and breathe naturally. Notice the tension. Now relax. (Notice how the pain goes away when you relax).

25. Now, let your eyes just lay there and keep your mouth open slightly.

26. Open your eyes as much as possible. Hold it. Now, relax your eyes.

27. Now wrinkle your forehead as much as possible. Hold it. Okay, relax.

28. Now, take a deep breath and hold it. Relax.

29. Now, exhale. Breathe all the air out . . . all of it out. Relax. (Notice the wondrous feeling of breathing again).

30. Imagine that there are weights pulling on all your muscles, making them flacid and relaxed . . . pulling your arms and body into the couch.

31. Pull your stomach muscles together. Tighter. Okay, Relax.

32. Now extend your muscles as if you were a Prize Fighter. Make your stomach hard. Relax. (You are becoming more and more relaxed).

33. Now, tense your buttocks. Tighter. Hold it. Now, relax.

34. Now, search the upper part of your body and relax any part that is tense. First the facial muscles. (Pause . . . 3–5 sec.) Then the vocal muscles. (Pause . . . 3–5 sec.) The neck region. (Pause . . . 3–5 sec.) Your shoulder . . . relax any part which is tense. (Pause) Now the arms and fingers. Relax these. Becoming very relaxed.

35. Maintaining this relaxation, raise both of your legs (to about a 45° angle). Now relax. (Notice that this further relaxes you).

36. Now bend your feet back so that your toes point towards your face. Relax your mouth. Bend them hard. Relax.

37. Bend your feet the other way . . . away from your body. Not far. Notice the tension. Okay, relax.

38. Relax. (Pause) Now curl your toes together—as hard as you can. Tighter. Okay, relax. (Quiet . . . silence for about 30 seconds).

39. This completes the formal relaxation procedure.
    Now explore your body from your feet up. Make sure that every muscle is relaxed. (Say slowly)—first your toes, . . . your feet, . . . your legs, . . . buttocks, . . . stomach, . . . shoulders, . . . neck, . . . eyes, . . . and finally your forehead—all should be relaxed now.
    (Quiet—silence for about 10 seconds).
    Just lay there and feel very relaxed, noticing the warmness of the relaxation. (Pause) I would like you to stay this way for about one more minute, and then I am going to count to five. When I reach five, I want you to open your eyes feeling very calm and refreshed.
    (Quiet—silence for about one minute).
    Okay, when I count to five, I want you to open your eyes feeling very calm and refreshed. One . . . feeling very calm; Two . . . very calm, very refreshed; Three . . . very refreshed; Four . . .; and, Five.

Adapted in part from Jacobson (1938), Rimm (1967, personal communication), and Wolpe and Lazarus (1966).

warm, heavy and relaxed."; "Notice how relaxed your _____ (*particular muscle group*) feels in contrast to when you were tensing them."; "Notice how you are becoming more and more relaxed—feeling relaxation throughout your whole body."

For various reasons, sometimes a few clients have difficulty relaxing with this procedure. No matter how motivated they are, they just find it difficult to respond.

They report, for example, having difficulty closing their eyes for longer than a few seconds (or minutes), or feel very uneasy when they lie back in a recliner chair or lie down on a couch while someone is watching them. In an attempt to deal with this problem effectively, some writers (e.g., Brady, 1966, 1972; Friedman, 1966) have recommended the use of drugs (like Brevitol) to help their clients relax during relaxation training and desensitization. Others have suggested the use of hypnosis or carbon dioxide-oxygen (e.g., Wolpe and Lazarus, 1966; Wolpe, 1973) or the use of a modified shaping procedure called "relaxation programming" (Morris, 1973). The interested reader should consult the original published papers for a detailed description of these approaches.

Development of the Anxiety Hierarchy

Upon completion of the initial interview and during relaxation training the therapist begins planning out an anxiety hierarchy with the client for each of his fears. This hierarchy is based on the fear(s) that the therapist and client have agreed upon as requiring changes and which the therapist has consented to treat.

At the end of the first relaxation training session (assuming the initial interview has been completed), the client is given ten 3×5 index cards and asked to come to the next session with the cards filled out—each containing a description of a situation which produces a certain level of anxiety in him. Specifically, he is asked to identify those situations that are related to his fear, and which produce increasingly more anxiety and tension. He is asked to divide his fear on a zero to one-hundred scale and assign an anxiety-provoking situation to every tenth value (100 representing the most anxiety-provoking situation). Examples of some initial anxiety hierarchies are listed in Table 8.4.

Table 8.4.   Sample—Initial Anxiety Hierarchies.

Fear of being alone

10. Being with a group of people at the lab either at night or during the day.
20. Being alone in a room with another female.
30. Thinking about the possibility of being alone in my house during the day.
40. Walking to class early in the morning when there are few people outside.
50. Actually alone in my bedroom at home and it's daylight.
60. Driving a car alone at night and feeling a man is following me.

70. Walking alone on a city street downtown at night with a girl-friend.

Fear of driving in high places

10. Entering a ramp garage on ground level.
20. Going up to third level of the garage from the second level.
30. Riding with a friend in a car and approach the bridge over the Chicago River on Michigan Avenue.
40. Driving my car with a friend and begin to approach the bridge over the Chicago River.
50. Driving my car over the Chicago River bridge.
60. Driving with a friend and crossing the bridge over the Mississippi River near Moline.
70. Driving my car on the bridge over the Mississippi River near Moline.

Table 8.4. (Continued).

Fear of being alone	Fear of driving in high places
80. Being alone in a house with a young child for whom I am baby-sitting.	80. Driving my car with a friend on a hilly road in Wisconsin.
90. Thinking about being alone at night a few hours before I will actually be alone.	90. Driving my car with a friend on a hilly road in Wisconsin going halfway up a fairly steep hill.
100. Sitting alone in the living room of my house at night with the doors closed.	100. Driving my car with a friend up to the top of a fairly steep hill. We get to the top and get out of the car and look around at the valley below— then go into a restaurant nearby— and later drive back down the hill.

Fear of flying in airplanes	Fear of leaving the house
10. Watching a movie of a plane moving up and down and banking.	10. Going out the front door to my car to go to the store.
20. Sitting in a private plane—on the ground with the motor idling.	20. Getting in the car and starting it up.
30. Sitting in a private plane on the ground and the pilot begins to taxi down to the runway.	30. In the car and pulling out of the driveway.
40. Sitting in a private plane on the ground, taxiing, and the pilot revs the engine.	40. On the street and pulling away from my house.
50. Planning a trip with a friend on a commercial jet and it's three months before the trip.	50. Two blocks from my house on way to the store.
60. One month before the trip on the jet.	60. Arrive at the store and park.
70. Three weeks before the trip by jet.	70. Enter the store.
80. Three days before the trip by jet.	80. Get a shopping cart and begin looking for items on my list.
90. In a private plane at take-off.	90. Have all the items and go to check-out girl.
100. In a commercial jet over land.	100. Have all the items and have to wait in a long slow line to go through check-out

The exact nature of a hierarchy will vary depending on the client's particular fear and perception of the various situations. For example, someone who has a fear of being criticized may describe a number of very different situations when this fear occurs—each differing in the level of fear that it arouses in him. Someone else may have a very specific fear, where the descriptions of the increasing anxiety-provoking situations differ on a spatio-temporal dimension. This was the case of the woman in Table 8.4 who had a fear of leaving her house. The hierarchy can also vary in terms of the number of people present in a particular situation (e.g., an elevator), the perceived attitudes of others toward the client, as well as a combination of some of these dimensions (see the fear of flying hierarchy in Table 8.4).

When the client returns with his prepared hierarchy, the therapist goes through it with him and adds intermediary items where it seems appropriate. The final hierarchy should represent a slow and smooth gradation of anxiety-provoking situations, each of which the client can easily imagine. Most hierarchies contain 20–25 items. It is not unusual, however, for those hierarchies that represent a very specific fear (e.g., fear of driving on the highway at night) to contain fewer items, while those representing a more complex fear (e.g., fear of being alone) to contain more items. In Table 8.5, we have listed a few final hierarchies.

The therapist should also determine what is a very relaxing scene for the client; one which would be zero on the hierarchy. This is often called the *control scene*. The scene should be unrelated to the fears, and totally satisfying and comforting to him. Some common "zero-level" scenes are the following:

"Walking through the forest on a nice sunny day with my wife (husband)."
"Laying on the beach by the ocean on a sunny, warm day."
"Laying in bed and reading an interesting novel."
"Sitting in a lounge chair in my backyard on a beautiful spring day—watching the clouds go by."

Hierarchy development usually occupies at least part of two or three sessions, though less time may be spent with those cases which involve a single phobia.

Systematic Desensitization Proper

Desensitization proper usually begins about three or four sessions after the completion of the initial interview. By this time the client has had the opportunity to practice relaxation at home as well as in the therapist's office, and has been able to construct his anxiety hierarchy. If the client has developed a number of hierarchies, the therapist should first work on the one which is most distressing and troublesome to the client. If time allows, the therapist can also work on other hierarchies during the hour, but he probably should not go beyond exposing the client to more than three *different* hierarchies in a given session.

The first desensitization session starts with having the client spend about three to five minutes relaxing himself on the couch or in the recliner chair. During this time, the therapist suggests to the client that he is becoming increasingly more relaxed and is achieving a deeper and deeper level of relaxation. The therapist might add the following comments during this phase:

Your whole body is becoming heavier . . . all your muscles are relaxing more and more. Your arms are becoming very relaxed. (*Pause*) Your shoulders. (*Pause*) Your neck. (*Pause*) Now the muscles of your jaws . . . your tongue . . . (*Pause*) and your eyes . . . very relaxed. Your forehead . . . very relaxed . . . noticing that as you become more relaxed you're feeling more and more calm. (*Pause*) Very relaxed . . . relaxing any part of your face which feels the least bit tense. (*Pause*) Now, back down to your neck . . . your shoulders . . . your chest . . . your buttocks . . . your thighs . . . your legs . . . your feet . . . very, very relaxed. (*Pause*) Feeling very at ease and very comfortable.

Table 8.5. Sample—Final Hierarchies.

Driving
1. Husband driving 70 down fast lane on freeway, 50 feet behind car in front. Heavy but fast traffic
2. Driving to store at own pace
3. Driving 55 on freeway in light traffic, increase gradually to 70
4. Driving 35 in 35 mile zone to the store. Someone is 30 feet behind you
5. Driving on freeway starting at 65 with light traffic, traffic becomes increasingly heavy
6. Riding on El Camino (a city street) with mother and she breaks unnecessarily
7. Riding with father on a freeway and he is a little angry and following too close
8. Driving 65 mph on Bayshore Freeway as it gets darker and darker
9. Driving 65 mph on Bayshore Freeway at night. It rains harder and harder. You slow down as safety indicates
10. Driving in the mountains in the dark
11. Driving through mountains in dark and rain

   (from Marquis, Morgan, and Piaget, 1971)

Elevators
*1. At my (therapist's) office and seeing the elevator as you walk down the stairs
 2. Pushing button to summon elevator at my office (on second floor)
 3. Elevator comes to second floor...doors open...and you go inside and down to first floor
*4. In the new elevator with others at the Acme building below the fourth floor—going down
 5. You enter the elevator at my office, the doors close, and there is a slight pause before it begins going down
 6. Alone in the elevator in my office building going up from the first to the third floor
*7. In a new elevator alone at the Acme building, going up between the first and fourth floors
*8. In the new elevator with others at the Acme building going down between the fifteenth and fourth floors (15 story building)
 9. In the elevator at my office going down. As the elevator reaches the first floor there is a slight pause before the doors open
*10. In a new elevator with others at the Acme building and going up between the fourth and fifteenth floors
 11. In the elevator alone at the Acme building, going up between the fourth and fifteenth floors and as you reach the twelfth floor to get out there is a momentary pause before the doors open
*12. You're on the fifth floor of the Marshall building (a very familiar old building to the client) and you enter the elevator alone, push the button, and it starts to go down to the first floor
 13. As you are going down in the elevator you begin hearing a few noises from the elevator machinery
*14. You enter the Marshall building and walk up to the elevator, step inside, and press the button to go up to the fifth floor
*15. You enter the elevator alone at the Ajax building (30 floors) and you take it up to the 10th floor
 16. ...to the 15th floor
 17. ...to the 20th floor
*18. You enter the elevator alone at the Thomas building (50 floors) and you take it to the 20th floor
 19. ...to the 30th floor
 20. You are in the elevator alone in my office building and press the button to go up to the fifth floor and it doesn't stop until the seventh floor
 21. You are in the elevator alone at the Marshall building, going down to the first floor, and it stops between the second and first floors. You press the first floor button again and the elevator goes to the first floor
*22. You are in an elevator alone in the Thomas building going up to the 45th floor and it gets stuck between the 20th and 21st floors—and then starts up a while later after you pressed the alarm button

---

*Indicates original items which client developed.

The client is also asked by the therapist to indicate, by raising his right index finger, when he has achieved a very relaxing and comfortable state.

After he signals, the therapist says that he is now going to ask him to imagine a number of scenes from the hierarchy that the two of them developed over the past few sessions. He also asks him to imagine each scene as clearly and as vividly as possible—"As if you are really there!"—while still maintaining a very relaxed state. If the client feels the least bit of anxiety or tension when he imagines a particular scene, he is told to signal immediately with his right index finger.

At this point, the therapist asks the client to indicate with his index finger if he is still feeling very calm and relaxed. If he signals, the therapist presents the control scene. If he does not signal, the therapist reviews with him the earlier relaxation sequence until he no longer indicates feeling tense.

The control scene is presented for approximately 15 seconds. The therapist then proceeds with the desensitization procedure. An example of a desensitization session with a test phobic individual is presented below.

> ...Now stop imagining that scene and give all your attention once again to relaxing...Now imagine that you are home studying in the evening. It is the 20th of May, exactly a month before your examination. (Pause of 5 seconds). Now stop imagining the scene. ...[Pause of 10–15 seconds]. Now imagine the same scene again—a month before your examination. ...[Pause of 5–10 seconds]. Stop imagining the scene and just think of your muscles. Let go, and enjoy your state of calm. (Pause of 15 seconds). Now imagine again that you are studying at home a month before your examination. ...[Pause of 5–10 seconds]. Stop the scene and think of nothing but your own body. ...[Pause of 15 seconds]. (Wolpe, 1969, p. 126.)*

Each hierarchy scene is presented three to four times with a maximum exposure time of five seconds for the first presentation, and a gradual increase up to ten seconds for subsequent presentations. The hierarchy items are presented in ascending order, starting with the lowest feared item first, with relaxation periods between each scene varying from 10 to 15 seconds. In most cases, three to four *different* scenes are presented per session. This means that a particular desensitization session will last between 15 and 20 minutes. The remainder of the hour can be devoted to discussing issues related to the client's fear (e.g., what occurred during the week regarding his fear) and/or to the desensitization of another hierarchy, or to working on some other problem with the client.

After the last scene is presented for a particular session, and if the decision is not to go onto another hierarchy, the therapist usually asks the client to relax for a short period of time. He then starts the *ending phase* of the session by saying the following:

> ...Just relax...feeling very comfortable and at ease. I would like you to stay this way until I count to five. When I reach five, I want you to open your eyes feeling very calm and refreshed. (*Pause*) One...feeling very calm; two...very calm, very refreshed; three...very refreshed; four...; and, five.

The same general format is followed for all subsequent desensitization

---

*Sections in brackets have been added by the present author.

sessions. The scenes should not be presented in a rapid manner; rather, they should be presented in a conversational manner which conveys both understanding and concern for the client. In order to keep track of which scenes the client passes, how many times he has passed a scene, and where on the hierarchy each session started and stopped, it is advisable to follow a procedure outlined in Table 8.6.

Table 8.6.   Suggested Notational System.

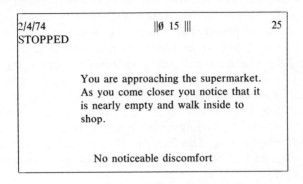

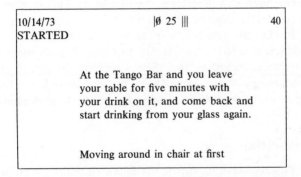

The date refers to when the scene was presented. The words "stopped" and "started" indicate whether the session stopped or started with the scene. The "hash marks" help the therapist recall how often the scene was presented—one mark per presentation. The circle through the mark indicates that the client signalled anxiety, and that the scene was stopped and followed by a relaxation period of the number of seconds indicated next to the circle. Comments are also made at the bottom of the card about the client's observed comfort level while imagining the scene.

The therapist should present each scene until the client has three consecutive successes. If, however, the client has two consecutive failures (indications of anxiety), the therapist should go back to the previous successfully passed scene and work back up again. If failure persists, the previously successful scene should be presented again so that the client ends the session with a positive experience. The ending phase of the procedure should then begin. The problems associated with the scene should be discussed with the client and modifications made either in the scene or in other aspects of the procedure.

Even if a client does not signal anxiety, it is often helpful during the conduct of desensitization (especially during the first session) to determine if he was disturbed by a particular scene, whether he was able to fully imagine the scene, or if he continues to feel very relaxed. To do this, the therapist asks the client between scene presentations "If you were not the least bit disturbed by that scene (or, "If you were able to imagine that scene very clearly . . . ," or "If you continue to feel very relaxed . . .") do nothing; otherwise raise your right index finger." If he raises his finger, the therapist then takes appropriate action (e.g., he might go through additional relaxation enhancing suggestions, or present either the scene or the control scene again and suggest that the client vividly imagine the detail in it). If, after re-presenting a particular scene, the client indicates again that he was disturbed by it or could not vividly imagine it, the session is stopped using the ending phase described above. The therapist then explores in detail the difficulty the client is having, and makes any modifications necessary in the hierarchy or relaxation procedure.

A second useful procedure involves assessing the client's overall level of relaxation before, during, and after a particular desensitization session. This usually takes place after desensitization has been completed for the day. The client is asked to rate his relaxation level on a 10-point scale—where zero is "Extremely" relaxed and 10 is "Not At All" relaxed. This approach not only gives the therapist feedback regarding the client's relative change in relaxation level from pre- to post-treatment across sessions, but also provides information to the client regarding his own progress and what he can do to make himself feel more relaxed.

Additional Considerations

Throughout desensitization proper, the client should be watched for signs of fatigue. In this regard, it may be helpful to ask the client whether he feels too many scenes (or hierarchies) are being presented at each session. It is also advisable to be sensitive to any discomfort the client is showing during either relaxation training or desensitization proper. Some of the ways clients express discomfort while laying on the couch are the following: moving their bodies around as if to find a comfortable position; rapid movement of their eyelids; excessive yawning; or, unsolicited verbalizations while their eyes are closed.

Occasionally, as in the following example, discomfort can be unrelated to the client's fear.

Mrs. Farber was well into her fifth desensitization session, progressing slowly, but steadily up her hierarchy concerned with a fear of being alone in her house. She fluttered her eyelids sporadically, but did not indicate any anxiety to the scenes being presented. During subsequent relaxation enhancing instructions, she began crossing her legs and shifting her body around. Just as the therapist was about to inquire about her relaxation level, she opened her eyes, sat up in the recliner chair and said, "You'll have to excuse me, I had a lot to drink today and must go to the washroom. I forgot to go before I came here."

At other times, as in the next example, deep relaxation may set the occasion for a very tense client to begin thinking about his problem.

Mr. Martin had difficulty learning how to relax. Several sessions passed with him unable to achieve a relaxation level lower than four on the 10 point rating scale. In the fourth session, a relaxation enhancing technique was used. He became very relaxed, more relaxed than on previous occasions, and seemed to be pleased with his success. Within a few minutes, he began moving his head from one side to the other and tears began falling down his cheeks. He then started crying and said that he apologized for the disruption but that this was the first time he has ever "let [himself] . . . really think about" the difficulties he has had with his impotence "and all the turmoil it has caused in my life."

Similar events can also contribute to a client's repeated failure of an item in a session. In the following example, the particular hierarchy item did not produce the signalled anxiety; rather, the anxiety was triggered by a telephone call that day from an old friend of the client.

Mrs. Carol was progressing steadily through her hierarchy concerned with a fear of leaving her home by herself—and driving more than a mile from the house. During the ninth session, an item was presented concerned with driving by herself nine miles to the therapist's office. As soon as the item was presented, she signalled anxiety and repeated this action until the session was stopped. Upon inquiring about her repeated signalling, she began crying and said she had received a telephone call that day from an old college friend with whom she was very close but had not seen for 10 years. The friend ended up at the airport unexpectedly, was between planes, and asked Mrs. Carol to come out (20 miles) to see her. Mrs. Carol wanted to go very much but was afraid to take a chance and declined, but did talk to her friend for a long time. She felt terrible and angry at herself for having such a "stupid problem."

Another reason for repeated failure of a hierarchy item may be the psychological distance between the last passed item and the next failed one. Two examples of this situation are the following:

Client A.
Item passed. Flying in the plane after leveling off at 30,000 feet and not hearing any change in the sound of the engines.
(60 on the hierarchy)
Item failed. Feeling the tilt of the plane as it is banking, and not hearing any change in the sound of the engines.
(65 on the hierarchy)

Client B.
Item passed. Planning a trip on an airplane with a close friend to the Bahama Islands, and it's nine months before the trip.
(20 on the hierarchy)
Item failed. Reviewing plans of airplane trip to the Bahamas with close friend, and it's one month before the trip.
(25 on the hierarchy)

In example A, the client and therapist decided on an intermediary scene that described a change in the noise of the airplane engines which the client could hear just before she felt the plane banking. A temporal dimension, on the other hand, was inserted between the two scenes in example B. Specifically three additional scenes were developed: ... six months before the planned trip; ... four months before; ... two months before .... In both cases these additions to the respective hierarchies facilitated successful passage of the heretofore failed items.

Just as some clients signal repeated difficulty with one or more hierarchy scenes, others never signal anxiety about particular scenes. In some cases, this is good because it suggests that the hierarchy represents a smooth, even, gradation of the client's fear. In other cases, this means that the client feels reluctant to signal that he is indeed experiencing anxiety. To reduce the possibility of the client not signalling anxiety when, in fact, he should, it is a good idea for the therapist to mention at various times throughout the session: "Remember to signal whenever you feel the slightest amount of anxiety." The therapist should also make every effort neither to convey dissatisfaction with a client's signalling of anxiety *nor* satisfaction that a client did not signal anxiety at all during a particular session. In both instances, the client may begin to feel that the therapist does not really want him to signal anxiety.

It is also important for the therapist to end each desensitization session with a positive experience for the client (i.e., ending on a hierarchy item which was passed successfully). Moreover, he should leave sufficient time at the end of the session (as well as before the session begins) to discuss any issues or concerns that the client has, or how things went for him during the week.

Most desensitization sessions last from 30 minutes to one hour, depending on the number of different hierarchies presented. Some researchers, however, have reported successfully treating a phobia by conducting a massed desensitization session which lasted 90 minutes (Wolpin and Pearsall, 1965) while others (e.g., Richardson and Suinn, 1973) have reported success after a three hour massed session. The spacing of most desensitization sessions varies from once to twice a week, though Wolpe (1973) reports that some clients have received two or more sessions per day.

During the initial stages of desensitization, the client is encouraged to avoid the temptation of entering the actual feared situation. Since this may be an unrealistic request for some clients, they are asked to try to avoid entering the feared situation at "full throttle." As desensitization progresses, however, they are encouraged to enter aspects of the feared situation which correspond to lower hierarchy items which have been passed successfully and for which the client now feels little, if any, tension or anxiety.

Finally, for some clients, whether or not they report being phobic, the therapist may decide to *only* use relaxation training with them. Though there is little empirical data to support this approach, there is some evidence from clinical case studies which suggests that relaxation training alone can be useful in helping anxious clients become more relaxed and report feeling more at ease.

Variations of Systematic Desensitization

Various alternatives to desensitization have been proposed by researchers. In *in vivo desensitization* (e.g., Sherman, 1972), the client is exposed to the items on the hierarchy in the real situation rather than through imagination. Relaxation training is not used as the counter-conditioned response to the situation. Instead, those feelings of comfort, security, and trust that the client has developed for the therapist (which have emerged from the therapeutic relationship) are used as the counter-conditioning agent. The therapist goes into the real-life situation with the client and urges him to gradually go through each item on the hierarchy. An example of this procedure is the following:

> Mr. Kay is a very successful salesman in a large metropolitan area, and often must attend business meetings in high rise office buildings in the downtown area. But, he is extremely afraid of elevators. Lately, his fear has become so intense that he has avoided attending meetings which occur on a level higher than the fourth floor. *In vivo* desensitization entailed having Mr. Kay and the therapist approach various elevators throughout the city, ride up and down in them, and purposely get stuck in them—following a hierarchy sequence developed earlier with the therapist. Mr. Kay was also encouraged to go up elevators, etc. on his own while the therapist waited for him at various floors.

A similar technique called *contact desensitization* is used with both children and adults. This technique also involves a graded hierarchy, but adds to it a modeling and touch component in addition to the therapist's encouragement and interpersonal relationship with the client. The procedure is outlined in the next example.

> In the application of this method to the elimination of snake phobia, at each step the experimenter himself performed fearless behavior and gradually led subjects into touching, stroking, and then holding the snake's body with first gloved and then bare hands while he held the snake securely by the head and tail. If a subject was unable to touch the snake after ample demonstration, she was asked to place her hand on the experimenter's and to move her hand down gradually until it touched the snake's body. After subjects no longer felt any apprehension about touching the snake under these secure conditions, anxieties about contact with the snake's head area and entwining tail were extinguished. The experimenter again performed the tasks fearlessly and then he and the subject performed the responses jointly; as subjects became less fearful the experimenter gradually reduced his participation and control over the snake until subjects were able to hold the snake in their laps without assistance, to let the snake loose in the room and retrieve it, and to let it crawl freely over their bodies. Progress through the graded approach tasks was paced according to the subjects' apprehensiveness. When they reported being able to perform one activity with little or no fear, they were eased into a more difficult interaction. (p. 185.)*

A third variation is very similar to desensitization proper, but involves the use of a tape recorder. It is called *automated desensitization*. In this procedure, the client goes through the desensitization process by listening to a series of tape recorded scene presentations prepared by the therapist with the client's assistance. Developed by Lang (Wolpe, 1969) and later used by Migler and Wolpe

---

*From Bandura, A. *Principles of behavior modification*. New York: Holt, Rinehart and Winston, 1969. Reprinted by permission.

(1967), this procedure allows the patient to pace himself in the desensitization process and to desensitize himself in the privacy of his home. This method has been found to be as effective as live desensitization. (See Baker, Cohen, and Saunders, 1973.)

The last variation to be discussed is *emotive imagery*. This method was first used by Lazarus and Abramovitz (1962) to adapt desensitization proper to children. It involves the use of those anxiety-inhibiting images which arouse feelings of excitement associated with adventure, as well as feelings of pride, mirth, etc., and consists of the following steps:

(a) As in the usual method of systematic desensitization, a graduated hierarchy is drawn up.
(b) By sympathetic conversation and inquiry, the clinician establishes the nature of the child's hero images and the wish fulfilments and identifications which accompany them.
(c) The child is asked to close his eyes and imagine a sequence of events which is close enough to his everyday life to be credible, but within which is woven a story concerning his favorite hero or alter ego.
(d) When the clinician judges that these emotions have been maximally aroused, he introduces, as a natural part of the narrative, the lowest item in the hierarchy. If there is evidence that anxiety is being inhibited, the procedure is repeated as in ordinary systematic desensitization until the highest item in the hierarchy is tolerated without distress. (Wolpe and Lazarus, 1966, p. 143.)

ASSERTIVE TRAINING

A second procedure for reducing fears is called *assertive training*. This method is especially useful in helping people reduce their fear of acting appropriately in social and interpersonal situations. It is utilized when the therapist believes that the client (1) is presently unable to stand up for himself in situations where he feels he has been treated unjustly, (2) cannot respond, or has difficulty responding, in his own best interests to those events which directly affect his life or the lives of his family, and (3) has difficulty expressing feelings of love and affection toward significant persons in his life.

Unlike the assertive individual, the unassertive person does not feel confident in social situations and interpersonal relationships, is not spontaneous in his expression of emotions and feelings, often feels tense and anxious in social situations, and typically allows others to make decisions for him. The following example describes a situation in which Mr. A. is behaving in an unassertive manner.

Mr. and Mrs. A. are at dinner in a moderately expensive restaurant. Mr. A. has ordered a rare steak, but when the steak is served, Mr. A. finds it to be very well done, contrary to his order . . . Mr. A. grumbles to his wife about the "burned" meat, and observes that he won't patronize this restaurant in the future. He says nothing to the waitress, responding "Fine!" to her inquiry "Is everything alright?" His dinner and evening are highly unsatisfactory, and he feels guilty for having taken no action. Mr. A's estimate of himself, and Mrs. A's estimate of him are both deflated by the experience. (Alberti and Emmons, 1970, pp. 26–27.)

The decision to initiate assertive training with a client is usually based on information gathered during the initial interview. In listening to the client, the therapist learns how he interacts with people, and from questionnaires like the Willoughby Schedule (see Appendix 2), the therapist can confirm some of his speculations about the client.

The therapist may also wish to ask a series of questions like those listed below and/or have the client fill out the *Rathus Assertiveness Schedule* (Rathus, 1973—this questionnaire is presented in Appendix 4) or *The College Self-Expression Scale* (Galassi, Delo, Galassi, and Bastien, 1974). Each of these assessment procedures helps delineate further those areas in which the client has difficulty being assertive.

> When a person is blatantly unfair, do you usually fail to say something about it to him?
> Are you always very careful to avoid all trouble with other people?
> Do you often avoid social contacts for fear of doing or saying the wrong thing? . . .
> When a clerk in a store waits on someone who has come in after you, do you call his attention to the matter?
> Do you find that there are very few people with whom you can be relaxed and have a good time? . . .
> If a person keeps on teasing you, do you have difficulty expressing your annoyance or displeasure? . . .
> If someone keeps kicking the back of your chair in a movie, would you ask him to stop?
> If a friend keeps calling you very late each evening, would you ask him or her not to call after a certain time?
> If someone starts talking to someone else right in the middle of your conversation, do you express your irritation?
> In a plush restaurant, if you order a medium steak and find it too raw, would you ask the waiter to have it recooked?
> If the landlord of your apartment fails to make certain necessary repairs after promising to do so, would you insist upon it?
> Would you return a faulty garment you purchased a few days ago? . . . (pp. 132–133.)*

Conducting Assertive Training

Assertive training is based on the general assumption that assertive behavior gradually *counterconditions* the fear and anxiety that a person associates with a particular situation. This change, in turn, helps him develop confidence in appropriately expressing his feelings in these situations, because he begins to notice that his assertive behavior does not lead necessarily to negative reactions by others (Salter, 1949; Wolpe, 1973).

Assertive training consists of three primary components: role playing, modeling, and social reward and coaching. *Role playing* is used to help the client rehearse how he should act in a particular situation, e.g., what he should say to his demanding wife, what his facial expression should be like, etc. The client usually plays himself and the therapist plays the individual to whom the client reacts. *Modeling* and role-reversal are used to help the client observe how a more assertive person would behave in the same situation. In most cases, the therapist

---

*From Lazarus, A. A. *Behavior therapy and beyond.* New York: McGraw-Hill, 1971. Reprinted by permission.

plays the client, and the client plays the person to whom the therapist reacts. Some therapists, however, have hired professional actors/actresses to play the various roles and have utilized this occasion to point out to the client what he should be doing in the same situation. *Social reward and coaching* from the therapist are also important. The therapist not only comments about how good the client is doing and how well he is progressing, but also makes suggestions and gives him feedback on his behavior to facilitate further improvement in his assertiveness.

Assertive Training Proper

The steps in conducting assertive training are:

1. The therapist and client work out in a graduated fashion a series of situations in which the client feels increasing difficulty being assertive. Like the anxiety hierarchy items used in systematic desensitization, these situations should be described in sufficient detail (including the use of a script in some cases) so that the client can adequately portray what goes on in real life. The events described at the lower end of the series should be such that there is a high probability the client will have no trouble being assertive and that no negative consequences will occur as a result of his assertiveness. This success will build up and strengthen his self-confidence and help reduce his fear and anxiety concerning the expression of his feelings.

2. The therapist and client act out each of the scenes through role playing. The therapist then comments on the client's behavior and offers suggestions about improvement—especially concerning facial expression, posture, gait, arm movements, tone of voice, eye contact, etc. Modeling also takes place during this stage. The number of situations role played and modeled per session varies, and is based on the severity of the client's nonassertiveness as well as the client's tolerance level for practicing assertive behavior.

3. Upon completing the role playing stage and feeling confident in what he should do in certain situations, the client and therapist then decide on alternative responses which can be made in these situations. For example, they may discuss what the client should say or do if a negative reply is given in response to his assertive statement, or what would be a more empathic and warm response instead of a mildly aggressive one. Once these alternatives are decided upon, role playing and modeling again occur until the client has mastered these alternatives, too.

4. Once the assertive responses have been mastered, and the therapist and client agree that the client is aware of when he should be appropriately assertive, he is encouraged to practice his assertiveness in the real situation. Since this is a difficult step to take for many clients, he should be encouraged to rehearse the behavior at home and to write down any feelings he has about performing the behavior, as well as what about the situation produced these feelings. He should also take notes on how he felt after he performed the behavior, or what prevented him from being as assertive as he wanted to be. The purpose of notetaking is to

help the client recall to the therapist any problems he had since the last session so that they can be worked out and prevented from recurring.

5. At the next session, the client's performance since the previous session is reviewed. If he behaved appropriately, he should be enthusiastically rewarded with praise. His notes should be discussed and any problems worked out. He should be encouraged to continue practicing his assertiveness in these situations and continue his notetaking on his performance. The therapist should then go on to the next situation where the client has had difficulty being assertive—following the above steps.

If the client had difficulty being assertive, the reasons for his difficulty (i.e., what in the situation prevented him from being assertive) should be discussed, and appropriate retraining take place—reviewing with him steps 1–4.

An example of assertive training is described in the following case.*

Mr. P. R., aged 38 years, complained of depression and described himself as an "occupational misfit." Although highly qualified in accountancy and economics, he held only junior positions in his work. He stated that he felt frustrated and demoralized. At the time that he sought behavior therapy, he had received promotion to the position of Assistant Chief Ledger Clerk in a large organization. This slight elevation in status, utterly absurd for a man with his excellent qualifications, tended to reactivate his personal misgivings about his station in life, and led him to behavior therapy "as a last resort." During the initial interview it became clear that Mr. P. R. was grossly deficient in assertive behavior . . .. The therapist stressed [at the next session] that Mr. P. R.'s lack of assertiveness was responsible for his occupational failures and that vocational advancement would have to follow rather than precede increased assertiveness. It was clear, however, that Mr. P. R. would use the work situation as the sole criterion for gauging his general improvement. A careful analysis showed that opportunities for advancement in his firm were extremely limited. It was obvious that Mr. P. R. would have to go elsewhere to achieve the desired elevation in occupational status, but he rationalized that he would feel less secure in an unfamiliar work milieu. Further inquiries revealed that Mr. P. R. abhorred the idea of being interviewed by prospective employers. This area was then made the focus of attention for assertive training by means of behavior rehearsal.

Mr. P. R. was told to pretend that the therapist was a prominent business executive who had advertised for an experienced accountant to take charge of one of his companies. Mr. P. R. had applied for the position and had been asked to present himself for an interview. The therapist instructed Mr. P. R. to leave the consulting room, to knock on the door and to enter when invited to do so . . . .

At the therapist's deliberately resonant "come in!" Mr. P. R. opened the door of the consulting room and hesitantly approached the desk. The therapist interrupted the role-playing procedure to mirror the patient's timid posture, shuffling gait, downcast eyes, and overall tension. Mr. P. R. was required to sit at the desk and to play the role of the prominent business executive while the therapist re-enacted Mr. P. R.'s entry into the room. The patient was asked to criticize the therapist's performance. The therapist then modeled the entry of an "assertive individual," asking the patient to note the impact of variations in posture and gait and the all-important absence or presence of eye-contact.

The "correct" entry was rehearsed several times until Mr. P. R.'s approach to the prominent-executive-behind-the-desk was completely devoid of any overt signs of timidity or anxiety. He was then taught to deal with a variety of entries—being met at the door; the employer

*From Wolpe, J. and Lazarus, A. A. *Behavior therapy techniques.* New York: Pergamon Press, 1966. Reprinted by permission.

who makes himself incommunicado while studying important-looking documents; and the overeffusive one who self-consciously tries to place him at ease.

Next the content of the interview was scrutinized. Mr. P. R.'s replies to questions concerning his background, qualifications, and experience were tape-recorded. Mr. P. R. was instructed to place himself in the position of the prospective employer and asked to decide whether or not he would employ the applicant on the basis of his recorded interview. It was clear from the recording that the elimination of Mr. P. R.'s hesitant gait and posture had not generalized to his faltering speech. Above all, it was noted that Mr. P. R. tended to undersell himself. Instead of stressing his excellent qualifications he mumbled rather incoherent and unimpressive generalities about his background and training. The therapist demonstrated more efficient verbal responses which the patient was required to imitate. In this manner, Mr. P. R. was able to rehearse adequate replies to specific questions, and to prepare an impressive-sounding discourse for use in unstructured interviews.

The above mentioned procedures were employed during five therapeutic sessions held at weekly intervals. Mr. P. R. cancelled his sixth appointment and did not communicate for approximately two months. He then made another appointment. On entering the consulting room he said, "You are looking at the Chief Accountant of . . . . He then described how he had replied to the advertisement, been exposed to three separate interviews . . . . and how he was finally offered the post at an even higher salary than advertised.

Mr. P. R. proclaimed himself "cured." Although the therapist felt that many remaining facets of Mr. P. R.'s interpersonal dealings warranted additional assertive training, he did not discourage him from terminating therapy (on the understanding that he was free to resume should he even deem it necessary).

Five years later Mr. P. R. telephoned the therapist to report that he had become principal economic advisor to an important mining concern. (pp. 48–50.)

Additional Considerations

The client should not be pushed by the therapist into being assertive. Such activity will only threaten him and contribute further to his nonassertiveness. Assertive training, like desensitization, should take place within a therapeutic environment which facilitates learning and growth—where the therapist shows concern for the client, warmth, and understanding of his problem. In this regard, assertive training should progress slowly, with enough time allowed for the client to practice his new behavior. The therapist should therefore plan to have no more than one or two sessions per week with the client.

In addition, before initiating treatment, the therapist should explain to the client the rationale behind the use of assertive training. For example, he should be told that the assumption made in this treatment method is that nonassertive behavior is learned. And, by teaching him to be assertive in various situations, this will countercondition the anxiety and fear he has associated with these situations—so that the end result will be that he feels satisfied with himself for acting appropriately.

It is also important to begin assertive training with situations in which it is highly probable that no adverse consequences will occur to the client and that his expectancy for success will be rewarded. The client, however, should not be given a 100 percent guarantee that his efforts will not be met with negative consequences. He should be made aware of this possibility, and told that though it is unlikely that such consequences will occur, he should be prepared to give one of the alternative responses discussed in step 3 above.

In some cases, a client will be very reluctant to act in an assertive manner—even in a situation where it is highly probable that no negative consequence will result from assertiveness. When this occurs, the therapist should use systematic desensitization (see pp. 230 to 252) to help the client feel more calm and relaxed in these situations.

Finally, the therapist should not assume that successful assertive training in one situation, or applied to one area of the person's life (e.g., his interactions with his colleagues at work) will *generalize* to other important areas (e.g., his interactions with his wife and/or children). The experience of the present author as well as others (e.g., Lazarus, 1973) is that generalization does not usually occur. Assertive training, therefore, should also be performed in those other areas of the person's life in which he is behaving in a nonassertive manner. The result of such training will be that the client will be able to appropriately demonstrate love, affection, warmth, and aggressive behavior.

IMPLOSIVE THERAPY

The third method which will be discussed is called *implosive therapy*. Like systematic desensitization, this procedure makes use of the imaginal presentation of anxiety-provoking material. But unlike desensitization, this procedure from the very beginning requires the client to imagine a very fearful and threatening scene for a prolonged period of time without undergoing any previous relaxation training.

The purpose of implosive therapy is to produce a frightening experience in the person of such magnitude that it will actually *lessen* his fear of the particular situation rather than heighten it. Developed by psychologist Thomas G. Stampfl (e.g., Stampfl, 1961; Stampfl and Levis, 1967), this method utilizes principles from both learning theory and psychodynamic theory (e.g., Freud's psychoanalytic theory). Though Stampfl maintains that fears and their associated anxiety are learned, he does not assume that such fears can be most effectively reduced by using a counterconditioning approach. Rather, he believes that a person can best unlearn his fear by using a procedure based on an *extinction model*. Here, extinction refers to the gradual reduction in the occurrence of an anxiety response, as a result of the continuous presentation of the fear producing stimulus situation in the absence of the reinforcement which perpetuates the fear. In therapy, this extinction process is accomplished by having the therapist "...re-present, reinstate, or symbolically reproduce the stimuli (cues) to which the anxiety response has been conditioned..." without presenting the concomitant reinforcement which maintains the response (Stampfl and Levis, 1967, p. 499.)*

---

*In this statement, Stampfl and Levis (1967) are using the term "reinforcement" in the classical conditioning sense of the word, i.e., the procedure of following a conditioned stimulus (CS) with an unconditioned stimulus (UCS).

The Development of the Avoidance Serial Cue Hierarchy

From information gathered during the initial interview, the therapist develops hypotheses concerning what are the important cues involved in the client's fear. Many of these cues are situational events in the client's life and can be readily identified. For example, in the case of those people who have a fear of heights, the situational events may be the sight of high-rise office and apartment buildings, winding roads in the mountains, airplanes, bridges, etc.

The remaining cues are formulated by the therapist, and are based on psychodynamic theory and on his knowledge of common reactions by clients with similar problems. They are derived from the client's statements in the initial interview as well as from his nonverbal behavior, and represent those psychodynamic areas which the therapist believes are relevant to the client's fear(s). These cues are usually related to themes of aggression and hostility, oral and anal activity, sexual activity, punishment, rejection, bodily injury, loss of impulse control, and guilt. For example, Stampfl and Levis (1967) describe four of the hypothesized dynamic cues in the following manner:

> *Aggression*. Scenes presented in this area usually center around the expression of anger, hostility, and aggression by the patient toward parental, sibling, spouse, or other significant figures in his life. Various degrees of bodily injury are described including complete body mutilation and death of the victim.
>
> *Punishment*. The patient is instructed to visualize himself as the recipient of the anger, hostility, and aggression of the various significant individuals in his life. The punishment inflicted in the scene is frequently a result of the patient's engaging in some forbidden act.
>
> *Sexual material*. In this area a wide variety of hypothesized cues related to sex are presented. For example, primal and Oedipal scenes and scenes of castration, fellatio, and homosexuality are presented.
>
> *Loss of control*. Scenes are presented where the patient is encouraged to imagine himself losing impulse control to such an extent that he acts out avoided sexual or aggressive impulses. These scenes usually are followed by scenes where the individual is directed to visualize himself hospitalized for the rest of his life in a back ward of a mental hospital as a result of his loss of impulse control. This area is tapped primarily with patients who express fear of "becoming insane" or concern about being hopeless and incurable. (p. 501.)*

Those cues which are lowest on the hierarchy are assumed to be the situations and events which the client can associate with his fear. The highest cues are those internal dynamic cues that the therapist believes are closely associated with the client's basic psychological problem. The particular dynamic themes emphasized in the hierarchy will depend on the client's problem and the information obtained in the initial interview.

The hierarchy scenes are developed by the therapist after the initial interview is completed. They are not developed by the client and therapist as in systematic desensitization. Overall, the hierarchy is quite different from the one developed in systematic desensitization. For example, the Avoidance Serial Cue Hierarchy

---

*From Stampfl, T. G. and Levis, D. J. Essentials of implosive therapy: A learning-based-psychodynamic behavioral therapy. *Journal of Abnormal Psychology*, 1967, 72, 496–503. Reprinted by permission.

only contains items which are thought to be capable of producing a maximum level of anxiety in the client. This is not the case for the desensitization hierarchy. The latter hierarchy is developed for a different reason, namely, to proceed gradually up the hierarchy in order to minimize the possibility that the client will experience any anxiety. The Avoidance Serial Cue Hierarchy starts with items which produce maximum anxiety in the person and proceeds from external stimuli that evoke anxiety to hypothesized internal stimuli which also produce maximum levels of anxiety.

An example of this type of hierarchy is presented below:

Fear of Rats
Imagine that you are touching a rat in the laboratory . . . it begins nibbling at your finger . . . and then runs across your arm. The rat suddenly bites you on your arm, and then you feel it run rapidly over your body . . . It begins biting your neck and swishing its tail in your face . . . then it claws up your face into your hair . . . clawing in your hair . . . you try to get it out with your bloody arm, but you can't. It then goes for your eyes . . . you open your mouth and it jumps in and you swallow it . . . It then begins to eat away at various internal organs—like your stomach and intestines, causing you great discomfort and pain . . . etc.*

In the next example, Stampfl (1970) discusses a hierarchy concerned with a fear of enclosed spaces.

. . . The client is instructed to imagine that he is entering a closed room. He remains there and is instructed to imagine that he is slowly suffocating to death . . . [the therapist supplies many details about suffocation and then, based on information obtained in the interview, might present] scenes involving wrongdoing, with a parental figure supervising confinement to the closed space as a punishment. The parental figure might beat and scold the patient while he suffocates. Early traumatic incidents that appear to be related to the phobia may also be introduced, as represented in teasing sequences by being covered and held under blankets. If the patient appears to have been involved in a typical Oedipal situation in childhood, the therapist may suggest scenes that include sexual interaction with a mother figure followed by apprehension by a father figure, who places the patient in a closed space and castrates him . . . the cues related to bodily injury are vividly described. (p. 200.)†

Implosive Therapy Proper

After the hierarchy has been planned, the therapist describes implosive therapy to the client. This usually occurs at the beginning of the third session. It involves telling the client that a number of scenes will be presented to him, and that he is to sit back in the recliner chair and make every effort "to lose himself" in that part of the scene he is playing and to "live" the scenes with genuine emotion and feeling. The goal then is ". . . . to reproduce in the absence of physical pain, as good an approximation as possible, the sights, sounds, and tactual experiences originally present in the primary . . ." situation in which the fear was learned (Stampfl and Levis, 1968, p. 33).

---

*From Hogan, R. A. and Kirchner, J. H. A preliminary report of the extinction of learned fears via short term implosive therapy. *Journal of Abnormal Psychology*, 1967, 72, 106–111. Copyright 1967 by the American Psychological Association. Reprinted by permission

†From Stampfl, T. G. Implosive Therapy: An Emphasis on Covert Stimulation. In D. J. Levis (Ed.), *Learning approaches to therapeutic behavior change*. Chicago: Aldine, 1970. Reprinted by permission.

The client is neither asked to accept the accuracy of what he is imagining nor to agree that the scenes are representative of his fear(s). The scenes are then described by the therapist and are elaborated on in vivid detail. The more dramatic the presentation of the scenes the easier it is for the client to participate fully in the experience. Then, as Stampfl and Levis (1967) state,

> .... an attempt is made by the therapist to attain a maximal level of anxiety evocation from the patient. When a high level of anxiety is achieved, the patient is held on this level until some sign of spontaneous reduction in the anxiety-inducing value of the cues appears ... the process is repeated, and again, at the first sign of spontaneous reduction of fear, new variations are introduced to elicit an intense anxiety response. This procedure is repeated until a significant diminution in anxiety has resulted. (p. 500.)*

One way of determining if the scenes are producing anxiety in the client is to observe if the client is either flushing, sweating, grimacing, moving his head from side to side, or increasing his motoric activity in the chair. The implosion procedure is maintained for about 30–40 minutes. After a scene has been presented a few times and upon observing that the client experiences anxiety to this scene, he is given the opportunity to present the scene to himself through imagination, and is encouraged to act-out fully in his imagination his part in the scene. The therapist continues to monitor the presence of anxiety and aids the client by suggesting that he imagine the scene vividly. Sometimes the client will mention to the therapist a few additional events in his life which produce his fear response. These should be noted by the therapist and included in the next implosive therapy session.

The session ends after 50–60 minutes and after the client has demonstrated a diminution in his anxiety response to the implosive scene(s). The client is then told to practice imagining the implosive scenes at home about once a day until the next session. This practice not only extends treatment outside the therapist's office, and therefore aids in the generalization of the treatment effects, but it also helps the client realize that he, himself, can effectively deal with his fears by using the implosive therapy procedure. In fact, it "... is hoped that at the termination of treatment the patient will be able to handle new anxiety-provoking situations without the therapist's help" (Stampfl and Levis, 1967, p. 500).

The following excerpt from a therapy session with a snake phobic woman demonstrates how implosive therapy has been used.

> Close your eyes again. Picture the snake out in front of you, now make yourself pick it up. Reach down, pick it up, put it in your lap, feel it wiggling around in your lap, leave your hand on it, put your hand out and feel it wiggling around. Kind of explore its body with your fingers and hand. You don't like to do it, make yourself do it. Make yourself do it. Really grab onto the snake. Squeeze it a little bit, feel it. Feel it kind of start to wind around your hand. Let it. Leave your hand there, feel it touching your hand and winding around it, curling around your wrist.

In this second excerpt the level of anxiety is raised and the tempo of the presentation is increased.

---

*Reprinted by permission.

Okay, now put your finger out towards the snake and feel his head coming up. No, it is in your lap, and it is coming up. Its head towards your finger and it is starting to bite at your finger. Let it, let it bite at your finger. Put your finger out, let it bite, let it bite at your finger, feel its fangs go right down into your finger. Oooh, feel the pain going right up your arm and into your shoulder. You want to pull your hand away, but leave it there. Let the snake kind of gnaw at your finger. Feel it gnawing, look at the blood dripping off your finger. Feel it in your stomach and the pain going up your arm. Try to picture your bleeding finger. And the teeth of the snake are stuck right in your finger, right down to the bone. And it is crunching like on your finger there. Let it. Feel it biting, it is biting at your finger, it is biting, now it is coiling around your finger, and it is biting at your hand. Again and again and again . . . .

In the third section the level of anxiety is increased as the animal begins to attack the person's face or vital organs. This material is closer to the real fears of such Ss.

Okay, feel him coiling around your hand again, touching you, slimy, now he is going up on your shoulder and he crawls there and he is sitting on your chest and he is looking you right in the eye. He is big and he is black and he is ugly and he's coiled up and he is ready to strike and he is looking at you. Picture his face, look at his eyes, look at those long sharp fangs. He is staring at you, he is evil looking, he is slimy, he is ready to strike at your face. Feel him sitting there, just staring at you. Those long sharp teeth with the blood on them. He strikes out at you, (T slap hands). Feel him bite at your face. Feel him bite at your face, let him bite; let him bite; just relax and let him bite; let him bite at your face, let him bite; let him bite at your face; feel his fangs go right into your cheeks; and the blood is coming out on your face now. And the poison is going into your body and you are getting sick and nauseated and he is striking at your face again and again. Now he coils up on this shoulder and he is ready to strike again at your face. Feel him bite, put your head down towards him, put your head down, let him bite at your face, let him bite as much as he wants. Feel him bite, he is putting his head, his little head up by your ear and he is snapping at your ear. Feel him snap at your ear. Now he is going up by your eyes and he is starting to bite at your eyes, feel him bite at your eyes. Feel him bite, let him bite, feel his fangs go into your eyes and he is pulling at them and tearing at them and ripping at them. Picture what your face looks like. Get that sick feeling in your stomach and now he is gnawing at your nose, and biting at your mouth. Just take a deep breath and let him do it. Now he is coiling around your neck, slimy and wet and dirty, and he is squeezing you. He is choking you, feel him choke you, feel the breath come out of you, that sick feeling in your stomach. He snaps out at you, feel him snap at you. Now he is crawling across your face. Can you feel him? He is wet and slimy and he's touching your face, he is crawling up into your hair. Feel him up in your hair, coiled around up there . . . Feel him snap at you. Feel him snap; that sick feeling in your stomach, feel him biting you; he is gnawing at your cheeks now feel him, bluhh—and just picture how ugly you're looking and terrible, and he's enraged and he's biting and biting and biting and biting and biting and biting and biting.

And later the following scene:

Feel it up by your eye and it is going to bite it, it is going to pull it right out. Feel it is biting your eye and it is going to pull your eye right out and down on your cheek. It is kind of gnawing on it and eating it, eating at your eye. Your little eye is down on your cheek and it is gnawing and biting at your eye. Picture it. Now it is crawling into your eye socket and wiggling around in there, feel it wiggling and wiggling up in your head. Feel it wiggling around, uhhhh uhhhhh, feel it wiggling. And now it wiggles out of your eye, and now it is wiggling up into your nose. Feel it crawling right up into your nose, into your head, wiggling around and it is gnawing out through the other eye, from the inside. Feel it biting its way out.

For the most I do not let the S verbalize at will, because speech is often used as a defense to avoid anxiety. I am satisfied with a nod of the head or a brief comment to verify a clinical hypothesis. The reader will note that the therapist frequently goes right on after a comment by the client.

With clinical cases this next sequence would include greater sexual emphasis. I might have the snake swallowed by the S, and later it might exit from her vagina. I would have her play a male sexual role, or she might be castrated in an attempt to relive, in imagery, Freudian-related conflict.

> *Therapist*: I want you to picture yourself getting ready to get into your bed and there in your bed are thousands of snakes. Can you see them there crawling around in your bed? I want you to lay down with them. Get down with them. Feel yourself moving around with the snakes and they are crawling all over you. And you are moving and turning in bed and they are touching you. Feel them crawling on you, touching you, slimy and slithering. Feel yourself turn over in your bed, and they are under you and on you and around you, and touching your face and in your hair. And they are crawling across your face. Can you feel them touch you? Describe the feeling.
>
> *Subject*: Kind of cold.
>
> *Therapist*: Feel, you are now cold and clammy like a snake and they are touching you with their cold, clammy, wet, slimy, drippy, cold bodies that are wiggling and touching your skin and feel them. Uhhhh how can you feel them touch you. They are touching you. Can you feel them touch you? Move around so you can get greater contact. Move your body like that woman in the Seely ad and feel them touch you, uhhh, wiggly and slimy, they are crawling on you, on your face. Uhhh!

Because of this S's overt responses to the series of imagery in which we had her swallow the snake, and in view of our clinical judgment that she had oral conflicts, (she is overweight and seemed to be an oral aggressive personality) we included the material in this final section.

> *Therapist*: Squeeze it now, softly, kind of get the squish of it. Feel it bite, feel it bite. Squeeze it harder. Does that bother you to do that? Kind of knead its body like it was dough. Stick your nails into it and break open its skin. Feel its insides start to squish out. Squish it between your fingers. Kind of squish it up now in little pieces like it was dough. Squish it, take that sloushy stuff and put it up by your face. Go on up by your face. Rub it on your face quickly. Feel it, uhhhh, you don't like that part of it do you? Put it down, uhhhhh, squish it some more. Now rub your hands in that mess, and put that by your face and leave it there. Up by your nose, uhhh smell it, feel it. It is cold come on, put it on your face. You are pulling away from it, okay put your hand down. Pick up the snake; pick it up, put it up by your mouth. Bite its head off. Bite its head. Bite it! Bite it! Did you bite it? Chew its head. Feel it. Chew it! Chew it! Chew it! Chew it hard. You are not chewing it. Chew it. Now swallow it, uhhh, it is inside you, the poison and uhhh it is dripping down in your stomach. Do you feel it in your stomach? Its head is down there. It is laying in your stomach, the head is biting now, it is biting down in your stomach. It is moving around and biting. Feel it down in your stomach. Uhhh! It is wiggling around, it is wiggling by itself, that head. Pick up another snake, pick it up. Bite its head off, bite it. Now chew it. Chew it! Chew it! Chew it! Chew it! Chew it! Feel its crunching in your mouth. Feel its crunching hard, bite it, swallow it; uhhh it's down in your stomach, can you feel that sick feeling in your stomach? . . .

Alternatives to Implosive Therapy

A variant of implosive therapy is called *flooding*. The major difference between this method and implosive therapy is in the type of scenes to which clients are exposed. Instead of exposing clients to horrifying scenes in which certain consequences occur (e.g., eating flesh, castrating people, death, etc.), scenes are described in which the feared external stimuli are presented for an extended period of time.* For example, compare the implosive therapy scene described above (about the rat) with the following flooding scene:

> While studying at your desk in the laboratory you suddenly become aware of a large rat crawling up your leg. You jump up and try to shake it off, but it runs up your side . . . across your face . . . into your hair and is caught there. In an attempt to get loose, its tail falls down onto your face and touches your lips. You try to get him off your head, but you fail . . . etc. (Adapted from Rachman, 1966, p. 3.)

Thus, psychodynamic cues and/or interpretations are not used in the formulation of the scenes; rather, the therapist uses only the external cues and vividly describes the scenes in a way similar to implosive therapy. Scenes are presented for about the same period of time as in implosive therapy, and an attempt is made at also maintaining the client's anxiety arousal at a maximum level throughout the session.

Limitations of Implosive Therapy

Stampfl and Levis (1967) state that "the more accurate the hypothesized cues and the more realistically they are presented, the greater the extinction effect . . . will be" [p. 499]. This statement suggests that the therapist should be quite knowledgeable in psychodynamic theory, especially psychoanalytic theory. If he is not, he should probably refrain from using this approach. A possible substitute for this therapy is the flooding procedure, but this, too, should be used with caution unless the therapist is very familiar with identifying anxiety cues, formulating highly anxiety-provoking scenes, and is capable of dealing with a client who might have a very negative experience to the anxiety-provoking scenes that are presented.

CONCLUSION

The three methods discussed in this chapter have been widely used in the reduction of fears. The major question, however, which has not been answered is "Which one should I use in reducing a client's fear?" The question is not easily answered, but we will attempt to provide a guideline regarding when the therapist should use each method.

Without doubt the most useful and most heavily researched fear reduction method is systematic desensitization. It has been shown in many studies to be very effective in reducing various types of fears.

Its only limitation is that it is extremely time consuming when the client has a great number of fears. Even considering this limitation, it appears that systematic desensitization is the treatment of choice for most fears.

---

*This distinction between flooding and implosive therapy has been questioned by Levis (1974).

On the other hand, if a client's fears are strictly related to social situations—where he is afraid to act in his own behalf—then assertive training should be tried first. If, however, the client is afraid to practice his assertiveness training in the real situation, then desensitization should be used to help him relax in this situation.

Finally, because of the limitations mentioned at the end of the Implosive Therapy section and because implosive therapy has not been generally found to be more effective than systematic desensitization (see Morganstern, 1973), implosive therapy should not be used as the first treatment of choice.

REFERENCES

Alberti, R. E. and Emmons, M. L. *Your perfect right.* San Luis Obispo, Calif.: Authors, 1970.

Baker, B. L., Cohen, D. C., and Saunders, J. T. Self-directed desensitization for acrophobics. *Behaviour Research and Therapy*, 1973, **11**, 79–89.

Bandura, A. *Principles of behavior modification.* New York: Holt, Rinehart and Winston, 1969.

Brady, J. P. Brevital-relaxation treatment of frigidity. *Behaviour Research and Therapy*, 1966, **4**, 71–77.

Brady, J. P. Systematic desensitization. In W. S. Agras (Ed.), *Behavior modification: Principles and clinical applications.* Boston, Mass.: Little, Brown, 1972.

Friedman, D. E. A new technique for the systematic desensitization of phobic symptoms. *Behaviour Research and Therapy*, 1966, **4**, 139–140.

Galassi, J. P., Delo, J. S., Galassi, M. D., and Bastien, S. The college self-expression scale: A measure of assertiveness. *Behavior Therapy*, 1974, **5**, 165–171.

Hogan, R. A. The implosive technique. *Behaviour Research and Therapy*, 1968, **6**, 423–431.

Hogan, R. A. and Kirchner, J. H. A preliminary report of the extinction of learned fears via short term implosive therapy. *Journal of Abnormal Psychology*, 1967, **72**, 106–111.

Hull, C. L. *Principles of behavior.* New York: Appleton-Century-Crofts, 1943.

Jacobson, E. *Progressive relaxation.* Chicago: University of Chicago Press, 1938.

Lazarus, A. A. *Behavior therapy and beyond.* New York: McGraw-Hill, 1971.

Lazarus, A. A. On assertive behavior: A brief note. *Behavior Therapy*, 1973, **4**, 697–699.

Lazarus, A. A. and Abramovitz, A. Learn to relax—A recorded course in muscular relaxation. Johannesburg: Troubadour Records, 1962.

Levis, D. J. Implosive therapy: A critical analysis of Morganstern's review. *Psychological Bulletin*, 1974, **81**, 155–158.

Marquis, J. N., Morgan, W. G., and Piaget, G. W. *A guidebook for systematic desensitization.* (2nd ed.) Palo Alto, Calif.: Veterans Workshop, 1971.

Migler, B. and Wolpe, J. Automated self-desensitization. A case report. *Behaviour Research and Therapy*, 1967, **5**, 133–135.

Morganstern, K. P. Implosive therapy and flooding procedures: A critical review. *Psychological Bulletin*, 1973, **79**, 318–334.

Morris, R. J. Shaping relaxation in the unrelaxed client. *Journal of Behavior Therapy and Experimental Psychiatry*, 1973, **4**, 353–354.

Morris, R. J. and Suckerman, K. R. The importance of the therapeutic relationship in systematic desensitization. *Journal of Consulting and Clinical Psychology*, 1974, **42**, 148. (a)

Morris, R. J. and Suckerman, K. R. Automated systematic desensitization: The importance of therapist warmth. *Journal of Consulting and Clinical Psychology*, 1974, **42**, 244–250. (b)

Mowrer, O. H. *Learning theory and personality dynamics.* New York: Roland Press, 1950.

Paul, G. L. *Insight vs. desensitization in psychotherapy.* Stanford, Calif.: Stanford University Press, 1966.

Pavlov, I. P. *Conditioned reflexes*. London: Oxford University Press, 1927.

Rachman, S. Studies in desensitization, II: Flooding. *Behaviour Research and Therapy*, 1966, **4**, 1–6.

Rathus, S. A. A 30-item schedule for assessing assertive behavior. *Behavior Therapy*, 1973, **4**, 398–406.

Richardson, F. C. and Suinn, R. M. A comparison of traditional systematic desensitization, accelerated massed desensitization, and anxiety management training in the treatment of mathematics anxiety. *Behavior Therapy*, 1973, **4**, 212–218.

Salter, A. *Conditioned reflex therapy*. New York: Farrar, Strauss, 1949. Republished: New York: Capricorn Books, Putman, 1961.

Sherman, A. R. Real-life exposure as a primary therapeutic factor in the desensitization treatment of fear. *Journal of Abnormal Psychology*, 1972, **79**, 19–28.

Skinner, B. F. *The behavior of organisms*. New York: Appleton-Century, 1938.

Skinner, B. F. *Science and human behavior*. New York: MacMillan, 1953.

Stampfl, T. G. Implosive therapy: A learning theory derived psychodynamic therapeutic technique. Paper presented at the University of Illinois, 1961.

Stampfl, T. G. Implosive therapy: An emphasis on covert stimulation. In D. J. Levis (Ed.), *Learning approaches to therapeutic behavior change*. Chicago: Aldine, 1970.

Stampfl, T. G. and Levis, D. J. Essentials of implosive therapy: A learning-based-psychodynamic behavioral therapy. *Journal of Abnormal Psychology*, 1967, **72**, 496–503.

Stampfl, T. G. and Levis, D. J. Implosive therapy—A behavioral therapy? *Behaviour Research and Therapy*, 1968, **6**, 31–36.

Wolpe, J. *Reciprocal inhibition therapy*. Stanford, Calif.: Stanford University Press, 1958.

Wolpe, J. The experimental foundations of some new psychotherapeutic methods. In A. J. Bachrach (Ed.), *Experimental foundations of clinical psychology*. New York: Basic Books, 1962.

Wolpe, J. *The practice of behavior therapy*. New York: Pergamon Press, 1969.

Wolpe, J. *The practice of behavior therapy*. (2nd ed.) New York: Pergamon Press, 1973.

Wolpe, J. and Lazarus, A. A. *Behavior therapy techniques*. New York: Pergamon Press, 1966.

Wolpin, M. and Pearsall, L. Rapid deconditioning of a fear of snakes. *Behaviour Research and Therapy*, 1965, **3**, 107–111.

APPENDIX 1

FEAR SURVEY SCHEDULE*

The items in this questionnaire refer to things and experiences that may cause fear or other unpleasant feelings. Write the number of each item in the column that describes how much you are disturbed by it nowadays.

	Not at All	A Little	A Fair Amount	Much	Very Much
1. Open wounds					
2. Dating					
3. Being alone					
4. Being in a strange place					
5. Loud noises					
6. Dead people					
7. Speaking in public					
8. Crossing streets					
9. People who seem insane					

*Adapted from Wolpe, J. *The practice of behavior therapy* (2nd ed.) New York: Pergamon Press, 1973.

	Not at All	A Little	A Fair Amount	Much	Very Much
10. Falling					
11. Automobiles					
12. Being teased					
13. Dentists					
14. Thunder					
15. Sirens					
16. Failure					
17. Entering a room where other people are already seated					
18. High places on land					
19. Looking down from high buildings					
20. Worms					
21. Imaginary creatures					
22. Strangers					
23. Receiving injections					
24. Bats					
25. Journeys by train					
26. Journeys by bus					
27. Journeys by car					
28. Feeling angry					
29. People in authority					
30. Flying insects					
31. Seeing other people injected					
32. Sudden noises					
33. Cockroaches					
34. Crowds					
35. Large open spaces					
36. Cats					
37. One person bullying another					
38. Tough looking people					
39. Birds					
40. Sight of deep water					
41. Being watched working					
42. Dead animals					
43. Weapons					
44. Dirt					
45. Crawling insects					
46. Sight of fighting					
47. Ugly people					
48. Fire					
49. Sick people					
50. Dogs					
51. Being criticized					
52. Walking on dark streets alone					
53. Being in an elevator					
54. Witnessing surgical operations					
55. Angry people					
56. Mice					
57. Blood					
(a) Human					
(b) Animal					

	Not at All	A Little	A Fair Amount	Much	Very Much
58. Parting from friends					
59. Enclosed places					
60. Prospect of a surgical operation					
61. Feeling rejected by others					
62. Airplanes					
63. Medical odors					
64. Feeling disapproved of					
65. Harmless snakes					
66. Cemeteries					
67. Being ignored					
68. Darkness					
69. Premature heart beats (Missing a beat)					
70. Nude men (a) Nude women (b)					
71. Lightning					
72. Doctors					
73. People with deformities					
75. Looking foolish					
76. Losing control					
77. Fainting					
78. Becoming nauseous					
79. Spiders (Harmless)					
80. Being in charge or responsible for making decisions					
81. Sight of knives or sharp objects					
82. Becoming mentally ill					
83. Being with a member of the opposite sex					
84. Taking written tests					
85. Being touched by others					
86. Feeling different from others					
87. A lull in conversation					
88. Laboratory rats					
89. Taking any type of test					
90. Public speaking (speaking in front of groups)					
91. Looking down from high places					

APPENDIX 2

REVISED WILLOUGHBY QUESTIONNAIRE FOR SELF-ADMINISTRATION*

Instructions. The questions in this schedule are intended to indicate various emotional personality traits. It is not a test in any sense because there are no right and wrong answers to any of the questions. After each question you will find a row of numbers whose meaning is given below. All you have to do is to draw a ring around the number that describes you best.

0 means "No," "never," "not at all," etc.
1 means "Somewhat," "sometimes," "a little," etc.
2 means "About as often as not," "an average amount," etc.
3 means "Usually," "a good deal," "rather often," etc.
4 means "Practically always," "entirely," etc.

1. Do you get anxious if you have to speak or perform in any way in front of a group of strangers?—0 1 2 3 4
2. Do you worry if you make a fool of yourself, or feel you have been made to look foolish?—0 1 2 3 4
3. Are you afraid of falling when you are on a high place from which there is no real danger of falling—for example, looking down from a balcony on the tenth floor?—0 1 2 3 4
4. Are you easily hurt by what other people do or say to you?—0 1 2 3 4
5. Do you keep in the background on social occasions?—0 1 2 3 4
6. Do you have changes of mood that you cannot explain?—0 1 2 3 4
7. Do you feel uncomfortable when you meet new people?—0 1 2 3 4
8. Do you daydream frequently, i.e. indulge in fantasies not involving concrete situations?—0 1 2 3 4
9. Do you get discouraged easily, e.g. by failure or criticism?—0 1 2 3 4
10. Do you say things in haste and then regret them?—0 1 2 3 4
11. Are you ever disturbed by the mere presence of other people?—0 1 2 3 4
12. Do you cry easily?—0 1 2 3 4
13. Does it bother you to have people watch you work when you do it well?—0 1 2 3 4
14. Does criticism hurt you badly?—0 1 2 3 4
15. Do you cross the street to avoid meeting someone?—0 1 2 3 4
16. At a reception or tea do you go out of your way to avoid meeting the important person present?—0 1 2 3 4
17. Do you often feel just miserable?—0 1 2 3 4
18. Do you hesitate to volunteer in a discussion or debate with a group of people whom you know more or less?—0 1 2 3 4
19. Do you have a sense of isolation, either when alone or among people?—0 1 2 3 4
20. Are you self-conscious before 'superiors' (teachers, employers, authorities)?—0 1 2 3 4
21. Do you lack confidence in your general ability to do things and to cope with situations?—0 1 2 3 4
22. Are you self-conscious about your appearance even when you are well-dressed and groomed?—0 1 2 3 4
23. Are you scared at the sight of blood, injuries, and destruction even though there is no danger to you?—0 1 2 3 4
24. Do you feel that other people are better than you?—0 1 2 3 4
25. Is it hard for you to make up your mind?—0 1 2 3 4

*From Wolpe, J. *The practice of behavior therapy* (2nd ed.). New York: Pergamon Press, 1973, by permission.

APPENDIX 3

BERNREUTER S–S SELF-SUFFICIENCY INVENTORY*

1. Yes No ? Would you rather work for yourself than carry out the program of a superior whom you respect?
2. Yes No ? Do you usually enjoy spending an evening alone?
3. Yes No ? Have books been more entertaining to you than companions?
4. Yes No ? Do you feel the need of wider social contacts than you have?
5. Yes No ? Are you easily discouraged when the opinions of others differ from your own?
6. Yes No ? Does admiration gratify you more than achievement?
7. Yes No ? Do you usually prefer to keep your opinions to yourself?
8. Yes No ? Do you dislike attending the movies alone?
9. Yes No ? Would you like to have a very congenial friend with whom you could plan daily activities?
10. Yes No ? Can you calm your own fears?
11. Yes No ? Do jeers humiliate you even when you know you are right?
12. Yes No ? Do you think you could become so absorbed in creative work that you would not notice the lack of intimate friends?
13. Yes No ? Are you willing to take a chance alone in a situation of doubtful outcome?
14. Yes No ? Do you find conversation more helpful in formulating your ideas than reading?
15. Yes No ? Do you like to shop alone?
16. Yes No ? Does your ambition need occasional stimulation through contacts with successful people?
17. Yes No ? Do you have difficulty in making up your mind for yourself?
18. Yes No ? Would you prefer making your own arrangements on a trip to a foreign country to going on a prearranged trip?
19. Yes No ? Are you much affected by praise, or blame, of many people?
20. Yes No ? Do you usually avoid taking advice?
21. Yes No ? Do you consider the observance of social customs and manners an essential aspect of life?
22. Yes No ? Do you want someone with you when you receive bad news?
23. Yes No ? Does it make you uncomfortable to be 'different' or unconventional?
24. Yes No ? Do you prefer to make hurried decisions alone?
25. Yes No ? If you were to start out in research work, would you prefer to be an assistant in another's project rather than an independent worker on your own?
26. Yes No ? When you are low in spirits do you try to find someone to cheer you up?
27. Yes No ? Have you preferred being alone most of the time?
28. Yes No ? Do you prefer traveling with someone who will make all the necessary arrangements to the adventure of traveling alone?
29. Yes No ? Do you usually work things out rather than get someone to show you?
30. Yes No ? Do you like especially to have attention from acquaintances when you are ill?
31. Yes No ? Do you prefer to face dangerous situations alone?
32. Yes No ? Can you usually see wherein your mistakes lie without having them pointed out to you?
33. Yes No ? Do you like to make friends when you go to new places?
34. Yes No ? Can you stick to a tiresome task for long without someone prodding or encouraging you?
35. Yes No ? Do you experience periods of loneliness?
36. Yes No ? Do you like to get many views from others before making an important decision?

*From Wolpe, J. *The practice of behavior therapy* (2nd ed.). New York: Pergamon Press, 1973, by permission.

37. Yes No ? Would you dislike any work which might take you into isolation for a few years, such as forest ranging, etc.?
38. Yes No ? Do you prefer a play to a dance?
39. Yes No ? Do you usually try to take added responsibility upon yourself?
40. Yes No ? Do you make friends easily?
41. Yes No ? Can you be optimistic when others about you are greatly depressed?
42. Yes No ? Do you try to get your own way even if you have to fight for it?
43. Yes No ? Do you like to be with other people a great deal?
44. Yes No ? Do you get as many ideas at the time of reading as you do from a discussion of it afterwards?
45. Yes No ? In sports do you prefer to participate in individual competitions rather than in team games?
46. Yes No ? Do you usually face your troubles alone without seeking help?
47. Yes No ? Do you see more fun or humor in things when you are in a group than when you are alone?
48. Yes No ? Do you dislike finding your way about in strange places?
49. Yes No ? Can you work happily without praise or recognition?
50. Yes No ? Do you feel that marriage is essential to your happiness?
51. Yes No ? If all but a few of your friends threatened to break relations because of some habit they considered a vice in you, and in which you saw no harm, would you stop the habit to keep friends?
52. Yes No ? Do you like to have suggestions offered to you when you are working a puzzle?
53. Yes No ? Do you usually prefer to do your own planning alone rather than with others?
54. Yes No ? Do you usually find that people are more stimulating to you than anything else?
55. Yes No ? Do you prefer to be alone at times of emotional stress?
56. Yes No ? Do you like to bear responsibilities alone?
57. Yes No ? Can you usually understand a problem better by studying it out alone than by discussing it with others?
58. Yes No ? Do you find that telling others of your own personal good news is the greatest part of the enjoyment of it?
59. Yes No ? Do you generally rely on your judgment?
60. Yes No ? Do you like playing games in which you have no spectators?

APPENDIX 4

RATHUS ASSERTIVENESS SCHEDULE*

Directions. Indicate how characteristic or descriptive each of the following statements is of you by using the code given below.

+3 very characteristic of me, extremely descriptive
+2 rather characteristic of me, quite descriptive
+1 somewhat characteristic of me, slightly descriptive
-1 somewhat uncharacteristic of me, slightly nondescriptive
-2 rather uncharacteristic of me, quite nondescriptive
-3 very uncharacteristic of me, extremely nondescriptive

_____ 1. Most people seem to be more aggressive and assertive than I am.*
_____ 2. I have hesitated to make or accept dates because of "shyness."*

*Reversed item. From Rathus, S. A. in *Behavior Therapy*, Vol. 4, 1973, pp. 399–400. Reprinted by permission from author and Academic Press for research purposes only.

_____ 3. When the food served at a restaurant is not done to my satisfaction I complain about it to the waiter or waitress.

_____ 4. I am careful to avoid hurting other people's feelings, even when I feel that I have been injured.*

_____ 5. If a salesman has gone to considerable trouble to show me merchandise which is not quite suitable, I have a difficult time saying "No."*

_____ 6. When I am asked to do something, I insist upon knowing why.

_____ 7. There are times when I look for a good vigorous argument.

_____ 8. I strive to get ahead as well as most people in my position.

_____ 9. To be honest, people often take advantage of me.*

_____ 10. I enjoy starting conversations with new acquaintances and strangers.

_____ 11. I often don't know what to say to attractive persons of the opposite sex.*

_____ 12. I will hesitate to make phone calls to business establishments and institutions.

_____ 13. I would rather apply for a job or for admission to a college by writing them letters than by going through with personal interviews.*

_____ 14. I find it embarrassing to return merchandise.*

_____ 15. If a close and respected relative were annoying me, I would smother my feelings rather than express my annoyance.

_____ 16. I have avoided asking questions for fear of sounding stupid.*

_____ 17. During an argument I am sometimes afraid that I will get so upset that I will shake all over.*

_____ 18. If a famed and respected lecturer makes a statement which I think is incorrect, I will have the audience hear my point of view as well.

_____ 19. I avoid arguing over prices with clerks and salesmen.*

_____ 20. When I have done something important or worthwhile, I manage to let others know about it.

_____ 21. I am open and frank about my feelings.

_____ 22. If someone has been spreading false and bad stories about me, I see him (her) as soon as possible to "have a talk" about it.

_____ 23. I often have a hard time saying "No."*

_____ 24. I tend to bottle up my emotions rather than make a scene.*

_____ 25. I complain about poor service in a restaurant and elsewhere.

_____ 26. When I am given a compliment, I sometimes just don't know what to say.*

_____ 27. If a couple near me in a theatre or at a lecture were conversing rather loudly, I would ask them to be quiet or to take their conversation elsewhere.

_____ 28. Anyone attempting to push ahead of me in a line is in for a good battle.

_____ 29. I am quick to express an opinion.

_____ 30. There are times when I just can't say anything.

Total score obtained by adding numerical responses to each item, after changing the signs of reversed items.

CHAPTER 9

Aversion Methods

JACK SANDLER

INTRODUCTION

The control of undesirable behavior by means of aversive methods is probably the oldest of all forms of behavior modification. No doubt, the earliest observers of human behavior noted the essential common characteristics of all such techniques: undesirable behavior can be terminated if a sufficiently painful event is brought to bear on the behavior in question. It is a practice which has probably been repeated by every parent and teacher concerned with child discipline.

More recently, the general principle underlying the use of aversive control (applying a painful stimulus "contingent" on undesirable behavior) has been most frequently used as a treatment technique in the modification of self-reinforcing problem conditions which are extremely resistant to change. Perhaps the best example is alcoholism, although, as we shall see, almost the entire range of undesirable behavior is now being treated by aversive methods as our knowledge expands and our techniques improve.

These developments have also produced a mounting tide of furor and debate. In fact, if the behavior modification movement, in general, has initiated a great deal of controversy, perhaps no one topic focusses the arguments, both pro and con, more than the use of aversion therapy. Antagonists view these practices as the quintessence of all the "evils" of behavior therapy; it is simplistic, theoretically questionable, potentially dangerous, and possibly unethical. The protagonists, on the other hand, refer to the reports in the literature which reveal quick and efficient changes induced by such techniques, especially with problem conditions which have been resistant to treatment by traditional methods.

Perhaps this controversy is analogous to other complex social dilemmas: for example, the arguments pro and con relating to the use of DDT and the controversy regarding pollution control, to name just two of the weighty issues facing society. In each case, the disadvantages must be balanced against the advantages, and the short-term gains must be considered in the light of long-term risks.

The same problems and emotional debates arise with regard to aversion therapy. Somewhere between our concern for employing techniques which are currently effective for dealing with the multitude of cases that require immediate action, and our concern for employing techniques which are universally acceptable, some guidelines must be formulated to help the practitioner decide *when* such techniques should be employed. However, there are probably only a few cases in which the answer is readily formulated. Consider a situation in which we are dealing with a profoundly retarded, institutionalized deaf child who has started to poke sharply at his eyes with his fingers. Medical examination further reveals that such behavior will shortly result in a permanent loss of vision. Conventional wisdom can be invoked to determine the decision—immediate intervention designed to stop the eye-poking behavior as quickly as possible must be employed and probably only aversion therapy will accomplish this objective. *Not* to do so, in such a case, given the existing knowledge of the efficacy of such procedures, might even be considered a neglect of professional responsibility. Donald Baer (1970) has offered an excellent treatise on the moral imperatives involved in such decisions. In brief, Baer has argued that the use of aversion therapy should be made on the basis of scientific evidence, and not on the basis of preconceived biases. To refuse to use aversive methods on the latter grounds could conceivably relegate otherwise treatable patients to a lifetime of maladjustment.

Unfortunately, few situations are this clearcut. In the vast majority of cases, the decision to use or reject aversion therapy must be made despite the fact that all of the relevant information is not at hand. Thus there is no simple answer to the question "when to use aversion therapy?"

Perhaps a more fruitful approach to the use of aversion therapy might be obtained through an analysis of the advantages and disadvantages involved. In this fashion, we can direct our attention to the issue of maximizing the effectiveness of such techniques when they are employed.

There is nothing magical or mysterious about aversive forms of behavior control. As we have seen, techniques of this nature have been employed since antiquity. In fact, such practices are so prevalent that the point scarcely requires elaboration. Suffice it to say that many authorities agree that most attempts to control or regulate undesirable behavior are accomplished by means of aversive methods, from the parent who spanks a naughty child, to the teacher who chastises an unruly student, to the judge who fines a reckless driver. Such practices have been widely accepted and employed, at least in large part, because they "work" in the vast majority of instances, i.e., they get people to stop engaging in undesirable behavior.

If terminating undesirable behavior were the only question to be considered, we could simply detail the circumstances under which such control might be optimized and, in this fashion, develop a set of aversive procedures which would be maximally effective. Unfortunately, the actual situation is much more complex. The fact of the matter is that aversive methods of controlling behavior do *not* always work, and even when they do there are many additional problems generated by such techniques. Although such observations have been made by many students of human behavior, it is only recently that a relatively clear understanding of the limitations of aversive techniques has emerged, primarily as a result of laboratory studies with animals.

Perhaps the strongest critic of the use of aversive methods for behavioral control has been B. F. Skinner. Skinner has argued that while it is indeed true that aversive controls are "effective," the effects are often transient; furthermore, the techniques frequently result in counter aggression, and produce other forms of undesirable behavior. Thus, the net effect of such experiences might be other problem behaviors which are at least as serious as the target behavior (Skinner, 1953).

Additional reservations have been expressed by other writers, and there is a long-standing taboo in clinical psychology and psychiatry against the use of any techniques which allegedly treat only observable symptoms while ignoring the underlying cause. Both this position and the Skinner argument would predict that the reduction of some target behavior through aversion therapy might result in another form of (perhaps even more) undesirable behavior. More recently, these traditional criticisms of aversive controls have been questioned on the grounds that they are merely popular myths (Solomon, 1964) and overextended generalizations (Johnson, 1972). Part of the reason for these differences of opinion stem from the fact that, for the most part, aversion therapy has involved physically painful stimuli. As we shall see, this need not necessarily be the case and perhaps some of the reservations about conventional aversion therapy can be circumvented through the use of nonpainful physical methods.

One further complicating factor in assessing the advantages versus the disadvantages of aversion therapy stems from the fact that many clinical studies in the aversion therapy literature do not permit any reliable and valid conclusions about treatment effectiveness (Johnson, 1972). Perhaps the current situation can be summarized as follows: although many of the traditional reservations against the use of aversive methods may be questionable, only further research will provide answers. In the meantime, considering the present state of knowledge, a conservative rule of thumb may be offered when considering the modification of behavior. *Depending on circumstances, nonaversive techniques designed to counter undesirable behavior should be considered as the treatment of choice.* If aversive methods are invoked, when possible, nonphysical painful techniques should be attempted before resorting to painful stimulation. Thus, *with relatively mild, non-threatening or non-dangerous problem conditions, highly aversive techniques should rarely be employed. Conversely, given a serious condition in which an individual's biological or psychological integrity is in jeopardy, aversive techniques must be immediately considered.*

It should be emphasized that this merely represents a general guideline. Departures will depend upon a host of specific individual circumstances and will vary from one end of the continuum to the other.

General Description

At the practical level, a description of aversive procedures appears to be relatively straightforward and uncomplicated. For the most part, such arrangements involve an undesirable and/or maladaptive behavior on the part of the patient and the presentation of an unpleasant stimulus or event in close time relationship with the behavior. All forms of aversive treatment reflect these characteristics, whether commonplace and informal as in the case of the parent who spanks a child for playing with matches, or unusual and more systematic as in the case of administering shock to the fingertips of a child molester while he is handling children's clothing. The objective in each case, of course, is to reduce the future probability of occurrences of the maladaptive behavior.

A detailed analysis of the procedures which have been used, however, would quickly reveal the complexities which are involved in aversion therapy. Although it is not the intent of this chapter to analyze the theories underlying these efforts, the interested reader should at least be acquainted with the issues.

Briefly stated, there are two major theoretical positions which have attempted to explain such processes. Although there are areas of overlap between the two, they start from different assumptions and more often than not are *designed* to generate divergent treatment practices. Most of the aversion therapy reports in the literature reflect either one or the other theoretical assumption, although in actual practice, the differences between the two are often blurred.

The first of these emerged out of Pavlov's well-known research on conditioned responses in dogs. In this system, a previously *neutral stimulus* such as a buzzer, or a flashing light, is presented in close temporal contiguity with an *unconditioned stimulus*, i.e., a stimulus which naturally elicits a reflex reaction. After a sufficient number of such pairings, the previously neutral stimulus also acquires the power to elicit the reflex. Thus, when an organism is exposed to an aversive stimulus, certain physiological reflexes are evoked which are typically identified as the fear response. Furthermore, under appropriate circumstances, neutral stimuli which are present on such occasions also acquire the power to evoke the same or similar response. In this fashion, the fear response is "conditioned" to these previously neutral stimuli. Although this is by necessity an over-simplification of the conditioned fear hypothesis, these observations have been invoked to suggest both the manner in which certain maladaptive responses may be *acquired*, as well as the manner in which certain pathological responses may be *modified*. Thus, if an alcoholic is required to drink liquor while exposed to a painful stimulus which elicits the fear response, after a sufficient number of such experiences, the fear will become conditioned to the liquor. In the future, the sight, taste, and smell of liquor will elicit the physiological changes associated with the fear responses and the patient will be repelled by such substances. Indeed, as we shall see, procedures of this sort have been employed in a variety of problem conditions with varying degrees of success.

An alternate theory has been proposed by operant conditioners who focus their attention on the *consequences* of a response rather than on the events which precede a behavior. In this system (see Chapter 7 for an extensive discussion of the operant conditioning paradigm) the theory specifies that virtually all behaviors, abnormal as well as normal, are maintained or at least heavily influenced by reinforcing events. Thus, when a response produces a positively reinforcing event or avoids a negatively reinforcing event, the probability of future occurrence of that response increases. Conversely, when a response produces an aversive stimulus or is followed by no consequences, the probability of future occurrence of that response decreases. These arrangements are respectively defined as punishment and extinction. Again, such procedures have been employed in actual clinical practice. Thus, if a child who is a headbanger (a form of self-injurious behavior often observed in disturbed and retarded children) receives shock "contingent" on the undesirable behavior, that is, if each headbanging response "produces" the aversive event, after a sufficient number of such experiences, the response will decline in frequency.

It must be remembered that the above description represents the procedures and results obtained in the laboratory. In the clinical situation, there may be considerable departure from these arrangements such that an accurate analysis of the *actual* procedures is precluded. Thus, Pavlovian procedures may be inadvertently combined with operant procedures, and vice versa. For example, a Pavlovian procedure may dictate the use of shock paired on every occasion with alcohol-related stimuli, *independent* of the patient's behavior. The *actual* arrangement, however, may deviate from this procedure by virtue of the patient's response, thus confounding the procedure with operant conditioning. For this reason, it would appear that many techniques ostensibly designed within the context of one of the above systems frequently may be interpreted as involving processes from the alternate system.

Maximizing the Effects of Aversion Therapy

Once the decision to use aversion therapy has been made, it is the therapist's responsibility to apply the chosen technique in the most efficient manner possible, i.e., his efforts should include all of the ethical and scientific safeguards which are part of any therapeutic procedure. Ideally, then, the procedure should be designed to eliminate the problem condition permanently, as quickly as possible, and without undesirable residual effects.

Although it is impossible at the present time to specify all the conditions which would aid in reaching this objective, the therapist should attempt to approach the ideal as closely as possible. Since most of the recommendations for the effective use of aversive techniques have emerged from the operant literature, the assumption is made that most problem conditions encountered by clinicians can be regarded as the unfortunate learning of undesirable operants that create problems for the individual or the failure to learn those operants which enable a satisfactory adjustment in daily life.

First and foremost, at least at the beginning of treatment, the aversive event should be completely coincident with the problem behavior. That is, it should be administered each time the response occurs and it should not be administered in the absence of the response. This rationale stems from research which indicates that response reduction occurs most rapidly when the aversive stimulus is paired with the response whenever it occurs.

In many instances this principle can be easily applied without fear of error because of the specific characteristics of the response. A pronounced facial tic, for example, is usually easily identified (i.e., has discrete characteristics) and is of brief duration. With such a condition it is a relatively simple task to insure that the aversive event will be paired with each response and that it will never be presented under other circumstances.

A slightly more complex situation is encountered with head banging which may actually encompass a variety of responses with different topographies and durations. Thus, the head banger may involve different muscle groups from time to time; he may move the head forward, backward, or from side to side, or strike with different intensity. Furthermore, the head banging response also involves components of *normal* head movement which may be misinterpreted as precursors to the head banging. In practice, such subtle variations may result in the delivery of stimulation when unwarranted and/or in failure to deliver such stimulation when appropriate.

Even more difficulties are presented by the aversive treatment of alcoholism which involves elaborate response chains which are subject to considerable variation from time to time and place to place.

One way to resolve these problems is to circumscribe the variability of the behavior, for example, in head banging, by applying a mechanical device which enables only a forward thrust of the head, thus increasing the reliability of treatment. The disadvantage of this approach is that the treatment regime becomes somewhat artificial since it will differ from the natural circumstances under which the response occurs. This problem is dealt with in detail later on.

A *second* recommendation for maximizing treatment is to continue treatment until the problem behavior is no longer evident, thus enhancing the durability of the effect. This may appear to be so obvious as to require no elaboration. The fact of the matter, however, strongly suggests that aversion therapy is frequently ineffective precisely because the clinician has failed to continue treatment beyond some limited time range. "How long should therapy be maintained?" can only be answered empirically, i.e., it may be terminated after some reasonable length of time has elapsed (two weeks, six months) during which time the response has not occurred *under nonclinical circumstances.* A good criterion (and one which is unfortunately rarely employed) is the appearance of adaptive behavior under circumstances in which the problem behavior had previously occurred.

A *third* recommendation is to employ a stimulus or an event which is *in fact* aversive (in the sense that it would ordinarily be avoided) and not merely a stimulus which is *alleged to be* aversive on the basis of some *a priori* consideration. Again, the obvious requires explanation. Many ostensibly aversive stimuli may lose their noxious qualities with repeated occurrences. In fact, under special circumstances, they can even acquire reinforcing properties, thereby producing an effect which is directly opposite to the goal of aversion therapy. For example, there are numerous instances in the clinical literature referring to individuals who continually expose themselves to normally painful stimuli. Such "masochistic" behavior has been the subject of considerable interest in clinical psychology (Sandler, 1964). In general, most socially offensive stimuli such as threats, ridicule, insults, and menacing gestures are characterized by such limitations, but even physically painful stimuli may on occasion become reinforcing. It is probably for this reason that more and more aversion therapists are turning to the use of electric shock. The advantages of shock have been described on numerous occasions and require little elaboration (Azrin and Holz, 1966). Suffice it to say that electric shock may be considered as an almost universal aversive stimulus when used appropriately. Furthermore, shock has none of the brutal characteristics associated with conventional physical punishment such as paddling, beating, or slapping.

More recently, the search for nonphysical aversive events has produced several new techniques which appear to be extensions of traditional fines and penalties. These are more fully described in the section on operant procedures.

There are, of course, many other aspects of aversion therapy procedures which will enhance their effectiveness, especially when they are combined with other techniques as described in a later section. To paraphrase Johnson, the successful use of aversion therapy cannot be reduced to a concise summary of principles; the basic principles must be expanded in application to a variety of procedural details, the importance of any one of which will vary with each situation. Ignoring any of these variables will not doom necessarily any particular therapeutic endeavor; rather the probability of maximal effectiveness is increased to the extent that such factors are carefully considered in the therapeutic attempt (Johnson, 1972).

PROCEDURES AND TECHNIQUES

Pavlovian Procedures

It has been suggested that the therapeutic uses of aversive methods have generally followed one of the two learning paradigms: the Pavlovian model and the operant model. In the former case the procedure generally involves pairing an attractive stimulus with an aversive stimulus that ordinarily elicits pain, nausea, muscular retraction, etc. Although many such attempts are reported in the literature, they are subject to serious methodological and conceptual criticism (Feldman, 1966; Franks, 1963; Kushner and Sandler, 1966; Rachman, 1965).

We have already mentioned the major difficulty in this connection; that is, applying the Pavlovian model to responses which have pronounced operant components. In addition, Franks has argued that some Pavlovian procedures (especially those used in the treatment of alcoholism) may actually involve "backward" conditioning (see below); a tenuous form of learning, at best. Finally, a number of writers have indicated that Pavlovian effects may not be as durable as effects generated by means of operant conditioning procedures.

Perhaps the weight of these criticisms explains the increasing shift away from Pavlovian techniques in favor of operant techniques. Consequently, this review will be restricted to several representative reports.

By far, the most extensive body of literature based on Pavlovian aversive methods has been reported by investigators concerned with alcoholism. Of these, Lemere and Voegtlin (1950) present the most extensive and systematic series of observations. In their procedure, patients are administered emetine or apomorphine (unconditioned stimuli) which frequently elicit nausea and vomiting within thirty minutes. Shortly before vomiting occurs, the patient is instructed to drink his preferred alcoholic beverage. This procedure is repeated several times each day for ten days. Occasional "booster" sessions are administered after the patient is discharged. Voegtlin (1947) reports that about half of the patients treated in this fashion remain abstinent for at least two years.

The Pavlovian rationale is evident in the procedure. Ostensibly, after a sufficient number of pairings with emetine, the taste, sight, and smell of liquor should elicit nausea and vomiting. A similar rationale is offered in the treatment of alcoholism with antabuse, a drug which causes a violent physiological reaction when mixed with alcohol. Obviously, the validity of the rationale depends upon how closely these procedures approximate the Pavlovian paradigm. In fact, it would appear that such techniques may involve considerable departure from the classical conditioning procedure (Franks, 1963). Among other problems is the variation in individual responses to the drug. If a patient responds very quickly or very slowly (and this is hard to determine with certainty) the alcohol may be delivered too early or even after the patient experiences nausea.

Somewhat better control over the relevant events can be provided when the aversive event is electric shock, but even here methodological problems are still encountered. Pavlovian type procedures have also been used in a variety of therapeutic attempts designed to modify sexual deviancy. Close inspection of these procedures strongly suggests that operant processes were also involved and for this reason they are reviewed under that heading.

Operant Procedures

The second major category of aversion therapy techniques generally reflect the characteristics of the operant model. The rationale here stems from the assumption that behavior which results in unpleasant consequences will decrease in frequency. While there are important exceptions to this rule, the assumption has been well documented.

As we have seen, there are a number of conditions which must be taken into account, perhaps the most important of which is the close temporal relationship between the response and the aversive event (the contingency). For this reason, operant conditioners frequently describe such arrangements as examples of "response produced" aversive stimulation, even though the noxious event may be administered by an external agent.

This requirement can be properly implemented in the laboratory situation when the appropriate procedural controls are available. In clinical practice, however, limitations arise that frequently require some departure from the laboratory procedures. The degree of departure depends upon a variety of circumstances, the most important of which is the nature of the problem condition. For example, if therapy is designed to reduce the frequency of a writer's cramp, then the "real-life" circumstances in which such behavior occurs can be reasonably represented in the clinic, enabling the use of a contingency with the same or a similar response. The situation changes quite drastically, however, in the case of other problem conditions. For example, it is difficult (but not impossible) to recreate a reasonable approximation of the real-life circumstances related to alcoholism, and even greater problems are encountered with certain sexual deviations and aggressive behavior. Consequently, practitioners have devised a number of methods designed to circumvent this problem. For example, homosexuals are provided with problem-related stimuli such as pictures of same-sex nudes. They are then shocked in the presence of these stimuli. Or, patients are asked to imagine a "real-life" scene and then shocked when they signal the imagined presence of the scene. Although such techniques are by now almost standard practice, it must be acknowledged that these procedures involve (perhaps, at best) *problem-related* events rather than the actual problem behaviors themselves. That is not to imply that such techniques are therefore ineffective. On the contrary, many of these efforts have resulted in profound constructive changes in behavior. The reasons for this success, however, remain to be identified since they involve processes beyond those specified by a strict response-contingency model.

This section describes several techniques which are organized from the least physically aversive to the most physically aversive.

1. Time Out from Positive Reinforcement

Over the last few years, increasing attention has been turned to an aversive technique which has been termed Time Out from positive reinforcement (TO). This procedure assumes that a decrease in frequency can be effected if the opportunity to obtain positive reinforcement is denied the individual on the basis of some target behavior, for example, separating a child from the opportunity to receive peer reinforcement contingent on "show-off" behavior.

There are two major TO procedures: (a) removing the reinforcer from the individual and (b) removing the individual from the reinforcing system. In most instances, the choice will be made on the basis of practical considerations. In the first case, the major changes involve the removal of reinforcement with little change in the individual's status. A commonplace example is turning off the TV set as a result of an argument between children over a program preference. This makes the reinforcement inaccessible for a while. Or, in the case of a clinical example, turning away from a child during a rewarding activity when the child begins to engage in a temper tantrum. Thus, the adult's potential reinforcing stimuli are temporarily removed.

In the second case, the major changes usually involve the physical removal of the individual from the potentially available reinforcers. The teacher who isolates an aggressive child from the positive effects of classroom presence exemplifies a commonplace use of TO.

TO can be applied successfully with individuals of differing ages, personal characteristics, and problem conditions. Several examples are given in a later section of this chapter. In each case, the successful use of the technique depends upon (a) identifying the positive reinforcement; and (b) ensuring that the interruption of positive reinforcement is immediately and precisely contingent on the target behavior. In other words, *before* considering the use of TO, the practitioner must specifically isolate the positive reinforcement and develop a procedure which ensures the response-contingent nature of the arrangement. When these rules are neglected in actual practice, the effectiveness of TO will be reduced. The teacher who removes an aggressive child from a class activity which the child *dislikes* is not fulfilling the requirements of TO. Moreover, if he is sent to the office and becomes the target of individual attention on the part of the guidance counselor or principal, the undesirable behavior may increase rather than decrease in frequency. Similarly, the parent who sends a misbehaving child to a room in which there is a TV, games, and toys, has not deprived the child of positive reinforcement and therefore failed to maximize TO.

Some question has also been raised regarding the duration of TO. That is, once the undesirable response-reinforcement relationship has been determined, how long should the individual remain in TO? Although there is no simple rule of thumb, the duration should be established on the basis of combining practical and behavioral criteria. If a child is placed in TO, for example, in general he should remain there until he has lost several reinforcement opportunities and the undesirable behavior has stopped. In actual practice, it is probably best to limit TO to 10 to 15 minutes (although occasionally longer durations may be required initially), and then to gradually reduce the duration, thus more clearly defining the response consequence relationship.

In some cases, the difference between TO and an extinction procedure (see Chapter 7 for a detailed discussion) may be obscure. For example, the popular current practice of "turning away" from a child during a temper tantrum is frequently regarded as an attempt to extinguish such behavior, but may also be regarded as Time Out, primarily depending upon whether or not the reinforcement is completely withdrawn, as in extinction, or is merely withheld, as in TO. Obviously, in actual practice, it is difficult to distinguish between such arrangements.

In any event, the TO technique makes available to the clinician concerned with reducing the frequency of undesirable behavior an important addition to the more conventional aversive methods. When used as described above, there are many clinical problems which are amenable to such treatment.

2. Response Cost

A second aversive procedure which has received increasing attention has been termed response cost (Weiner, 1962). These arrangements are analogous to the conventional penalty technique in which an individual is fined for undesirable behavior. The major difference between the two is in terms of the systematic nature of response cost. Thus, driving illegally may *occasionally* result in a fine under the assumption that the loss in money will serve as a deterrent to such future behavior. The fact of the matter, however, is that these efforts frequently do not produce the desired outcome or are effective for only a limited duration.

Response-cost, on the other hand, requires a clear explication of the relationship between each undesirable response and the appropriately assigned penalty. When these requirements are maximized, the effectiveness of response cost as a deterrent is maximized. Perhaps for this reason, the clinical application of response cost has usually involved a loss of rewards earned for appropriate behavior.

For example, hospitalized patients may be operating under a token economy in which several different dimensions of constructive behavior earn tokens exchangeable for tangible rewards or privileges. Additional rules may be involved in which behavioral infractions result in the loss of tokens. Such combined reward, response-cost arrangements are usually very effective in generating desirable changes in constructive behavior.

On the other hand, if the ratio between amount earned and amount lost results in an overall deficit, the incentive of working for reinforcement decreases and the system may break down. It is important, then, for the practitioner to continuously monitor the effects of response cost in relation to earnings and to adjust the values of each accordingly.

3. Feedback

Several behavior modification techniques include the monitoring of behavior for the purpose of recording the frequency of a response. The monitoring procedure may take a variety of forms which range from a patient observing his own heart rate on an oscilloscope to the mere act of making a mark on a sheet of paper as in the case of an individual recording the number of cigarettes he has smoked.

Under such circumstances, and independent of any formal treatment, the mere act of "alerting" the individual to the response occurrence may influence the rate of the response (see discussion of self-monitoring in Chapter 10). Such effects have been termed *feedback* since they essentially provide information not ordinarily available to the person that a particular response has occurred. With certain problem conditions, feedback may result in a decrease in the frequency of a response. Although the causes of these effects are not well understood, the changes which are produced may have implications for aversion therapy.

Subsequently, a number of investigators have suggested procedures designed to enhance the effectiveness of feedback for reducing the frequency of a response. Thus, there are several examples in the behavior modification literature which demonstrate that self-charting resulted in a reduction in the frequency of smoking, drinking, overeating, or arguing. In these cases, it would appear that merely bringing attention to the high incidence of the behavior in question was sufficient to effect a constructive change. The client who suddenly realizes he is smoking three packs per day rather than the two initially reported must make an adjustment to this new information.

In still other situations, the effectiveness of feedback can be enhanced if it is systematically presented in connection with an appropriate change in behavior. Several investigators, for example, have found that stuttering rates can be suppressed if each dysfluency was immediately followed by delayed auditory feedback (Siegel, 1970). In these cases, since delayed auditory feedback is regarded as aversive by most individuals, the procedure seems to be analogous to the punishment paradigm described in greater detail below.

There are still many questions which remain to be answered about response-feedback techniques; heir major role as a treatment device would seem to be largely in terms of generating initial changes, but these changes will probably be transitory unless buttressed by other techniques.

4. Unconditioned Aversive Stimuli

By far the bulk of the operant aversion therapy literature involves the use of stimuli which are physically unpleasant or even painful. In these techniques, the noxious event occurs in a response-produced or correlated arrangement. A wide variety of stimuli have been employed for this purpose, most of which usually elicit the withdrawal response (for example, foul odors, uncomfortable sound, and painful stimuli such as slaps, hair pulls, and electric shock applied to an area of the limbs). Sometimes these stimuli have been paired with explicit conditioned stimuli such as shouts, reprimands and, disapproving gestures and facial expressions.

The vast majority of these efforts have employed shock, since it complies with the requirements for maximizing the effects of aversion therapy as described earlier. In addition, the intensity and duration of shock can be adjusted in the light of treatment requirements. For these reasons, the current review is largely restricted to shock procedures.

Considerable research with shock, both in the laboratory and in clinical situations, has been conducted, providing good descriptions of the manner in which the effectiveness of shock can be maximized.

In brief, in order to achieve the optimal aversion therapy effect, initially the shock should be delivered at a high intensity (rather than gradually increased), relatively briefly (0.05 seconds, for example), and coincident with the onset of each target response. At some later stage in treatment, a shift to a variable schedule of shock delivery (see Chapter 7 on operant conditioning) might be considered in order to enhance the durability of the suppression effect.

The variety of problem conditions which have been treated via such procedures range across a wide behavioral spectrum, from relatively commonplace responses, such as cigarette smoking, to broad dimensions of complex pathological behaviors, such as child molesting and disturbing obsessions. A review of several clinical investigations and case sudies is presented in the section below entitled Practical Applications.

Combining Aversion Therapy with Other Techniques

This section is concerned with the manner in which the techniques described above can be used with additional procedures in order to maximize treatment effectiveness.

Although they are usually a part of any behavior change program (and as such they are also described in other chapters), the emphasis here is upon their use in conjunction with aversion therapy.

There are two reasons for including such practices. First, practically speaking, as we have seen, any attempt to apply a laboratory procedure to clinical situations usually results in some departure from the use of the technique under "pure" circumstances. Secondly, there is increasing evidence that the effects of aversion therapy can be enhanced if the practitioner *systematically* includes other learning techniques. That is, a more rapid and longer lasting reduction of the undesirable behavior can be achieved under such circumstances than would be true if time-out, response cost, etc. were used alone.

1. Including Response Alternatives

Several studies have shown that a change in target behavior can be expedited if an alternative response is available to the patient. In some cases, the therapist may explicitly encourage such "new" learning, and if this technique is combined with a procedure designed to eliminate an undesirable response, positive treatment results can be maximized. Although such procedures have been variously termed *counter-conditioning*, *differential reinforcement of other behavior* (DRO), or *reinforcement of incompatible behavior*, they share the practice of *concurrently manipulating more than one response dimension in a treatment program*. Thus, a counter-conditioning program might involve shock contingent on an undesirable response such as aggressive behavior and, at the same time, provide positive reinforcement for an adaptive alternative response, for example, cooperative behavior.

While it may be assumed that some new response will emerge in every aversive procedure, the response alternative technique requires that the alternative response be identified prior to treatment. For this reason, we distinguish between those programs which formally and explicitly incorporate a response alternative and those procedures in which this process might have occurred but was not planned for. Obviously, the clinician interested in such techniques should acquire some understanding of general learning principles beyond those which are limited to aversive conditioning.

The advantages of the response alternative procedure are numerous: it can be used with all of the techniques described above; it enhances the treatment process thereby reducing the number of aversive experiences required to modify behavior; it enhances the durability of the effect; and, perhaps most important of all, it offers an adaptive alternative to the individual which may generalize outside the clinic arena. The common practice of substituting Life Savers for cigarettes reflects some of the features of the alternative response technique.

2. Fading

As we have seen, constructive changes which occur in one situation may not necessarily generalize to other situations. The child who is trained to cooperate in the classroom may continue to be aggressive at home or on the playground. Such "limited" change effects are particularly characteristic of attempts to treat certain problem conditions, such as alcoholism. It is not unusual, for example, for patients in a hospital treatment program to show a reduction in alcoholic behavior while in the hospital, only to break down soon after return to the environment in which the original drinking behavior occurred. The problem may be construed as an example of different reactions to different circumstances.

Obviously, then, the most effective treatment is that which accomplishes the greatest generality of change and the "fading" technique offers distinct advantages in this connection (also described in conjunction with operant methods in Chapter 7).

Essentially, fading involves a gradual change in the treatment situation such that either (a) reduction in undesirable behavior is maintained in the presence of new (and preferably more "relevant") circumstances, or (b) new circumstances are introduced in order to enhance changes in behavior. Such techniques have been used informally for many years.

A growing practice in penology, for example, involves a gradual series of "discharge experiences" in which a prisoner is first placed on a work-release program for limited duration, while readjusting to the requirements of normal life. He may also at first see his parole officer perhaps several times a week. If he is successful, he may be advanced to a half-way house and the number of parole visits reduced. In this fashion, the transition from prison life to normal life is gradually effected, under the assumption that constructive changes in behavior will be better maintained in the process.

Similarly, improving psychiatric hospital patients are first allowed several week-end passes at home, and if no problems arise, advance to a month's "trial visit." This may subsequently be extended depending upon the patient's adjustment outside the hospital.

The difference between these practices and a fading technique involves the greater degree of detail and rigor in the latter case. An ideal fading technique would provide for a gradual exposure to the patient's real-life physical and social stimuli so that all of the natural events relevant to the problem behavior are ultimately reflected in the treatment situation.

The closer the fading technique approaches the ideal, the greater the generality of treatment effects. One growing practice in the modification of children's behavior involves first instructing parents in treatment skills, and then gradually increasing their share of responsibility for treatment. Similarly, in aversion therapy, parents may be instructed in the use of a shock procedure to be applied in the home situation. In this fashion, the fading technique incorporates those individuals and those situations which will ultimately determine the durability of any constructive changes which first occurred in the treatment setting.

3. Schedules

Another technique which in some respects resembles fading involves changes in reinforcement schedules. It was mentioned earlier that treatment is initially most effective if the aversive event is applied to each instance of the undesirable response since this will result in the most rapid reduction of behavior. Greater durability of the desired reduction, however, can probably be achieved if the schedule of aversive events is unpredictable, e.g., every third or fourth response on an average. The frequency of aversive stimulation can be further gradually reduced if desired, although at some stage the practitioner will obviously be dealing with events which occur only infrequently. Thus, a cigarette smoker may initially receive ten shocks distributed over thirty cigarettes per day, but as the smoking rate declines to perhaps three or four cigarettes per day, adjustments in the shock schedule will also be required.

4. The Use of Significant Others

Where possible and appropriate, individuals who bear an important relationship to the patient may be incorporated into the treatment program. The rationale here again is similar to that underlying the use of fading, i.e., enhancing the durability of the change. Some instruction is obviously necessary, including specifically designating a Time-Out area, a response-cost system and even the use of response-contingent shock. As we shall see in the next section where this has been attempted and depending upon the degree of instruction and preparation, the results have been most impressive. For example, self-injurious behavior in disturbed children is very effectively controlled when parents are instructed to use the treatment technique in the home environment.

5. Self-Control

Finally, and perhaps most important, considerable attention has increasingly turned to the use of techniques designed to make the patient himself responsible for change (see Chapter 10 on self-management). The rationale here scarcely requires any explanation, although this is a development representing, in many respects, a radical departure from some conventional treatment practices which covertly, if not overtly, place the major responsibility for change on the therapist.

Techniques of this sort were first initiated in conjunction with problem behaviors which were difficult to analyze publicly, such as cigarette smoking, drinking, obsessions, compulsions, etc. More recently, self-control techniques have been employed with a wider variety of problem behaviors, including aggression, family arguments, temper tantrums, etc. Essentially, the procedure requires instructing the patient in a variety of techniques which are designed to alter one or more of the following: (a) typical undesirable reactions to particular occasions, (b) the sequence of responses which comprise the aggregate response (breaking up the chain), (c) the consequences of the undesirable behavior. Thus, an analysis of the relevant components of an undesirable behavior may reveal that it occurs under certain identifiable circumstances; that it is comprised of several discrete responses; and that it produces certain reinforcing events. Cigarette smoking, for example, usually occurs at regular intervals and in typical stimulus situations. This would provide a picture of the frequency of the smoking behavior. The chain for one smoker may be characterized by removing the package from the shirt pocket, withdrawing a cigarette with the right hand, tapping it on a hard surface, inserting it in the mouth, lighting it, taking several deep drags, keeping it dangling from the lips, alternating between deep drags and knocking off the ashes, and smoking it down rapidly to a short butt before extinguishing the cigarette. This would provide a picture of the topography of the response. Finally, an attempt might be made to analyze the response-reinforcement relationship.

With this information, the patient can be instructed in self-control techniques which would enhance the aversion therapy effects. For example, he might be instructed to avoid some of the circumstances in which smoking occurs with high frequency; he may be instructed to change some of the components of the chain, such as holding the cigarette in the left hand, placing the cigarette in an ashtray between drags, smoking less rapidly, etc. Finally, the patient may also be instructed in the self-administration of aversive events which could range anywhere from accumulating all the butts and inhaling the stale aroma, and placing a picture of a diseased lung in the pack, to self-imposing fines, denying privileges, and delivering shock.

Kanfer and Karoly (1972) recently offered a learning theory analysis of the issues related to self-control processes. Among other things, they suggest the manner in which relevant events can be employed to enhance clinically relevant changes. They point out the necessity for increasing client motivation, for example, through a contractual negotiation between the client and therapist which represents a statement of the client's intention or a promise of performance on his part.

There are probably additional procedures which should be considered along with those described above. In practice, there is sufficient overlap between the techniques such that the distinctions may be blurred. For the most part, the practitioner need not be concerned with the theoretical "purity" of the technique. What is probably more important is that as many as possible should be employed in a *systematic* fashion thereby optimizing the chances of a successful outcome.

SUMMARY

In brief, the information advanced in the preceding sections suggests several important steps that the therapist must take in any program using aversion methods. First, he should provide evidence that the event to be employed is indeed aversive; that it be applied on a response-contingent basis, and that it be maintained long enough to suppress the behavior for as long as possible.

Furthermore, durable changes can be insured if an alternative (adaptive) response is available, if ordinary, real-life circumstances are represented in the treatment setting, and if self-control techniques are integrated into the treatment program.

PRACTICAL APPLICATIONS

Up to now, the discussion has focussed on general principles and guidelines. Representative applications of the above from the operant aversion therapy literature will be described in the present section.

An arbitrary distinction is offered between: (a) those problem conditions which are relatively "circumscribed" and easily defined and, (b) problem behaviors which are more complex in their response dimensions and are less accessible to a "public" analysis. The term "compulsion" has been traditionally applied to many of the problem behaviors in the latter category under the assumption that there is an internal drive which compels the individual to engage in such behavior despite the maladaptive consequences. The behavior modification movement has called this assumption into question.

In any event, there is some reason to believe that, at least in our present state of knowledge, greater success has been realized with problems in the first category. This conclusion must be qualified by the fact that aversion therapy is a relatively young approach, and by the fact that successful treatment is determined not only by the complexity of the problem condition, but also by the precision and rigor of the treatment technique.

Where possible, examples contrasting each major aversion therapy technique within a problem condition are described.

Discrete and/or Easily Defined Problem Conditions

1. Self-Injurious Behavior

One of the problem behaviors frequently encountered in extreme forms of pathology are various forms of self-injurious behavior (SIB). Although many other problem conditions such as smoking, alcoholism, and gambling reflect similar characteristics, the SIB label is usually reserved for those behaviors which, if left unchecked, would *shortly* threaten the biological welfare of the individual. Thus, they require immediate intervention including physical restraint. Unfortunately, most of these interventions are temporary and ineffective.

In the clinical literature, the term SIB usually implies the involvement of the "voluntary" motor-response system as manifested by head banging, self-mutilation, pulling one's hair out, etc. In the present review, we shall also include examples possibly involving "involuntary" (or autonomic) processes.

(a) Head banging, self-biting, and similar problem behaviors. By far the most extensive application of aversion therapy with discrete problem conditions has involved the use of painful shock, contingent on head banging and self-mutilation in children. There are now a sufficient number of observations which confirm the effectiveness of such procedures, especially when compared with non-aversive techniques, in terms of rapid suppression of the behavior. Furthermore, when additional measures are incorporated in the procedure (for example, treatment

administered by parents of SIB children in the home) the suppressive effects generalize, thereby enabling the emergence of other more productive responses.

Perhaps the most impressive evidence of the efficacy of aversion therapy in such cases is provided by Lovaas and Simmons (1969). In this study, three severely retarded children displaying extreme forms of SIB (thereby requiring long periods of time in physical restraints) were exposed to response-contingent shock. In each case SIB was effectively and completely suppressed in the treatment setting after only a few shocks. The same treatment was also successfully applied by other individuals in other situations in order to maximize the generality of the effects.

Similar results have been reported by a number of other investigators. Tate and Baroff (1966) administered response shock to a blind nine-year-old boy who employed a wide assortment of SIB (head banging, face slapping, self-kicking, etc.). During 24 minutes prior to the treatment condition, 120 instances of SIB were recorded. For the next 90 minutes, a half-second shock was administered for each SIB and only five SIB responses occurred. The child was also praised for non-SIB. As the treatment progressed, the child was moved from restraints for increasing time intervals (fading). The rate of SIB continued to decline and no such responses were observed for 20 consecutive days. Interestingly enough, an increase in pro-social behavior emerged during this time.

Risley (1968) attempted to eliminate dangerous climbing behavior in a six-year-old retarded girl who was constantly injuring herself due to numerous falls. After several other techniques proved to be ineffective (DRO and TO) the use of response shock combined with verbal reprimands completely eliminated the climbing behavior in the treatment setting. After instruction, the child's mother employed the same technique in the home setting with the result that climbing behavior declined from about twenty responses to two responses per day. Once again, these changes were accompanied by a concurrent increase in constructive behavior in terms of attending and responding to social stimuli.

These efforts have been followed by a host of similar procedures with highly successful outcomes. Corte, Wolf, and Locke (1971) almost immediately and completely reduced SIB (including self-slapping, eye poking, hair pulling, and scratching the skin) in four retarded adolescents with response contingent shock, after an extinction procedure and a DRO procedure proved ineffective. Again, the treatment had to be applied outside the first treatment setting to enhance generalization.

A similar procedure was employed by Scholander (1972) for reducing a response in which a 14-year-old male continuously placed his hands around his neck. This behavior (which evidently emerged out of an epileptic condition) occurred with such high frequency that it was interfering with many normal ordinary activities, such as eating or dressing. The shock procedure resulted in a change from about 25 responses per day to zero in four and a half weeks, after which the shock apparatus was removed. No further responses occurred during a nine month follow-up.

Merbaum (1973) reduced SIB (beating face with hands) in a psychotic boy from an average of about 221 responses per 10-minute period to virtually zero in a two-hour treatment period. Similar results were obtained by the child's teacher and mother who were also instructed in providing positive reinforcement for non-SIB (differential reinforcement for other behavior or DRO). These effects were maintained over a one-year follow-up period and were accompanied by improvement in a variety of behavioral dimensions.

Finally, Greene and Hoats (1971) showed that "tickling" could be used to suppress SIB in one adolescent girl and aggressive behavior in a second. The procedure involved approaching the girl from the rear while she was engaged in the undesirable behavior, and tickling her beneath the arms forcefully and somewhat aggressively. This usually resulted in attempts to escape, on the part of the girls, thereby interrupting the undesirable behavior. If the target response was resumed, the tickling procedure was repeated and continued until the episode subsided. In each case, there was a substantial decrease in the frequency of the undesirable behavior, but this behavior did not completely disappear from the girls' repertoires.

This survey represents only a small sample of the breadth and variety of aversion therapy with SIB. Suffice it to say that, at least in this one area, aversion therapy has been highly successful in not only rapidly reducing the frequency of undesirable behavior but also establishing long term constructive changes. We have also seen that some of the reservations regarding the use of shock procedures are not supported by the evidence. On the contrary, it would appear that once control over the SIB is established, the path is clear for the development of other more adaptive responses.

(b) Self-induced vomiting. Perhaps as a result of the growing confidence in aversion therapy with SIB several clinicians have attempted to use similar procedures with other serious problem conditions which have been traditionally resistant to treatment.

One potentially dangerous but fortunately rare problem behavior involves self-induced vomiting. This is a condition characterized by the absence of physiological determinants as well as resistance to drug therapy, thus suggesting the influence of psychological factors. In extreme cases such conditions may result in a severe loss of weight, retarded development, and even threaten loss of life. For these reasons, immediate intervention is required and three studies report the successful cure of excessive nonorganically determined vomiting behavior.

Luckey, Watson, and Musick (1968) employed a response contingent shock with a chronic six-year-old retarded vomiter, after standard medical treatment failed to produce any constructive changes. The child was observed throughout the day, and one-second uncomfortable shock was administered whenever vomiting or its precursors occurred. By the fifth day, the treatment was reduced to two hours at each meal. Further reductions were introduced at later stages as the frequency of the behavior decreased.

Except for a minor reversal several days after the treatment was initiated, no evidence of vomiting was observed on the last nine days of the treatment. Again, this marked reduction in maladaptive behavior was accompanied by improvement in a variety of pro-social and self-care dimensions.

Lang and Melamed (1969) employed a similar procedure with a nine-month-old chronic vomiter whose life was threatened by continuation of the behavior. In this case, the vomiting act was preceded by sucking behavior and accompanied by vigorous throat movements. The aversion therapy procedure involved a one-second shock which was administered as soon as vomiting occurred and continued until the response was terminated.

The vomiting response was substantially reduced after two brief sessions and by the third session only one or two responses occurred. These changes were accompanied by a substantial weight gain and increased alertness and responsiveness to the environment.

After approximately three weeks, the child was discharged from the hospital and continued to do well one year after treatment.

Kohlenberg (1970) reported similar success in treating excessive vomiting in a 21-year-old severely retarded female. In this case, shock was administered contingent on the presence of stomach tensions which served as the precursor to the vomiting response.

(c) Seizures. As in the case of vomiting, seizures are generally considered to be the result of some physiological dysfunction. However, some investigators have argued that such conditions may also be induced or influenced by external factors. In any event, if left unchecked, the frequency and severity of seizures may constitute a serious threat to the individual and a recent report by Wright (1973) suggests that at least some forms of seizure-related events may be suppressed by aversion therapy, thereby resulting in a decrease in seizure activity.

Wright worked with a five-year-old retarded boy who induced his own seizures by moving his hand back and forth before his eyes and blinking, while looking at a light source. Observation and EEG recordings confirmed the correlation between these events and seizure episodes. They further revealed the occurrence of several hundred self-induced seizures per day.

Consequently, shock was delivered contingent on each "hand-eye" response in five one-hour sessions extending over a three-day period. All responses were suppressed by the third session. However, five months later the child was again inducing as many as 400 seizures per day by blinking. Shock was then administered contingent on the blinking response, resulting in a substantial reduction of seizures by the fourth session. A seven-month follow-up revealed a 90 percent decrease from the pre-treatment frequency of hand-eye responses.

2. Enuresis

Several examples of aversion therapy have also been employed for the purpose of reducing nocturnal bed wetting (enuresis). Tough, Hawkins, McArthur, and Ravenswaay (1971) found that a cold bath contingent on bed wetting, plus praise for bladder control (DRO) completely eliminated the enuresis problem in a retarded eight-year-old boy but was less effective for his younger brother.

Atthowe (1972) found that a combination of aversive events could reduce enuresis in even severely disabled elderly patients. Chronically enuretic patients (who otherwise participated in a token reward program) were moved to a generally aversive environment: crowded ward, lights turned on for 10 minutes four times each night, and patients escorted to the bathroom for 10 minutes. These procedures were maintained for two months after which continence was rewarded (DRO), while incontinence resulted in loss of reward (response cost). By the eighth month of the program all of the patients were continent, including some who were severely neurologically disabled, an effect which was maintained almost four years after the study was initiated.

By far the largest number of successful attempts to treat enuresis have used a variety of the "Mowrer alert system" in which bed wetting results in a signal which arouses the individual. After a number of such experiences most children begin to wake up prior to wetting the bed and are then encouraged to urinate appropriately.

When the apparatus was first described by Mowrer (1938) he invoked a Pavlovian model in explaining the effectiveness of the technique. Thus, the distended bladder served as the conditioned stimulus (CS) which was paired with the unconditioned stimulus (UCS, the alerting stimulus). By means of Pavlovian conditioning, the CS alone would result in arousal. More recently, Jones (1960) has suggested that the technique relies upon an operant aversion therapy model.

3. Sneezing

Kushner (1970) has shown that excessive sneezing may also be controlled by means of aversion therapy. This case involved a 17-year-old girl who had been vigorously and rapidly sneezing (approximately one response per 40 seconds) for six months with no relief. Extensive medical examinations failed to isolate the cause of this condition and a variety of treatment techniques had not produced any substantial improvement.

During treatment, a microphone was placed around her neck which was connected to a voice key and a shock source. Each sneeze activated the voice key and automatically delivered a shock to the fingertips (response-contingent shock). Following an adjustment of the shock procedure, in which the electrodes were taped to her arm, thereby insuring better contact, the patient stopped sneezing after four hours of treatment. There was no evidence of a relapse during a thirteen-month follow-up period.

4. Functional ("Hysterical") Paralysis

In an unpublished study conducted at the Veteran's Administration Hospital in Miami, a modified aversion therapy program was employed for the purpose of treating a functional paralysis. The patient was a middle-aged male whose presenting complaint was a loss of feeling and impaired locomotion in the lower half of the left limb, causing him to be confined to a wheelchair. Extensive neurological examination ruled out the possibility of any organic dysfunction. The aversion therapy procedure was conducted as follows: electrodes were placed on the patient's leg and on two fingertips. He was then informed that a mild shock would be administered to his leg, followed in five seconds by a stronger shock to his fingers. If he felt the leg shock he was to press a switch which he held in his hand. No further instructions were provided, although each switch response enabled the patient to avoid the shock to the fingers.

This procedure was presented for three trials in the first session, during which time no avoidance responses occurred. The second session was interrupted after the first trial because the patient became nauseated. In the third session, the patient emitted two switch-press responses and verbally indicated that feeling had returned to his leg, whereupon the electrodes were removed and the patient walked back to the ward. He was discharged several days later without complication. Although the results in this case were successful, the procedure employed represents a departure from the typical response-contingent paradigm and seems to be more similar to the "anticipatory avoidance" procedure described more fully in the next section.

5. Writer's Cramp

Two studies have appeared which report on attempts to treat various forms of writer's cramp by means of aversion therapy. This form of motor impairment is usually characterized by muscular contractions or spasms and prevents the individual from continuing in tasks which require the use of hand muscles such as writing, typing, etc. The condition is usually attributed to fatigue or emotional problems. In any event, sufferers of writer's cramp are frequently capable of performing other tasks even though such tasks may involve the operation of the same or similar hand muscles.

Liversedge and Sylvester (1955) identified 39 cases of writer's cramp as a function of either hand tremors or muscular spasms; each of these conditions was separately treated with a different apparatus. The tremor patients were required to insert a metal stylus into a series of progressively smaller holes in metal chassis. Deviations (striking the side of the hole) resulted in shock. The contraction response was treated by delivering shock to the patient whenever excessive thumb pressure (as measured by a gauge) was applied to a pen. Normal writing was regained after three to six weeks of treatment in 24 of the patients. These improvements were maintained for up to four and a half years.

Kushner and Sandler (1966) used a similar procedure for treating a hand contraction response in a 42-year-old male teletype operator. The patient was required to operate a typewriter in the clinic and pre-treatment observations revealed a high frequency of rapid, spasmodic contractions of the right hand, resulting in errors at the keyboard. The patient was then seen for twelve 30-minute sessions with shock delivered contingent on each contraction response. The electrodes were removed during the next three sessions and no contractions were observed. Shortly thereafter, however, the contraction response recurred and his performance remained erratic and gradually declined through the 46th session. Consequently, the number of weekly sessions was increased. No contractions were observed by the 61st session and the patient was then switched to a teletype machine. Almost immediately, he was functioning effectively even when the electrodes were removed.

6. Stuttering

The behavior modification literature reveals a long and continued interest in the use of aversive techniques for improving the speech of stutterers. Numerous response-contingent events have reduced the frequency of stuttering, including delayed auditory feedback, response-cost arrangements, time out arrangement, and electric shock. Since only a brief overview of these efforts is provided in the present account, the interested reader is referred to Siegel's comprehensive review (Siegel, 1970). In each of the studies described, stuttering is defined in terms of the frequency of speech dysfluencies (repetitions, interjections, prolongations, interruptions, etc.).

Adams and Popelka (1971) employed a Time Out technique with eight young, adult stutterers. Essentially, the procedure imposed a nonspeaking period contingent on each dysfluency under the assumption that the opportunity to speak was positively reinforcing. Although the dysfluency rate decreased during the TO condition, it seems apparent that the results are subject to alternative explanations.

Kazdin (1973) compared the relative effectiveness of response-cost, loud response-contingent sound and feedback on the suppression of dysfluent speech in 40 retarded patients. In the response-cost procedure, tokens which could be exchanged for tangible rewards were removed upon the occurrence of dysfluencies. In the second condition, a loud noise was presented contingent on each dysfluency; and in the feedback condition, each dysfluency was marked by a light being turned on. The results indicated that both response-cost and aversive stimulation procedures reduced dysfluencies, but response cost was more effective in every respect including generalization of treatment effects during a post-test.

Delayed auditory feedback (DAF) has also been studied in this connection since such events seem to reflect aversive properties. Typically, the DAF procedure usually involves a brief delay of the dysfluency which is then transmitted through the client's earphones during a speech task. This requires the individual to reduce his verbal rate while simultaneously speaking and listening for dysfluencies. Goldiamond (1956) has shown that such treatment produces fluent and rapid speech. Soderberg (1968) obtained similar results with eleven student stutterers, and, in addition, observed that these effects generalized beyond the experimental condition.

Finally, Daly and Frick (1970) employed a shock procedure with 36 adult male stutterers. Stuttering expectations as well as actual stuttering responses were treated independently in some patients and simultaneously in others. The results indicated that shocking stuttering expectancies did not reduce the frequency of stuttering responses but the other conditions did produce a constructive change. Furthermore, these effects were maintained during a 20-minute post-test period.

Complex Problem Conditions

1. General Compulsions

As noted previously, there is by now an extensive literature describing attempts to deal with chronic, long-standing compulsive-type problem conditions via aversion therapy. Perhaps it is natural for behavior therapists to turn in this direction, since most conventional treatment efforts in this area have not been very successful. The literature is replete with examples of treated alcoholics who have fallen off the wagon, dieters who eat more after treatment than before, cigarette smokers who quit during treatment only to smoke again at higher rates after discharge, etc.

One of the problems encountered with some of these conditions (especially the first of the following three) is that they are directly promoted and reinforced in certain (sometimes many) circumstances. Drinking and smoking are for the most part socially acceptable and, in fact, abstinence may even result in social disapproval. Eating, of course, is a biological necessity and the rewards are built in to the response. It is only when they occur at *excessive* frequency and/or under *inappropriate* circumstances that they represent problem behaviors. Under these circumstances, such conditions may be considered as a breakdown in discrimination. The current review is not an attempt to survey the entire range of activity, but rather a sampling of representative efforts.

(a) *Alcoholism*. The history of the aversive treatment of alcoholism surprisingly stretches back to the Roman era. It is only within recent years, however, that these techniques have achieved an advanced level of sophistication. Starting in the early and middle 1960's, behavior therapists began to employ aversive controls under carefully planned conditions. Many of the early studies clearly reflected a Pavlovian methodology but the more recent investigations are more congruent with operant procedures. Furthermore, they are characterized by attempts to find alternatives to shock and their objectives are to establish controlled (moderate socially appropriate) drinking rather than complete abstinence. A study by Blake (1965) is perhaps representative of the earlier aversion therapy efforts involving operant processes. In this procedure, electric shock was presented at the same time the patient complied with instructions to sip his drink. The shock was increased until the patient spat out the drink, thus terminating the shock (escape behavior). In addition, the shock was presented only 50 percent of the time in a random manner. When this treatment was combined with relaxation training, Blake found that approximately 50 percent of the 37 patients in the program remained abstinent one year after follow-up.

In a similar procedure, Vogler, Lunde, Johnson, and Martin (1970) served liquor to alcoholic patients in a simulated bar arrangement. Each drinking response was accompanied by a shock, which was maintained until the patient spat out the drink. Although again, it is difficult to isolate the punishment effects (the shock for drinking) from the escape effects (the cessation of shock contingent on spitting the drink out), these investigators did include several control conditions and also provided for "booster" treatments after discharge. The results indicated that abstinence was engendered by the treatment.

The Vogler technique in which treatment was conducted in a naturalistic setting represents an important development and is evidently being used with increasing frequency. Wards are converted such that they reflect many of the characteristics of settings in which the drinking response actually occurs. Obviously, the effects produced under these conditions stand a better chance of generalizing to the patient's real-life situation than would seem to be true when more artificial circumstances are used.

A more clearly operant approach has been reported by Davidson (1973). Actual alcohol-related responses are assessed by an automated device which dispenses 2 cc. of preferred liquor per 30 responses in a half-hour period. The patient is given the opportunity to drink the liquor at each delivery interval. Once his response rate stabilizes, the patient receives a shock as he actually picks up the drink. Shock intensities are maintained until the effects at a given intensity (whether an increase or decrease in response rates) can be reliably demonstrated and then a new and higher shock intensity is employed until the patient's response rate is completely suppressed. Once this criterion is achieved, the patient is allowed to respond to liquor in the absence of shock (the electrodes are removed). Following these observations, the patient is discharged and requested to make follow-up visits during which time measurement is continued. Over 80 percent of the patients did not respond in the follow-up visits and information from the patient as well as other sources suggested a substantial reduction in drinking behavior in over 65 percent of the patients for at least one year after discharge. Such techniques seem to offer genuine promise for the treatment of what many authorities consider to be the most serious behavior problem of our times.

(b) *Cigarette smoking.* Almost from the beginning, in the 1960's, therapists have revealed a strong interest in the use of aversive methods for cigarette smoking. By now, the number of suggested techniques which incorporate some form of aversive control probably runs into the thousands. Unfortunately, this burgeoning development has not been accompanied by a comparable interest in providing evidence to support the efficacy of the various techniques. Probably everyone knows someone who has tried to stop smoking even through various aversive means, only to have failed. Without a proper scientific analysis, it is impossible to assess the effectiveness of the technique. In a recent issue of a major psychological journal devoted entirely to the topic of behavioral approaches to smoking, a review of a variety of modification efforts (including aversive methods) found that at least 75 percent of the individuals treated had started to smoke again (Hunt and Matarazzo, 1973). With this observation in mind, let us consider several of the aversion therapy studies and their effectiveness.

Gendreau and Dodwell (1968) applied the "increasing shock-escape response" technique to reduce the frequency of cigarette smoking. Patients received shock as soon as they complied with instructions to light up a cigarette. Shock intensity was gradually increased until the patient extinguished the cigarette. Differences in smoking rates between treated and nontreated smokers were observed both at the end of treatment and two years later.

By the late 1960's, a whole series of studies was reported involving techniques and equipment designed to enhance the effects of aversion therapy with smokers. Perhaps the most sophisticated of these involves a portable shock apparatus which automatically administers shock at some point during the cigarette smoking period. The assumption which seems to underlie such efforts is that if the patient complies with the instructions he will receive response shock contingent on each smoking response, and in every smoking situation. This will result in a satisfactory treatment outcome. Although the assumption is a reasonable one, appropriate controls have not been exercised and the assumption remains to be verified. The limitation of these procedures is that they rely completely upon the cooperation and reliability of the individual patient.

Elliot and Tighe (1968) offered an aversive alternative to the shock procedure, but again with ambiguous results. Their procedure involved a modified response cost-avoidance technique in which volunteer patients posted money for a twelve-week or sixteen-week period. The money was refunded to those patients who abstained from smoking during this time. Of 25 patients, 21 abstained through the duration of the study. Furthermore, 38 percent of the patients remained abstinent at a 12-month follow-up. Although far from a satisfactory success index, the rate compares very favorably with the results reported by investigators using other techniques.

At the present time it would appear that most therapists engaged in reducing smoking behavior have applied a bewildering assortment of techniques including aversive methods with only limited success.

(c) *Overeating*. As with cigarette smoking, prematurely applied aversive treatment methods are now widely used for the treatment of obesity, resulting in the emergence of questionable practices and undocumented claims of effectiveness. Again, because of the lack of rigorous studies, only several examples from the aversion therapy literature are presented.

Perhaps the earliest example of a response-contingent shock procedure with two overweight women is described by Meyer and Crisp (1964). Temptation food (food for which the patient had most craving as distinguished from food on a prescribed diet) was displayed for increasing periods of time, and the patients received shock for approach responses. The shock contingency was gradually faded while weight changes were constantly monitored. Any increase in weight resulted in a return to the treatment regime. Although the results for one patient were highly satisfactory (a weight reduction of about 75 pounds during six months which was maintained almost 2 years after discharge), no durable constructive change was observed in the second patient.

Although this procedure appears to have been adapted by a substantial number of behavior therapists, an alternative approach is offered by other investigators employing non-physically painful aversive events. Ferster *et al.* (1962) described a procedure which involved a variety of techniques, including emphasizing the ultimate aversive consequences of overeating. Obese women met in groups and discussed the expected outcome of their problem behavior (putting on weight, undesirable appearance, etc.). In addition they were required to monitor their own food intake and weight changes. All of the women reported weight losses although these effects were not maintained for any great length of time.

(d) *Other compulsive conditions.* Other investigators have reported the successful treatment of gambling (Barker and Miller, 1968) and shoplifting (Kellam, 1969). Although it is clear that operant aversive techniques were intimately involved in these efforts, the complexity of the procedures makes it impossible to analyze the relative contribution of each component.

2. "Covert" Problem Conditions

Another interesting development which has emerged over the last several years involves the use of aversion therapy in the treatment of covert problem conditions. In such cases, the patient's verbal complaint is usually regarded as the external concomitant of disturbing thoughts frequently involving sexual or aggressive ideations. Despite this commonly accepted assumption, the following review suggests that such conditions are also amenable to aversion therapy.

Kushner and Sandler (1966) used a shock procedure for treating suicidal thoughts in a 48-year-old male. These obsessions were characterized by persistent, daily ruminations focussing upon six different suicidal images. The patient was instructed to imagine a particular scene and received shock upon a signal that the image was clear. Fifteen to twenty such trials were presented in each session and after the twelfth session, the patient reported that only one image was still present. Treatment was temporarily discontinued after three more sessions because of a death in the family, but reinstated after his return. (No suicidal ruminations occurred during this time). Treatment was terminated after five more sessions and a total of 350 trials. A three-month follow-up revealed no recurrence of the former problem.

Bucher and Fabricatore (1970) employed a self-shock procedure in an attempt to reduce the frequency of hallucinations in a 47-year-old hospitalized patient diagnosed as a paranoid schizophrenic. The hallucinations were described as frequent, obscene, and critical voices which occurred from four to seven times per day and lasted for as long as 20 minutes.

The patient was supplied with a portable shock device and instructed to administer shock to himself at the onset of the hallucinations. This resulted in an apparent immediate and virtually complete cessation of hallucinatory episodes during 20 days when the shock device was abruptly removed, and the patient was unfortunately discharged without his consent. He was returned to the hospital 2 weeks later and the voices appeared to have "returned."

Haynes and Geddy (1973) showed that hallucinations could also be suppressed by means of a Time Out procedure. The patient was a 45-year-old hospitalized female diagnosed as schizophrenic. She showed a high incidence of loud and incomprehensible verbal behavior which was considered to be evidence of hallucinations. During treatment, each hallucinatory episode resulted in a staff member informing the patient that she had to go to the TO room because she was talking to herself, then leading the patient to the TO room, closing the door and then opening the door 10 minutes later. Two treatment periods were separated by a non-treatment interval to observe the effects of discontinuing treatment.

The results indicated that the hallucinatory behavior decreased by about one-half during the two TO procedures. Even more pronounced changes were produced in a second patient displaying similar problems.

Reisinger (1972) showed that depression-related behavior could be treated by a non-physically aversive treatment procedure. The patient in this case was a 20-year-old institutionalized female diagnosed as anxiety-depressive. Her behavior was characterized by a high frequency of crying without any apparent provocation and little or no positive emotional behavior. The treatment consisted of presenting tokens (exchangeable for tangible rewards) contingent on smiling and removing tokens contingent on crying. Thus, the procedure involved a DRO plus response-cost arrangement. Two treatment periods were interspersed with a reversal condition, in which the contingencies were withdrawn. Appropriate changes in both response systems accompanied the various conditions. Finally, the tokens were faded and ultimately replaced by social reinforcement (praise, compliments, etc.) in order to maintain the positive changes under more natural conditions.

3. Sexual Deviations

An extensive variety of aversion therapy techniques have been employed for the purpose of modifying deviant sexual behavior. The work in this area has been particularly susceptible to the criticisms described in the introduction of this chapter. Once again, many of these criticisms do not appear to be warranted in the sense that a large number of previously unhappy individuals have achieved a more satisfactory level of sexual adjustment as a consequence of such treatment. Nevertheless, the concern for better controlled observations is genuine and one can only hope that this will be resolved by future research.

As was true in the case of alcoholism, many of the earlier efforts were formulated in the context of the Pavlovian model although it shortly became apparent that operant processes (frequently uncontrolled) intruded into the procedures. The major value of this work is more of a heuristic and historic nature rather than in terms of contributing any hard knowledge to theory and practice. Moreover, the initiative displayed by these investigators in attacking complex problems via previously suspect methods, thereby challenging many prevailing myths, should not pass unmentioned.

One of the first attempts to apply an operant aversion therapy procedure with sexual deviations is reported by Blakemore, Thorpe, Barker, Conway, and Lavin (1963). Prior to this study most of these efforts used nausea-producing drugs in order to produce a conditioned aversion in the presence of stimuli related to the deviant practices.

The particular problem condition treated in the Blakemore study was a long-standing transvestism. A variety of such activities was reported by the patient which usually led to sexual gratification. Marital and legal circumstances served as the impetus for his seeking assistance.

The treatment was conducted in a private room of a hospital which housed a full-length mirror and an electric grid floor. The patient's "favorite outfit" of female clothing was placed on the chair.

The procedure involved a series of trials in which the patient was instructed to start dressing with the female clothes. At some point during a trial, he received a signal to start undressing. The signal was either a buzzer or shock to the feet. These were randomly presented and occurred at varying time intervals while all the female clothes were removed. Following a one-minute rest, the procedure was repeated for a total of five trials in each treatment session. A total of 400 trials was administered over six treament days. Since no transvestite behavior was reported six months after treatment, the procedure was evidently successful.

It is difficult to classify the Blakemore procedure since it involves mixed components of different paradigms. It seems clear that a response contingency was involved since shock occurred in connection with at least some transvestite responses, and the patient could escape shock by undressing. In any event, this study represented a transition procedure from earlier aversion therapy efforts with sexual deviations and within the next several years a host of similar efforts was reported.

Thorpe, Schmidt, Brown, and Castell (1964) applied an "aversion relief" procedure to a variety of sexual problems including homosexuality (in individuals who desired to change) and transvestism. This technique relies upon the "relief" experienced by an individual who has escaped a painful event. Furthermore, if an aversive stimulus, such as shock, is removed in the presence of another stimulus, the latter stimulus may acquire positive properties in the process. In the Thorpe study a series of problem behavior-related words were presented, followed by shock. At the end of the series an opposite and "normal" stimulus (e.g., female breasts) was presented which was not accompanied by shock, and therefore produced "relief." Although the procedure is a complicated one, the constructive changes in the patients' sexual behavior may be at least partially attributed to the use of response-contingent shock.

Further refinement of the aversion therapy procedure with sexual problems was reported by Marks and Gelder (1967) in a study detailing the treatment of five patients with fetish and/or transvestite related behaviors. In addition to other pre-treatment measures, each patient's penile reactions to problem-related stimuli was assessed by means of an instrument which measures penile volume (plethysmograph).

The procedure involved two one-hour sessions each day for two weeks. During the first stage of treatment, the patient was instructed to imagine performing the deviant behavior and shock was delivered whenever a clear image was indicated. On about the third or fourth day, the patients were asked to actually practice the problem behavior and shock was delivered on a contingent basis on 75 percent of the trials.

In general, the results showed that the clients experienced increasing difficulties in fantasizing the deviant acts, and, what is probably more important, a reduction in penile reactions to the relevant stimuli.

Thus, this procedure used well-defined pre- and post-treatment measures and introduced the technique of partial and random shock which may have increased the durability of the suppression effect, as described earlier.

During approximately the same period of time, several studies employing aversion therapy exclusively with homosexuals (who desired to change their sexual preferences) were also reported. Again, although the procedures were complicated and therefore make analysis difficult, the results ranged from moderately to highly successful. Perhaps the most extensive of these efforts was reported by Feldman and MacCulloch (1965) and MacCulloch, Birtles, and Feldman (1971). Their procedure, termed "anticipatory avoidance" involved response-contingent shock, negative reinforcement (avoidance of shock), fading, probably DRO. In any event, anywhere from 50 percent to 70 percent of these patients treated showed complete cessation of homosexual behavior and an increase in heterosexual behavior during therapy. Moreover, these effects were maintained for as long as 24 months.

Additional reports have also suggested that fetishism (Kushner, 1965), exhibitionism (Kushner and Sandler, 1966), and voyeurism (Bancroft et al., 1966) can all be reduced or eliminated via the "shock-contingent-on-fantasy" procedure.

Finally, a more clearly operant procedure was reported in the treatment of a pedophilia (i.e., child molesting) which was so serious, the patient was being considered for brain surgery (Bancroft, Jones, and Pullan, 1966). The procedure attempted to recreate the natural conditions in which the pedophilia-related behaviors occurred. Pictures of young girls were presented to the patient and when a penile reaction occurred (as measured by the penile plethysmograph) a painful shock was administered to the arm. These were continued until there was a reduction in the response. Each trial lasted ten minutes with no shock administered in the absence of a criterion response. Six to eight trials were administered each day over a period of eight weeks for a total of 200 shock trials. In addition, on every fourth trial, the shock apparatus was disconnected and the patient saw photographs of adult women while encouraged to engage in normal sexual fantasies.

Although the investigators did not consider their results to be a complete therapeutic success, there was a marked reduction in pedophilia-related activities and an increase in normal heterosexual behavior.

In any event, the study represents the continued refinement of the aversion therapy procedures with sexual deviations. It employed a discrete response-shock contingency; the procedure was repeated often enough until a marked reduction in undesirable behavior was realized; and an alternative response was incorporated. Although it is not clear which of these components contributed to the final outcome, the general procedure represents an important advancement of the aversion therapy paradigm for such problem conditions.

4. Generalized Asocial Behaviors

The last problem condition to be considered represents a category which encompasses a wide variety of socially deviant acts from mild forms of nuisance and asocial behaviors to dangerous acts of aggression directed at objects and other people.

The literature in this area is quite extensive and only a brief overview is presented here.

There are by now a whole series of studies indicating the effectiveness of Time

Out for reducing a wide assortment of aggressive, asocial, negativistic behaviors. In addition, these studies have been conducted with a wide variety of people of various ages and sexes in a diversity of institutional settings. Bostow and Bailey (1969) for example, reduced severe disruptive and aggressive behaviors (loud abusive vocalizations, attacking others) in two retarded female adults by making a brief TO contingent on such responses. White, Nielsen, and Johnson (1972) extended these observations to 20 retarded children. Ramp, Ulrich, and Dulany (1971) reduced out-of-seat behaviors and inappropriate talking in a classroom situation, and Wahler (1969) demonstrated that similar techniques could be employed in the home environment through parental instruction. Tyler and Brown (1967) found that aggressive asocial behavior (throwing objects, physical assault, etc.) in 15 adolescent males could be similarly treated.

Aggressive behavior has also been effectively reduced by means of response cost. Winkler (1970) for example, suppressed episodes of violence and loud noise in chronic psychiatric patients by removing tokens contingent on such responses. Kazdin (1972) provides a review of the relevant literature in which he describes the variety of problem behaviors successfully treated by response cost (smoking, overeating, stuttering, psychotic talk); the durability of such procedures in terms of long-range effects; and several aspects of response-cost procedures which may enhance their efficacy.

Finally, response-contingent shock has also been employed, especially where the problem conditions are highly dangerous. In this fashion, Bucher and King (1971) suppressed the rate of highly destructive acts in an 11-year-old psychotic boy in the treatment setting as well as at home where the treatment was continued by the child's parent. Royer, Flynn, and Osadca (1971) also used a shock procedure to reduce the frequency of fire setting in a severely regressed disorganized psychiatric patient. In this case, shock correlated with arson-related words had no effect on the patient's actual behavior. Subsequently, the patient was required to rehearse a series of fire setting activities with shock administered on a response-contingent basis. This procedure resulted in a marked reduction of the problem behavior and a complete absence of such acts during a four-year follow-up assessment.

SUMMARY—AVERSION THERAPY

In a relatively short period of time, the aversion therapy literature has increased at an astounding rate. Each new review attests to the growing elaboration of techniques and to the expanding list of problem conditions which have been at least to some degree ameliorated by such techniques. What is perhaps even more impressive, is that this progress has been accomplished despite the fact that few if any of these procedures have incorporated all of the techniques designed to maximize the effectiveness of treatment.

In the light of these developments, it no longer seems appropriate to dismiss such practices out of hand. On the contrary, knowledge of these procedures would seem to add an important dimension to the total range of skills which the behavior therapist can bring to bear on the problems encountered in clinical settings.

Aversion therapy is indeed a legitimate treatment modality, especially when dealing with problems which require immediate intervention. Anyone who has observed the dramatic improvement produced in a head banger, for example, is almost forced to accept this conclusion. Furthermore, in the process of expanding our knowledge, it appears that many of the traditional reservations and criticisms are being laid to rest. True, there have been excesses in the other direction, especially in the indiscriminate and unsystematic use of electric shock by unrestrained enthusiasts. But the alleged horrors that have been linked to the use of aversion therapy expressed by many critics have been greatly exaggerated—they are not a necessary and irresistible outcome of such practices as long as the proper safeguards, as described in preceding sections, are exercised.

What is needed—desperately needed—are better controlled clinical investigations which more closely correspond to the well-designed efforts emerging from the laboratory. Moreover, we need to devise better behavior change measures, to extend outcome assessment, to use more realistic treatment techniques, to make comparison studies of the relative effectiveness of different treatment methods, within the same problem condition—the list is a long one.

The behavior modification movement is proud of its alleged reliance upon scientific rigor. Perhaps in this area more than any other, the opportunities are presently available to justify this claim.

REFERENCES

Adams, M. R. and Popelka, G. The influence of "time out" on stutterers and their dysfluency. *Behavior Therapy*, 1971, **2**, 334–339.

Atthowe, J. M., Jr. Controlling nocturnal enuresis in severely disabled and chronic patients. *Behavior Therapy*, 1972, **3**, 232–239.

Azrin, N. H. and Holz, W. C. Punishment. In W. K. Honig (Ed.), *Operant behavior: Areas of research and application*. New York: Appleton-Century-Crofts, 1966.

Baer, D. M. A case for the selective reinforcement of punishment. In C. Neuringer and J. L. Michael (Eds.), *Behavior modification in clinical psychology*. New York: Appleton-Century-Crofts, 1970.

Bancroft, J. H., Jr., Jones, H. G., and Pullan, B. R. A simple transducer for measuring penile erection, with comments on its use in the treatment of sexual disorders. *Behaviour Research and Therapy*, 1966, **4**, 239–241.

Barker, J. C. and Miller, M. E. Aversion therapy for compulsive gambling. *Journal of Nervous and Mental Disorders*, 1968, **146**, 285–302.

Blake, B. G. The application of behavior therapy to the treatment of alcoholism. *Behaviour Research and Therapy*, 1965, **3**, 75–85.

Blakemore, C. B., Thorpe, J. G., Barker, J. C., Conway, C. G., and Lavin, N. I. The application of faradic aversion conditioning in a case of transvestism. *Behaviour Research and Therapy*, 1963, **1**, 29–34.

Bostow, D. E. and Bailey, J. B. Modification of severe disruptive and aggressive behavior using brief time-out and reinforcement procedures. *Journal of Applied Behavior Analysis*, 1969, **2**, 31–38.

Bucher, B. and Fabricatore, J. Use of patient-administered shock to suppress hallucinations. *Behavior Therapy*, 1970, **1**, 382–385.

Bucher, B. and King, L. W. Generalization of punishment effects in the deviant behavior of a psychotic child. *Behavior Therapy*, 1971, **2**, 68–77.

Corte, H. E., Wolf, M. M., and Locke, B. J. A comparison of procedures for eliminating self-injurious behavior of retarded adolescents. *Journal of Applied Behavior Analysis*, 1971, **4**, 201–215.

Daly, D. A. and Frick, J. V. The effects of punishing stuttering expectations and stuttering utterances: A comparative study. *Behavior Therapy*, 1970, **1**, 228–239.

Davidson, R. S. Alcoholism: Experimental analyses of etiology and modification. Personal communication, 1973.

Elliot, R. and Tighe, T. J. Breaking the cigarette habit. *Psychological Record*, 1968, **18**, 503–513.

Evans, D. R. Masturbatory fantasy and sexual deviations. *Behaviour Research and Therapy*, 1968, **6**, 17–20.

Feldman, M. P. Aversion therapy for sexual deviation: A critical review. *Psychological Bulletin*, 1966, **65**, 65–79.

Feldman, M. P. and MacCulloch, M. J. The application of anticipatory avoidance learning to the treatment of homosexuality. I. Theory, technique and preliminary results. *Behaviour Research and Therapy*, 1965, **2**, 165–183.

Ferster, C. B., Nurnberger, J. L., and Levitt, E. B. The control of eating. *Journal of Mathetics*, 1962, **1**, 87–109.

Franks, C. M. Behavior therapy: The principles of conditioning and the treatment of the alcoholic. *Quarterly Journal of Studies on Alcohol*, 1963, **24**, 511–529.

Gendreau, P. E. and Dodwell, P. C. An aversive treatment for addicted cigarette smokers: Preliminary report. *Canadian Psychologist*, 1968, **9**, 28–34.

Goldiamond, I. Stuttering and fluency as manipulative operant response classes. In L. Krasner and L. P. Ullman (Eds.), *Research in behavior modification*. New York: Holt, Rinehart and Winston, 1965.

Greene, R. J. and Hoats, D. L. Aversive tickling: A simple conditioning technique. *Behavior Therapy*, 1971, **2**, 389–393.

Hamilton, J., Stephans, L., and Allen, P. Controlling aggressive and disruptive behavior in severely retarded institutionalized residents. *American Journal of Mental Deficiency*, 1971, **71**, 852–856.

Haynes, S. M. and Geddy, P. Suppression of psychotic hallucinations through Time-out. *Behavior Therapy*, 1973, **4**, 123–127.

Hunt, W. A. and Matarazzo, J. D. Three years later: Recent developments in the experimental modification of smoking behavior. *Journal of Abnormal Psychology*, 1973, **81**, 107–114.

Johnson, J. M. Punishment of human behavior. *American Psychologist*, 1972, **27**, 1033–1054.

Jones, H. G. The behavioral treatment of enuresis nocturna. In H. J. Eysenck (Ed.), *Behavior therapy and the neuroses*. Oxford: Pergamon Press, 1960.

Kanfer, F. H. and Koroly, P. Self-control: A behavioristic excursion into the lion's den. *Behavior Therapy*, 1972, **3**, 398–416.

Kazdin, A. E. Response cost. The removal of conditioned reinforcement for therapeutic change. *Behavior Therapy*, 1972, **3**, 533–546.

Kazdin, A. E. The effect of response cost and aversive stimulation in suppressing punished and non-punished speech dysfluencies. *Behavior Therapy*, 1973, **4**, 73–82.

Kellam, A. P. Shoplifting treated by aversion to a film. *Behaviour Research and Therapy*, 1969, **7**, 125–127.

Kohlenberg, R. J. The punishment of persistent vomiting: A case study. *Journal of Applied Behavior Analysis*, 1970, **3**, 241–245.

Kushner, M. The reduction of a long-standing fetish by means of aversive conditioning. In L. Ullmann and L. Krasner (Eds.), *Case studies in behavior modification*. New York: Holt, Rinehart and Winston, 1965.

Kushner, M. and Sandler, J. Aversion therapy and the concept of punishment. *Behaviour Research and Therapy*, 1966, **4**, 179–186.

Kushner, M. Faradic aversive controls in clinical practice. In C. Neuringer and J. L. Michael (Eds.), *Behavior modification in clinical psychology*. New York: Appleton-Century-Crofts, 1970.

Lang, P. J. and Melamed, P. G. Case report: Avoidance conditioning therapy of an infant with chronic ruminative vomiting. *Journal of Abnormal Psychology*, 1969, **74**, 1–8.

Lebow, M. D., Gelfand, S., and Dobson, W. R. Aversive conditioning of a phenothiazine-induced respiratory stridor. *Behavior Therapy*, 1970, **1**, 222–227.

Lemere, F. and Voegtlin, W. L. An evaluation of aversion treatment of alcoholism. *Quarterly Journal of Studies on Alcohol*, 1950, **11**, 199–204.

Liversedge, L. A. and Sylvester, J. D. Conditioning techniques in the treatment of writer's cramp. *Lancet*, 1955, **2**, 1147–1149.

Lovaas, O. I. and Simmons, J. Q. Manipulation of self-destruction in three retarded children. *Journal of Applied Behavior Analysis*, 1969, **2**, 143–157.

Luckey, R. E., Watson, C. M., and Musick, J. K. Aversive conditioning as a means of inhibiting vomiting and rumination. *American Journal of Mental Deficiency*, 1968, **73**, 139–142.

MacCulloch, M. J., Birtles, C. J., and Feldman, M. P. Anticipatory avoidance learning for the treatment of homosexuality: Recent developments and an automated aversive therapy system. *Behavior Therapy*, 1971, **2**, 151–169.

McGuire, R. J. and Vallance, M. Aversion therapy by electric shock: A simple technique. *British Medical Journal*, 1964, **1**, 151–153.

Marks, I. and Gelder, M. Transvestism and fetishism: Clinical and Psychological changes during faradic aversion. *British Journal of Psychiatry*, 1967, **119**, 711–730.

Merbaum, M. The modification of self-destructive behavior by a mother-therapist using aversive stimulation. *Behavior Therapy*, 1973, **4**, 442–447.

Meyer, V. and Crisp, A. Aversion therapy in two cases of obesity. *Behaviour Research and Therapy*, 1964, **2**, 143–147.

Mowrer, O. H. and Mowrer, W. M. Enuresis. A method for its study and treatment. *American Journal of Orthopsychiatry*, 1938, **8**, 436–459.

Rachman, S. Aversion therapy: Chemical or electrical? *Behaviour Research and Therapy*, 1965, **2**, 289–300.

Ramp, E., Ulrich, R., and Dulaney, S. Delayed timeout as a procedure for reducing disruptive classroom behavior: A case study. *Journal of Applied Behavior Analysis*, 1971, **4**, 235–239.

Reisinger, J. J. The treatment of "anxiety-depression" via positive reinforcement and response cost. *Journal of Applied Behavior Analysis*, 1972, **5**, 125–130.

Risley, T. R. The effects and side effects of punishing the autistic behavior of a deviant child. *Journal of Applied Behavior Analysis*, 1968, **1**, 21–34.

Royer, F. L., Flynn, W. F., and Osadca, B. S. Case history: Aversion therapy for fire-setting by a deteriorated schizophrenic. *Behavior Therapy*, 1971, **3**, 229–232.

Sandler, J. Masochism: An empirical analysis. *Psychological Bulletin*, 1964, **62**, 197–204.

Schaefer, H., Sobell, M. K., and Mills, K. C. Some sobering data on the use of self-confrontation with alcoholics. *Behavior Therapy*, 1971, **2**, 28–39.

Scholander, T. Treatment of an unusual case of compulsive behavior by aversive stimulation. *Behavior Therapy*, 1972, **3**, 290–293.

Siegel, G. M. Punishment, stuttering, and disfluency. *Journal of Speech and Hearing Research*, 1970, **13**, 677–714.

Skinner, B. F. *Science and Human Behavior*. New York: Macmillan, 1953.

Soderberg, G. A. Delayed auditory feedback and stuttering. *Journal of Speech and Hearing Disorders*, 1968, **33**, 260–267.

Solomon, R. L. Punishment. *American Psychologist*, 1964, **19**, 239–253.

Solyom, L. and Miller, S. A differential conditioning procedure as the initial phase of the behavior therapy of homosexuality. *Behaviour Research and Therapy*, 1965, **3**, 147–160.

Tate, B. G. Case study: Control of chronic self-injurious behavior by conditioned procedures. *Behavior Therapy*, 1972, **3**, 72–83.

Tate, B. G. and Baroff, G. S. Aversive control of self-injurious behavior in a psychotic boy. *Behavior Therapy*, 1966, **4**, 281–287.

Thorpe, J. G., Schmidt, E., Brown, P. T., and Castell, D. Aversion-relief therapy: A new method for general application. *Behaviour Research and Therapy*, 1964, **2**, 71–82.

Tough, J. H., Hawkins, R. P., McArthur, M. M., and Ravenswaay, S. V. Modification of neurotic behavior by punishment: A new use for an old device. *Behavior Therapy*, 1971, **2**, 567–574.

Tyler, V. O., Jr. and Brown, G. D. The use of swift, brief isolation as a group control device for institutionalized delinquents. *Behaviour Research and Therapy*, 1967, **5**, 1–9.

Voegtlin, W. L. Conditioned reflex therapy of chronic alcoholism. Ten years experience with the method. *Rocky Mountain Medical Journal*, 1947, **44**, 807–812.

Vogler, R. E., Lunde, S. E., Johnson, G. R., and Martin, P. L. Electrical aversion conditioning with chronic alcoholics. *Journal of Consulting and Clinical Psychology*, 1970, **34**, 302–307.

Wahler, R. G. Oppositional children: A quest for parental reinforcement control. *Journal of Applied Behavior Analysis*, 1969, **2**, 159–170.

Weiner, H. Some effects of response cost upon human operant behavior. *Journal of the Experimental Analysis of Behavior*, 1962, **5**, 201–208.

White, G. D., Nielsen, G., and Johnson, S. M. Timeout duration and the suppression of deviant behavior in children. *Journal of Applied Behavior Analysis*, 1972, **5**, 111–120.

Winkler, R. C. Management of chronic psychiatric patients by a token reinforcement system. *Journal of Applied Behavior Analysis*, 1970, **3**, 47–55.

Wright, L. Aversive conditioning of self-induced seizures. *Behavior Therapy*, 1973, **4**, 712–713.

CHAPTER 10

Self-Management Methods

FREDERICK H. KANFER*

In Chapter 7, techniques of behavior change were presented which rely heavily on modification of the environment. For example, appropriate delivery of reinforcement, use of particular events as signals or cues for behavior, and combinations of operant and discrimination techniques were described as means of change by environmental control. In all of these instances the change requires the cooperation of another person—a teacher, helper, therapist, or friend. In extreme cases, environmental control has to be fairly extensive. Institutionalization often provided the only opportunity for systematic behavior control. However, many problems, varying from small personal annoyances to relatively severe disturbances that interfere with daily life, are not easily brought under environmental control for a number of reasons: (1) The behavior may not be sufficiently public to permit modification by others—intimate sexual behaviors or thinking about oneself occur in privacy. (2) The behavior may be infrequent or only incidental in the person's life, and continuous supervision by a therapist would be uneconomical and bothersome. For instance, a weight control program could be carried out by operant shaping of eating behaviors while the person is confined to a hospital. But this strategy is uneconomical and unduly restrictive. (3) The target behavior for change may be verbal, relating to the person's self-evaluation, his self-control or his self-reactions. For example, a person's constant self-critical behaviors may remain hidden from the observer. They may go on while the person is engaged in productive activities. (4) Ultimately, a person has to assume responsibility for changing and maintaining his own behavior. Although environmental controls may be effective in the beginning stages, eventually the new behavior has to be carried out in the individual's daily life and in the absence of the therapist. In some cases, the social setting can be changed and modification of behavioral contingencies in a family or school environment may be sufficient. But in many instances the changed

*The author wishes to express his appreciation and thanks to the graduate students and undergraduates who critically read the manuscript, among them Larry Grimm, Bryce Kaye, Marian MacDonald, and Charles Spates.

behavior must be maintained not only by the environment but also by the client himself.

These limitations in environmental control programs have led behavior modifiers to search for new techniques. The common element in the various forms of self-management techniques lies in the fact that the therapist serves the role of an instigator and motivator to help the client in starting the change program. The responsibility for carrying out the program and for maintaining the effectiveness of the procedures ultimately lies with the client. The therapist provides the support needed by the client. Sometimes he makes special arrangements to insure that the client's new efforts are further supported by his natural environment at home, at school, or at work. However, in working with his client, the therapist clearly arranges the interaction as one in which the client consults with the therapist, obtains aid and directions for setting up a particular program, carries it out, and reports progress to the therapist so that the program can either be changed or continued. Thus at the very outset of the change program the client must be made aware that it is not *within* the session with the therapist, but *between* these sessions that the change occurs. While self-management techniques permit a much wider range of application of behavior change principles, their success demands greater commitment and higher motivation by the client than do programs based solely on environmental control.

In summary then, self-management techniques supplement other behavior change methods by permitting the extension of behavior modification methods to persons whose problems do not interfere with many of their daily activities, whose difficulties are not easily observable, who do not require interruption of their life routine by placement in institutions, who have sufficient motivation and skill to benefit from direction and instructions of the therapist to execute their own programs, and whose problems may include a wide range of verbal and fantasy behaviors that produce discomfort not only in relation to other persons but also in the client's relationship with himself.

Early behavior modification techniques have disregarded the role of a client's past history, his thoughts and his fantasies in modifying the effects of environmental controls. Under circumstances in which the individual has no choice, i.e., behavioral contingencies are thoroughly and consistently applied by the entire social or physical environment, the role of these private behaviors is indeed relatively unimportant. For example, relatively strict control of behavior is exercised by clearly established rules in some institutions, in military organizations, and in some cases where the individual is totally dependent on his social or physical environment for survival. In such highly programmed (and often inflexible) environments the person's reactions to such control or his attitudes about himself contribute little to the shaping of his behavior. A small child who is totally dependent for satisfaction of his physical needs on the adults in his environment can easily be taught to change his behavior by re-arrangement of reinforcement contingencies. Similarly, a person whose social environment consistently reinforces wearing of a particular uniform and executing behaviors in a strictly prescribed fashion will adopt the necessary behavior patterns to avoid trouble and pain and to obtain what positive reinforcement the environment offers.

In our everyday experiences environmental controls are much less stringent and often contradictory. For example, a child may be rewarded or punished for the same behavior (e.g., telling a funny story) on different occasions and sometimes even in similar situations. Verbal instructions conveyed by teaching and preaching, examples seen on television and in the everyday surroundings, frequently demonstrate both the punishments and benefits of aggressive behavior. Similarly, assertiveness, sexual behaviors, smoking, alcohol consumption are under control of conflicting social and physical consequences. A still larger group of behaviors, often called neurotic and including many interpersonal strategies for controlling the behavior of other persons or for reducing anxiety or discomfort of conflicting self-reactions, are determined by combinations of both positive and aversive consequences. All too frequently these inefficient behaviors are maintained by some positive effects on the environment, while punished by others. It is in the case of conflicting behavioral controls that the person's thinking, fantasies, and other covert reactions, show the greatest influence in modifying the simple input-output relationships, that is, the relationship between environmental, discriminative and reinforcing stimuli and the behavior which they aim to regulate.

The Skinnerian framework, from which many of the techniques described in this chapter have been derived, views self-regulatory behaviors as having their origin in the person's earlier learning experiences. These skills can free the individual, at least temporarily, of immediate control by the current environment. It is assumed that the social and physical environment ultimately must support such self-regulation. It is useful to differentiate between *momentary external* and *self-generated* sources of control for the purpose of providing more efficient behavior change methods.

A THEORETICAL FRAMEWORK OF SELF-REGULATION

In order to understand the general framework from which various self-management techniques have been derived, it is helpful to consider first some of the psychological processes that occur in self-regulation. Social learning theory assumes that much of everyday behavior consists of chains of reactions that have been built up so that a response is cued by completion of the immediately preceding response. For example, typing, walking, driving a car, shaving, preparing breakfast, and many other activities do not consist of discrete acts which require continuous decisions among alternate responses, based on the person's judgment of the adequacy of each discrete component. However, when these smooth activities are interrupted, or fail to produce the effects to which the person has become accustomed, the activity will stop and a *self-regulation* process will begin. On the basis of laboratory research and some theorizing, this self-regulation process has been described as a sequence in which three distinct stages can be identified (Kanfer, 1970). To illustrate these, imagine that a person drives to work. As he turns a corner he finds himself in an unfamiliar street. A behavior disruption occurs. The driver might first pay closer attention to what he is doing. He may ask himself how he happened to get into this street. This first stage is called the *self-monitoring* or *self-observation* stage and is essentially described as deliberately and carefully attending to one's own behavior. On the basis of past experience with driving to work the person has built up expectations for what *should* happen when he drives down certain streets and makes a given turn. These might be called *performance criteria* or *standards*, the expectations of what will happen when a well rehearsed behavior is carried out.

The second stage of self-regulation consists of a comparison between the information obtained from self-monitoring and the criteria for the given behavior. This stage has been called the *self-evaluation* stage. It is a discrimination response, a matching which reveals the discrepancy between what one is doing and what one ought to be doing. A close match between performance criteria and information from feedback should result in some satisfaction with oneself, while a large discrepancy would yield dissatisfaction. For example, our driver might note that the corner is familiar but he has turned too soon. He might comment on his foolishness and then correct his behavior.

The third stage in the self-regulation process is motivational. It consists of the administration of *self-reinforcement*, contingent upon the degree to which the behavior diverges from the performance standards. Positive self-reinforcement should result in continuation of the interrupted behavior chain. For example, our driver might note that he is not really on a strange street but that only a store sign had been changed. He might then be satisfied that he is on the correct route and continue on his way. However, if his expectations (standards) are not met, he would begin a series of behaviors intended to correct the error. Each time a new response is tried out, the same process is repeated until the standard is approximated, or the person gives up the whole sequence.

The self-regulation model then suggests that persons tend to be alerted when their behavior has unexpected consequences, or when a decision needs to be made about how to proceed. Such interruptions are most common when learning a new activity, finding oneself in a strange situation, or when an environmental reaction has changed. Overall behavioral efficiency is reduced to the extent that any of the three psychological processes that we have described above are carried out inefficiently. For example, if our lost driver were to become panicky because he is late for work he may fail to *self-monitor*. He may fail to observe where he is and how he got there, trying instead to correct his path by turning at the next street corner without much consideration. If he has not traveled this route very often his *performance criteria* may be vague, that is, he may not remember where he should have been after the turn and his performance will be erratic. If our lost driver is an individual who has been very critical of himself for the slightest errors in the past, this tendency toward self-criticism (self-punishment) might lead him to become agitated and upset. In clinical situations, numerous methods have been used to increase the effectiveness of behavior at each of the stages of the self-regulation process. Most self-management programs combine techniques that involve *standard-setting*, *self-monitoring*, *self-evaluation*, and *self-reinforcement*. We will describe these methods as separate elements in the following sections, remembering that the design of an individual program would focus on any of these components, depending on the client's skills and his particular problem.

A sketch of this working model is given in Fig. 10.1. It should be noted that this is only a framework that guides our thinking. It has been derived from laboratory research and it has been useful in developing clinical techniques. This does not mean that the model represents the actual and universal presence of these discrete psychological processes. In fact, it is quite likely that the total sequence of criterion-setting, self-observation, evaluation, reinforcement, and planning of new actions proceeds rather quickly, often without much thought by the person. Nevertheless, it can help us to organize some of the essential features of the process by which an individual manages his own behavior. The model also helps us to understand that the task of maintaining one's behavior by reward is much more complex than the learning of operant responses that are selectively reinforced by the environment. In environmentally arranged contingencies, no critical decisions need to be made by the person. For comparison we can alter the example of our driver to one in which his behavior is under external control. Assume that a friend who knows the city very well is sitting next to the driver. As the driver proceeds, the friend confirms correct directions and warns the driver prior to making an incorrect turn. Shaping and external control thus are in the hands of the guide.

When the question of self-regulation involves behavior that is under strong conflicting consequences, a change process is complicated further by the need to establish acceptable standards. Prior to engaging in self-correcting behavior the individual has to make a *commitment*. But the commitment to alter a behavior is itself influenced by the variables that lead a person to state such intentions. Various environments provide favorable or unfavorable settings that can determine whether the intentions (the behavior standards) will be achieved. Table 10.1 describes some of the factors that might lead a person to make intention statements. A separate set of factors however, relates to the question of whether or not the person will initiate and execute a change program. Therefore, when a person comes

Table 10.1. Factors That May Influence the Commitment to Execute a Self-Control Program.*

Commitment Easier	Commitment Difficult
1. Delayed Program Onset	1. Program begins immediately
2. History of pos. Rf. for promise-making	2. Past failure to keep promises was punished
3. Recent indulgence to satiation	3. Problematic behavior is not perceived to be under client's control—"can't be helped"
4. Guilt, discomfort and fear over action (aversive effects of response) is high	4. Pos. Rf. for problem behavior is high
5. Escape from social disapproval	5. Criteria for change too high
6. Presence of others making promises (modeling and social pressure)	6. Consequences of non-fulfillment are harsh
7. Behavior to be changed is private and cannot be easily checked	7. Behavior is publicly observable
8. Promise is vaguely phrased	8. Support for program planning is not anticipated
9. Promise-making leads to social approval or immediate benefits	

*Note: Expression of commitment does not guarantee execution of the program. Other factors, e.g., program requirements and reinforcement for execution in its early stages, determine fulfillment of a commitment after it is made.

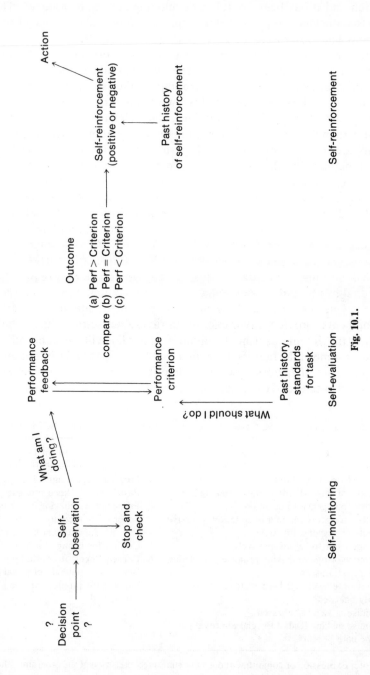

Fig. 10.1.

314

to ask for help, a major consideration is how to motivate the client to make a decision to change, and to initiate the program. Techniques for handling these problems in helping relationships are discussed in later sections of this chapter. Equally important is the reduction of external support for maintaining the problem-behavior, at least during the beginning of the program. A drug-addict in his old environment or a spouse who is dominated at home may never muster sufficiently strong self-reinforcers to overcome the environmental rewards for continuing old behaviors. Of course, in some instances the reduction of the environmental contingencies alone may suffice to permit the client to solve the problem. If not, self-management techniques can be taught. Their range of effectiveness, however, is greatest when the beneficial effects of the problem behavior are only moderate, or at least not increased by persons who would benefit by the client's remaining unchanged (e.g., a dominating spouse whose control would be disrupted when the partner becomes more assertive).

The term "self-regulation" applies to the general case in which a person directs his own behavior. The behavior may not be very conflictful, such as in the learning of a new skill that has previously been witnessed or in some problem-solving. (Chapters 4 and 11 cover methods that include training in self-regulation.) When the behavior to be executed or avoided is conflictful, we speak of the redirection as "self-control." In clinical problems, it is this special case of self-regulation that is most frequently encountered, and to which self-management methods are most often applied.

In self-management problems the client who seeks help is usually enjoying some aspect of the problem of which he complains. For example, the sexual exhibitionist, or the alcoholic, or the shoplifter may protest endlessly about his unhappiness and speak of his earnest desire to change. Indeed, some of the effects of their behavior may be aversive, for example, social rejection, job loss, or police action. At the same time these activities also yield some satisfactions that keep them going. Since the positive consequences are usually immediate while the aversive consequences may not occur until a later time and may be uncertain, attempts to change such behaviors often require the assistance of a helper.

Self-Control as a Special Case of Self-Management

In common speech, such terms as self-control, will power, and self-discipline are used interchangeably. Such behavioral dispositions have been considered to be personality traits resulting from the person's biological constitution, or his experience in learning to control his actions and impulses. On the other hand, the behavioral view advocated in this chapter, reserves the term self-control to describe a person's actions in a *specific* situation, rather than a personality trait. Specifically, our definition of self-control requires: (1) that the behavior in question is one that has relatively *equal positive and aversive consequences*; (2) that prior to the occurrence of the behavior, i.e., earlier in the chain leading up to it, a *controlling response* is introduced that alters the probability of the response to be controlled; and (3) that although the individual may have been trained in self-control techniques by others, at the time that he performs the controlling response it is *initiated by self-generated cues* and is not under direct control of the social or physical environment. Thus, when a person exercises self-control we talk about the fact that, in the absence of immediate external constraint or urging, he engages in the behavior (the controlling response) that originally had a lower probability than that of a more tempting behavior (the controlled response), in such a way that the controlled response is less likely to occur (Kanfer, 1971; Thoresen and Mahoney, 1974).

But this does not mean that self-control is viewed as behavior that unfolds in individual development, independent of environmental influences. On the contrary, its history is related to the person's earlier training and its success is related to the ultimate consequences supplied by the social environment. It is only at the moment of initiating the response that the person is not under direct environmental control. However, the likelihood that a person will begin a self-control program can be influenced by his environment, and the factors that lead him to the decision to control his own behavior will influence the probability that he will do so. The decision to start a weight control program can be heavily influenced by numerous factors. For example, the information from a physician that excessive weight is affecting her health, the after effects of overeating during a holiday period, the inability to fit into most of her dresses, the decision of a friend to diet, are strong influences in moving a woman to initiate a weight control program. Thus, even the commitment to a course of action, regardless of how well it is carried out later, is subject to environmental influences. In a later section we will discuss techniques by which such commitments can be enhanced by means of contracts, and the steps necessary to insure that the contract requirements are met.

To the client the main obstacle at first is to overcome the attractive aspects of the problem behavior. For example, a sexual exhibitionist may find himself in a tempting situation with the promise of sexual fulfillment by carrying out the act. Although the prospect of apprehension by the police and the possible consequences of losing his job or going to jail may make him anxious, these possible outcomes are distant and not very certain. It is at this point that training in self-regulation may alter the balance. The client finds himself in a conflictful situation and stops momentarily, wavering between giving in or controlling the behavior. If he is tending toward a course of action that could violate the standard that he has previously established for his conduct, it is likely to result in self-criticism, anxiety, or other aversive consequences. As a result it becomes more probable that he will escape from the tempting situation rather than to give in. The exhibitionistic client may expose himself if there is little danger of being caught, the target is attractive, his previous experiences have all been pleasant and never followed by the capture, and he has not risked grave consequences by previous commitments to his spouse or friends. But he may also call a friend, say a prayer, or take a cold shower if the expectations of dire consequences outweigh the attractions of the approach response.

Our discussion should make it clear that training in self-management requires strong early support from the helper, with the client gradually relying more and more on his newly developed skills. These include skills in (1) self-monitoring, (2) establishment of specific rules of conduct by contracts with oneself or others, (3) seeking support from the environment for fulfillment, (4) self-evaluation, and (5) generating strong reinforcing consequences for engaging in behaviors which achieve the goals of self-control. The concept of self-control implies that an individual can be taught to rearrange powerful contingencies that influence behavior in such a way that he experiences long range benefits, even though he may have to give up some satisfactions or tolerate some discomforts at first. This approach suggests that self-control is a transitory concept. If an individual fully enjoys an activity, even though it may have long range aversive consequences, no conflict is created and the question of self-control does not apply. For example, the person who indulged in heavy smoking prior to his knowledge of the aversive consequences of such behavior, or fully recognizes the dangers but is unwilling to sacrifice his immediate pleasure for a longer life, is not engaging in behavior that falls within the self-control analysis. He is not "failing to exercise self-control." Similarly, the person who had on one occasion engaged in excessive eating but who, over many years, has acquired new eating habits and rarely finds himself torn between dieting and indulging in heavy food, is not exercising self-control when he is eating in moderation. In other words, we speak of self-control *only* when the person initiates some behavior, that attempts, successfully or not, to alter the probability of a problematic act.

In clinical situations it is often necessary to introduce variables that may produce or increase a conflict before treatment can begin. For instance, discussion of the aversive consequences which the person has disregarded may facilitate the client's acceptance of a treatment program. Although research on this problem is just beginning, there have been some studies (Kanfer and Zich, 1974; Mischel, Ebbesen, and Zeiss, 1972) showing that control depends on the joint action of the three sets of variables (external, self-generated, and physiological) that we have discussed, rather than the manifestation of a long and enduring personality characteristic. Individuals who have difficulties in resisting temptation in one situation do not necessarily experience such difficulties in others. However, it is presumed that training an individual in methods that make the tempting response less likely may have some utility in later situations for which no specific training had been undertaken. While this "generalization effect" has been noted in the clinic, it remains to be demonstrated in the research laboratory.

Self-management techniques frequently involve methods of self-control. From what we have said, it should be apparent that the helper's role can be concentrated in three different areas: (1) In helping the individual to establish favorable conditions for carrying out a self-control program and providing initial reinforcement to alter the balance in favor of changing the undesirable behavior (motivation); (2) In helping the individual to acquire specific behavior change techniques that ease the process of change (training); and (3) By reinforcing the client's efforts and successes in carrying out a self-management program (support and maintenance). The importance of the helper's role in the early stages of treatment suggest that the various factors that influence the helper-client relationship (and have been reviewed in Chapter 2) should also be considered here.

The Role of Self-Attribution in Self-Management Methods

In addition to the practical advantages of involving a client in the change program, there have been indications from different areas of research that a person's emotions, actions, and attitudes may be influenced by beliefs about the causes of his behavior. The most important distinction appears to be due to a person's attribution of these causes to his own actions or to the invention of another person. These effects have been noted regardless of the actual truth of the person's belief. The direction of the effects of an attribution depends on the setting in which the attribution takes place. In the medical literature, it has been known for a long time that patients may respond favorably to harmless and inactive medication (placebo) when the patient has strong faith in the doctor's prescriptions and harbors high expectations that the physician will help him. In fact, the term "placebo" is derived from the Latin meaning "I will please," indicating the important element of suggestion and compliance that is an ingredient in the therapeutic effects of some doctor-patient interactions. However, while this effect may bring about changes while the placebo is taken, the beneficial changes tend to disappear when the drug is stopped. Changes believed to be due to the person's own effort last longer than those associated with belief in the drug effect.

In a recent study by Davison, Tsujimoto, and Galros (1973), subjects complaining of insomnia were given a treatment package composed of chloral hydrate (a drug that tends to shorten the time to fall asleep), self-produced relaxation, and specific suggestions for regulating their sleep schedules. The authors argued that, according to an attributional analysis, treatment changes which are perceived by the subject as due primarily to a drug do not generalize once the drug is withdrawn. Following treatment, half of the subjects were told they had received an optimal dosage of the sleep aid, while the others were informed that the doses were too weak to have been responsible for any improvement. All subjects then discontinued the drug but continued relaxation and scheduling procedures. It was found that subjects who were led to attribute their improvement less to the drug than to a self-produced relaxation procedure maintained these gains to a significantly greater degree than subjects who believed their dosage had been optimally effective in helping them sleep. These results are consistent with an earlier report by Davison and Valins (1969) who found that after administration of a vitamin compound, allegedly a pain reducer, the subjects who were later told that they had received an inert substance endured a pain stimulus to a greater degree than those who were told that they had received an effective pain reducer. Thus, behavior changes which a person attributes to an external influence, such as a drug, would be expected to be less enduring than changes attributable to one's own efforts.*

---

*Wilson and Thomas (1973) evaluated the effects of self- vs. drug-attributed relaxation on systematic desensitization. In this and several related studies, different attributions failed to affect the outcome. In part this may be due to the fact that their studies used these attributions during generating *initial* treatment effects while the positive results were obtained when a behavior change *maintenance* was the desired result. Further, the self-attribution effect may be limited to situations in which the *method* effect itself is not very strong, or motivational variables are of overriding importance.

Other research has shown that achievement motivation is related to the person's attributing the causes of his success and failure to himself or to external sources (Kukla, 1972); that attitude formation and changes are influenced by the locus of attribution (Ross, Insko, and Ross, 1971; Valins, 1966, 1967); and that improved performance in learning new skills and on social and perceptual tasks is associated with the subject's thinking, that his success depended on his own efforts, rather than on chance or the experimenter's actions (Rotter, 1966). A person's belief that he has control over the occurrence of aversive events can also alter his pain tolerance. The greater effects of self-generated control of pain have been explained as due to the subject's ability to predict the timing of the stimulus, which is greatest when he administers it himself. Since therapeutic programs often require taking steps that are initially aversive or anxiety-arousing, one would expect that a person who paces his own progress through the program should do better than when the pace is controlled by another person. However, in a review of studies on the role of personal control of aversive stimuli, Averill (1973) has pointed out that the context of the behavior is critical in predicting the person's reaction. Averill concludes "the stress inducing or stress reducing properties of personal control depend upon the *meaning* of the control response for the individual; and what lends a response meaning is largely the context in which it is embedded" (1973, p. 301).

The importance of attributing the sources of emotional arousal to different stimuli has been pointed out in a series of studies by Schachter and his co-workers (Schachter and Singer, 1962; Schachter and Wheeler, 1962; Schachter, 1964). Schachter proposed that two components are necessary for the occurrence of emotional behavior: (a) a degree of emotional arousal that the person can recognize; and (b) a casual attribution of the arousal to some relevant source. The quality of the following emotion is determined by the label that the individual bases on the casual attribution. For example, the effect of an arousing drug may be labelled anger or anxiety, depending on the structure of the situation. Since behavioral problems often involve emotional components, the implications of these studies have been of interest to clinicians. For example, once a client can be helped to identify his own arousal state and attach a realistic label to its genuine source, the subsequent behavior may be considerably altered. A common clinical example is offered by some sexual problems presented by adolescents. At times, these clients mislabel sexual arousal as due to anxiety, and respond to increasing intimacy with escape or avoidance responses learned previously for control of anxiety. Relabeling of the emotional cues can aid these clients to acquire appropriate sexual responses.

Another series of studies has relevance to the motivational aspects of self-management. Reports by Deci (1971), and Lepper, Greene, and Nisbett (1973) suggest that a person's intrinsic interest in an activity may decrease after it has been rewarded by other persons and the reward is then withheld. These studies can be interpreted to demonstrate the effects of establishing a discrimination reinforcement. When reward is withheld, the S^D for the activity is no longer present and the response no longer occurs. In self-management methods, these results suggest that the helper guard against excessive use of reinforcement for behaviors that the client already enjoys. It emphasizes the importance of using the client's self-reinforcement to maintain behaviors which the client has learned and can carry out without external support.

METHODS FOR THERAPEUTIC CHANGE

Providing the Conditions for Change

Self-management techniques are most easily applied when the client is concerned about his present problem and can anticipate some improvement by its resolution. However, clients are frequently not strongly motivated to engage in a program. Some may feel that it is really hopeless to expect a change after so many years of suffering. Others are afraid that they will have to give up some satisfying behavior patterns in favor of an unknown and possibly unpleasant style of life. Still others expect the change to happen through the helper's magic and without effort on their part. In the use of self-management techniques it therefore becomes crucial to make change appear possible and desirable. The helper must communicate very early the limitations of his own role to the client. He must convey his expectation that the client will carry out some of the exercises associated with the program, and will take responsibility for initiating and maintaining behavior changes. At the same time the helper assures the client that he will be available to train the client in techniques that make change easier, that he will provide guidance in formulating the change program and treatment goals. Self-management therapy can be structured by giving the client information about the nature of the program but it must also be bolstered by the helper's actions throughout the program. Among these are consistent efforts to facilitate the client's handling of decisions and choices that promote the overall change plan. A helper would not respond to direct inquiry by the client, for example, about the advisability of changing a job or selecting a friend. However, he works with the client so that the elements of a decision are clearly labeled, the outcomes of each alternative are reviewed in terms of their effects on the client and on other people. The choice is then made by the client.

Several methods are available that accomplish the dual purpose of structuring the course of self-management treatment and helping the client to clarify his goals. In this section, three of the most widely used methods will be discussed: contracts, self-monitoring, and task assignments.

Contracts

Legal and social contracts form the basis of our systems of social control. Mutual agreement to work toward a specific goal or to exchange services and goods usually takes the form of some general statement of expectation by each party. In most *social* contracts the specific consequences of fulfillment or nonfulfillment of the contract by either party are not described. For example, an arrangement to meet a friend can be broken with consequences that are usually not clearly spelled out in advance. On the other hand, a contract to deliver merchandise at a specified time might include provisions for a fixed penalty for nonfulfillment of the contract.

Psychological contracts generally emphasize the positive contingencies for achieving the stated goal. In behavior change programs they are used (a) to help the client initiate specific actions, (b) to establish clear-cut criteria for achievement, and (c) to provide a mechanism for clarifying the consequences of engaging in the behavior. Contracting provides both the helper and the client with a record of what has been agreed upon and an opportunity to evaluate progress by comparison against the terms of the agreement. It also provides the client with a set of rules that govern the change process.

Contracts can be unilateral, that is, one party obligates himself toward a change program without expecting specific contributions from the second party, or they can be bilateral. Bilateral contracts, commonly used in marriage counseling, or in families, or between teacher and child, specify the obligations and the mutual reinforcements for each of the parties. Contracts can also be made by an individual with himself, with the helper, with others when the helper serves as a monitor and negotiator, or with a group such as a classroom or a family.

There are seven elements that should be contained in every good behavioral contract. Each of these elements should be spelled out in detail, arrived at by negotiation and accepted fully by the client. Good contracts should have short range goals and should be written. The behaviors required in the contract should be rehearsed prior to commitment by a client, and all efforts should be made to avoid a contract that might be difficult or impossible for the person to attain. The seven elements in the contract are:

1. A clear and detailed description of the required instrumental behavior should be stated.
2. Some criterion should be set for the time or frequency limitations which constitute the goal of the contract.
3. The contract should specify the positive reinforcements, contingent upon fulfillment of the criterion.
4. Provisions should be made for some aversive consequence, contingent upon nonfulfillment of the contract within the specified time or with the specified frequency.
5. A bonus clause should indicate the additional positive reinforcements obtainable if the person exceeds the minimal demands of the contract.
6. The contract should specify the means by which the contracted response is observed, measured, recorded; and a procedure should be stated for informing the client of his achievements during the duration of the contract.
7. The timing for delivery of reinforcement contingencies should be arranged to follow the response as quickly as possible.

Stuart (1971) has suggested that behavioral contracting in interpersonal relationships rests on four assumptions. Positive reinforcement in interpersonal exchanges is a privilege rather than a right. It follows that setting certain reasonable standards for obtaining positive reinforcements is not punishing or excessively restrictive. The rules should simply systematize an interpersonal relationship. A second assumption is that effective interpersonal agreements are mutually binding.

A third principle is that the value of an interpersonal exchange is a direct function of the range, rate, and magnitude of the positive reinforcement mediated by the exchange. Therefore, an interpersonal contract encourages the highest possible rate of mutual reinforcement between the contracting parties. The final assumption is that rules create freedom in interpersonal exchanges. This implies that the knowledge of the available reinforcers for particular actions permits the individual to make better choices, since he knows the probable outcome of each alternative. A definition of mutual obligations removes the uncertainty of the partner's response to a particular act.

Behavioral contracts are most frequently used in combination with other self-management techniques. However, they serve not only to establish conditions for motivating a person. They may also be viewed as a behavior change technique that structures and clarifies the progress of the treatment process. Finally, they offer a common framework for assessing progress to both the helper and the client. We will illustrate their adaptation to three types of situations: classrooms, families, and adult clients who continue their normal life during treatment.

Contracts with Children

Homme (1969) has described in detail how contingency contracting can be used with individual children and in the classroom. Ten basic rules are suggested on the use of reinforcement in contracting and contract procedures.

Rule 1. The contract payoff should be immediate. With children it is especially important that the required behavior be simple and easy to identify and that the reward follow immediately.

Rule 2. Initial contracts should call for and reward small approximations. It is essential to specify and break the behavior into small components. For example, a contracted target behavior should not be "keeping the room clean." Instead, the first target behavior might be to remove all articles of clothing from the floor and put them in their proper place. A second step might be added later, requiring the child to make his bed. A third contract might require him to organize his play area or his desk in a pre-arranged way. Thus, the contract requirements are gradually increased after each successive target behavior is well established.

Rule 3. Reward frequently with small amounts. It is important to use rewards with children not only for their intrinsic value, but also as information that clearly tells the child when he has carried out the proper activity.

Rule 4. Contracts should specify rewards for accomplishment and not for obedience. This rule suggests that a contract with a child should not define target behaviors in terms of unspecified activities that are evaluated only by the adult in each instance. Determination if a criterion has been reached should not depend on the adult's judgment alone, but on standards that the child can also verify.

Rule 5. Reward the performance after it occurs. Often called grandma's law, this rule simply reflects utilization of the reinforcement principle: the target behavior comes first, the consequence later. The child is *never* permitted to engage first in a rewarding activity and then required to carry out the target response. For example, it is incorrect to establish a contract which permits a half hour of play if the child promises to do his homework afterwards.

Rule 6. The contract must be fair. This rule emphasizes the importance of the child's acceptance of the conditions, and the balance between the magnitude of reinforcement and the required behavior.

Rule 7. Terms of the contract must be clear. The child must always know *how much* performance is expected and *what* he can expect as payoff.

Rule 8. The contract must be honest. When parents engage in contingency contracting, they will often reinforce the target behaviors at the beginning. Gradually, however, they may resent continued payoff for something the child should be doing "naturally." While it is true that a good contingency contracting program aims toward eventual reduction of external reinforcement and increase in self-reinforcement, it is essential that the terms of the contract be carried out by the adult as long as it is in force. In several instances we have observed serious deterioration in slowly built up target behaviors, because the parent failed to fulfill a contract condition.

Rule 9. The contract must be positive. The basic message to the child should not be that the contract involves a threat of punishment but that its fulfillment represents a positive contribution to the child's growth and development.

Rule 10. Contracting as a method must be used systematically. The very essence of the effectiveness of the contract procedure, as of many other self-management techniques, lies in the fact that it becomes a rule for everyday conduct. Neither contract management nor other methods can be reserved for use only on special occasions, on weekends, or in difficult situations. As much as possible, contract conditions should be adhered to without exception.

In the classroom, contingency management has been used mainly to encourage improved academic performance and to decrease disturbing classroom behaviors. Establishment of classroom contracts requires first a list of reinforcing events that would be effective incentives for most students in the class. The teacher then must pinpoint the particular responses that he wishes to alter, such as rate of solving problems, participation in class, disturbing comments to other students during class periods, or physical aggression toward others. The teacher then explains the system to the children and allows them to experience the reinforcing events for a short period. Tokens or a point system can be used so that each child can choose among a variety of backup reinforcers. For younger children free playtime, engagement in a favorite activity, or privilege to choose among various activities are effective group reinforcers. The teacher must explain the means by which changes in the target behavior are monitored, and he must explain the precise contingency relationship.

Contracts with Marriage Partners

In a detailed research report, Patterson and Hops (1971) describe a technique for training marriage partners in behavior negotiations aimed at reducing the rate and intensity of their conflicts. The underlying assumption is that there is an increased escalation of discord among marriage partners as a result of a series of minor irritations. Since it is likely that each partner will attempt to control the irritating behaviors of his mate by delivery of aversive stimuli, a series of coercive interchanges results in which each partner strengthens the irritating behavior of the other (Patterson and Reid, 1970). Over a series of interactions, one partner may learn to avoid confrontations and submit early in the sequence, or he may increase the aversiveness of his control, or a confrontation may temporarily reduce irritations only to start the cycle over again later. In training marriage partners to reduce the rate of aversive behaviors, Patterson and Hops used videotapes of a couple's interactions, modeled non-aversive interactions, and supervised practice. The couple was also taught to pinpoint the target behaviors (irritations). The desired behavior changes, with the hoped-for consequences to each partner, were recorded in the original contract. The procedure described by Patterson and Hops involves initial interviews, some discussion of the critical problems and some information and required reading of material assigned from Lederer and Jackson (1968). The couple was asked to discuss one of their conflicts, and their attempts were videotaped and replayed. The concept of aversive stimuli was explained to them and two experimenters role played the problem interchange, but dealt with the same problems in a nonaversive way. The couple was asked to repeat their performance, pinpointing the behavior that they thought required change in the other person. The couple was trained to be highly specific in their complaints and in their negotiations in setting up contracts for behavior change. Figure 10.2 gives an example of the first contract. Subsequent contracts included more specific daily activities that had been sources of irritation to the couple.

Contracts with Individual Clients

Contingency contracting is also widely used with individual clients. For example, a graduate student came for help because she felt inadequate, had difficulty asserting herself with her roommate, and felt that she was wasting too much time in activities other than her studies. After initial discussion it was decided to focus first on her feelings of inadequacy. A behavioral analysis suggested that this complaint referred mainly to the client's tendency to look back on most social situations and emphasize her failure to have acted decisively or effectively in comparison to others. First, a list of positive self-statements was made up to give the client a ready set of self-reinforcers. A contract was then set up in which the client agreed to review her interpersonal activities twice daily, specifically after her lunch hour and before going to bed, and to find at least three positive actions in which she had engaged during a social interchange. After recording these events, she attached positive statements to them and recorded their frequency. The accumulation of 25 contingent positive self-statements was the

Betty's request for changes in Bill:

1. Discuss money only once a week for about 15 minutes.
2. Nag only once a month.
3. No nagging about the job unless the routine is changed.

Consequence. If he slips up and does more nagging than agreed upon, then Betty can buy a dress on the household account ($20.00). However, if he nags more than three times in the week, this is now a down payment on a $100 dress.

Bill's request for changes in Betty:

1. No deviations from the present work routine. At present, this includes: Mon. 9–5:30, Tue. 5–9; Wed. off; Thurs. 5–9; Fri. 9–1; no Sat. or Sun. Consequence: If the routine is broken, i.e., Betty comes home after the specified hours or works on a weekend, it will cost her $5 from her personal checking account.
2. When Bill can afford to give Betty $100 per month for herself then she quits working.

Betty	Bill

Fig. 10.2.   Agreement No. 1. (Adapted from Patterson, G. R. and Reid, S. Coercion, a game for two; intervention techniques for marital conflict. Technical Report #6, ONR Project, University of Oregon, 1971. With permission.)

occasion for her engaging in reading a short story, an activity that she enjoyed very much. The conditions of the contract were gradually increased so that up to 10 positive incidents and contingent self-statements per day were required before she could read a short story. After improvement with this problem, behavioral contracts were established that required a minimum of one assertive response, defined as expressing the client's thoughts and attitudes during social interactions. After success in this area, behavioral contracting was extended to rearranging the client's nonproductive but enjoyable activities so that they always followed a period of study or work. Progress in the client's behavior change was followed in interview sessions by considerable encouragement and praise from the helper. The use of contingency contracts in this case was supplemented by relaxation training and practice during periods when the client felt increases in tension. In the process of negotiating and evaluating each of the contracts (which were set up for periods of two to three weeks) the client was taught self-monitoring and practiced pinpointing the effects of her own behaviors on others and herself. In 14 weekly sessions, the client's behaviors and her satisfaction with them had sufficiently changed so that treatment was no longer necessary.

Clinical examples of successful behavioral contracting, combined with other self-management techniques, come from the treatment of overweight, excessive smoking, homosexual fantasies, and alcoholism. In each case, the behavioral contracting can be helpful because the client is not faced with the overwhelming task for eliminating the undesirable behavior all at once. For example, one client reported excessive worries about sexual potency. However, at first the man could not even accept the notion that he would ever be sexually competent. A contract with him and his wife introduced stimulus control that did not attempt to eliminate but only to limit the periods of worry to times when they would not directly interfere with his marital sexual behavior. Sexual courtship behaviors that were specifically unrelated to achievement of orgasm were contracted. Following the general approach proposed by Masters and Johnson (1970) and others, gradual increase in the instrumental behaviors that constitute the early part of the lovemaking chain was practiced. In this case, the behavioral contracts served primarily to reduce the client's fear that he would never be able to change by requiring only small behavior changes at first and by providing a framework within which other self-management techniques could be carried out. Reports of successful contract use are available in cases of drug addiction (Boudin, 1972; Wisocki, 1972), weight control (Tobias, 1972), excessive smoking (Russell and Sipich, 1973) and many other behaviors.

Behavioral contracts can be enhanced if the contract is associated with public commitment either to a friend, a spouse, a class, or a group of co-workers. However, in use of such public commitments, caution must be exercised because of the danger that the client might set the criterion for the contracted behavior higher than he can achieve in order to impress others. Furthermore, the client's difficulties in fulfilling the contract may lead him to avoid a person who knows of the commitment, or to engage in actions that might even endanger the relationship with the "witness" of the client's unfulfilled contract. This effect is related to the problem of reactance or counter-control discussed at the end of this chapter.

Self-monitoring

As we indicated in the discussion of the conceptual model of self-management, self-monitoring is an operation that parallels the measurement of behavior in situations where a client is under continuous observation of a therapist or experimenter. Treatment methods which rest primarily on instigating behavior change in the client outside the range of observation of the helper therefore demand some recording of the behavior. And if only the client has access to the behavior, self-monitoring, a refined version of self-reporting, would seem to be the most practical method to assess the client's execution of the self-management program. Our conceptual framework suggests that self-monitoring (SM) however, is not isolated from the person's self-evaluation, nor his tendency to attach contingencies to his behavior. A person who is asked to observe and record his own behavior is helped immediately to become more aware of its occurrence. He also has objective evidence of the change in his monitored behavior over time. Therefore, self-monitoring may be a *reactive* measure, that is, its very occurrence may alter the behavior which is observed.

In establishing SM as a behavior change procedure, there is an implicit or explicit statement of the criterion for the desirable level of the observed behavior. The client may expect that the SM data will be praised or criticized by the helper, and the client himself may show satisfaction or displeasure as he observes a change or no change in a monitored behavior. Therefore it is critical to separate various functions of SM in self-management practice. SM has often been used only to obtain a record of the frequency of the response prior to the introduction of *any* treatment procedure. When a client is taught to categorize a target behavior and is then asked to monitor its frequency, the helper may be interested only in assessing the severity of the problem or the conditions under which the target behavior occurs. However, available research literature suggests that the reliability of self-monitoring, when compared to independent measures of the same behavior, varies widely in different situations (cf. Kazdin, 1974). While some researchers have reported high correspondence between SM and independent observations, others have found that subjects vary greatly in the accuracy of SM. As an assessment instrument therefore, SM may be useful only when independent observations are used to check on the client's reports.

    When SM was first used, it was intended only to provide a record of baseline behavior. However, it was noted in some instances that the observed behavior changed in a favorable direction. Subsequent research and clinical practice have therefore attempted to utilize SM as a therapeutic technique. Several studies, with obese patients (Stuart, 1971), with smokers (McFall, 1970), with school children (Broden, Hall, and Mitts, 1971), and with study problems (Johnson and White, 1971) have reported reductions in undesirable behaviors. However, other investigators (Mahoney, Moura, and Wade, 1973) have failed to reproduce these findings. Our current understanding of the effects of SM on the observed behavior suggest that an effect can be expected at the beginning of treatment, but it weakens over time. The magnitude and direction of this effect varies considerably under different treatment conditions and with the behavior which is monitored. For example, when SM is introduced as a therapeutic technique and clear value statements about the desirability of a change in the monitored behavior are made, SM effectiveness is increased. However, the active elements in producing the effect probably consist not only of the monitoring activity. Changes in the monitored behavior would be enhanced by the implied expectations of progress by the helper and the client's increased self-reinforcement for meeting a therapeutic criterion. The client who has been impressed with the absolute necessity of reducing his caloric intake, who has been taught techniques of self-reinforcement for refusing food, and who may have a contract to engage in reduced eating is likely to respond to self-monitored eating behavior of high caloric foods with more than a simple mark on his monitoring sheet.

    Another important feature of SM, often deliberately used by helpers, is the fact that SM may be incompatible with continuation of an undesirable behavior. For example, the author has used SM of aggressive responses and of thoughts of physical violence to interrupt the habitual sequence of behavior which constituted the client's problem. When SM thus represents a behavior that is incompatible with the target response and strongly reinforced by the therapist and the client, its beneficial influence on changing the undesirable behavior clearly cannot be attributed to SM alone. For example, in a case by the author, SM of hostile and aggressive thoughts toward a spouse was assigned to a couple with severe marital problems. The monitoring task included making a tape recording of any interactions which threatened to develop into a fight. The couple reported reduced frequency of fighting, explaining, laughingly, that on several occasions the tape recorder had not been handy. The clients then jointly set up the recorder. By that time, the hostile interpersonal interaction had been interrupted and the couple could no longer remember what they were going to fight about.

Another critical feature of SM lies in the particular behavior selected for monitoring and the time relationship between the behavior and the monitoring. Investigators have reported use of SM for ruminating thoughts, for urges to engage in a problematic behavior, for simple motor behaviors like skin picking or throwing objects, for complex social behaviors such as self-depreciatory statements and many others. SM can also be carried out prior to the occurrence of the undesirable behavior, immediately following it, or at the end of a long interval. There is insufficient research to guide the helper in deciding whether intention or urges to engage in the undesirable behavior should be monitored, or acts should be recorded after their occurrence, for maximal effects. Summary recording of the target behavior after several hours or at the end of the day would introduce a long delay, and surely would weaken the beneficial effects of the recording act alone. From our considerations it is clear that SM is not a sufficiently powerful technique for use as a primary vehicle for lasting behavior change. However, SM procedures can be used quite successfully to increase the client's motivation for change. In discussion with the helper, the achievement of a criterion as represented by the behavioral graph, can serve both as an incentive and later as an occasion for reinforcement by the helper as well as the client himself. For example, various common self-indulgences, such as buying a luxury item, engaging in a pleasurable activity, or taking a brief rest can be tied directly to the achievement of a change in the target behavior. Thus, the monitoring chart can serve as a visual guide for administration of self-reinforcement.

Rules for Self-Monitoring

In introducing SM to the client the following steps are suggested:

Step 1. Discuss the importance of accurate record keeping with the client and give examples of the utility of SM in the therapeutic program.

Step 2. Together with the client, clearly specify the class of behaviors to be observed and discuss examples to illustrate the limits of this class. Be sure to use frequency counts for behaviors that are easily separable, e.g., smoking of a cigarette or making a specific positive self-statement, and use time intervals for behaviors that are continuous. For example, duration of studying is indicated by the time started and stopped. Durations of interpersonal exchanges, or of obsessive ruminations are clocked.

Step 3. Discuss and select an unobtrusive and convenient method for recording, taking care to select a recording instrument that is always available where and when the behavior is likely to occur. For this purpose, golf counters, worn like wrist watches, can be used for frequency counts. For low frequency behaviors a client can carry a small supply of pennies in his right pocket and move one to the left when the behavior occurs, transferring the score to a written record at regular intervals

(Watson and Tharp, 1972). Similarly, toothpicks, small plastic tokens or other devices can be used. Small note pads, previously ruled for ease of recording a score, can be conveniently carried in a purse or pocket.

Step 4. Show the client how a set of frequency recordings or time intervals can be graphed for visual inspection.

Step 5. Role play and rehearse the entire sequence of recording with the client. It is also advisable at first either to provide the client with record sheets or to have him purchase the necessary items so that he can rehearse the actual procedure with the instruments at hand.

It is advisable to begin SM by selecting relatively simple responsive classes and monitoring only one class of behaviors. As the client becomes more adept, he can be asked to record additional information. For example, a coding system can be developed so that the conditions under which the behavior occurred are also recorded. It is usually necessary to limit these to a few easily distinguishable situations. For example, behavior in the presence of others or when alone can be differentiated by entering the score in two different columns, or by using a second position on a golf counter for tallying one of the two conditions, or by putting items into two different pockets on the same side. In general, clients to whom the mechanics and purpose of the SM procedure has been explained will contribute specific suggestions that are most consistent with their own practices.

Self-monitoring assignments should be reviewed during interviews following the session in which they were assigned. Clients are frequently tempted to bring in long essays or verbal descriptions of the behavior and the circumstances under which critical incidents occur. Such records are not quantifiable and should be discouraged. If the target behavior is very frequent or extends over a long time, it is possible to use a time sampling technique. This method requires that the person make self-observations only during previously specified time intervals. To assure adequate sampling of the behavior, the helper can develop a program, best based on randomization of all the periods during which the behavior occurs and then ask for SM for specified periods only. For example, with persons who interact with others during much of their working day as part of their occupation, the occurrence of particular responses, e.g., aggressive behaviors or subassertive responses, may be sampled by randomly selecting half hour periods during each of a number of days for observation. Care must be taken however that no biases are introduced if the client's activities systematically vary from day to day and his problems are limited to specific situations.

Other variations of SM include the use of the graph for display, either as a reminder to the client or for social recognition and support in a small group. For example, SM data have been displayed by institutionalized clients at their bedside, by family members in an accessible part of the home, or by children in classrooms. Rutner and Bugle (1969) report a case of behavior change with SM in a hallucinating patient who recorded the duration of his hallucinations and posted the graph on the wall. Social reinforcement for progress can certainly add to the effectiveness of this technique.

There are several other modifications of SM techniques that require somewhat more elaborate recording techniques. A series of studies have been reported that use audio and video tape playback as a means by which the client can observe his own behavior. Later these self-observations serve as a base for attempts to improve the actions. Generally, this type of self-observation is an integral part of a more complex intervention program. It often involves participation of group members or several helpers who initiate a self-correcting process by helping the client to discriminate and pinpoint particular problematic aspects of his interaction behavior. Other helpers then model more desirable behaviors and reinforce the client's approximation to these (see Chapter 5 for discussion of these techniques).

A more sophisticated SM technique consists of biofeedback procedures. Clients are helped to recognize variations in physiological activities by means of visual or auditory displays of their heart rate, electrical skin resistance, brain waves, or other physiological outputs. Both in research and in clinical studies this technique has been hailed as an important discovery because of its potential utility in psychological and medical treatment. However, review of the literature suggests that the use of biofeedback alone has not yet successfully achieved large scale changes in patients with psychological or medical problems by providing voluntary control over bodily functions that are problematic (Schwartz, 1973). SM of physiological activities has been shown to be effective in producing small and time limited changes of physiological functions in laboratory animals as well as in men (Barber, DiCara, Kamiya, Miller, Shapiro, and Stoyva, 1971) but has not yet been shown to persist over long periods of time nor be of the magnitude necessary for long range therapeutic effects.

In summary, SM is a useful component of a total self-management program. It is not sufficiently reliable to serve by itself as an assessment technique, nor has its effect as a behavior change technique been substantiated when it is applied alone, under different conditions, and to different types of behaviors. It can serve as an important program component and motivating device, when combined with contracts, self-evaluation, and self-reinforcement. Its application requires training the client to recognize instances of the target behavior, to record and graph the data and to use the visual data display both as an incentive and as a cue for self-reinforcement contingencies.

Tasks and Assignments

The assignment of particular tasks has long been used as a therapeutic technique (Herzberg, 1945). However, in a self-management program this feature takes on a central role. The assignment of tasks that are graded in difficulty gives meaning to the helper's structure of self-management methods as procedures that require the client to take responsibility for changing his own behavior. In addition, they stress the importance of the gradual change of habitual behaviors *outside* the helping relationship. The procedure also has the purpose of reducing the client's belief that change is impossible. It further provides opportunity for self-observation and clarification of the problems which the client encounters as he engages in the new and more desirable behaviors. In addition, the execution of these small changes by the client himself should add to his motivation for increased contributions toward the change process, on the assumption that self-attribution should enhance the process. The assignments usually consist of new behaviors which the client is urged to attempt in his everyday activities as a step toward expanding his repertoire.

Homework assignments are presented as tentative efforts to progress toward new behavioral repertoires. Sometimes they can also be presented in the guise of tryouts for which there are no aversive consequences. It is important that the client participate in planning the particular forms that the assigned behavior takes. Goals should be realistic to minimize the possibilities of failure.

When the client seems fearful toward some component of a total situation, the helper may emphasize a contrived purpose in order to bring about initial emission of the behavior. For example, a client with severe fears of social interaction may be given a highly specific task that would help him to overcome the initial fear. With an extremely withdrawn client we have used such contrived tasks as going to a drug store for a cup of coffee and specifically recording the number and types of interactions of people sitting at the counter for a 15 minute period. A shy and insecure young woman was asked to go to a social gathering for the specific purpose of obtaining information about the occupational background and current jobs of several (two male and one female) guests. A heavy wine-drinker was asked to go to a tavern, order one bottle of beer, and keep a count of the number, approximate age and sex of customers who entered and left the bar. In all of these cases, the tasks served several purposes. First, they provided an opportunity for execution of behaviors that had been a problem in the past. At times this helps to dispel the client's expectations that something terrible will occur. Secondly, the client's self-observation and later discussion with the helper can give the client greater efficiency and comfort in his newly acquired role. The client can also be asked to say what he thought his impact was on the behavior of others and to discuss his feelings during the interactions that he witnessed (cf. Kopel and Arkowitz, 1972). These new experiences permit the individual to reevaluate himself and his skills. They also make possible the utilization of problem solving skills, acquired in the interview sessions, in his daily life.

In all cases it is important that the assigned behaviors be role played in the presence of the helper and discussed in detail prior to execution. Furthermore, self-monitoring and recording of observed events in written form is highly desirable. Finally, the helper's encouragement and reinforcement should be offered not for those accomplishments that depend on the reaction of others, but only for the client's execution of the previously planned behaviors. Client observations and comments are often helpful in preparing the ground for designing later tasks. In fact, as the change program progresses, the client should be encouraged to plan himself and carry out tasks that contribute to his overcoming his problems.

Modification of the Environment

The client whose problems are suitable for treatment by self-management techniques has probably made repeated previous attempts to alter his behavior. His failure may have been due to lack of environmental support, lack of knowledge of specific behavior change methods, or lack of sufficient self-generated reinforcement for trying to change. The techniques described in the following two sections require only a minimal self-initiated step by the client, namely to trigger a change in the environment in such a way that many subsequent behaviors would naturally follow. For example, once a person steps off the edge of a swimming pool, subsequent events are programmed by the laws of physics and no longer require self-regulation. Similarly, the alcoholic who calls a fellow AA member to accompany him on a walk through the park is programming environmental conditions that will reduce the need for generating self-controlling responses to compete with a quick trip to the liquor store.

The techniques to be described here can be summarized under the concept of *stimulus control*. These procedures set up environmental conditions that either make it impossible or unfavorable for the undesired behavior to occur. Stimulus control methods include such extremes as *physical prevention of the undesirable behavior*, for example by voluntary confinement in an institution, locking oneself in a room, or turning the car keys over to a friend. In each case, some undesirable behavior is avoided simply by the fact that the individual has relinquished control over the required behavior to an external controlling agent. Unfortunately, such control is often only temporary in its effectiveness. In addition, it frequently leads to development of avoidance or hostility toward the agent who has now been given control. At the other extreme, stimulus control methods include training of *self-generated verbal responses* without changing the physical environment, nor the physical possibility of executing the undesirable behavior. For example, repeated self-instructions that emphasize long-range aversive consequences of the behavior, statements about the positive aspects of tolerating an unpleasant situation or resisting a temptation, self-rewarding statements about one's "will power," or similar verbal cues can serve as stimuli that exert powerful control over subsequent action. Self-generated verbal instructions are discussed in detail in Chapter 11 and will not be elaborated here.

In the following section we will consider stimulus control techniques that involve manipulations of the physical environment, rearrangement of the social environment and self-generation of controlling stimuli and controlling responses. They are similar in principle to those discussed in the chapter by Meichenbaum but somewhat different in method. The techniques to be covered in a later section on covert conditioning overlap considerably with stimulus control methods, since training a person to generate stimuli in fantasy or imagination represents an example of altering controlling stimuli. However, unlike the alteration of external physical stimuli or reprogramming of the social environment, the covert conditioning methods require continued activity by the person in rearranging *his own* behavior and in reorganizing his habitual ways of thinking.

The introduction of physical controlling stimuli is best accomplished early in the problematic sequence when the elements in the chain leading to the undesirable behavior are relatively weak and many alternate behaviors are competing. Since attempts to alter conflicting behaviors by stimulus control have only transitory effectiveness, in most cases additional self-management techniques are needed to help the individual after external control has temporarily reduced the undesirable behavior.

Stimulus control techniques can be separated according to the function of the technique in (a) altering the physical environment so that the execution of the undesirable response is impossible, (b) altering the social environment so that the opportunities for target behaviors are heavily controlled by other persons, (c) changing the discriminative stimulus functions so that the target behavior is specifically restricted to particular physical environments or the presence of distinctive external cues stimuli, (d) altering the physical or physiological condition of the person so that changes in the target behavior are produced. It should be remembered that, as in all self-control techniques, these methods may reduce the problem behavior. But their effects are substantially increased if a new behavioral repertoire is built up at the same time. This dual approach is especially important when the target behavior can be suppressed or eliminated only through temporary rearrangement of the environment.

Physical Stimulus Control

Numerous clinical reports have described the use of alteration of physical environments to prevent a response. For example, cigarette cases or refrigerators have been equipped with time locks that make access impossible, except at preset intervals. Persons on weight reduction programs have been advised to keep only as much food in the house as can be consumed in a short time, thus eliminating late evening snacking. The ancient use of chastity belts (and other confining garments) represents a use of stimulus control to make sexual contact impossible by altering the physical circumstances. In everyday life most persons use this technique incidentally. Mothers put mittens on small children to reduce thumb sucking, students find isolated areas for study, some persons reject opening charge accounts or carrying charge cards, others play loud music, or flee from houses that hold past memories in order to control undesired behaviors or fantasies.

For most people, the presence of other persons is a strong determinant of behavior. By selecting the right person or environment, the client can relieve himself of much of the burden of generating his own controlling responses. For instance, handing a pack of cigarettes to a friend who has agreed to help you stop smoking makes it more likely that you will quit. With one client who was under indictment for shoplifting, the author established a contract that she would not go to stores except when accompanied by her husband or daughter. Most young adults are familiar with various dating rituals, such as double dating or planning an evening in public places which are designed to control exposure to unwanted sexual advances.

Stimulus Narrowing

A frequent clinical method is to encourage the clients toward gradually decreasing the range of stimulus conditions in which an undesirable behavior occurs, i.e., the behavior is put under S^D control. For example, overweight clients are requested to eat *only* in the dining room, at a table with a particular colored tablecloth, or in the presence of other family members (cf. Ferster, Nurnberger, and Levitt, 1962; Stuart and Davis, 1972). Over a period of time the numerous cues previously associated with eating gradual lose control over the response. Similarly, smoking behavior can be brought under S^D control by restricting smoking to a particular environment. For example, smoking can be gradually eliminated while driving, in the office, in various rooms of the house, or in the presence of certain individuals. Such techniques have been reported by Nolan (1968), and Roberts (1969) who treated excessive smoking by restricting that behavior to a special "smoking chair." Frequently, this technique is combined with the method of making the response execution impossible by keeping cigarette packs or food only in those areas that have been chosen for S^D control. Study habits have been considerably improved by setting up specific environments in which no other activities take place (Fox, 1962). In establishing S^D control, the client is asked to leave the study area when daydreaming or when engaging in other activities. Sexual relations of married couples have been improved by establishing particular rituals such as candle light or other mutually shared love making cues in which both partners focus their attention solely on each other. Among the most powerful and convenient S^D's are clocks and watches. Specific time intervals have been employed as cues for engaging in assertive behaviors, smoking, daydreaming, worrying, skin picking, or nail biting. These techniques can be used for two purposes: to reduce the frequency of the behavior by gradually restricting the environment and time during which it occurs, or to increase a response because of its frequent and exclusive association with a particular environment or time interval.

Stimulus control techniques are frequently combined with the method of *increasing response cost* if the frequency of the target behavior is to be reduced. For example, in addition to requiring that the behavior occur only in a certain place or at a given time, one can gradually increase other demands so that preparation for execution of the behavior becomes more and more cumbersome. Ultimately, the ritual is sufficiently aversive so that the effort outweighs the anticipated positive consequences of the target behavior. For example, in establishing stimulus control over smoking, clients may deliberately place the pack in a distant place, remove matches from the usual location, be required to chew a stick of gum prior to engaging in smoking, put on a "smoking cap," and finally seat themselves in a smoking chair. On several occasions, clients who have been helped to arrange these procedures have reported that the undesirable behavior gradually dropped out, "because it was just too much trouble to go through all that." The establishment of stimulus control requires a slow acquisition period, with small steps of increasing difficulty. Care must be taken that no new elements are added until the prior step is fully mastered.

The use of bodily cues for stimulus control is somewhat more difficult, because such cues are not easily differentiated. However, let us remember that the discriminated function of a set of stimuli is built up because the person has had previous experience in which behaviors emitted in the presence of such S^D's were always followed by either positive or aversive consequences. Thus, characteristic events surrounding or preceding the physiological stimulation may be used to make the S^D's more distinct. The use of antabuse in the control of excessive drinking, and of placebo pills to reduce pains or to increase sexual potency, represent examples of stimulus control procedures, either by actual physiological alteration or by altering only the client's interpretation that bodily changes are occurring. Although satiation or deprivation of an individual have often been considered separately as motivational techniques, these methods can also be used for control of physiological stimuli. For example, low calorie, high bulk foods can reduce cues for eating; for an alcoholic the high intake of nonalcoholic fluids prior to a party may serve to control some of the internal thirst cues that justify drinking.

Techniques of stimulus control are generally used in combination with other methods described in this chapter. For example, if you publicly announce your intention to change, the presence of the persons before whom the commitment is made becomes an S^D affecting the target response. Further, techniques of stimulus control are designed only after a behavioral analysis that reconstructs the chain of events preceding the problem behavior. Some distinct cue for the new (controlling) response is set up *early* in the chain, when proximity of the target response, high response strength, and the presence of immediate positive reinforcers are not so great that they cannot be overcome. While many of these techniques have been used for centuries, it is their systematic application that permits the client to reorganize his environment in such a way that a problem behavior is most easily altered.

All of the methods mentioned so far have dealt with the reorganization of a person's external environment. Stimulus control techniques have also been developed in which the individual changes the nature of self-generated verbal cues. In contrast to the preceding methods, the control of self-generated stimuli is relatively tenuous, since the individual can easily "remove" or shut out such cues as verbal instructions, imagined sequences, or thoughts. In altering external controlling stimuli the individual needs only to make one step, the initiation of a chain of events. The subsequent sequence is then determined by the natural environment or by the behavior of others. In the case of self-produced controlling stimuli, the individual must often maintain them despite the presence of temptations in an environment that encourages and supports the problem behaviors. We will be dealing with these self-control methods in a later section of this chapter, and they are also described in Chapter 11.

Changing Self-Generated Behavioral Consequences

In the course of an adult's daily life, only a few of his actions appear to have immediate external consequences. Many others seem to be maintained by the person himself. Despite the accumulation of much research on the conditions that affect the self-reinforcement (Bandura, 1969; Kanfer, 1968), many issues concerning the processes by which self-reinforcement (SR) operates have not yet been clarified. For practical purposes, we can deal with SR operations as paralleling the motivating operations carried out in the application of external reinforcement (see Chapter 7 on Operant Conditioning). Self-reinforcement of operants represents a special type of self-initiating behaviors that permit the individual to maintain or alter his actions with relatively little dependence on the immediate environment. Skinner (1953) has defined one property of self-rewards by stating that it "presupposes that the individual has it in his power to obtain reinforcement but does not do so until a particular response has been emitted (pages 237–238)." While this definition emphasizes the contingency of SR on preceding S^D's, it does not provide a complete description of the classes of behavior to be discussed here.

Positive self-reinforcement encompasses two different operations: (a) approaching or consuming a material reinforcer that is available in the person's environment. For example, when a person "rewards himself" for hard work by a cup of coffee or by treating himself to a good meal, he is applying a positive *self-administered* consequence, or (b) delivery of contingent *verbal-symbolic* self-reinforcement, such as self-praise for a completed task. In addition, aversive SR may follow a response, delivered in the form of self-criticism, self-punishment, or withholding of positive SR. The aversive SR operation will be discussed later. The self-administered SR procedures involve the administration of external reinforcement by the client himself and to himself. The self-administered positive SRs can be further divided into two groups: (1) self-presentation of a new and commonly unavailable reinforcer that is usually outside the everyday life of the client; such as a luxury item of clothing or attendance at a special event; and (2) the initial denial of some pleasant everyday experience and later administration of it only as a contingent reinforcer for a desired behavior (Thoresen and Mahoney, 1974). For example, making an enjoyable phone call, going to a movie, talking to a friend, or a cup of coffee may be initially postponed, and carried out only as a reward for accomplishment of a prescribed task. As Thoresen and Mahoney suggest, this requires that the person initially deny himself the experience, introducing a preliminary aversive component in the self-management of behavior. When such easily available reinforcers are contingently administered, then the period of delay and postponement of gratification introduce the conflict elements of a self-control situation, that is, one in which the self-administration of rewards is a behavior to be controlled until a given contingency is met.

Verbal-symbolic SRs consist of such verbal statements as "I did well," "That was good," and other positive self-statements by which the individual communicates his own satisfactions with his achievement. These types of self-reinforcing statements are extremely difficult to examine in the laboratory, since they are usually said quietly or only in fragments and are difficult for a client to describe or remember. However, in a change process, deliberate programming of such verbal-symbolic self-rewards can be carried out by first asking the person to say them aloud, and to make them contingent only upon a specified event. A further problem with this last class of SRs lies in the fact that some events may represent the equivalent of verbal-symbolic SRs in abbreviated form. For example, a self-satisfied smile, a feeling of satisfaction, or even a slight righting of one's posture all may represent self-generated reinforcing operations contingent on successful <u>accomplishment of a task</u>. The parallel of external negative reinforcement can also be set up for self-administration. A person can present himself with an aversive stimulus that is removed or terminated only when the self-prescribed escape or avoidance response is carried out. Similarly, a positive event can be contingently removed. For example a person can plan to stop watching television until he completes preparation for the next day's work. Finally, self-punishment may be carried out by administering a strong aversive consequence following the occurrence of a target behavior. Withholding of a positive SR after previous continued administration, and self-imposed extinction also have been used in self-management programs (see covert extinction). Extinction differs from punishment in that a person stops the pleasant consequence but does nothing else. For example, in an effort to reduce the frequency of ruminations about a lost lover a client may train himself to continue thinking about the person but not fantasize any positive consequence of meeting and interacting with her, or to impose deliberately some unrelated and neutral consequence after the thoughts occur. Figure 10.3 summarizes the possible combinations of these operations, paralleling the various external reinforcement contingencies.

Consequence-Operation

Quality of Consequence	Give	Take Away
Positive	Positive Self-Reinforcement (a) self-administered (b) verbal-symbolic	Covert Extinction self-imposed time-out (temporary)
Aversive	Self-Punishment (a) self-administered (b) verbal-symbolic	Negative Self-Reinforcement (a) self-administered (b) verbal symbolic

Fig. 10.3.   Some combinations of self-reinforcement.

Although training the administration of SR contingencies is more difficult than exposure of a client to external consequences, SR procedures have the great advantage that the individual can eventually apply them independently of the helper, and that he can also use the same procedures for other problems which may not be related to the central complaint. Laboratory research with children and adults has demonstrated that self-reinforcing operations show the two characteristic properties of reinforcing stimuli, i.e., they alter the probability of occurrence of the response that precede them, and they motivate new learning (Bandura and Perloff, 1967; Kanfer and Duerfeldt, 1967; Montgomery and Parton, 1970). In comparisons with administration of the same reinforcement by another person, positive SR has been shown to be generally equal, if not slightly superior in effectiveness (Johnson and Martin, 1973; Lovitt and Curtiss, 1969; and others). The growing literature on the self-reinforcement concept, most of it carried out with positive SR, has also demonstrated that self-reinforcement is not always independent of the environment. While SR operations make it possible for a client to be *temporarily* independent, ultimate positive consequences from the environment, i.e., some success in pursuing behaviors that are self-reinforced and some consistency with the models in the client's environment who demonstrate SR patterns, would seem to be necessary to maintain the newly developed behavior in the long run. Numerous studies have clearly shown that the patterns of self-reinforcement and self-criticisms themselves can be modified by learning. They are probably acquired in childhood by direct training and by observation of contingency relationships and self-reinforcing activities in the social environment (cf. Bandura, 1969; Kanfer and Phillips, 1970, for summaries).

Establishing SR in Individual Adult Programs

As we have suggested, the goal of the helper is to start a behavior change program that is carried out by the client, and to achieve changes that are maintained without continuing social reinforcement. Thus, most self-management programs incorporate SR as a treatment component. In some cases the deficit in positive self-statements is itself the target behavior. For example, a behavioral analysis may reveal that low rates of positive SR limit the client in achieving his goals. Or, the client may be excessively self-critical, show excessively high criteria for achievement so that positive SR rarely occurs, or he has learned that self-praise is undesirable or immodest.

The following four steps summarize the usual procedures in aiding an individual toward effective use of positive SR.

Step 1. Selection of appropriate reinforcers. Although some questionnaires can aid in the preliminary selection of reinforcers (Cautela and Kastenbaum, 1967), it is generally desirable to discuss and negotiate individual reinforcers in interviews with the client. Asking the client about his current practices of self-reward, both symbolic and material, inquiring about "luxury items" that the client would like to acquire, obtaining verbal statements that would express self-satisfaction frequently yield suggestions for appropriate SRs. What is often most effective is a rearrangement of behavioral contingencies for self-rewards that the person normally administers noncontingently or only in conjunction with behaviors other than the problem responses. To this, some novel material SRs are added as special incentive for a prolonged program. The list of material reinforcers, enjoyable activities and positive self-statements is compiled on the basis of the client's current behaviors. For example, acquisition of inexpensive luxury items that the client has wanted but never obtained might include purchase of a paperback book, a small item of jewelry, clothing acessories, or cosmetics. Among activities, the individual's preference might be a trip to a museum, a rock concert, a weekend vacation, or time spent in hobbies.

Verbal-symbolic reinforcers include positive self-statements that are employed in self-praise, reaffirmation of one's adequacy or self-worth, congratulating oneself on physical appearance, physical strength, social attractiveness, interpersonal skill, or any other appropriate content. It is crucial that the selected reinforcers relate to the client's personal history. They must be acceptable to him as something that he wants, could easily acquire or do, and that would make him feel good. If a complex and long-range program is designed, several reinforcing stimuli should be equated for approximate value so that they can be interchanged. This prevents satiation with a single item or statement. In a long-term program, a series of small reinforcers should also be exchangeable for one large reinforcer at infrequent intervals. A person who has accumulated a predetermined number of symbolic SRs because he has shown improvement in the target response might work toward a larger material reinforcer, such as purchase of a luxury item, contingent upon achievement of a desired goal within a fixed time period. The list of exchangeable reinforcers, therefore, should contain both small items obtained from the person's current daily activities and larger items that may be just outside his current reach.

Step 2. Specific response-reinforcement contingencies are defined. The client is encouraged to list variations within the target response class and to indicate the precise conditions and methods for delivery of SR. For example, if the person is on a weight control program, a verbal-symbolic reinforcer might be used for such target behaviors as rejecting offers of food, staying within the allotted daily caloric intake, or choosing an alternate low calorie food. In addition, a larger SR, such as buying a new dress or wardrobe accessory, might be made contingent upon achieving a predetermined weight loss within a specified time period. In establishing the response-reinforcement contingency care must be taken to select a good match. For example, not all SRs are equally appropriate for all responses. It would obviously be foolish to choose eating a large meal as an SR for weight loss in an obese client. It has been pointed out (Seligman, 1970) that there are predispositions for some reinforcers to be more effective with particular behaviors. Whenever possible, the SR should be one that is essentially compatible with the target behavior. For example, the obese client might select purchase of a new dress as an SR because such a possession emphasizes the positive aspects of weight loss in terms of physical attractiveness or body size. An appropriate reinforcing stimulus for assertive behavior might be one that enhances the person's feelings of adequacy, or self-worth, or physical attractiveness, consistent with the goal of helping the person to develop a sense of equality and personal confidence in relation to others. After the appropriate contingencies are established, specific provisions should be made for the occurrence of both the delivery and recording of SR. On occasion, high frequency of the desirable behavior or involvement in a long-term program may require use of intermittent schedules of reinforcement. For instance, one client who had set small material SRs as his rewards for improving his study habits decided to add both interest value and effectiveness to his SR schedule by setting up an intermittent reinforcement schedule. He accomplished this by using a deck of playing cards. He assigned SR values only to cards with values above ten. Prior to administering a material SR he would shuffle and cut a deck of cards and reward himself only if a ten or higher card appeared.

Step 3. Practice of procedures. After selecting appropriate reinforcers and establishing reward contingencies, the helper should rehearse with the client several instances of occurrence of the target behavior and the self-reinforcing sequence. In these role playing sessions the helper can improve, simplify and reinforce the client for execution of the behavioral sequence until it is performed smoothly. These role playing sessions are also important because they provide the client with a model and the initial experience in an activity about which he may have doubts or in which he may feel uncomfortable. Of course, the helper's presence and his encouragement and approval not only strengthen the likelihood that the client will carry out the behavior but might also eliminate the common misconception that such simplistic mechanics for self-management require no effort nor careful programming, nor diligent practice.

Step 4. Checking and revising procedures. The client should bring in records of the target behavior and contingent SRs for discussion with the helper and for necessary adjustments in the procedure. For example, if the target is the general increase in verbal-symbolic SRs, it would be desirable to change responses rather frequently in order to extend the program over a wide range of the client's daily activities. The monitoring sessions also can be used by the helper to model administration of SRs under different conditions. This aids the client to develop a repertoire of appropriate verbal-symbolic stimuli and permits the gradual decrease of small material reinforcers. The ultimate goal of the program is not to eliminate long range "luxury" reinforcers completely, but to make them sufficiently infrequent, and to increase the demand for achievement to the point where they can be maintained by the client himself. In fact, the purpose of the program is to help the client to utilize the techniques of self-produced reinforcers as a means of handling psychological difficulties that may arise after his contact with the helper is terminated.

Several research projects have reported that the addition of SR improves behavior change programs (Jackson and Van Zoost, 1972; Mahoney, Moura, and Wade, 1973). There have been reports of effective use of self-reinforcement to improve study habits, enhance weight reduction, increase dating skills and assertive behavior, raise activity levels in depressed patients, and reduce homosexual fantasies. The SR procedures represent primarily the motivational component of a self-management program; other techniques are also required to provide the mechanical procedures in which SR can be embedded.

Establishment of Self-Reinforcement Programs with Children

Although young children can be taught to establish contingencies for self-reinforcement (cf. Masters and Mokros, 1974 for summary of research) some modifications are required. Clinicians and researchers have reported studies in which an adult first models SR contingencies in detail. Gradually, support and probes are faded as the child shows an increased ability to execute the required behavior sequence alone. Initially, verbal-symbolic SRs are given aloud. For example, a teacher asks a child to repeat a positive self-statement if, after comparing the results of his academic performance with a key, he sees that he has achieved the criterion. Gradually, matching the teacher's performance is neither encouraged nor required, and the teacher fades out of the picture. Both with the individual child and in training a classroom, it is often desirable to use token reinforcers initially because of their distinctiveness and because the use of back up reinforcers for the token avoids boredom and satiation.

Self-Generated Aversive Consequences

There are essentially two different types of self-generated aversive consequences that can be used in the control of behavior, *self-punishment* and *negative self-reinforcement*. These two sets of operations differ in that self-punishment is aimed at interrupting or decelerating a response while in negative reinforcement a response is increased. In negative reinforcement, a continuing unpleasant stimulus is escaped or avoided by engaging in an alternate or competing behavior. It has been assumed that the reduction of the unpleasantness or anxiety serves to reinforce the newly learned escape behavior. Verbal-symbolic SRs such as self-criticism or self-depreciating statements, can serve either function. In addition, just as in operant conditioning, an aversive consequence can also consist of programming the removal of a positive stimulus following a response, and it can be used either to decrease the preceding response or to increase a new target behavior. The former is illustrated by leaving a party as self-punishment for having acted foolishly. The negative SR is exemplified by depriving oneself of the company of a lover to enhance studying for an examination. In the second case, the absence of the lover is the unpleasant stimulus escaped by completing one's work.

A somewhat more complex procedure involves levying a fine (removal of money, widely held to be a generalized positive reinforcer) following a response that has been targeted for decrease. For example, in the control of smoking behaviors, some clinicians have requested the client donate a one dollar bill to their most disliked political organization after smoking a cigarette. But the use of withdrawal of a positive reinforcer has been infrequently reported. In a weight control program, Mahoney, Moura, and Wade (1973) found that this procedure is not very effective when used alone. However, there are some logical advantages to this technique, even though there is limited evidence that it works. Since aversive stimuli are not used, the many problems associated with such techniques as self-administered punishment are avoided. At the same time, the practical problems of persuading a person to discontinue a pleasant situation, or to give away or destroy a valuable item, are still not known. Thus, this technique has not been sufficiently explored for widespread clinical application.

In self-punishment, a variety of procedures have been used. Self-critical verbal statements, presumably conditioned to earlier aversive consequences, can be systematically attached to the undesired behavior. Unfortunately, self-punishing responses are often common in a client's repertoire and very frequently do not decelerate target behavior. Instead they merely remove the guilt and anxiety accompanying performance of the target behavior. The author saw a client for whom mild electric shock (administered by a portable battery operated device) was used as a self-punishment. The student, who had complained of sexual rumination during study, was instructed to give himself mild shocks whenever the fantasies occurred. Initially, he reported a decrease in ruminations with this procedure. However, after several days he found their frequency increasing again. He also tended to increase both the number and intensity of the self-administered shocks. A closer analysis of the procedure indicated that the client had begun to reverse the sequence. He would shock himself briefly after the start of ruminations. Then, feeling that "he had already paid the price for his bad behavior" he would continue his fantasies and shock himself at intermittent intervals.

Many clients have a long history of childhood experiences in which they discovered that one way to "have your cake and eat it too" is to carry out the undesirable behavior and suffer punishment as well. Helpers who work with mothers are familiar with the problem of children who fail to respond to physical punishment. Frequently, the externally administered—and eventually self-generated—punishing response simply serves to alleviate guilt and anxiety associated with the behavior, clearing the way for repetition. Also, unusual individual histories in which punishment served as a positive reinforcer, or as an S^D for affect, lead some clients to use physical self-punishment excessively. For these reasons both verbal-symbolic and physical methods of self-punishment should be used only whenever no alternative is possible. When the physical self-punishment is continuously monitored by a helper, its application may be less problematic. In fact, good results have been reported with this method, using self-administered mild electric shock in variations of aversion therapy (see Chapter 9).

A simple but effective technique has been suggested by Mahoney (1971). A client was instructed to wear a heavy rubber band around his wrist. Upon occurrence of obsessive ruminations that were the target for deceleration, the client snapped the rubber band to produce some pain. This self-punishment procedure has also been used by the author and his students with good results. Self-administered aversive consequences, much like other SR, may owe part of their effectiveness not so much to their high value as pain producers but because they help to make the undesirable response clearly stand out in the total flow of behavior. Finally, they serve as cues for the self-evaluation and self-correction processes that we have described earlier.

Another example of self-administered punishment is the use of an aversive conditioned reinforcer in the *thought-stopping* technique (Cautela, 1969). The client is asked to think about the ruminations, hallucinations, or fantasies that need to be decelerated. When he is well into the behavior he raises his finger and the helper shouts: "Stop," loudly enough to evoke a startle reaction from the client. After several trials and explanation of the procedure, the client initiates this behavior, first aloud, then imagines himself yelling "Stop" at the top of his voice. Frequent practice is suggested at first, in addition to actual use of the procedure whenever the problem behavior occurs. This method has been widely reported to be helpful in eliminating disturbing thoughts.

The utilization of aversive SR in escape paradigms is best illustrated by *covert sensitization*, a procedure that is described in detail in a later section. In essence, the client is trained to imagine an unpleasant event and make its removal contingent upon carrying out the desired behavior. A simpler use of aversive SRs has been made in some weight control programs. The client is instructed to buy a heavy piece of lard or beef fat and to place it in the refrigerator as a continually present aversive stimulus. With successive weight losses the client cuts away pieces of the lard, gradually removing the aversive stimulus.

When a response of excessive frequency is to be modified, *satiation* has been suggested as a behavior change technique. This procedure consists of deliberate repetition of a behavior even when the client no longer wants to do it. For example, an excessive cigarette smoker may be instructed to light and smoke cigarettes continuously until he feels physically ill. Thus, the positive stimulus may lose its reinforcing properties with frequent repetition and acquire an aversive character. After a long and intensive smoking session, lighting a cigarette may actually become a cue for feeling ill or dizzy. The procedure is most frequently used in conjunction with other aversive stimuli, such as confining the person in a small room where the increased smoke level itself becomes noxious, or in conjunction with relief responses (see discussion of the aversion-relief technique in Chapter 9). We have already noted that self-deprivation may constitute a self-imposed aversive consequence. This procedure is illustrated by the withholding of various positive reinforcers when a person feels that he has not behaved appropriately. Giving up an invitation to a dinner, imposing a ban on smoking, on sexual activity, or alcohol intake all may be used as self-imposed aversive consequences.

Covert Conditioning

A widely used technique of behavior modification is Wolpe's systematic desensitization (see Chapter 8). This method of anxiety reduction utilizes self-presented imagery as a substitute for reproducing the actual physical conditions under which a client experiences intense fears. The demonstrated effectiveness of this technique has suggested that behavior changes may be brought about by visual representation of the problem situation while the client is in the helper's office. The major difference between the use of verbal stimuli and visual imagery lies in the fact that the helper has very little control over the self-presented imaginal stimuli. He cannot specify the characteristics of these stimuli and therefore cannot study their direct effects in a clinical setting or in research. Homme (1965) has suggested that covert operants, or coverants, can be treated very much like operant responses, even though the exact nature of these coverants is difficult to ascertain because they are not publicly observable. Out of these trends and under the leadership of Cautela (1969) a series of covert conditioning procedures have been developed. All of them employ client imagery as stimuli, as responses, or as reinforcing events. The various paradigms of covert conditioning parallel those of operant conditioning. We have differentiated these techniques from the use of verbal stimuli because covert processes usually include verbal, symbolic, and imaginal representations that are produced by the client on instruction of the helper. In this section we will illustrate examples of the most widely used techniques, including *covert sensitization, covert reinforcement, covert extinction, and covert modeling*.

Covert Sensitization

In covert sensitization, the client is asked to imagine a scene that portrays the undesirable behavior and that currently offers some satisfaction to the client. After the positive image is built up to high intensity and vividness, the client is requested to change abruptly into imagining a highly aversive event. Both physical and social aversive stimuli are usually used and modified according to the client's personal history. Then, the client is asked to imagine fleeing the problem situations and the aversive events associated with it. After the escape he visualizes relief and reduction of discomfort. Strong positive reinforcement by the helper, and eventually by the client himself, is offered for escaping or avoiding the situation, and verbal statements are used to summarize the implications of the experience. Thus the maladaptive behavior is paired with aversive consequences and escape from the total situation is rewarded by the relief experience. All of these events take place with guidance from the helper.

To illustrate the specific procedure, consider a case in which the target behavior is excessive alcohol consumption. After the helper explains the rationale to the client, positive and aversive consequences are selected that are especially suited for the client. The helper then obtains a description of the usual setting in which the drinking occurs, including many details about the physical setting and the social environment. A preliminary test should be given to be certain that the client has sufficient skills in visualizing critical scenes upon instruction. If the client is deficient in this skill, it can be deliberately built up by practice and training in imagining and describing various events.

An alcoholic client may then be asked to imagine a scene in which he is comfortably seated at a favorite bar. As the helper describes and outlines the scene he asks the client to imagine and visualize all the details of it. When a client appears immersed in the imagery, perhaps imagining that he raises a full glass to his lips, the helper asks him to imagine the aversive event. For instance, it can be suggested that the client gets sick to his stomach and begins to vomit. The helper describes this aversive feature in all its details and asks the client to imagine, visualize, smell, and feel all aspects of it. When the client appears to be experiencing the aversive consequences, the helper then suggests that the client imagine turning away in disgust from the bar and rushing out to get a breath of fresh air. As he does so, a previously established positive event is imagined. For example, a pretty young woman smiles at him, the client experiences the relief of having escaped from his alcohol habit. Favorable summaries are offered that the client can use as a self-statement, such as "why do I do silly things like drinking; it only gets me sick." At first, the scenes are worked out together in about ten trials for each scene. Scenes are also varied to encompass different settings and consequences. The client takes alternate turns with the helper in presenting the scene to himself aloud. Some scenes might also involve training in avoidance. For example, the alcoholic might imagine being offered a drink and saying "no, I won't take any alcohol" and then sensing relief. After practice with the helper the client is instructed to practice the scenes repeatedly between sessions. Some variations of the procedure have been to provide taped recordings of scenes that might be sufficiently general to appeal to several clients and to carry out in groups whose members share similar target behaviors.

Clinical reports and some research evidence point to the effectiveness of this technique. However, it requires careful preparation of the client to become proficient in imagining the suggested scenes. The client must be highly motivated and cooperative, and the scenes must be varied sufficiently to provide generality of the effect. Finally, it is important that strong personal reinforcers be used. For instance, if the alcoholic in our example is socially oriented, his vomiting may be portrayed as accidentally soiling an outraged pretty girl on a barstool next to him. Similarly, relief stimuli may include social acceptance or approval after he imagines leaving the bar.

Covert sensitization has been found to be clinically useful with numerous problems, including various addictive behaviors that are generally difficult to attack. Most often it is combined with other behavior change methods. Unfortunately, only few reports are available in which the procedure was submitted to rigorous scientific analysis. Several methodological problems make evaluation difficult. First, the stimulus events and the behaviors said to constitute the process of covert conditioning, by their very nature, are inaccessible to objective observation and measurement. Secondly, in clinical practice the helper who suggests the scenes modifies their intensity, rate of presentation and duration as he watches the client for signs of the effectiveness of his instructions. As a result, individual administrations vary considerably. Finally, an essential ingredient in covert sensitization is the disruption of the imagined sequence. For instance, the image of sitting comfortably in the bar and consuming large quantities of alcohol is interrupted. In effect, similar results might be obtained by interposing any competing response. Perhaps the interruption of the habitual chain by imagining a more satisfying behavioral sequence rather than an aversive one might accomplish the same results (cf. Foreyt and Hagan, 1973). Nevertheless, this technique has provided a potentially powerful clinical tool for behavior change since it requires no particular stimulus settings, it can be carried out fairly unobtrusively by the client, and it has been reported to be effective in few sessions.

Covert Reinforcement

This method generally parallels the operations carried out in self-reinforcement. The technique differs only in that it involves the self-presentation of an imagined scene rather than a verbal statement. The client is trained to imagine a well practiced scene that is subjectively experienced as happy or pleasant. Cautela suggests further that the helper attach a verbal cue such as the word "reinforcement" to call forth the scene. The imagery is then evoked, as any reinforcing stimulus, contingent on the occurrence of a target response. As in covert sensitization, the imaginal scenes are first practiced with the helper and eventually the client is instructed to deliver the reinforcement to himself.

Covert negative reinforcement consists of practice in imagining an unpleasant situation that can later be used in the place of other aversive reinforcers. In addition to using covert negative reinforcement for deceleration of a target response, Cautela suggests that it may be used as a noxious stimulus for escape conditioning. In this procedure the client first imagines the rehearsed unpleasant scene. Subsequently he imagines the response to be increased. For example, after imagining himself experiencing a very distasteful situation, the client visualizes walking into a room full of people and feeling comfortable, calling up a girl for a date, or engaging in whatever behaviors represent the deficiency in the client's repertoire. Covert negative reinforcement should be used judiciously, since aversive scenes that leave a residual of the unpleasant feeling might actually have the opposite effect, if the behavior to be increased becomes associated with the aversive after effects. For instance, a client who selects as an aversive event feeling anxious or vomiting in a situation, might not be able to terminate the imagery quickly. If the desirable escape response is one which had previously produced intense anxiety, detrimental effects might follow. Thus, this technique must be used with great caution.

Covert Extinction

Parallel to operant extinction procedures, the client is asked to present himself with the target response to be decelerated and to imagine a neutral effect rather than the usual pleasant consequences. For instance, in order to reduce high calorie food intake, the client is asked to imagine himself eating his favorite dish of ice cream but finding it to be tasteless and having no pleasant effects whatsoever.

The use of imagery in covert conditioning can be extended to include not only scenes that the person has actually experienced but also imagery about ideal situations, feared situations, or other fantasy constructions. In all of these procedures care must be taken to rehearse the self-presented scenes in great detail in the presence of the helper to ascertain that the necessary elements are indeed self-presented. Despite rehearsal, however, the problem in dealing with imagery techniques remains. Control over the stimuli and responses which the client presents to himself is limited, and corrective interventions by the helper are difficult to carry out.

Covert Modeling

Recent papers (Cautela, 1971; Kazdin, 1973) have reported the use of imaginal stimuli as substitutes for live or film models in the reduction of fearful behavior. The procedure combines the covert methods with those of modeling techniques (see Chapter 5). The client practices imagining the aversive scene in detail for a series of trials. Then, the client is asked to imagine another person, the model, performing the feared behavior, such as stroking a dog, or entering a crowded room. The helper describes the model as confident, and together with the client sketches the positive characteristics of the model during early constructions of the scene. In a study with snake phobic students, Kazdin (1973) found covert modeling to be highly effective in producing enduring changes in avoidance behavior. Further, his experiment suggests that the same variables that enhanced the effectiveness of live or film modeling may also be important in facilitating the behavior change with covert modeling.

A variation of covert modeling has been described by Susskind (1970) as the *idealized self-image* technique. The client is asked to imagine some desirable change in his own behavior that is within practical reach. He first describes this behavior, then he actively superimposes his idealized self-image on his current image and observes the gradual enhancement of his self-image. To help in the attainment of the self-idealized image, an incident or experience is recalled which yielded a feeling of accomplishment or success. This feeling is then extended to efforts toward accomplishing the set goal. The client is requested to act, feel, and see himself in his daily routines in ways that are consistent with his idealized self-image. Thus, some imagined changed portion of one's behavior serves as the basis for covert modeling and for initiating behaviors that are congruent with this model. Both the idealized self-image and other covert modeling methods bear some relationship to the use of role play and Kelly's fixed role therapy (1955). A basic assumption is that imagining oneself acting differently and eventually carrying out such behaviors, even if they are first tried out in artificial situations, eventually brings about changes in everyday life. Thus, imagined scenes may serve as standards toward which the client aspires. Eventually they may serve as cues in actual situations.

OTHER SELF-MANAGEMENT PROCEDURES

Anxiety Management

Several techniques have been proposed that differ from systematic desensitization in that the client is not exposed to a specific phobic or anxiety arousing stimulus, either in real life or in imagination. Instead, anxiety is first induced by suggestive instructions or reconstruction of an anxiety arousing scene. After the client shows increased restlessness and tension he is taught to relax. In theory, these approaches (Bornstein and Sipprelle, 1973; Sipprelle, 1967) use anxiety responses as S^D's to which responses that are antagonistic to anxiety are conditioned.

Suinn and Richardson (1971) describe several major steps in an anxiety management training. First, the client is told the principles underlying the procedure and their purpose. Deep muscle relaxation training is then introduced. Specific cues for anxiety arousal and for relaxation are identified and rehearsed. Anxiety is induced and quickly followed by imagination of a relaxing and happy scene. Deep breathing serves as a cue for relaxation. After the client is relaxed, anxiety cues are presented and terminated again, a rapid shift to relaxation is introduced. Suinn and Richardson used tape recordings with instructions and appropriate background music or sounds for presenting these sequences. During this process, anxiety cues are labeled for easier discrimination. In essence, these procedures are intended to provide the client with means for terminating anxiety, no matter how produced, in situations where the fear stimulus is not clearly identifiable. In contrast to desensitization methods, which intervene before the occurrence of any anxiety, in anxiety management methods it is the discriminated onset of feeling anxious that leads the client to initiate a self-relaxation sequence. The methods have been found to be successful in reducing the frequency of anxiety attacks in clients. However, once the feeling of anxiety has progressed, the technique does not seem to be effective on that occasion.

Self-Directed Desensitization

Modifications of desensitization procedures (see Chapter 8) include the initial establishment of hierarchies with a helper, followed by self-administered presentation of taped relaxation instructions. Some standard tapes that include hierarchy scenes appropriate for many different clients have also been prepared for clients with common complaints. In essence, variations of this procedure consist of assigning the client the task of learning relaxation and hierarchy presentations from taped guides. The details of the procedure are generally similar to the contents of the particular technique which is self-directed. As with other self-management procedures however, additional features of the self-directed program include the use of self-monitoring, self-reinforcement and reports to the helper, who must then maintain the client's progress by encouragement and support. The underlying rationale in self-directed densensitization differs from the more common desensitization procedure (in which the client is relatively passive), in that active coping and anxiety reduction are emphasized, rather than the gradual reduction of the fear attached to an object or situation. Numerous variations of the systematic desensitization procedure have been developed by clinicians and researchers. Many of these combine Wolpe's original method with self-management methods by enlarging the role of the client in recognizing and coping with anxiety situations and in using internal cues that signal the beginning of an anxiety episode.

Systematic Rational Restructuring

Goldfried has suggested a procedure that is based on Ellis's rational-emotive therapy. After exposure to imagined anxiety provoking situations the client is asked to label the degree of arousal and to use his anxiety state as cue for exploring and describing self-defeating attitudes or expectations about the fear arousing situation. The self-defeating statements are then reevaluated rationally, first with the helper and then by the client himself, and reduction in anxiety is noted after rational reevaluation has taken place. The anxiety provoking situations are arranged hierarchically. Goldfried, Decenteceo, and Weinberg (1974) describe this procedure as one in which the client learns to control his anxiety by modifying the cognitive set with which he approaches potentially upsetting events. In theory, the process is somewhat similar to that in the anxiety management techniques, in that the client is taught to utilize internal cues of anxiety as cues for executing newly learned anxiety reducing responses.

Self-Management and Self-Control

In our introduction we have indicated that there was a difference between problems of self-control and problems of self-regulation. Now that the reader is familiar with a variety of techniques for self-management, let us review the applicability of self-management techniques to self-control problems. When we speak of self-control problems we usually emphasize the client's dilemma in embarking upon a behavior change when his current actions give him at least some degree of gratification. It is the building of a controlling response and the conflicting consequences of the current behavior that differentiate self-control problems from those in which self-management is used to rearrange behavioral schedules, to learn how to identify and solve problems, to acquire new skills, or to engage in activities that do not alter the behavioral consequences very much. First, increases in self-control can be obtained by *providing a controlling response* that eventually replaces the undesirable activity and becomes a habitual response. We have summarized numerous techniques which can be used to achieve this goal, such as stimulus control, strengthening of competing responses, and contingency management. The second feature of the self-control problem is the fact that a problem behavior has *conflicting consequences*. Self-generated aversive consequences for an undesirable response, increased positive SR, or similar techniques can be used to help the individual alter the balance of these response contingency conflicts. A third feature of self-control concerns the fact that the individual must *initiate the new behavioral sequence by himself*. Self-instructions, discrimination training and labeling, and self-monitoring, among other methods, may be used to accomplish this. Thus we see that self-control may utilize many of the methods described here, but that it is applied to problems that fit the specific definition of the self-control phenomenon. In all self-control programs, many essential elements of self-management are employed. For example, helping the client to set his own goals, to monitor his behavior, to evaluate it, and to reward himself are common features in most programs. Invariably it is the helper's task to provide the initial motivation for behavior change, by interviews, contracts, self-monitoring, and other methods, and to withdraw support gradually as the client becomes more proficient in self-management methods. It is because of their overlapping similarity that we have not distinguished between self-control techniques and self-management methods. What differentiates self-control from self-management methods is the nature of the problem to which they are applied, not the methods themselves.

LIMITATIONS AND CAUTIONS

We have already suggested that self-management techniques cannot be applied unless the client accepts the treatment goals as desirable and is motivated toward their achievement. Research evidence for the effectiveness of the programs described in this chapter, although still limited, is generally favorable. Nevertheless, the theoretical framework on which self-management techniques rest is still tentative and incomplete. As we have indicated, some investigators have achieved success with procedures that are derived from common theoretical assumptions while others, using slightly different procedures, have not been able to achieve similar results. In part, the difficulty lies in the fact that a self-management program requires the skillful combination of several elements in matching the program to the needs of each individual client, while research usually tests the effects of only one element at a time. Interactions between various components can produce effects that could not have been foreseen from the research evidence on the separate elements.

The combination of individual elements into a program requires a thorough behavioral analysis of the problem before the program is undertaken, as well as a helper-client relationship that can promote the change process. Since targeted behaviors for self-management are often behaviors that are difficult to observe, the helper's reliance on the cooperation of the client is greater than it is in other behavior change methods. It is not infrequent that clients, because of their past history, are either unwilling or ashamed or afraid to describe target behaviors that are of greatest concern to them until they are sure that they can trust the helper. If the circumstances under which the client is referred for help are unfavorable for a trusting relationship, for example when a client is referred by a court, pressured into treatment by others, or too disturbed to enter interpersonal relationships, self-management methods are not immediately applicable. Under these conditions it is still possible to work toward creating an atmosphere in which the prerequisites of self-management are met. However, the appropriate self-management methods can be introduced only after this prior goal is accomplished.

In our society, there has been strong emphasis on the concepts of freedom and self-determination (Skinner, 1971). If a person perceives himself as giving up control over his behavior to another, he might oppose such efforts. We have stressed at the beginning of the chapter the importance of self-attribution in the self-management program. If a client perceives himself as controlled by the helper, the active cooperation necessary to accomplish the treatment goals may in fact turn into opposition. Research from social psychology (Brehm, 1966) has led to a description of the nature and the effects of *reactance*, the development of opposition to influence. With increased skill in management of behavior control, more attention has been paid to the conditions under which counter control can and should be exercised (London, 1969). Self-management techniques essentially are based on the assumption that the helper plays only a temporary and supportive role in guiding the client toward changing his own behavior. However, in applying the strategies described in this chapter it is quite possible, and often tempting, for the helper to assume too much of the burden of arranging the environment, or establishing reinforcement contingencies, or influencing criteria and goals without first obtaining the client's cooperation or at least his agreement. In such a case, a client's opposition to the helper's influence may appear in the guise of failure to carry out the program. It is therefore of prime importance that the helper, at the very beginning of treatment, work to insure that the choice of target behaviors and techniques is acceptable to the client.

SUMMARY

In this chapter we have presented methods of behavior change, based on the assumption that a client can alter his own behavior by the use of certain newly learned skills and by rearrangements of his environment. A brief outline of the theoretical framework of self-regulation was presented, and it was pointed out that even in self-management the client requires initial support and help from his environment. The importance of the client's perception of himself as controlling the behavior change process was discussed. Self-control problems were defined as relating to situations in which the person is enjoying positive consequences of a behavior that has both positive and aversive consequences for him. The resolution of such problems was outlined as consisting of the establishment of controlling responses that eventually change the occurrence of the response that needs to be controlled. Such situations may involve the execution of a response, such as smoking or overeating, or the avoidance or withdrawal from a necessary but unpleasant activity, such as working or tolerating mild pain.

Prior to the training of particular self-management techniques, the conditions for instigating behavior change must be created. Contracts, self-monitoring, and assignment of tasks can aid in motivating the client toward change. Operations parallel to control by external reinforcements have been presented that use positive or aversive self-reinforcement, either of the material or verbal-symbolic type. Similarly, self-produced satiation and deprivation have been described as techniques in the service of behavior change.

One group of change strategies have been classified under the term stimulus control. They may involve rearrangement of the social and physical environment (so that the probability of executing a target behavior is altered) or the use of self-generated behaviors. A special case of rearrangement of self-generated reinforcing consequences has been discussed for imaginal presentation of stimuli and responses, subsumed under the concept of covert conditioning. Several additional methods have been noted that incorporate features of self-regulation.

Most effective self-management programs incorporate the following features, although their particular sequence may be different in each case.

Step 1. A behavioral analysis, including a description of specific problem behavior, positive and negative reinforcers appropriate for the client's strengths and skills, and the resources in the client's environment that can be enlisted to aid the behavior change process.

Step 2. Observation and self-monitoring of the target behavior.

Step 3. Development of a plan for behavior change. Negotiation of a contract that includes clear specification of the goals to be achieved, the time allowed for the program, and the consequences for achieving it, as well as the methods for producing the behavior change.

Step 4. A brief discussion with the client on the underlying assumptions and rationale of the techniques to be used.

Step 5. Frequent external verification of progress and of factors that have retarded progress, as well as reevaluation of the contract.

Step 6. Recording and inspection of qualitative and quantitative data documenting the change.

Step 7. A self-reinforcement program that relies increasingly on the person's self-reactions, is sufficiently varied to avoid satiation, and is effective in changing the target behavior.

Step 8. Execution of new behaviors by the client in his natural environment with discussion and correction of his behavior as needed.

Step 9. Frequent verbalization of the procedural effects, the means by which they are achieved and situations to which they can be applied in the future.

Step 10. Continuing strong support by the helper for any activity in which the client assumes increasing responsibility for following the program accurately or extending it to other problematic behaviors.

REFERENCES

Averill, J. R. Personal control over aversive stimuli and its relationship to stress. *Psychological Bulletin*, 1973, **80**, 286–303.

Bandura, A. *Principles of behavior modification*. New York: Holt, Rinehart and Winston, 1969.

Bandura, A. and Perloff, B. Relative efficacy of self-monitored and externally imposed reinforcement systems. *Journal of Personality and Social Psychology*, 1967, **7**, 111–116.

Barber, T., DiCara, L. V., Kamiya, J., Miller, N. E., Shapiro, D., and Stoyva, J. (Eds.), *Biofeedback and self-control*. New York: Aldine-Atherton, 1971.

Bornstein, P. H. and Sipprelle, C. N. Group treatment of obesity by induced anxiety. *Behaviour Research and Therapy*, 1973, **11**, 339–341.

Boudin, H. M. Contingency contracting as a therapeutic tool in the deceleration of amphetamine use. *Behavior Therapy*, 1972, **3**, 604–608.

Brehm, J. W. *A theory of psychological reactance*. New York: Academic Press, 1966.

Broden, B., Hall, R. V., and Mitts, B. The effect of self-recording on the classroom behavior of two eighth grade students. *Journal of Applied Behavioral Analysis*, 1971, **4**, 191–199.

Cautela, J. R. The use of imagery in behavior modification. Paper presented to the Annual Meeting of the Association for the Advancement of Behavior Therapy, Washington, D.C., September 1969.

Cautela, J. R. Covert extinction. *Behavior Therapy*, 1971, **2**, 192–200.

Cautela, J. R. and Kastenbaum, R. A reinforcement survey schedule for use in therapy, training and research. *Psychological Report*, 1967, **20**, 1115–1130.

Davison, G. C. and Valins, S. Maintenance of self-attributed and drug-attributed behavior change. *Journal of Personality and Social Psychology*, 1969, **11**, 25–33.

Davison, G. C., Tsujimoto, R. N., and Galros, A. G. Attribution and the maintenance of behavior change in falling asleep. *Journal of Abnormal Psychology*, 1973, **82**, 124–133.

Deci, E. L. The effects of externally mediated rewards on intrinsic motivation. *Journal of Personality and Social Psychology*, 1971, **18**, 105–115.

Ferster, C. B., Nurnberger, J. I., and Levitt, E. B. The control of eating. *Journal of Mathetics*, 1962, **1**, 87–109.

Foreyt, J. P. and Hagan, R. L. Covert sensitization: Conditioning or suggestion? *Journal of Abnormal Psychology*, 1973, **82**, 17–23.

Fox, L. Effecting the use of efficient study habits. *Journal of Mathetics*, 1962, **1**, 75–86.

Goldfried, M. R., DeCenteceo, E. T., and Weinberg, L. Systematic rational restructuring as a self-control technique. *Behavior Therapy*, 1974, **5**, 247–254.

Herzberg, A. *Active psychotherapy*. New York: Grune and Stratton, 1945.

Homme, L. E. Perspectives in psychology—XXIV Control of coverants: The operants of the mind. *Psychological Record*, 1965, **15**, 501–511.

Homme, L., Csanyi, A. P., Gonzales, M. A., and Rechs, J. R. *How to use contingency contracting in the classroom*. Champaign, Ill.: Research Press, 1969.

Jackson, B. and Van Zoost, B. Changing study behaviors through reinforcement contingencies. *Journal of Counseling Psychology*, 1972, **19**, 192–195.

Johnson, S. M. and Martin, S. Developing self-evaluation as a conditioned reinforcer. In B. Ashem and E. G. Poser (Eds.), *Behavior modification with children*. New York: Pergamon Press, 1973.

Johnson, S. M. and White, G. Self-observation as our agent of behavioral change. *Behavior Therapy*, 1971, **2**, 488–497.

Kanfer, F. H. Verbal conditioning: A review of its current status. In T. R. Dixon and D. L. Horton (Eds.), *Verbal behavior and general behavior theory*. Englewood Cliffs, N.J.: Prentice-Hall, 1968.

Kanfer, F. H. Self-regulation: Research, issues and speculations. In C. Neuringer and J. L. Michael (Eds.), *Behavior modification in clinical psychology*. New York: Appleton-Century-Crofts, 1970.

Kanfer, F. H. The maintenance of behavior by self-generated stimuli and reinforcement. In A. Jacobs and L. B. Sachs (Eds.), *The psychology of private events*. New York: Academic Press, 1971.

Kanfer, F. H. and Duerfeldt, P. H. Motivational properties of S-R. *Perceptual and Motor Skills*, 1967, **25**, 237–246.

Kanfer, F. H. and Phillips, J. S. *Learning foundations of behavior therapy*. New York: Wiley, 1970.

Kanfer, F. H. and Zich, J. Self-control training: The effects of external control on children's resistance to temptation. *Developmental Psychology*, 1974, **10**, 108–115.

Kazdin, A. E. The effect of response cost and aversive stimulation in suppressing punished and nonpunished speech disfluencies. *Behavior Therapy*, 1973, **4**, 73–82.

Kazdin, A. E. Self-monitoring and behavior change. In M. J. Mahoney and C. E. Thoresen (Eds.), *Self-control: Power to the person*. Monterey, Calif.: Brooks/Cole, 1974.

Kelly, G. A. *The psychology of personal constructs*. New York: Norton, 1955.

Kopel, S. A. and Arkowitz, H. The role of attribution and self-perception in behavior change: Implications for behavior therapy. Paper presented at Sixth Annual Meeting of the Association for Advancement of Behavior Therapy, New York, 1972.

Kukla, A. Attributional determinants of achievement-related behavior. *Journal of Personality and Social Psychology*, 1972, **21**, 166–174.

Lederer, W. J. and Jackson, D. D. *The mirages of marriage*. New York: Norton, 1968.

Lepper, M. R., Greene, D., and Nisbett, R. E. Undermining children's intrinsic interest with extrinsic reward: A test of the "overjustification" hypothesis. *Journal of Personality and Social Psychology*, 1973, **28**, 129–137.

London, P. *Behavior control*. New York: Evanston, and London: Harper and Row, 1969.

Lovitt, T. C. and Curtis, K. A. Academic response rate as a function of teacher and self-imposed contingencies. *Journal of Applied Behavioral Analysis*, 1969, **2**, 49–53.

Mahoney, M. J. The self-management of covert behavior: A case study. *Behavior Therapy*, 1971, **2**, 575–578.

Mahoney, M. J. and Thoresen, C. E. *Self-control: Power to the person*. Monterey, Calif.: Brooks/Cole, 1974.

Mahoney, M. J., Moura, N. G. M., and Wade, T. C. Relative efficacy of self-reward, self-punishment, and self-monitoring techniques for weight loss. *Journal of Consulting and Clinical Psychology*, 1973, **40**, 404–407.

Masters, J. C. and Mokros, J. R. Self-reinforcement processes in children. In H. Reese (Ed.), *Advances in child development and behavior*, vol. 9. New York: Academic Press, 1974.

Masters, W. H. and Johnson, V. E. *Human sexual inadequacy*. Boston: Little, Brown, 1970.

McFall, R. M. The effects of self-monitoring on normal smoking behavior. *Journal of Consulting and Clinical Psychology*, 1970, **35**, 135–142.

Mischel, W., Ebbesen, E. B., and Zeiss, A. R. Cognitive and attentional mechanisms in the delay of gratification. *Journal of Personality and Social Psychology*, 1972, **21**, 204–218.

Montgomery, G. T. and Parton, D. A. Reinforcing effect of self-reward. *Journal of Experimental Psychology*, 1970, **84**, 273–276.

Nolan, J. D. Self-control procedures in the modification of smoking behavior. *Journal of Consulting and Clinical Psychology*, 1968, **32**, 92–93.

Patterson, G. R. and Hops, H. Coercion, a game for two: Intervention techniques for marital conflict. Technical Report # 6, ONR project, University of Oregon, 1971.

Patterson, G. R. and Reid, J. Reciprocity and coercion: Two facets of social systems. In C. Neuringer and J. Michael (Eds.), *Behavior modification in clinical psychology*. New York: Appleton-Century-Crofts, 1970.

Roberts, A. H. Self-control procedures in modification of smoking behavior: Replication. *Psychological Report*, 1969, **24**, 675–676.

Ross, M., Insko, C. A., and Ross, H. S. Self-attribution of attitude. *Journal of Personality and Social Psychology*, 1971, **17**, 292–297.

Rotter, J. B. Generalized expectancies for internal vs. external control of reinforcement. *Psychological Monographs*, 1966, **80**, 1–28.

Russell, R. K. and Sipich, J. F. Cue-controlled relaxation in the treatment of test-anxiety. *Journal of Behavior Therapy and Experimental Psychiatry*, 1973, **4**, 37–49.

Rutner, I. T. and Bugle, C. An experimental procedure for modification of psychotic behavior. *Journal of Consulting and Clinical Psychology*, 1969, **33**, 651–653.

Schachter, S. The interaction of cognitive and physiological determinants of emotional state. In L. Berkowitz (Ed.), *Advances in experimental social psychology*, vol. 1. New York: Academic Press, 1964.

Schachter, S. and Singer, J. E. Cognitive, social and psysiological determinants of emotional state. *Psychological Review*, 1962, **69**, 379–399.

Schachter, S. and Wheeler, L. Epinephrine, chlorpromazine, and amusement. *Journal of Abnormal and Social Psychology*, 1962, **65**, 121–128.

Schwartz, G. E. Biofeedback as therapy: Some theoretical and practical issues. *American Psychologist*, 1973, **28**, 666–673.

Seligman, M. E. P. On the generality of the laws of learning. *Psychological Review*, 1970, **77**, 406–418.

Sipprelle, C. N. Induced anxiety. *Psychotherapy, Theory, Research and Practice*, 1967, **4**, 36–40.

Skinner, B. F. *Science and human behavior*. New York: Macmillan, 1953.

Skinner, B. F. *Beyond freedom and dignity*. New York: Alfred A. Knopf, 1971.

Stuart, R. B. A three-dimensional program for the treatment of obesity. *Behaviour Research and Therapy*, 1971, **9**, 177–186.

Stuart, R. B. and Davis, B. *Slim chance in a fat world: Behavioral control of obesity*. Champaign, Ill.: Research Press, 1972.

Suinn, R. M. and Richardson, F. Anxiety management training: A non-specific behavior therapy program for anxiety control. *Behavior Therapy*, 1971, **2**, 498–510.

Susskind, D. J. The idealized self-image (ISI): A new technique in confidence training. *Behavior Therapy*, 1970, **1**, 538–541.

Thoresen, C. E. and Mahoney M. J. *Behavioral self-control*. New York: Holt, Rinehart and Winston, 1974.

Tobias, L. L. The relative effectiveness of behavioristic bibliotherapy, contingency contracting, and suggestions of self-control in weight reduction. Unpublished Ph.D. dissertation, University of Illinois, Champaign, Ill., 1972.

Valins, S. Cognitive effects of false heart rate feedback. *Journal of Personality and Social Psychology*, 1966, **4**, 400–408.

Valins, S. Emotionality and information concerning internal reactions. *Journal of Personality and Social Psychology*, 1967, **6**, 458–463.

Watson, D. L. and Tharp, R. G. *Self-directed behavior: Self modification for personal adjustment*. Monterey, Calif.: Brooks/Cole, 1972.

Wilson, T. G. and Thomas, M. G. W. Self-versus drug-produced relaxation and the effects of instructional set in standardized systematic desensitization. *Behaviour Research and Therapy*, 1973, **11**, 279–288.

Wisocki, P. A. The successful treatment of a herion addict by covert conditioning techniques. *Journal of Behavior Therapy and Experimental Psychiatry*, 1972, **4**, 55–61.

CHAPTER 11

Self-Instructional Methods

Donald Meichenbaum

PROLOGUE

After reading several chapters in this book, some readers will probably be wondering about the variety of therapy procedures available to the would-be therapist. Should the therapist relax the client or provide him with practice in assertive training by means of modeling and role-playing? Is the proper focus of therapy teaching new skills or trying to change thinking? Should the therapist use a variety of techniques and, if so, in what order? If only there were a sure-fire checklist that could help the therapist match the presenting problem with the "right" technique! But then the dilemma is that problems which bring people to therapists rarely turn out to be simple.

Other readers may be thinking that the techniques they have been reading about sound promising, and indeed may be fine with motivated, cooperative clients who have easily defined or limited problems. However, most clients don't seem to fall into that category. A frequent problem is how to get the patient motivated to practice the self-control procedures and to comply with the behavioral contract. The reader may think, "I'd like to see Dr. so-and-so try his procedure on my client!"

Still other readers may be devotees of behavior modification procedures and have approached this chapter with the set "What are self-instructional procedures? How, when, and by whom can they be employed? By the way, what is the purpose of this prologue?"

The purpose of the prologue is to capture the thinking processes of the reader as he begins this chapter. For I will try to illustrate that the therapist's recognition of his client's thinking style can provide an important avenue for behavior change. The therapist's ability to *anticipate* and *change* what the client will say (or fail to say) to himself is an important component of self-instructional training procedures. If the therapist follows the client's thinking patterns, he will find that the therapy procedures described in this book can be applied to the modification of the client's thinking style. The therapist can, therefore, use a self-instructional approach for the treatment of many different clinical problems, or to help the client learn methods that he can later apply to new problems. Indeed, the research on self-instructional training has highlighted the fact that it is not only the manipulation of environmental consequences *per se* which are of primary importance in the therapy process, but what the client says to himself about those consequences. However, what the client says to himself, that is, how he evaluates and interprets these events, is explicitly modifiable by many of the behavior therapy techniques which have been used to modify maladaptive behaviors. The following set of clinical examples will help illustrate these points.

Clinical Examples of Clients' Internal Dialogue

Picture the following scene. Two individuals, both of whom possess the *same* speaking skills, are asked on separate occasions to present a public speech. The two individuals differ in the degree to which they fear speaking in public: one has high speech-anxiety, while the other has low speech-anxiety. During each speaker's presentation some members of the audience walk out of the room. This elicits quite different self-statements or appraisals from the high and low speech-anxiety individuals. The high speech-anxiety individual is likely to say to himself: "I must be boring. How much longer do I have to speak? I knew I never could give a speech," and so forth. These self-statements produce anxiety and result in the very speech-anxiety behavior that the person fears (i.e., they become self-fulfilling prophecies). On the other hand, the low speech-anxiety individual is more likely to view the audience's departure as a sign of their rudeness or to attribute their leaving to external causes. He might say something like: "They must have a class to catch. Too bad they have to leave; they will miss a good talk."

A similar pattern of different thinking styles can be seen in high and low test-anxiety individuals. Consider an exam situation in which some students hand in their exams early. For the high test-anxiety individual this event gives rise to worrying-type self-statements, namely, "I can't get this problem. I'll never finish. How can that guy be done?," resulting in increased anxiety and further irrelevant and self-defeating thoughts. In comparison, the low test-anxiety student readily dismisses the other students' performance by saying to himself: "Those guys who handed in their papers early must know nothing. I hope they score this exam on a curve."

Note in each of the above examples that the same event (in the first case people walking out in the middle of a speech, in the second, students handing in their examinations early) elicits different perceptions, attributions, and self-statements in high- and low-anxiety individuals. Such thinking styles are not limited to the high test- or speech-anxiety individual. One can find similar examples of negative self-statements contributing to maladaptive behaviors in many situations and among different clients (e.g., depressives, phobics).

The client's thinking style, or what he says to himself, has an important role in the definition of the presenting problem. As we will see in the description of the therapy procedures, there is an important interplay between the client's behavioral repertoire and what he says to himself. Self-instructional therapy procedures are designed to modify *both* the cognitive and behavioral components of the problem. Self-instructional therapy is designed to make clients aware of their thoughts and to train them to produce incompatible self-instructions and incompatible behaviors.

Perhaps a more convincing example is the case of the phobic client who must eventually confront the threatening situation. What the client says to himself may well influence the outcome of treatment, whether the form of treatment is *desensitization*, *modeling*, or *flooding*. Prior to treatment, the phobic client's internal dialogue has probably included statements reflecting a sense of helplessness, of being embarrassed by his incapacity, feelings of losing control, images and thoughts of catastrophe, and so forth. Training him to produce a set of coping self-instructions in the phobic situation fosters behavior change. For example:

> One step at a time, relax. Good, I can psych myself up to do it. This tenseness and anxiety is just what I thought I might feel. I'm supposed to label my fear from 0 to 10 and watch it change. Good. My tenseness and heavy breathing are cues for me to use my coping techniques.

Interestingly, investigators who have treated phobics with different treatment procedures have all suggested that a common mediating mechanism underlying the therapy process is a change in the client's self-statements. Writers who have attempted to reduce phobic behavior by means of desensitization, modeling, flooding, and altering cognitions about internal reactions have all commented on the importance of the client's self-statements in the change process, even when no direct effort is made to change these statements. Marks, Boulougouris, and Marset (1971) related that following flooding therapy some clients spontaneously reported that they talked themselves out of feelings; others reported telling themselves that reality never matched up to the horrors of fantasy, while the self-statements of others emphasized the elements of challenge they felt (e.g., "I'll show the therapist."). Geer and Turtletaub (1967) hypothesized that a possible mechanism mediating behavior change from modeling treatment is the client's self-instruction, "If the other client could do it, so can I." In a similar vein, Lang (1969) has suggested that changes in the client's self-statements may mediate behavioral change resulting from desensitization. Lang stated that "desensitization is designed to develop the response 'I am not afraid' (or a potentially competing response such as 'I am relaxed') in the presence of a graded set of discriminative stimuli. When well learned, the response could have the status of a 'set' or self-instruction, which can then determine other related behaviors" (1969, p. 187).

If the hypothesis that the client's self-instructions mediate behavior change is valid, we would expect explicit self-instructional training to enhance treatment effectiveness.

Two additional types of examples are offered to illustrate the role of the client's self-statements in the change process. The first is the treatment of clients who have self-control problems with smoking, overeating, alcohol intake, etc. The content of the client's self-statements must also be considered in treatment. Perceptions, attributions, and self-statements accompany any attempts to change the client's behavior and should be included as targets for change. The individual who is working to control his urge to smoke faces critical moments when his internal dialogue may well influence the therapy outcome, whether he is being treated by means of aversive conditioning, relaxation, or role-playing. Upon reaching for a cigarette, the client's internal dialogue may be:

> Damn it, there I go again. Well, what's the use, I'll never be able to quit . . .. Don't give yourself that line. Make the effort! The urge does seem to be getting less.

This is consistent with Premack's (1970) analysis of the self-control mechanisms that contribute to the termination of smoking behavior. Premack proposed that the decision to stop smoking results in a *self-instruction* that interrupts the automatic quality of the behavioral chain that constitutes the act of smoking. An increase in self-monitoring of smoking behavior sets the stage for such self-instructions, and the development of self-instructions proves efficacious in treatment. An illustration that the inclusion of the smoker's cognitions in the therapy enterprise enhances treatment efficacy is the study by Steffy, Meichenbaum, and Best (1970). They modified the aversive conditioning treatment paradigm so that the onset of the punisher (electric shock) followed the smokers' reporting the descriptive thoughts and images of the settings in which they engaged in smoking. The termination of shock was contingent upon the expression of self-instructions to put out the cigarette, or such self-statements as not wanting a "cancer weed." The addition of making the onset and offset of shock contingent upon the verbalized covert processes that accompany smoking was highly effective in reducing smoking behavior. (Other examples of this treatment paradigm are offered in a later section).

In the case of the high speech- and test-anxiety individuals, the content of their negative self-statements was a contributing factor to their problem. In the case of the phobic and the smoker, the therapist has to take into account the client's internal dialogue in critical situations. In all of these instances the self-instructional therapist attempts to make the client aware of the content of his self-defeating internal dialogue. It is the awareness of this internal dialogue that is the cue for producing constructive, incompatible self-statements and behaviors.

The final example concerns a somewhat different clinical problem, namely, clients whose behavioral deficits seem to result from what the client *fails* to say to himself, and not so much from the production of negative self-statements. The inability to or tendency *not* to generate and use cognitive and behavioral strategies is a major contributor to the presenting problem. Two groups of people who seem to have this problem are adult schizophrenics and hyperactive, impulsive children. We can illustrate the nature of the deficit by using the Continuous Performance Task (CPT) (Rosvold, 1956). Interestingly, both impulsive children (Sykes, Douglas, and Morgenstern, 1973) and schizophrenics (Orzack and Kornetsky, 1966) have marked difficulty in sustaining attention on this task. The requirements for the CPT are given in the following instructions:

> When the machine starts, you will see letters appearing one at a time. Your job is to press the key when you see an X that follows right after an A. Don't press the key for any other letter, only when X follows A.

Both schizophrenics and impulsive children have difficulty in maintaining attention on this task over a prolonged period of time (15 minutes). The therapist who is working in a self-instructional framework goes about explaining the deficit in this way:

1. In order to speculate about what leads to a poor performance on the CPT, the therapist takes the task himself. Upon completion of the CPT the therapist introspects about thoughts and strategies he employed in order to maintain attention. The therapist may wish to take the CPT once again, focussing on the cognitive and behavioral strategies he is employing.

2. The next step is to have other individuals examine their strategies. During each performance the therapist is watching for cues that may indicate the use of particular strategies.

Subjects who do well on the CPT report that they attempt to monitor their performance and note when attention is waning. This recognition of their attention wandering from the task triggers a variety of cognitive and behavioral strategies, such as trying to visualize the $A-X$, setting more stringent response standards and self-instructing, or producing motor responses such as shaking themselves in order to remain vigilant. In other words, the self-instructional therapist performs an analysis of not only the behaviors, but also the thinking that is necessary to perform the task. Thus, inadequate performance on the CPT may result from the number of task interruptions and the way in which the subject notices and copes with these interruptions.

3. The therapist can then translate each of the cognitive and behavioral strategies into specific self-statements and rules which can be modeled by the therapist for the client and eventually rehearsed by the client.

Another task which has been used with both schizophrenics and impulsive children is the reaction time task. (The task requires the subject to press a telegraph key as quickly as possible after a signal light turns on.) Interviews with normal subjects indicate that they often enhance their performance by inventing cognitive games. When confronted by a boring, repetitive task such as reaction time, many people set challenging goals for themselves or use imagery to make the task more meaningful (e.g., the signal light may be thought of as an oncoming enemy plane and pressing the telegraph key triggers antiaircraft fire). Such imagery facilitates performance by helping to maintain a high level of attention. The adult schizophrenic and impulsive child who have attentional deficits seem unable to spontaneously mobilize such imagery and self-instructions. If attention can indeed be sharpened by engaging in controlled, playful fantasy and self-instructional challenges, the therapeutic implications are intriguing. Meichenbaum and his colleagues (Meichenbaum and Cameron, 1973a; Meichenbaum and Goodman, 1971) have shown that self-instructional training procedures, which involve cognitive modeling and rehearsal, can be used to teach schizophrenics and impulsive children to initiate and control task-relevant cognitions that facilitate task performance.

How these training procedures are implemented is described below. For now it is sufficient to conclude that what the client says, or fails to say, to himself is the proper domain of the therapist. The next section describes the alternative therapy strategies available to modify the client's internal dialogue.

Therapy Strategies Used to Modify Clients' Self-Statements

Which therapy technique is used to modify the client's internal dialogue and maladaptive behavior in large part depends upon how one views the client's thinking style. Different conceptualizations lead to different therapeutic interventions. One popular view is put forth by semantic or cognitive therapists such as Jerome Frank (1961), Albert Ellis (1962), and Aaron Beck (1970). They view the client's negative self-statements and maladaptive behaviors as the result of the client's faulty belief system and faulty thinking patterns. According to Frank (1961), psychotherapy involves the use of the therapist's influence in changing the client's assumptions (i.e., the complex set of images, values, and expectations). For example, an individual may assume that he must be perfect in order for anyone to love him. Therapy would involve an attempt to change the assumptions, perceptions and attributions that the client has about himself and the world.

The semantic therapist tries to make the client aware of his own thinking style and conveys to him that he can control such thinking. Secondly, the therapist attempts to teach the patient, by means of rational analysis, information giving, or other procedures, a set of self-statements incompatible with his previous negative self-statements and a more adaptive behavioral style. Often included in the treatment package are such things as self-monitoring, behavioral and imaginal rehearsal via hierarchically arranged stressful situations, modeling, and therapist praise and support. Semantic therapists differ in how directive they are and in how much they utilize behavioral techniques. Perhaps the saying, "If you are not feeling well you are probably not thinking right" captures the spirit of this approach. (See Chapter 4 in this book and Meichenbaum (1974b) for a more complete description of these procedures).

In contrast to the semantic therapist, the behavior therapist approaches the task of modifying the client's cognitions or self-statements in a different way. Two general treatment strategies seem to characterize the behavior therapy approach. The first views the client's cognitions explicitly as behaviors to be modified in their own right. The client's covert behaviors, private events, and higher mental processes, such as ideas, self-statements, and images, are viewed as behaviors. Thus they are subject to the same "laws of learning" as overt or nonprivate behaviors. In fact, Homme (1965) has offered the concept of "coverants" (covert operants) to include covert behaviors within a learning framework, even though they are not observed by others. Thus the behavior therapist can affect the strength of the client's thoughts by pairing them with either reinforcers or punishers.

The second strategy of behavior therapists is to focus treatment on the client's maladaptive overt behaviors, and *not* on the client's faulty thinking style. The focus of this treatment is on teaching the client a set of adaptive overt behaviors that are incompatible with his previous maladaptive behaviors. It is assumed that as the client learns new behavioral skills and receives reinforcement for these from significant others in his environment, his thinking style in turn will change. The latter treatment approach is illustrated by the saying: "It is easier to act your way into a new way of thinking than it is to think your way into a new way of behaving."

However, it has become more and more obvious that it is *impossible* to proceed therapeutically along a single dimension, cognitive or behavioral. Perhaps the unique advantages of both the semantic and behavior therapy procedures could be combined. One could use the behavior therapy procedures of modeling, behavioral and imagery rehearsal, operant and aversive conditioning, and others, to modify the client's self-statements and belief system. With this in mind, a "shaky" marriage between the technology of behavior therapy and the clinical concerns of semantic therapists was conceived. The offspring has been the development of self-instructional training procedures.

The following sections describe how self-instructional training procedures may be applied to adults and children, respectively.

Self-Instructional Methods with Adults

The therapy process can be viewed as consisting of three phases. These phases do not form a lock-step progression and can be repeated or returned to as necessary for therapy progress. The first phase is concerned with *understanding the nature of the client's presenting problem(s) and formulating an initial treatment plan*. In this phase the client and therapist begin to evolve a common view of the presenting problem from which a variety of therapeutic interventions naturally follow. A motivating factor for a number of clients is the need to make sense of their behaviors, to understand what is happening and why, to receive assurances that they are not going to "lose their minds," and that something can be done to help them change. It is partly in response to these concerns and also as a way of preparing clients to actively engage in the change procedures that the conceptualization process receives so much attention. During the *second* phase of self-instructional training the therapist *helps his client to explore, try on, and consolidate the conceptualization of the presenting problem*. The variety of methods available to the therapist during these two phases are described below.

Whereas the first two phases of therapy involved preparing the client for change, it is during the third phase of self-instructional training that the therapist *helps the client to modify his self-statements and to produce new, more adaptive behaviors*.

The length of time for each of these phases varies depending on the client's presenting problems, therapist style and skill, goals of therapy, and other factors. In research studies with clients who had common problems the three phases were successfully completed in eight sessions, whereas some individual therapy required 40 sessions.

PHASE I. CONCEPTUALIZATION OF PROBLEM

The role of the conceptualization process in therapy has received insufficient attention from behavior modifiers. For example, what goes on in therapy before the behavior therapy such as desensitization begins is rarely discussed. How do we prepare the patient to accept the rationale and the treatment intervention? One way is to try and modify what the client says to himself about his presenting problem or symptom, that is, modify his perceptions and attributions. The client usually enters therapy with a conceptualization or definition of his problem. If he is depressed and obsessing he may complain that he is a victim of his thoughts and mood changes; if anxious and phobic, external events are viewed as causing his malady. Rarely does the client see the role of his own thinking processes and/or the interpersonal meaning of his behavior as sources of disturbance. One goal of this initial conceptualization phase of therapy is for the therapist and patient to redefine the client's problems in terms that will give the client a sense of control and a feeling of hope, particularly in terms that will lead to specific behavioral interventions. Thus the therapist tries to understand the client's description and definition of his problem, but does not merely uncritically accept the client's view of the problem. Instead, the therapist and client attempt to redefine the problem in terms that are acceptable to both of them. It is this reformulation or conceptualization phase that provides the basis for behavior change.

It is suggested that *any* client has sufficient life experiences to provide data to support any therapy conceptualization. If the therapist has a psychoanalytic orientation, he can elicit from the client's life experiences that support his conceptualization. The same applies for a Jungian, Rogerian, Gestalt, or semantic therapist. The human life condition provides sufficient experience to maintain the employment of a host of therapists of different persuasions. The more essential variables that determine therapy outcome are the degree to which the client and therapist evolve a common conceptualization with common expectations, and the degree to which a given conceptualization leads to specific behavioral changes that can be transferred to the real-life situations. This section describes how the therapist and client evolve a common conceptualization.

Exactly how one proceeds depends on whether the self-instructional treatment is conducted on a group or individual basis. Our previous work (Meichenbaum, 1972; Meichenbaum, Gilmore, and Fedoravicius, 1971) has indicated that group treatment was as effective as individual therapy. Indeed, group treatment proved easier, and more valuable in fostering behavior change. The advantage in terms of therapist hours is obvious. Moreover, in group treatment clients can benefit from a group discussion of their faulty thinking styles and self-statements and by the group discussion of the incompatible thoughts and behaviors they must employ to reduce anxiety and change their behavior. Other factors such as group cohesion and group pressure can be readily employed in a group treatment process.

Thus, for illustrative purposes let's assume that therapy will be conducted on a group basis. Moreover, we will make the therapist's life somewhat easier by including only patients who have a similar presenting problem—such as interpersonal anxiety, or lacking in assertion. Since the clients have similar presenting problems, the therapist can have the clients, prior to treatment, individually undergo a similar behavioral assessment situation, such as making a speech, taking an exam or confronting a phobic situation. Then, in the initial therapy sessions the group can explore the feelings and thoughts they experienced in the behavioral assessment situation. Note, that this creates a new potential use of behavioral assessment procedures in terms of fostering group identity, group cohesion (i.e., something like rites of initiation into a fraternity or club) and it also provides the group with a common experience which they can share in therapy. The sense of group process and identity (at the outset of therapy) may be further enhanced by the knowledge that clients will be asked to participate in a post-treatment assessment.

There are a variety of ways in which the client and therapist can evolve a common conceptualization. Some therapists are very directive in forcing upon the client a particular conceptualization by power of their personality, jargon, or position. In some cases such a "hard sell" approach may prove successful.

A preferred way to proceed is to have the client and therapist evolve a common conceptualization, so that the client feels that he is an active participant and contributor. The initial phase of self-instructional therapy with adults is designed to have such a common conceptualization evolve. The manner in which the therapist discusses the presenting problem, the kinds of questions he asks, the type of assessment procedures employed, the content of the therapy rationale, and the kinds of homework assignments given are all used to evolve a common client-therapist conceptualization.

The initial session of self-instructional training begins with the therapist exploring the extent and duration of the client's presenting problem. The therapist performs a *situational analysis* of the client's presenting problems. (Table 11.1 describes such an interview.) The therapist has the group discuss their problems not only in a general context, but also in terms of the specific assessment situation in which all clients participated. Clients can discuss the feelings and thoughts they experienced in the behavioral assessment situation. In some cases it may be helpful to have a client close his eyes and "run a movie through his head" of a recent incident involving his problem, reporting the sequence of thoughts and behaviors. Such an imagery procedure has proved a useful adjunct to the standard interview in eliciting self-statements. Another interesting supplement has been the use of videotaping. Clients are asked to perform their maladaptive behaviors (e.g., making a speech, handling a phobic object) while being videotaped. Immediately after the taping both the client and therapist view the tape while the client tries to reconstruct the thoughts he was experiencing on the tape.

Following a discussion of the clients' thinking process in the specific assessment situations, the clients explore the range of situations in which they have the same or comparable self-statements. Throughout this first phase, the therapist has to determine the degree to which each client's problem is illustrative of a characteristic thinking style. In a recent case, a client was obsessive and

Table 11.1. Clinical Interview.*

A. Definition of problem behavior
  1. Nature of the problem as defined by client
     "As I understand it, you came here because..." (discuss reasons for contact as stated by referral agency or other source of information) "I would like you to tell me more about this. What is the problem as you see it?" (Probe as needed to determine client's view of his own problem behavior, i.e., what he is doing, or failing to do, which he or somebody else defines as a problem.)
  2. Severity of the problem
     (a) "How serious a problem is this as far as you are concerned?" (Probe to determine perceived severity of problem.)
     (b) "How often do you...?" (Exhibit problem behavior if a disorder of commission, or have occasion to exhibit desired behavior if a problem of omission. The goal is to obtain information regarding frequency of response.)
  3. Generality of the problem
     (a) Duration "How long has this been going on?"
     (b) Extent "Where does the problem usually come up?" (Probe to determine situations in which problem behavior occurs, e.g., "Do you feel that way at work? How about at home?")
B. Determinants of problem behavior
  1. Conditions which intensify problem behavior
     "Now I want you to think about the times when... (the problem) is worst. What sorts of things are going on then?"
  2. Conditions which alleviate problem behavior
     "What about the times when... (the problem) gets better? What sorts of things are going on then?"
  3. Perceived origins—"What do you think is causing... (the problem)?"
  4. Specific antecedents
     "Think back to the last time... (the problem occurred). What was going on at that time?"
     As needed:
     (a) Social influences—"Were any other people around? Who? What were they doing?"
     (b) Personal influences—"What were you thinking about at the time? How did you feel?"
  5. Specific consequences
     "What happened after... (the problem behavior occurred)?" As needed:
     (a) Social consequences—"What did... (significant others identified above) do?"
     (b) Personal consequences—"How did that make you feel?"
  6. Suggested changes
     "You have thought a lot about... (the problem). What do you think might be done to... (improve the situation)?"
  7. Suggested leads for further inquiry
     "What else do you think I should find out about to help you with this problem?"

*From Donald R. Peterson, *The Clinical Study of Social Behavior* © 1968, pp. 121–122. By permission of Prentice-Hall, Inc., Englewood Cliffs, New Jersey.

somewhat phobic of crossing streets. The therapist had to determine to what degree such indecisiveness was a characteristic thinking style evident in a variety of situations. The therapist has to decide whether to focus therapy on making the client aware of and changing such a thinking style, *or* to focus treatment on the specific presenting problem (i.e., inability to cross streets). The severity and duration of the presenting problem, goals of therapy, and other factors influence this decision. For the moment, we have few clear rules to guide us in the decision whether we should treat the presenting problem directly or merely employ that problem as an illustration of the client's general thinking style.

During this initial phase of therapy the therapist helps the clients to realize the irrational, self-defeating, and self-fulfilling aspects of their thinking style and self-statements. For example, we have found that clients have specific behavior rituals to cope with stress and anxiety. On an exam day, a high test-anxiety client knew exactly which seat she would sit in, arrived early in order to avoid the fear of being late, but remained isolated in order not to hear what other students were talking about. These overheard conversations would trigger anxiety-producing thoughts. During the initial sessions, after the clients have offered descriptions of such behavioral patterns, the therapist can wonder aloud about what purpose behavior such as the seating ritual would serve. A plausible answer that the group may produce is that the ritual controlled negative self-statements.

Another way of having the group appreciate the role of negative self-statements is to give a homework assignment of having clients listen to themselves with a "third ear." The purpose of the homework assignment is to strengthen the client's belief that self-statements contribute to problems. Therapists differ in how demanding and structured this homework assignment should be. Some therapists encourage monitoring, recording, and graphing specific behaviors, thoughts, urges, moods, etc. In part, how one proceeds concerning homework and the other aspects of therapy depends on how one views the role of self-statements. Before treatment it is *unlikely* that the client tells himself various things consciously or deliberately when confronted by problem situations. Rather, as Goldfried, Decenteceo, and Weinberg (1974) have indicated, because of the habitual nature of one's expectations or beliefs it is likely that such thinking processes become automatic and seemingly involuntary, like most overlearned acts. The client's negative self-statements become a habitual style of thinking, in many ways similar to the automatization of thought that accompanies the mastery of a motor skill such as driving a car, skiing, etc. However, the therapist can make the client aware of such thought processes and increase the likelihood that the client will in the future notice similar self-statements.

Note that the client's faulty cognition may take a pictorial form instead of the verbal form. Beck (1970) reports a woman with a fear of walking alone found that her spells of anxiety followed images of her having a heart attack and being left helpless; a college student discovered that her anxiety at leaving the dormitory was triggered by visual fantasies of being attacked.

In summary, the purpose of the four steps in this initial phase of therapy: (a) the assessment procedures, (b) group discussion, (c) situational analysis, (d) homework assignment, is to secure information about the client's problems, to lay the groundwork for the therapist and client to evolve a common conceptualization of the presenting problem, and to decide upon the means of therapy intervention. Once the client comes to accept the possibility that what he says to himself influences his behavior, self-instructional treatment can be easily introduced.

PHASE II. "TRYING ON" THE CONCEPTUALIZATION

The second phase of self-instructional training with adults is designed to have the clients "try on" and consolidate the conceptualization of their problem. Included in this phase is a discussion of the therapy rationale and therapy plan.

The phase begins with the clients reporting on their homework assignment of "listening" to their self-statements. As the clients begin to report these, the therapist can begin to take a more passive role by asking tactfully, "Are you saying that part of your problem is what you are telling yourself? How so?" This ploy should not be used until the group has first explored the content of their self-statements and the self-defeating and self-fulfilling prophecy aspects of this style of thinking. In fact, one can use the client's behavior in the therapy session as a basis to explore self-statements. For example, if the client does not participate in the group, the therapist may ask the client to describe how he is feeling and to then explore the thoughts which are keeping him from participating. In this manner, the group members will work to convince the therapist, each other, and themselves, that a key aspect of their problem is their thinking styles. The clients are beginning to discover that their fears and anxiety are *not* a property of the external events, but rather that it is their own *thoughts* that elicit anxiety.

At this point the therapist may introduce the therapy rationale. Throughout presentation of the rationale, there is a dialogue between the therapist and the group. The following rationales are offered as examples. The exact wording, vocabulary level, and format can be adapted to each group.

The first rationale offered was used in the cognitive behavior modification treatment of test-anxiety (Meichenbaum, 1972). The therapist says to the group:

"As I listen to you discuss your test-anxiety I am struck by some of the similarities in how each of you is feeling and what you are thinking. On the one hand there are reports of quite a bit of tenseness and anxiety in exam situations and in evaluative situations. This seems to take many forms such as stomachs and necks becoming tense, pounding hearts, sweaty palms, heavy breathing, etc. (the therapist should use the specific reactions offered by group members). At the same time, and correct me if I am wrong, several of you described how difficult it was for you to focus attention on only the task before you. Somehow, your attention wandered away from what you had to do (such as studying, or taking the exam) to something irrelevant. (Once again the therapist should use reactions offered by group members.) Your thinking or self-statements seem to get in the way of what you had to do. Your thoughts about catastrophes, and how awful the consequences will be because of your not doing well got in the way. (Pause.) Have I heard you correctly?"

The therapist may decide to have the group return to the description of their text-anxiety; specifically, to the test assessment situation in which each member participated. What kinds of thoughts and feelings, what self-statements did the clients emit in that situation?

Note that the therapist shares with the clients the theory that led to the development of the treatment procedure. In this case, the two factors of emotionality and worry which characterize the high test-anxiety individual's behavior (Morris and Liebert, 1970) and the problems with focusing attention (Sarason, 1973; Wine, 1971) constitute the basis of the therapy rationale.

The therapy rationale continues:

"In the therapy sessions we are going to work on ways to control how you feel, on ways of controlling your anxiety and tenseness. We will do this by learning how to relax.

"In addition to learning relaxation skills, we will learn how to control our thinking processes and attention. The control of our thinking, or what we say to ourselves, comes about by first becoming aware of when we are producing negative self-statements, catastrophizing, being task irrelevant, etc." (Once again, the therapist should give examples of the client's thinking style.) "The recognition that we are in fact doing this will be a step forward in changing. This recognition will also act as a reminder, a cue, a bell-ringer for us to produce different thoughts and self-instructions, to challenge and dispute our self-statements. In this way we will come to produce task-relevant self-instructions and new, adaptive behaviors. (Pause.) I'm wondering about your reactions to what I have described. Do you have any questions?" (The therapist should determine how the rationale matches the clients' expectations and conceptualization for change.)

Perhaps a better illustration of how the therapist incorporates and shares the theory for change with the client is offered in the description of a "stress inoculation" training procedure for the treatment of clients with several intense fears (Meichenbaum and Cameron, 1973c). The training was designed to accomplish three goals: (a) to "educate" the phobic clients about the nature of stressful or fearful reactions, (b) to have the client rehearse various coping behaviors, and (c) to give the client an opportunity to practice his new coping skills in a stressful situation.

The educational phase of the stress inoculation treatment began with a discussion of the nature of the client's fears. Discussion topics included how he felt and what he thought about when confronted by the phobic objects, and how he was coping with stress in general as well as his phobias in particular. Interestingly, even clients who appear incapacitated can describe coping techniques that they have employed in other stressful areas (e.g., visits to the dentist). The therapist had the group discuss these skills and explore why they were not employed in overcoming the presenting problem.

As part of the therapy rationale, the therapist conceptualized the client's anxiety in terms of Schachter's model of emotional arousal (Schachter, 1966). That is, the therapist stated that the client's fear reaction seemed to involve two major elements: (a) his heightened physiological arousal, and (b) his set of anxiety-producing, avoidant thoughts and self-statements (e.g., disgust evoked by the phobic object, a sense of helplessness, panic thoughts of being overwhelmed by anxiety, a desire to flee). After laying this groundwork, the therapist noted that the client's fear seemed to fit Schachter's theory that an emotional state such as fear is in large part determined by the thoughts the client engages in when he is physically aroused.

It should be noted that the Schachter and Singer (1962) theory of emotion was used for purposes of conceptualization only. Although the theory and the research upon which it is based have been criticized (Lazarus, Averill, and Opton, 1970; Plutchik and Ax, 1967), the theory has an air of plausibility which clients tend to accept: the logic of the treatment plan is clearer to clients in light of this conceptualization.

The therapy rationale then continued, indicating that treatment would be directed toward (a) helping the client control his physiological arousal and (b) substituting positive coping self-statements for the anxiety-engendering self-statements which habitually occupied his mind under stress conditions. The client was told that he would be taught a set of physical relaxation exercises that would provide the basis for reducing physiological arousal. It was also pointed out that if he used these exercises in anxiety-provoking situations, his concentration upon doing something positive about his discomfort (i.e., relaxing) would in itself tend to eliminate the negative self-statements. (How one conducts such relaxation exercises has been described by Paul (1966) and Meichenbaum (1974).)

In order to further prepare the client for self-instructional training, the therapist helped the client change his perception of how he behaved in the phobic situation. Instead of viewing his response as a massive panic reaction, the therapist suggested that the client's response seemed to include several stages. In the course of the discussion the following four stages were suggested: preparing for, confronting or handling a stressor, possibly being overwhelmed by a stressor, and, finally, reinforcing oneself for having coped.

The client was encouraged to offer examples of self-statements which he could use for coping during each phase. With some support, a package of self-statements similar to that listed in Table 11.2 emerged. During the next few sessions, clients practiced self-instructing, initially aloud and subsequently silently. This was done in conjunction with the relaxation and breathing exercises.

The self-statements encouraged clients to: (a) assess the reality of the situation; (b) control negative, self-defeating, anxiety-engendering ideation; (c) acknowledge, use, and possibly relabel the anxiety they were experiencing; (d) "psych" themselves up to perform the task; (e) cope with the intense fear they might experience; and (f) reinforce themselves for having coped.

Once the client had become proficient in the relaxation exercises and the self-instructional techniques, the therapist suggested that the client should test and practice his coping skills by actually employing them under stressful conditions, such as receiving an unpredictable electric shock, watching gruesome films, or imagining frightening scenes. The more varied and extensive the application training, the greater the likelihood that the client would develop a general learning set, that is, a general way of coping.

In summary, the stress inoculation training involved discussing the nature of emotion and stress reactions, rehearsing coping skills, and testing these skills

Table 11.2.   Examples of Coping Self-Statements Rehearsed in Stress Inoculation Training.

Preparing for a stressor

　　What is it you have to do?

　　You can develop a plan to deal with it.

　　Just think about what you can do about it. That's better than getting anxious.

　　No negative self-statements: just think rationally.

　　Don't worry; worry won't help anything.

　　Maybe what you think is anxiety is eagerness to confront the stressor.

Confronting and handling a stressor

　　Just "psych" yourself up—you can meet this challenge.

　　You can convince yourself to do it. You can reason your fear away.

　　One step at a time; you can handle the situation.

　　Don't think about fear; just think about what you have to do. Stay relevant.

　　This anxiety is what the doctor said you would feel. It's a reminder to use your coping exercises.

　　This tenseness can be an ally; a cue to cope.

　　Relax; you're in control. Take a slow deep breath.

　　Ah, good.

Coping with the feeling of being overwhelmed

　　When fear comes, just pause.

　　Keep the focus on the present; what is it you have to do?

　　Label your fear from 0 to 10 and watch it change.

　　You should expect your fear to rise.

　　Don't try to eliminate fear totally; just keep it manageable.

Reinforcing self-statements

　　It worked; you did it.

　　Wait until you tell your therapist (or group) about this.

　　It wasn't as bad as you expected.

　　You made more out of your fear that it was worth.

　　Your damn ideas—that's the problem. When you control them, you control your fear.

　　It's getting better each time you use the procedures.

　　You can be pleased with the progress you're making.

　　You did it!

under actual stress conditions. In some sense the emphasis of treatment switches from trying to totally reduce the client's anxiety to training him to function despite his anxiety. If this is achieved, then continued practice would probably lead to anxiety reduction. This is illustrated by the statements made by a phobic client following self-instructional treatment. She reported that following treatment she reassured herself by talking to herself. She said:

> It (self-instructing) makes me able to be in the situation, not to be comfortable, but to tolerate it . . . . I don't talk myself out of being afraid, just out of appearing afraid . . . . You immediately react to the thing you're afraid of and then start to reason with yourself. I talk myself out of panic.

Following a series of such successful attempts, she reported that even the feeling of fear dissipated and the amount of anxiety was reduced.

　　Given the increasing demand on individuals to deal with daily stress, the possibility of using inoculation training for prophylactic purposes is most exciting. The possibility of explicitly teaching persons to cope cognitively by such diverse techniques as information seeking, anticipatory problem solving, imagery rehearsal, task organization, altering attributions and self-labels, shifting attention, or using cognitive re-evaluation and relaxation seems to hold much promise. An explicit training program that would teach coping skills and then provide training in handling various stressful situations contrasts sharply with the haphazard way in which most individuals now learn to cope with stress.

An illustration of the potential of this approach is a recent study by Langer, Janis, and Wolfer (1973) in which they successfully trained patients about to undergo major surgery to use such coping devices as cognitive reappraisal of anxiety-provoking events, calming self-talk, and cognitive control through selective attention. The surgery patients were told that people are somewhat anxious before an operation, but people can often control their own emotions if they know how. It was explained that it is rarely events themselves that cause stress, but rather the views people take of them and the attention they give to these views. Consistent with these introductory remarks, patients were given several alternative ways of viewing seemingly negative events, including undergoing surgery. Patients were asked to rehearse realistic positive aspects whenever they started to feel upset about the unpleasant aspects of the surgical experiences. They would be asked to interpret the event, "Suppose that some emergencies have come up so that your operation has to be delayed for a few days. How would you view this positively?"

Such reappraisal training, combined with preparatory information concerning post-surgery discomforts and operative care resulted in significant reduction of pre- and postsurgical distress as indicated by nurses' observations and requests for sedatives.

PHASE III. MODIFYING SELF-STATEMENTS AND PRODUCING NEW BEHAVIORS

The first two phases of self-instructional treatment served the purpose of having the therapist understand the client's problems and concerns and of having the client and therapist evolve a common conceptualization. The third phase of self-instructional treatment is designed to help the client modify his self-statements and to produce new behaviors. There are a variety of therapy procedures that can be employed in changing the client's self-statements.

Perhaps the most popular therapy procedure is semantic therapy in the form of Albert Ellis' Rational-Emotive Therapy (RET). As mentioned above, the RET therapist views the client's self-statements as a product of irrational attitudes due to the acceptance of faulty beliefs. These biased thoughts lead to emotional, maladaptive reactions. How RET is conducted varies greatly with the therapist's style. Semantic therapy procedures vary widely among different therapists, even when called by the same name. The "semantic therapist" who wishes to modify his client's self-statements by group discussion may follow the lead of Ellis (1962) and "attack" the client's belief system. Or he may instead wish to follow the lead of Beck (1970) and try to alter his client's thinking style, making the client aware of such processes as overgeneralization, dichotomous reasoning, arbitrary inference, and the like. Or, the semantic therapist may wish to focus attention on making the client aware of specific negative self-statements and on training specific coping self-instructions and adaptive behaviors. At this time we do not know the relative merits of each of these approaches.

As suggested at the outset of this chapter, a number of behavior therapy procedures can be readily adapted to modify the client's self-statements. In fact, when behavior therapy procedures have been modified to include a self-instructional component, greater treatment generalization and greater persistence of treatment effects have been observed (Meichenbaum and Cameron, 1974). The following sections describe how each behavior therapy procedure can be used to alter the client's internal dialogue.

Systematic Desensitization

The basic procedures in desensitization have been described in Chapter 8. Both the relaxation and imagery phases of the desensitization process can be altered to include self-instructional components. After reviewing the literature on desensitization, Rachman (1967) concluded that the major contribution of relaxation to the desensitization process is a matter of mental rather than physical relaxation. Consistent with this is the suggestion that during the relaxation phase the therapist should use the following instructions:

"You can deepen the relaxation and relax away feelings of tension by thinking silently to yourself the words 'relax' and 'calm' as you relax. Think or picture these words to yourself as you slowly exhale. This is especially helpful between sessions when you practice relaxing or whenever you feel tension and anxiety."

A number of years ago, Dorothy Yates (1946) described a similar process under the title "association set technique." Essentially, it involved helping the client to relax by thinking of a soothing word such as "calm" or a pleasant image. Clients were encouraged to rehearse concentrating on the key word or image, such as a peaceful landscape, while relaxed, and to summon up the word or image in disturbing situations to counteract stress. Similarly, Cautela (1966) taught clients to say to themselves, "I am calm and relaxed," while giving themselves a relaxation session, especially in anticipation of a stressful situation. The clients reported that "in a while the mere words calmed them down." Kahn, Baker, and Weiss (1968) used a similar procedure in the treatment of insomniacs, and Chappell and Stevenson (1936) successfully treated peptic ulcer patients by having them imagine a pleasant scene whenever they experienced anxiety.

The imaginal component of the desensitization treatment can also be improved by including self-instructions. In standard desensitization treatment, the client is instructed to imagine a scene while relaxed and if the client experiences anxiety he signals the therapist, who then instructs the client to terminate the image and to continue relaxing. These procedural steps are based on the premise that the success of the treatment depends on principles of counterconditioning (see Chapter 8).

In contrast to the standard desensitization procedure, in which a mastery-type image is employed, a self-instructional approach to desensitization employs coping imagery. The coping-imagery procedure requires that while visualizing a scene from the hierarchy, the client is to see himself coping with anxiety by slow deep breaths, relaxing, and self-instructions. In other words, in the coping-imagery procedure the client visualizes the experience of anxiety and also ways to handle and reduce this anxiety. This is in contrast to standard desensitization, in which there is no suggestion that the client will experience anxiety in the life situation outside of treatment.

The modification to the desensitization procedure is based on the premise that when desensitized clients imagine hierarchy scenes, they are in fact providing themselves with a model for their own behavior. The greater the similarity between the imagined scenes and the real-life situation, the greater the likelihood of treatment generalization.

The coping-imagery procedure can be used in two situations. First, if the client imagines a scene from a standard hierarchy and signals the therapist that he is anxious, the therapist can have the client continue imagining the scene while seeing himself using the coping techniques to reduce the anxiety. For example, upon receiving the client's signal of anxiety, the therapist can say:

"See yourself coping with this anxiety by use of the breathing procedures which we have practiced. See yourself taking a slow deep breath, slowly filling your chest cavity. Good. Now slowly exhale. As you see yourself exhaling, note the feeling of relaxation and control you have been able to bring forth. Fine. Now stop the image and just relax."

A second situation that allows employing coping imagery results from the therapist's presenting an item from the hierarchy, but this time including in the scene the client's becoming tense and anxious and then seeing himself coping with these feelings and thoughts. For example, in the treatment of test anxiety the therapist can say:

"See yourself taking an important exam and as you are thumbing through the exam booklet, you feel some tenseness in the pit of your stomach. Your eyes begin to wander about the room, your thoughts wander, etc." (The therapist can employ specific instances of his client's experiences.) The image continues: "Now notice what you have been feeling and doing. These are the reminders, the cues to cope. (Therapist pauses.) Good. See yourself taking a slow deep breath, hold, hold. See yourself parting your lips and as you are breathing out you are telling yourself what to do." (The therapist can tailor the self-instructions and coping devices to his particular client.) A detailed therapist manual of how to conduct such coping desensitization has been prepared by Meichenbaum (1974).

Several investigators (Debus, 1970; Kazdin, 1974; Meichenbaum, 1971, 1972) have provided evidence that such coping procedures are more effective than mastery based procedures. For instance, one outcome of including such coping procedures in treatment is that clients tend to view the experience of anxiety following treatment as positive and not debilitating, (i.e., as a cue for employing their coping mechanisms). Thus, the client's anxiety, his presenting problems and symptoms act as reminders to use the newly learned coping techniques. In short, the therapist attempts to modify what the client says to himself about his symptoms. Whereas before treatment such behaviors led to more anxiety and maladaptive behaviors, following treatment the client's symptoms are to be cues to cope, to function in spite of anxiety. In this way treatment generalization is built into the therapy package. The client's symptoms are the reminder to use the procedures he has learned in therapy.

These changes in the desensitization process are consistent with (a) observations that desensitization should be viewed as an active means of learning coping and self-control skills, and (b) notions of the therapeutic value of the "work of worrying." The "work of worrying" is the anticipatory problem solving and cognitive rehearsal that individuals employ in preparing for stress such as surgery (Marmor, 1958). The addition of self-instructional components to the desensitization procedure attempts to strengthen such skills.

Another interesting variant of the desensitization procedure has been offered by Feather and Rhoads (1972) in what they call "Dynamic Behavior Therapy." Instead of having the client imagine real-life scenes while relaxed, the client is asked to picture the fantasy that often underlies the anxiety. The therapist elicits the client's fantasies by asking him what is the worst thing that could happen if he were confronted by the phobic situation. A speech-anxious client might offer the fantasy of getting so angry with himself and the audience that he loses control and hurts someone. It is to this fantasy that the client is then desensitized. Feather and Rhoads argue that in many instances the client is afraid of his own thoughts and that much of the client's behavior is a learned avoidance of having such thoughts. The distinction between reality and fantasy, and the control of fantasy are achieved by having the client imagine the fantasy scene in a controlled manner while relaxed.

Modeling

It is mainly within the last ten years that the full therapeutic potential of behavioral, cognitive and imaginal modeling has begun to be realized (The basic modeling paradigm has been described in Chapter 5). Part of the impetus for this has been the growing realization that modeling or observational learning should *not* be equated with mimicry or exact matching or superficial imitation. Instead, the exposure to a modeling display permits the discrimination and organized memory of relatively complex and integrated behavior chains which may then be retrieved to satisfy environmental demands.

Bandura (1965, 1969) has emphasized that the information which observers gain from models is converted to covert perceptual-cognitive images and covert mediating rehearsal responses that are retained by the observer and later used by him as symbolic cues to overt behaviors. It then follows from a self-instructional viewpoint that the explicit modeling of such mediating responses in the form of self-statements will facilitate the learning process Bandura has described.

A few examples will illustrate the manner in which modeling procedures may be changed to incorporate and emphasize a self-instructional component. The first involves the use of coping modeling films for the treatment of adults who are afraid of snakes (Meichenbaum, 1971). Although, the treatment of such a circumscribed problem is limited, the study illustrates the clinical potential of a cognitive modeling treatment approach which can be applied to more significant clinical problems.

In a self-instructional modeling treatment, the therapist enhances the perceived similarity between the observer and model by including models who demonstrate coping behaviors (i.e., initially modeling fearful behaviors, then coping behavior, and finally mastery behavior). The models begin by commenting on their anxiety and fear and the physiological accompaniments (sweaty palms, increased heart rate and breathing rate, tenseness, etc.). But at the same time, the models attempt to cope with their fear by such means as instructing themselves (1) to remain relaxed and in control by such activity as slow, deep breaths, (2) to take one step at a time, (3) to maintain a determination to forge ahead and overcome their fear. The models were—to use the colloquial term—"psyching" themselves up to perform each task and, upon completion of that task, they emitted self-rewarding self-statements and positive affective expressions for having performed the task. One model in the snake study talked to the snake:

"I'm going to make a deal with you. If you don't scare or hurt me, I won't scare or hurt you," and after concluding the final step added, "Wait until I tell my mom I was able to handle a snake barehanded for a full minute; she won't believe it. I'm so happy with myself. I was able to overcome my fear."

It is interesting to note that two subjects who observed this series of coping verbalizing self-statements, upon return to the post-treatment assessment room, stated aloud (in essence):

"You (referring to the snake) made a deal with her (referring to the model); I will make a similar deal. If you don't hurt me, I won't hurt you. I'm going to pick you up."

We believe that additional therapeutic benefits can be gained if models demonstrate coping rather than mastery behavior. The perceived similarity between models and observer is enhanced by having the model portray at first the behaviors, thoughts, and feelings that are similar to those of the client. The models then demonstrate the sequence of coping skills that can be employed in overcoming the client's deficit.

The models demonstrate not only desirable behaviors, but also coping cognitions, re-evaluations, and ways of coping with feelings of frustration or self-doubt. In the final stage they demonstrate self-reinforcing statements.

The models' cognitions can be included in videotaped presentations in many ways. In each case, the observing client is told that the model was asked to share his thoughts or think aloud as he was performing the task. In one instance the model can talk aloud to himself while performing the task. Another possibility is having the videotaped model perform the task, but have the cognitions spoken offstage. At present there has been little research to indicate the best procedures for conducting such treatment.

Another illustration of a cognitive modeling procedure is provided by the work of Sarason (1973) on test anxiety. Sarason had models explicitly demonstrate the process by which they arrived at overt responses. Sarason found that the opportunity to observe a model who verbalized general principles while working on an anagram task resulted in high test-anxiety subjects solving anagrams more quickly than low test-anxiety subjects. The Sarason models, while doing an anagram task, used such verbalizations as: "I want to be sure not to let myself get stuck on just one approach to letter combinations. At times it looks like a hopeless group of letters, but I'm sure I'll hit on something." Richardson (1973) has developed a semi-automated, self-study manual to teach self-instructional skills to high test-anxiety students.

Such observational opportunities promote restructuring of the clients' thought processes. The inclusion and modeling of the covert responses related to performance seem to enhance the change process. More research is required in order to tailor the particular modeling technology to individual clients. It is possible that with children a mastery model may prove more effective than a coping model in helping overcome fears. Zimmerman and Rosenthal (1974) have described other procedural steps which must be included in modeling of rule-governed behaviors with children. For example, young children need to use an "alternation" format, in which the model performs one instance and then the child is allowed to respond to the same instance before the model performs on the next item.

In the treatment of adults, Kazdin (1974) has extended the coping modeling procedure to imaginal or covert modeling and has shown that modeling effects can be achieved by imagination. The modeling cues are presented to the client by means of instructions and the client imagines a model engaging in the various behaviors. Kazdin found that a coping imaginary model was more effective than a mastery model.

Modeling provides the therapist with an opportunity to include in therapy the thoughts and feelings the client will likely experience. In the treatment of nail biting or a similar self-control problem, the therapist can have a videotape model portray the following:

The model is about to bite her nails when she says, "There I go again. Just this one nail, then I'll stop . . . . I knew the treatment wouldn't help me. I just can't control myself. Cut it out. You always make excuses for yourself. Take a slow, deep breath, Relax. Just think of myself sucking my finger in front of everyone. What a picture! etc."

The therapist can show the client several such models coping with their urges and exerting self-control. This exposure serves several purposes: it teaches specific cognitive and behavioral skills; it provides models of others who have mastered their problems and demonstrates the reinforcements that they accrue; and it alerts the client to the style of thinking she may likely engage in. Thus, when she has such thoughts they will have a "déja vu" flavor (namely, "those are the thoughts that we discussed in therapy. They are the reminders to cope.").

Other behavior therapy procedures, including behavioral rehearsal and role-playing, can be modified to include a self-instructional coping process. One can teach clients to notice which interpersonal cues elicit negative self-statements and can then train them to produce incompatible self-statements and behaviors. Meichenbaum and Cameron (1973a) have described how this procedure can be applied to schizophrenics. The schizophrenic client was taught to self-instruct initially on simple, structured, sensorimotor tasks (e.g., digit symbol substitution task, finger maze task) and then on more demanding cognitive tasks (e.g., proverb interpretation). In this way an effort was made to have the schizophrenic develop with some proficiency a set of self-instructional responses to focus attention and improve performance. He was then taught to employ these coping self-statements in more anxiety-producing interpersonal situations. In interview situations the schizophrenic was trained to note the impact of his behaviors on others, especially the impact of his maladaptive, inappropriate verbal and nonverbal behaviors. This recognition was to be a cue to use the self-instructional controls which he had developed. The self-instructions included: "Be relevant; be coherent; make yourself understood." In addition, he was taught to appropriately use such interpersonal statements as "I'm not making myself understood," "Its not clear, let me try again." Whereas, in the past the behaviors of significant others often elicited anxiety and schizophrenic thinking, the present training procedure attempted to break this cycle. By means of teaching the schizophrenic to recognize when such a pattern was underway, he could then use his repertoire of self-instructional and interpersonal behaviors.

Interestingly, in such a treatment approach the client's own maladaptive behavior is the cue, the reminder, to use the cognitive coping and behavioral techniques. In the past the client's symptoms were the occasion for worry, anxiety, depression, and maladaptive behaviors, whereas following self-instructional training what the client says to himself about his symptoms has changed to a more adaptive way of functioning.

Anxiety Relief Conditioning and Aversive Conditioning

In both desensitization and modeling, the procedures were altered to include self-instructional components. The client's cognitions (i.e., thoughts, images, and fantasies) were viewed as sets of coping skills that were rehearsed both imaginally and behaviorally. The client's self-statements were viewed as part of a complex repertoire to be practiced.

In contrast to this emphasis on altering the client's cognitive process to provide direction for new behaviors, a number of behavior therapy procedures view the client's cognitions as behaviors to be modified in their own right. As previously mentioned, the client's covert behaviors are viewed as behaviors and thus are subject to the same "laws of learning" as are overt behaviors.

From such a viewpoint, one can influence the frequency and strength of the client's cognitions by having (1) the client pair his cognition with the onset, offset, or avoidance of an externally administered aversive consequence such as electric shock or the administration of an external reward; (2) the client pair two covert events, such as two images in the Cautela (1973) covert sensitization process; (3) the client pair his cognition with an overt behavior such as physical relaxation. Thus, the therapist can influence what the client says to himself, and in turn his overt behavior, by pairing various events with the client's cognitions.

Three illustrations of behavior therapy procedures used to influence directly what the client says to himself are *anxiety relief conditioning*, *aversive conditioning*, and *thought stopping-covert assertion*. The rationale for the *anxiety relief* procedures is offered by Wolpe and Lazarus (1966).

> If an unpleasant stimulus is endured for several seconds and is then made to cease almost immediately after a specified signal, that signal will become conditioned to the changes that follow cessation of the uncomfortable stimulus. (p. 149.)

Typically, the word "calm" is the signal which is paired with the offset of aversive stimulation (usually electric shock). Theoretically, the self-instruction "calm" takes on counterconditioning, anxiety-relief qualities which generalize across situations. The notion is that the client will be able to reduce his anxiety level in virtually any situation by instructing himself to be "calm," thus evoking the conditioned "relief" response. A number of investigators (Solyom and Miller, 1967; Thorpe, 1964) have presented data which demonstrate the therapeutic value of such anxiety-relief techniques in alleviating phobic and obsessive behaviors.

Meichenbaum and Cameron (1973b) have extended the anxiety relief procedure by making the onset and offset of the electric shock follow, respectively, the client's expression of anxiety-engendering and coping self-statements. In the treatment of snake phobic clients the anxiety relief procedure was as follows: the therapist said the word "snake"; the client then verbalized the self-statements, thoughts, and descriptive images which he experienced when confronted by a snake (e.g., "It's ugly; it's slimy; I won't look at it."). The client was encouraged to emit the personal self-statements that he had experienced in previous encounters with the phobic object. Following the expression of these self-statements shock was administered, thus punishing the anxiety-related self-statements. The instrumental response which the client used to terminate shock (and in later sessions avoid shock onset) was a set of positive coping self-instructions (e.g., "Relax, I can touch it; one step at a time."). Throughout the training all self-statements were made in a meaningful, personalized manner. This training was successful in reducing the persistent avoidant behavior.

The *aversive conditioning* treatment procedure can also be modified to include the client's self-statements. Typically, aversive conditioning involves showing the client a taboo stimulus or its representation (e.g., a slide) and when the client responds (as indicated by physiological measures of arousal) he is shocked. Shock is terminated by the reduction of autonomic arousal or by an instrumental response such as choosing another slide. In some paradigms the onset and offset of shock is made contingent upon the start and termination of an instrumental act such as drinking alcohol or smoking. From a self-instructional viewpoint the aversive conditioning can be expanded to include the client's self-statements. For example, if we were treating a child molester by means of aversive conditioning and the conditioned stimuli were slides of young children, the therapist could make the onset of shock contingent upon the meaningful expression of the set of self-statements and descriptive images, feelings, and fantasies the client experiences when confronted by a real child. Shock offset could then be made contingent upon incompatible self-statements which may involve self-instructions that he is mistaking his arousal as sexual, or that he should remove himself from the playground, or that he is not that kind of person.

Thought Stopping and Covert Assertion

The therapist quite often meets clients whose major problems involve obsessive thinking and ruminations about events which are very unlikely to occur. The content of these clients' thinking is usually not conducive to problem solving; but rather it focuses upon the imagined negative and catastrophic aspects of the situation.

One behavior modification approach used to treat such problems is thought stopping. In this procedure, the client is asked to concentrate on his obsessive, anxiety-inducing thoughts and then the therapist suddenly and emphatically shouts "stop," or produces some other interruption by means of a loud noise or electric shock. This procedure is repeated several times until the client reports that his thoughts were successfully interrupted. Then the responsibility for the intervention is shifted to the client, so that the client now tells himself "stop," initially aloud and then subvocally whenever he begins to engage in self-defeating rumination.

Rimm and Masters (1974) have supplemented the thought stopping technique with a *covert assertion* procedure. In addition to having the client learn to interrupt his obsessive thoughts with self-instructions, the client is encouraged to produce a positive, assertive-like statement which is incompatible with the content of the obsession. These authors report that a client who kept ruminating about having a nervous breakdown or becoming mentally ill (when there was no basis in fact for such thinking) adopted the covert assertion "Screw it! I'm perfectly normal," to combat such ideation.

The thought stopping, covert assertion procedure includes the following steps:

1. The frequency and impact of the client's irrational self-verbalizations (and images) are determined. The self-defeating nature of such thinking process is discussed.

2. Thought stopping procedure begins with the client's closing his eyes and imagining himself in a real-life situation and beginning to verbalize his obsessive

thoughts aloud. The therapist shouts "stop" at the beginning of the obsessive thought. After several successful trials, the responsibility is turned over to the client.

3. Now the client begins his obsessive thoughts, saying them to himself subvocally and then the client shouts "stop" aloud in order to interrupt the obsessive thought sequence. This is repeated for several trials, initially aloud and then covertly.

4. In order to strengthen the client's ability to interrupt and sense that he can control his thinking processes, he is encouraged to produce an assertive statement to himself that is incompatible with the content of the obsession. Initially, the expression of "stop" and the assertion is made aloud. Over a number of trials they are gradually made in lower and lower tones and eventually faded out to a covert level.

Mahoney (1973), as part of a comprehensive treatment program to develop self-control in overweight clients included covert assertion and thought management exercises. Using the term "cognitive ecology" he trained clients "to clean up what they say to themselves" about losing weight. Mahoney taught his clients to become aware of such weight relevant self-verbalizations as, "I just don't have the will power"; "If I don't lose my two pounds I'll never make it." The clients were encouraged to use covert assertion to combat these thoughts. The cognitive ecology component was only one important aspect of the treatment. The other components included self-monitoring of relevant behaviors, nutritional counseling, exercise management, regulation of cues which influence eating, relaxation training, self-reward training, and family support.

A great deal of research is required to determine if one can, indeed, treat client's cognitions in the same fashion as overt behaviors. A number of recent studies have questioned the adequacy of a learning theory explanation of behavior therapy procedures. For example, Marks (1973) reports that thought stopping, when applied to neutral nonobsessive nonphobic thoughts, proved as effective as the contingent application of the procedures. Thus, obsessive clients who were trained to use the thought stopping procedure only with their nonobsessive everyday thoughts showed as much improvement following treatment as did clients who were trained to use the thought stopping procedure with obsessive thoughts. The results of the Marks study raises the question, What is the client really learning when he uses the thought stopping procedure? In other words, what mechanisms mediate the efficacy of the specific treatment?

This question also arises in another of Marks' studies (Marks et al., 1971). Here the treatment procedure is imaginal flooding or implosion treatment of phobics. The flooding procedure requires the phobic client to imagine highly emotional fear-producing scenes related to their phobic area. For example, a spider phobic client may be asked to imagine spiders climbing all over his body, etc. In order to investigate the mechanisms involved in the treatment procedure, Marks and his colleagues included a second treatment group who imagined highly emotionally arousing scenes that were not related to the phobic scene. Thus, the spider phobic was asked to imagine that while he is visiting a zoo, a tiger escapes and attacks the client. Interestingly, both groups demonstrated comparable treatment improvement. Once again the question of what mechanisms mediates treatment efficacy is raised.

A "learning theory" explanation to explain treatment efficacy is also questioned in a series of treatment studies which have investigated the importance of the contingency of electric shock. The anxiety relief and aversive conditioning treatment paradigms (which were described above) were subjected to investigation. The investigators' strategy was to compare the efficacy of the standard treatment approach, where the onset and offset of electric shock was appropriately contingent upon behavior *versus* a treatment group where the contingent use of shock was inverted or made backwards. If both treatment groups were found to show comparable improvement, then a learning theory explanation for treatment outcome would be strained and an alternative explanation would have to be considered. Three illustrative studies which have examined this question are described. Meichenbaum and Cameron (1973b) reported that an "inverted" anxiety relief procedure, which punished the expression of coping self-statements and rewarded anxiety-producing thoughts, proved just as effective as the standard anxiety relief procedure. Carlin and Armstrong (1968), with smokers, and McConaghy and Barr (1973), with homosexuals, have reported that inverted or noncontingent aversive conditioning were found to be as effective as straight aversive conditioning. Much more research is required to replicate and extend these studies. However, in the interim these results should give pause to behavior therapy devotees and cause them to question the assumptions underlying the treatment approaches.

SELF-INSTRUCTIONAL TRAINING WITH CHILDREN

The major use of self-instructional procedures with children has involved the training of self-control skills, especially with hyperactive, impulsive children. Other behavioral and academic problems which have been treated by self-instructional procedures include resistance to temptation, delay of gratification, problem solving, reading, and creativity. In this section the major focus will be on the work with impulsive children.

Hyperactive, Impulsive Children

A major social problem in schools is the high incidence of hyperactive, impulsive children, i.e., some five to ten percent of school aged children are diagnosed as hyperactive (O'Malley and Eisenberg, 1973). It has been estimated (Grinspoon and Singer, 1973) that some 200,000 school children in the United States daily receive some form of medication for treatment of hyperactivity. The second major mode of treatment for these children is environmental control by such means as operant conditioning. A self-instructional treatment approach was developed to treat hyperactive, impulsive children. Further research is required to determine the relative efficacy of the three different treatment approaches and how they can be used to supplement one another.

The impetus for the self-instructional training procedure was the theoretical work of the Soviet psychologists Luria (1961) and Vygotsky (1962). On the basis of his work with children, Luria (1959) has proposed three stages by which the initiation and inhibition of voluntary motor behaviors come under verbal control. During the first stage, the speech of others, usually adults, controls and directs a child's behavior. The second stage is characterized by the child's overt speech becoming an effective regulator of his behavior. Finally, the child's covert or inner speech comes to assume a self-governing role. From this hypothetical developmental sequence we developed a treatment paradigm which was successfully used to train impulsive children to talk to themselves as a means of developing self-control (Meichenbaum and Goodman, 1971).

The self-instructional training procedure was administered on an individual basis and proceeded as follows: (a) first, the child observed a self-verbalizing model perform on a task such as a finger maze task; (b) then the child performed the same task while following the verbal instructions of the model; (c) the child was then instructed to talk aloud while doing the task, approximating the model's verbalizations; (d) the child was instructed to employ covert self-instructions in a final stage to consolidate the internalization process. The verbalizations that the therapist modeled and the child subsequently used included (a) questions about the nature of the task, (b) answers to these questions in the form of cognitive rehearsal and planning, (c) self-instruction in the form of self-guidance, (d) ways of coping with frustration and failure, and (e) self-reinforcement. In this way, the impulsive child is trained to develop a new cognitive approach or learning set in which he can "size up" the demands of the task, cognitively rehearse, then guide his performance by means of self-instructions, and, finally, appropriately reinforce himself.

The following is an example of the therapist's modeled verbalizations which the child subsequently used:

"Okay, what is it I have to do? You want me to copy the picture with the different lines. I have to go slowly and carefully. Okay, draw the line down, down, good; then to the right; that's it; now down some more. Good, I'm doing fine. Remember, go slowly."

Such instructions were modeled by the therapist and then practiced by the child on a variety of tasks, ranging from simple sensorimotor abilities to more complex, problem-solving abilities. Recently, Butter (1971) has demonstrated that a tactile discrimination task can be successfully employed to alter an impulsive cognitive style. On such tactile tasks the child is asked to select from behind a screen one object from a set which is identical to the standard. This task lends itself very nicely to cognitive modeling and self-instructional rehearsal.

One can imagine a similar training sequence in the learning of a new motor skill such as driving a car. As Henry Murray (1938) noted some years ago, "When one is learning to drive an automobile, one is, at first, aware of every accessory intention and subsequent motor movement, but later, when proficiency has been attained, the details of the activity are seldom in consciousness" (p. 51). The self-instructional training procedure follows a similar sequence with the fading of verbalizations as proficiency at the task increases.

There are two major concerns with regard to the self-instructional training of children. The first involves the question of what the child has learned from training that involves cognitive modeling and overt and covert self-instructional rehearsal. Do changes following such self-instructional training represent true alterations in the child's cognitive style, or merely superficial changes in specific responses that are demonstrated on a particular task? We cannot equate cognitive development with the child's merely memorizing a strategy that the therapist has differentiated for him, or the child's repeating the mere mechanical integration that the therapist has demanded. The research (Bem, 1967; Egeland, in press; Meichenbaum and Goodman, 1971; Palkes *et al.*, 1968, 1972) thus far conducted on self-instructional training and cognitive modeling with children is promising in terms of transfer of training to other tasks, across situations, and over time, which suggests that the cognitive changes are indeed general.

A second concern about self-instructional training with children is more practical in nature and has to do with how one actually engages the young child to talk to himself. One way to conduct self-instructional training is to use the child's medium of play. The self-instructional treatment can begin in the midst of ongoing play activities. The therapist can teach the hyperactive, impulsive child the concept of talking to himself and gain the child's attention by using his play activities. For example, while playing with one hyperactive child, the therapist said, "I have to land my airplane, now slowly, carefully, into the hangar." The therapist then encouraged the child to have the control tower tell the pilot to go slowly, etc. In this way the therapist is able to have the child build up a repertoire of self-statements to be used on a variety of tasks. Training begins on a set of tasks (games) in which the child is somewhat proficient and for which he does *not* have a history of failures and frustrations. The therapist employs tasks that lend themselves to a self-instructional approach and have a high "pull" for the use of cognitive strategies. For example, the therapist can have the impulsive child verbally direct another person (e.g., the therapist) to perform a task such as a finger maze while the child sits on his own hands. In this way, the child has to learn to use language in an instrumental fashion in order to direct another person to perform the task. Another technique designed to enhance self-control is to have an older, impulsive child teach a younger child how to do a task. The impulsive child, whose own behavior is actually the target of modification, is employed as a "teaching assistant" to model self-instructions for the young child.

In using such self-instructional procedures, it is important to insure that the child does not say the self-statements in a relatively mechanical, rote, or automatic fashion without the accompanying meaning and inflection. This would approximate the everyday experience of reading aloud or silently when one's mind is elsewhere. One may read the paragraph aloud without recalling the content. What is needed instead is modeling and practice in synthesizing and internalizing the meaning of one's self-statements.

The rate at which the therapist proceeds with the self-instructional training procedure can be individually tailored to the needs of each child. Some children require many trials of cognitive modeling and overt self-instructional rehearsal, whereas others may proceed directly to the state of covert rehearsal after being exposed to a model. For some children, the phase of having the child do the task while the therapist instructs the child tends to foster a dependency. In such cases cognitive modeling followed by covert rehearsal may suffice. In some cases it is *not* necessary to have the child self-instruct aloud. One strength of the training procedure is its flexibility.

The self-instructional approach also provides some flexibility in how quickly the therapist and the child rehearse comprehensive packages of self-statements. Usually, the self-instructional training follows the principle of successive approximations. Initially, the therapist models and has the child rehearse simple self-statements such as "Stop! Think before I answer." Gradually the therapist models (and the child rehearses) more complex sets of self-statements.

The self-instructional training regimen can be supplemented with imagery manipulations, especially in treating young children. One can train the impulsive child to imagine and to subsequently self-instruct, "I will not go faster than a slow turtle, slow turtle." Schneider (in press) has used such a turtle imagery procedure in an ingenious way to foster self-control in hyperactive, disruptive school children. Schneider incorporates the turtle image into a story which is read to the class. Following the story, the students imitate the turtle who withdrew into his shell when he felt he was about to lose control. This was followed by relaxation, self-instructional and problem-solving exercises to teach self-control. In the Schneider study, the teacher spent 15 minutes each day for approximately three weeks in training and achieved reduced aggressive behavior and fewer frustration responses. One could use a variety of different stories and cognitive techniques to teach self-control behaviors. Imagine the story, cognitive and behavioral modeling films, self-instructional training techniques one would use with children who have a high incidence of social withdrawal and introversion (O'Conner, 1972).

The self-instructional approach to treat impulsivity focuses on the child's conscious self-regulatory ability. This also applies to the treatment of impulsive adolescents and adults. The child's behavior pattern is broken down into smaller manageable units and in this way the therapist tries to make the subject aware of the chain of events (i.e., environmental situations and behavioral and cognitive reactions) which set off the impulsive and often explosive behavior. This process is enhanced by performing a diagnostic evaluation of the conditions under which self-control is deficient. By making the child aware of the sequence of events, he can be helped to interrupt them early in the chain and to employ coping procedures.

The self-instructional approach may be contrasted with other therapy approaches employed with problems of impulsivity. As Bergin (1967) has indicated: "Impulse control problems are often treated by aversive methods, by analysis of

psychodynamics via transference, by modification of self-perceptions and relationships with others, by altering values, etc., but seldom are they dealt with by
direct treatment of the self-regulatory defect per se" (p. 116).

Treatment of Academic Problems

Recently there has been increasing research on the possible application of
self-instructional training procedures with traditional academic concerns, such as
reading, problem solving, creativity. At this point we can share the general
training strategy that is being employed and make a call for more research to
assess the pedagogical potential of self-instructional training procedures.

In the same way that the origins of the self-instructional procedure with
hyperactive children found impetus in the work of Soviet psychologists, the
training approach toward academic problems got its start in the work of the
American psychologist Gagne. Gagne (1966) uses a task-analysis approach by
beginning with a behavioral statement of the instructional objective. Then he asks
what are the prerequisite behaviors the child must possess in order to perform the
desired terminal behaviors. For each of the identified behaviors the same question
is asked, and a hierarchy of objectives is thereby generated. Gagne is proposing
that an individual's learning of a complex behavior is contingent on his prior
acquisition of a succession of simpler behaviors. Thus, the instruction can be
based on the cumulative learning process.

The self-instructional training approach follows a similar strategy, except each
step in the hierarchy is translated into self-statements or cognitive strategies
which can be modeled and rehearsed. Practically, this means that the teacher must
be sensitive in performing a task analysis of not only the behaviors, but also the
cognitions, strategies, and rules required to do a task.

When put into operation self-instructional training requires the teacher to
determine the strategies and self-statements necessary to perform a given task.
The teacher can discover the hierarchy of cognitive abilities required by such
means as observing his own thinking processes as he performs the task, or by
observing and interviewing children who do poorly or well on the task. He can
then translate these cognitive strategies into sets of self-statements that can be
modeled and then rehearsed by the student. Moreover, the teacher can cognitively
model not only task-relevant, problem-solving self-statements, but also the coping
self-statements. Teachers (this includes professors as well) very infrequently, if at
all, model how they cope with frustrations and failures while doing a particular
task (i.e., they are mastery, not coping models). They rarely share with their
students the thinking processes and other events which are involved in how they
performed the task.

The student is told to perform a task, but rarely is shown (a) how to break the
task down into manageable units, (b) how to determine the hierarchy of skills
required to do the task, or (c) how to translate these skills into self-statements
which can be rehearsed.

One demonstration of the potential of self-instructional procedures to academic problems is a recent study that attempted to enhance creativity by explicitly modifying what college students say to themselves (Meichenbaum, 1973b). Each of three major conceptualizations of creativity represented in the literature was translated into a set of self-statements that could be modeled by the therapist and then practiced by the subjects on meaningful self-selected tasks. Table 11.3 illustrates the variety of self-statements used in training. The use of

Table 11.3.   Examples of Self-Statements Used in Creativity Training.

Self-statements arising from an attitudinal conceptualization of creativity

Set inducing self-statements

What to do:

Be creative, be unique.

Break away from the obvious, the commonplace.

Think of something no one else will think of.

Just be free wheeling.

If you push yourself you can be creative.

Quantity helps breed quality.

What not to do:

Get rid of internal blocks.

Defer judgments.

Don't worry what others think.

Not a matter of right or wrong.

Don't give the first answer you think of.

No negative self-statements.

Self-statements arising from a mental abilities conceptualization of creativity

Problem analysis — what you say to yourself before you start a problem

Size up the problem; what is it you have to do?

You have to put the elements together differently.

Use different analogies.

Do the task as if you were Osborn brainstorming or Gordon doing Synectics training.

Elaborate on ideas.

Make the strange familiar and the familiar strange.

Task execution — what you say to yourself while doing a task

You're in a rut—okay try something new.

How can you use this frustration to be more creative?

Take a rest now; who knows when the ideas will visit again.

Go slow—no hurry—no need to press.

Good, you're getting it.

This is fun.

That was a pretty neat answer; wait till you tell the others!

Self-statements arising from a psychoanalytic conceptualization of creativity

Release controls; let your mind wander.

Free-associate, let ideas flow.

Relax—just let it happen.

Let your ideas play.

Refer to your experience; just view it differently.

Let your ego regress.

Feel like a bystander through whom ideas are just flowing.

Let one answer lead to another.

Almost dreamlike, the ideas have a life of their own.

---

self-statements not only enhanced performance on creativity measures, but engendered a generalized set to handle life situations more creatively. Following training the clients reported that they had spontaneously applied the creativity training to a variety of personal and academic problems. This observation suggests that psychotherapy clients may benefit from such a self-instructional creativity or problem-solving regimen. A similar suggestion has been offered by D'Zurilla and Goldfried (1971) in their article on a problem-solving approach to psychotherapy.

It should be noted that clients are *not* given a list of self-statements and not told that just saying these things to themselves will make everything better. This strategy reminds one of the exhortative statements made popular by the French psychiatrist Emile Coué, who in the 1920's encouraged everyone to say, "Every day in every way I'm getting better and better." Instead, the present treatment approach is designed to have the client (1) become aware of the negative thinking style that impedes performance and that leads to emotional upset; (2) generate, in collaboration with the therapist, a set of incompatible, specific self-statements, rules, strategies, etc., which he can then employ; and (3) learn specific adaptive, cognitive and behavioral skills.

The self-instructional training procedure is presently being applied to such academic problems as reading comprehension, critical thinking, and interpersonal problem solving. Indeed, the cognitive behavior modification technology may have a great deal to offer teachers.

EPILOGUE

Perhaps the present chapter has not dealt with each of the concerns and self-statements of the reader, but by now there should be a greater appreciation of the role self-statements can play in the change process. Quotes from two quite different observers of human behavior further underscore this process. The first quote is from no less a therapist (of sorts) than Don Juan, the quixotic philosopher in Carlos Castaneda's writings. Don Juan, in his inimitable manner, advises:

> The world is such-and-such or so-and-so only because we tell ourselves that that is the way it is . . . . You talk to yourself. You're not unique at that. Every one of us does that. We carry on internal talk . . . . In fact we maintain our world with our internal talk. (Castaneda, *Separate Realities*, 1972, pp. 218–219.)

Perhaps more familiar is the quote by Farber:

> The one thing psychologists can count on is that their subjects or clients will talk, if only to themselves; and not infrequently, whether relevant or irrelevant, the things people say to themselves determine the rest of the things they do. (1963, p. 196.)

Self-instructional training procedures are designed to influence the nature of the client's internal dialogue.

REFERENCES

Bandura, A. Vicarious processes: A case of no trial learning. In L. Berkowitz (Ed.), *Advances in experimental social psychology*, Vol. 2. New York: Academic Press, 1965.

Bandura, A. *Principles of behavior modification*. New York: Holt, Rinehart and Winston, 1969.

Beck, A. Cognitive therapy: Nature and relation to behavior therapy. *Behavior Therapy*, 1970, **1**, 184–200.

Bem, S. Verbal self-control: The establishment of effective self-instruction. *Journal of Experimental Psychology*, 1967, **74**, 485–491.

Berenson, B. and Carkhuff, R. *Sources of gain in counseling and psychotherapy*. New York: Holt, Rinehart and Winston, 1967.

Bergin, A. A self-regulation technique for impulse control disorders. *Psychotherapy: Theory, Research and Practice*, 1967, **6**, 113–118.

Butter, E. Visual haptic training and cross modal transfer of a reflective cognitive strategy. Unpublished dissertation, University of Massachusetts, 1971.

Carlin, A. and Armstrong, H. Aversive conditioning: Learning or dissonance reduction? *Journal of Consulting and Clinical Psychology*, 1968, **32**, 674–678.

Castaneda, C. *A separate reality: Further conversations with Don Juan*. New York: Pocket Books, 1972.

Cautela, J. A behavior therapy approach to pervasive anxiety. *Behaviour Research and Therapy*, 1966, **4**, 99–111.

Cautela, J. Covert processes and behaviour modification. *Journal of Nervous and Mental Disease*, 1973, **157**, 27–35.

Chappell, M. and Stevenson, T. Group psychological training in some organic conditions. *Mental Hygiene*, 1936, **20**, 588–597.

Debus, R. Effects of brief observation of model behavior on conceptual tempo impulsive children. *Developmental Psychology*, 1970, **2**, 202–214.

Denny, D. Modeling effects upon conceptual style and cognitive tempo. *Child Development*, 1972, **43**, 105–119.

D'Zurilla, T. and Goldfried, M. Problem solving and behavior modification. *Journal of Abnormal Psychology*, 1971, **78**, 107–126.

Egeland, B. Training impulsive children in the use of more efficient scanning techniques. *Child Development*, in press.

Ellis, A. *Reason and Emotion in Psychotherapy*. New York: Lyle Stuart Press, 1962.

Farber, I. The things people say to themselves. *American Psychologist*, 1963, **18**, 185–197.

Feather, B. and Rhoads, J. Psychodynamic behavior therapy: I. Theory and rationale. *Archives of General Psychiatry*, 1972, **26**, 496–502.

Frank, J. *Persuasion and healing*. Baltimore, Md.: Johns Hopkins Press, 1961.

Gagne, R. Elementary science: A new scheme of instruction. *Science*, 1966, **151**, 49–53.

Geer, J. and Turtletaub, A. Fear reduction following observation of a model. *Journal of Personality and Social Psychology*, 1967, **6**, 327–331.

Goldfried, M., Decenteceo, E., and Weinberg, L. Systematic rational restructuring as a self-control technique. *Behavior Therapy*, 1974, **5**, 247–254.

Grinspoon, L. and Singer, S. Amphetamines in the treatment of hyperkinetic children. *Harvard Educational Review*, 1973, **43**, 515–565.

Homme, L. Perspectives in psychology: Control of coverants, the operants of the mind. *Psychological Record*, 1965, **15**, 501–511.

Janis, I. *Psychological stress: Psychoanalytic and behavioral studies of surgical patients*. New York: Wiley, 1958.

Kagan, J. Reflection-impulsivity: The generality and dynamics of conceptual tempo. *Journal of Abnormal Psychology*, 1966, **71**, 17–24.

Kahn, M., Baker, B., and Weiss, J. Treatment of insomnia by relaxation training. *Journal of Abnormal Psychology*, 1968, **73**, 556–558.

Kazdin, A. Covert modeling and the reduction of avoidance behavior. *Journal of Abnormal Psychology*, 1973, **81**, 87–95.

Kazdin, A. Covert modeling, model similarity, and reduction of avoidance behavior. *Behavior Therapy*, 1974, **5**, 325–340.

Lang, P. The mechanics of desensitization and the laboratory study of human fear. In C. Franks (Ed.), *Assessment and status of behavior therapies*. New York: McGraw-Hill, 1969.

Langer, E., Janis, I., and Wolfer, J. Effects of cognitive coping device and preparatory information on psychological stress in surgical patients. Unpublished manuscript, Yale University, 1973.

Lazarus, A. *Behavior therapy and beyond*. New York: McGraw-Hill, 1971.

Lazarus, R., Averill, J., and Opton, E. Towards a cognitive theory of emotion. In M. Arnold (Ed.), *Feeling and emotion*. New York: Academic Press, 1970.

Luria, A. The directive function of speech in development. *Word*, 1959, **15**, 341–352.

Luria, A. *The role of speech in the regulation of normal and abnormal behavior*. New York: Liveright, 1961.

Mahoney, M. Clinical issues in self-control training. Paper presented at the meeting of the American Psychological Association, Montreal, 1973.

Marks, I. New approaches to the treatment of obsessive-compulsive disorders. *Journal of Nervous and Mental Disease*, 1973, **156**, 420–426.

Marks, I., Boulougouris, J., and Marset, P. Flooding versus desensitization in the treatment of phobic patients. *British Journal of Psychiatry*, 1971, **119**, 353–375.

Marmor, J. The psychodynamics of realistic worry. *Psychoanalysis and Social Science*, 1958, **5**, 155–163.

McConaghy, M. and Barr, R. Classical, avoidance, and backward conditioning treatments of homosexuality. *British Journal of Psychiatry*, 1973, **122**, 151–162.

Meichenbaum, D. Examination of model characteristics in reducing avoidance behaviour. *Journal of Personality and Social Psychology*, 1971, **17**, 298–307.

Meichenbaum, D. Cognitive modification of test anxious college students. *Journal of Consulting and Clinical Psychology*, 1972, **39**, 370–380.

Meichenbaum, D. Cognitive factors in behavior modification: Modifying what clients say to themselves. In C. Franks and T. Wilson (Eds.), *Annual review of behavior therapy: Theory and practice*, New York: Bruner-Mazel, 1973. (a)

Meichenbaum, D. Enhancing creativity by modifying what subjects say to themselves. Unpublished manuscript, University of Waterloo, 1973. (b)

Meichenbaum, D. Therapist manual for cognitive behavior modification. Unpublished manuscript, University of Waterloo, 1974.

Meichenbaum, D. A self-instructional approach to stress management. A proposal for stress inoculation training. In C. Spielberger and I. Sarason (Eds.), *Stress and anxiety in modern life*. New York: Winston, in press (a).

Meichenbaum, D. *Cognitive behavior modification*. Morristown, N.J.: General Learning Press, 1974.(b)

Meichenbaum, D. and Cameron, R. Training schizophrenics to talk to themselves: A means of developing attentional controls. *Behavior Therapy*, 1973, **4**, 515–534. (a)

Meichenbaum, D. and Cameron, R. An examination of cognitive and contingency variables in anxiety relief procedures. Unpublished manuscript, University of Waterloo, 1973. (b)

Meichenbaum, D. and Cameron, R. Stress inoculation: A skills training approach to anxiety management. Unpublished manuscript, University of Waterloo, 1973. (c)

Meichenbaum, D. and Cameron, R. Clinical potential of modifying what clients say to themselves. In C. Thoresen and M. Mahoney (Eds.), *Self-control: Power to the person.* Palo Alto: Brooks/Cole, 1974.

Meichenbaum, D. and Goodman, J. The nature and modification of impulsive children: Training impulsive children to talk to themselves. Paper presented at the Society for Research in Child Development Conference, Minneapolis, Minnesota, April 1971.

Meichenbaum, D., Gilmore, B., and Fedoravicius, A. Group insight vs. group desensitization in treating speech anxiety. *Journal of Abnormal Psychology*, 1971, **77**, 115–126.

Morris, L. and Liebert, R. Relationship of cognitive and emotional components of test anxiety to physiological arousal and academic performance. *Journal of Consulting and Clinical Psychology*, 1970, **35**, 332–337.

Murray, H. *Explorations in personality*. New York: Oxford Press, 1938.

O'Conner, R. Relative efficacy of modeling, shaping, and the combined procedures for modification of social withdrawal. *Journal of Abnormal Psychology*, 1972, **79**, 327–334.

O'Malley, J. and Eisenberg, L. The hyperkinetic syndrome. *Seminars in Psychiatry*, 1973, **5**, 95–103.

Orzack, M. and Kornetsky, C. Attention dysfunction in chronic schizophrenia. *Archives of General Psychiatry*, 1966, **14**, 323–326.

Palkes, H., Stewart, M., and Freedman, J. Improvement in maze performance of hyperactive boys as a function of verbal training procedures. *Journal of Special Education*, 1972, **5**, 337–342.

Palkes, H., Stewart, M., and Kahana, B. Porteus maze performance of hyperactive boys after training in self-directed verbal commands. *Child Development*, 1968, **39**, 817–826.

Paul, G. *Insight vs. desensitization in psychotherapy: An experiment in anxiety reduction*. Stanford: Stanford University Press, 1966.

Peterson, D. *The clinical study of social behavior*. Englewood Cliffs, N.J.: Prentice-Hall, 1968.

Plutchik, R. and Ax, A. A critique of "Determinant of emotional states" by Schachter and Singer (1962). *Psychophysiology*, 1967, **4**, 79–82.

Premack, D. Mechanisms of self-control. In W. Hunt (Ed.), *Learning and mechanisms of control in smoking*. Chicago: Aldine, 1970.

Rachman, S. Systematic desensitization. *Psychological Bulletin*, 1967, **67**, 93–103.

Richardson, F. Coping with test anxiety: A guide. Unpublished manual, University of Texas at Austin, 1973.

Rimm, D. and Masters, J. *Behavior therapy: Techniques and empirical findings*. New York: Academic Press, 1974.

Rosvold, H. A continuous performance test of brain damage. *Journal of Consulting Psychology*, 1956, **20**, 343–350.

Sarason, I. Test anxiety and cognitive modeling. *Journal of Personality and Social Psychology*, 1973, **28**, 58–61.

Schachter, S. The interaction of cognitive and physiological determinants of emotional state. In C. Spielberger (Ed.), *Anxiety and behavior*. New York: Academic Press, 1966.

Schachter, S. and Singer, J. Cognitive, social and physiological determinants of emotional state. *Psychological Review*, 1962, **69**, 379–399.

Schneider, M. Turtle technique in the classroom. *Exceptional Child* (in press) 1972.

Solyom, L. and Miller, S. Reciprocal inhibition by aversion relief in the treatment of phobias. *Behaviour Research and Therapy*, 1967, **5**, 313–324.

Steffy, R., Meichenbaum, D., and Best, A. Aversive and cognitive factors in the modification of smoking behavior. *Behaviour Research and Therapy*, 1970, **8**, 115–125.

Sykes, D., Douglas, V., and Morgenstern, G. Sustained attention in hyperactive children. *Journal of Child Psychology and Psychiatry*, 1973, **14**, 213–220.

Thorpe, J. Aversive-relief: A new method for general application. *Behaviour Research and Therapy*, 1964, **2**, 71–82.

Vygotsky, L. *Thought and language*. New York: Wiley, 1962.

Wine, J. Investigations of attentional interpretation of test anxiety. Unpublished doctoral dissertation, University of Waterloo, 1971.

Wolpe, J. and Lazarus, A. *Behaviour therapy techniques*. New York: Pergamon Press, 1966.

Yates, D. Relaxation in psychotherapy. *Journal of General Psychology*, 1946, **34**, 213–238.

Zimmerman, B. and Rosenthal, T. Observational learning of rule governed behavior by children. *Psychological Bulletin*, 1974, **81**, 29–42.

CHAPTER 12

Expectation, Hypnosis, and Suggestion Methods

WILLIAM C. COE AND LINDA G. BUCKNER

THE ROLE OF EXPECTATION IN THERAPEUTIC CHANGE*

The importance of a person's expectations for the outcome of treatment has long been recognized. Similarities among healers from many persuasions, including witchdoctors and psychotherapists, have been pointed out, and the importance of expectations may overshadow effects of the treatments they claim to administer. Drugs and other therapies appear at times to be no more effective than the patient's "faith" in the treatment. These curative effects are often called "placebo" effects, indicating they are not specific to the "treatment" effects. They exist nevertheless, sometimes to a remarkable degree, and should therefore be considered in administering helping procedures.

Three General Principles

Torrey (1972) suggests that a patient's "faith" and motivation for improvement are determined by several factors: (1) the degree to which the therapist's ability to name the disease and its cause agrees with the views of the patient, (2) the degree to which the therapeutic techniques employed are considered by the patient to be of value in helping him, and (3) the degree to which the therapist's personal qualities match the patient's expectations of what a therapist should be like.

For a clearer understanding of the operation of placebo principles in specific

---

*Our task for this chapter is twofold: clarifying the role that expectation plays in enhancing positive change, and demonstrating the use of hypnotic and suggestive techniques to help people change. These topics are only related through the general effects which expectations have on all therapies. The reader should not have the impression that the effectiveness of hypnotic or suggestive therapies rests more on expectancy effects than do other forms of therapy. While they offer examples of the use of expectancy in psychotherapy, other approaches could as easily have been used for the same purpose. While expectation effects are pointed out whenever appropriate, only a part of the chapter emphasizes them. Most of the text is devoted to hypnosis and other suggestive psychotherapies.

techniques, we will examine each of these general principles in more detail. All contain strong cultural and subcultural components for both the therapist and the patient. Therapists should be aware of the effects of cultural factors, adjusting their approach in order to maximize their therapeutic potential. It is not unusual for a therapist to find himself in the position of trying to persuade a client into accepting his views. In some cases, in fact, it is desirable to refer him to another therapist who is more familiar with his cultural beliefs and values.

Naming the Problem and Its Cause

Naming the disease entity may in and of itself be effective in alleviating many of the client's problems. Being able to assign a label and point out a cause, indicates to the client that there is someone who understands what is happening to him. Labelling also implies that something can be done to alleviate the suffering. However, when the healer's label does not agree with the client's view of "mental illness" (or psychological maladjustment), further therapeutic contact is less likely to be helpful. If, for example, the client views psychological problems as being related to unconscious repression of traumatic childhood experiences, the label of a therapist who shares these views is much more likely to be perceived as competent, and thereby enhance the client's faith. For a therapist of a different persuasion to be effective, he must at least begin by working from the client's viewpoint, or spend a considerable amount of time re-educating the patient.

Another example is the very religious person who attributes his maladjustment to a punishment inflicted by God for his sins. This person might profit more by seeing a priest for confession and atonement than he would by seeing a psychotherapist who views the problem in behavioral and environmental terms. The client is likely to view the therapist as an incompetent heathen who does not understand the "workings of God."

Therapeutic Technique

The therapist's treatment procedures logically follow from his views of causation. The behavioral therapist employs techniques for learning and unlearning habits; the psychoanalyst uses techniques for discovering unconscious conflicts, and so on. Likewise, the client has expectations about the kind of techniques that will benefit him, depending on his beliefs of why he is suffering. The client's cultural or subcultural milieu are often important in this respect.

Illustrative is the problem found in anglo clinics trying to help Mexican-Americans. Therapists who do not recognize the importance of Mexican-American social norms will have difficulty as helpers. For example, if a Mexican-American couple is being counseled because of marital problems, it is important to recognize the accepted roles of men and women within their subculture. Teaching the woman to enjoy sexual intercourse, and to become more dominant in her relationship with her husband, will most likely serve no useful function in maintaining their marriage. The Mexican woman generally expects and is expected to be submissive and not to enjoy sexual intercourse. A dominant wife threatens the male's masculine identity, and a woman who enjoys sex is suspected of being promiscuous (Torrey, 1972, Chapter 10). It is unlikely that this couple would return for therapy with such a "naive, degenerate" therapist. The *curandero* of the Mexican-American subculture, the priest of the church, would probably be of more help. He is more likely to share the couple's views on how things should be, and to implement steps to change them for the better.

Personal Qualities of the Therapist

Everyone has his own view about how a psychologist or psychiatrist should look and behave. Views vary a great deal from, "They're all crazy!" to "They're all wise, knowledgeable and helpful." In general, people who contact a therapist do so on the assumption that he is an authority and that he holds competencies that will help them. This expectation itself may enhance the client's ability to resolve his problems. The therapist's office has its effects. Diplomas, certificates of membership in prestigious professional organizations, licenses, and other emblems establishing the therapist as a legitimate healer in American culture, enhance the client's expectancies of being helped. The location of the office may also be a factor. Clients who hold usual middle-class values may be quite impressed by a "plush" office as it indicates financial success, and by association, professional success. Clients who are less conforming may have an opposite reaction, categorizing the therapist as "straight" and as someone who is unable to understand their views. The dress and grooming of the therapist will have similar effects. Long hair, styled hair, mod clothing or business suits among other characteristics, will tend to label the therapist for the client initially, and the client's impression may help or hinder therapy. Whatever the case, the physical surroundings and the therapist's appearance have their effects. The alert therapist will recognize these effects and work to arrange (or rearrange) them in his favor.

Therapist qualities of warmth, genuineness, and understanding have been emphasized by Lazarus (1971) among others. As a general rule, these qualities seem desirable regardless of the therapist's theoretical orientation. However, people differ about the degree of activity they expect of a therapist, how directive or passive he should be, and the relative amount of time he should spend talking during the session. For example, a business man who expects to unload his tensions through cathartic sessions would expect the traditional listening therapist as opposed to the activity of a behaviorally-oriented therapist. It is up to the therapist to recognize these expectations and to employ them to his advantage.

Perhaps one of the most important therapist variables is his belief that a given client can be helped. A recent study by Lerner and Fiske (1973) showed that the therapist's belief that he could help the client was possibly a better predictor of outcome than client attributes, like socio-economic level, that have been claimed to predict outcome in the past. It seems quite likely that the therapist subtly communicates his optimism or pessimism to the client, thus affecting the client's expectations.

Finally, and related to the therapist's expectations for a client's success, is the convincingness of his techniques to the client. That is, if the client can be convinced that *this* particular procedure will alleviate his suffering, the probability of success is substantially raised. For example, McReynolds (1973) found that systematic desensitization, a behavioral technique for treating phobias, was no more effective than other techniques presented in an equally convincing way. The degree to which a technique is convincing to a client is influenced by all of the variables we have discussed and it illustrates the importance of such variables in therapy.

Techniques for Enhancing Expectation Effects

All of the variables described above may be important in enhancing a client's expectations of being helped. Torrey (1972) discusses three suggestive techniques that are widely utilized in our culture for enhancing expectations: direct suggestion symbolism, and magical formulas.

Direct suggestion is often unintentionally employed by physicians and psychotherapists in the course of their contact with their client. While writing a prescription for a drug the physician may say, "Take this and you will feel better." In so doing he gives a direct suggestion that the drug is effective, thereby raising his client's expectations for success. As a behavior therapist outlines a program for change, he may add something like, "This program will help you accomplish your goals," or "You will find this program easy to follow and effective in . . ..". Again, a direct suggestion to expect success is given. The antithesis of positive suggestion would be something like: "Well, we might as well try such and such, what have we got to lose?" At best, the client hopes whatever it is will work, even though the therapist seems doubtful.

As Americans become more familiar with Eastern cultures and religions, the use of *symbolism* is gaining in importance. Symbolism exists in the form of rituals that are believed to bring about certain desired end-states, such as relaxation, symptom-removal or contact with God. Hypnosis and relaxation training are the most popular forms of symbolism employed in American psychotherapy and will be covered more extensively in later portions of this chapter. Meditation approaches also include symbolic rituals; however, as yet they are not so widely accepted. Humanistic and psychoanalytic procedures include rituals as well.

Symbolic rituals are of tremendous importance in enhancing the effectiveness of therapy for some people. The performance of the hypnotic induction ritual, for example, is a signal that something profound and of great importance might occur. Rituals not only enhance the client's expectations, but therapists are often equally as convinced of their effectiveness, enhancing further the effect for the client. Rituals are only effective, however, in so far as they meet with other expectations and beliefs of the client. When they are counter to his beliefs, they may have a detracting effect.

Magical formulas in our society exist mainly in the form of psychoactive prescription drugs. The middle-class housewife will attest to the effectiveness of tranquilizers prescribed by her family physician, even when they are really sugar pills (placebos). They help her through the drudgery of housework, and to be more patient with her children. Mental health propaganda has convinced her that her stress is caused by a "nervous condition"—and her physician has confirmed her diagnosis. He has also prescribed an acceptable cure in our culture, a pill, accompanied with the statement, "Almost without exception, these conditions are helped by taking one of these tablets each morning."

In another culture the physician might find the formulae effective in a different way. A tribesman in a "primitive" society may profit more by wearing the prescription around his neck, in the manner of his society's rituals for healing, than he will by ingesting it. The tribesman's expectations about illness and treatment are quite different from the housewife's, but just as important to the outcome of treatment.

In sum, suggestion may be a major consideration for enhancing the effectiveness of many therapies. They may be of considerable benefit, providing they are congruent with the client's view of the world, and his expectations for therapy.*

Applying Placebo Therapy

Fish (1973) describes how the foregoing variables may be applied in the therapy setting. His entire book, *Placebo Therapy*, is devoted to ways of applying placebo principles.

Fish describes therapy in major stages: pre-therapy, therapy, and post-therapy. The third stage, post-therapy, deals less directly with expectancy, but the pre-therapy and therapy stages necessitate the consideration of these variables if they are to be implemented successfully. We will only outline Fish's stages here and refer the reader who wishes detail to his work.

Considerations during the *pre-therapy* (the placebo formulation stage) include the qualities of the therapist along with the client's problems, expectations, and world-view. Knowledge of these factors is essential in drawing up a therapeutic contract that takes advantage of placebo principles. In the *therapy stage*, the strategies devised in the pre-therapy stage are implemented. It is communicated to the client that a cure will result if he does certain things, the "healing ritual" begins. Once positive changes begin, the therapist can refer to them as proof of the treatment's effectiveness, creating further expectancies that enhance the client's response to treatment.

The *post-therapy stage* consists of steps meant to maintain the cure. Self-reliance is emphasized as are changes in the client's environment.

The remaining portion of the chapter will be concerned with the use of hypnosis and other suggestive therapies. Many of these approaches include logical extensions of applying the variables we have just discussed.

---

*Jerome Frank's book, *Persuasion and Healing* (1961 and 1972), is another excellent source of material along this same line. He presents evidence for the importance of expectancy variables in both medical and psychological therapies. His major thesis is to show that any treatment which reduces anxiety and arouses hope, can effect a cure.

HYPNOSIS AND HYPNOTIC TECHNIQUES

Hypnosis has characteristically been associated with the mystical, the strange, the unusual, and the dramatic. The mass media and popular literature nearly always report hypnotic experiences as the ultimate of wonderment—the dramatic cure, the multiple personality, or the powerful influence of the hypnotist. From the "mesmerizer" of the 18th century to the stage hypnotist of the present, the lay public has been exposed to hypnosis as a phenomenon of power and influence. The more conservative views of hypnosis, although present since its beginnings, have been given scant attention. In recent times hypnosis is being increasingly viewed as a legitimate therapeutic tool in medicine, dentistry, and psychotherapy. Less dramatic expectations are replacing the overstated ones, but an aura of mystery and sensationalism nevertheless remains. Unfortunately, the image of hypnosis as mysterious and bordering on the occult has caused some practitioners to avoid using it, and persons who might benefit from it to shy away. These same expectations, on the other hand, open its practice to otherwise unqualified persons who take advantage of people looking for the "instant cure."

What is hypnosis? Although the most common conception involves a one to one relationship between a hypnotist and his subject, the behaviors it subsumes may range from self-suggestive techniques to large-group phenomena. The hypnotist performs certain actions and says certain things, which in turn appear to bring about the client's responses. It appears as though he has power over the subject.

The usual procedure is to begin by administering an "induction," instructions that lead the subject from his normal "waking" state into the "trance" state. The client is often requested to gaze at an object while the hypnotist repeats a variety of suggestions, including those leading to relaxation, heightened awareness of sensations, and tiring of the eyes. After the clients eyes close, the "hypnotic state" is deepened with further suggestions. In response to the hypnotist's requests, a good subject, one who becomes involved in the task, may perform striking behaviors, like suggested changes in bodily sensations, induced paralyses, imaginings of vivid quality, heightened awareness, selective forgetting, dissociative-like phenomena, and posthypnotic tasks.

Induction procedures and hypnotic behaviors are similar whether in group hypnosis, individual hypnosis, or autohypnosis, the main difference lies in the number of people participating, and the presence or absence of the hypnotist.

Describing the usual operations in hypnosis is, of course, an incomplete answer for the scientist as regards the nature of hypnosis. The conditions accounting for the observations are still not fully understood. Many of the questions have not been answered with finality but most of the earlier notions about a "trance state," the excessive power of the hypnotist, and so on, are being replaced by less exaggerated, naturalistic explanations based on psychological and social psychological concepts (Hilgard, 1965; Sarbin and Coe, 1972.)

The uses of hypnosis and autosuggestion have expanded and become more refined, but in many instances they are still quite similar to those employed a hundred years ago. Often the same old techniques are labelled differently on the basis of new rationale. The same procedures that one person calls autohypnotic, for instance, are also found in yoga, autogenic training, psychocybernetics, and sleep teaching. It often seems that independent investigators have simply rediscovered the usefulness of self-suggestions, or interactive suggestions, only to relabel them so they fit within their preferred theoretical framework.

As we look at the procedures and applications of suggestive therapies, the use of expectation, conviction and commitment should become clear. Methods of building the client's hope and positive attitude play an important part. Depending on the therapist's preference, however, specific therapeutic techniques are also included, and presumably add to the goal of positive change.

Who Employs Hypnosis

Although it is thought that hypnosis is used principally for psychotherapy, it is interesting to note that this does not appear to be the case. Levitt and Hershman (1963) mailed a questionnaire to the membership of the two major hypnotic societies in the United States. While their results should be considered with caution because of the rather small proportion of the questionnaires that were returned, they offer some indication about what kinds of professionals use hypnosis, and for what purposes.

Only seven percent of the respondents were psychiatrists and psychologists. Physicians composed 70 percent of the memberships, dentists 19 percent, other doctorates four percent, and nondoctorates seven percent. General practitioners accounted for 61 percent of the physicians, and apparently their primary use of hypnosis is as an analgesic agent in minor surgery. The single best represented medical speciality was obstetrics-gynecology (11 percent). They reported using hypnosis with 12 percent of their patients to ease childbirth. On the average they claimed a three hour reduction in labor and a 60 percent reduction of chemical anesthesia. Surgeons made up four percent of the medical respondents and used hypnosis primarily as an analgesic agent. They estimated a 50 percent average reduction in the use of chemical anesthetics, and significantly reduced bleeding. It appears that the use of hypnosis as an anesthetic overshadows all others; its application reduces the need for chemical anesthesias which carry a significant risk for some patients. However, the use of hypnosis in solving problems of adjustment will be our focus. Some of the ways that it is being applied will be examined in later sections.

Historical Background

It is impossible to date exactly the first appearance of hypnotic or hypnotic-like techniques. It seems likely that they began very early in man's history, probably at the time tribal groups were formed with their related values, customs, and ceremonials—a time when it became important to influence one's fellow man through verbal means. Certainly, trance-like states and suggestive influence occurred with early religious beliefs and their emotionally arousing ceremonials. Some religions still incorporate the power of suggestion in creating dramatic occurrences, voodoo influence and "medicine men" being examples. Eastern cultures have long recognized the usefulness of meditative procedures and self-suggestion, but the acceptance of hypnosis into Western practice began less than 200 years ago.

The earliest attempt to bring hypnotic phenomena under scientific study has been attributed to a Viennese physician, Franz Antoine Mesmer (1734–1815). His techniques came to be known as "mesmerism." We still use the term to describe the act of placing a person in a trance-like state.

In the middle 1700's science was still strongly influenced by a dualistic philosophy, the belief that the mind and body were separate entities. The study of the "mind" was relegated to religion and philosophy, the study of the body and inanimate objects to the natural sciences. Since matters of the mind were not tampered with by men of science, it was only after Mesmer explained his observations on a physical basis that they became interested.

Astrology's postulates about the power of the stars and astral bodies in affecting human behavior were popular in Mesmer's time, and early advances in the study of electricity and magnetism had made concepts related to these phenomena available. From the tenets of astrology, Mesmer believed that some principle must permeate the universe, a force that could be identified with electricity or magnetism. His thinking led him to experiment with the effects that magnets might have on his patients. He tried different methods, passing magnets over them, stroking their bodies, and so on. His efforts resulted in some cures, mostly afflictions that later came to be considered hysterical. To his surprise, however, he found that the magnet was not necessary. Simply making passes with his hands or stroking his patients produced similar effects. His experiments led him to believe that he had discovered a source of universal force, and in some way he was able to redistribute his patients' bodily fluids in a curative way. He called his process "*animal magnetism*," postulating an animal fluid, a life force similar to magnetism, that he was able to redistribute and thus bring about a cure. That is, the source of cure lay in his capacity to redistribute the fluids, the first theory to attribute the client's response to the power of the hypnotist.

Mesmer reported his findings to a number of scientific societies in 1775, but his claims were ignored. Discouraged, but still convinced that he had made a great discovery, he moved to Paris and established a place where he could treat a large number of patients at the same time, his famous *Baquet*. The Baquet was a large tank containing "Mesmerized" fluid. His healing force could be transmitted into the patients' bodies through metal rods immersed in the fluid. The patients gathered round the Baquet in a dimly lighted room, music in the background, and held the metal handles as Mesmer in flowing cape moved from one to the other, making passes over some, fixating another with his eyes, and stroking another. It was usually not long before one of the patients would fall into a swoon, to be followed shortly by dramatic responses from others. Mesmer had helpers who massaged and worked with the patients once they had fallen into a trance. The effects were highly emotional and varied, and often appeared to result in a number of cures.

Mesmer gained a great deal of notoriety in Paris and eventually scientific commissions were appointed to examine his claims. Their findings did not support his theory and he eventually fell into disrepute, but his followers continued to teach and practice the art of animal magnetism for many years throughout Europe and America.

Some 50 years after Mesmer's attempts, John Elliotson, a professor and senior physician at the University College in London, was led to believe that mesmerism had potential as a medical tool. He established a mesmeric infirmary at the hospital, but became embroiled in a struggle with the University administration over it, ending with his resignation. Although he suffered continual harassment and professional ostracism, he continued to carry on his fight for mesmerism and established the first journal devoted entirely to the study of "cerebral physiology and mesmerism." This journal was the only formal means of communicating reports from mesmeric clinics that began to be established during the mid 1800's.

Because of the medical profession's earnest desire to alleviate surgical pain in the 1800's (chemical anesthetics were as yet undiscovered), one might have thought that mesmerism would find acceptance for this use. A British surgeon working in India, James Eisdale, began using mesmerism for anesthetic purposes. But it was not until he had reported over 100 operations, with the patients apparently free from pain, and the death rate from surgical shock greatly reduced, that the medical profession investigated his work. The outcome was sufficiently favorable for the approval of a small mesmeric hospital supported by the Indian government. His work, however, was cooly received by medical journals. About the same time, Ward, a physician in England, reported the amputation of a leg under mesmerism with no apparent pain. There was much furor over his report, with claims of deception marking its objective examination.

Considering the pressing need, and the apparent validity of at least some of the reports, it would seem that mesmerism might have been admitted as a valid medical tool, and it may have been, were it not for three historical accidents. Nitrous oxide (laughing gas), ether, and chloroform were all discovered at about the same time. These agents could be explained on a physiological basis, their effects were more reliable, and they were available without a great deal of special training. Not having the mystical connotations of mesmerism they were much more acceptable to the medical profession.

Mesmerism's acceptance came with a new theoretical explanation and a change of name. James Braid (1795–1860), a Scottish physician, became interested in mesmeric phenomena about the same time that Eisdale and Elliotson were performing their work. While attending a public demonstration of mesmerism he concluded that the entire proceedings were a fraud. But, at a second session, after he had examined the mesmerized subject, he changed his opinion. He was impressed by the fact that the subject was unable to open his eyes, that a paralysis of the eye muscles had apparently taken place. He began to experiment with friends and found that he was able to produce most of the same phenomena by having them look steadily at a spot slightly above eye level. After some minutes their eyes would tear and close, whereupon they would appear to fall into a sleep-like state. Braid reasoned that a change in the nervous system had occurred because of the fatigue and paralysis of the nervous centers controlling the eyes. Thus, he reinterpreted mesmeric behavior in concurrently understandable, neurophysiological terms, naming the phenomena "nervous sleep" or "neurohypnotism"; later abbreviated to "hypnotism." Greco-Latin terms were acceptable scientific procedure and a physiological explanation was in keeping with the scientific knowledge of the times. Braid's reinterpretation of mesmerism also caused the mesmerists to reject him, which in turn prevented him from being a central target of the orthodox, medical group.

Hypnotism had finally been admitted to the arena of scientific controversy and study. The primary disputes from then on centered about its nature rather than whether or not it occurred. Since that time, many important men of science—Charcot, Bernheim, Janet, Freud, Binet, Wundt, Hull, Sarbin, Hilgard—have studied hypnotic phenomena, and the various helping professions have slowly added it to their armamentarium of therapeutic tools.

Considerations for Enhancing Expectancy

The potential hypnotic subject has already developed characteristics that will in part determine the way in which he will respond to hypnosis. He has cognitive abilities to help him focus his attention and others that aid in vivid imagery. It is likely that these abilities are in part inherent; however, past experiences with hypnotic-like behaviors, for example, absorption in literature or music, practice in experiencing or creating emotional states, or other experiences requiring focus on bodily and cognitive functioning, contribute to the development of abilities that are called upon in hypnosis. Further, the subject brings beliefs and expectations with him that act to motivate him positively (or negatively) toward the hypnotic role. Subjects who have a liking for strange, unusual, or exciting experiences are likely to be more willing to cooperate with hypnotic instructions and become more involved in the role. Almost everyone has preconceived ideas about hypnosis and the behaviors that occur in the hypnotic setting—the more their expectations are in agreement with the hypnotists, the more likely it is that they will be good hypnotic subjects. It behooves the hypnotist to clarify what he expects.

If a person is unwilling to cooperate with the hypnotist's requests (such as those presented later on the Stanford Scale) he cannot be hypnotized. It is necessary to overcome his trepidations or fears before he is going to try to follow instructions and put his abilities to work. That is, the potential hypnotic subject must be motivated to enter the relationship. And, the closer his expectations for his own conduct match the requests of him by the hypnotist, the more likely it is that he will be a good hypnotic subject. Coupled with motivational factors are certain abilities that appear to be required in hypnosis, e.g., concentration, imagination. The greater they are, the more likely the subject is to become involved in hypnosis and to report that his subjective experience was different and convincing. It is also clear, however, that a number of individuals will simply comply with the hypnotist's instructions and not experience their conduct as unusual.

The conditions of the environment and the characteristics of the hypnotist will make a difference in responsiveness as well. Usually, both the setting and the appearance of the hypnotist are designed to encourage the subject's cooperation. The setting is often a laboratory with decor that indicates serious scientific purposes, or a private office with furnishings complimenting the professional qualities of the hypnotist and the services to be rendered. Consequently, the environment tends to motivate the subject favorably and to reduce his apprehensions. The appearance of the hypnotist is also important. In the first place, it is necessary for the subject to recognize him as a hypnotist. This is usually clear through verbal interchanges during their meeting, or else the subject has already learned that he is to work with a professional identified as a hypnotist. A number of cultural symbols are also nearly always associated with the hypnotist to establish his status as a trustworthy professional. His dress, his age, and his general professional manner all add to the perception that he is a competent, trustworthy person. Few persons would subject themselves to a hypnotic induction by a person who is unkempt, coarse in language, and appears to be irresponsible. Thus, before the hypnotic induction has begun a number of factors have entered into the relationship to modify the subject's response.

The wording of the induction is aimed at increasing the subject's motivation and to provide cues indicating what is expected of him. Typically, the induction is organized in a way to create the impression that the subject is *expected* to respond to the hypnotist's suggestions. The initial suggestions are usually quite easy to follow, for example, body relaxation, closing of the eyes, heaviness of the body. The subject is gradually led toward behaviors that are more difficult and require higher levels of imaginal ability and concentration. Suggestions are also given to increase the subject's physiological involvement in the role. His attention is turned toward stimulus inputs from bodily processes, or in a therapeutic setting, to circumstances that carry emotional associations. The more the subject becomes involved, the more likely it is that he will experience a subjective loss of control and allow responses to occur that would normally be suppressed.

The termination of hypnosis again provides clear instructions of the hypnotist's expectations. He tells the subject that a shift in roles is forthcoming and that the subject is again to enact the experimental-subject role, or the non-hypnotized client role.

Subjects who respond well may be "trained" to enter hypnosis upon a brief signal. Again, the hypnotist communicates his expectations that upon a predetermined signal the subject is to turn his attention toward performing the behaviors he has experienced previously in hypnosis. Thus, the need to repeat time consuming induction procedures is eliminated.

Induction of Hypnosis

To investigate any behavior it is necessary to agree upon its characteristics, i.e., it must be measured in a reliable way. Hypnosis is no exception. In recent times its study has been greatly facilitated by the development of standard measuring instruments that operationally define what is meant by hypnosis. Although some investigators do not agree that the standard scales "really" measure hypnosis (that is, that the scales are valid) the scale items have typically been associated with hypnotic behavior since Mesmer's time.

The development of the Stanford Hypnotic Susceptibility Scales (SHSS) has provided investigators with a reliable measure of hypnotic behavior (Weitzenhoffer and Hilgard, 1959). They are a work sample of hypnosis in that the subject is actually hypnotized and his response to typical hypnotic suggestions are recorded. His total score (range of 0–12) indicates the degree to which he responds to hypnotic procedures. Administration requires approximately 45 minutes. The hypnotist reads the instructions verbatim, and detailed scoring criteria provide high inter-rater reliability. Norms based on the responses of a large number of subjects are available for comparing the individual's response to the distribution of responses in the general population. Because these scales are very structured, they are especially useful for the novice hypnotist who is still unsure of induction procedures.

Administration of the scale, as with nearly all hypnotic approaches, begins with a general discussion of hypnosis. It is an open-ended exchange where an attempt is made to reduce any fears or hesitancies the subject might have about hypnosis. The purpose is to put him at ease and thereby enlist his cooperation. A "waking suggestion" is then demonstrated. The subject is told that hypnosis is primarily the response to suggestion and that the waking suggestion is an example of what it is like. This suggestion, "postural sway," is the first item on the scale. The hypnotist stands behind the subject, asks him to close his eyes and hold his hands at his sides with his feet together, and that in a moment he is going to ask him to think of falling backwards. The hypnotist continues to suggest "swaying and falling" until the subject falls into his arms, or until the standard instructions have been completed. (Some hypnotists use this suggestion to induce hypnosis: After the client falls into the hypnotist's arms, he is moved to a chair with suggestions to relax and go even deeper into hypnosis.)

The subject is then asked to seat himself in a comfortable chair. A spot on the wall, slightly above eye level, serves as a point of concentration. (A lighted candle or other artifact is often used for this purpose clinically. It tends to raise the expectations of the client that something more unusual is to take place. When hypnosis is used with insight therapy approaches, unusual focal objects may facilitate the later focus on unusual psychological associations.) The subject is to concentrate on the spot until his eyes close. The hypnotist then begins reading a standard induction procedure that leads to eye closure. The first part of the induction includes a further explanation of hypnosis, instructions to elicit cooperation, increasing suggestions on heaviness, drowsiness and relaxation, and finally suggestions of eye heaviness and lid closure. If the subject closes his eyes before the hypnotist completes the 14-minute induction he is scored as passing the second item. After the subject's eyes are closed the hypnotist gives suggestions to "deepen" the trance—counting backwards from 20 to 1 with the suggestion that with each count the subject will go deeper and deeper into a pleasant state of hypnosis. After the "deepening," 10 hypnotic suggestions are presented. In the standard administration of the scale these suggestions are scored by predetermined criteria for passing or failing. For clinical purposes, you may not want the client to "fail" and believe that hypnosis is not working for him. Many therapists do not "test" the depth of hypnosis for this reason, although the expectations of a good subject may be increased when he responds positively to your suggestions. For example, "Your eyes are tightly shut, glued together, you cannot open them—try!"

Another Stanford scale, SHSS, Form C (Weitzenhoffer and Hilgard, 1962) includes more cognitive items that may be useful in clinical practice, like age regression, hypnotic dream, and positive and negative hallucinations. Again, the structure of the scale may be reassuring to the neophyte hypnotist.*

Milton H. Erickson has been one of the major proponents of the use of hypnosis in psychotherapy. He has made many contributions in the form of unique induction and therapeutic techniques. It will be illustrative to examine one of his induction techniques because it points out the wide variety of ways that influence communications may be phrased during hypnotic transactions. Erickson (1964) and Haley (1967) describe a *confusion technique* which is reported to be effective for a variety of purposes. It is claimed to be very helpful with resistant subjects who try to analyze what is happening during induction and therefore do not concentrate and respond well. A flow of words that is very difficult to understand is presented to the subject in a serious, intent manner. Erickson uses plays on words, changes in verb tenses, and irrelevancies that are meaningful out of context, but in the context of the verbal flow they are confusing and distracting. The point of the technique is described as follows: "Thus the subject is led almost to begin a response, is frustrated in this by then being presented with the next idea, and the whole process is repeated with a continued development of a state of inhibition, leading to confusion and the growing need to receive a clear-cut comprehensible communication to which he *can make* a ready and full response." (p. 183)

He has used the confusion technique for inducing hypnosis when age regression was to be the goal. Specific incidents taken from the patient's history are appropriately interspersed in a historical context that will lead the patient to a specified age by the end of the suggestions. The following illustration will show how well he incorporates irrelevant material, verb tenses, and so on to create confusion in the subject until he is ready to accept any clear path of understanding, and consequently, the hypnotist's suggestions.

> I am so very glad you volunteered to be a subject. You probably enjoyed eating today. Most people do though sometimes they skip a meal. You probably ate breakfast this morning, maybe you will want tomorrow something you had today, you have eaten it before, perhaps on Friday like today. Maybe you will next week. Whether last week, this week, or next week, makes no difference. Thursday always comes before Friday. This was true last week, will be true next week and is so this week. Before Friday is Thursday and before June is May, but first there is "whan that Aprille with its shoures soote," and March followed the snows of February but who really remembers the 6th of February. And January 1st is the beginning of the New Year of 1963 and *all that it will bring.* But

---

*In a later section on autohypnosis, another induction technique is presented in some detail. It should be especially helpful where teaching relaxation is considered an important part of therapy.

December brought Christmas. But Thanksgiving preceded Christmas and all that shopping to get done and what a good dinner. (p. 188.)*

These communications are then continued, introducing more factual material from the patient's history and progressively moving him backwards in time. (In the above example the quote from Chaucer about April was personally relevant to the patient. It carried associations with a definite date in his history.) Although most of Erickson's work is based on clinical report, his examples are usually convincing and offer new ideas for more stringent testing.

Evaluative Uses (Diagnosis)

Hypnosis may be employed as a diagnostic tool in cases where physical complaints cannot be attributed to organic pathology. One approach is to hypnotize the patient and suggest that his symptoms will disappear. If they do, the difficulty is felt to be functional (nonorganic). Dramatic results have been observed in some cases. A patient whose arm is paralyzed, for instance, may have complete freedom of movement following hypnotic suggestions to that effect. In the absence of medical evidence to the contrary, the diagnostician assumes that the disorder has a psychological basis.

There is a problem with this technique because it is possible that hypnotically induced analgesia will mask real pain from a physical disorder. Suggesting to a patient who complains of back pain that he will no longer feel the pain and be able to stand upright may accomplish its purpose during the hypnotic session; however, the possibility of a physical cause of pain cannot be eliminated on this basis alone.

Another diagnostic method, following from dynamic theories of personality, seeks to use hypnosis as a vehicle for uncovering psychological conflicts behind a physical disorder. Rosen (1953) has applied hypnosis in this manner to patients whose physical difficulties had not responded to medical diagnosis and treatment. He often does not inform the patient that he is to be hypnotized, but explains that he is going to demonstrate a method that will help him to relax. The patient may be told that his tenseness and his ability to relax are to be tested, that they wish to determine the degree of his tenseness and his ability to dispense with it. The patient is told to focus on the bodily region of his discomfort, that his attention may wander but that it will return. The hypnotist then uses the patient's reactions to help induce hypnosis. He times his speech to the patient's breathing and comments upon behaviors that occur spontaneously as soon as he notices them (flushing, tremulousness, foot tapping, and so on), sometimes before the patient has become aware of their existence. These comments are made in a way to lead the patient to believe that they are physiologically based. Even though these behaviors increase with the hypnotist's description, the patient is not made aware that he is responding to suggestions. The patient is also told that other phenomena, which the hypnotist

---

*From Erickson, M. H. The confusion technique in hypnosis. Originally published in *The American Journal of Clinical Hypnosis*, 1964, **6**, 183–207. Copyright 1964 by the American Society of Clinical Hypnosis.

describes in minute detail, will occur. These behaviors are impossible on the basis of natural physiological and anatomical factors and when they show themselves they must be in response to the hypnotist's suggestions. The patient is led into hypnosis in this manner. The hypnotist then proceeds in various ways to uncover the psychological reasons behind the difficulty.

Fantasy evoking methods are often used to uncover the patient's psychological dynamics. One technique is to suggest that the patient has seated himself in a theater whereupon the master of ceremonies appears before the curtain. It is suggested in detail that the master of ceremonies is experiencing the same symptoms as those of the patient. The suggestions continue until it is felt that the patient has developed a clear image of the scene. The hypnotist then suggests that the curtains are opening and a shocked look crosses the face of the master of ceremonies—a look of surprise because on the stage he sees what causes his symptoms. The hypnotist then waits for signs of emotional response before asking the patient to describe the scene. The scene may have personal relevance to the patient's difficulties and help to direct further psychotherapeutic efforts.

A technique often used in conjunction with the theater fantasy is the "intensification of emotion." The hypnotist suggests that the patient become aware of his current emotional response, that it will build until it is so strong that he cannot stand it any longer. When it reaches high intensity he will remember another time in his life that held great meaning for him when the feeling was equally as strong. The hypnotist then continues to encourage the building of the emotion until the patient experiences a new fantasy which furnishes more information for future therapeutic purposes. The following case is an example of this technique:

> One patient, for instance, with what for years was diagnosed as asthma found himself forced to cease work because of the increasing frequency of his severe and incapacitating gasping spells. He became obsessed with memories of the drowning three years before of a close friend, and expressed not-too-vague suicidal thoughts because of guilt in not having affected a rescue. When his emotion of the moment was hypnotically intensified, he developed a pronounced rage reaction and acted out his desire to bash in the head of the girl friend to whom he was engaged and with whom he had just started having intercourse, knock her to the floor and kick her to death in the abdomen. On the non-hypnotic level, he remembered that this was how he once felt about his alcoholic sister and wondered if he had originally wished to kill both her and his now dead friend whose drowning had precipitated his symptoms. His gasping spells ceased immediately after this abreaction, and he found himself able to return to work. He slowly became somewhat depressed, however, and showed some mild free-floating anxiety. Since he realized that it was "about time" to quote his own words, for him "to do something constructive about his underlying pattern," therapy continued although a symptom cure had been affected. (Rosen, 1953, p. 260.)*

Therapeutic Uses

Suggestive Approach

It would seem that the most direct therapeutic use of hypnosis would be to suggest that the patient's symptoms would disappear when he is not hypnotized as

---

*From H. Rosen, *Hypnotherapy in clinical psychiatry.* Julian Press, 1953.

well as when he is hypnotized. This technique is an old approach, and was typical of Freud's early work with hypnosis. Numerous reports indicate that symptoms are effectively eliminated by this method. However, there is still a good deal of controversy about the technique because many therapists, especially psychoanalytically oriented ones, feel that the symptom may be replaced by one that is more debilitating, or its loss may bring on a severe underlying psychological disorder and only worsen the patient's condition.

Mainly on the basis of this controversy, and because of reports that appear to verify "symptom substitution," an alternative technique has been developed. Rather than suggesting that the patient will be symptom free, a less debilitating symptom is suggested in its place. That is, the hypnotist gives the patient a substitute symptom to serve the function of the original one. A salesman with a facial tic might be treated by suggesting the tic would move into a less obvious part of his body, such as his toe or finger. Then, instead of his face twitching, his toe would twitch and not interfere as much with his occupation.

Direct suggestion and symptom substitution sometimes appear to produce dramatic cures although they are much rarer than the popular literature would lead one to believe. If pain is hypnotically relieved, there is also the danger that a real physical disorder may be masked and, to the patient's detriment, go untreated.

Hypnosis and Insight Psychotherapy

Hypnosis may be used as an adjunctive technique to speed the progress of traditional psychotherapy. The general hypothesis of these approaches is that hypnosis offers a condition that facilitates the awareness of unconscious material. How it is combined with therapy will depend upon the therapist's overall strategy and technique.

Wolberg (1948) uses hypnosis in conjunction with psychoanalysis—a technique he terms *hypnoanalysis.* Because unconscious material may be more readily obtained with hypnosis, he sees it as a useful tool in breaking through therapeutic resistance and speeding insight. Before analysis begins the patient is trained to enter deep hypnosis upon a signal from the analyst. Although this may take a number of sessions, Wolberg believes it is a necessary step because later in treatment the patient may build up resistances and refuse to be hypnotized. Hypnosis is called upon when resistances are encountered and the therapist wishes to pass through them quickly. He signals the patient to become hypnotized, then applies one of many techniques to uncover the unconscious material that is the basis of the resistance. The patient is also trained in these techniques before the formal analysis begins. Some of these will be described below:

1. Hypnotic Dream

In this procedure the patient's fantasies are used to provide meaning to a

---

*See Gill and Brenman, 1959, for another reference on the use of hypnosis from a psychoanalytic viewpoint.

particular class of stimuli. For instance, if the patient seems to block during free association around material associated with his mother, he would be hypnotized and the analyst would suggest that he will have a dream showing the significance of the material to him. The content of the dream is interpreted in the same light as other dreams and used in the regular session.

2. Automatic Writing

After being hypnotized the subject is given a paper and pencil with the suggestion that he will write the important elements associated with some analytic material. He is apparently unaware of what he is writing and his response appears to occur as if his hand were dissociated from his conscious thoughts. The resulting message is interpreted for its significance to the patient's conflicts.

3. Age-Regression and Revivification

The hypnotist suggests that the subject is becoming younger and younger, returning to a specific time period of his life. It is then suggested that he is reliving these experiences at that time and the content he reports is again used as grist for the psychoanalytic session.

Jacob Conn (1968) uses hypnosis in dynamic psychotherapy in a way he terms *hypnosynthesis*. The basic premise is that the patient will use hypnosis to synthesize and bring together disparate aspects of his life. As a result, his functioning will become more harmonious. Conn does not emphasize the past nor does he direct his patient toward recalling forgotten memories. He supports the importance of the patient's preconceived ideas about psychotherapy and his picture of the ideal therapist. Thus, Conn sees the patient as the active factor in his own recovery and therapy is aimed at helping him to liberate the natural strengths he has in resolving his own difficulties. He does not seek to induce deep levels of hypnosis but rather allows the patient to determine his own level on the basis of his needs in the here-and-now situation. Hypnosis for Conn is a permissive procedure. The patient is not challenged while in the trance, nor is it necessary that he act out his conflicts with extreme emotionality. He believes that patients who do so are pleasing the doctor because they believe that that is the way they will improve. Conn finds that patients can speak quietly about even very traumatic events if instructed accordingly. The following excerpts from a case show the nature of Conn's therapeutic use of hypnosis.

> John B., age 32, was first seen because he had been "nervous and jumpy and nauseated especially in the morning" for four years. He described himself as being a very conscientious individual who was fearful of "talking up" to his supervisors. He had been with the same company for the past fifteen years. For the previous ten years, the patient had been "too much in a hurry" to eat breakfast. During the initial interview the patient stated that his father, whom he described as being "hardboiled," had "resented" him since birth. He blamed this on the fact that his mother was pregnant when his father married her. Mr. B. is the eldest of four children. He recalled how he had avoided his father on every possible occasion, and had preferred living at the home of his maternal grandmother, where he spent most of his time. His brother and two sisters, however, seemed quite content to live in their own home.

The patient promptly went into the trance state and spontaneously brought up the fact that he had been having "nightmares" since boyhood. "It was as if someone was after me, and I woke up frightened. It was a ghost who seemed to be eavesdropping," then "the ghost was coming after me. I had a sense of fear of being caught, a sense of wrong-doing. I remember I swiped a quarter when I was seven years old. What stands out most is running away." (Tell me about the ghost?) "It reminds me of the Canterville ghost. Charles Laughton played that part [in the movie of that name and] my father has the same build. I was afraid of him as a child. I was afraid he'd catch me masturbate; he never did. In the dream I made him the villain. It just popped into my mind." (Go on.) "One time my sister [age eight] was asleep; I tried to examine her body. I heard him walking upstairs. I hid under the bed; I was twelve then. I want to see your face." (Why?) "I want to know how *you* feel about it." (Go on.) "Could that also explain the lions that chase me in the dreams. They are the kings of the jungle, the big courageous animals; could that be my father too?" (When you are a kid you naturally feel that your father is a big, powerful person.) "Underneath I am still afraid of him." (Not only of him.) "I am afraid of life, afraid to trust myself." (When you were examining your sister's body, why didn't you take a good look?) Patient smiled. (What is wrong in learning about a girl's body like every other boy does? You were afraid; you felt you never had a right to look.) "That's a pretty good idea. I feel like I am going to float. I am so much at ease." The patient was then told that he could open his eyes by counting to five (which he did), and again expressed his satisfaction at being so relaxed.

During the next session (the hypnotic interviews occurred twice weekly), the patient spoke of feeling better. His eyes closed in about a minute and he began breathing deeply and regularly. When asked what he would like to say he said, "I was afraid of my father. I still am. I am afraid of all superiors, that's why I am so uncomfortable on my job after fifteen years. My father *made* me feel uncomfortable." (You can't *make* a man feel uncomfortable. It could only have been ____?) "Myself, I get it, I was inferior because I thought I was. I agreed with my father to keep him from becoming angry. It is much easier to say, "Yes you are right."

In September, six months after the treatment began (34th session), Mr. B. abruptly said, "This method doesn't work for me." (What method? It is you who are doing what you want to do. What do you really want? You know that you can change to suit yourself.) "I honestly think I have to quit the job. I've known the decision for a long time. Today, I was able to say it."

Mr. B. could give no reason for leaving; he had been with the same company for fifteen years and every possible consideration had been shown him. The patient just felt that he had to leave. He then was told, while still in the trance, that the reason would come to him without any effort on his part and that he must trust this impulse even if he had no "reason" at present for doing so. A week later the patient called to say that he had quit his job after bawling out his superior for having pushed him around all these years. He had been doing the actual work while his immediate superior had been taking all the credit. The patient had felt quite pleased with himself only to be called back a few days later and offered a better position with an increase in salary, which he accepted. He now knew the "reason" why he had left. He had to be as "free" on the job as he had been at home, in the Bible class, and in accepting himself as he really was. He felt as if now he could effectively express himself. He ended the last interview (September 17) saying, "One thing sticks out. I know—I am positive—I can do what I want to do, what I really what to do; and that's the difference between knowing what I want to do and what other people want me to do!"

A follow-up interview two years later revealed the patient to be free of complaints, normally self-assertive, and well adjusted at home and at work. (pp. 17–20.)*

Hypnosis in Behavior Therapy

Behavior therapists most often employ hypnosis for enhancing relaxation and/or imagery. Wolpe (1969) recommends that behavior therapists learn several

---

*Quoted from Conn, J. H. Hypnosynthesis: Psychobiologic principles in the practice of dynamic psychotherapy utilizing hypnotic procedures, in the January 1968 *International Journal of Clinical and Experimental Hypnosis.* Copyrighted by The Society for Clinical and Experimental Hypnosis, January 1968.

techniques for inducing hypnosis. Furthermore, Weitzenhoffer (1972) points out that hypnotherapists have employed methods for some time that are quite similar to techniques now called behavior therapy, the main difference being that the use of learning principles has been largely unrecognized by hypnotherapists, or not applied systematically when they were.

In Wolpe's technique of *systematic desensitization* (see Chapter 8) the client who experiences a phobia (1) is trained to relax deeply, (2) develops a list of scenes in ascending order based on the degree to which they arouse his fear, and (3) imagines these scenes in the same order while remaining relaxed. The goal is to desensitize the client's fear to the actual situations. Relaxation techniques that utilize hypnosis (like those to be described later) may be used. The hypnotic techniques may be more successful than nonhypnotic techniques for some clients; however, there is no certain way to predict at present which clients respond more favorably. It is also possible that the induction of hypnosis will enhance the imaginative capacity of some clients. Imagined scenes should therefore be more similar to actual settings, thereby increasing the generalization of learning to real-life circumstances.

Cautela's (1967) *covert sensitization* technique (see Chapter 10) is also quite similar to methods that have been, and are being employed by hypnotherapists (Weitzenhoffer, 1972, pp. 73–74). The basic idea is to associate noxious imagery with an undesired habit or object. The alcoholic, for example, imagines he is becoming nauseous when he approaches alcohol. It is the therapist's task to administer suggestions that will help the client create a vivid image of the aversive conditions. Cautela does not speak of hypnosis, but the procedures are undeniably similar. Overeating, smoking, homosexuality and presumably other undesirable habits may be weakened with this technique, although other techniques are often included as well.

Coe* combines aversive imagery with fattening foods as part of a more comprehensive approach to weight control. The client is required to associate the aversive stimulus and the desired food in actuality before attempting to use them in autosuggestion. For example, a client who "loves" chocolate cake is requested to pour castor oil over it and *try* to eat it. The point is to use the memory of the experience to enhance the vividness of the imaginary stimulus.

Whether the induction of hypnosis will enhance the effectiveness of covert sensitization, or any "behavioral" technique for that matter, is not definitely established. In our opinion, however, the choice of calling the therapeutic approach hypnotic or nonhypnotic (relaxation training, for example) should be made on the basis of the client's expectations and attitudes toward hypnosis. Exactly the same procedures can be employed whether or not the word "hypnosis" is mentioned. Although we offered some suggestions earlier about the expectations and attitudes of people who seem to be more acceptable of "hypnosis," we know of no fool-proof way of deciding whether or not a particular client's expectancies will be enhanced

---

*An unpublished manuscript of this technique, "A Behavioral Approach to Weight Control," may be obtained from W. C. Coe, Ph.D., Department of Psychology, California State University, Fresno, California.

by the term hypnosis. It remains a clinical skill at this time to reach that decision. Nevertheless, we should be aware that simply calling techniques "hypnotic" may enhance therapeutic progress in some cases.

Weitzenhoffer (1972) presents a number of other hypnotherapy approaches which may be interpreted as using a learning theory paradigm. He also points out that hypnosis may add to therapy by increasing client motivation and helping to establish a strong relationship between the client and the therapist.

AUTOHYPNOTIC TECHNIQUES

Autohypnosis, variously called autosuggestion or self-hypnosis, is a technique in which the client learns to give suggestions to himself. A therapist-hypnotist usually trains him initially, although in some cases phonograph records and literature may be the only source of instruction. In nearly all of these approaches the client is expected to practice in order to increase his responsiveness to suggestions. Explicit, or at least implicit, is the message that the hypnotist will be necessary for a short time, perhaps only two or three sessions, and that the main burden for therapy will rest on the client.

After an initial interview, most autohypnotic approaches begin with relaxation training. In general, relaxation training starts with the induction of hypnosis, either through standard techniques or progressive relaxation. Regardless, at some point the subject is usually shown that he can relax all the muscles of his body by focusing on one small group of muscles at a time. While thinking of specific muscles, suggestions are given that they will relax, they will become limp and heavy, hang loosely, allow the tension to flow out, and so on.* With practice, he learns to concentrate on his body and to bring about relaxation with self-suggestions. Many people appear to be able to accomplish rather complete relaxation in a relatively short time, or at least they learn to relax much more than they had before.

Teaching Relaxation and Deep Concentration

A technique that the senior author has found helpful in introducing his clients to the use of imagination and concentration will be described in detail.

The technique is presented to the client as one that will help him to reduce his general level of tension and also teach him to apply self-suggestions in the most effective way. You begin with a demonstration meant to show him that he can be successful in taking suggestions, giving them to himself, and bring about positive changes by doing so.

Emphasize that what he is about to learn can best be viewed as a skill, and as with other skills, he will become more adept at it with practice. Expectations of an

---

*Other methods of teaching relaxation are presented in Wolpe (1969, p. 100) and Lazarus (1971, p. 273). It is a good idea for the therapist to be familiar with several techniques because clients vary as to which suits them best.

instant cure or dramatic effects are nearly always played down. Stress that it is a matter of employing certain natural abilities which are normally not used by people in a systematic way; however, these abilities are available for use once they are recognized.

With the client sitting across from you, or beside you, begin by saying that you wish to explain the most effective way to take suggestions, whether he gives them to himself, or you give them to him. Say something like:

> There are several things I would like to explain about taking suggestions, or giving them to yourself, so that they will be most effective. To begin with, there are a couple of things you should try and avoid. The first is trying to work too hard at the task. It is an easy-feeling sort of task, not one requiring what we ordinarily think of as hard concentration, or hard work. If you take the attitude that you must work hard, you will find that thoughts about working, instead of the suggestions you wish to use, will become the dominant thoughts. A second common problem is that when suggestions begin to have their effects, especially when you are first learning, it may seem a bit unusual, or interesting. The tendency is to try and analyze what is going on—to figure it out—but when you do, the suggestions are broken-up, and their effects cease. If you will think of your mind as a river that flows along at a steady pace, allowing your thoughts to progress at the same pace, over and over again—easy, not forced, just flowing along at a nice easy pace—your suggestions will become the dominant thing of interest, and will have their greatest effects. The whole thing is really a rather easy, relaxed technique. If you should become distracted, that's alright, just go back to your thoughts, letting them flow through, over and over, so that they become the only thing of importance for that time. Don't worry about distractions. They are likely to occur, especially when you are first learning. Simply recognize that you have been distracted and redirect your attention back to the slow, easy flow of suggestion you were giving.

At this point you should answer any questions the client might have, essentially reiterating what you have already told him.

The next step is to introduce a suggestive task that almost everyone can respond to to some degree. Thus, the client is very likely to have a success experience with his first introduction to suggestions. The suggestion I use is called the Chevrul Pendulum. A thread, or light string, approximately the length of your elbow to your fingertips, with a moderately heavy bob of some sort attached, like a small key, is all the equipment needed. The client rests his elbow on the desk and holds the loose end of the thread between his thumb and forefinger with his wrist bent at approximately a right angle. The bob then hangs straight down and away from his arm, an inch or so above the surface of the desk. The suggestion itself is to have the client focus on the bob and think of it doing different things, like making circles, swinging back and forth in predetermined directions, and so on. The following is a verbatim demonstration of its administration:

> I want you to hold this little bob just the way I am. (Demonstrate the proper way to hold the thread.) That's it, just hold it so you can sit there comfortably and relax. Now I want you to take the attitude just for a moment or so that that little bob is the only thing of importance to you. That's it, just focus your gaze on it, and begin trying to discover all you can about it. (It is helpful if the bob has designs, colors, or other irregularities on it.) That's it, look at it carefully, trace all around its outline, notice any geometric shapes that may be on it, like circles—squares—perhaps you can even find rectangles if you look carefully. Just try to learn everything you can about that little bob, think of it as a new and different experience, something unique, something you would like to know everything about. Notice its colors—notice how even in the same color it seems to vary from place to place,

different shades of the same color, even where it seems like one—notice how the light plays upon it—notice how this varies from spot to spot, and how it changes—as you become more interested in the bob, you notice that in fact it becomes more the center of your attention. Your vision narrows, things in the side of your vision tend to grey out, to become less important. The bob in fact becomes the center of your attention—now watch it very closely, because in a moment it is going to begin doing something—it will begin moving back and forth, back and forth, back and forth.

At this point the bob may be naturally moving in one direction or another. It is helpful and encouraging to the subject to increase the natural movement that is occurring. Continue with the same suggestions, trying to time your suggestion to the tempo of the movement of the bob.

Back and forth, back and forth, more and more, farther each time, back and forth, back and forth, freer and freer, freer and freer, back and forth, back and forth, etc. (Once the movement is well established you are ready to change to a new movement.) Now the bob will change its direction—it's going to begin making a round, round circle. Round and round, round and round, round and round. There, it's beginning to go now, round and round—rounder and rounder, rounder and rounder. You can imagine a circle below it, and it's tracing right around that circle, rounder and rounder, rounder and rounder, etc.

Subjects vary a good deal as to their magnitude of response. However, even a very small response in the suggested direction can be quite a convincing experience. But at this point you have demonstrated to the client that he is able to take suggestions. It is time for him to find that he can give them to himself.*

"Now I want *you* to think of the bob going back and forth again." When he has changed the direction of the bob into a stable movement, ask him to think of a circle again. After he creates a circle, suggest that he think of the bob slowing down and coming to a stop. When it is almost stopped, take it from him and proceed in the following way.

"What was that like for you?" The usual response is one of amazement or surprise, indicating that it has been a new and unusual experience. If the client does not voluntarily say that it seemed like his thoughts were moving the bob, ask him directly if he had that impression. Most people feel that their thoughts were controlling the bob at least a little, although clients vary on the degree that they report being aware of their fingers moving. Go on to explain:

There is nothing really so unusual about this. You did not notice your fingers moving for two reasons. First, your attention was very much focused on the bob; therefore, you did not notice the small movements in your fingers. Had you focused on your fingers, you would have noticed the movements. This is a characteristic of being able to take suggestions well. Your attention becomes focused upon them, and other things are less likely to be noticed. Secondly, the small movements in

---

*Some subjects seem unable to respond to this task, but it is usually apparent that they are breaking their thought train, most often indicated by jerky movements of the bob. If this is happening, it is good to stop and ask him what he is doing, what he is thinking. You will usually find that he is committing one of the errors you have already cautioned him about. A brief discussion of the problem and returning to the task is often enough. When the difficulty is still not overcome, you can start the bob in the direction suggested, letting the client follow the swing with his thoughts in order to grasp the tempo. As his thoughts fall into the rhythm of the bob, suggestions for change of direction are usually effective, and he will have learned something about taking suggestions.

your fingers were exaggerated by the length of the string, such that the movement of the bob seems quite large compared to the very small muscle movement necessary to create it. The movement of the bob demonstrates how your thoughts can affect your muscles or other organs of your body. Your nervous system sends a message to the proper places in the body, in this case the muscles of your hand and fingers, and the appropriate actions result. At any rate, you have had a chance to see how you can take suggestions, and the effects they might have. You have also seen that you can give yourself suggestions with the same results. Now I would like you to move to that comfortable chair and we will continue teaching you how to relax completely, and to place yourself in a state where suggestions will have their maximum effect for you.

At this point the client moves to a comfortable chair that will support his entire body. A recliner, a couch, or other furniture that will completely support the client's body is most appropriate for this part of the training. Once he is seated explain that it is always important to practice relaxing in a position where all of his muscles are able to "let go." They should not have to support any part of his body so that all muscular tension can be released completely. Caution the person against crossing his legs, or resting his hands on his stomach, a normal practice for many people when they sit or lie down. Explain that the weight of one part of his body on another makes it necessary for the lower part to retain some muscular tension in order to support the one on top.

Once he is comfortably settled, begin by demonstrating a suggestion that is easy to follow, explaining that you start with an easy suggestion because responding to one suggestion tends to increase the responsiveness to further suggestions. I often refer back to the way he became more adept during the Chevrul Pendulum once he started following those suggestions.

A fast and easy suggestion to respond to is to ask the client to look at a spot between his eyes, at his hairline. This forces him to roll his eyes way up, creating strain. Begin by touching the spot with your finger, telling him to remember it. Then explain that he is to try and see that spot, to imagine an "X" near his hairline, and to focus on it. Before going on, be certain that he demonstrates by rolling his eyes up into the proper position. Explain that as he looks at the spot, the natural strain in his eyes becomes an easy thing to focus upon. By focusing on the strain, it will become greater than it ordinarily would, his eyes will become tired, his eyelids will become heavy, and his eyelids will soon close. Caution the client not to fight the suggestion. Tell him to let his eyes close as the suggestions have their effects and to await your instructions after his eyes have closed. Move back to your chair, ask the client to focus on the spot, and proceed as follows:

> I want you to look right at that spot, keep your attention right on the spot—notice the strain in your eyes, how it seems to grow and grow—straining more and more, the strain in your eyes becoming greater and greater, more and more strain, more and more strain, eyes becoming tireder and tireder, tireder and tireder. (If you notice that the client's eyes are beginning to blink slightly, suggestions of blinking can be included also.) Your eyes are blinking, becoming heavier and heavier—eyes tired, tired from straining, straining more and more, greater and greater strain—eyelids becoming heavier now, heavier and heavier, heavier and heavier, wanting to close, feeling heavier and heavier, etc.

Most people will close their eyes within a few minutes. If you notice that the client is looking away, or blinking excessively as if to reduce the strain, caution him that he should not fight the response—"let it occur, let the heaviness creep in, let your eyelids close slowly as the heaviness takes over." If the client is taking some time in responding, you may want to suggest that as you count his eyes will become heavier and more and more strained. Then you can simply begin counting, continuing to suggest strain and heaviness in between counts. As long as they continue to focus on the spot and create strain, you should be able to outlast even the most nonsuggestible clients by counting.*

As the client's eyes close, you continue

—fine, now leave your eyes closed and let your eyes roll forward. Feel the strain going out of your eyes, and as you feel the strain going out of your eyes, think of the strain going out of your *entire* body—your body just *letting go*, dropping into the chair, going limp, limp, heavy and relaxed. As your eyes close and roll forward, and you feel the strain going out of your eyes, that is a cue for the strain to begin going out of your entire body. Think of the strain as flowing right out of your body—from your eyes, throughout your body, right out of your toes. Your body loosening, dropping into the chair—relaxing.

Now I want you to think only of your right foot. Turn all your attention to your right foot. Think of nothing but your right foot—your right foot is the only thing that is important. As you turn your attention to your right foot, you become more aware of it than you were a moment ago. You notice any small changes in sensation—perhaps a slight tingling—or changes in temperature—you become more aware of your right foot than you were before. Notice the shoe on your foot, feel its pressure around your toes—on the ball of your foot—on your arch—on your heel—over the top. As you become very aware of your right foot, think of it going *limp, limp and loose.* Your right foot relaxing, letting go, dropping down, loosening, letting go, relaxing. Feel your toes spread slightly as the muscles let go, loosen and drop, letting all the weight of your foot onto the chair, the chair supporting your foot entirely—your foot becoming heavy, heavy and limp, limp and relaxed—more and more relaxed, loose, limp and relaxed. Your right foot just letting go, letting go completely—looser and looser, more and more relaxed. With each thought of relaxation, the muscles let go just a little bit more, just a little bit more. The tension flows out of the muscles as they loosen, loosen and let go. Now think of the muscles in your lower right leg loosening, dropping going limper and limper, more and more relaxed, more and more relaxed. The muscle on top letting down, dropping down right on through the calf muscle, letting go, hanging, hanging loosely and limply—relaxed.

The same sorts of suggestions are given for various muscle groups as you progress through the client's body. My usual order is as follows: right foot, lower right leg, upper muscles of the right leg, then the *entire* right leg and foot.

Now I want you to imagine your entire right leg and foot. Think of it as being separated off from the rest of your body—as if it is off by itself, completely relaxed, limp and loose, all the muscles hanging, letting go, loosening and letting go—your entire right leg and foot relaxing, more and more relaxed with each thought. The chair doing all the work, your leg and foot letting go, letting go.

The point of starting with smaller muscle units like the foot, lower leg and upper leg, and then incorporating the entire leg and foot, is to show the client the type of progress he can expect. That is, at the beginning, before he has much practice, he

---

*A few clients seem not to respond well to this suggestion. They constantly look away, they blink a good deal, and they tend to stop their eyes from closing naturally. I often stop the procedure with these people and tell them that responding to this suggestion is not really necessary for our purposes. Simply have them close their eyes and go on with the rest of the training.

will only focus on small muscle groups where he is more likely to be successful. As he becomes more adept at relaxing, he should be able to relax increasingly larger groups of muscles at the same time. The eventual goal is for him to sit down, close his eyes, and relax his entire body in a matter of seconds.

The order proceeds: left foot; lower left leg; upper left leg; *entire* left leg and left foot; *both* legs and both feet; right hand; right forearm; upper right arm; right shoulder; *entire* right shoulder, arm and hand; left hand; left forearm; upper left arm; left shoulder; *entire* left shoulder, arm and hand; area across both shoulders; *both* shoulders, arms, and hands; chest; breathing; stomach; hips; lower back; middle back; upper back; *entire* body from shoulders to the feet; neck; jaw; lips; nose; right cheek; left cheek; eyelids; eyebrows; forehead; *entire* face; scalp and ears; *entire* head and neck; *entire* body. It is quite helpful if the therapist also experiences these muscle loosenings. His own feelings act as a guide in saying the proper things, such as "dropping," and "letting go."

The neck and shoulder muscles are often sources of tension. The following sorts of suggestions seem to be helpful:

> Now think of the area right across your shoulders, right across your shoulders, from shoulder to shoulder, and letting those muscles drop, drop right down into the chair. Let your arms and hands just *hang* from your shoulders. Let your shoulders just *drop* into the chair—loose, looser, letting go, dropping down, relaxing—shoulders dropping and relaxing—now think of your chest. Think of your chest relaxing, dropping down, loosening, letting go. As you notice your chest, you notice that your body can breath by itself. Your body will simply take care of itself, and you can let all of your muscles relax. Imagine yourself standing off watching your body take care of itself, breathing by itself. As you let your muscles relax, letting all your muscles go, your body just takes care of itself. Think to yourself, "my body breathes itself, my body breathes itself," and you notice that your body will just take care of itself. Your muscles can loosen and relax, you can let go all the tension in your body, and your body simply takes care of itself.

The following suggestions are useful for the neck region.

> Now let your neck relax, loosen, let go. Let your head move slightly, slightly from side to side as you feel the muscles in your neck letting go and loosening. Let the chair do all the work in holding your head up. Let your head rest on the chair and let your neck muscles loosen and relax, loosen and relax, letting go completely, letting go completely.

The face is important also. You can suggest that the jaw is going slack, "slack and limp, loose, slack and relaxed." If the client is responding well, his mouth will open slightly. Many people are hesitant to be observed with their mouth open, and it may take some encouragement to have them let their jaw go, to let their lips part. It is helpful to suggest this specifically, even thinking of their tongue lying on the bottom of their mouth, loosening and relaxing.

Once you have progressed through the entire body, the next step is to help the client deepen his concentration on his thoughts. The basic technique is to have him imagine himself going downward, having everything "come in" around him so that his thoughts and your words become the center of importance. There are a number of ways to suggest deepening, like going down an elevator or a stairway, or floating on a cloud, and so on. Presenting a rather neutral suggestion, like "you are floating downward," may be best. Some clients are afraid of elevators, stairways, or other things; it is difficult to predict what things might be negative for a particular person. I usually suggest something like the following:

> Now that you have relaxed your entire body, part by part, I want you to imagine that you are standing off, as if watching yourself just sitting in the chair. With each breath your body loosens a little bit more, becomes more and more relaxed, and you begin to float downward—downward, deeper and deeper. With each breath you are moving down, down—deeper and deeper—more and more attention to your thoughts. Your body is taking care of itself. Your muscles are completely relaxed. All the tension is flowing out and you are able to attend more and more to your thoughts. Attending more and more to your thoughts, so that suggestions you give to yourself will have maximum effect. Down, deeper and deeper, deeper and deeper, more and more relaxed, more and more concentrated on your thoughts. With each breath your thoughts become more and more the center of your attention, where what you suggest for yourself will have its maximal effect.

After several minutes, suggest that the client will be able to practice and have no difficulty arousing himself whenever he wishes.

The session can be finished in the following way:

> Now you are deeply relaxed, paying complete attention to your thoughts and my voice, you will be able to do this for yourself with practice, and your thoughts will have maximum effect. In a moment I am going to count from 5 to 1. When I reach 1, I want you to open your eyes and to arouse yourself. With each count, however, I want you to suggest to yourself that by practicing this technique you will be able to overcome your difficulties more readily, more sensibly, and through your own control. I am now going to count from 5 to 1, with each count suggest to yourself that by practicing this technique you will gain control over your difficulties and resolve them more readily. Ready now, 5—4—3—2—1!

Most clients arouse themselves rather slowly. They will usually look at you, smile, stretch, and rub their faces, showing that they have been relaxed. Once in a while a person falls asleep. It is usually easy to tell during the procedure, but if you are not certain, and they have not opened their eyes, simply say in a louder voice, "Wake up!!" I have never had any great difficulty in arousing a person. Once your client is aroused, ask him what the experience was like. Ask if he had any difficulty at particular points, and if he has any questions. Discuss ways that should help him to overcome any difficulties he may have experienced. Reiterate the technique, including the purpose of starting with small groups of muscles and progressively moving to larger ones, until in a very short time he should be able to imagine his entire body relaxing and his concentration deepening. He should practice the technique twice a day if at all possible, and he should contact you if he runs into any problems.

Once a person has learned to relax and to focus on his thoughts, the groundwork has been set for the application of many special techniques. There is the initial benefit of relaxation itself, and the client is ready to participate in other insight or behavioral methods.

Relaxation on a Signal

Relaxation training in itself may prove beneficial for clients who suffer from chronic tension states and their associated psychophysiological disorders (migraine headaches, ulcers, asthma, and so on). Training may take the form described above, until the client is able to attain deep relaxation in a relatively short period of time. Or, training may take the form of a more direct hypnotic procedure.

One approach is to hypnotize the client with suggestions of deep relaxation, then give him a posthypnotic suggestion that when he awakens and the hypnotist says "relax," he will again experience relaxation. That is, the client is trained to become hypnotized on a signal, and the hypnotic state is defined as one of deep relaxation. After he shows that he will respond to the hypnotist's signal, it is suggested that *he* may say "relax," and go into the same deep state of relaxation. The final step is to suggest that all he need do is to think "relax," and relaxation will follow.

Whatever method is used, the final objective is for the subject to respond to his own mental signal. When he thinks "relax," his body will automatically begin to relax. A tense individual should derive a great deal of benefit from this approach. When he notices the first signs of tenseness, he can think "relax," and prevent its buildup. In the process he reduces the physiological responses associated with tension states, thereby reducing their irritating effects on his body. Early signs of an impending migraine headache, or the tensing of the bronchial tubes in the asthmatic, may serve as cues to begin relaxing. A busy executive with stomach problems, for example, can think "relax" during a hectic part of his schedule. The crippling, physiological side-effects of emotional arousal should therefore decrease.

The same procedure can be used to ease and facilitate childbirth. Relaxation is almost always an integral part of a natural birth program although other aspects of childbirth are usually incorporated as well. Suggestions that pain is completely normal, and that its occurrence during childbirth is not especially important, tend to reduce the client's negative experience of it. Training also usually includes teaching the movements associated with labor and what to expect during birth. By the time the client is ready to deliver, she will have developed the ability to relax, she will have learned when to expend energy "bearing down," and she should not be afraid of what is going to happen. She becomes a partner in the delivery, with practical skills and a positive attitude.

OTHER SUGGESTIVE TECHNIQUES

Autogenic Training

Shultz and Luthe (1959) developed a rather detailed method of therapy which makes major use of auto-suggestion. Their approach is to teach the client how to control his bodily and imaginal functions through auto-suggestion. The therapist maintains rather close control throughout training (which may take a considerable amount of time) and carefully watches the progress of the patient, helping him to overcome any difficulties that he may encounter.

Therapy starts with simple suggestions that one's left arm will relax. Gradually, more limbs and muscle groups are incorporated. When satisfactory control is gained over the muscles, suggestions for controlling various organ systems are added, like his body "breathes itself," "my body breathes itself," "my body breathes itself." As the client gains control over his musculature and internal functioning, he moves toward the production of suggested fantasy, such as controlling colors, sounds, and so forth. Once he learns the skills of concentrated fantasy, they may be used to focus on problems in living and resolution of psychological conflicts.

Yoga

Yoga refers to a system of beliefs. Its practice has the purpose of obtaining a "union" with the supreme reality, a universal self, or God. There are several systems of Yoga, but all have in common the purpose of achieving a final trance state to obtain the "union." The belief systems will not be detailed here although they are felt to be the most important part of training by those who practice Yoga.* Some of the exercises are included because many of them take advantage of auto-suggestions. One of the first steps in Yoga is autosuggestive relaxation training. However, physical positions and postures are emphasized as well. Various breathing exercises are also associated with self-suggestions.

Meditation is an important part of Yoga. Techniques quite similar to those used for the induction of hypnosis are employed for teaching meditation, with the exception that they are self-administered. Specific postural positions believed helpful in maximizing nervous system functioning are also recommended. The aim in meditation is to relax "the mind," and to facilitate a growth of "personal spirit," eventually leading to the mystical "union."

The following is an example of meditation instructions (Devi, 1963). The subject uses a candle as a fixation point.

> Now keep your eyes steady upon the flame and don't let them wander. Start breathing rhythmically. Next close your eyes, and try to retain the impression of the flame. You can visualize it clearly, hold the picture, but if the light eludes you, open your eyes for another look at the light. Close them again and see if you are able to envision the flame this time. Repeat this until you are able to capture *and hold* the impression.
>
> If you are still unsuccessful, try the same procedure again the following day, and continue trying until you have succeeded. Do not hurry or force anything—do not try too intensively. Not only will such an approach not expedite matters but it may even retard everything. Remember that it is most important to remain inwardly relaxed and motionless. (pp. 104–105.)†

The subject is instructed further to contemplate the light and to ponder upon its characteristics, like its shape, color and so on. The light is to be thought of as something of "goodness" and "divinity," and meditation upon those ideas should follow. Progression moves to imagining the light within one's self, contemplating its goodness which disburses "the darkness of ignorance, of loneliness, of fear, hatred, lust, jealousy, greed, anger, envy." The purpose is to reach an inner harmony, a peace with one's self, through the use of positive self-suggestions.

---

*See Eliade (1969) for a more comprehensive treatment of Yoga and its practice.

†From *Renew Your Life Through Yoga* by Indra Devi. Englewood Cliffs, N.J.: Prentice-Hall, 1963. © 1963 by Prentice-Hall, Inc. Reprinted by permission.

Exercises to relieve tension are also taught, and healthful, well-rounded diets are recommended. Some Yoga postures are meant to promote good health by stimulating the endocrine glands. The "Reverse Posture," for example, is said to have a rejuvenating effect on all of the body organs and a beautifying effect on the skin and general appearance. The subject's weight is supported on his neck, shoulders, and back of the upper arm with his hands supporting his buttocks and legs above him. "Such apparent magic is due to the influence of this exercise on the thyroid and especially the sex glands, whose secretions keep us looking young and feeling vital. While practicing this posture you should concentrate on becoming healthier, calmer, younger, and stronger" (Devi, 1963, p. 174). Again, the accompaniment of self-suggestions are apparent.

Psychocybernetics

Psychocybernetics (Maltz, 1960), one of the most popular "do-it-yourself" techniques currently, employs self-suggestion. Maltz's system is based on the importance of a person's "self-image," and its effects on attitudes, motives, and behavior. He believes that the self-image holds a position of primary importance in guiding and directing a person's life. The purpose of his method is to help people develop realistic, positive self-images.

The self-image is developed and changed, according to Maltz, through experiences. Experiences come from direct interaction with the environment, *or* through imagination, both being effective modifiers of how a person views himself. It is the effect of imaginative experiences that, in part, justify the use of self-suggestive techniques in his system. His rationale for how imaginative stimuli are effective is based on a cybernetic model. Like machines, the human subconscious can be thought of as a mechanism—"a goal-striving, 'servo-mechanism' consisting of the brain and nervous system, which is *used by*, and *directed* by mind" (p. 12). That is, consciousness (mind to him) operates an automatic mechanism (the old subconscious mind), that like electronic servo-mechanisms serves to furnish feedback information to solve a problem. A guided missile utilizing feedback impulses to stay on course would be an electronic analogy. The mechanism is neutral, however, and works to achieve whatever goal is set for it by consciousness. It will work for failure goals as well as success goals.

Maltz writes in a convincing way. He cites many case examples to clarify his notions, and supports his ideas with medical reports, scientific findings, and quotes from great men and the Bible. His personal conviction is also notable throughout the book. The expectancies and hopes of most readers should be enhanced by his style.

As the reader progresses through the book, he is exposed to a number of exercises and formulas for successful living. We will present some of these to show how self-suggestion is employed, and to demonstrate the general flavor of the approach.

The first exercise is to reread the second chapter at least three times per week, for the first 21 days. This chapter tells the reader how his brain works as an automatic servo-mechanism in finding answers, and how man has a success instinct that through creative imagination can become actual. The purpose is to "set you free of an old inadequate self-image . . . (p. 25)."

The next exercise is to use your imagination for 30 minutes each day, making the images as vivid and detailed as possible (imagining a motion picture screen may be helpful) because your imaginings are actually practice experiences that can affect your self-image, and as such, they will have more impact the closer they approach actual experiences. The task is for the person to imagine himself behaving successfully. A shy person, for example, imagines he is very outgoing and successful in a group situation. Another exercise teaches the person to relax by imagining "mental pictures," like concrete legs sinking into the bed, your body like a limp doll, or a setting that has been personally relaxing in the past. Learning to relax is then employed to create a relaxed feeling during daily activities. The reader is instructed to remember how relaxed he was while practicing. A relaxed attitude should become a habit in time, and conscious practice will become unnecessary.

Maltz offers constructive ideas about such things as happiness, success, failure, emotional hurts, inhibition, self-tranquilizing, crisis, and a winning feeling. For each, he points out positive activities and suggests that the person practice them in his daily living and in imagination.

In presenting the "success-type" personality, for example, he uses the word "SUCCESS" as a memory aide for its essential ingredients:

S-ense of direction
U-nderstanding
C-ourage
C-harity
E-steem
S-elf-confidence
S-elf-acceptance

Each concept is discussed in some detail and its importance to the self-image is pointed out. Often a specific technique is suggested. For example, to build self-confidence the person should deliberately picture himself in a past success experience and recall the feelings associated with it, especially when he is to begin a new task. The entire program is aimed at changing a person's beliefs that he is a helpless victim of his world, and to demonstrate that to a great extent he is capable of controlling and choosing his destiny.

OTHER CONSIDERATIONS

The Powers of Hypnosis?

Inevitably people ask, "Can hypnosis cure me of my smoking? of my obesity? of my bad habits? of my uncontrollable fantasies?, and so forth." The content of the question most often relates to some extraordinary power that has been attributed to hypnosis through the mass media. The performances of stage hypnotists encourage the public to believe hypnosis is a strange and powerful influencing technique—that people can be made to surpass their normal capacities or to change in ways that are so dramatic as to seem unbelievable. Newspaper reports of medical hypnosis emphasize the dramatic cases while at the same time ignoring less dramatic clinical results and experimental investigations. The historical origins of hypnosis as a magical, influencing power, plus the indiscriminate reporting of spectacular individual cases, has led a large percentage of the general public to regard hypnosis either as a cure-all or something to be feared and avoided. Obviously, if hypnosis were so effective in changing behavior as the scattered claims imply, every helping professional would be taught hypnotic techniques, and in a short time the prisons, the mental hospitals and the welfare agencies among others, would be freed of their clients through the dramatic changes invoked with hypnotic power. If a hypnotist could whisk away a craving for alcohol, the debilitating effects of psychosomatic illnesses, or the performance of anti-social behavior simply by suggesting it, personal adjustment would certainly be a simple matter. Nevertheless, professional hypnotists are constantly sought out because of the idea that they hold some magic power to relieve painlessly, quickly, and inexpensively all of the stubborn problems in living.

Before examining two areas of "power" that have been subjected to more careful investigation, it should be stated categorically that *hypnosis is not a cure-all*; *the hypnotist has no mysterious powers*, and *most of the dramatic reports can be accounted for by variables other than the induction of hypnosis*.

Anti-Social Behaviors

An often-asked question is, "Can a person be made to do something against his will while under the influence of a hypnotist?" There is no sense denying that unethical hypnotists at one time or another have induced their subjects into immoral actions, such as public exhibitionism, sexual intercourse, and theft. However, it is just as likely that other nonprofessionals and unethical helpers (friends, teachers, bartenders, drug pushers, and others) have taken advantage of persons in the same way. The difference lies in how one chooses to explain the behavior, whether it is attributed to some inner, mentalistic concept like the hypnotic trance, or to other, more understandable variables.

The stage hypnotist, for instance, has people perform amusing and sometimes ridiculous acts leading the audience to interpret his subjects' behavior on the basis of his hypnotic technique. There is no denying that it makes his act more appealing and entertaining, and it is indeed unlikely that the stage hypnotist would explain that it is just such beliefs about hypnosis that give the subject the excuse to perform. Most of them enjoy being on stage and having the attention of the audience anyway, or they would not have volunteered in the first place. Nor is he likely to explain that propriety norms place demands on his subjects to comply with his requests so as not to embarrass him. He does not tell the audience either that his selection of subjects (he usually selects two or three from 10 to 15 volunteers) for his performance is aimed at picking people who are showing their willingness to comply with his requests, and that they will most likely continue to do so as long as he recognizes the limits to which they will go. If he tells the audience what he is doing at all, it is very likely that he says he is selecting those who reach a "deep hypnotic state" with the implication that they are then essentially helpless to resist his commands. I do not mean to imply that stage hypnotists are simply out to dupe the audience; on the contrary, many have firm and deep beliefs that the hypnotic trance is the important aspect of their performance. But, strange and unusual powers come to be attributed to hypnosis simply because of the explanatory concepts used to account for the observations.

Two arguments are generally submitted to support the notion that subjects *will* commit acts against their will, or perform feats of strength and ability beyond their capacity, under hypnosis. The first is presented in some modified form of the following hypothesis: "If a subject is deeply enough hypnotized, he will perform acts against his will." Such a statement, without accompanying quantitative measures of "how deep" is necessary, is a statement that can never be proved nor disproved. If the subject performs an anti-social act, apparently against his will, then he must have been hypnotized enough. However, if he does not perform the act, the hypnotist simply states that he was not hypnotized enough. Such reasoning can only serve the purpose of supporting a belief—it can never be submitted to a crucial test.

The second hypothesis is stated as follows: "The hypnotized person will perform acts that are apparently against his will if he has an unconscious desire to do so." Again, such a statement is only useful to support a belief and can never be empirically validated. If the subject performs an act that seems to be against his will, then the hypnotist states that he had an unconscious desire to do so. On the other hand, if he refuses, it is claimed that he did not have an unconscious desire. By definition, it is impossible to measure an unconscious wish and therefore impossible to establish its presence.

Experimental Evidence

Orne (1962) reviewed the evidence relating to hypnosis and anti-social behavior. One group of studies approached the question on the assumption that suggestions to the effect that an act to be performed is criminal, when in fact it is not, are sufficient to state that the subject perceived it as criminal. The subject is given a rubber knife, for example, with the suggestion that it is a real knife, then told to stab one of the experimenters. If the subject performs the act, it is assumed that he did so in the belief that he would actually stab the person. In interpreting such studies, the obviously important variable is the assumption that the hypnotic suggestions actually established the belief that the act was criminal. A more parsimonious explanation for these studies could be that the subject perceived that he was expected to comply with the instructions, but knew very well he was not going to hurt the other person. When similar situations are made real, such as asking a girl to undress in public, they almost always refuse.

Another approach attempts to redefine an anti-social act as an acceptable one by inducing hallucinations and false beliefs, then to observe whether or not the subject performs the act. As one example, a subject in a military setting was made to attack his superior officer, a serious breach of military law, by suggesting that the officer was a Japanese soldier who would attack and kill him. It was necessary to restrain the subject to prevent him from harming his superior officer. Other experiments based on similar techniques have been carried out in college settings, and the findings appear to support the hypothesis that anti-social behavior is possible under hypnotic distortion. But all of these studies are subject to a telling criticism. The entire context of the experiment must be evaluated before drawing conclusions. In the first place, it is highly unlikely that the subject believes an ethical experimenter will allow him to harm somebody else or himself. The important part of the communication, as opposed to the claim of distortion is that the subject decides the experimenter does in fact want him to perform the behavior. Once he has determined the experimenter's desires, there is little reason for him to believe that actual harm will be allowed. Further, the suggestions of hallucinations and delusions may not be very important even though they sound convincing. Many of these studies have been repeated without using distortion producing suggestions and subjects will perform the same acts anyway. The important aspect, therefore, appears to be that the subject actually determines that the experimenter wants him to perform the act and *not* that his beliefs or perceptions of the act have been changed through hypnotic distortion.

In a recent study, we attempted to overcome many of the weaknesses in design recognized in earlier work (Coe, Kobyashi, and Howard, 1973). The anti-social request was to help a graduate student hypnotist sell heroin off-campus. While our results were not definitive, the important variable appeared to be whether or not the subject saw the act as against his personal values. Hypnosis apparently had no facilitating effect in and of itself.

Criminal Cases

The criminal literature on hypnosis and anti-social behavior are of two main types: sexual offenses committed against the subject by the hypnotist, and the commission of acts by the subject that led to the hypnotist's material benefit.

The individual cases will not be detailed except to note that the protesting individuals claimed that hypnosis was the reason they performed the acts. In regard to sexual advantage, especially in a psychotherapeutic setting, a number of other possible explanations may be offered. First, the sexual relationship may simply have been a fantasy relationship on the part of the patient and, in that sense, it is simply the subject's word against the therapist's. Secondly, it is probably more common than is widely known that therapists and patients become sexually involved in therapy, with or without the use of hypnosis. In the context of a doctor-patient, teacher-student or pastor-parishioner relationship, sexual contacts occur that are considered improper, but would be acceptable under different social circumstances. Consequently, it is impossible to evaluate the significance of hypnosis over and above the other emotional and interpersonal factors in operation.

In the cases where the person claimed that he was forced to do anti-social acts for the benefit of the hypnotist (there are only a few of these cases), the factor of a long-term relationship has also been involved. That is, in each of these cases the hypnotist and the subject have experienced a close relationship of long standing. The influence of the relationship could just as easily account for the subject's behavior as hypnosis. It is also questionable that the real facts in these cases have been established. They are often determined by hypnotizing the subject again (by a proper authority of course) and requesting him to recall what happened. It would be naive to believe that recall under hypnosis is not affected by unwitting confabulation or deliberate lies.

It would be inappropriate to say, in summary, that the question has been answered beyond any reasonable doubt. However, the more sophisticated the design in controlling variables like the personal relationship, the expectations that the request is part of an experiment, and the subject's moral stance toward the act, the less likely does it appear that hypnosis plays a crucial part in influencing the commission of anti-social acts.

Exceptional Ability

People often ask if a hypnotized subject can be induced to show superhuman capacities. A common demonstration of super strength is often performed by stage hypnotists. They suggest that a subject's body will become completely rigid and then suspend him between two chairs with his neck on one, and his heels on the other. By itself, the suspension seems impossible, but the hypnotist may test the audience's credibility further by standing on the subject's stomach (chest usually). The convincingness of this demonstration fades away when it is known that any man of robust physique can duplicate the same event without hypnotic suggestion, and most people can suspend themselves in this manner anyway for a short time, without undue discomfort.

Other behaviors seem to support the superhuman feats of hypnotic subjects, for example, suggested blindness, color blindness, deafness, and so on. These studies will not be detailed (by and large, they have not included adequate control groups) except to point out that Barber's experiments with highly motivated control subjects who are not hypnotized result in the same kinds of behaviors (Barber, 1969).

Increases in memory, learning, and physical endurance, and freedom from pain are other behaviors attributed to the power of hypnosis. When adequate controls are utilized these behaviors lose their startling effects. For instance, when testing an increase of physical endurance that was supposedly due to hypnotically suggested analgesia (no pain to the tiring muscles) it was found that by offering the subjects a sum of money to continue their performance that they were able to surpass the level obtained in the hypnotic condition. Studies in learning have been variable, although none shows very significant increases in ability because of hypnosis. In fact, in some studies, hypnosis has been shown to *reduce* the speed of learning.

Is Hypnosis Dangerous?

Another question is often asked, "Isn't hypnosis dangerous?" Probably the greatest danger involved with hypnosis is the subject's *belief* that it is dangerous, and/or similar beliefs held by the hypnotist. Certainly, in the hands of competent professionals, the use of hypnosis is much less dangerous than the administration of drugs or most other medical procedures. To the best of my knowledge, there are no reported cases where an "overdose" of hypnosis resulted in suicide or accidental death. On the other hand, untrained individuals who attempt to deal with emotional difficulties and problems of living, whether they employ hypnosis or not, may inadvertently create a good deal of unnecessary stress for the individual. If a person chooses to consult with a pseudo-professional (clairvoyant, metaphysicist, palmist, medium, fortune teller, card reader, hypnologist) there is always an element of risk in the relationship.

Because of the public and professional prejudices against hypnosis its greatest danger is probably *to the hypnotist*, not the subject! Even though there is no definitive evidence that hypnosis is harmful, it may be used as an explanation for unfortunate complications. Hollow arguments are often proffered by professionals against the use of hypnosis simply on the basis of their own misinformation, their naive beliefs, or their fears. For example, one anti-hypnosis psychiatrist made the claim that patients under hypnotic therapy commit suicide. But, the percentage of suicides is equally high, or higher in patients under the care of general psychiatrists or psychoanalysts. Such claims are as ridiculous as the statement that hospitals are dangerous because many people die there.

The untenable claims made for hypnosis spring largely from the belief in some special, inner state which makes the hypnotized person somehow different from other persons. His behavior must therefore be explained by special propositions, and, as a consequence, almost any act that would normally be explained on more rational grounds is attributed to some esoteric, inner agent.

Qualifications for Hypnotic Techniques and Training

As we have shown throughout the chapter, hypnosis may be employed by psychotherapists of varying persuasions as well as professionals from other areas (medicine and dentistry especially). In proper perspective, hypnosis or the induction of hypnosis is employed as an auxiliary procedure to other therapeutic goals. It is not a method of therapy in and of itself. The general qualifications for someone who uses hypnosis, therefore, should be the same qualifications required for whatever purposes it is to be employed—psychotherapy for example.

The use of hypnosis has been legitimized by medicine and psychology for only a little over ten years. The American Psychological Association has a separate division for persons interested in hypnosis, and the medical, dental, and psychological professions have board qualifications for users of hypnosis. Some states have enacted laws controlling its use, usually attempting to restrict its application to the professions of medicine, dentistry, and psychology. The prospective user of hypnosis should check his state regulations before employing it.

Assuming a person has the necessary professional training to practice whatever it is he wishes to combine hypnosis with, it remains for him to learn hypnotic techniques. Rosen, Kaufman, Lebensohn, and West (1962) have discussed views of training for hypnosis in medicine, and Moss, Logan, and Lynch (1962) have discussed the same topic for psychology. In general, there appears to be a conservative view toward who is qualified to employ hypnosis and what is considered proper training in hypnotic techniques. The problem seems to result from the misconceptions about the dangers of hypnosis. Nevertheless, as we have repeatedly pointed out before, expectations can lead to actions, and in the case of hypnosis the actions are often negative. Perhaps unfortunately, the induction of hypnosis is quite simple to learn. A tape recorded induction, for example, can produce results very similar to that of an experienced hypnotist. While there are many ways to induce hypnosis (Haley, 1967; Weitzenhoffer, 1957), all seem to be about equally effective, claims to the contrary notwithstanding. It is not difficult for otherwise untrained persons to induce deep hypnosis in susceptible persons, even though they do not know what to do after the person is hypnotized. Given the dramatic expectations that many people have about hypnosis (including hypnotists), it is not too surprising that things can get out of hand when an untrained person employs it.

Formal courses are difficult to find in universities although some are offered around the United States. Workshops and courses are sponsored several times a year by the two main hypnosis societies in the United States. Information may be obtained by writing the Society for Clinical and Experimental Hypnosis, 140 West End Ave., New York, New York, 10023, or the American Society of Clinical Hypnosis, 800 Washington Ave. S.E., Minneapolis, Minnesota, 55414. The workshops range from the beginner's level to specialized, advanced uses of hypnosis.

Coe (1964) has recommended a way to teach yourself hypnotic techniques for experimental purposes. It requires background reading, a qualified person on-call, and actual experience administering waking suggestions and a standard hypnotic scale. While its purpose is to qualify persons to carry out research, it would seem a reasonable way for clinicians to begin their early training.

The Effectiveness of Hypnotherapy

Evaluating the effectiveness of hypnosis is no less difficult than evaluating the effectiveness of any kind of psychotherapy. The same research problems are present. Among others, how is improvement defined and measured? What constitutes an adequate control group(s)? It is not our purpose to discuss this important issue here, but the interested reader may pursue the topic in detail in Bergin and Garfield (1971).

However, indications that hypnosis is effective in therapy have been reviewed by Barrios (1970). Using the results from published case studies, he points out that psychoanalysis results in a 38 percent recovery rate after an average of around 600 sessions, Wolpean behavior therapy a 72 percent recovery rate after an average of 22 sessions, and hypnotherapy a 93 percent recovery rate after an average of six sessions. We cannot, of course, simply accept these figures as valid comparisons among the three therapies, but they should at least alert us to the positive potential of including hypnotic techniques among our other therapeutic skills.

The specific techniques employed in the outcome reports were not what many professionals usually expect of hypnosis, that is, direct symptom removal or uncovering. "The current trend is to use hypnosis to remove the negative attitudes, fears, maladaptive behavior patterns, and negative self-images underlying the symptoms. Uncovering and direct symptom removal are still used to a certain extent, but usually in conjunction with this new main function" (Barrios, 1970, p. 4). Also, "light" hypnosis is probably sufficient in these reconditioning approaches. Therefore, there is little limitation on application because of the client's susceptibility.

Barrios notes that the range of clients who have benefited from hypnotherapy is quite large. Diagnostic categories included psychophysiological disorders, neurotic disorders, personality disorders, and some psychotic disorders.

In keeping with the concept of expectancy, Barrios views the hypnotic induction as an effective method for establishing confidence and belief in the therapist. In turn, a strong interpersonal relationship should develop where the therapist's words will be more effective in bringing about constructive change.

CONCLUSIONS AND SUMMARY

We have attempted to present two topics in this chapter. One was the enhancing effects that expectancies can create in psychotherapy, and the other was the therapeutic uses of suggestive techniques.

Expectancy is related to all forms of psychotherapy, not just the suggestive therapies, and should be taken into account by all therapists. While expectancy alone cannot account for therapeutic outcome, it probably plays a part in all techniques. The placebo effect with drugs is an example of a major expectancy effect. The application of operant conditioning principles in institutional settings is probably an example where it plays a comparatively minor role, and suggestive therapies most likely fall some place in between. Nevertheless, when a client comes to a professional he expects certain things. How these expectations are met and dealt with will have an impact on the outcome of their relationship. The more a therapist is aware of expectancy effects, the more likely he is to use them to his advantage.

Various uses of hypnosis and self-suggestion were presented in some detail. These techniques have been employed in many ways for many kinds of difficulties. "Depth" therapists have claimed that hypnosis speeds the progress of therapy when used as a tool for uncovering unconscious material and overcoming resistances. They may also employ it as a psychodiagnostic technique in discovering underlying, dynamic causes. Hypnosis is applied in behavior therapy to bring about relaxation and to enhance imagination ability. While the same theoretical backgrounds are not presented, many hypnotherapeutic techniques appear to be quite similar to those employed by behavior therapists.

Since its introduction by Mesmer in the 16th century, hypnosis has had its difficulties in being accepted by recognized healing professions. An aura of magic, mystery, and mysticism has surrounded it, even to the present, although it has now been formally recognized as a legitimate therapeutic tool. These magical expectations about hypnosis can be an advantage or a disadvantage. Clients may expect miracles on the one hand, or be very apprehensive on the other. In either case, such expectations can reduce therapeutic effectiveness. The person expecting miracles, while positive expectations may be enhanced, is nearly always disappointed if the therapist's magic does not work, and the fearful client cannot enter into therapy. Having been exposed to the same popularized misconceptions, many professionals are no more realistic about hypnosis than the layman.

Several approaches that take advantage of self-suggestions were discussed. In common, they all emphasize the client's use of his imaginal abilities and the power of his own thoughts. Autohypnosis, autogenic training, Yoga, and psychocybernetics served as examples of these techniques.

The chapter concluded with topics of interest related to hypnosis. Namely, the "powers" of hypnosis, training, and qualifications for employing hypnosis, and a look at its effectiveness as a psychotherapeutic agent. Evidence is available to suggest that hypnotic approaches may be quite effective, and therefore, they should be considered seriously as a part of every therapist's armamentarium.

REFERENCES

Barber, T. X. *Hypnosis: A scientific approach.* Princeton, N.J.: Nostrand, 1969.

Barrios, A. Hypnotherapy: A reappraisal. *Psychotherapy: Theory, Research and Practice*, 1970, **7**, 2–7.

Bergin, A. E. and Garfield, S. L. (Eds.), *Handbook of psychotherapy and behavior change.* New York: Wiley, 1971.

Cautela, J. Covert sensitization. *Psychological Reports*, 1967, **20**, 459–468.

Coe, W. C. A procedure for teaching one's self-hypnotic techniques for experimental purposes. *International Journal of Clinical and Experimental Hypnosis*, 1964, **13**, 144–148.

Coe, W. C., Kobyashi, K., and Howard, M. L. Experimental and ethical problems in evaluating the influence of hypnosis in antisocial conduct. *Journal of Abnormal Psychology*, 1973, **82**, 476–482.

Conn, J. H. Hypnosynthesis: Psychobiologic principles in the practice of dynamic psychotherapy utilizing hypnotic procedures. *International Journal of Clinical and Experimental Hypnosis*, 1968, **16**, 1–25.

Devi, I. *Renew your life through Yoga.* New York: Prentice-Hall, 1963, (Also Paperback Library, New York, 1969.).

Eliade, M. *Yoga: Immortality and freedom.* Princeton, N.J.: Princeton University Press, 1969.

Erickson, M. H. The confusion technique in hypnosis. *American Journal of Clinical Hypnosis*, 1964, **6**, 183–207.

Fish, J. M. *Placebo therapy.* San Francisco: Jossey-Bass, 1973.

Frank, J. D. *Persuasion and healing.* Baltimore, Md.: Johns Hopkins Press, 1961, 1972.

Gill, M. M. and Brenman, M. *Hypnosis and related states: Psychoanalytic studies in regression.* New York: International Universities Press, 1959.

Gordon, J. E. *Handbook of clinical and experimental hypnosis.* New York: Macmillan, 1967.

Haley, J. (Ed.), *Advanced techniques of hypnosis and therapy: Selected papers of Milton H. Erickson, M.D.* New York: Grune and Stratton, 1967.

Hilgard, E. R. *Hypnotic susceptibility.* New York: Harcourt, Brace, and World, 1965.

Lazarus, A. A. *Behavior therapy and beyond.* New York: McGraw-Hill, 1971.

Lerner, B. and Fiske, D. W. Client attributes and the eye of the beholder. *Journal of Consulting and Clinical Psychology,* 1973, **40**, 272–277.

Levitt, E. E., and Hershman, S. The clinical practice of hypnosis in the United States: A preliminary survey. *International Journal of Clinical and Experimental Hypnosis,* 1963, **11**, 55–65.

Maltz, M. *Psychocybernetics.* Englewood Cliffs, N.J.: Prentice-Hall, 1960. No. Hollywood, Calif.: Wilshire, 1970.

McReynolds, W. T., Barnes, A. R., Brooks, S., and Rehagen, N. J. The role of attention-placebo influences in the efficacy of systematic desensitization. *Journal of Consulting and Clinical Psychology,* 1973, **41**, 86–92.

Moss, C. S. *Hypnosis in perspective.* New York: Macmillan, 1965.

Moss, C. S., Logan, J. C., and Lynch, D. Present status of psychological research and training in hypnosis: A developing professional problem. *American Psychologist,* 1962, **17**, 542–549.

Orne, M. T. The nature of hypnosis: Artifact and essence. *Journal of Abnormal and Social Psychology,* 1959, **58**, 277–299.

Orne, M. T. Antisocial behavior and hypnosis: Problems of control and validation in empirical studies. In G. H. Estabrooks (Ed.), *Hypnosis: Current problems.* New York: Harper and Row, 1962.

Rosen, H. *Hypnotherapy in clinical psychiatry.* New York: Julian Press, 1953.

Rosen, H., Kaufman, M. R., Lebensohn, Z., and West, L. J. Training in medical hypnosis. *Journal of American Medical Association,* 1962, **180**, 693–698.

Sarbin, T. R. and Coe, W. C. *Hypnosis: A social psychological analysis of influence communication.* New York: Holt, Rinehart and Winston, 1972.

Shultz, J. H. and Luthe, W. *Autogenic training.* New York: Grune and Stratton, 1959.

Torrey, E. F. *The mind game: Witchdoctors and psychiatrists.* New York: Emerson Hall, 1972.

Weitzenhoffer, A. M. *General techniques of hypnotism.* New York: Grune and Stratton, 1957.

Weitzenhoffer, A. M. Behavior therapy techniques and hypnotherapeutic methods. *American Journal of Clinical Hypnosis,* 1972, **15**, 71–82.

Weitzenhoffer, A. M. and Hilgard, E. R. *Stanford Hypnotic Susceptibility Scale, Forms A and B.* Palo Alto, Calif.: Consulting Psychologist's Press, 1959.

Weitzenhoffer, A. M. and Hilgard, E. R. *Stanford Hypnotic Susceptibility Sacle, Form C.* Palo Alto, Calif.: Consulting Psychologist's Press, 1962.

Wolberg, L. R. *Medical hypnosis, Volume I and II.* New York: Grune and Stratton, 1948.

Wolpe, J. *The practice of behavior therapy.* New York: Pergamon Press, 1969.

CHAPTER 13

Group Methods

Morton A. Lieberman

INTRODUCTION

In today's urban (and even not so urban) America, almost any bulletin board contains testimony that groups are "in" as a medium of choice for changing people. It has been estimated that upward of five million Americans have at one time or another participated in some type of group activity aimed at personal growth or change in *encounter groups*. A few million others are members of *self-help groups*; tens of thousands have been patients in some form of *group psychotherapy*. What sorts of groups, what sorts of members, what sorts of problems, and what sorts of people assume the function of helping others to change? These four questions require somewhat lengthy answers to convey some sense of the current scene, because the range of applications, methods, participants, and agents of change has increased geometrically over the last two decades.

Who Comes to Groups and Why Do They Come?

The most reasonable answer is, nearly every kind of person with almost every conceivable psychological or social complaint. The goals of group clients vary all the way from reducing juvenile delinquency in others to reducing weight in themselves. Some among the clientele of current-day healing groups bring problems once taken almost exclusively to mental health professionals—severe personal or interpersonal concerns. Others face no immediate serious stress, but seek the group in hope that it will provide them with clues to personal enrichment—that participation in a shared effort at growth will help them actualize unused but available personal potential. Another sizable part of the clientele are those who see themselves as limited not by general aspects of their own personalities or personal situations, but by specific problems that impinge on them because of their relationship to a social order which they feel suppresses them because of sex, sexual mores, race, age, and so on. Finally, groups can be found which contain members who claim no motive for belonging other than to widen their experience, to share, to enjoy, or to learn to enjoy communion with others.

When one turns to the question of *what sorts of groups* make up the current scene, the divergence seen is equal to that of the type of clients and their goals. The litany of labels—Gestalt, Transactional Analysis, Confrontation Therapy, Marathon, Encounter, Sensory Awareness, T-Groups, self-help groups, consciousness-raising groups, all in addition to the more traditional forms of group psychotherapy—does not aid in clarifying what sorts of things are thought by each school to be the essential ingredients of change or cure. Some group leaders on the current scene believe passionately in the healing qualities of group-generated love; others believe just as passionately in the curative powers of hate, seeing the basic stuff of change as stemming from the experience of primary rage. Some depend solely on talk therapy; others use music, lights, and the clench of human bodies. And many groups have no appointed or formal leaders.

Can the Current Use of Groups Be Described by Who It Is Who Leads Them?

Can the sense of confusion be reduced by organizing the array of forms and techniques according to the background, education, or professional discipline of those who purvey group people-changing services? No, for those who have made themselves available to lead such groups may have been prepared by long years of training in prestigious professional institutions, by participation in two-week institutes, or purely by personal commitment. Nor would a sense of order stem from examining the location of such activities. Many personal change-oriented groups are to be found in traditional help-giving institutions, such as mental hospitals, schools, or social agencies; some take place in the offices of mental health practitioners in private practice. Many are found in growth centers, a new institution specifically formed for conducting such groups. Church basements, dormitories, and living rooms have also become the scene of people-changing groups.

The diversity of goals, clientele, form of activity, leadership, and setting of people-changing activities in groups may suggest why attempts to evaluate the consequences or effects of all these activities have yielded equal diversity. These effects range from ably-documented findings suggesting major behavioral attitudinal and personality changes—the reconstruction of individuals—to equally well-documented examples of the severe debilitation of individuals growing out of their participation in change-oriented groups.

This chapter aims to apprise the reader, both descriptively and analytically, of the current use of groups in all their diversity, and to establish some reasonable signposts which may help to organize the vast array of activities now characteristic of healing groups. What are the historical as well as current forces that have shaped the practices so abundant in our society? Why do therapists, leaders, or organizations place people in groups for healing purposes? What theories underlie group-based healing? What assumptions underlie each of these theories with respect to who are appropriate clients; what definitions of illness or pathology are implicit or explicit in various theoretical perspectives; what events do diverse theoretical perspectives imply as necessary for growth, development, or positive change? What is seen as the role or task of the leader or therapist? And finally, how do these divergent theories assess the role of the group in the curative process? The last half of this chapter will focus on a general theory of group-based healing which starts with an examination of the *unique properties of the group* for helping people in psychological distress as the base from which to discuss answers to questions of what the leader or central person must do in order to accomplish the task or goal of the group. Particular emphasis is placed on how to read or diagnose groups in order to make appropriate, helpful interventions. Finally, the critical events that must transpire in order for people to use the group as a meaningful personal learning environment are examined.

Why Use Groups?

The use of groups for systematically helping individuals in distress is of relatively recent origin in modern mental health practice. It is perhaps helpful to recall, however, that small groups have always served as important healing agents; from the beginning of recorded history, group forces have been used to inspire hope, increase morale, offer strong emotional support, induce serenity and confidence, or counteract many psychic and bodily ills. Religious healers have always relied heavily on group forces, but when healing passed from the priestly to the medical profession, the deliberate use of group forces fell into a decline concomitant with the increasing sanctity of the doctor-patient relationship.

The strangeness experienced by many seekers of psychiatric help when confronted with the help-giving conditions of groups is the resultant of a complex process affecting both those who seek the help as well as those who give it. The development of psychiatry as an entrenched part of modern medicine was, in part, predicated on the idea that "scientific medicine" must at all costs distinguish itself from healing which stemmed from nonscientific traditions. Modern Western psychiatry was even more plagued than other branches of medicine with the need to become "scientific." In its beginnings, the medical treatment of psychological problems required, for its legitimization as a branch of medical science, a clear differentiation between its methods and those that preceded it in folk societies, where highly developed group-based techniques were used for curing psychological illness within the framework of the family, the group of similar sufferers, the village, or the religious community. This association of "pre-scientific" therapies with group forms perhaps influenced psychiatry away from utilization of group techniques.

Until the recent advent of the *new group therapies*, it has been expected in Western culture that personal help be given by *one* person—it may be the corner bartender, a personal friend, or a professional, such as lawyer, doctor, or clergyman, but what is important is that it is expected that the context in which it is rendered will be private, intimate, and exclusive. Even in such congregate bodies as the family or the church, it is generally assumed that personal help will be offered and received in a private, two-person relationship, not through the congregate as a whole. The genesis of modern psychiatry within the general Western cultural context in the first half of the twentieth century did not, in other words, contain conditions suitable for the flourishing growth of group-based healing technologies.

In the early 1900's, Joseph Pratt, a Boston internist, organized classes for tubercular patients—"The class meeting is a pleasant social hour for members . . . made up as a membership of widely different races and different sexes, they have a common bond in a common disease. A fine spirit of camaraderie has developed. They never discuss their symptoms and are almost invariably in good spirits . . . ." (1907). Pratt's therapy had many similarities to current-day inspirational group psychotherapy; he hoped to overcome the pessimism of the patients, to discourage neurotic secondary gains from illness, and to encourage self-confidence.

Isolated individuals in the early 1900's reported similar sets of experiences to those of Pratt. In Europe, for example, Alfred Adler established guidance centers that used group concepts in treating working-class patients. An early and important influence in the development of group psychotherapy was the use of the healing group by Jacob L. Moreno, who is best known for his development of psychodrama (1953). The analogies between Moreno's approach to the healing groups and those described in anthropological literature is impressive. The patient is provided the opportunity to express himself freely through drama, trying the role of himself or others he feels are significantly related to his present problems. The patient often enacts scenes from his past, while other persons (whom Moreno called alter egos) articulate feelings, moods, responses, and so on which may not be evident to the patient himself (a kind of Greek chorus orchestrated by the therapist). In England, the work of Trigant L. Burrow was an important, but unfortunately unrecognized, influence in the area of the use of groups. Burrow, a psychoanalyst, became dissatisfied with the emphasis psychoanalysis placed on the individual, an emphasis that he felt excluded examination of social forces. In the early twenties, Burrow initiated the use of the group context for the analysis of behavioral disorders in relationship to social forces and coined the term "group analysis" to describe the treatment setting (1927).

Thus, the techniques characteristic of current group treatment practices were clearly evident in the first quarter of the century. The inspirational character of Pratt's groups has many modern counterparts in the self-help movement, such as Alcoholics Anonymous, Recovery Inc., and Weight Watchers. The employment of the expressive part of the person through dramatization as part of the curative process forms a major component of many current group methodologies. Finally, the use of the group social context for psychoanalytically-oriented analysis is still very visible as a major direction in current practice. By and large, however, the efforts of the early proponents of group methods were isolated; their predominantly pragmatic concerns did not lead them or others to explore the conceptual grounds underlying the use of groups for therapeutic benefit.

By the time the reader has reached this chapter and has noted that out of all the preceding chapters only one discusses the use of groups for change (therapeutics), it would seem to be reasonable to question, why place clients in groups? It should perhaps be noted that at different times and in different cultures the forces might be just the opposite, and it would seem "abnormal" or unusual to have one healer and one patient. The examples of healing cults in folk societies amply express that in many societies the ordinary or the usual way of healing may be within a social or multi-person context. It does seem sensible to ask, nevertheless, how it is that patients began to be placed in groups for treatment in this culture. Although there is no single answer to this question, there are several important factors which have helped to accelerate the use of groups for healing purposes.

The current use of group psychotherapy did not develop in full force until the 1940's. Although, as the history of the forces impinging upon group therapy indicates, there were clear-cut signs of a movement to the use of groups for healing functions prior to that time, these were small and isolated attempts without much reverberation within psychiatric circles. Foremost on the list of reasons are the simple pragmatics or economics of the situation. In time of short supply of psychiatric personnel, such as during World War II, and increased need for service, the "reasonableness" of treating patients in groups came to fore. This "discovery" has been made over and over again in various segments of the healing professions—the spread of group forms was much influenced by the social pragmatics of picking professionals to treat larger numbers of people, and, to some extent, shaped by the economics of fee structures—forces that cannot be ignored in explaining the development and spread of groups for healing functions.

A second major impact directing the professional to the use of groups developed out of the changing nature of theory with regard to both the nature of man and the genesis of his psychological ills. An increasing emphasis on an interpersonal view of man and the suggestion that psychological disturbance might be intrinsically related to problems of relationships among people—a social rather than intra-psychic phenomenon—made the jump from a dyad (a two-person interaction) to multi-person treatment situations an easy transition.

The practice of the healing professions is littered in its history with examples of serendipity—the chance discovery that groups seem to be potent constructive forces in the healing of psychological illness. This is a theme that cannot be omitted when examining the question of why therapists do place patients in groups. Psychotherapists are a restless lot, and the practice of healing is never stabilized. Inner doubt, feelings of failure, discouragement, and frank therapeutic despair are the common lot of the mental health professional. The search after new techniques, modalities, or procedures is unending, a theme that may explain in part the current popularity of group practice.

Finally, the personal needs and gratification of the healer, a topic fraught with apprehension, concern, and frequent avoidance, also is present as one of the factors that move therapists to place patients in groups rather than dyads. The excitement, stimulation, the need for novelty, are a few of the "reasons" that have directed therapists toward the use of groups. For many practitioners, the sanctity and the privacy and the ability to concentrate totally on one other human being, and the opportunity that such an intimate relationship offers for exchange, is a prime attraction of the individual psychotherapeutic relationship. There are others, however, who need different arenas, for whom an audience, a chance to observe rather than hear about behavior, an opportunity to wield a different form of influence, are more attractive.

An Illustration of the New and Not So New

Before proceeding to examine the various systems of people-changing that occur in groups, it may be useful to have some image of group psychotherapy both as it has commonly been practiced within traditional mental health settings and in some of the "newer therapies." The initial session of a traditional therapy group, for example, would be something like this:

About nine people file into a room slowly, tentatively. Each has seen only one other person in the room: the therapist, a week earlier in a diagnostic interview. Some appear reluctant, some enthusiastic, but all have come to this first meeting with at least the willingness to go along with the therapist's belief that the group could be useful to them. They sit in a circle, quiet and expectant. Their posture seems anxious. What will go on here? What can go on here? What will the therapist do? Several in the group have had previous psychotherapy. One woman begins the interaction by describing the disappointments she has experienced in previous treatments. A note of desperation and near panic is discernible in the responses of others to her wail of self-negation and helplessness. Sympathetic offerings of similar tales of woe are heard from various people in the room. From time to time the therapist comments, pointing out the fearful expectations of the various group members.

Underneath the "stories" and histories offered by various members, the therapist "hears" the patients asking each other a set of questions only hinted at in what they are saying. And underneath the questions about others in the room lie still another set all having to do with the person himself. Why did you come? What are your hopes? What forms does your "illness" take? Do you feel that this may do me any good at all? Are you as sick as I? Am I as sick as you? How strange, perhaps even insane, is the arrangement whereby I come to a group of neurotics to get better. Above all what is the "doctor" over there planning to do for me? I don't like people—why must I be here? Who are these others and what have I to do with them?

Thus, group therapy begins. The patients begin an experience in treatment which they may understandably feel violates expectations they bring from their experience in other doctor-patient relationships. Often group therapy patients cannot see what good it will do an unhappy neurotic person to share his "problems" with other neurotic sufferers. Is it enough to reassure him, as some therapists indeed believe, that "a problem shared is a problem helped," or to provide a context founded on the assumption that misery not only loves but is relieved by company? What of the therapist? Will he, by virtue of some rare professional training and intuitive attributes, be able to understand, diagnose, and change the troublesome personality problems of a lifetime? And, at that, of a roomful of people simultaneously? He—the therapist—obviously expects something useful to come from the interactions of these people, but how does he see the members to be of use to each other when he remains silent and passive so long? What does he expect will happen?

At the other end of the group treatment continuum, we can imagine another group of people temporarily migrating to a growth center. Their arrival is noisier, more buoyant, more playful; they are in vacation garb, their talk is more free and more reminiscent of the first evening of summer camp than the still, anxious scene of the group therapy session. They are likely to have a speaking knowledge of Maslow, Rogers, Berne, and Perls, and of the latest people-changing procedures. They express their desire for change freely and seem eager to get to know one another. They seem hardly able to await the morning's beginning; if some appear a bit anxious, others are enthusiastic about the drama that will unfold. All know in general what they can expect to happen but seem restless to generate the specific emotions and events which will form the content of their shared experience.

What will the leader, whom they have never met, be like? What will he do or expect of them? In the back of their minds are the accumulation of images based on what they have heard from friends and the popular press—images which are mixed with desires to become changed people. Will it work for me? What about the others? Will they really get to know me? Can I trust them? Will they help me?

They do not have long to wait: the leader begins with an explosion of his inner feelings. He may be sleepy this morning, he may not have wanted to come, he may look around and find the group full of "unattractive people" and "tell it like it is" without pausing. On the other hand, he may express his total positive regard for all and quickly exhibit a readiness to accept any behavior expressed. He may then launch into a set of instructions, perhaps suggesting, "all of you look so 'up tight' that we ought to loosen up and begin by playing a childhood game."

The images evoked by these two settings are intended to suggest that the group-based people-changing business in our society today has diverse assumptions, allegiances, and expectations, to an extent that it might appear sheer folly to consider them under the same rubric.

COMPARISONS AMONG CURRENT-DAY HEALING GROUPS

A scanning of the field of group-based activities whose central task is the psychological and behavioral alteration of individuals and the relief of human misery would suggest that the range of such activities might be grouped under four major types which are distinguished from one another mainly by whom they see as appropriate clientele and what they regard as the major function(s) of the group. At one end of the continuum would be those activities that formally fall within the purview of societally sanctioned, professionally-led groups—*group psychotherapy*. Group therapy explicitly employs a *medical* model. Its avowed public goal is "cure," or the production of mental health, and sees as its relevant population those who define themselves as seeking release from psychological misery. The group members are generally called "patients," who are thought by the therapist (and probably themselves) to be psychologically "ill" and to exhibit "sick" behavior. An important implication of this emphasis is that some individuals would be considered as appropriate candidates for the method and others (the "psychologically healthy") would not.

At the opposite end of the professional continuum are a variety of *self-help movements*—Alcoholics Anonymous, Synanon, Recovery Inc., and so forth, up to perhaps as many as 216 separate organizations. By intention these groups are not professionally led. As lay movements, however, they share with group psychotherapy some restrictive notions of appropriate clientele. The definition of appropriate clientele is usually much narrower than in group psychotherapy, but there are clear-cut inclusion-exclusion principles. One must be an alcoholic, an abuser of drugs, a child abuser, a parent of a child who has a particular disease, and so forth. The range for any particular self-help movement's attention is limited to individuals who have a common symptom, problem, or life predicament.

A third set of healing groups occur under the rubric of the *Human Potential Movement,* including such variously labeled activities as sensitivity training, encounter groups, and so on. Although there are many instances where such groups are led by non-professionals, they usually do involve professionals, whether legitimized by traditional psychological and psychiatric training or by newer short-term training institutions. A major distinction between the previously-mentioned activities and encounter or growth groups is that the latter view themselves as having universal applicability. Unlike group therapy which implies psychological illness and patient status, or self-help programs which are directed at a common problem of members, the encounter movement considers its activities relevant to all who want to grow, change, and develop.

Finally, we come to *consciousness-raising groups,* which share with the self-help groups the insistence on non-professional orientation and peer control, but unlike the self-help groups have broad criteria for inclusion. Although they do not take in everyone, as does the Human Potential Movement, consciousness-raising groups are formed on the basis of such certain *general* demographic similarities as sex, race, ethnicity, age, or sexual behavior. The tie that binds is not a common psychological syndrome but a general social characteristic of a large sub-group of people; the membership criteria, in other words, permit wide latitude regarding personal particularities.

STRUCTURAL AND TECHNICAL DIFFERENCES AMONG GROUPS

Perhaps the most important technological change reflected in the newer forms of healing groups as compared to more traditional psychotherapeutic groups is reflected in techniques for *lessening the psychological distance* between the leader and the participants. A variety of methods serve this function: the transparency of the therapist (he reveals his own personality), the use of informal setting, the trend of leaders to assume the stance of participant, the diminution of the importance of expertise of the leader, his presentation of self more nearly as a peer and, finally, the use of physical contact—touching—are all innovations which seem calculated to reduce the psychological distance between the changer and the changing.

Few guides exist to assess the importance of such a change from the traditional patient-therapist relationship. Perhaps all that can be said for sure is that such changes reflect current changes in social mores, which have increasingly moved away from emphasis on the priestly status of healing professionals and other experts. The new forms, having developed more recently, could be said to be more sensitive than the old to current cultural expectations.

A second major distinction between therapy and encounter groups, on the one hand, and most self-help and consciousness-raising groups, on the other, relates to their conception of the function of the group as a mechanism for personal change. Both psychotherapy and encounter groups of almost all theoretical persuasions share, as a fundamental assumption, a view of the group as a *social microcosm*, a small complete social world, reflecting in miniature all of the dimensions of real social environments. It is this aspect of the group—that is, its reflection of the interpersonal issues that confront individuals in the larger society—that is most highly prized as the group property which induces individual change. Varying types of encounter and psychotherapeutic schools of thought of course differ over which transactions are most important—those between patient and therapist or those *among* patients. They also differ regarding which emotional states are most conducive to positive change. But underneath all the activities that fall into these two types lies the assumption that cure or change is based on the exploration and reworking of relationships in groups.

Self-help groups and consciousness-raising groups develop a rather different stance to the issue of the group as a social microcosm. The interaction among members as a vehicle for change appears to be somewhat de-emphasized. The group is a supportive environment for developing new behavior not primarily within the group, but outside. The group becomes a vehicle for cognitive restructuring, but analysis of the transactions among members is not the basic tool of change.

Another characteristic that contrasts these four systems is the degree to which they stress *differentiation* versus non-differentiation among their members. "Being neurotic," having psychological difficulty, or being a patient, are vague and relatively unbound identifications, compared to being a member of a racial minority group or a woman in a consciousness-raising group. Being interested in growth and development is obviously a more vague, indistinct basis for forming an identity with a communal effort than being an alcoholic or a child abuser. It is easier for consciousness-raising groups and self-help groups to stress identity with a common core problem than it is in psychotherapy and other groups. Although it is typical for a psychotherapeutic group to go through a period of time in which similarities are stressed, this is usually an early developmental phase and represents an attempt of the group to achieve some form of cohesiveness. It is not the *raison d'etre* of the group, as it may be for a consciousness-raising or self-help group. In fact, there is some evidence that encounter group participants who remain committed to a sense of similarity are less likely to experience positive change. The potency of both self-help groups and consciousness-raising groups, on the other hand, appears to stem from their continued insistence on the possession of a common problem; their members believe themselves to derive support from their identification with a common core issue.

An obvious distinction among the various systems of group-based healing rests in their *attribution system*—the interpretive theories explicitly and implicitly communicated regarding the source of human misery and how one resolves it; for example, the degree to which the systems emphasize internal versus external sources of the problem. Psychoanalytically-oriented psychotherapeutic groups attribute the source of psychological difficulty to the personal past. Women's consciousness-raising groups emphasize an external locus of the problem: an impersonal, sexist society. In our attempt to understand what processes may be psychotherapeutic, I believe we have paid too little attention to the effect of varying attribution systems on change. In comparing several theories of personal change employed in encounter groups (Gestalt, Transactional Analysis, Rogerian, and so forth) it was found that it made little difference which theory was "taught," as long as some cognitive structure was taken away from the group to explain one's problems and how to resolve them. Whether this observation would fit the larger differences in attribution systems one can assume between, for example, psychotherapeutic groups and women's consciousness-raising groups, is a major unknown.

APPROACHES TO HEALING

The student interested in learning how to lead healing groups faces a far more complex task than he would have less than ten years ago. Theories, techniques, client systems, and goals have expanded to an extent which enormously complicates the process of learning how to conduct such groups. Which theory to choose, how to sort among techniques, how to apply appropriate methods to particular clients, may appear to the beginner to require the wisdom of Solomon.

It would be foolhardy to assume that the reader has arrived at this chapter *tabula rasa* regarding theories of changing people. It is more likely that most readers have been exposed to ideas about personal change that represent some amalgam of behaviorism, humanistic psychology, and probably also dynamic theories of personality and therapeutic technique. It may, therefore, be useful to review briefly ideas stemming from these three orientations and examine their influence on group-based healing activities. In so doing, it is crucial to recognize that nearly every theory or set of ideas about changing people in groups has been derived from theoretical systems related to dyadic models of therapy.

Behavioral Models

Behavioral models, perhaps best expressed in social learning theory terms, advance various mechanisms as essential for change induction—arousal enhancement and reduction, modeling, cognitive restructuring, and so forth. The specific mechanisms and their operations are delineated in several chapters of this book, so that the reader need not be treated to yet another review of behavioral approaches. Behavioral approaches, however well they may serve in dyadic contexts, involve some serious theoretical as well as technical problems when they are applied to groups. By choosing to place several individuals into a group setting for change induction, we construct a social system that has a number of important properties that do not characterize dyads. These unique properties of the group fundamentally alter the relationship between the central person (leader, therapist) and members in ways which mere technical adaptations on his part will not overcome.

Those who have attempted to use a behavioral orientation in groups assume implicitly that the leader is in precise control of the situation—that he has the power to change, to desensitize, to model, and so forth, all the behavior that is desired. This implicit assumption limits the utility of behavioral approaches in the group context. Power and influence are considerably more diffused in a multi-person relationship than they are in a dyad. The sources of power and the ability to wield it become complex issues where more than two are gathered together. The nature of the reward-punishment system in groups may differ from dyads in some important aspects: for example, the ultimate punishment in a dyad is withdrawal of love; in a group, it is exclusion, a punishment more under the control of the group than of the leader. Thus, the precision that so attracts people-changers to be-havioral therapies is probably considerably reduced in a group context, where influence is a function of how the social system takes place. Another example is the dilemma inherent in behavioral theories in talking about the role of the others in the group. Statements like, "The members will reinforce, will model, will vicariously learn," are commonplace in this approach. It is as if the theoreticians assume that the group members will do just the right thing at the right time so that they will be facilitative, and that producing these responses in the collectivity is open to strategies in accordance with social learning theory.

Most social psychologists would agree that which behaviors become reinforced in groups can perhaps be best explained in terms of group norms—those shared but unexpressed agreements among members about what is appropriate and inapprop-riate behavior. Again, there is an implicit assumption among behavioral technicians that group norms will be harmonious with the intention of the central person. Recent studies, however, indicate that group norms are not necessarily or primarily a function of leader behavior or leader desires. Thus, approaching change induction in groups with a behavioral orientation presents some tricky theoretical and technical issues which tend, as yet, not to be addressed in the behavioral literature. As with most other theories of change derived from examination of dyadic experience, the failure of behavioral approaches to take account of the most salient feature of groups, namely that they represent a complex social system not only with unique properties for change, but also with unique problems, reduces the power of change strategies that have demonstrated success in the dyadic context.

Humanistic Approaches

There are a number of ideas and ways of looking at people-changing that have their roots in the humanistic-existential perspective. As in both the dynamic and behavioral perspectives, there are differences among various positions which can be broadly classified under this rubric. They all, however, share a common view of the nature of man, the source of his plight, and what is required for him to grow or change. The elements of this perspective are what most distinguish the humanistic orientation from behavioral as well as dynamic views. Emphasis is placed on the human being as a developing person and the goal is actualization of latent potential. The most widely known humanistic system is that developed by Carl Rogers (1970), originally for group therapy and later applied to encounter groups. The core set of ideas in Rogers' thinking relate to how the therapist or leader can be a facilitative human being. Rogerians regard three general conditions as crucial in a relationship between facilitator (therapist-leader) and client(s): the acceptance (unconditional positive regard) of the client or the group; the empathetic understanding of another human being; and genuineness as a way of communicating to others, which necessitates trusting one's own feelings. These three conditions have been amply portrayed in an impressive series of research studies begun in the fifties by Rogers and his students. Truax and his colleagues (1967) have reasonably established that these three basic conditions of relationship between therapists and clients in dyadic relationship are facilitative and lead to positive outcome. Of interest here is that few new concepts have been developed within the humanistic framework to take account of the social forces introduced when change induction takes place in the group. It is apparently assumed that the leader, facilitator, or therapist can establish these three conditions with each individual in the group and copy the situation he institutes in a dyad. Yet, what is of importance here is that Truax and Carkhuff indicate that in their own studies the same three therapist-induced conditions which were shown to be robust in their positive influence in individual therapy were nowhere near as powerful in the group situation. Among practitioners stemming from the Rogerian perspective, the group is used for support, for a sense of communion, and for a source of feedback. The theoretical system, however, contains no means of analyzing group forces or of relating therapist interventions to the dynamics of the group as a social system. The approach of such leaders to the group is reminiscent in many ways of the great man view of history. Implicit in the emphasis on the establishment of basic trust and acceptance and empathy is the assumption that the leader will be able to be facilitative to the group by the force of his own person and, perhaps, set an example as well as directly aid people in changing.

Although it uses the group quite differently, the Gestalt approach also embraces a fundamentally positive view of the nature of man and his psychosocial needs. As compared to Rogerian-oriented leaders, Gestalt leaders are much more active, make far more use of techniques of confrontation, and generally involve their members in many more structured exercises or games. Nevertheless, in much the same way as Rogerian practitioners, they make minimal use of group forces beyond communion and support. Thus, these approaches clearly differ in their techniques and in their assumptions about conditions which induce change; they share, however, the underlying perspective that human problems arise more from the social experience of man than from negative inner forces. They also are alike in their tendency to make limited use of the whole group as a source of change-induction.

Dynamic Approaches to Person-Changing

As with the behavioral and humanistic-existential approaches, there are many theoretical and technological contributions that can be broadly classified as fundamentally dynamic orientations. Their historical roots are psychoanalytic, so that what most distinguishes this set of approaches from those already discussed is their view that the source of human misery is intrapsychic—inner conflicts which an individual has carried over a lifetime. Therapy involves the cognitive mastery, both generically and currently, of these conflicts. Two major processes are involved in therapeutics, the interpretation of resistance and the analysis of transference. Resistance is viewed as stemming from the fundamental ambivalence of the person and is felt necessary to defend against discovering aspects of himself that he fears will be painful. Ambivalence is also expressed in that change is desired yet also resisted. Transference in a classical sense, of course, refers to the set of feelings about current people that have their roots in significant early relationships. These core ideas have been translated into group therapy *in toto*, so that the classic set of operations of dynamically-oriented group therapists are the interpretation of resistance and the analysis of transference. They view the group as a major source of stimulation of the lifelong conflicts and issues confronting the members. From this perspective, the fundamental contribution of the group to the treatment process is that it permits the patient to better understand and observe the nature of his neurotic operations. The content of transference is handled by viewing the group as a place where multiple transference distortions can take place, although by and large the focus is still on the person of the therapist. In practice, groups conducted within a psychoanalytic framework appear to take on the special coloration of the tradition; for example, in such groups it is common to observe the interpretive role traditionally played by the analyst in the dyad being taken over by members of the group.

Other dynamic theorists have made much more considerable use of the group. Because Alfred Adler and his students conceived of man's main problems as fundamentally social, Adlerian group psychotherapists attribute greater potency to the group, not only because it reveals or highlights members' conflicts and maladjustments but also because it offers corrective influences. The *social* nature of psychopathology, the conception that psychological illness is a product of interaction with others, also underlay the work of Harry Stack Sullivan (1953). Sullivan saw most of therapy as having to do with acquainting the patient with the various processes and techniques which are his maneuvers for minimizing or avoiding anxiety responses derived from early social interactions. The group as social microcosm, then, offers for the Sullivanian group therapist the basic stuff of analysis, the important interactional components.

It is important to recognize that these three general orientations to person change—behavioral, humanistic-existential, and dynamic—all have been derived from theory and experience generated in dyadic therapeutic relationships. By and large, as these orientations have been increasingly adopted for use in group therapeutic contexts, there has been extensive innovation in techniques for applying them. There has been virtually no examination, however, of whether crucial differences between group and dyadic change contexts may not make theoretical reexamination and development a requisite for effective selection of techniques.

THE UNIQUE POWERS OF THE GROUP*

What then are the special properties of groups, as opposed to dyads, which are not to be overlooked when groups are used as the medium for personal change? Five capacities of groups are particularly important in their influence on the therapeutic experience of the client: (1) the capacity of the group to develop *cohesiveness* or sense of belonging; (2) the capacity of the group to *control*(reward and punish) behavior; (3) the capacity to define *reality* for the individual; (4) the capacity to induce and release powerful feelings (*emotional contagion*); and (5) the capacity to provide a contrast for *social comparison* and *feedback*. What are the implications of these properties for the induction of productive, psychotherapeutic experiences in the group context?

The Capacity of Groups to Develop Cohesiveness

This capacity reflects the phenomenal experience of communion or belonging-ness which is most often operationally defined as the attractiveness of the group to its participants. Roughly, cohesiveness plays the same role in group therapy as the positive "transference" relationship between the doctor and patient in dyadic therapy. In recent years, there has been a marshalling of evidence on studies of individual psychotherapy that point to the importance of the transference relation-ship between the therapist and patient. Researchers such as Truax and Carkhuff (1967) have presented findings which support the thesis that qualities of this relationship, such as high levels of accurate empathy, non-possessive warmth and genuineness, or patients who are liked or consider themselves liked by the therap-ist, are more likely to improve in psychotherapy. The group context does not as readily offer the opportunity to establish such relationships between each member and a single leader. The group property of cohesiveness, however, plays the same role, for it is this sense of belongingness that motivates the members to stay in the group and to work with it, and that eases the pain associated with therapeutic exploration. Cohesive groups are those which offer a member almost unconditional acceptance no matter what his history and behavior have been outside of the group. They offer support for risk-taking; they provide the psychological "glue" that permits the members to reveal themselves; as a social microcosm they provide a setting for public esteem and consequently for one's own esteem.

---

*The section on the unique powers of the group is a summary of material presented in a paper: Lieberman, M. A., Lakin, M., and Whitaker, D. S. The group as a unique context for therapy. *Psychotherapy: Theory, research and practice.* Vol. 5, No. 1. Winter, 1968.

The Capacity of the Group to Control Behavior

Closely associated with and dependent on the level of cohesiveness is the group's capacity to control behavior and to provide a system of rewards and punishments. As microcosms of a larger society, groups develop their own cultures and depend on special rules and standards which they establish as they extend their lives. How much one talks, what one talks about, what one doesn't talk about, even "the way" one talks about certain things, are aspects of how members behave over which the group wields influence. Such control over individual behavior is a central property of a group, including a therapy or growth group. The group member is almost inevitably confronted with pressure from others to change his behaviors or his views. The need to be in step, to abide by the rules, is a powerful factor inducing conformity in the group. Disregard for the rules means the potentiality of punishment. The ultimate punishment available to the group is the power of exclusion—either psychological or physical. In dyadic therapy, the patient does not fear exclusion if he does not go along with the therapist, but loss of the therapist's respect or love. Note then that we are dealing with two very different psychological experiences leading to similar behavior—conformity. A strong force additionally pulling members toward conformity is the group's most prized reward—its *power to offer the authenticating affirmation of one's peers.* The experience of "consensual validation" (approval by members who have become important) appears to be the most salient and gratifying experience in group therapy, more powerful than the affirmation of the therapist. The power of groups to exact conformity also frequently induces fear in people, and there is much evidence not only that groups have a very real capacity to induce conformity, but also that members fear punishment for departure from the group's "rules." It is important to note, however, that the norms that are developed which determine what characteristics of behavior are open to group influence, are never generated by a single person in the group, but are shared agreements. It is the person's belief that he has some power to influence the development of norms and standards in a group that reduces, to some extent, the fears and other negative feelings stemming from the capacity of groups to induce conformity.

The Capacity of the Group to Define Reality for Its Members

In dyadic psychotherapy, one of the major roles of the therapist is to contribute meaning to the patient's behavior—to provide *labels* for his thoughts, his feelings and fantasies, and his transactions with others, both current and past. Most schools of verbal psychotherapy view *understanding* by the client as a prime effect to be sought through psychotherapy; developing understanding (insight) is of course not simply a matter of the therapist labeling or lending meaning, which produces this sought-after state, but a goal to which a variety of therapist interventions are directed.

An important group property is the influence the group exerts on how each person should view himself, the group as a whole, and others in the group; thus in a group situation it is not only the leader who has a salient role in providing insight and understanding, or attributing meaning; the social system, the collection of participants, also adds to that meaning collectively. The group's capacity to define reality is dramatically illustrated by an incident in a group therapy course given by the author in which psychiatric residents observed two classmates working as therapists with an ongoing group. The observers watched from a darkened observation room and discussed the proceedings afterward with the two therapists. Before the eighth session began, the window blinds were removed for cleaning, so that the patients could see the observers through the one-way mirror. The two student therapists felt that since all the patients knew they were being observed there was no need to call off the observation. As the patients arrived one by one, each looked particularly closely at the large observation mirror and then took his seat. The meeting began with members talking about how difficult it is to communicate with people, "particularly when you couldn't see them—in telephone conversations, etc." They referred to the observers (which they had not done in previous sessions) with statements like, "It's uncomfortable. I don't like being observed because it's one-sided. The observers can see the patients but the patients cannot see the observers." The meeting went on in this vein for about a half hour and then shifted to other topics. After the session, when the two therapists joined the other residents to discuss the session, the observers asked the therapists why they had not intervened and brought some sense of "reality" to the group by pointing out that the observers could be seen for the first time. They answered that the light had shifted and the observers couldn't really be seen. Their belief was so strong that several of us had to accompany them into the therapy room to demonstrate that obviously the group could see the observers—perhaps not every facial gesture, but clearly their outlines at least.

This illustrates an instance of a group's capacity to define its own, special reality. The two therapists, who had entered the session knowing the observers could be seen, and the patients, who collectively upheld as "reality" the illusion that the observers could not be seen, had *consensually* redefined reality to meet their own needs.

The Capacity to Induce and Reduce Powerful Feelings

Historically, emotional contagion was the first phenomenon to interest investigators of groups. LeBon (1960) and Freud (1940) pointed out that powerful, primitive affects can be released in groups. Individuals may get carried away, experience feelings which they later believe are uncharacteristic of themselves and act on feelings without displaying their typical controls. This potential of groups can have either positive or negative effects on therapy. An individual may experience previously frightening feelings, with a new acceptance rather than his old sense of terror; he experiences, in other words, the corrective emotional experience of finding that the feelings are not overwhelming or that the feared consequences do not occur. Negative affect may occur when an individual is overwhelmed by affect and must defend himself against a group by literal or psychological withdrawal, or by the invocation of undesirable psychological defenses. The potential to stimulate emotionality, although, again, not peculiar to therapeutic groups, is an important quality of groups which bears directly on the sorts of personal learning or changes which take place in group people-changing contexts.

The Capacity of the Group to Provide a Context for Social Comparison

This fifth characteristic of groups is also an important influence in the therapeutic contexts. Group therapy patients frequently compare their attitudes toward their parents, husbands, wives, children; their feelings about things that are happening in the group; what makes them sad, happy, guilty, and angry; the ways that each typically deals with and expresses anger, affection, and so on. Such comparisons occur naturally and facilitate revision of the patient's identity by suggesting to him new possibilities for feeling, perceiving, and behaving. The availability in a group to examine a number of perspectives because different individuals present new vantage points is an important property inherent in the group situation. It occurs perhaps most powerfully in the therapeutic context because we have placed individuals in a social system which expects, often demands, that they talk about their behavior. Social comparisons occur as a natural outgrowth of these demands.

These group properties create conditions that engage the group member in a number of activities and concerns which differ from those of the patient in dyadic treatment. In comparison with the latter, the group member gets little practice in reflecting about himself and his interactions with others, in associating about his own feelings, in analyzing dreams, in linking present and past experiences, or penetrating covert meanings; he is too busy actively interacting and finding a viable place for himself in the group. He gets greater practice, however, than the patient in dyadic treatment, in expressing his feelings to peers, in noting the consequences of such expressions, in attempting to understand and empathize with others, in hearing from others about his impact on them, and in comparing himself with others.

Do these differing balances in experience lead to differences in outcome? It is commonly assumed that the group member should end up getting help of much the same order as he would have obtained in a dyadic relationship. It is perhaps helpful to test this assumption against, first, the end-state of the person at the close of the change process (symptoms, conflicts, defenses, interpersonal patterns, and the like); and second, the meta-learning achieved (learning how to approach problems, how to confront and resolve conflicts, and how to cope with anxiety).

Three aspects of the individual's end-state are relevant: (1) the symptoms or presenting complaint; (2) the revision of maladaptive patterns, the relinquishment of neurotic defenses, or the resolution of neurotic conflict; and (3) the unsought, positive side-effects. Symptom relief, for example, may be achieved at different rates. The "placebo" effect, (see Chapter 12 for detailed discussion), critical in many instances of rapid symptom relief, seems to us unique to the dyad. Particular behavior changes or conflict resolutions may be accomplished better by one or the other of the two settings depending on the nature of the problem, the composition (if a group), and so on. For example, a therapy group whose composition encouraged a patient to maintain an established neurotic pattern might be less effective than individual therapy. On the other hand, a group which led a patient to experience positively a previously-feared emotion through emotional contagion, might be more effective than individual therapy.

Finally, the two treatment contexts may be conducive to different secondary benefits. For example, difficulty in giving to others may be only peripherally related to the person's presenting complaint or core conflicts but, nevertheless, an issue. Since giving to others is often a focal concern in a group, many opportunities appear for each member to note the nature of his anxieties about giving and to try out new forms of giving behavior. Thus, changes in "giving" behavior may occur sooner, or more directly, than in individual therapy.

The two contexts may also call attention to different aspects of humanness. In group contexts, members are likely to be struck by the common needs for basic kinship, for sharing with others, of persons who on the surface appear quite different. They may be impressed both by the difficulties in communicating meaningfully to others, and by the profound rewards experienced when such communication proves possible. The dyad, in contrast, does not directly facilitate such experiences.

The differences for meta-learning may be even greater than the differences in end-state outcomes. In any form of treatment the person often adopts a style of approaching problems which reflects the emphases of the treatment orientation to which he has been exposed. It is not unusual for a patient to emerge from psychoanalysis with an increased tendency to pay attention to his dreams, to deduce emotional meaning from forgetting, to search out unrecognized feelings when he notes inconsistencies in his behavior. A person who has undergone group treatment may be more likely to seek out feedback from others, to make social comparisons, to test out behavior interpersonally. An appreciation of the intensive positive and negative forces inherent in the face-to-face social microcosm that is the group treatment context is perhaps the single most helpful guide in developing a realistic picture of both the problems and potentials inherent in using groups for personal change.

Although some theorists such as Bion (1961) and Ezriel (1950) have in fact initiated their explorations of group therapeutic processes on the premise that groups have unique properties, most examples of this orientation predate recent developments in the group people-changing enterprise. They are based solely on observations of traditional settings, and have not as yet been extended to account for the changed conceptions of clients and functions which the new forms represent. These social systems-oriented theorists have attempted to take both group properties and individual dynamics into account in developing a unified theory of group therapy. Of interest is the role that the therapist is seen to play under such conditions. The English school has used the word "conductor" to explain the function of the therapist in the group; perhaps a more descriptive, if less human, concept which has also been applied is that the group therapist or leader acts as a social engineer whose most important function is to help the social system (the group) to develop norms and other systems properties which will permit effective psychotherapy to take place. Perhaps a useful way of describing systems-oriented conceptions of group psychotherapy is to distinguish between what have been called therapeutic conditions and therapeutic mechanisms. The former implies the *context* for change or learning—in a dyad it is the characteristics of the relationship, in the group it is the characteristics of the social system. In both situations the role of the therapist is considered to be to enhance the positive aspects of the condition so that change can occur. This is not the same as saying that the therapeutic relationship is in itself therapeutic. It *is* to say that certain events that facilitate growth must happen to the person in treatment. It is these events that we have labeled therapeutic mechanisms.

LEADERSHIP FUNCTIONS IN THE GROUP SETTING

It is but a small step from a consideration of the unique properties of groups that are relevant to therapeutics to the issue of how therapists or leaders must behave in such a context to maximize the group potentials for participants in the group. Essential to the process of effective therapeutics is the ability of the therapist to gauge the feeling-states and progress of his client. Effective group therapy can take place only in a setting in which the leader or therapist has access to sufficient feedback about the state of his clients to diagnose their needs and adjust his behavior accordingly. The group therapist in essence has two clients—the social system he has helped to create that forms the context for therapeutics or change, as well as each individual in that system. Without feedback, it is impossible for a therapist or leader to diagnose individual and group needs to an extent where he can be helpful. One needs to know when to intervene, in what way, what needs to be done, when the group is working well and when it is not, when it is being useful and when it is not.

A moment's reflection will probably suffice to indicate that such a requirement places considerable demand on the central person. What does he listen to in order to "read" the group, and derive relevant feedback to gauge his interventions? Does he rely on his feelings—if he is bored, then perhaps everyone in the group is bored, and he must do something about it. If he is angry, perhaps all are angry. Such a course is obviously fraught with danger, for one of man's unfortunate traits is his great capacity for projection, a capacity that seems to be magnified when facing a group. It is difficult to disentangle one's own feelings from those of the others around him, and more often than not, trusting one's own feelings in a group situation may simply mean ascribing one's feelings to a collectivity that does not share them. On the other hand, the therapist may be able to distinguish between what it is he feels and what the others feel, yet decide that the most relevant source of feedback is the level of enthusiasm, aliveness, or vibrancy that the group is expressing. The assumption here is that when people are expressing or experiencing intense positive feelings, the group is on target; conversely, when these feelings are at low ebb, the group is in trouble and needs new inputs. Level of enthusiasm as expressed by group members, however, is a poor gauge of how well the group is serving its participants in their quest for change. Group members may be highly enthusiastic about their experience; yet the group may be a poor learning environment, inducing very little positive change.

Another cue the therapist might wish to attend to is the participant's indications that he is doing okay—that he is perceived by them as competent, helpful, and so forth. Again, unfortunately, members' perceptions of competence, expertise, and so forth, have not proven to be useful to gauge how helpful the group actually turns out to be. Leaders can, for example, substantially increase members' impressions of their expertise or competence simply by involving them in a large number of structured exercises or games. These activities prove to be interesting to participants, but not to be highly useful learning experiences.

What diagnostic tools, then, can therapists or group leaders use to "read" the group and determine when and how to intervene? Descriptions follow of two approaches which take account of the social forces that have powerful effects in group-based people-changing contexts. Each of them looks at somewhat different aspects of the group social system and derives from somewhat different theoretical perspectives. The first (Focal Conflict Model) offers a diagnostic tool to help translate the conversations, themes, and so on that make up the activities of the group into an orderly explanation of the real, but far more covert, concerns of the groups. The second concept is an approach to understanding what particular groups consider important, as indicated by agreements shared among participants regarding appropriate and inappropriate behavior, thoughts, and feelings in the group. Group norms are the rules or guidelines which may be observed to operate in any social system but which participants are often unaware of until someone expresses them. These two conceptual frameworks are not presented as exhaustive, for there are many perspectives for systematically examining social systems. These two have been chosen because of their importance in relation to groups designed to achieve personal change. There are other well-researched models that describe problem solving, role-assumption, and other characteristics of groups that may be more useful for diagnosing work groups than therapeutic groups.

A FOCAL CONFLICT MODEL*

In any therapy group in which the therapist does not control the content or the procedure, a session is likely to take the following form. As the patients gather, there is a period of unofficial talk—perhaps about some event from the preceding session, perhaps about an experience that someone has had since the last meeting, or perhaps about some neutral outside happening. Several conversations may go on at once, with the patients talking in pairs or threes; one or two may be silent. The conversation may be general. The atmosphere might suggest depression, tension,

---

*Material on the focal conflict model is abridged from Whitaker, D. S. and Lieberman, M. A. *Psychotherapy through the group process.* New York: Aldine-Atherton, 1964, Chapter 1.

distance, or casual friendliness. Then at some signal—perhaps the closing of a door, the arrival of the therapist, or simply the clock indicating that the starting time has arrived—the session "begins."

After a pause or a longer silence, an initial comment is made. It may reflect some personal concern, some reaction to the previous session, or some reference to the current situation. The speaker may direct his comment to the therapist, to another patient, or to the entire group. The initial comment is followed by another which may or may not appear related to the first. If it seems related, it may be a response to the topic just introduced, or it may be stimulated by the emotion of the original statement and have little to do with the content. It may be a response to some relationship established earlier in the group's history. Comment follows comment, and a conversation develops. There is some coherence to this conversation, so that the group can be described as talking "about" something. Occasionally the conversation may become disjointed. There may be abrupt shifts in logic, lapses into silence, and illogical elements. The mood may shift, and the rhythm and pace of the discussion may vary. Some patients may talk a great deal, others very little. From time to time, the therapist may enter the discussion, directing his remarks to one person or to the group in general. He may comment about the mood of the group, the character of the interaction, or a problem of a patient.

Some comments get "lost" in the group, as if no one hears them; others are built upon and form the predominant topics and themes. The patients may express such emotions as anger, delight, suspicion, nervousness, or superiority. Some feelings and attitudes are expressed in words; others come through in non-verbal behavior. Certain patterns may emerge in terms of who dominates, who is silent, who talks to whom, and who expresses what feelings. After about an hour of complex interaction, the therapist will signal that the time is up, and the group will disperse. It will meet a few days later for another session.

What has happened? We assume that the diversity observed during a group-therapy session is apparent rather than real and that the many different elements of the session "hang together" in relation to some underlying issue. For example, the first session of an inpatient group was marked by long tense silences, brief staccato periods in which the patients compared notes about physical ills but seemed careful to avoid references to psychological worries, and an animated period in which the patients discussed the architecture of the hospital and wondered whether it was well designed and built on solid ground. On the surface these elements are diverse and unrelated, but they gain a certain coherence if one assumes that they all refer to some shared underlying uneasiness about having been placed in a group, and a shared concern about the competence and strength of the therapist. As another example, a group of patients which had been meeting for some time were told that the sessions were to be interrupted for the therapist's vacation. They warmly wished him a good time, ignored him for the rest of the session, and turned to an older member for information about college admission procedures and policies about "dumping" students after the end of the first year. Again, these elements gain coherence if one assumes that they all refer to shared underlying feelings about the impending separation from the therapist.

In this view, the observable elements of the session constitute the manifest material. These elements include not only content, but also non-verbal behaviors, mood, pace, sequence, and participation pattern. Thus, an animated period in which everyone joins the discussion is an element of the session, as is a period of desultory conversation or a period of sober but ritualistic "work" on one patient's problems. A seating pattern in which the chairs on either side of the therapist are left vacant is an element of the session, as is a seating pattern in which male and female patients take chairs on opposite sides of the room. Non-verbal behaviors—looking only at the floor when speaking, directing oneself exclusively to the therapist, or directly engaging one another—are also important elements.

We assume that a subsurface level exists in all groups, but is hardest to detect in groups in which the manifest content is itself relatively coherent and internally consistent. When a group is talking about something, one might assume that this is all that is happening. In the brief illustrations just presented, one group was talking about architecture, and the other about college policies. Yet, even when the group situation consists of a conversation which is coherent in itself, we assume that another level of meaning also exists, for, even in such a group, breaks and shifts occur in the topic under discussion. There are reversals and non-verbal accompaniments, suggesting that to assume that only a conversation is going on is to miss an important aspect of the situation. In therapy groups, covert levels are most apparent in groups of sicker patients, where there is less capacity to maintain coherence on an overt, public level. However, even in non-therapeutic groups, one can observe the same phenomenon.

The covert meaning of the manifest material is not likely to be within the patients' awareness. From the patients' point of view, the conversation *is* about architecture or college admission policies. But an observer is in a position to grasp the underlying issue. Once he "sees" the core issue, aspects of the session which might on the surface appear diverse, contradictory, or meaningless, gain coherence and meaning.

This view assumes that the successive manifest elements of the session are linked associatively, and that they refer to feelings experienced in the here-and-now situation. Whatever is said in the group is seen as being elicited not only by the strictly internal concerns of the individual, but by the interpersonal situation in which he finds himself. Of all the personal issues, worries, impulses, and concerns which a patient *might* express during a group session, what he actually expresses is elicited by the character of the situation. Moreover, a comment is likely to include a number of elements and is responded to selectively by others. An individual may make a comment which includes a half-dozen elements. As the others listen to an individual's highly personal contribution, they will respond to certain aspects and ignore others. The aspects which are picked up and built upon are in some way relevant to the other patients and gradually become an emerging shared concern. As this suggests, the group-relevant aspect of an individual's comment is defined by the manner in which the other patients react to it. To cite an example, in an inpatient group a patient told a story about a man who had been misunderstood when he used the word "intimate." It was known that this was a personal concern of this patient, who was always apologizing for his sexual thoughts. However, the comments by other patients elaborated on the "misunderstood" aspect of his comment and ignored the "intimate" aspect. We therefore assume that being misunderstood was the shared concern and that the issue of intimacy was not a common concern.

We assume that the content of the session, no matter how seemingly remote, refers to here-and-now relationships and feelings in the group. The patients who worry about the competence of the architect and the strength of the building are really worrying about the competence and strength of the therapist. The patients who complain about college administrators who "dump" their students after the first year are really expressing resentment toward the therapist. The same is true for elements of the session other than the manifest content. Non-verbal behavior, such as a seating arrangement in which male and female patients sit on opposite sides of the room, might reflect concern about heterosexual contact in the group. A participation pattern in which one patient is allowed to dominate might mean that the others are using him to protect themselves from having to participate.

We view the covert, shared aspects of the group in terms of forces and counterforces, particularly those involving the shared impulses, wishes, hopes, and fears of the patients. For example, in a session presented in detail later, there emerged scattered clues that many of the patients in the group wished to be unique and to have special close relationships with the therapists. At the same time, there was awareness that the other patients would not permit this and then, more strongly, fear that the therapists would punish them or retaliate in some way. As the session went on, the patients seemed to search for things that they had in common, finally agreeing that they were all alike in some surface traits. Such a session can be understood in light of the force of the wish to have a uniquely gratifying relationship with the therapist, and the counterforce of the fear of retaliation. The wish and the fear constitute opposing forces; the fear prevents the wish from being expressed directly or perhaps even recognized. The wish cannot be pursued actively or thoroughly satisfied. At the same time, the wish cannot quite be given up and keeps the fear in the foreground. This situation creates tension in the group. The patients are beset with strong, conflicting feelings and impulses which are, at best, only dimly perceived. Strong impulses are exerting pressure, yet the patients can neither express nor recognize them. Under such circumstances, the patients attempt to find some way of dealing with their conflicting wishes and fears. In the above illustration, the search for things in common and the final agreement that everyone is alike can be seen as an attempt to allay their fears. It is as if the patients were saying, "Don't punish me; I didn't ask the therapist for anything special." Of course, such a solution cannot really be satisfying, since it involves renouncing the wish. It might temporarily reduce anxiety, however.

In attempting to describe the covert, shared aspects of the group's life, we have adopted a theoretical language which utilizes the key terms "group focal conflict," "disturbing motive," "reactive motive," and "solution." The events of a group therapy session are conceptualized in terms of a slowly emerging, shared covert conflict consisting of two elements—a disturbing motive (a wish) and a reactive motive (a fear). These two elements constitute the group focal conflict. The term "group focal conflict" summarizes the key features of this view of groups, indicating that the disturbing and reactive motives conflict, pervade the group as a whole, and are core issues engaging the energies of the patients. Concomitant with the group focal conflict, one sees various attempts to find a solution. A group solution represents a compromise between the opposing forces; it is primarily directed to alleviating reactive fears but also attempts to maximize gratification of the disturbing motive.

No two group sessions are exactly alike in the group focal conflict which emerges. Even when similar feelings are involved, they are expressed in unique imagery. The solution may also vary in the manner in which it copes with the patients' fears and in the extent to which it satisfies and expresses the disturbing motive.

The impulses and fears involved in a group focal conflict exist outside the awareness of the patients. Although an outside observer can perceive and link the covert references to a shared concern, the individual who is in the focal conflict does not have this perspective. Under some circumstances, the patients may become aware or may be helped to become aware of these feelings. Ordinarily, however, and especially during the period in which the focal conflict is emerging, the patients are not in a position to recognize the character of the disturbing or reactive motives. A solution differs in character from either a disturbing or a reactive motive. It is usually expressed in more direct terms and is more readily observed. The patients may be aware of the content of the solution, although they are not likely to perceive its relevance to the underlying focal conflict.

Solutions may be successful or unsuccessful; in order to be successful, a solution must be unanimously accepted and must alleviate anxiety. Unanimity is necessary, for if one patient fails to accept such a solution as "all be alike," it cannot be effective. If one patient opposes asking the therapist to rule against a deviant patient, he is interfering with the solution. But unanimous acceptance does not imply that everyone must indicate overt willingness to abide by the solution. Most typically, acceptance is implicit, and some patients indicate through silent acquiescence that they will not interfere. Solutions also vary in the manner in which they deal with the associated conflict. Some solutions concentrate on the reactive fears; it is as if the patients are so concerned about their fears that they adopt a solution which copes with their fears at the expense of satisfying the associated wish. For example, the solution "all be alike" was established in response to this focal conflict: "wish to be unique and singled out by the therapists for special gratification" versus "fear of retaliation." This solution dealt exclusively with the fear. It reduced the fear of retaliation by renouncing the wish for a uniquely gratifying relationship with the therapist. Other solutions alleviate reactive fears and still allow some gratification or expression of the disturbing motive. The solution in which the patients banded together to express angry compliance was of this type—it relieved fears of abandonment by making it impossible for anyone to be singled out for abandonment and rejection and, at the same time, allowed the disguised expression of resentment toward the therapists. In this case, the solution allowed for the disguised rather than direct expression of the disturbing motive. In other instances, one sees solutions which reduce fears and simultaneously permit the direct expression of the disturbing impulse.

The detailed illustration to be presented now should not be regarded as typical, except insofar as it demonstrates how the manifest material of a session refers to covert concerns and how a single group session may be summarized in focal-conflict terms.

The session to be described is the first of a reorganized inpatient group which included eight male patients, three female patients, and two female therapists. Only one patient was regarded as psychotic, two were alcoholics, and the rest were suffering from acute anxiety which had reached incapacitating proportions. Five of the patients had previously been in group therapy with Dr. T. The other six, as well as the other therapist, Dr. E., were participating in the group for the first time.

> Dr. T. made a general statement about the purposes of the group. She commented that the group presented an opportunity for the patients to talk about whatever was important to them—events in the hospital, personal problems, or things that happened in the group. She introduced Dr. E. and announced the meeting schedule.

Such an opening offers little structure, yet communicates to the patients that they are expected to attend and to take responsibility for determining the content of the sessions.

> Carl said that he would drop a bombshell into the group by asking Dr. E. how her hair could look like she combed it with an egg-beater and yet look so good.

When Carl uses the term "bombshell," he is calling attention to the daring and perhaps potentially dangerous quality of his comment. His comment has both an aggressive and a sexual flavor. It focuses the attention of the group immediately on the new therapist.

> There was a brief silence. Tim said, "That was a left-handed compliment," and there was general laughter in the group. Carl said that his wife was too fussy about her hair, and Tim made some comment about his wife's hair. Margaret defended Carl's wife by saying that he should either compliment her or coax her into changing her hair style.

Apparently Carl was right, and his comment was really a bombshell, because the group seemed momentarily stunned into silence. Tim's comment seemed to provide tension release for the group by making explicit both the hostile and complimentary aspects of Carl's bombshell. Carl then felt impelled to take back the hostile elements of his comment by comparing Dr. E. to his wife, to Dr. E.'s benefit. With Margaret's attack on Carl there is a suggestion of a battle drawn on sexual lines.

To this point in the session, several potential focuses have appeared, but it is difficult to see which way the group will move. There has been a direct approach to one of the therapists which seems to have both sexual and hostile elements to it, but in any case emphasizes the femaleness of the therapist. It certainly brought Carl to the forefront of the group and focused attention on him. There followed a retreat toward a discussion about outside persons and a hint of contention within the group. But so far, an underlying trend is not apparent.

Dr. T. suggested that there might be some feeling in the group because there were women patients present for the first time. The group did not respond to this comment but continued talking in a general way about hair styles.

This was a premature intervention—a guess at a focus which seems to have missed the point. Underlying this intervention was some assumption that the heterosexual problem being introduced had to do with feelings among peers. In a sense, the comment asks the patients to focus on their feelings for one another. The patients are not prepared to do this and continue their discussion of hair styles, which could be seen as a displaced and symbolic expression of sexual interests.

A trend toward focusing on sexual interests and impulses seems to be emerging, but neither the target nor the implications for the group are clear.

Melvin, who had been silent up to this time, commented that he wanted a medal for being in a therapy group for the third time. Carl said that this was the fourth time he had been in a group, and Melvin said that he would have to back down.

On the face of it, this is an abrupt shift in content and focus. Although in a different area, this comment, too, has a bombshell quality. Melvin seems to be wanting to gain some kind of recognition or attention, either from the therapists or from the patients, by pointing out that he is special. He points to the difference between himself and all the others and perhaps, secondarily, reminds the group that there are both old and new members present. Carl immediately attacks Melvin's claim to specialness and superiority. He is competitive and effectively gains the upper hand by implying that, if anyone is special and deserving of recognition, it is he and not Melvin.

Jean commented that she was an alcoholic and therefore had different problems from all the other patients. Carl said, "We're all addicted," but Tim argued that this was not true. A discussion followed in which the patients tried to arrive at a definition of "addiction." Carl suggested that Tim might be addicted to sleep. Carl said that his wife thinks he is an alcoholic.

Jean makes her own claim to distinction. Like Melvin, she is immediately countered by Carl, who, this time, rather than suggest that he himself is superior, suggests that everyone in the group is the same and that Jean, therefore, has no claim to being special. It is interesting that it is always Carl who insists that everyone is alike and no one is special. Others in the group are not ready to agree with him.

At this point in the session, one might hypothesize that an issue is developing as to whether people are unique or the same. Two patients, Melvin and Jean, have made distinct bids to be singled out. Carl's first comment—the bombshell—might also be regarded in this light. By that comment, Carl was clearly lifting himself out of the mass of patients and making himself conspicuous; in particular, he was bringing himself to the attention of one of the therapists. From a focal-conflict point of view, a disturbing motive may be emerging which involves a wish to be unique and to receive special attention. The object of the wish is not clear. For Carl, it is the therapist; for Melvin, it is probably the therapist (a medal from whom?); for Jean, it is less clear. The reactive motive—the force which keeps the wish from fruition—is not clear. All we can see is that one of the members, Carl, will not allow anyone to satisfy this wish. Whenever anyone makes a bid for uniqueness, Carl interferes. It is uncertain how the rest of the group feels about this issue. Perhaps they don't care; perhaps they care very much but are letting Carl fight their battle for them. In terms of focal-conflict theory, Carl is also suggesting a solution—"let's all be alike;" it is as if he is saying, "Let's not let anyone win this competition." But there is no evidence yet that anyone else supports this view.

> Tim and Melvin (both old members) began to talk about Dr. Y. (a psychiatrist who had been permitted to sit in as an observer of several previous sessions). They referred to an argument the group had had at that time about the cost of psychiatric treatment.

If one paid attention only to the content of this portion of the meeting, it might appear that these two patients are wondering whether the feelings stirred up in the group may be too much to handle. Perhaps they are indirectly questioning whether the group sessions will be worth while. However, the interactive characteristics of this episode suggest another line of thought.

Both Tim and Melvin were old members. By discussing a topic which was meaningless to the new people in the group, they excluded the new members from the conversation and brought sharply into focus the difference between the old and the new. Entirely apart from the content of their conversation, this behavior might be regarded as an interesting variation on the theme of claiming uniqueness. Before, each member has made a personal bid for attention or uniqueness. Now, two members collaborate in their attempt to establish a special place for themselves in the group. This behavior may be seen as a solution to the developing focal conflict. One might conceptualize such a focal conflict in the following manner:

disturbing motive	*reactive motive*
wish to be unique and singled out for special gratification from the therapists	interference by other patients

The behavior of Tim and Melvin partly involves giving up the wish to be unique, but still attempts to reserve a special place in the group for themselves as old members. The reactive motive does not involve feelings of fear or guilt, or the like, but simply indicates that, thus far, any bids for uniqueness have been blocked by another patient.

> Two of the new patients, Sam and Margaret, began to ask Dr. E. questions. Sam asked whether tranquilizing drugs would help him. Dr. E. asked whether they had helped him in the past. Margaret asked whether tranquilizers were sedatives. Dr. E. responded with medical information. At this point, both Tim and Melvin reacted with exaggerated pleasure. Tim said, "For the benefit of new personnel, doctors do not answer questions in this group, so this is really something."

Here, Sam and Margaret interrupted the conversation between Tim and Melvin. In effect, they did not permit reminiscences about special experiences. At the same time, they made their own bid for attention. These two new patients were seeking attention from the new therapist in the group. When it looked as if they were succeeding, Tim and Melvin interfered. Although they were ostensibly telling Sam and Margaret that they were getting something special, they were also implicitly telling both the patients and the new therapist that an old standard was being violated. Thus they are not only interfering with Sam and Margaret's bid to gain special notice from the therapist, they are also re-emphasizing the differences between the old and new members. Here one sees a repetition of what has occurred earlier: a bid for a therapist's attention is blocked by other patients. Such repetition strengthens the hypothesis that a disturbing motive which involves a wish to receive something special from the therapists is operating. It also strengthens the assumption that the other patients will not allow anyone to be singled out in this way.

This interpretation re-emphasizes the interactive characteristics of the group. Turning to the content, one might wonder why the patients focus on tranquilizers rather than on something else. It is not clear whether this focus carries a symbolic implication, whether it expresses some wish to have things calmed down in the group, or whether it merely grows out of some private assumption that this is what doctors are for.

> Melvin referred to a discussion the group had had a number of meetings previously about automobiles. He then told Carl that this meeting would be a good opportunity to sell chances (again referring to something that had happened in a previous session). There was some talk among Carl, Tim, and Melvin about the cost of the chances and about Ford, Mercury, and Lincoln cars (all these were topics which had been discussed in previous sessions).

This conversation involves strengthening ties among old members and excluding the new members. Earlier it was suggested that in the group a solution was developing which would reserve a special place for the old members. It is as if the old members were saying, "Perhaps we cannot be unique and receive special attention as individuals, but at least let us band together to exclude these newcomers." The car conversation suggests that this solution is gaining adherents and being put into practice.

> Dr. T. suggested that the group was asking Dr. E. a lot of questions in order to find out what sort of person the new doctor was. The group responded with laughter. Dr. T. then suggested that the group was concerned about the new members versus the old members and pointed out that some of the conversations introduced by old members could not possibly be understood by new members.

The first portion of this comment appears irrelevant to the shared concerns which seem to be developing in this group. The reference to curiosity about Dr. E. does, however, touch on the wish, which several patients have revealed, to get close to Dr. E. and obtain special help from her. More clearly, however, the second portion of the therapist's comment directly confronts the old members with the alliance they are establishing and makes one aspect of the developing focal-conflict pattern—the solution—explicit.

> Tim said he really wanted an answer to the question he was about to ask and asked Dr. E. about a shot he had had which produced anesthesia in his arm. Dr. E. did not answer this question directly. The group began to discuss spinal taps. They expressed considerable apprehension about this procedure and wanted to know why it was used. The gist of the conversation was that spinal taps were about the most painful and horrible treatment that one could undergo.

Again, this constitutes an abrupt shift in topic. It might seem that the patients have not heard Dr. T.'s intervention or at least are not responding to it. But interactive characteristics show the patients turning away from Dr. T. and toward Dr. E. In terms of content, the discussion about injections and spinal taps may be a symbolic expression of the patients' feeling that doctors are potentially dangerous and capable of inflicting great pain in the guise of aid. It seems reasonable to suppose, then, that the patients actually are reacting to Dr. T.'s intervention. This intervention had blocked a developing solution by communicating disapproval. Perhaps it has elicited some covert angry reaction which the patients now express by turning to Dr. E. The content also suggests that the patients perceive Dr. T.'s intervention as a punitive one. Perhaps they are indicating indirectly and symbolically that the therapist's previous comment was as punitive as actually performing a spinal tap. Perhaps—although this is more speculative—they feel that their angry reaction deserves punishment. It is not clear which aspect of the therapist's comment they are responding to—whether it is the exposure of their solution to exclude the new members or whether it is the exposure of their curiosity about Dr. E. In any case, the reaction is a strong one, as is demonstrated by the primitive quality of the symbolism—spinal taps and anesthesia.

From a focal-conflict point of view, the therapist's intervention has led to a shift in the reactive motive. Previously the wish was held in check by an awareness that other patients would block any bid for uniqueness; now it is held in check by a fear that the therapist will punish the patients. It is as if the therapist will disapprove of not only the wish to be special, but even of the modified solution—a special place in the group for the old members.

It is interesting to note, parenthetically, that in this instance Dr. E. did not respond directly to the patients' questions. She appears to be responding to the earlier suggestion that to answer questions is to violate a custom of the group.

The group began to talk about the value of their meetings.

> Alan said that he might learn to get along with this group, but added, "What good will it do me with friends and relatives?" Jean said, "I am a stranger, and yet you talk to me." Carl said, "This is because we've been through the same thing." Jean talked about Alcoholics Anonymous and said that the value of the group was that "you think you are alone, but you're not." Carl said that he would feel free to talk about anything in this group.

This portion of the session displays a drop in morale and then a recovery. The first part, in which the group is devalued, may express veiled anger toward the therapist; it may also suggest the patients' sense of despair when confronted with difficult issues and feelings. Then, rather abruptly, there is a shift in mood. The patients become more friendly to one another. For the first time, they begin to break down the barriers between the old and new members. (Jean, a new member, tells Carl, an old member, "I am a stranger, and yet you talk to me," and Carl responds, "This is because we've been through the same thing.") There is a new emphasis on the value of peers and the possibility of closeness among them.

From the point of view of the group's focal conflict, this shift suggests a renunciation of the wish to be unique (the disturbing motive), as well as the adoption of a new solution. The patients' friendly overtures may indicate that they will no longer insist on being unique, nor will the old members insist on being a special subgroup. It seems reasonable to suppose that the shift in the reactive motive—from the threat of active interference by other patients to the fear of punishment by the therapist—has led to this change. With such intense, primitive fears involved in the reactive motive, it seems that the only solution is to renounce the wish.

> Dr. T. responded to Carl's comment by saying that an important issue in the group would be what people felt that they could talk about and what they felt they could not talk about. Alan said that the group might be a place where he could learn to understand himself. Tim said he did not know what his problems were, but he did know his symptoms. He described them as eating, sleeping, and indefinitely postponing any attempt to do his job. Jean said she felt the same way and described a drinking pattern in which she drank alone until she was stuporous, ate nothing, and sipped straight whisky for weeks at a time. There was some conversation between Jean and Tim, identifying common problems.

The therapist's comment seems to be an attempt to slow down the headlong rush into complete trust and suggest to the group that it is appropriate to move more slowly. The interaction between Tim and Jean is a continuation of the previous friendliness but has now shifted to sharing the content of problems. In part, the patients seem to be turning to one another for support; in part, they may be mollifying the therapist by doing what they assume the therapist wants them to do. In either case, this portion of the session may be seen as a solution which focuses largely on the reactive motive. It is an attempt to deal with fears about the therapist's displeasure.

> Melvin brought up the subject of hypnotism. He said that he trusted his individual therapist, Dr. J., and would let him do anything, even hypnotize him. Jean said that Dr. J. had tried to hypnotize her once and that it had not worked. Ella said the same thing. Several patients asked Melvin about hypnotism, expressing a good deal of skepticism. Sam asked whether the pills he took produced the same effect as hypnosis. Alan suggested that sleeping was really like being hypnotized. Dr. T. asked, "You mean that everyone has been hypnotized?" Alan described blackout spells he had had. Jean and William were asking him questions about his spells as the session ended.

GROUP NORMS

As a shared idea of appropriate behavior in a particular social system, norms not only influence participants, but are perceived by each member as being accepted by most others in the system. Behavior which violates such ideas of what is the "right way" to behave is ordinarily treated as deviant, and is sanctioned by some means or another to reduce its occurrence, and thus to return the system to its prior equilibrium. Ordinarily, sanctions do not need to be exerted frequently or vigorously; rather, the anticipation of sanctions is often as effective in controlling deviant behavior as is actual application.

Norms and associated sanctions provide a certain amount of stability and predictability in social life; members of the social system know what to expect of each other. Although group members seldom discuss the norms which characterize the group, the group norms nevertheless serve as a simple substitute for interpersonal pressures and *ad hoc* influence tactics; they are, in effect, an unwritten social contract which can be invoked when troublesome behavior arises. Norms can be seen to be a crucial aspect of the culture of people-changing groups. The success of such groups depends, in large respect, on the creation of a tiny society which is separated from and marked off from the surrounding culture. In most day-to-day contacts it is widely accepted as a violated norm if one openly objects to the appearance or behavior of other persons, or reveals his own feelings about issues culturally-defined as private or too personal. Such behavior is usually defined as "rude," "sick," or "weird," and occurs rarely even among intimates. People-changing groups, however, generally create norms which may be counter to those of the larger culture; talking about interpersonal or inner feelings is generally viewed as a decisively good idea, and avoidance of such behavior is ordinarily defined as bad. Similarly, people-changing groups often support norms which encourage closer relationships than are typical of ordinary social transactions. It is difficult to conceive of a personal change group, regardless of type, which does not develop norms that are distinctive from and often opposite to the normative culture of the larger society. For whatever one's view of appropriate mechanisms for personal change, most change systems are predicated on the assumption that, to be successful, they must present differences compared to the participants' ordinary life; otherwise one would need to ask why positive changes are not made, at least for the people who come into such groups, in their ordinary life situation.

The group leader or therapist who has chosen to work with his clients in a group situation must ask himself how he can develop group norms which are conducive to treatment or change. It is not a matter of introducing norms into the group situation, for all groups develop norms. It is as unthinkable to imagine a social system without norms which define appropriate and inappropriate behavior as it is to imagine an earth without gravity, for in a normless society, no one would know what to do or what to expect of others. The issue for the group leader is one of using whatever influence he has to help develop norms which will facilitate the therapeutic goals of the group. Before he can do so, however, he must be able to "read" the group correctly; he must know what the norms are as the members perceive them. He must also be cognizant that although certain norms may be discernible in most personal-change groups, they may take on special colorations depending on the particularities of composition and so forth of each group as a social entity. It is imperative, therefore, that the leader develop methods or strategies for understanding the specific norms in the system he is working in. Most germane to change induction are the norms that relate to the boundaries of the system, the criteria for group membership, what can and cannot be talked about, what emotional expressions are legitimate and illegitimate. It is these areas of regulation that directly affect the therapeutics of any change-directed group.

How to Determine Group Norms

Although the concept of norms may be foreign to most people, almost everyone engages in adjustive behavior or accommodations based on some assessment of what norms are at work in the contexts in which they find themselves. Most people, upon entering a new group or a new culture, "automatically" engage in search behavior directed toward determining what is appropriate and inappropriate behavior in this situation. Most of us usually scan the scene in a new situation; we observe what others appear to be doing, and how it differs from what we are accustomed to. We probably seek, although implicitly, to determine regularity of behavior in the new group or new culture. We probably note that certain things get talked about and others do not, that certain attitudes or emotions are "okay" to express and others are not; we may note that people seem to take turns and that at the end of a specified period of time almost all the members of the group have talked about equally. We are, in a word, studying the norms of the group. We are attempting to find out what is expected of us; what is appropriate and what is prohibited behavior.

One approach to "diagnosing" the norms of a group or any social system is to look, more consciously than we would in everyday life, for regularities of behavior, both behaviors that are present as well as those that are absent. Such a process of observation, akin to the familiar methods of anthropologists, allow norms to be discerned. Over time, in a group, other types of observations will produce information about the normative characteristics of that particular social system. We will note over some period of time that certain members appear to become the focus of the group's attention. We may note at such times that there is considerable intensity involved in focusing on particular members. More often than not, it seems as if most of the group members are ganging up on a particular member and trying to change or alter his behavior. As events progress a little further, the group may become even more intense; what were at first relatively benign attempts to get a particular member to change his behavior now become a more charged group effort, with anger predominating. If all these efforts of the group do not succeed in getting the member to alter his ways (which they usually do not), the group begins to "withdraw" its attention from this member to the point where he almost becomes a nonperson in the group—ignored, isolated, as if he were not there.

What has happened? More likely than not, the member in question violated a basic group norm. He may have taken a point of view that was considered offensive in this particular group, or he may have expressed an intense positive or negative feeling for another member of the group, or done any one of a number of other things that this group considered inappropriate. Group norms are most easily discerned when they are violated by a member. When a group works hard on one member to get him to alter his attitudes or behavior, then gets aggressive toward him and, finally, abandons him, it is a safe bet that the group is out to protect a norm it considers vital. Observation of repeated incidents of the sort just described is likely to reveal the group's norms in their rawest form. Without being aware of it, these sorts of cues are quite similar to those most people use in everyday life to determine "what goes on" or what doesn't in a particular setting; frequently it is what they conclude from such observations that helps them decide whether or not the group is one to which they want to belong.

There is still another way to discern group norms that can be analogized to what people often do when they enter an unfamiliar setting—a new college, a new social group, a new job, a foreign country, or whatever. If they want to "fit in," they ask a friend or acquaintance such things as, "what to wear," "what's the usual tip around here," and so forth. In so doing they are in actuality asking the other person's help in determining what the norms of the new situation are. They are applying the anthropologist's time-honored method of using an informant to discover the unwritten and generally unarticulated social regulations that govern the culture under investigation. In much the same way, a group leader or therapist can determine norms he may be unaware are influencing a group by asking each participant, through administration of a simple questionnaire, what array of behaviors the group would find acceptable or unacceptable. Although all three methods just described may be used, the last is the simplest and most quickly enables the leader or therapist to ascertain the norms of the groups he works with.

A concrete example of this approach was the use, in studying encounter groups (Lieberman, Yalom, and Miles, 1973), of a questionnaire on which leaders and participants checked how they thought their groups would feel about 48 behavioral items. Each group member (or leader) was asked to imagine that he was speaking to a new member who wanted to have an idea of what, in general, went on in the group. The respondent was asked to explain to the imaginary new member whether the group would see a particular behavior, such as being repeatedly late, as appropriate or inappropriate by most members of the group. These behavior items referred to underlying normative characteristics of such groups. As a handy rule of thumb, in using such information to determine group norms, it is useful to remember that group norms are shared agreements among members. Thus at least two-thirds of the members ought to agree that a particular behavior is appropriate or inappropriate before one should consider it a norm. Table 13.1 shows the items arranged, by factor and cluster analyses, into five normative dimensions.

Table 13.1. Factor Analysis of Norm Instrument.

Item	Factor Loading
Factor 1 Intense Emotional Expression (27% of Variance)	
Warmly touched another member	0.96
Kissed another member	0.94
With strong feelings, told another member how likable he is	0.91
Told another member how much he cared for her	0.89
Cried	0.81
Pleaded for help	0.77
Hit another member	0.76
Asked for reactions or feedback ("How do you see me in this group?")	0.65
Made threatening remarks to other group members	0.61
Focused his comments on what was going on in the group	0.58
Talked a lot without showing his real feelings	−0.56
Frankly showed sexual attraction to another person in the group	0.61

Table 13.1. (Continued).

Item	Factor Loading
Factor 2 Open Boundaries: Expression of Outside and Personal Material (17% of Variance)	
Frequently joked	0.88
Talked about the details of his sex life	0.81
Kept bringing in topics from outside the group	0.70
Brought up problems he had with others who weren't in the group	0.66
Disclosed information about the group on the outside	0.64
Refused to be bound by a group decision	0.60
Described his dreams and private fantasies	0.57
Brought a friend to the group session	0.46
Factor 3 Hostile, Judgmental Confrontation (11% of Variance)	
Said another member's behavior was wrong and should be changed	0.81
Challenged the leader's remarks	0.82
Kept on probing or pushing another member who had said, "I've had enough"	0.78
Talked about killing himself	0.76
Put down another member who had just "opened up" with some personal feelings	0.70
Shouted with anger at another member	0.73
Told another member he was unlikable	0.72
Interrupted a dialogue going on between two people	0.67
Gave advice to other members about what to do	0.62
Tried to convince people of the rightness of a certain point of view	0.61
Told another member exactly what he thought of him	0.55
Factor 4 Counterdependence/Dependence (9% of Variance)	
Said he thought the leader should have the biggest responsibility for planning and guiding group activities	−0.82
Said he thought the group should take more responsibility for deciding what activities should go on	−0.77
Appealed to the leader to back him up	−0.66
Said little or nothing in most sessions	−0.47
Factor 5 Peer Control (7% of Variance)	
Tried to take over the leadership of the group	−0.92
Tried to manipulate the group to get his own way	−0.84
Dominated the group's discussion for more than one session	−0.74
Said little or nothing in more sessions	−0.54
Wrote another member off saying he didn't matter	−0.52
Acted indifferently to other members	−0.51
Was often absent	−0.50

From Lieberman, M. A., Yalom, I., and Miles, M. *Encounter groups: First facts.* New York: Basic Books. Reprinted by permission.

Less exhaustive questionnaires of this sort are easy to construct, and although the items may differ for any particular set of circumstances, they offer a handy approach to finding out where the leader or therapist needs to concentrate his efforts in order to create a better learning or therapeutic climate. In the encounter study, norms were significantly related to the effectiveness of groups. Groups which forbade discussion of events that took place outside the group, for example, tended to be far less productive learning environments than groups which were more permissive about what members could talk about. Groups with a large number of norms, regardless of the content, were more productive than groups with a smaller number. Whether these findings are generalizable to other types of change groups is unknown at this time; what is important is that norms have been shown to affect the quality of the learning or therapeutic environment. Thus, for a leader to ignore the normative structure of a group is to ignore a major variable in change-induction.

THERAPEUTICS AND THE ROLE OF THE LEADER

Up to this point, we have talked about how groups have come to be used as a medium for personal change. Still, we have skirted the main question—what is it that occurs in such settings that is essential to changing people. The fundamental assumption underlying all theories of changing people through groups is that as time passes the group, as a social microcosm, will increasingly generate in each member those feelings, thoughts, or behaviors that are at heart troublesome to him. Whether one begins with a psychoanalytic assumption that dynamic conflicts are at issue, or looks at interpersonal relationships as the source of personal problems, or takes a strictly behavioral position, fundamentally each position views—as the initial step in change—the *elicitation, directly or indirectly, of the issues that are troublesome to the participant.* The display, internally or overtly, of these troublesome issues in a context that is in some important ways different from ordinary life constitutes the first step in the therapeutic process.

In a most general way, the next step in this sequence of change is that the *behavior, thought, or feeling must be experienced by the person in a way that is different from his previous history.* The person has to "learn" that what he had feared or expected if he behaved, thought, or felt in a particular way will not necessarily occur, that a calamity will not befall him, that getting close to people, depending on them, fighting with them, or whatever, does not always bring dire consequences; that there are more ways of achieving sought-after goals or fulfilling needs than he had previously thought, and so forth. What has to happen in a group for members to reap such benefits is what the business of change induction in groups is all about. It is most important for the reader to recognize that the current state of knowledge about people-changing is primitive; no formula has been advanced that will suffice for every case. The evidence that can be brought to bear all leads to the conclusion that people-changing is complex. Whether in groups or dyads, no single method or set of techniques has been shown to change all, but few have been tried that will not change someone. It is this observation that some are changed by almost any kind of system people have thought about, and not everyone is changed by any system ever developed, that creates the complexity (as well perhaps as the excitement) of developing more sophisticated theories about the essential ingredients of individual change.

Some people are helped by seeing others go through an experience; the elicitation of their own related problems is indirect rather than direct. They experience new learnings through watching others try out feared behavior rather than by doing so themselves. Some learn through an internal cognitive response—a new recognition that the conflict they previously felt between their wants and fears is not as certain as they had once thought. Still others may observe that some group members are able to meet their needs by using behaviors that never occurred to them and are encouraged by these "good examples" to try the same. Some are unburdened to discover that no one is shocked by their deep hidden secrets which have always made them feel ashamed or guilty. Still others experiment with new behaviors in a situation that may be the first to appear safe and supportive to them and are thereby encouraged to change.

What, then, is the therapist's or leader's role in facilitating change for group members? How will he insure that the group setting will elicit the troublesome thoughts, feelings, and behaviors that people bring? How can he help the members experience new thoughts, feelings, and behaviors in ways that release them from the fears with which they previously associated them?

An examination of the variety of theoretical positions about people-changing in groups would reveal a large number of terms or concepts to describe things therapists or leaders do: interpreting resistance, confronting, reflecting, supporting, developing role-playing scenes, acting as the observing ego, precipitating crises for the group by not acting in accord with ordinary patient expectations, reinforcing, modeling, making contracts, setting up ground rules, protecting, expressing acceptance, communicating genuineness and positive regard, analyzing transference, teaching, being a whole person, disclosing personal feelings, expressing feelings, interpreting group dynamics, interpreting individual dynamics, challenging, being provocative, and so forth. The descriptive and conceptual labels used to describe the work of a therapist are indeed broad and far-ranging. It is possible, however, to bring some order to the vast array of descriptive titles of leader behavior and function.

Sensitivity group leaders see their role as helping members understand themselves and others through understanding the group process. Such leaders characteristically focus on the group as a whole, and on the members' transactions with each other. They attempt to explain what the group as a whole is doing, focusing on such issues as group maintenance, cohesiveness, power and work distribution, sub-grouping, scapegoating, and so on.

Gestalt therapy leaders stress the wholeness of the individual. Change is viewed as a sub-intellectual process which is mediated by helping the individual get in touch with the primitive wisdom of the body. There is little use of the group or, for that matter, the other group members. In the classical practice of this methodology, there is an empty chair, "the hot seat," next to the leader, to which the members come one by one to "work" with the leader. In Gestalt groups, much emphasis is placed on heightened emotionality, or understanding what the body is telling one by its posture or by its numerous autonomic and musculoskeletal messages. The leader often helps members to resolve inner conflicts by holding dialogues between the disparate parts of the psyche. The participation of the other members is minimal; often their primary function is simply to verify what the leader says by their presence, like the all-seeing Greek chorus.

Transactional analysis leaders work with each of the group members in turn. The term transactional analysis refers to the transactions among ego states (parent, child, and adult) within one individual, rather than transactions among individuals. Establishing learning contracts (the setting of specific goals) is a typical characteristic of this approach. Formal teaching of the analytic model is stressed, so that patients in the group can apply this conceptual system to themselves and to the behaviors of others.

Basic encounter group leaders emphasize the experiencing and deepening of interpersonal relationships and the liberating of somatic restrictions. They believe that by breaking free of social and muscular inhibitions, people can learn to experience their own bodies and other people in a different and fuller sense. The group leader's focus is on both the individual and the interpersonal relationships within the group. The basic encounter leader often suggests exercises for members to perform to help shuck constricting inhibitions. The emphasis is on doing and experiencing; the cause or meaning of the persisting restrictions is of minor consequence.

Client-centered group therapy is an adaptation of Rogerian individual psychotherapy. Most of the leader's attention is centered on interpersonal or intrapersonal dynamics; he rarely focuses on the group as a whole. He is to behave as a model of personal development, establishing the conditions of genuineness, unconditional positive regard, and empathy, that are received in Rogerian therapy as the basic ingredients of the therapeutic relationship.

Attack therapy emphasizes the expression of anger; each member in turn is systematically attacked and explored by the others in the belief that if one is attacked long enough in his weak areas he will strengthen them. This procedure is called "the game" in Synanon because, once the group meeting is over, the atmosphere changes quickly to one of warm support. The Synanon form of attack therapy differs from other models having a similar emphasis in that the Synanon groups are composed of both experienced and inexperienced members, so that much of the work of the system is done not by the leader but by several "experienced game players." In other forms of attack therapy, the leader is almost exclusively the confronting agent.

Psychodramatic approaches to group-based change induction are adaptations of ideas developed by Jacob L. Moreno, the founder of psychodramatic therapy. The basic format is the construction of role-playing or psychodramatic exercises, directed toward providing a means for participants to act out heretofore blocked behaviors or feared emotional relationships in a "safer" setting. The technology involves the assumption that a person can learn from direct experience (if he plays a role in the exercise) or vicariously (if he observes the psychodrama).

As discussed earlier, psychoanalytically-oriented group therapy focuses on the inner dynamics, especially the early history, of the individual as they are expressed in the group. Such groups tend to be less emotionally charged, more rationally based, with heavier focus on intellectual mastery of inter- and intrapersonal forces operating in the group. The therapist acts as an observing ego, interpreting resistance and analyzing defenses of individuals as they are played out in the group social microcosm.

Through studying 16 leaders (Lieberman, Yalom, and Miles, 1973) representing these eight theoretical orientations as they actually worked in groups, using observers' ratings as well as members' perceptions of their behavior, four fundamental functions were isolated that described most of the behavior of all these leaders: emotional stimulation, support, meaning-attribution, and executive functions. All leaders, no matter what their theoretical orientation, employ some behavior in these four areas, although they differ widely with regard to the amount and the particular emphasis on any one—some leaders are primarily emotionally stimulating, others spend the majority of their time involved in executive functions, and so forth. Other leaders combine support with meaning attribution, others emphasize stimulation and support, and so on.

Emotional Stimulation

All personal change groups emphasize the emotional participation of the participants. At its most elemental level, the stimulation function of the leader is response-demand behavior. The leader uses some tactic or strategy to engage participants and elicit emotional responses. The tactics involved in exercising this function are varied and range from the leader revealing his own feelings (leader transparency) to challenging, confrontation, participating as a group member rather than the leader, exhortation, drawing attention to self, demonstrating or modeling on the leader's part by risk-taking, expressing anger, warmth, and love, and so forth. Other strategies leaders use to stimulate emotions among the members may involve role-playing scenes, simulated games, or various "structured exercises," arrangements the leader suggests to involve the members in activities such as "trust walks," "break-in," and the like.

Each of these leader tactics varies with regard to the intensity of the demand for response. Leader strategies also vary in the degree to which they involve direct relationship to a particular participant as opposed to the generation of more elaborate structures involving many participants for invoking emotional responses. Some leaders employ relatively low levels of stimulating behavior, using invitations, elicitations, and questions; others evoke high-intensity responses through challenging, confrontation, and personal revelation. *What is important is that all leaders, no matter what their theoretical persuasion, act as if one fundamental function of their role is to elicit emotional responsiveness in the participants.*

The historical change with regard to this form of behavior is of interest. A fundamental difference between personal change groups that stem from traditional psychotherapeutic orientations and the so-called newer therapies is the degree to which each type emphasizes emotional stimulation. Classical forms of group therapy stem from a tradition that suggests that just placing participants in small face-to-face groups for personal change creates high levels of excitement and stimulation, so that the major function of the therapist is seen to be to manage this potent climate. In traditional forms of group therapy it is also assumed that change takes a long time, a perspective that probably minimizes the importance of emotional stimulation. The newer change systems generally view change as possible in relatively brief periods of time, and perhaps emphasize intensity of stimulation as a means of "speeding up the process." Despite these differences, however, it is important to recognize that all forms of therapy perceive emotional involvement and responsiveness as central to the change process and all provide techniques for seeing to it that participants come forth with such responses.

Support-Caring Function

Any group designed to effect personal change is bound to create anxiety or tension in its members. Personal change groups are fraught with potential for anxiety-induction—no one is sure what may happen next, exceedingly personal topics often get discussed, and interactions among members may evoke highly emotional events. Finally, although members may deeply desire to change, they may feel apprehensive about giving up old ways of behaving for new ones. Thus, a basic function of every leader of a people-changing group is to teach the group to manage the anxiety inherent in the change process. Although all leaders exhibit behaviors directed toward supporting and caring for group participants, the variation in both the amount and kind are large. Some theories of group-based people-changing, for example those growing out of Rogerian tradition, are in good part characterized by the emphasis placed on the establishment of supportive relationships to members with whom the leader works. Genuineness, positive regard, empathy, are the terms of this framework, and such leaders emit greater amounts of such behavior.

Therapists influenced by the English Tavistock school of group analysis consider a relatively high degree of anxiety a necessary condition for change, and other differences among various theoretical positions with regard to the support-caring function can be seen in whether leaders institute supportive processes directly or indirectly. Some leaders offer warmth, caring, support, affection, praise, and encouragement through their own activities. Other leaders perceive provision of an accepting setting and manage the tensions that the change-producing situation induces as a basic function. Such leaders are more likely to operate indirectly, attempting to create situations in which the group members themselves offer the greatest source of support. Direct observations of leaders suggest, however, that no matter what their school of orientation or theoretical position, all are involved to some extent in providing direct support, affection, friendship, encouragement, praise, and support to others.

Meaning Attribution

The unknown or unrecognized has always been fearful to men. Since time immemorial, the basic function of healers in society has been to aid man to conquer fear by making the unknown feel knowable or at least less threatening. Leaders of people-changing groups are no different. A fundamental function they perform is to create meaning. They label feelings and events that participants may undergo without full awareness. They attribute meaning to experiences occurring in the group or to a particular member with the intention of rendering a higher level of understanding of what lies beneath the experience. Whether they embrace the more traditional therapeutic concepts such as insight or speak in terms of the newer, more experience-based, people-changing movements, all leaders perform this function. How they do it and what particular meanings or labels they ascribe to experience differ widely. The methods of transmission also vary considerably. Some leaders use modeling as their primary means of giving cognitive structure to salient emotional experiences; other leaders make use of more formal educational methods traditionally employed to upgrade conceptual internalization. Some directly teach general systems of how to understand behavior, others label experiences as they occur, so that participants will view them with a new perspective. Some teach about how to change by providing exercises intended to leave participants with new views about themselves and their relationships to others—ideas which they can apply to achieve more effective behavior patterns away from the group. Other leaders focus the attention of participants more on the processes they believe underlie the achievement of change, introducing concepts which may range from classic Freudian to more socially-oriented Lewinian to those deriving from far more contemporary biopsychic frameworks. The methods and the labels of course vary, but what is important is that all leaders of people-changing groups provide members with some means of translating feelings and behavior into *ideas*.

Executive Function

Theories and theorists differ widely about how to use the social properties of the group for therapeutic benefit. Some theories ignore consideration of group-level phenomena; the leader's relationship with individual members is presented as sole source of change; other theories acknowledge that one is obviously constructing a social system when working with groups, yet provide no concepts about the social system nor techniques using the social system as a therapeutic force. A smaller number of theories and theorists see the *major* work of the therapist or group leader to be centered around developing a viable and therapeutically productive social system. Nevertheless, all leaders of personal change groups direct some of their attention to the management of the group as a social system.

Anything the leader does that has to do with the workings of the group as a social system are aspects of the leader's executive function. Some leaders are *laissez-faire* with respect to this function; they do very little to alter how the group is functioning. Other leaders rely little on the usual forms of executive function as a therapeutic means for confronting the group with its need to develop its own resources. Such leaders do not totally abrogate the executive function but rather spend much of their efforts on helping the group to reflect on the meaning of the absence of ordinary executive functions to them as a group as well as to each individual in it.

It is helpful to examine the leader's executive functions with regard both to direct and indirect interventions. Direct interventions are those behaviors he carries on during the course of the group which are directed toward how the social system is functioning. Indirect interventions are things leaders do when they organize groups which are intended to enhance the therapeutic qualities of the group. Direct interventions include such leader acts as suggesting or setting rules (which may range from simple rules regarding the time and place of the group's meeting to strictures about the relationships among members outside of the treatment or group situation), discussing the group's goals with the members, suggesting that the group has spent enough time on a particular topic, stopping or blocking, for example stopping the group from "scapegoating" one member, or getting the group to reflect what it is doing. Behaviors directed toward aiding the group to make a decision or suggesting various procedures that the group can follow are other forms of the executive function.

The most powerful indirect executive functions of the leader or therapist involve the selection of persons to be in the group, the "preparation of the person" before he enters the group, and the composition—the array of individuals who make up the group. The principles and controversies that govern these three considerations are beyond the scope of the current chapter to cover in any detail. Suffice to say here, with regard to selection, a considerable body of clinical observation would suggest (although the empirical evidence is inconsistent) that some types of individuals can work better in a group situation than in a dyad, and *vice versa*. With regard to preparation, clinical observation and empirical research both strongly indicate that the expectational sets of individuals entering groups can be altered by various procedures prior to the beginning of the group, and that the nature of the expectational sets and the view the person has of what to look for in the group and what to expect can make a difference in the functioning of the group, particularly in its initial stages. Finally, composing the group membership in some ordered way has also been clinically and empirically demonstrated to be a powerful strategy for affecting the productivity of a change group.

EXPERIENCES THAT MAKE FOR CHANGE

The overall process of change through group methods can be thought of in terms of two central and interdependent aspects of the group experience. The group characteristics already discussed prescribe the conditions which define the context in which the sought-for changes are to take place. The other important aspect of the group change-induction system is the "package" of events or change mechanisms, such as self-disclosure, getting and giving feedback, or expressing strong emotions, which are expected to effect alterations in members' feelings, thoughts, or behavior. If one imagines how frightening such experiences can be under certain conditions, the interdependence of these two aspects of people-changing groups can be readily recognized. Many leaders and participants in group change programs assume that self-disclosure, for example, is unconditionally therapeutic. Yet it is a safe bet that certain members will not engage in such behavior unless they feel a certain degree of confidence in the group. The group conditions, in other words, must be such that members need not feel chronically anxious and can "afford" to drop their usual defensive maneuvers at least to some of the events which take place in the group.

A number of the types of events usually witnessed in people-changing groups have been often regarded as inherently productive of positive change. Some change mechanisms will be quite familiar to anyone acquainted with dyadic helping relationships; others can only take place in a multi-person situation. None of these events has been shown to be necessarily successful with all people, nor under all conditions. They represent a distillation of what is regarded in the people-changing groups as generally being important.

Expressivity

Emotional expression is an important element of the change process in most theories of group change. In some theoretical systems the expression of positive feelings is stressed; in others, the expression of negative feelings, especially hostility and anger. Expression of feelings about important life events is sometimes viewed as crucial. Theories differ considerably both with regard to the kind of emotional expressions considered important and to the importance placed on this change mechanism. Freud initially considered catharsis an important mechanism of change; he saw stifled emotions as a major impediment to mental health and a major source of symptoms. Later Freud and psychoanalytic theorists who followed him considerably de-emphasized the cathartic dimension in the change process. In sharp contrast, in some of the "new therapies" (Gestalt, various encounter techniques, and certain self-help groups such as Synanon) considerable emphasis is placed on emotional expression as a central element of change. The assumption is that unless the person is freed to express both negative and positive feelings toward others directly and openly, the road to change will be blocked. A number of distinctions can be made with regard to the function of expressivity in particular orientations. Intense feelings may be considered important only when they are cathartic (get out previously blocked feelings), or only when they are expressed toward others in the "here and now" group, or only when they involve re-living critical events from the person's life outside the group. Theoretical systems also differ with regard to whether emotional expression is received as an end in itself or simply a necessary step in a more complex change process involving other elements, such as cognitive mastery. Gestalt therapists, for example, see the expression of intense affect as an end in itself, and frequently encourage emotional expression toward current figures in the group. In contrast, women's consciousness-raising groups may emphasize emotional expression, particularly of an angry variety, much more in a cathartic fashion, directing such emotional expression toward society, rather than the members of the group itself. On the other hand, self-help movements like Alcoholics Anonymous do not view emotional expression as central to changing people. In general, the more traditional group psychotherapists place less emphasis on emotional expression (although they do not ignore it) as compared to leaders of the new orientations, which have highlighted expressivity as a mechanism of change. Clients in many group-based change systems report the ability to express both angry and positive feelings in the group as important in their view of the experience. It is of interest that frequently other people's intense emotional expressions are viewed by participants in groups as being more important to them, a phenomenon that will be discussed under a different mechanism (spectator therapy).

Self-Disclosure

Self-disclosure is the explicit communication of information that a group participant believes other members would be unlikely to acquire unless he told it to them, and which he considers so highly private that he would exercise great caution regarding whom he told it to. Although the experience of self-disclosure in individual psychotherapy has been discussed by several theorists, it is important to recognize that disclosure to a single paid professional is quite different in meaning from disclosure to a group of peers. It feels less dramatic and is less anxiety-laden to reveal private information to a single professional than to a group. Group participants imply that it is easier to reveal themselves in a one-to-one relationship than in a group; yet they indicate more exhilaration over such acts in a multi-person situation. Some theorists, such as Jourard (1964) and Mowrer (1964), see self-disclosure as the primary therapeutic mechanism, the *sine qua non* of growth. Group change systems in which guilt is perceived as a primary issue confronting people also stress self-disclosure as a curative mechanism. For example, revelation plays an important role in many of the self-help movements, particularly Alcoholics Anonymous. In general, the newer therapies place more emphasis on self-disclosure than the more traditional theories of group therapy. As with emotional expression, self-disclosure can be considered a primary mechanism in terms of its effect on the person who discloses, as well as a secondary mechanism in the sense that frequently the self-disclosure of other people appears to be a salient therapeutic experience for certain individuals.

The particular content of self-disclosure—what sort of information gets disclosed—probably depends on the values of the particular change system. In some groups, events associated with guilt or shame appear to be stressed; in others, revelations are more geared to the person's feelings, thoughts, and fantasies about other group members. What is important, however, is that generally the content makes little difference when compared to the sense that persons who self-disclose have engaged in a risky and essentially social act; self-disclosure appears to be useful only when the initiator's intention of sharing of deeply personal material is understood, appreciated, and correctly interpreted by the group collectivity. In other words, the power of self-disclosure is *not* that what is said has been said for the first time. (This is rare; in one study participants indicated that only 14 percent of all self-disclosures were first-time disclosures.) It is the sense of well-being and confidence in other human beings and the feeling of acceptance that seem to be the active ingredients in making self-disclosure an important mechanism of change. Finally, it is worth noting that self-disclosures may be seen as cathartic events, much like the expression of intense emotions. It is the sense of relieving oneself in the social context that characterizes some self-disclosures, while others appear to be valuable to the participant when the act of self-disclosing leads to some cognitive mastery, some sense that the person achieves an understanding of the meaning and implications of what he has disclosed. As with most change mechanisms that are seen as generally productive, the context is overriding. In a context where it is not appreciated or accepted, self-disclosure is negatively rewarded; when it is accepted and appreciated by the other group members, it is more likely to have therapeutic benefit. There is some evidence that when self-disclosure occurs prior to the building of a cohesive group, it is less beneficial than when it occurs after some sense of trust and sharing has developed.

Feedback

Of all the learning mechanisms associated with personal change and development through groups, feedback—the receipt of information about how one is perceived by peers—is unique to the group situation. Theories wherein psychopathology is viewed as social in origin tend to emphasize feedback as a curative mechanism more than theories that emphasize intrapsychic determinants of pathology. It appears, however, that some form of feedback is seen as important in almost all theories of group-induced change. It appears also that feedback responds to a very basic human need, the need to find out where we stand, how we are seen by others. Group members perceive feedback to be one of the most salient experiences in their participation in groups. Generally, the closer (in time) feedback is given on a specific behavior, the more effective it is. The form in which it is transmitted also seems to be an important factor in determining its utility. Feedback appears to be helpful to the degree that it is concrete, that is, easily understood by the person because it is related to a particular event and given within a relatively unthreatening context.

Leader strategies vary widely with regard to feedback. Some leaders stress feedback as a central mechanism; they engage in a considerable amount of active teaching about the nature of feedback, frequently model feedback behavior, and use other strategies to encourage its occurrence. Other leaders appear less active in encouraging or teaching about feedback, but generally seem to support it when it occurs. As with the expression of emotions, there probably are differences with regard to the content and valence of feedback among different systems—some seem to generate more negative or critical responses; others, more positive-supportive observations.

The Experience of Intense Emotions

All theories of therapy involve deeply the emotional life of the person. The experience of strong affects is closely related to the expressive mechanism already discussed, but does not necessarily require that the person engage in the direct expression of feelings; in this view, it is sufficient to experience strong positive or negative emotions whether or not they are expressed. The concept of the "corrective emotional experience" articulated by Franz Alexander (1946) describes the function of the experience of intense emotions. The basic principle of treatment advanced by Alexander is to expose the patient, under more favorable circumstances, to emotional situations which he could not handle in the past. For Alexander, *corrective* emotional experience involves the experience of strong affect *accompanied by* reality-testing. The change group offers innumerable stimuli to generate intense emotions in members. The events of the group life activate issues in the individual's core problem areas — competition, intimacy, dependency, and so forth. It is likely that during the course of any healing group, affective issues will come up among members that are related to the person's problem area. Other characteristics of the group, for example the frequent contagion of affects in which individuals are "carried away" by the emotional expression of others, may unleash feelings certain members have been previously unable or unwilling to experience. Among different theories of people-changing in groups somewhat different aspects of emotional experience are emphasized. Psychoanalytically-oriented group psychotherapists are prone to emphasize and select out strong emotional experiences that recapitulate characteristics of earlier experiences; those who emphasize the interpersonal aspects of groups are more likely to stimulate intense experiences revolving around interpersonal relationships in the group without seeking directly to relate them to the re-living of past events. The newer therapies are, in good part, based on the diagnosis that much of the plight of modern man stems from the mutilation of the ability to experience intense emotions. Hence, their technology has been built to design devices which increase sensory awareness through the stimulation of physical feelings and emotion-provoking experiences. Many of the structured exercises which are practiced repeatedly in the newer therapies and which are used to induce meditation, inner fantasy, heightened interpersonal responsiveness, and so on, are partly aimed at revitalizing what are considered atrophied pathways to intense feelings about one's inner life, one's body, and one's relationship to others. Again, in some theories curative forces are assigned to negatively-toned emotions (anger, rage, and so forth), while others are more directed toward inducing positive emotions, especially love.

The Experience of Communion

The unique attribute of the group to provide its members with a feeling of oneness with others, a sense of belonging to a collectivity, has become increasingly emphasized in recent years, perhaps in response to the view that contemporary society lacks the ability to provide for such needs. Communion appears to be one of the driving, if unverbalized, needs of participants in personal change groups. The achievement of a sense of communion can be seen as a primary therapeutic mechanism insofar as individuals who first experience it through groups learn that it is possible to feel toward others in a way they had previously not experienced. In many theories the experience of communion is seen as an important step and is emphasized more as a condition which can lead to increasing trust and openness and, in turn, to facilitating change processes. Phenomenologically, many participants in groups emphasize communion as a primary aspect of their learning. Women's consciousness-raising groups, for example, particularly emphasize communion as a core element of the change process because they ascribe modern women's problems in part to alienation from other women. In general, while more traditional psychotherapists perceive the experience of communion as an important byproduct of the group, they do not emphasize it as having primary therapeutic value. Groups that are usually outside the professional tradition, such as many self-help and consciousness-raising groups, are more likely to place primary emphasis on the experience of communion as a mechanism of personal change.

Altruism

Although participants do not enter change-induction groups to be helpful to others, a common experience unique to the group is that individuals can be genuinely facilitative for others. The low self-esteem and poor conceptions of self so characteristic of neurotic patients often prevent them from feeling they can be genuinely helpful to other human beings. Yet, they frequently do feel helpful to others in the group to an extent that appears critical and, in this sense, a primary therapeutic mechanism.

Spectatorism

It is not uncommon in a psychotherapeutic group or in other change-inducing groups to note that a few people have been quiet and inactive throughout the history of the group. Yet, such individuals may clearly express a sense of having benefitted from the group and have been shown to have achieved gains on empirical measures of outcome. Apparently, such people can learn something useful just by being in a situation where others are having critical and significant emotional experiences. The most likely explanation of this process is that such situations clarify issues which are critical to the spectator. The work of Bandura (1969) on imitative learning may have relevance to understanding the nature of spectatorism (see Chapter 5 on modeling). Personality characteristics are also relevant to understanding this mechanism of change, for it appears that not all participants in a group are equally able to identify with others and make use of their experiences. When one asks group participants at the end of a meeting what were the most important events, more often than not they select strong emotional experiences or meaningful self-disclosures of others as being personally most significant for them. Although it is not fully understood as a mechanism of change, spectator-derived gains occur very frequently in groups. It is reasonable to assume that the spectator employs some cognitive processes to make use of what others are experiencing in connection with his own problematic areas. Many self-help groups capitalize on this phenomenon; for example in Alcoholics Anonymous the formal process of telling others "how it is with me" appears to provide some opportunity for identification for non-active participants, as well as serving other functions.

Discovering Similarity

The relief that group participants so frequently experience when they discover that their problem is not unique appears to be one of the more positive subjective experiences offered to individuals through groups. Many of the self-help and consciousness-raising groups are purposely organized around maximizing the experience of similarity as a basic mechanism of support and alleviation of problems. Other group change-induction systems differ considerably in the degree to which a sense of similarity among participants is viewed as curative. Nevertheless, in most newly-formed groups the discovery of similarity seems important to the participants regardless of how much use the leader makes of it through particular interventions. The process by which this experience is change-inducing is rather opaque. Phenomenologically, it seems to be an important experience for the person and appears to offer relief from a negative image of self. As with many mechanisms of change, it is difficult to isolate its specific contribution to outcome or change.

Experimentation

A unique property of a group situation is the setting it offers participants to experiment with new forms of behavior under low risk. All formal systems of group psychotherapy and many of the newer group therapies are maximally constructed to encourage participants to try out new behaviors. Experimentation tends to be viewed as an important mechanism of change to the degree that a theoretical position views the group as a social microcosm. Experimentation seems to be less stressed in most self-help and consciousness-raising groups. Some group change-induction systems have developed formal procedures for encouraging experimentation—role playing is a prime example. Many proscriptive interventions of leaders—suggestions for trying out new ways of relating, and so forth—are aimed at inducing change through experimentation. The assumption is that having done something once under the protection of the group, the person may be more fortified to do it in the outside world. It is clear that this mechanism is highly dependent on group conditions. The ability of individuals to experiment implies that the group offers a sense of safety and lower threat than the real world. It also requires some specification of the person's problem and of alternative ways of behaving. Often, participants get ready to adopt a new stance in the outside world through a long chain of events, perhaps beginning with discovering through watching others that there are alternative ways to achieve a desired goal; this discovery may lead to thinking over, then trying out alternative behavior in the group and, finally, in the external stiuation. For this complex chain of events to occur, many properties of the group must be conducive. The group norms, for example, must support decisions to experiment.

Modeling

The concept of modeling has been well described and discussed in other chapters (see Chapters 5 and 6). That it does occur in groups is not questioned; little is known, however, about the conditions under which modeling is enhanced, or to what degree modeling implies what the participants do or only what the leader does. There is some evidence that modeling may work as a prime mechanism for maintaining change. In following up individuals who made positive gains in encounter groups, it was found that modeling, an internalization of how particular participants or leaders would have handled the situation, proved to be an important element in the change-maintenance process. Thus, although modeling is clearly an important mechanism, it is a poorly understood mechanism in the group situation. There is little knowledge available about under what conditions it occurs, what characteristics of leaders encourage modeling, and how one determines what behavior is to be modeled and what is not.

The Inculcation of Hope

Group situations often generate events that inspire hope in participants. Jerome Frank (1961) has more than adequately described the importance of hope as a factor in change. Simply put, hope is a feeling that one can change and that the group (or the individual) can be responsible for such change. Group situations offer many stimuli to increase hope; for example, seeing other members in the group success-fully grapple with problems or seeing others who have changed as the result of their participation in the group. The leader or therapist is probably less important in inculcating hope in the group than in the dyadic situation. The evidence of what is happening to others which is before the eyes of most group participants is probably more powerful than the hope-inducing behavior generated by leaders. Some group therapeutic systems employ hope as a central change-induction mechanism. This is particularly characteristic of self-help and consciousness-raising groups. The type of "game group" practiced by Synanon, in which new and experienced members are mixed, provides a classic example of seeing others who have been in the same boat, who have shared the same misery, and have conquered it. Opportunities to hear testimonials of those who have conquered their problems as offered in Alcoholics Anonymous and the positive belief systems presented by many self-help movements, clearly are intended to inculcate hope.

Cognitive Factors

For many of the therapeutic mechanisms that have been reviewed, there is an implicit suggestion that some cognitive aspects are involved. Yet, there has been much confusion and considerable debate concerning the role of cognitive factors in the group curative process. Traditional psychotherapeutic systems growing out of dynamic psychiatry have clearly emphasized the role of cognitive factors, usually expressed in terms of insight into the neurotic processes at work. The more modern group therapies have generally placed less emphasis on cognitive factors in learning. Some theories stress cognitive mastery, but view it as understanding or discovering previously unknown or unacceptable parts of the self which need not relate to historical events in a person's life. Some systems of treatment overtly train their participants to use a particular cognitive model. For example, in transactional analysis groups, leaders frequently use traditional educational modes for teaching participants the framework for analyzing experience. Other systems rely on more incidental or less formal educational processes, which are usually generated by the leader "pointing out" or interpreting events as they occur. Some systems of change see cognitive mastery as being generated both directly when a person is involved in some experience in the group, as well as indirectly by seeing others have experiences and partaking and identifying with their experiences for cognitive mastery. Most systems of psychotherapy and many self-help groups stress cognitive mastery with regard to personal life history, and understanding is sought in that arena. Groups such as women's consciousness-raising provide cognitive mastery not so much for understanding personal life histories but rather for understanding oneself in the light of societal models. In general, there have been a wide variety of devices for inculcating cognitive mastery, and an even wider range of frameworks through which to understand experience.

Although cognitive learning has been de-emphasized in some of the newer therapies, recent evidence (Lieberman, Yalom, and Miles, 1973) suggests that the most effective mechanisms for learning in encounter groups involve some elements of cognitive mastery. For example, it was found that the degree of frequency of self-disclosure in and of itself was not salient in explaining who experienced positive outcomes, but that self-disclosure which involved some sort of cognitive mastery or understanding of the self-disclosure was highly related to positive outcome. In general, the cognitive mastery of experience was established as a positive force. Experiences in and of themselves seem to be less important than when they were mediated through cognitive factors. The degree to which the particular kind or nature of cognitive mastery is important is a major unanswered question. To what degree is the proposition advanced by psychoanalytic theoreticians about genetic cognitive mastery valid, compared to cognitive mastery of current interpersonal operations? Does it make a difference whether the person understands himself and his experiences with a psychoanalytic framework or a framework stemming from interactional systems or even a socio-cultural system? It may be that any consistent system which the person finds useful for understanding experience is a crucial element, and the particular content of the system is less relevant.

EXPERTISE

Even after one cuts his way through the jungle of theoretical and technical issues about healing groups, another major hurdle is presented regarding what one needs to know to be a healer. It is possible to amass considerable opinion in the group-based healing field which suggests that a long and arduous route must be traversed to master the role. Many, on the other hand, feel that training is almost irrelevant to practice. Unlike the relatively developed steps that behavioral approaches to change provide, group technologies appear opaque from the perspective of a newcomer. Most traditional group therapists consider that preparation for conducting people-changing groups involves training and apprenticeship.

Over the past ten years a diametrically opposite view has emerged. The roots of this new view are several—the lack of available manpower to serve demands for mental health services, a substantial egalitarian theme among some sectors of our society which denigrates the priestly function (wherever it may be found), the sense among many disenfranchised groups that only those who have undergone their experience (with, for example, addiction, sexual or racial discrimination, parenthood of a handicapped child) can understand them enough to help them, the explosive growth of the human potential movement which has developed a myriad of techniques that can be passed on to participants (who often assume leader roles very soon after they have been participants). The consequence of such themes has been a decided shift away from the use of professionally-trained persons to conduct change-induction systems.

The beginner may legitimately ask, when so many people are conducting groups for personal change without passing through elaborate and time-consuming educational pathways, what is the appropriate route to take if one wants to learn to conduct people-changing groups. Those who are empirically-minded might wonder whether this question can be aided by available research data. Unfortunately, the studies are few, of limited scope, and frequently contradictory. Some researchers have formally tested the question of whether professionally-trained leaders do better than untrained leaders, and have presented data which suggest that there is no significant difference in impact. Other studies have demonstrated the efficiency of nonprofessional leaders in conducting psychotherapy (primarily individual psychotherapy). Other reports have shown the value of the nonprofessional in the helping area. Various systems have been set up in which individuals are given a modicum of training and then seem to function reasonably well as leaders. However, the data base is thin, and it would be premature to draw reasonable inferences from this material. One of the inherent problems with many of the studies in the group area is that groups have inherent capacities for facilitating growth and change, so that positive gains may not be a simple function of the degree of expertise of the leader but, to an unknown extent, a function of the inherent facilitative capacities of groups. In this view, the question of the expertise of the leader becomes considerably more complex, for unless we know (and none of these studies has really asked this question) whether the leader utilized the group forces, it may very well be that in those few studies contrasting professional and nonprofessional leaders, the professional leaders may have worked in ways which interfered with the inherent properties of groups that can facilitate human change.

Can expertise be operationally defined? One of the major impediments to quality studies of skill in people-changing groups has been the inability of the field to define the meaning of expertise. Many are satisfied with the definition of an expert as one who applies the right intervention at the right time to the right person.

Changing people involves a complex sequence of events, and what evidence is available suggests very clearly that no particular experience will be uniformly profitable to all people. The appropriateness of a particular experience to a particular person is highly dependent on the state of the person at that point and on the context (the characteristics of the social system) in which the person finds himself. Such a view of skill implies that the leader be able to gauge more accurately the states of both person and social system, have within his grasp a wide variety of intervention strategies, and be able to diagnose both the individual and the group so that what he does can be useful to both. The social microcosm that is the group is a complex, dynamic, changing entity. It can be, even to the highly experienced leader, an often bewildering set of contradictions and frank mysteries of what is going on. Cognitive maps are difficult to find in groups, and the leader must work hard in order to make sense of the myriad of behaviors, thoughts, and feelings that are rapidly generated in any group aimed at personal change. Groups offer a great opportunity for projective error—the ascription by the leader of his own thoughts or feelings to the amorphous, complex, supercharged collectivity that is the group. More often than not, leaders will ascribe their own inner state, their boredom, their anger, their warm feelings, to the group.

Groups have considerable persuasive force, and it is not uncommon for the leader to find himself carried along by particular group emotions. The example offered earlier of both leaders and participants accepting an illusion illustrates this point. Groups generate primitive fears in their members and can do so in leaders as well. A common error made by many who conduct groups is to join the members when they focus in on a particular member in scapegoat fashion; this is an easy error to make in change groups because the goals are to try to get the person to change, to reveal himself, and so forth. Examples like this could be multiplied tenfold, but the essential issue that the supercharged collective feelings that so often characterize people-changing groups cannot help but impact on the leader. Crucial, therefore, is the ability of the leader to disentangle his own feelings and thoughts from those that dominate the group at a particular time, so that he maintain enough distance to observe what is happening and be useful to the participants. Such skills are not automatic to most people; education and training and the development of a perspective on one's role and position are critical to their development.

Skill or expertise also implies the ability to develop adequate sources of feedback. One cannot be useful to the group or to the individuals in it without having some means of knowing how his interventions have affected the group. The leader must develop some way of assessing the impact of his interventions. Again, this is a most important skill that requires training and expertise.

Perhaps the most useful way of illustrating some of the problems of circumventing expertise would be to review briefly some of the newer assumptions of the "new group therapies." In a very real sense, the human potential movement has attempted to shortcut training issues by developing strategies for conducting groups that minimize training requirements. The human potential movement assumes that everyone who comes to encounter or sensory awareness groups has the same underlying needs because all moderns are alienated, isolated, and cut off from their feelings. Groups can provide a sense of communion and relatedness to others without the aid of highly-trained leaders. The generalized view that all people need the same thing serves to diminish the attention to the complexity of the change process, for it obviates the problem of determining particular needs of a particular person. Change then becomes a simple matter of providing a context through the group for expressing those feelings assumed to be blocked; leadership becomes simply a matter of providing experiences for psychological and physical closeness to allow participants to sense that they are not alone. Such a monothematic approach to people and their needs and how they can be changed flies in the face of considerable evidence to the contrary.

A second solution has been to develop a highly specific set of techniques (usually termed structured exercises), which are primarily sets of proscriptive behaviors by which the leader creates particular feeling states and experiences in the members. Numerous books presenting such techniques have appeared in the last five years. They also serve to simplify the task for the leader, for he now has a set of highly specific activities which he can offer the group in order to be facilitative. When such leader interventions were studied (Lieberman, Yalom, and Miles, 1973), it was found that they were not highly successful and served more to increase the group's esteem for the leader than to change individuals in the group. Leaders who used such devices were both liked and perceived by the participants as competent, but they were not particularly successful in changing people.

Probably the most serious error of the newer therapies is the assumption that what group members like is what is useful and productive. The new therapies generally generate enthusiasm in their members—it is common for those who have engaged in encounter and other growth-oriented groups to proselytize, to tell their friends they should join a group led by their leader. Thus leaders are caught in a closed cycle in which they increase their behavior to produce enthusiastic responses from members. By and large, they are successful in such interventions, and do create enthusiastic groups. Unfortunately, the evidence at hand is that level of enthusiasm is not equivalent to productive learning and change. In fact, they are orthogonal; some of the most enthusiastic participants are among the least changed. Change and enthusiasm are not the same thing; when they are confused the leaders endanger their chances to provide a setting where people can learn and grow.

Thus, despite the absence of direct evidence that expertise is a crucial element in facilitating change in groups, some of the solutions which have been designed to bypass the issue of expertise have not proven to be useful. The question is still open and demands sophisticated research on the elements of expertise, and on how much expertise in the person of the leader contributes to developing the social microcosm in which the change process is to take place.

REFERENCES

Alexander, F. and French, T. M. *Psychoanalytic therapy.* New York: Ronald Press, 1946.
Bandura, A. *Principles of behavior modification.* New York: Holt, Rinehart and Winston, 1969.
Bion, W. R. *Experiences in groups.* London: Tavistock Press, 1961.

Burrow, T. The group method of analysis. *Psycho-analytic Review*, 1927, **14**, 268–280.

Ezriel, H. A psychoanalytic approach to group treatment. *British Journal of Medical Psychology*, 1950, **23**, 59–74.

Frank, J. *Persuasion and healing*. Baltimore: Johns Hopkins Press, 1961.

Freud, S. *Group psychotherapy and the analysis of the ego*. New York: Boni and Liveright, 1940.

Jourard, S. M. *The transparent self: Self-disclosure and well-being*. Princeton, N.J.: Van Nostrand, 1964.

LeBon, G. *The crowd: A study of the popular mind*. New York: Viking, 1960.

Lieberman, M. A., Yalom, I., and Miles, M. *Encounter groups: First facts*. New York: Basic Books, 1973.

Moreno, J. L. *Who shall survive?* New York: Beacon House, 1953.

Mowrer, O. H. *The new group therapy*. Princeton, N.J.: Van Nostrand, 1964.

Pratt, J. H. The class method of treating consumption in the homes of the poor. *Journal of the American Medical Association*, 1907, **49**, 755–759.

Rogers, C. R. *Encounter groups*. New York: Harper and Row, 1970.

Sullivan, H. S. *The interpersonal theory of psychiatry*. New York: Norton, 1953.

Truax, C. B. and Carkhuff, R. R. *Towards effective counselling and psychotherapy: Training and practice*. Chicago, Ill.: Aldine, 1967.

CHAPTER 14

Automation Methods*

David L. Elwood

INTRODUCTION

The professional psychological community is showing steadily increasing interest in use of automated techniques for study of research questions and for delivery of mental health services to individual clients. Nevertheless, I write this chapter with the awareness that some readers interested in *helping people change* may have little or no interest in automated methods. Buttons, knobs, switches, machines, computers, etc. tend to turn them "off" rather than to turn them "on." For these readers, I would like to say three things. First, a lack of interest in automated methods is understandable. Notwithstanding the steadily increasing emphasis on automation, most of the practice, research, and theorizing in psychological treatment does not focus on automation. Second, it may be that lack of interest in automation is related to a lack of information about the ways automation can increase one's capacity to help people change. If lack of information is a problem, this chapter will help meet the need. Third, it is my intention in presenting the material in this chapter to write, as much as possible, in a direct, nontechnical manner. I hope this approach will help some "low interest" readers become "high interest" readers who will look for ways of applying automated techniques in their own work with individual clients.

Some readers will start this chapter having high interest *and expertise* in psychological instrumentation. For these readers, I want to say this discussion is intended only as an introduction to automation methods. There will be no attempt to

*The preparation of this chapter was supported by funds received from the National Institute of Mental Health, Grant # R01 MH 14864. The author expresses his appreciation to Lowell E. Engelking, George C. Weinland, M.D., M. Eugene Hall, Thomas B. Orr, Ph.D., and the Quinco Consulting Center Board of Directors for their support, encouragement, and interest in the work of the Automated Psychology Laboratory. Also, the author wishes to thank Mary L. Muckler for typing this chapter and Carolyn L. Clark for her perceptive suggestions that improved the readability of this presentation. Drs. Frederick H. Kanfer and Arnold P. Goldstein made numerous valuable suggestions that improved both the readability and organization of this chapter, and the author gratefully acknowledges their help.

make a systematic, comprehensive survey of the entire field of automation, as related to psychology, and few if any extensive discussions of technical details of equipment will be included. Nevertheless, it is my hope that enough new and useful information has been included to maintain the interest of the initial "high interest" reader.

What is meant by *automation methods?* In this chapter, we have reference mainly to electromechanical devices used to present treatment stimuli to individual clients. It is not necessary for a device to be programmable to qualify as an automated method. Thus, we define both a commercially available audiotape recorder and a computer as automated techniques. Our essential concern is whether or not the device, whatever its complexity, is used (or might be used) to deliver psychological treatment stimuli to individual emotionally disturbed clients. The definition we have offered is broad; but it is not meant to include daily use of the telephone to talk to clients, nor to include prosthetic devices such as hearing aids, notwithstanding the potential contribution of such devices to positive behavior change. For the most part, the devices reviewed here will have been described in case studies or controlled experiments involving subjects with emotional adjustment problems. We will report illustrative applications of automated techniques and will describe the different psychological interpretations of behavioral changes resulting from use of these techniques.

HISTORICAL OVERVIEW

The use of instrumentation to present stimuli and record responses has a long tradition in experimental psychology. Hardware played a sufficiently important role in the early work of experimental psychologists that these scientists were sometimes referred to as "brass instrument" psychologists. Later on, the phrase was used disparagingly to refer to the psychologist judged to be "too interested" in instrumentation, the same as the phrase "armchair psychologist" was used pejoratively to describe the psychologist "too interested" in theorizing and not interested enough in experimental data. The history of clinical psychology, by comparison, has been largely void of any emphasis on instrumentation. The use of hardware, mechanical apparatus, or electromechanical devices in psychotherapy has been the exception rather than the rule. We should note that materials such as pictures, puzzles, and painted blocks have traditionally been standard tools in intelligence tests, but in psychotherapy the emphasis has been on the human relationship. As a result, therapist characteristics and their operations, rather than standard tools or devices, have been the center of attention.

In recent years, the picture has changed greatly in clinical psychology. There are now numerous and varied examples of sophisticated instruments that have been introduced directly into the treatment process. There is no easy, fully reliable way to estimate the number of automated treatment devices in use, but tabulation of the dates of articles cited in Schwitzgebel's (1968) "Survey of Electromechanical Devices for Behavior Modification" suggests the number of devices and/or applications reported for the eight year period from 1960 through 1967 was approximately twice as great as for the 94 year period from 1866 through 1959.

There are at least three reasons for this dramatic increase in the use of automated instruments in psychological treatment. First, there has been a widespread increase in the use of technology and computers in all fields of human knowledge. A practical impact has been that psychologists have found it increasingly easy to imagine ways that technology might be used to improve psychological treatment techniques. Second, the widespread availability of high quality, economical, audiotape recorders has greatly increased the psychologist's ability to record, store, and replay verbal stimuli for treatment purposes. For example, relaxation instructions can be conveniently recorded by the therapist and played again and again to different clients without need for the therapist to be present. The same things said about audiotape recording, plus storing and replaying the visual stimulus, can be said about videotape recording, although videotape recorders are less available and cost much more. Third, the success of behavior therapies, such as systematic desensitization (see Chapter 8) in sharply focusing psychological theory and treatment efforts upon specific responses and stimuli, has resulted in treatment approaches that are easily standardized and automated.

It appears clear that automation will play an increasingly important role in the delivery of psychological treatment services. We can expect the time to come when automated systems, with preprogrammed therapeutic material and complex subroutines making these systems responsive to client differences, shall constitute the *clinical standard* methods for treating certain specified adjustment problems in certain types of clients.

RATIONALE FOR AUTOMATED TREATMENT

The rationale for development of automated psychological treatment is based on scientific, professional, and client considerations which we shall now discuss. There are two basic scientific advantages that accrue from use of automated treatment methods: (1) achieving greater experimental control over interpersonal variables believed to be important in psychological treatment, and (2) making available for monitoring and therapeutic manipulation certain physiological and/or motor processes that ordinarily could not be worked with at all, because they are impossible to observe with the naked eye or too brief to be dealt with by the therapist.

A treatment program that is delivered via automation is controllable to the point of being objectively definable, fully standardized, and replicable with the same client or different clients. Thus, a more careful and valid analysis of the effectiveness of the treatment program is possible. An illustration may help clarify the point. It is known that emotionally "warm" therapists having soft, pleasant voices tend to be more effective in reducing phobic behavior in clients than do emotionally "cold" therapists with harsh, impersonal voices (Morris and Suckerman, 1974). A therapist may be trained to use a soft, pleasant voice, but the degree to which he actually is "warm" toward the client will be influenced by the therapist's attitudes, mood, temperament, and recent experiences. Also the way in which a therapist presents face-to-face therapy will be influenced by the reactions of the client. If the client is friendly and cooperative, it may be easy for the therapist to be warm and helpful, but, if the client is sullen and has a "chip on the shoulder" attitude, then it may be difficult for the therapist to be warm, especially if he cannot like the client. In contrast to these unpredictable and difficult to control aspects of face-to-face treatment, automated treatment programs are constant irrespective of changes in the thinking or feelings of the "live" therapist. Furthermore, automated programs can be made immune to client influences except under certain specific conditions when the therapist may want the program to change as a result of some particular response made by the client.

The advent of sophisticated instruments used in biofeedback applications, such as brain wave monitoring and detection of electrical impulses in muscle contractions, has created the possibility of therapeutic interventions that could never have been considered when all treatment was performed directly by the human therapist. Some aspects of behavior are easily observed and their manipulation may have some therapeutic significance, but they are too tedious to be worked with by the human therapist. For example, most clinical workers consider excessive motor movement to be a sign of anxiety and see diminished motor activity as indicating a lowering of anxiety and an increase in self-control. Elwood (1972a) described a device for detecting motor movements, as fine as hard eyeblinks, that sounded a noxious buzzer each time movement occurred. One client who complained of a nominally involuntary contraction of neck muscles causing her head to turn sideways periodically was treated with this device in a recliner chair in the clinic and reported that her condition improved.

The advantages of automated treatment methods for professional and paraprofessional practitioners are that these methods will increase the likelihood that: (1) quantitative bases will be used for therapist assessment of client improvement, resulting in more effective treatment management; (2) the range of variables available for therapeutic manipulation will increase, thus potentially widening the effectiveness of the therapist; (3) packaged treatment programs that can be *prescribed* for certain clients will become available; and (4) specifically trained technicians will be able to apply some types of treatment to the client. In many uses of automated treatment, the primary human therapist who manages the client's treatment plan and maintains needed face-to-face contact will be freed from some routine responsibilities and have greater time to see other clients. In research reports and articles describing clinical applications of automated methods, the most often cited, or implied, advantage of automation is the saving of therapist time.

The rationale discussed so far has concerned the advantages of automation to the scientist and to the therapist, but the client himself should be the ultimate beneficiary of automation. What are the advantages that automation brings to the client? As the client would see things, why use automated treatment?

A highly visible advantage of automated treatment is that it can and does cost less than equal time face-to-face therapy. In the Automated Psychology Laboratory, the cost of "automated practiced imagination therapy," which we shall discuss in detail later in this chapter, is 25 percent of the rate for equal time face-to-face therapy. An engineer in our laboratory estimated that an "automated treatment machine" we are building would have an amortized cost of less than 20 cents per treatment hour before needing repair (after 4000 hours) that would make it temporarily unavailable for service. Whether or not this estimate is accurate, the central point is that the use of machines to provide clinical services can result in large savings and that these savings can be passed on to the client.

Another advantage of automated treatment for the individual client is that it may be more conveniently available than other forms of therapy. Some automated treatments are "packaged" such that it is easy for the client to take the treatment home and apply it to himself at his own leisure, or according to some predetermined schedule that does not conflict with working hours. This treatment could be valuable to the hourly worker who has difficulty making arrangements to be away from his job for therapy appointments at an office.

Automated treatment may be particularly advantageous to a special group of clients who recognize they have problems and want help, but wish to avoid discussing their problems with another person. It appears that many of these clients continue to suffer from their adjustment problems because they are unwilling to yield to the traditional insistence that problems must be "talked out" with another person. Automated treatment may provide help to this special group of clients on terms they will accept. Improvement as a result of automated treatment could make later interpersonal therapy more acceptable to these clients. Probably every person has observed in himself the occasional tendency to talk to another person about a problem *after* he felt he himself had made some significant headway in handling it. We have observed that mentally handicapped clients sometimes prefer automated intelligence testing to face-to-face testing, possibly because they are spared the embarrassment of saying "I don't know" to another person. Some clients seen in our laboratory have stated frankly that they are more comfortable receiving automated treatment than talking with live therapists.

PARALLELS BETWEEN HUMAN AND AUTOMATED THERAPY

One way to understand the psychological theory underlying automated treatment methods is to begin by analyzing the functions of the human therapist. As seen from the humanistic viewpoint, the live therapist is a warm, understanding, compassionate person who listens carefully to each remark made by the client. He empathizes with the client, offers encouragement and support, and attempts to fully appreciate the uniqueness of each client. The humanistic interpretation of live therapist behavior reveals functions that cannot be performed by any device or machine.

A humanistic view of the live therapist is valuable in that it opens for discussion certain dimensions of feelings, thinking, and basic philosophical issues such as "what is man?" that are critical, in our judgment, to a full appreciation of the "human condition." Nevertheless, it is possible and desirable to analyze the functions of the live therapist from a perspective that (a) focuses sharply on a valid understanding of behavior change processes, and (b) leads to improvement of treatment procedures. An example may be helpful. In normal social interaction, we appreciate the "wholeness" of other people; but in medical contexts we do not hesitate to see persons as made up of systems and to draw analogies between human biological systems and inanimate physical systems. We know that hearts work like pumps, eyes work like cameras, arms work like levers, etc. These analogies assist in understanding and treating physical problems. In the same vein, we can see the psychotherapist as a "warm" human being and at the same time know that he functions like an information processor, response analyzer, reinforcement machine, computer, etc. The question to ask about analogies such as these is whether or not they help us develop effective treatment strategies.

What are some functions of the live therapist that are comparable to functions of automated methods? One major role of the live therapist is monitoring and storing (i.e., remembering) the client's behavior. He does this principally by listening to what the client says and observing what the client does. When he listens he hears words, statements, trends, feeling tones, loudness, and speed of talking; and as he observes he sees posture, gestures, unnecessary movements, facial expressions, perspiration, tremors, and eye contact with the therapist.

Automated methods also have the function of monitoring and storing, or recording client behaviors. For the most part, automated methods monitor a more restricted range of behavior than does the live therapist. As an example, an automated system might be devised that would present several different push buttons to the client. The client could be instructed to push different buttons to represent different responses. The control system associated with the different buttons could then record such variables as the number of button presses, duration of button presses, and even finger pressure on the button if it were a relevant concern. Also, electrodes could be attached to the client's arm to monitor galvanic skin response (i.e., electrical activity of the sweat glands often occurring in response to emotionally laden stimuli), a behavior that occurs essentially without the client's awareness or voluntary control. This method of recording vastly increases the reliability and specificity of behavioral observations. It permits easy monitoring of changes due to introduction of treatment procedures and can serve as a base for research and improvement of the individual program. On the other hand, what is lost is the richness of the patient's output that sometimes aids a clinician to gain clues about the patient's behavior, and at other times invites personal interpretations and judgments that can be distorted by the clinician's personal biases.

Either during or following behavioral monitoring, a therapist engages in some form of response analysis. This analysis may consist of the simple attempt to put a client's response into one of two categories: "Is the client making a statement, or asking me a question?" Or, the analysis may involve a complicated series of attempts to classify the client's behavior. It is convenient to think of the process as a series of questions that the therapist asks himself about the client's response: "Is this a statement or question? Is the statement about his understanding of things, or is he asserting some fact? Is the 'fact' likely to be true or false? Has he stated his thinking clearly, or is more information needed? Am I arousing his anger, or does he just find it convenient to express it toward me?" On the basis of his answers to these questions, the therapist formulates a response strategy, replies, and the interaction continues.

An automated treatment counterpart to the "response analysis" process of the live therapist is seen clearly in computer programs. Large numbers of pre-determined "questions" can be written into computer programs, stored in computer "memory," and then be used to evaluate client responses. For example, the amount of time a client talked could be measured, the time could be compared against some predetermined standard in computer memory, and then a decision could be made either to reward the client for talking (e.g., audiotape player would turn on and play message: "You are doing fine. Keep it up.") or provide some mild punishment if the client had talked too much (e.g., noxious buzzer turns on).

An informational analysis of what therapists say to clients would reveal that they give instructions, examples, guidelines, verbal models of how to say things, and that they attempt to coach clients to help them learn effective ways to analyze their problems. It is easy to see parallels between the live therapist and automated systems as givers of information. Most information given by the live therapist can be provided in an automated format that uses audiotape, videotape, moving pictures, or slides. Automated systems do not have as much flexibility as the live therapist to mix different kinds of information within the same treatment appoint-ment, but this may not be a significant handicap. For treatment of specific behavior adjustment problems, it may be more effective to have carefully developed treatment programs with rather fixed informational content, than to have the unlimited flexibility of the live therapist. The work in systematic desensitization suggests that this approach is clearly more effective than the totally flexible interview approach for treating phobias.

DESCRIPTION OF AUTOMATED METHODS

In order to give the reader a brief picture of a community mental health center setting in which automated methods and clinical services have been integrated, we will first describe the Automated Psychology Laboratory (APL). This description is intended to suggest that the atmosphere of concern, openness, and interest can be maintained in a center that uses automated methods for some clinical services. The APL is a clinical service and research unit located in Quinco Consulting Center, a comprehensive community mental health center. The clinical objective of APL is to make automated services available to individual Quinco clients on a routine basis. The research purpose is to work toward the development and evaluation of automated machines and programs that can be put directly into clinical service in this and in other clinical centers. In pursuing these dual objectives, laboratory personnel schedule regular appointments for clients to receive automated treat-ment programs and for research subjects to participate in experimental studies.

Figure 14.1 shows a schematic drawing of APL which includes a receptionist area, three offices, four treatment/testing rooms for clients, a shop/equipment room, and a storage room. Client rooms # 1, # 2, and # 4 are furnished with recliner chairs and are used principally for automated treatment. Room #3 is set up for automated psychological testing and can be used for a totally automated administration of the Wechsler Adult Intelligence Scale (Elwood, 1972b). Also, Room #3 could be used for automated administration of other psychological tests as well, with some additional minor work on the electrical circuits that control the testing procedures.

At this time, we are in the process of expanding and improving the electrical program control system that has been used to present psychological test stimuli and treatment stimuli to clients. The new system, which will use a Digital Equipment Corporation PDP-12 computer, will simultaneously regulate the administration of treatment programs in rooms #1, #2, and #4 while controlling testing functions in room #3. In addition to presenting stimuli at these different client terminals, the PDP-12 computer will collect and store, in "memory," data relevant to (a) the client's responses to treatment programs and (b) his answers to test question. The system will be capable of monitoring and analyzing both digital and analog data received from the client, and it will provide individually tailored feedback to the client through audio messages, lights, tones, buzzers, digital readouts, and a vibrating unit built into the recliner chair where the client will sit.

A block diagram of the major electrical systems in APL is shown in Fig. 14.2. It will be possible to generate computer programs to control this automated system by typing the program instructions into the keyboard of the ASR-33 Teletype. Once programs have been written and debugged, they will be stored in computer memory while in use and at other times will be stored on magnetic tape. The PDP-12 computer will be combined with the Universal Digital Controller and Behavior Research Systems units in order to monitor client responses and to present stimuli to clients. Computers often need an "interface," a network of circuits, switches, and relays, to be nested between the computer and (a) the conditions to be sensed (e.g., client presses a button) and (b) the devices to be operated (e.g., an audiotape recorder is to be turned on and lighted numbers are to be shown). The UDC and BRS units will be the major interface systems in the APL.

The Broadcast Electronics units include 17 remotely controllable audiotape players that use electronically cued closed loop tapes. Large numbers of individual messages can be recorded on these tapes and by the press of a button a "stop cue" can be placed at the end of each message. Thus, a tape player can be turned on remotely, play a pre-recorded message, and stop when the stop cue is sensed. Also auxiliary cues can be placed on these tapes so that as one message ends, another message begins from a different audiotape player. A practical application would be that one tape player could play the name of a client, stop at the stop cue, and then be followed immediately by a treatment item (i.e., a therapeutic statement) played from another tape player.

The "personalizing" of treatment items in this manner is not the most important use of the Broadcast Electronic tape units. Most importantly, these units create the

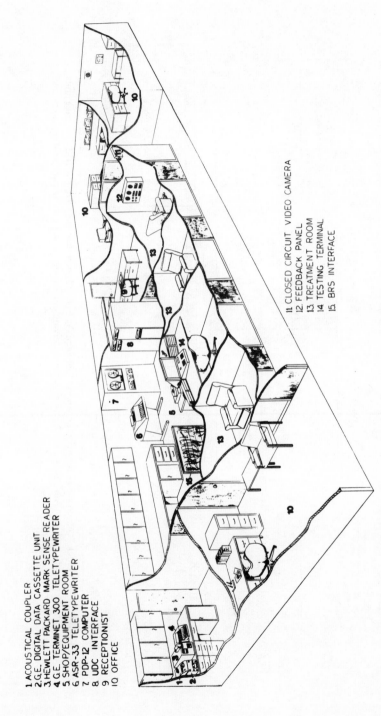

1 ACOUSTICAL COUPLER
2. G.E. DIGITAL DATA CASSETTE UNIT
3 HEWLETT PACKARD MARK SENSE READER
4 G.E. TERMINET 300 TELETYPEWRITER
5 SHOP/EQUIPMENT ROOM
6 ASR-33 TELETYPEWRITER
7 PDP-12 COMPUTER
8 UDC INTERFACE
9 RECEPTIONIST
10 OFFICE

11 CLOSED CIRCUIT VIDEO CAMERA
12. FEEDBACK PANEL
13. TREATMENT ROOM
14 TESTING TERMINAL
15. BRS INTERFACE

Fig. 14.1. This schematic drawing shows the general floor space and major pieces of equipment in the Automated Psychology Laboratory. The four rooms in the lower part of the drawing are used to provide clinical services to clients and to conduct clinical-experimental research.

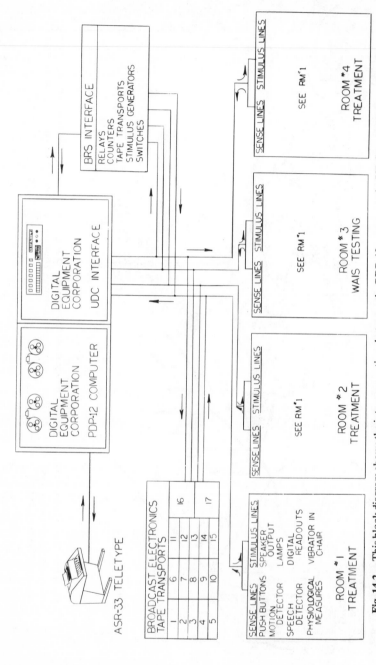

Fig. 14.2. This block diagram shows the interconnections between the PDP-12 computer, the UDC and BRS interface units, the tape transports, and the rooms in which clients sit while receiving clinical services, or while participating in research studies.

possibility of "random access audio." What random access means in this context is that any one of the 17 audiotape players can be played in any order. For example, a client could be receiving an anxiety reduction program from audiotape player #17. If the PDP-12 "decides" that the client's responses showed a need for a message of encouragement, it could activate player #14 that stores such a message. If a clarification of instructions is needed, player #15 would be activated, etc. Thus, the PDP-12 computer could instruct the UDC interface unit to suspend playing player #17, play one message from player #14 or #15, then return to player #17 to continue the anxiety reduction program.

A random access audio system will help make automated therapy more responsive or "sensitive" to client differences. Computer programs can include instructions that will help automated systems to detect whether or not a client is getting "hung up" on some particular program, and if alternative procedures need to be tried. As versatility of available programs increases, this "branching" procedure comes closer to the "flexible" therapist.

A cutaway drawing of a client seated in a recliner is shown in Fig. 14.3. The response panel held by the client is connected by cable to the UDC-BRS interface system and contains several back-lighted push buttons for the client to press in order to rate treatment items, select multiple choice options, indicate the presence of anxiety, etc. The specific functions the buttons have depends upon the nature of the automated treatment program to be presented. The feedback panel on the wall in front of the client contains speakers, programmable numerical readouts, and indicator lamps, all of which can be programmed to present a variety of feedback conditions to the client. As an example, a reticent client could be given the task of talking to earn points that could be exchanged for money. A voice operated relay would detect client speech. The amount of speech that had occurred would be constantly updated and displayed on a programmable numerical readout. Thus, the client could have constant "feedback" on the amount of money he had earned.

Whereas the APL includes a variety of devices that are being integrated into a total automated system, many therapists make use of single devices that they can operate alone. We wish now to describe some of these devices.

The most common automated treatment method used by the clinical psychologist is the ordinary audiotape recorder. There is a huge range of special features, functions, and specifications for these machines; but, for the most part, the applications that psychologists make of tape recorders do not require special features. However, two special features are desirable. First, units with stereo record/playback "heads" make it convenient to record therapeutic material on one track and to record program control cues on the other track. If the therapist desires that some condition (e.g., turning on a slide projector) be associated with a specific therapeutic message or response, he can record the needed cue on the program control track. When the cue is sensed while the tape is playing, (a) the indicated device will be turned "on," or (b) an electrical circuit will be "set" such that the device will be turned on *if* the client makes some specific response (e.g., presses a button to signify "I feel anxious."). If one wishes to use a recorder in this way, it is necessary to have a unit (e.g., Columbia Scientific Industries, Media Master, Model

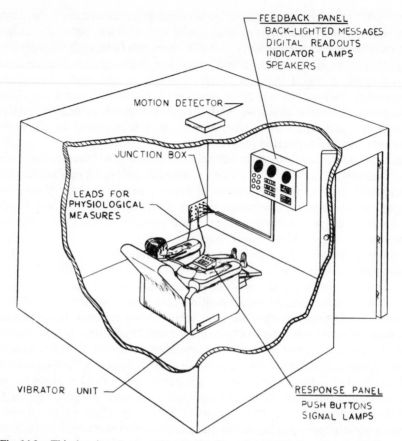

Fig. 14.3.   This drawing shows a client reclined in a chair, holding a response panel and looking toward a feedback panel. These units can be used either for testing or treatment purposes.

375) that will generate and record cues onto tape, and will sense these cues during playback and convert them into electrical energy that is appropriate to operate relays, lamps, etc. Some audiotape recorders have these encoder-decoder functions built directly into the recorder (e.g., Hitachi, Model AVA-1000).

Second, recorders with "solenoid operated pinch rollers" can usually be operated remotely to cause tape motion to start and stop very quickly without stopping the motor that drives the tape. These recorders are desirable because they are free from distorted speech sounds and time lags sometimes associated with motor slow-down and start-up.

By far the most popular tape recorder-player on the market is the cassette tape recorder and increasing numbers of them are finding their ways into psychological laboratories and treatment centers. These units, typically small and easy to handle, often operate from AC or battery power sources, are available from inexpensive models under $25 to high quality multi-function models over $500 and all of them use small enclosed reel to reel tape cartridges (cassettes) that are easy to store and handle. Most cassette units, excluding the very compact hand held types, reproduce the human voice with acceptable fidelity. Also, some suppliers offer closed loop cassette tapes making possible endless repetition of the same program or message without rewinding the tape.

Eight-track closed-loop cartridge recorders appear to be less convenient to work with than cassette units (possibly because recording and editing are more complicated), but they do have a potentially important advantage. These units may be modified for remotely controlled random access audio. As explained earlier, what this means is that any one of the eight tracks can be played in any order the operator, or a program, "decides." Some eight-track players are designed so that the cartridge which includes the pinch roller can be remotely pushed against or released from the "capstan," the small shaft that turns to drive the tapes. Thus, starting and stopping tape motion is possible without needing to start and stop the motor that drives the tape. Since it is routinely true that changing tracks in eight-track players is accomplished via a solenoid operated mechanism that moves the "head" across the tape, completely remote random access to any one of the eight tracks of the tape is feasible.

The RCA Mark 8 Stereo, MYC 555W is an example of a unit that could be used in the manner described above. This model can hold a stack of five cartridges, and, therefore, could offer complete random access to 40 different tracks, or channels, of information. If certain requirements were met which we shall not attempt to spell out here, it would be possible to divide each track into a large number of different audio messages (60 or more) that could be played sequentially, one message at a time. As an example, one might always hear a "strong positive reinforcement" from cartridge #1, track #1, but each time it would be worded or phrased differently until the tape loop had made a complete revolution. Track #2 might contain samples of "mild positive reinforcements." The availability of different verbal reinforcements would help clients to perceive automated treatment as approaching the variety of verbal output that characterizes the live therapist.

The radio broadcast industry uses audiotape "transports" suitable for psychological research and treatment applications. A tape transport is the motor, mechanical works, and supporting hardware necessary for tape motion, without the complete amplification electronics and speakers needed for sound reproduction. These tape transports are expensive, but they are usually well engineered, ruggedly constructed, reliable, easily available for remote control applications, easily available with built-in electronic cueing functions for stopping tape motion and triggering auxiliary devices, and most of these transports take standard sized closed-loop cartridges. Companies that manufacture these types of tape transports often advertise in trade magazines such as *Broadcast Engineering*.

The videotape recorder-player has been rapidly assimilated into many educational, training, and clinical service settings. As the demand for videotape recorders has increased in a broad range of educational, business, and industrial settings, prices have been driven down, special functions and options have become more common, and an important major development, the videocassette has become available. The ease of handling video equipment (assuming some practical experience to acquire the needed skills), the zoom lens, high resolution pictures, the convenience of videocassettes, color pictures, the ease of editing unwanted tape segments, and the impressiveness of instant playback of good quality pictures synchronized with good quality sound have all contributed to the rising popularity of this technique as a facilitator of therapeutic change. The widespread use of videotape recorders in therapeutic work with clients has been accompanied by numerous claims about the technique's value. Alger and Hogan (1970) stated "It may be no exaggeration to say video tape recording represents a technological breakthrough with the kind of significance for psychiatry that the microscope has had for biology." Woody (1971) continues this theme, after commenting on the importance of audio tape recording, by saying, *"further, it is preferable, if true maximum treatment potential is to be possible that every psychotherapist have access to video tape recording facilities and equipment for at least selected patients"* (Woody's italics). See Chapter 6 for comment on the therapeutic effectiveness of video playback.

The use of film is quite familiar in the study of psychotherapy, but traditionally it has played a minor role in treatment of individual behavior adjustment problems. Two important changes occurring in recent years have increased the attractiveness of film usage in individual treatment. *First*, the theoretical climate is now more favorable. Since the start of the behavior therapy movement, there has been increased willingness to break down complex behavior sequences into their component parts and to examine limited aspects of the environments in which these responses occur. Thus, it is now acceptable to consider using a 12 or 15 minute motion picture, or series of slides, as part of a therapeutic program. This can be done without fear of unwarranted criticisms that one is ignoring the "uniqueness of the client," or is treating "only a part of the client's problems." It needs to be understood that use of automated techniques does not rule out collateral face-to-face meetings in which the live therapist is compassionate and uses his full range of interpersonal skills. *Second*, technological improvements have made motion pictures easier to produce and use. The widespread availability of cameras that are battery powered, use electronic circuits to automatically regulate the lens opening and shutter speed, and that accept film cartridges simple to load and unload has made film production more appealing to the individual user. Film projectors are also improved. Projectors that are compact, self-threading, and can be synchronized with sound from audiotape cassettes are commonplace. Some projectors accept closed loop film cartridges that are simply plugged into a slot in the projector and shown without fuss or bother.

Slide projectors are an attractive means of presenting some types of stimuli. Most slide projectors are fairly trouble free devices that interface easily with other pieces of equipment. An appealing feature of some slide projectors modified by behavior research equipment manufacturers is that the slides can serve program control functions. As an example, showing slide #10 might always result in a tape recorder turning on and presenting a reassuring message, or instructions, to the client. This use of slides for program control purposes is achieved by punching small binary coded holes into the edges of the slides. Light shines through these holes activating photoelectric cells in patterns identical to the punched holes. In turn, electrical circuits are triggered that energize devices such as lights, buzzers, and tape recorders; or, circuits can be "set" so that if the client responds one way to the slide one thing will happen and if he responds another way something different will happen.

The biofeedback training field, which has grown very rapidly during the past decade, includes many different devices and areas of application. The devices range from (a) simple to operate, easy to carry, personally owned units that are advertised in popular magazines to (b) highly complex, relatively permanent feedback "systems" that require "on-line" computer programs in order for the feedback system to be most effectively applied to a client. On-line means that the computer is immediately and directly available to receive data, analyze the data, and then send signals, or instructions, back to the device that interacts with the client. Biofeedback training devices have been applied to help clients acquire voluntary control over heart rate, blood pressure, skin temperature, brain waves, and other biological processes that traditionally were felt to be impossible to influence using volitional techniques. Many biofeedback units are attractively packaged, designed to be controlled by an individual operator, and are desk mountable making them appealing to use in clinical offices.

Many automated procedures involve nothing more than the straightforward playing of an audiotape recorder which is turned off after the therapeutic material is completely presented. Other automated procedures are "responsive," or "interactive." What the automated technique does depends upon what the client does. Interactive automated systems require some type of program control capability. The most flexible, general purpose program control system is a computer. However, there are other less expensive and highly useful means of achieving program control. We should explain that two types of programs are implicit in this discussion. One is the "therapeutic program" that is comprised of the material to be presented directly to the client. The other is the "control program" which consists of the instructions or information that regulates the interaction between the automated system and the client himself. It is the latter, the "control program," that is our concern here.

As noted earlier in this discussion, audiotape and slides can be sources of program control information. Coded slides may offer a more flexible program control technique than is generally recognized. It is not necessary for the picture on the slide to be presented as therapeutic material. The projector lamp can be turned off so that the pictures are not shown, and coded information in the holes on the slides can still be used to operate devices such as buzzers, lights, and audiotape players, or to "set" circuits so that particular responses are required before certain treatment stimuli are presented. Entire programs may be changed in a few seconds by removing one tray of slides and inserting another tray of slides with different patterns of holes in them. Also, individual program steps may be changed by removing one slide and inserting a new one.

Stereo tape recordings that are electronically cued on one track may offer the most feasible form of program control for typical automated treatment methods. The parallel location of audio messages on one track and cues on the other track assures that what the client hears and what the equipment does will always be synchronized. The ease of editing these cues to correct errors and make improvements adds to the attractiveness of this form of program control. "Punched paper tape readers" offer considerable flexibility as program control devices, but their use tends to require a significant amount of support equipment that makes them unattractive for many clinical settings. Some program control systems are "hardwired" meaning that specific control functions are dependent upon specific components and wires that connect the components to each other. A totally hardwired system has very limited flexibility.

Implicit in much of this discussion has been the need for some rather complicated electrical circuits to handle various counting, timing, measuring, comparing, and "logic" functions. A considerable amount of effort may be required to fully understand these circuits. In this regard, I would like to say it is not necessary for a therapist to understand the electrical circuits that make automated methods operate. The main task for the therapist is to express his treatment strategies in language that is clear enough so that an expert in equipment design or selection can put the treatment into an automated format. It is important to know that all behavior research equipment manufacturers have application specialists on their staffs. These specialists work closely with potential customers to translate their psychological procedures into hardware-software configurations, to design the necessary electrical circuits, and to estimate costs for the proposed automated system.

CLINICAL APPLICATIONS OF AUTOMATED METHODS

Automated techniques appear to be compatible with any theoretical orientation, although the theory held by a therapist will undoubtedly influence his use of automated procedures. A behavior therapist who analyzes adjustment problems as undesirable stimulus-response connections may allow automated procedures to play a central role in treatment. A psychoanalyst who diagnoses problems as unresolved childhood conflicts that must be talked-out with an understanding person may limit the role of automation. The studies discussed below were selected to illustrate the wide range of psychological treatment procedures, adjustment problems, and theoretical orientations to which automated methods have been applied.

Interview Therapy

Interview therapy is characterized by face-to-face verbal interactions between therapist and client. Usually, the therapist attempts to communicate feelings of concern, warmth and understanding, tries to promote insight, seeks information, and gives the client a chance to talk. The client talks, seeks self-understanding, ventilates emotion, and looks for more effective ways to solve problems. The interactions between therapist and client are extremely complicated, but some investigators have attempted to apply automated methods to therapeutic interviewing.

One approach is to develop computer-based interview systems that use a teletypewriter for communication between the client and computer. The client types a statement or question into the keyboard, using his own spelling, punctuation, etc., then signals the end of the message. The computer program searches the client's message for "key words" which are used by the computer to compose a reply to the client. The computer prints the reply on the teletypewriter and then awaits further input from the client. As an example, a client might type the message, "I am unhappy because my children will not obey." The computer program might isolate *unhappy* as a key word and reply, "Please tell me more about your unhappiness." Samples of dialogues between clients and computers have a conversational tone, but, apparently, most clients finally become frustrated with the computer because it fails to "remember" everything it should remember and does not "appreciate" the full implications of client statements. In short, the client sees the computer program as "incompetent." The computer can "remember" all critical information obtained from the client and ascertain significant implications of client statements, but it must be programmed to perform these functions. We must await further developments in therapeutic programming before computers are indeed programmed to operate in fully acceptable and effective manners (Colby, Watt, and Gilbert, 1966; Colby and Enea, 1967).

A criticism of computerized interviewing is that the computer fails to note and make use of certain kinds of nonverbal information that may be important to understanding the client but that are not suitable for entry into a teletypewriter keyboard. For example, a client's gestures may provide useful information to the live therapist. Slack (1971) developed a program that not only monitored the client's keyboard responses but also measured and stored the response latency and heart rate for each response. These nonverbal data were available to influence the administration of the computer program (i.e., "branching") to make it more responsive to client differences. Other therapists have experimented with (1) standardized series of statements that are presented on a TV monitor that encourage the client to talk, (2) computer programs that sense the presence of speech and encourage the client to talk if he is silent too long, and, (3) the interposing of a "human translator" between the client and computer to facilitate the computer's "understanding" of the client. "Speech synthesizers" are now available and can be programmed to generate any words in any sequences. Thus, a client could type his message into a keyboard, and the computer would reply in an audible voice—the computer would literally "talk" to the client. These and other developments are making it feasible to start thinking of therapeutic computer programs that will be available via computer timesharing and can be used by any person who (a) knows the entry code to the computer, (b) has access to an ordinary telephone, and (c) has a portable teletypewriter terminal available for use in his own home, hotel room, office, hospital, etc.

Most of the approaches discussed above are heavily dependent on computer programs, but some attempts to automate interview therapy, or some aspects of it, have not relied upon computers at all. Lindsley (1969) developed a system in which the therapist and client sat in different rooms and viewed each other over closed circuit television. The client was given two handswitches that controlled whether he saw the therapist's image on the TV monitor and/or heard what the therapist said. If the client pressed one handswitch, he caught a glimpse of the therapist on the screen, but he had to press the switch at a high rate (about 60 times per minute) to obtain a continuous image of the therapist. The other handswitch worked similarly except that it controlled therapist voice input into the client's room. The client had to press both handswitches at high rates to continue to see the image of the therapist *and* hear everything he said. An important practical application of the system is that it could provide the therapist with instant feedback about whether his image and voice were reinforcing to the client (i.e., pressing the handswitches can be seen as operant responding). Thus, if the therapist saw that the client was procuring his image and voice at low rates, he could promptly attempt to modify his behavior to encourage more rapid client responses. The optimal rates of responding for different types of clients and whether low response rates would sometimes be desirable are questions to be decided by empirical research.

Cameron, Levy, Ban, and Rubenstein (1964) pointed out that automation might help reduce the "enormously time consuming" demands of psychotherapy, if the procedure could be used to "set into operation" one or more of the basic "mechanisms" of psychotherapy. Working from a psychodynamic perspective, they identified *uncovering* as one of these mechanisms. Uncovering consisted of attempts to elucidate childhood experiences and conflicts that the authors believed to be the basis for current adjustment problems. Automating consisted of recording the messages that encouraged the client to recall childhood experiences that could be related to his present problems. The client was instructed to listen to the tape several hours per week and to write down on paper his associations during built-in blank portions of the tape. The written associations were given to the therapist who used them as the basis for preparing new messages for the client to listen to. A number of other mechanisms such as problem identification, problem solving, and client-therapist interaction were activated also using this closed-loop tape technique. Cameron *et al.* kept face-to-face contact between the client and therapist at a minimum in their use of this technique, but we wish to encourage therapists to try any combination of face-to-face and automated treatments that they wish, consistent with sound clinical judgment.

Automated procedures may constitute the entire interview therapy process such as in some computer-based interviews, or automation may play a more limited role. For example, one therapist used a slide projector to treat sexually frigid women. To assist these women in learning to achieve orgasm through masturbation (a step that was felt to be helpful in preparation for penile-vaginal stimulation) a series of 19 "self-pleasuring" slides were shown in the therapist's office. The slides advanced automatically each 20 seconds and were presented as "instructional aids" that showed a woman touching her face, neck, thighs, breasts, and genital areas.

The technique was judged by the therapist to be valuable "in disinhibiting sexual attitudes and behaviors in orgasmically dysfunctional female clients . . ." Effectiveness of the procedure was attributed to probable desensitization, modeling, and vicarious learning influences (Lehman, 1974).

Social Modeling

The interest of clinical theorists and practitioners in social modeling is based on the common observation that some behaviors are learned more easily by watching another person perform the behavior than by hearing him explain it without seeing him perform it. For further discussion of social modeling, the reader is referred to Chapter 5 in this book. Chapter 6 on role playing is relevant as well.

Oftentimes, clients come seeking help for their adjustment difficulties, but they are unable to be interpersonally open and, consequently, do not maximally benefit from treatment. We discuss this lack of openness with the client and try to explain to him how to overcome it, but frequently we fail to bring about the desired change in the client's behavior. Automated modeling procedures may help us to deal with some problems of this type. Whalen (1969) used *audiotape* recorded instructions and *filmed* modeling to study interpersonal openness among small interacting groups of college students. Her principal finding was that the students who showed interpersonally open behavior were those who had heard "detailed instructions" on how to respond openly *and* had watched a filmed demonstration of openness. Students tending not to show interpersonal openness were those who (a) heard "minimal instructions" on how to respond openly and watched the film, (b) only heard "minimal instructions," (c) only heard "detailed instructions," or, (d) only saw the film.

An interesting aspect of this study is that two automated techniques, audiotape and film, were used, but neither one was sufficient alone to produce interpersonal openness. The combined use of the two techniques resulted in interpersonal openness. This use of audiotaped messages and filmed examples to promote interpersonal openness may be helpful in clinical situations. The procedure could be used to encourage clients to become more willing to talk about sensitive areas, to admit they misunderstand certain critical relationships, etc. The technique could be used to prepare clients to enter face-to-face treatment, or it could be the major behavior change method with interview therapy playing a supportive role only. We should note that the detailed instructions used by Whalen took less than five minutes and the film ran for only 12 minutes. The translation of this laboratory material into a therapeutic program for use in practice settings could involve expanding the material into a half dozen or more 30-minute programs. It would be desirable for such programs (a) to include specific skill training in the different aspects of interpersonal openness, and (b) to include feedback loops to enable the client to assess his progress as he went through the training procedure.

The usefulness of behavioral skills acquired through modeling is related to the variety of stimulus conditions that are present when modeling occurs. As an example, the ability to meet strangers may be learned best by watching many models meet many strangers. Automated treatment techniques may offer a potentially powerful advantage over face-to-face treatment methods as a means to present variable stimuli to the client. An endless variety of stimuli that includes words, people, animals, places, and conditions can be put onto slides, audiotapes, films, and videotapes. These stimuli can be used routinely in automated treatment. In contrast, it may be impractical in face-to-face therapy to arrange for the client to be exposed to any stimuli besides the live therapist. The point is illustrated in a study by Bandura and Menlove (1968). These psychologists treated children who were markedly fearful of dogs by showing them a wide variety of *filmed* models interacting nonanxiously "with numerous dogs varying in size and fearsomeness." Children treated in this way showed greater weakening of fear of dogs than another group of children who saw only a single filmed model interacting with a single dog.

Goldstein (1973) has attempted to meet the problem of traditional psychotherapy's failure to be a viable treatment method for many working class and poor clients by developing "Structured Learning Therapy." This therapy represents one of the most systematic and extensive efforts to (a) use automated techniques (mainly audiotaped and videotaped recordings) to present social modeling stimuli to clients, and (b) stress the importance of "prescriptive" psychological treatments that are tailor-made to fit individual client problems. Goldstein has developed a large number of audio- and videotapes to present series of social interaction situations that illustrate, or model, desirable social skills. A main significance of this work is that it points to the time when psychological treatment centers such as community mental health clinics will have "libraries" of treatment tapes that can be "prescribed" to fit the unique configuration of problems that a client brings into the clinic.

Assertion Training

The lack of an appropriate amount of assertive behavior can have debilitating effects on general social adjustment. The reader is referred to Chapter 6 in this book for further discussion of the theoretical and clinical issues involved in assertion training. Our discussion will focus on the ways that automated devices may be used to facilitate assertion training.

Serber (1972) outlined a way to use videotape playback to teach the "nonverbal" components of assertive behavior. The method is instructive and should be mentioned in some detail. He stated that the conditions favorable for nonverbal training were: (1) a clearly defined situation (i.e., the specific physical-social context in which problematic behavior is supposed to occur), (2) concentration on a limited number of nonverbal variables, and (3) use of audiovisual feedback, or playback. In implementing the approach, Serber picked a problem situation that could be repeated, asked the client to role play the behavior in question, videotaped the role playing, replayed the behavior back to the client, offered instruction and reinforcement as needed, had the client role play again, etc. He broke nonverbal assertive behavior into six categories: loudness of voice, fluency of spoken words, eye contact, facial expression, body expression, and distance from the person with whom one is interacting. As noted above, these specific behaviors tended to be dealt with (shaped) one at a time during the role playing-playback-instruction-reinforcement sequences.

Serber's use of videotaped playback to increase assertive behavior is appealing and he reported clinical improvement in the clients he treated; however, it must be noted that the procedure required the full time involvement of the therapist himself to operate the equipment, give instructions, and apply reinforcements. There are several steps that could be taken to more fully automate a nonverbal assertion training procedure. By purchasing appropriate electrical devices, or quite easily designing and building many of them himself, one could devise the following monitoring and feedback systems:

1. A unit whose sensitivity would be manually adjustable and would turn "on" a buzzer if the client's speech were too soft.
2. A manually adjustable "voice operated relay" that would activate an unpleasant tone if the onset of client utterances were too slow.
3. A headband containing a photoelectric cell that could detect head orientation (i.e., "looking") and trigger a circuit if the client's head orientation were incorrect—head is turned away from a desirable target such as the face of the therapist.
4. A system of gravity operated mercury switches that could be arranged on the client's head and shoulders and could trigger noxious feedback such as turning "on" electrical buzzers if the client failed to maintain erect posture.

Most of these monitoring and feedback systems would involve simple circuits that would either be "off" or "on." For example, the therapist could play a series of threatening messages from an audiotape (ideally these messages would be uttered by many different persons). The audiotape could be cued so that following each threatening message a circuit would be "set" requiring the client to say something very quickly in order to avoid hearing a loud noxious sound. The noxious sound would occur automatically, if after a predetermined latency, following the taped message, the client failed to speak. The latency could be adjusted by the therapist and might be set for a long duration in initial trials and made progressively shorter as the treatment session progressed. After the client had learned to speak quickly following each threatening message, an additional requirement could be imposed on him. In the next stage of treatment, the client could be required to speak quickly *and* to speak with specified loudness. If he failed to speak loudly enough, a "new" noxious sound could be triggered. As soon as the client was consistently speaking quickly and loudly in response to threatening messages, another requirement, etc. could be imposed upon him.

The clinical application of the approach described above could result in a very large number of client behaviors being made subject to control and manipulation by the therapist. The client's posture, gestures, where he looked, how loudly and quickly he talked, how long he talked, and so forth could be simultaneously controlled. It is important to note that the number of variables possible to control and the number that is clinically practical to control may not be the same. In other words, the use of instrumentation may result in more data being collected than the therapist can use effectively and the client may be unable to respond meaningfully to all feedback that could be offered to him. Also, it must be acknowledged that an approach such as this one does not attend, at all, to the content of the client's verbal responses. The therapist could attend to the content of what the client said and reinforce him according to how appropriate his statements were to the threatening messages he had heard. The optimal role of this automated approach, in the general scheme of assertion training therapy, must be decided by empirical studies.

McFall and his co-workers (e.g., McFall and Twentyman, 1973) have reported a series of experiments showing that an automated training technique consistently increased assertive behavior among college students. In essence, the automated technique involved using an audiotape player to present "stimulus situations" that included (a) miniature social situations in which assertive responses were appropriate, (b) opportunities for the subject to give his reaction, (c) social modeling, and (d) coaching as to what made a good assertive response. Longin and Rooney (1973) used a similar automated procedure in a successful effort to increase assertion among inpatients at a mental hospital. Potentially, it would seem that any social skill that could fit into this framework could be administered with automated techniques.

Extinction Processes

Another use of audiotape recorders is for presentation of implosive therapy, or flooding therapy. In essence, this treatment involves subjecting the client to a massive and unrelenting stream of stimulation (verbal descriptions, or real stimulus objects) that represents the situation, object, or person to which the client has phobic reactions. The consequence is that the client survives the situation even though he is unable to escape from it, and, apparently, the need to escape this type of stimulus situation is thereby diminished. The process is best understood as extinction of avoidance responses. Kirchner and Hogan (1966) reported using an audiotape recorder to provide implosive therapy to rat phobic subjects. They reported significantly greater improvement among treated subjects than among control subjects on a post test that consisted of picking up a rat. Dee (1972), in a well controlled study, used audiotape recordings to present implosive therapy to snake phobic subjects. She found no consistent differences between the treated subjects and control subjects who did not hear the implosive tapes. One problem in Dee's study was that her subjects were recruited on the basis of high snake phobia test scores rather than because these subjects requested treatment for snake phobia. Thus, they may not have been motivated to seek improvement. The ease of preparing verbal descriptions and recording this material onto audiotapes makes these tapes a highly attractive medium for automated implosion therapy, but videotapes and films as well can be used in implosion therapy (see Chapter 8). For example, some therapists have attempted to decrease snake phobia by showing moving pictures of snakes crawling around and over a person. Denholtz (1970) used audiotaped flooding to treat premature ejaculation in a 32-year-old man who feared verbal abuse from his wife and was terrified at thoughts of having a family. The therapist made an audiotape in which he asked the patient to see himself as being "locked" into an embrace by his wife while he uncontrollably and continuously ejaculated into her uterus. During this time the patient's wife was pictured as heaping verbal abuse on him and screaming out that he would become a father! The patient played the tape twice daily on a portable tape player in his car. The therapist reported the patient learned to hold back ejaculation until after his partner reached orgasm.

Avoidance Conditioning

Whereas the therapeutic use of extinction is often intended to help a client *approach* some stimulus object (i.e., overcome a phobia), other treatments are oriented to teaching clients how to *avoid* certain stimuli (e.g., an inappropriate sexual object). Feingold (1969) described an automated treatment of sexual deviations that used a tape recorder programmed to deliver electric shocks to the leg of the client. The audiotape programs consisted of series of descriptions of sexual stimulus situations, or scenes, (i.e., homosexuality, pedophilia, or exhibitionism) appropriate to each client's problem. Interspersed among these scenes (every three or four items) was a heterosexual scene in which a seductive female voice gave "verbal descriptions of arousing heterosexual situations . . .." The client listened to the description of a scene, stopped the recorder with a hand switch, and tried to imagine the scene clearly. Following the imagination of each problematic sexual scene, a shock was administered. The client was required to repeat the imagination of the scene (and receive the accompanying shock) as many times as necessary until he was able to imagine it without becoming sexually aroused. Feingold reported that the treatment sessions lasted from 45 to 90 minutes and that during the first week of treatment clients came in every day of the week. After treatment was concluded, it was possible for clients to come in for "booster treatments" if they needed them. Feingold reported that he "could never have given as many treatments as he did, and/nor ones as long as he did, without this automated device."

MacCulloch, Birtles, and Feldman (1971) described an automated device for assertive conditioning in homosexuality. The subject was shown a male slide which was used as a conditioned stimulus for the onset of electric shock which followed within 8 seconds if the subject did not press a button that removed the male slide and substituted in its place a female slide. The MacCulloch *et al.* system required the presence of a therapist who controlled the slide projector, adjusted the strength of electric shock, made judgments about how the client was progressing, etc. It would be possible to more fully automate this system with a minimum of electrical design work. MacCulloch *et al.* saw the desirability of additional automation and discussed this in their article. Birk, Huddleston, Miller, and Cohler (1971) described a procedure for the avoidance conditioning for homosexuality that is similar to the one used by MacCulloch *et al.* Two interesting aspects of their approach are that they asked subjects to bring their own sexual material to be reproduced as slides and that they used group psychotherapy concomitantly with automated avoidance conditioning.

It would seem easy to include an audiotape recorder to present appropriate verbal/other aural stimulation along with the slides. For example, one could make a simple classical conditioning approach to avoidance training. Aversive audio such as noxious sounds could be presented with some slides (e.g., male), and a soothing, enticing female voice could be coordinated with female slides. Uncomfortable electric shock could still be associated with male slides. We should note that (1) the increased availability of sexual treatment materials, (2) technical improvements in slide projectors and audiotape recorders, and (3) ease of interfacing and programming these units are helping make automated treatment more attractive to a wide range of psychotherapists.

Self-Control Paradigms

There is increasing interest among clinical theorists in finding ways to help clients achieve more effective control over their own behavior. Three major psychological processes assumed to be present during exercise of self-control are outlined in Chapter 10 of this book. These processes are *self-monitoring, self-evaluation*, and *self-reinforcement*. In this section, we wish to discuss ways in which automated devices can facilitate application of self-control treatment to individual adjustment problems.

Sims and Lazarus (1973) reasoned that a client who was prone to depression and daydreaming responded these ways partly because he failed to self-monitor positive feelings and to note pleasant elements in his current environment. In order to counteract this pattern, the client was given an "auditory stimulation device" that he carried with him. On random occasions the device would emit a high pitched tone that had been taught to the client as a cue for him to "self-monitor." For example, upon hearing the tone the client was asked to rate his feelings on a positive–negative scale from 1 to 5 and to record the most pleasant element in his current environment. According to the authors, use of this technique helped a depressed client develop a more positive outlook, think of himself in the present more than to daydream about the past, and improve his ability to single out rewarding elements in his present environment.

Cigarette smoking is said sometimes to occur "automatically." One could say that when this happens, self-monitoring did not occur for this response. Powell and Azrin (1968) devised a cigarette case that applied an electric shock to the user's arm each time the case was opened. Thus, the user was forced to self-monitor the action of "taking a cigarette." Many uses of audiotape and videotape recording may be said to facilitate self-monitoring, especially when playback occurs comparatively soon. For example, a client may be unaware of a rather chronic frown until after seeing himself on videotape replay a number of times. Also, any number of automated systems with feedback features may enhance self-monitoring processes. We should note that the mere activation of self-monitoring does not necessarily assure that constructive behavioral changes will follow. Self-monitoring for which the client is unprepared may be disruptive rather than helpful (see Bailey and Sowder, 1970).

Sometimes the reason a client fails to practice effective self-control is that he uses an inappropriately low rate of positive self-reinforcement. For example, a client wishes to overcome his depression, but he fails to recognize and self-reinforce his achievements; and he wishes to control his overeating, but he fails to recognize and reinforce his movements away from food. We wish now to develop an example of a treatment program that illustrates use of audiotape recorders to improve self-reinforcement practices for control of overeating. The following steps would be required to develop the program:

1. A script would be prepared depicting a series of social and nonsocial situations in which the client would be tempted to eat food inappropriately.
2. These situations would be recorded serially on an audiotape as "treatment items."
3. The tape would be "marked" with an electronic cue after each item which would make it possible for the recorder to stop after each item.
4. Another script would be prepared of a series of positive self-reinforcements such as: "Good, I made the correct decision," "I am on the right track now," "If I keep on thinking this way I will whip this problem," etc. (see Chapter 11 in this book). This material would be recorded *in the voice of the client* on a second audiotape.
5. Equipment which would be needed would include (a) two audiotape recorders that would play the electronically "cued" tapes, (b) *right* and *left* push buttons that the client would use, and (c) necessary control circuitry to make the system work.

In use, the automated system and program would work in this manner. The client would be seated alone in a room and would have *right* and *left* push buttons in front of him. The first treatment item would be presented over a speaker. As an example, it might go something like this:

> Imagine you are at a party and you have already had all the snacks you feel you should have, but then an impulse comes to you to walk toward the kitchen to talk to a friend, or to walk toward the family room to talk to another friend. Press the left button for the kitchen and the right button for the family room.

The control circuitry would be designed so that choosing the *right* button (the family room) would turn on the second tape recorder to deliver a self-reinforcement of the type described earlier. ("Good, I made the correct decision.") The reinforcement would be automatically followed by another treatment item from the first recorder. If the client had pressed the *left* button indicating he chose the kitchen, an aversive stimulus such as a loud buzzer could be sounded, or the next treatment item could be presented without comment.

This automated system would assure the client of prompt positive self-reinforcement each time he made decisions consistent with his aim to avoid overeating. The system would be easy to program and use, and would be applicable for treating a wide range of clinical problems in which the therapist wished to help the client acquire greater skill at applying positive self-reinforcements. Our experience in the Automated Psychology Laboratory suggests that treatment programs recorded in the voice of the client himself may be more reinforcing to him than programs recorded in another person's voice (see Kanfer and Zich, 1974).

Systematic Desensitization

Probably more attempts have been made to automate the administration of systematic desensitization therapy than any other type of psychological treatment. The reader is referred to the chapter by Morris for a full discussion of systematic desensitization. The present discussion assumes some familiarity with the general concepts and procedures of the SD technique. One of the best known automated procedures for administering SD therapy is Lang's DAD system (Lang, Melamed, and Hart, 1970). DAD (Device for Automated Desensitization) is an "interactive" system that can respond to the subjective emotional condition of the client—as indicated by pressing a push button. For example, if the client presses a button to indicate he feels fearful, the system stops presenting fearful stimuli (tape player #1 turns "off") and starts presenting relaxation instructions (tape player #2 turns "on"). If the client remains fearful (presses another push button), or is unable to relax, the system "backs up" and presents less fearful stimuli. There is some experimental evidence that DAD may be more effective than a live therapist in reducing snake phobia. Lang *et al.* suggested that the effectiveness of DAD may be related to the unyieldingly systematic nature of automated treatment.

Lang (1969) has described the development of a more complicated treatment system that uses a Digital Equipment Corporation LINC 8 computer, provides "random access audio" to as many as 36 channels of information, and is able to modify treatment program sequencing on the basis of continuous analyses of a client's physiological responses. For example, if physiological monitoring indicated respiration rate were too fast (a possible contributor to anxious feelings), the system might present an audio message intended to reduce respiration rate.

Mann (1972) successfully automated the systematic desensitization of test anxiety in junior high school students. He videotaped live SD and replayed the tapes as "vicarious desensitization." Students who watched these videotapes showed significant decreases in test anxiety, but other students who did not see the tapes failed to show any change in their anxiety levels. A technique such as this could be applied in a community mental health center for treatment of various anxiety reactions among adult clients. We know that some adults who are anxious will not enter face-to-face therapy—but they might be willing to watch videotapes showing *someone else* being treated for a problem similar to their own problem. Reppucci and Baker (1969) gave phobic students a kit to take home with them, instructions on how to construct their own hierarchy, and a log book to use in recording their daily progress. Also, they were given a long-play record having relaxation instructions on one side and a fear hierarchy administration framework on the other side into which the clients could insert their own specific fear items as they worked their way through the hierarchy. Reppucci and Baker found that energetic, outgoing, and well organized subjects were helped more by this self-desensitization procedure than were other subjects who tended to be thinkers rather than do-ers and who saw themselves as complex and sick. This study illustrates the need for careful attention to client characteristics that may predict the outcome of automated treatment. For example, a carefully constructed test instrument that would assess a client's reactions to buttons, switches, computers, and mechanization, and would tap his attitudes about the appropriateness of certain man-machine analogies might tell us a great deal about whether or not he will benefit from automated treatment.

Automated Practiced Imagination Therapy

As the reader has already learned from the earlier chapters by Meichenbaum, Goldfried, and Kanfer, changing self-talk can lead to important changes in one's actions. Automated Practiced Imagination Therapy (APIT) is a treatment technique, developed in the Automated Psychology Laboratory, based on the assumption that changes in self-talk can be accomplished by treatment that is administered via automated devices. There are two major advantages that we wish to note. First, use of automated procedures tends to result in treatments that can be defined more objectively, repeated more reliably, and controlled more easily than other kinds of treatment. These characteristics make automated treatment more open to scientific study. Second, the use of automated devices creates the possibility of "treatment programs" that can be *prescribed* by a therapist and administered by a technician. Thus, potentially there should be significant savings of professional time and effort. The therapist would be freed from some of the routine aspects of treatment and have greater time available for analysis and treatment of knotty clinical problems, seeing an increased number of clients, or planning research studies of the effectiveness of his treatment procedures.

The reader may be helped to understand APIT by seeing it as a client would see it. The client is taken to a small room where he relaxes in a recliner chair (see Fig. 14.3 in this chapter), and is given a push button switch to hold in his hand. He is told that pressing the button will cause a treatment item to be presented over a speaker located in the treatment room. The client is told to imagine being in the situation that is described, and to imagine that he thinks, feels, and behaves the way the item suggests. It is acknowledged to the client that he may not have always responded that way. Nevertheless, he is encouraged to *imagine* during the treatment session that he is actually in the described situation, and that he is thinking, feeling, and behaving in the adaptive manner suggested. After the client has fully imagined the treatment item, he presses the push button and a new item is presented. The client continues to procure messages, imagine that he is in the situations, etc. until the program is completed. The programs contain from 20 to 50 treatment items and all programs are designed to be completed in an hour, or less.

Readers enticed by the possibility of using automated methods to induce changes in patterns of self-talk (also, "self-emoting" and "self-visualizing") will recognize quickly that an audiotape recorder is probably required, but they may have questions about the steps to take in writing treatment items. How were the

APIT treatment items constructed? We have approached item construction in essentially three different ways. *First,* some items have been written from case history information to assist a client to overcome a specific adjustment problem. *Second,* many items have been written on the basis of a rational analysis of a problem area. We have attempted to identify the cognitive, "emotional," and interpersonal "skills" that we feel characterize the person who is competent and adaptable in a given problem area. Then we have tried to write treatment items that will give our clients opportunities to imagine that they possess these same skills. *Third,* many items have been based on standardized psychological test questions that measure the problem behavior we wish to treat. As an example, we have used questions contained in anxiety questionnaire scales to try to identify the *stimulus situations* and the *behaviors* that characterize one as being anxious. Next, we tried to write treatment items that we think reflect the various skills involved in non-anxious responding in these same stimulus situations.

In community mental health centers, there is an ever present need for improved treatment techniques that are easy to use, can reach larger numbers of clients, and are more effective than traditional techniques. Therefore, a main focus of our work with APIT has been to attempt to apply this procedure as a routine clinical tool. We have developed a variety of programs that have been put into direct service to help clients learn to solve adjustment problems. These APIT programs were designed for treatment of: anxiety, depression, negative self-concepts, inadequate social skills among adolescents, inadequate social skills among adult women, inadequate social assertiveness, overweight problems in males, overweight problems in females, parents' inadequacy in child management, etc. Also, special purpose programs have been written to deal with the idiosyncratic problems of individual clients.

The above programs are available to our staff members and they have selectively referred clients to receive specified APIT programs. Staff and administrative acceptance of APIT has advanced to the point that "automated treatment" is one of the codes used at Quinco Consulting Center to record the nature of the treatment service that is received by our clients. We must caution strongly against the conclusion that this kind of acceptance establishes the effectiveness of automated treatment, or any other treatment. What is important to note is that *automated approaches to providing professional treatment services to clients have been successfully incorporated into the day by day operations of a typical community mental health center.*

Evaluation of APIT, or any other treatment technique, may be performed from at least four perspectives: practical clinical usefulness, client acceptance, case studies, and scientific status. We wish now to consider each of these perspectives. The APIT technique has practical clinical usefulness. It is easy to understand, requires a minimum of hardware, and APIT program material is easy to prepare. A technician or secretary can administer APIT treatment programs. It is important for the person applying this treatment to use warmth and concern in relating to the client. As for client acceptance of APIT, the initial evidence suggests that client acceptance of this treatment is not significantly different from client acceptance of face-to-face therapy received from mental health professionals. Client acceptance of APIT has been inferred from client ratings of the "helpfulness" of this technique. A group of clients who had received APIT treatment were matched on age, sex, clinical diagnosis, and number of treatments with another group of clients who had received face-to-face therapy from experienced clinicians. Each client was asked to rate the "helpfulness" of his treatment on a five point scale ranging from "not helpful at all" to "very helpful." A statistical test (t test) showed that helpfulness ratings made by these two groups were not significantly different. We should note that "client ratings of helpfulness" of a treatment in no way establish the effectiveness of the treatment.

We wish to consider two clinical cases in which APIT treatment methods were applied. These case studies illustrate that automated techniques are applicable to different types of clinical problems, to clients varying in age and formal education, and that automated treatment can be used in combination with face-to-face treatment procedures.

Child Rejection

Mrs. Smith was a 29-year-old high school graduate who lived with her husband and three children in the country. Mrs. Smith's chronic rejection of her four-year-old daughter, Sally, was the reason for her self-referral into Quinco Consulting Center. She stated that her rejection of Sally began a few weeks after Sally's birth. She tended not to fondle or cuddle Sally, ignored her crying, jerked her and treated her gruffly, forced food back into her mouth when she spit up, made her eat burnt toast, denied giving her favors given to the other children, punished Sally when other adults showed her affection, etc. Mrs. Smith was seen for six sessions of face-to-face Practiced Imagination Therapy during which the therapist spontaneously generated treatment items intended to help Mrs. Smith overcome her rejection of Sally (e.g., "Mrs. Smith is a kind, generous person; Mrs. Smith has patience; Mrs. Smith is honest; Mrs. Smith wants to do what is right; Mrs. Smith can imagine hugging Sally; Mrs. Smith can imagine picking Sally up; Mrs. Smith can imagine kissing Sally; etc".). The treatment material developed in face-to-face meetings was recorded onto audiotapes. Mrs. Smith attended an additional 12 face-to-face interview appointments and attended 32 APIT treatment appointments that were divided about equally between working with child rejection audiotapes and weight control audiotapes. During therapy, the client reported that she no longer insulted Sally, no longer told her she was different, and the client became willing to engage in friendly play with Sally. According to weight measures made in the APL, Mrs. Smith lost 23 pounds. She terminated from therapy after approximately four months. Twenty-three months after termination, Mrs. Smith was seen for follow-up interviewing. She reported that her relationship with Sally had continued to improve. Now she takes initiative to defend Sally from unfair treatment, tries to make sure Sally's clothing is as pretty as the clothing of the other children, and she kisses Sally as she goes to school and when she goes to bed. Mrs. Smith expressed satisfaction with automated treatment and stated that some specific APIT treatment items still affected her behavior in specific ways.

Acrophobia

Mr. Brown, a 45-year-old mental health professional, referred himself for treatment of acrophobia that had been present since he was about 10 years old. Simply reading about situations of height made the client feel anxious. His self-referral was prompted by a planned business trip for which air travel was nearly mandatory. He had flown twice, 15–18 years earlier, and experienced intense discomfort and anxiety each time. In preparation for APIT treatment, Mr. Brown was interviewed by a research assistant* who collected personal history data that were used by her to write an APIT acrophobia treatment program specifically for Mr. Brown. After the program was written, Mr. Brown came to the Automated Psychology Laboratory to "record the program in his own voice." Next, he attended 10 appointments in the APL to hear his own APIT acrophobia program. After completing his program, Mr. Brown made an airplane trip during which he was free from anxiety, and he began deliberately exposing himself to situations of height such as to look over bridge rails, look out the windows of tall buildings, and to climb stepladders. He stated he would not hesitate to fly again if the need arose, and he mentioned specific ways in which he used coping mechanisms in APIT treatment items to talk himself out of feeling anxious about heights. Mr. Brown attributed his improvement to automated treatment.

We have examined APIT from the perspectives of practical clinical usefulness, client acceptance, and case studies and found encouraging information about the clinical value of this technique. We wish now to turn the reader's attention to the "scientific status" of APIT. By "scientific status" we mean, "are data available that were collected under controlled experimental conditions and were statistically analyzed which show APIT to have significant treatment effectiveness?" Bloch (1973) found significantly greater reductions in manifest anxiety for subjects who listened to APIT audiotapes that (a) described problem situations tending to arouse anxiety, (b) suggested ways of coping, and (c) suggested self-reinforcements as rewards for successful coping (subjects told themselves they were "doing a good job," were "on the right track," deserved a "cup of coffee," etc.) than for control subjects whose only participation was to receive pre- and posttesting. Another group of subjects who listened to audiotapes that were identical, except that the self-reinforcement component was omitted, were not significantly different from the control subjects in amount of anxiety reduction.

We have recently completed a study in the APL in which volunteer female subjects who listened to APIT anxiety treatment tapes that included *problem*, *coping*, and *self-reinforcement* components showed greater reductions of both covert and manifest anxiety than control subjects who only received pre- and

---

*Carolyn L. Clark.

posttesting. There were no significant differences between the control subjects and a group of treatment subjects who listened to tapes that included only *problem* and *self-reinforcement* components, or between control subjects and another group of treatment subjects whose tapes were essentially limited to descriptions of *problems* that aroused anxiety. This study and the Bloch (1973) study taken together suggested that APIT programs, in order to be maximally effective for anxiety reduction, needed to include (a) descriptions of problem situations in which anxious reactions were likely to occur, (b) suggestions about effective ways of coping with the problems, and (c) suggestions of self-reinforcement to serve as rewards for successful coping. In other words, if either the coping component, or self-reinforcement component, or both of these components were omitted from the audiotape programs, then treatment effectiveness appeared to be lessened.

In summary, our evaluation suggests that APIT is easy to use, is accepted by clients, and that the technique is a significantly effective treatment procedure.

RECOMMENDATIONS FOR USE OF AUTOMATED METHODS

What recommendations can be made regarding the use of automated treatment methods? We feel these recommendations should cover the wide range of experiences and problems likely to be encountered by the beginning therapist who desires to use automated methods in his clinical work, but has little or no prior experience in this field. Also, issues of interest to the experienced clinician should be raised and discussed.

Effectiveness of Automated Treatment

Answers to questions about the effectiveness of automated psychological treatment will depend upon the specific automated technique being used, the client, the nature of the adjustment problem, and many other variables. However, as a general statement, the experimental and clinical evidence on effectiveness of automated treatment is highly encouraging. Some automated devices appear to administer some treatments just as effectively, or more effectively, than the live therapist (see Lang, Melamed, and Hart, 1970). It may be, as Lang *et al.* suggested, that the unyieldingly systematic nature of automated treatment helps it be more effective. Other automated devices such as those used in some types of biofeedback training are able to detect certain "subtle response processes" and subject them to therapeutic manipulation. Some of these subtle response processes such as brain waves are not ordinarily worked with by the unassisted live therapist. Thus, it would seem that even tentative evidence of effectiveness is something "to get excited about." We must, however, avoid the uncritical acceptance of any automated technique or its claimed efficacy. Each automated device and procedure should be experimentally studied to determine its treatment effectiveness. Biofeedback techniques and research are too technical to discuss in detail in this chapter, but the interested reader may refer to an article by Blanchard and Young (1974) for a critical review of recent developments in this area.

There is much evidence to suggest that audiotape and videotape recordings, slides, films, and a variety of other electromechanical devices (see Schwitzgebel, 1968) can effectively produce desirable behavioral changes. There are a number of conditions that appear to facilitate the use of these materials/techniques for behavior change purposes. *First*, it is desirable to focus these techniques on "specific responses" that one wishes to modify and to develop well defined programs, or procedures, to produce the desired behavioral changes. *Second*, as much as possible, the automated procedure should be "interactive," i.e., have some feedback capability, to help the client be keenly aware of the appropriateness of his responses and to know when he is making progress. *Third*, care should be taken to avoid automated procedures that clients may perceive as "cold," impersonal, or indifferent to them as individuals (Morris and Suckerman, 1974). *Fourth*, it is probably desirable for a live therapist to maintain regular face-to-face contact with clients receiving automated treatments. Appointments with a therapist may be scheduled less frequently than appointments for automated treatment. *Fifth*, "transfer of training" procedures are desirable to help the client know how to apply in real life situations the skills he first learned in a laboratory, or clinical setting (Goldstein, 1973). *Sixth*, it is our impression based on experience in the Automated Psychology Laboratory that effectiveness of automated programs is enhanced when the client himself participates in preparation of the program.

What types of problems can be helped by automated treatment? In summary, these methods: (1) improve "chronic" social adjustment problems such as those that often are classified as neuroses, (2) bring about long term changes in cognitive processes for better approaches to analyzing problems and planning coping strategies for dealing with problems, (3) assist in development of specific interpersonal skills such as being more assertive, or showing greater empathy, (4) modify specific biological systems such as to relax a "chronically" contracted muscle group, and (5) improve self-control processes involved in monitoring, evaluating, and reinforcing one's own behavior.

Ethical Considerations

The ethical considerations relevant to automated psychological treatment are parallel, in a large degree, to the ethical constraints that apply to any psychological treatment. However, there are some significant differences. *First*, every reasonable attempt should be made when using automated methods to protect the client from any physical injury that could be caused by the equipment. The use of electric shock such as in aversive conditioning, occurrence of unexpectedly loud sounds, or attachments on the client's body could work singularly, or in combination, to cause injury. *Second*, efforts should be made to respect the dignity of the client. Clients should never be assigned to automated treatment if some form of face-to-face therapy would be more appropriate. However, it would be unwise to rule out the use of automated treatment simply because a client raised some initial question about it. Every effort should be made to help the client understand the rationale behind automated treatment and to accept it willingly. Nevertheless, there may be instances in which there is good reason to insist that a client try an unappealing treatment procedure, at least for a limited period of time. Many clients who are eventually helped by contact with mental health professionals had to be urged by family and friends to consider treatment. *Third*, the client should be aware that many automated techniques are still in the developmental stage. If an experimental procedure is tried with a client, he needs to be aware of this and have a choice whether or not to take the treatment.

Fourth, automated treatment may make the client more vulnerable to surreptitious observation with consequent embarrassment to the client and/or harm to his treatment program. The information gained from closed circuit TV monitors, intercom systems, and data print-outs, which are common in automated treatment settings, must be handled confidentially. As much as possible, the client should be informed of the different techniques that will be used to monitor his behavior during treatment. *Fifth*, the possibility that one therapist may *prescribe* automated treatment and another therapist administer the treatment sharpens the question of client responsibility. Is the therapist who prescribed the treatment, or the therapist who administers the treatment, primarily responsible for the client? This question needs to be clarified before automated treatment begins. *Sixth*, prescribed automated treatment raises the question of "program content" and whether or not it is fully appropriate for a given client. A therapist must inform himself of the contents and nature of automated treatment before prescribing it for his clients. *Seventh*, a therapist should make public his automated procedures so that he can have the benefits of both the judgment and criticism of the scientific community, at least his close colleagues, about the automated methods he is using. As these methods become more firmly established, it will be no more necessary to inform others about them than to inform the scientific community that one is using interview therapy techniques. For other pertinent discussions of ethical questions, see the *American Psychological Association Directory*, 1973 Edition, and especially Schwitzgebel (1973), Rubin and Franks (1969), and Berger (1970).

Qualifications for Appliers of Automated Treatment

The person who applies automated treatment techniques should have the same sensitivity, kindness, compassion, and good judgment that we wish to see in those who use interpersonal treatment methods. We know that some clients prefer automated treatment over face-to-face therapy, but other clients see automated treatment as an "unimportant" therapy that means they have been personally rejected. Thus, it is important for a therapist who uses an automated treatment procedure to communicate an attitude of interest and concern to the client who receives automated therapy. What about educational requirements? In the 1940s and 1950s, many Ph.D. psychologists who worked in mental hospitals were not permitted to perform individual psychotherapy. Now it is routine to hear about mental health technicians with B.A. degrees fulfilling a wide range of diagnostic and treatment roles. Thus, we see no need to impose arbitrary educational requirements onto practitioners of automated psychological treatment. It would be desirable for the applier of automated techniques to have some interest in technology or to have a background in audiovisual aids. It seems reasonable, since automated treatment is now in a formative, experimental stage, and there are numerous ethical questions to consider, that staff members with graduate training should have the prime responsibility for this treatment, even though lesser trained personnel may operate the equipment.

Administrative Considerations

There are steps a therapist can take to make sure his proposal to establish an automated psychological treatment program has the best possible hearing when being reviewed by administrative personnel. To begin with, it is essential for the therapist to have a measure of genuine, low-keyed enthusiasm for automated treatment. The idea is that administrators will be most likely to accept and support innovative proposals if they feel those making the proposals have some commitment to the things they propose.

This quality of enthusiasm is closely related to the range and depth of information the therapist has about automated psychological treatment. It is difficult to maintain a buoyant attitude about a new idea, especially if it is under fire, if one does not have a good grasp on factual information related to the idea. The detailed information potentially relevant in the hardware area could range all the way from such mundane items as to whether wall outlets are two pronged or three pronged to such highly technical considerations as the design of computer memories. Obviously, therapists cannot master all of this information and some practical choices must be made as to the things on which one will become informed. From the administrator's standpoint, the most needed information is that which bears directly upon the establishment, maintenance, usefulness, and cost of an automated treatment program. At some point, a detailed review will probably be needed of specifications and costs associated with personnel, consultants, equipment, supplies, travel, remodeling needs, floor space usage, and maintenance contracts for equipment. In many proposals, the therapist will limit the scope of the automated treatment program such that the only request he makes will be for a tape recorder-player, a supply of cassette tapes, and administrative approval to spend the time necessary to weave this treatment approach into the total agency operation. For these types of proposals, the details to be presented to the administrator will be limited. Other therapists will think in terms of a more comprehensive system including new personnel, pieces of specialized equipment, remodeling of floor space, use of consultants in the engineering and psychological specialties, and a significant budget that will need careful administrative review. In these cases, the formal proposal for establishing an automated psychological treatment program should include the range and depth of detailed information necessary for the administrator to evaluate the proposal and make a judgment about whether or not to support it.

"Getting One's Feet Wet" in Automated Treatment

Suppose one feels technology should play a more significant role in psychological treatment than it now does and he would like to make experimental use of some automated procedures, but he does not know where to begin. The purpose of this section is to provide diverse practical information that may not be conveniently available in any other single location. Psychological procedures and techniques that are already automated or easily lend themselves to automation tend to be described in behavior therapy journals. Also, many of the methods described in this book can be applied in an automated format. Some psychological journals (e.g., *Contemporary Psychology*) review new films and instructional aids that may be useful in some automated treatment applications. Some psychological equipment firms stock rather large selections of two by two inch slides designed for automated treatment applications. Also, automated psychological treatment systems that are "completely packaged" and shipped to the buyer ready to use are now available. The reader who would like to develop some knowledge of electronics as part of his approach to automated methods may want to refer to books by Hughes and Pipe (1961) and Cornsweet (1963). Sidowski (1966) has edited an excellent advanced text on instrumentation in psychology. One can keep abreast of many recent developments in psychological equipment by reading the journal, *Behavior Research Methods and Instrumentation*. The National Audio-Visual Aids Association publishes an annual equipment directory that provides pictures and technical specifications for a huge number of devices potentially useful in automated psychological treatment. *The International Journal of Instructional Media* and *Journal of Educational Technology Systems* publish articles that may be useful to the psychologist interested in automated treatment. Behavior research equipment manufacturers are one of the best resources for needed hardware. These companies regularly advertise in psychological journals, and often prepare specially designed electrical circuits as a customer service. Oswald and Wilson (1971) have written a small practical book that may be useful to those planning to use videotape as a treatment technique. Finally, we wish to support the legitimacy of "clinical psychologist" initiated requests for fiscal support to buy or lease needed equipment, to purchase supplies, to arrange for psychological and engineering consultations, to hire needed personnel, and to acquire, renovate, and furnish floorspace that is needed for automated treatment programs.

REFERENCES

Alger, I. and Hogan, P. The use of videotape recordings in conjoint marital therapy. In M. M. Berger (Ed.), *Videotape techniques in psychiatric training and treatment.* New York: Brunner/Mazel, 1970.

Bailey, K. G. and Sowder, W. T. Audiotape and videotape self-confrontation in psychotherapy. *Psychological Bulletin*, 1970, **74**, 127–137.

Bandura, A. and Menlove, F. L. Factors determining vicarious extinction of avoidance behavior through symbolic modeling. *Journal of Personality and Social Psychology*, 1968, **8**, 99–108.

Berger, M. M. (Ed.) *Videotape techniques in psychiatric training and treatment.* New York: Brunner/Mazel, 1970.

Birk, L., Huddleston, W., Miller, E., and Cohler, B. Avoidance conditioning for homosexuality. *Archives of General Psychiatry,* 1971, **25**, 314–323.

Blanchard, E. B. and Young, L. D. Clinical applications of biofeedback training: A review of evidence. *Archives of General Psychiatry,* 1974, **30**, 573–589.

Bloch, J. P. The automated presentation of practiced imagination therapy to reduce anxiety. Unpublished doctoral dissertation, University of Louisville, 1973.

Cameron, D. E., Levy, L., Ban, T., and Rubenstein, L. Automation of psychotherapy. *Comprehensive Psychiatry,* 1964, **5**, 1–14.

Colby, K. M. and Enea, H. Heuristic methods for computer understanding of natural language in context-restricted on-line dialogues. *Mathematical Biosciences,* 1967, **1**, 1–25.

Colby, K. M., Watt, J. B., and Gilbert, J. P. A computer method of psychotherapy: Preliminary communication. *Journal of Nervous and Mental Diseases,* 1966, **142**, 148–152.

Cornsweet, T. N. *The design of electrical circuits in the behavioral sciences.* New York: Wiley, 1963.

Dee, C. Instructions and the extinction of a learned fear in the context of taped implosive therapy. *Journal of Consulting and Clinical Psychology,* 1972, **39**, 123–132.

Denholtz, M. The use of tape recordings between therapy sessions. *Journal of Behavior Therapy and Experimental Psychiatry,* 1970, **1**, 139–143.

Elwood, D. L. Automated WAIS testing correlated with face-to-face WAIS testing: A validity study. *International Journal of Man-Machine Studies,* 1972, **4**, 129–137. (a)

Elwood, D. L. A device to record gross motor movements in human subjects. *Behavior Research Methods and Instrumentation,* 1972, **4**, 315–316. (b)

Feingold, L. An automated technique for aversive conditioning in sexual deviations. In R. D. Rubin and C. M. Franks (Eds.), *Advances in behavior therapy, 1968.* New York: Academic Press, 1969.

Goldstein, A. P. *Structured learning therapy: Toward a psychotherapy for the poor.* New York: Academic Press, 1973.

Hughes, R. J. and Pipe, P. *Introduction to electronics.* Garden City, New York: Doubleday, 1961.

Kanfer, F. H. and Zich, J. Self-control training: The effects of external control on children's resistance to temptation. *Developmental Psychology,* 1974, **10**, 108–115.

Kirchner, J. H. and Hogan, R. A. The therapist variable in the implosion of phobias. *Psychotherapy: Theory, Research and Practice,* 1966, **3**, 102–104.

Lang, P. J. The on-line computer in behavior therapy research. *American Psychologist,* 1969, **24**, 236–239.

Lang, P. J., Melamed, B. G., and Hart, J. A psychophysiological analysis of fear modification using an automated desensitization procedure. *Journal of Abnormal Psychology,* 1970, **76**, 220–234.

Lehman, R. E. The disinhibiting effects of visual material in treating orgasmically dysfunctional women. *Behavioral Engineering,* (Pub: Farrell Instruments, Grand Island, Nebraska), 1974, **1**(2), 1–3.

Lindsley, O. R. Direct behavioral analysis of psychotherapy sessions by conjugately programmed closed circuit television. *Psychotherapy: Theory, Research, and Practice,* 1969, **6**, 71–81.

Longin, H. E. and Rooney, W. M. Assertion training as a programmatic intervention for hospitalized mental patients. *Proceedings of the 81st Annual Convention of the American Psychological Association,* 1973, **8**, 459–460.

Mann, J. Vicarious desensitization of test anxiety through observation of videotaped treatment. *Journal of Counseling Psychology,* 1972, **19**, 1–7.

MacCulloch, M. J., Birtles, C. J., and Feldman, M. P. Anticipatory avoidance learning for the treatment of homosexuality: Recent developments and an automatic aversion therapy system. *Behavior Therapy,* 1971, **2**, 151–169.

McFall, R. M. and Twentyman, C. T. Four experiments on the relative contributions of rehearsal, modeling, and coaching to assertion training. *Journal of Abnormal Psychology,* 1973, **81**, 199–218.

Morris, R. J. and Suckerman, K. R. Therapist warmth as a factor in automated systematic desensitization. *Journal of Consulting and Clinical Psychology,* 1974, **42**, 244–250.

Oswald, I. and Wilson, S. *This bag is not a toy.* New York: Council on Social Work Education, Inc., 1971.

Powell, J. and Azrin, N. The effects of shock as a punisher for cigarette smoking. *Journal of Applied Behavior Analysis,* 1968, **1**, 63–71.

Reppucci, N. D. and Baker, B. L. Self-desensitization: Implications for treatment and teaching. In R. D. Rubin and C. M. Franks (Eds.), *Advances in behavior therapy, 1968.* New York: Academic Press, 1969.

Rubin, R. D. and Franks, C. M. (Eds.) *Advances in behavior therapy, 1968.* New York: Academic Press, 1969.

Schwitzgebel, R. K. Ethical and legal aspects of behavioral instrumentation. In R. L. Schwitzgebel and R. K. Schwitzgebel (Eds.), *Psychotechnology, electronic control of mind and behavior.* New York: Holt, Rinehart and Winston, 1973.

Schwitzgebel, R. L. Survey of electromechanical devices for behavior modification. *Psychological Bulletin,* 1968, **70,** 444–459.

Serber, M. Teaching the nonverbal components of assertive training. *Journal of Behavior Therapy and Experimental Psychiatry,* 1972, **3,** 179–183.

Sidowski, J. B., (Ed.) *Experimental methods and instrumentation in psychology.* New York: McGraw-Hill, 1966.

Sims, G. K. and Lazarus, A. A. The use of random auditory stimulation in the treatment of a manic-depressive patient. *Behavior Therapy,* 1973, **4,** 128–133.

Slack, W. Computer-based interviewing system dealing with nonverbal behavior as well as keyboard responses. *Science,* 1971, **171,** 84–87.

Whalen, C. Effects of a model and instructions on group verbal behaviors. *Journal of Consulting and Clinical Psychology,* 1969, **33,** 509–521.

Woody, R. H. Clinical suggestion in video taped psychotherapy: A research progress report. *American Journal of Clinical Hypnosis,* 1971, **14,** 32–37.

Author Index

Subject Index